TUTTLE
GUIDE TO
THE
MIDDLE EAST

Edited by
PETER SLUGLETT and MARION FAROUK-SLUGLETT

Charles E. Tuttle Company, Inc.
Boston • Rutland, Vermont • Tokyo

Published in the United States in 1992 by
Charles E. Tuttle Company, Inc. of Rutland, Vermont & Tokyo, Japan,
with editorial offices at 77 Central Street, Boston, Massachusetts 02109.

Library of Congress Cataloging-in-Publication Data

Tuttle guide to the Middle East / edited by Peter Sluglett and Marion
Farouk-Sluglett.
    p.   cm.
  Includes index.
  ISBN 0-8048-1814-2 (pbk.)
  1. Middle East. I. Sluglett, Peter. II. Farouk-Sluglett,
Marion. III. Title: Guide to the Middle East.
DS44.T881992
956.04—dc20   92-23053
                                              CIP

Typeset by Rowland Phototypesetting Limited, Suffolk, England
PRINTED IN THE UNITED STATES

The contributors

Peter Sluglett is Lecturer in Modern Middle Eastern History, Durham University, and visiting Professor of History, Harvard University.
Marion Farouk-Sluglett is Lecturer in Politics, University College of Wales, Swansea.

The book also includes contributions from
Martin Daly, Memphis State University
Sarah Graham-Brown
William Hale, SOAS, University of London
George Joffé, SOAS, University of London; Exeter University; and Southampton University
Homa Katouzian, specialist and writer on Iran
Helen Lackner
Robert Mabro, Fellow of St Antony's College, Oxford
Richard Owen, Deputy Foreign Editor, *The Times*
Charles Tripp, SOAS, University of London

Editors' foreword

It is too early to make an overall assessment of the impact that the great changes which have taken place in the world in the late 1980s and early 1990s have had upon the Middle East. One important recent consequence has been the series of events which have culminated in the announcement that the first Arab–Israeli peace talks will take place in Madrid early in November 1991. If these meetings manage to achieve even the modest objective of creating the framework for future diaologue, this will have been one of the most hopeful and positive developments in the Middle East for many decades. This volume is an attempt to place current events within an accessible historical framework; we hope it will serve as a useful starting point for those wanting to get to grips with what has happened in this region over the last few decades.

We should like to thank all the contributors for their commitment and enthusiasm. We should also like to thank Andrew Heritage, formerly of *Times Books* for having initiated the project, and Thomas Cussans, of *Times Books*, for having seen it through to completion with a remarkable combination of tact, determination, energy and good humour. We are particularly grateful to Shaalan for having endured several months of furious activity with tolerant and affectionate amusement, and to our families in Berlin, Bristol and North Carolina for understanding that we could not visit them as often as we and they would have liked.

CONTENTS

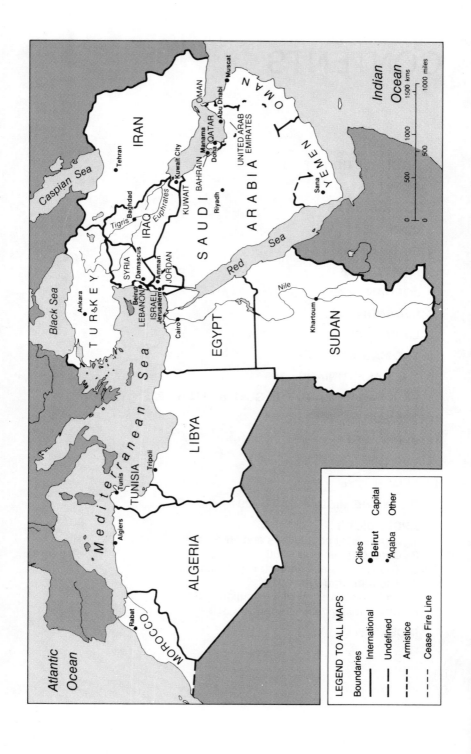

LEGEND TO ALL MAPS

Boundaries
International
Undefined
Armistice
Cease Fire Line

Cities
● Beirut   Capital
▪ Aqaba   Other

INTRODUCTION

At the beginning of the 19th century, almost all the Middle East and North Africa was, at least nominally, part of the Ottoman Empire. The Ottomans had conquered the area between what is now eastern Turkey and western Algeria in the 15th and 16th centuries; their rule extended over much of south-eastern Europe as well. In Iran, another dynasty, the Qajars, had ruled since 1779. By the time of the Treaty of Lausanne in 1923, which marked the end of the negotiations following the end of the First World War, the Ottoman Empire had disappeared—the last Qajar would be forced to abdicate in 1925—and most of the area between Morocco and Iran, with the exception of Saudi Arabia, northern Yemen, the Turkish Republic (founded in 1923) and Iran itself, had come under the control of Britain, France or Italy. Thus the 19th and early 20th centuries formed a period of great change. In the process, 'traditional' society and social structure was shaken to its foundations, new ways of life and institutions came into being, and a new intellectual and moral climate created. Yet, though the period was one of considerable ferment, the extent to which this was taking place was frequently unperceived or ignored by Europeans, whether politicians or colonial officials, who cherished notions of an 'unchanging East' which had little foundation in fact.

Collapse of the Ottoman Empire

Between the beginning of the 19th century and the end of the First World War, the Ottoman Empire disintegrated, despite extensive efforts to reform and modernise its structure. Steady European commercial and colonial penetration into the Near East and North Africa undermined its fragile economy, while growing demands for national independence among the subject peoples caused large areas either to break away or to fall effectively under foreign control.

The Napoleonic expedition to Egypt in 1798 was the first indication of the Great Powers' new concern with the area. In spite of his defeat by Britain, Napoleon's invasion marked the beginning of an extensive period of acculturation between East and West, which brought European technical, political and philosophical ideas to an area which had known neither the Renaissance nor the Enlightenment. In Egypt itself, 1798 marked the end of effective control from Constantinople, the seat of the sultan, the ruler of the Ottoman Empire. The Ottoman commander in Egypt, Mohammed Ali, sent in 1802 to restore order, founded a dynasty in 1805 which lasted until the revolution of 1952. Mohammed Ali's son, Ibrahim Pasha, led expeditions to Nejd, to subdue the Wahabis, adherents of a puritanical form of Islam, who had challenged Ottoman authority in the Hijaz and in Iraq. Ibrahim Pasha also conquered the whole area between Egypt and what is now Turkey between 1831 and 1839, and was only dissuaded from attempting to overthrow the central authority of the empire itself under pressure from Britain and France. Egyptian pretensions were subsequently confined to Egypt itself and Sudan, which had been ruled from Cairo since the early 1820s.

Faced with this and other challenges to its authority, the empire began a series of major reforms, in the armed forces, and in the fields of law, education, religion and administration. Previous efforts at reform had generally foundered on the intransigence of the traditional military forces, the janissaries, in the face of what they correctly perceived as a threat to their own position; Mahmud II (1808–1839) had dissolved the janissaries in a bloody battle in 1826, which meant that this obstacle no longer existed. Two edicts, in 1839 and 1856, stressed the subjects' rights to security of life and property, equitable taxation, and limited military service, and emphasised complete equality between Muslim and Christian subjects in the empire. Here, as in other spheres, the gap between the ideal and the reality was apparent, and opposition to the reforms soon developed. In addition, the stress on Muslim/Christian equality provided a ready excuse for the intervention of the European powers on behalf of their Christian and other protégés: the Orthodox, supported by Russia; the Maronites and other Catholics, protected by France; and the Druzes, under British protection. Foreign intervention contributed in particular to the Crimean War (1853–56) and the Lebanese crisis of 1860–61, while Russian and Austrian pressures were vitally important in securing the independence of most of the Ottoman lands in south-eastern Europe by 1878: Bulgaria, Montenegro, Serbia and Romania.

Thus by the outbreak of the First World War, the Ottoman Empire had been reduced to what is now Turkey, a small corner of south-eastern Europe, and the Arab provinces in Asia. Farther west, North Africa was completed dominated by the Powers; the French invaded Algeria in 1830, and by 1900 there were some 200,000 French settlers installed there. Similar developments took place on a smaller scale in Tunisia after the French invasion of 1881, in Morocco—itself never a part of the Ottoman Empire—after 1912, and in Libya, invaded and colonised by Italy after 1911. In Egypt, the rise of nationalism and the dangers which this posed to some £100 million of foreign investment served as the excuse for the British occupation in 1882.

In the other Arab provinces, there were stirrings of discontent, particularly during the long and oppressive reign of 'Abd al-Hamid II (1876–1909). Ideas of autonomy, encouraged by the revival of Arabic literature and campaigns to reform the Arabic language, gradually gained wider currency. 'Abd al-Hamid had prorogued the Ottoman parliament, itself one of the major achievements of the second wave of Ottoman reformers, in 1878, and opposition to his rule culminated in the Young Turk Revolution of 1908–9, which was supported by members of most of the ethnic groups in what was left of the empire. After the revolution, however, the Turkish element in the government proceeded to 'Turkify' all administrative, legal and educational institutions, a step which succeeded in alienating many Arabs and contributed in considerable measure to the willingness of many of them to seek accommodation with Britain in the war.

As the process of disintegration continued, new forms of trade and communications, largely funded by foreign capital, had begun to transform the empire. By 1914, Turkey and Egypt had substantial rail networks, with banks and mines and public utilities such as ports, tramways, water and electricity companies. North Africa and the Middle East became important markets for European goods, and Algeria began to export wine, Lebanon to produce silk, and, perhaps most spectacularly, Egypt to export cotton. Starting in 1822, demand for Egyptian cotton soared ten-fold during the American Civil War and almost trebled again, to £27 million, before 1914.

Parallel developments were taking place in Iran. The Qajars (1779–1924) had suffered constant British and Russian interference in their internal affairs, which culminated in the division of the country into British and Russian spheres of influence in 1907. However, the Tobacco Rebellion of 1891–92 and the Constitutional Revolution of 1905–11 served to arouse national consciousness and political awareness, although the Qajars were eventually to be overthrown by a military coup led by Reza Khan Pahlevi in 1924.

The First World War and the peace settlement

In 1914 the Ottoman Empire entered the war on the side of the Central Powers and thus emerged on the side of the vanquished. It was stripped of its Arab provinces and confined to Anatolia and eastern Thrace. However, the Turkish army was stung by further attempts on the part of the Allies to parcel out parts of Turkey proper, and its only undefeated general, Mustafa Kemal (Atatürk), rallied national feeling to his support, expelling French, Greek and Italian forces from the country by 1922. As first president of the Turkish republic he signed the post-war territorial settlement (the Treaty of Lausanne) in 1923, and abolished the caliphate in 1924. After the foundation of the Turkish republic, Turkey's fortunes became less closely involved with those of the rest of the Middle East, although this has changed again over the last two decades, during which Turkish trade, particularly in agricultural produce, with its Arab neighbours and Iran, has become increasingly important.

In the course of the war the Middle East became an important theatre of operations. Immediately after the declaration of war, Egypt, whose status had not been formalised after some 32 years of British occupation, was made a protectorate of the British Empire. Farther east, in order to protect the oil installations at Abadan in southern Iran, and to pre-empt a Turkish thrust towards the Gulf, British Indian troops invaded southern Iraq in the first weeks of the war, penetrating to Baghdad by March 1917. On the other side of the Fertile Crescent, Turkish resistance lasted rather longer, and Syria and Palestine remained in Turkish hands until the last months of the war.

The significance of the First World War to the Middle East was not confined to the final dismemberment of the Ottoman Empire. At least as important was the new political structure put up by the Allies in its place, the consequences of which are still with us today. In the first place, between March 1915 and May 1916, the British government conducted a protracted correspondence with the Ottoman governor of the Hijaz, Sharif Husain of Mecca. The outcome of these negotiations, known as the McMahon-Husain correspondence (McMahon was British high commissioner in Egypt), was that, in return for collaboration with the Allies against the Ottomans, Sharif Husain was promised 'Arab independence', albeit in somewhat vague terms:

'The two districts of Mersina and Alexandretta [both now in Turkey] and portions of Syria lying to the west of Damascus, Homs, Hama and Aleppo, cannot be said to be purely Arab, and should be excluded from the limits demanded . . . As for those regions lying within those frontiers where Great Britain is free to act without detriment to the interests of her ally France . . . Great Britain is prepared to recognise and support the independence of the Arabs.'

In June 1916 Sharif Husain and his sons accordingly launched the Arab Revolt, which was to culminate in the capture of Damascus from the Turks by an Arab-Allied force in September 1918 (see Chapter 13, Syria).

Meanwhile, over much the same period, Britain, France, Russia and Italy entered into a series of understandings, known collectively as the Sykes-Picot Agreement, under which, in the event of an Allied victory the Arab part of the Ottoman Empire would be divided into British and French spheres of influence; Palestine was to be under international control, while Russia was to receive Istanbul, the Straits, parts of Armenia and Kurdistan and Italy parts of south-west Turkey and the Dodecanese Islands. With some important reservations, France was to have paramount influence in Syria and Lebanon, and Britain was to have paramount influence in Iraq as well as control of the ports of Acre and Haifa. The precise form of government for these areas was not specified.

It is clear that the principles of the Sykes-Picot agreement and the offer accepted by Sharif Husain conflict. The one promises independence, the other some form of colonial rule. The episode has engendered heated, if

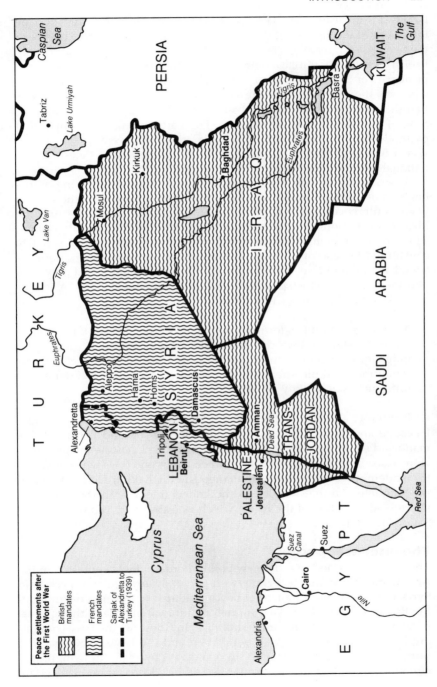

largely inconclusive, scholarly controversy: in addition, whatever the intentions of the authors of the documents themselves, the coexistence of the two sets of agreements is still felt to be a prime example of (particularly British) perfidy. It is not clear how far Sharif Husain was aware of the general principles of Sykes-Picot when he made his own agreement. However, whatever the motives behind the rival schemes, of greater significance was that the arrangements which actually materialised approximated more to Sykes-Picot than to McMahon-Husain. The matter was further complicated by another undertaking, the Balfour Declaration of 2 November 1917, under which Britain promised to facilitate 'the establishment in Palestine of a national home for the Jewish people' (p.308).

The war ended with Allied (almost entirely British) troops in occupation of most of the region. During and after it, in the course of the various peace conferences and in response to American and other pressures, the idea of direct colonial rule was discarded in favour of the mandate system, a form of international tutelage, which was to be supervised by the newly constituted League of Nations. The people of the region were not consulted as to the form of government they wished to have, and only very perfunctorily as to which power they wished to run their affairs. Article 22 of the League of Nations Charter reads:

> 'Certain communities formerly belonging to the Turkish Empire have reached a stage of their development where their existence as independent nations can be provisionally recognised subject to the rendering of administrative advice and assistance by a mandatory, until such time as they are able to stand alone.'

Naturally, any such 'advice' had to be taken. Britain took over Iraq, Palestine and Transjordan, while France took Syria and Lebanon. The mandated states were colonies in all but name. In Palestine the problems were exacerbated by the conflicts between Arabs and Jews which resulted from attempts to implement simultaneously the Balfour Declaration and the mandate. All that was left of the 'independent Arab state' was the short-lived Kingdom of the Hijaz, which was absorbed into what is now Saudi Arabia in 1925.

The inter-war period

The inter-war period saw the new political order widely contested in the Arab world. The mandate regimes were generally unpopular, especially in Syria and Palestine. In Iraq, after having set up a compliant government, the British felt able to make a formal withdrawal in 1932, although real independence was not obtained until 1958. In Palestine, there was mounting tension between the Arab population and the Jewish settlers, who formed 11% of the population in 1922 and 29% by 1936. (In 1939, Britain announced that Jewish immigration would be allowed to reach a certain ceiling and must then cease, which was seen as criminally generous by the Arabs and criminally restrictive by the Zionists.) In Syria and Lebanon, the French were welcomed by the Maronites and the other Catholic Christians (*see* Chapter 7, Lebanon) but by few others, since the new Lebanon had been carved out of Syria. In 1925–27 there was a major national rising in Syria, which the French had considerable difficulty in controlling; expectations were raised with the victory of the Popular Front government in France in 1936, although negotiations ceased when it fell, and independence was not to be granted until 1946.

Egypt escaped the mandate system, but had become a British protectorate. At the end of the First World War, a group of politicians wanted to send a delegation (*wafd*) to the Paris peace conference under the leadership of Sa'd Zaghlul. When permission was refused, there was a widespread rising in March 1919. In 1922, however, Britain agreed to a limited form of Egyptian independence, under which Britain retained ultimate control over four 'reserved points': the security of communications of the British Empire; defence; the protection of the interests of minorities and foreign powers; and matters relating to the Sudan. The Wafd won an overwhelming victory whenever there were free elections, but was never free to implement popular demands. Although an Anglo–Egyptian treaty enabling Egypt to enter the League of Nations as an independent state was signed in 1936, all but the third of the 'reserved points' remained. Indeed, there was a large British military presence in Egypt up to and even beyond the moment when Nasser seized power in 1952, when Egypt at last became fully independent.

Inevitably, Middle East politics underwent a series of important changes in the inter-war period. The struggles for local autonomy of the pre-war years gave way to a prolonged anti-colonial struggle against Britain and France and their local clients, who were running the governments in many of the new states. A new form of Arab nationalism developed, with appeals to the glorious Arab past and to an Arab world divided by British and French imperialism yet united by a common language and heritage. The anti-colonial struggle was temporarily halted by the Second World War, in which the Arab states generally supported the Allies, particularly after the Soviet Union joined the Allies in 1941. In the decades after the war the influence of France and Britain in the region gradually declined, to be replaced by that of the United States and the Soviet Union.

Although Iraq became nominally independent in 1932, Egypt in 1936, and Syria and Lebanon in 1936, strong economic and military ties bound the various states to their former European rulers. Further, though the constitutional arrangements of the new states were based on European models, they rarely extended to European political freedoms. Elections, for example, were rigged. Similarly, imprisonment without trial and the torture of political offenders (for the most part those suspected of 'communism', but also members of Muslim fundamentalist groups, particularly in Egypt, where the Muslim Brotherhood were founded in 1929) were not uncommon. At the same time, however, the establishment of national armies and easier access to education in almost all the states of the Middle East had the effect of creating a new and influential social group. Imbued with notions of social justice and national independence (and, in time, anti-Zionism), it is perhaps not surprising that many of its members came to believe that only a revolutionary break with colonialism would bring about genuine independence.

The revolutions of the 1950s

The first revolution came in 1952 in Egypt. It was masterminded, like so many of its successors in other Arab states, by disaffected elements in the armed forces. Like his Iraqi contemporary 'Abd al-Karim Qasim, Nasser was an army officer from a lower middle-class background, who had gained a commission in the new-style national army in the 1930s. Nasser's original intention seems to have been to force a radical change in the direction of Egyptian politics and then to return to the barracks, but it gradually became clear, at least to him, that his continued presence at the helm was indispensable. He remained in power until his death in 1970. His political philosophy was vague, pragmatic and somewhat naive. He believed that once liberated from the shackles of imperialism Egypt would be able to pursue her own destiny independent of power blocs and alliances. His practical solutions for Egypt's immense problems were somewhat amateur, and his early reform programmes for agriculture and industry showed evidence of hasty and inadequate preparation.

Nevertheless, Nasser managed to win the hearts if not the minds of many Egyptians and other Arabs by his populist rhetoric and by his appeal for a united front against colonialism and Zionism. Even though recent studies have shown that the middle classes rather than the very poor were the main beneficiaries of Nasser's domestic policies, it is clear that Nasser initiated a major turning point in modern Arab history. Syria, Iraq, Algeria and South Yemen went through comparable changes in the 1950s and 1960s.

Much of the early enthusiasm on which Nasser was able to capitalise derived from his emphasis on Arab unity, the premise that once the 'Arab nation' was free of colonialism and Zionism and (re)united in a single political entity, the Arabs would be able to resume their historic destiny. This powerful notion lies at the heart of both Ba'thism and Nasserism, though it largely ignores the considerable social, economic and political differences that exist within and between the various Arab states. Naturally, an internal social transformation that would have required coming to terms with the inequalities, problems and tensions within Egyptian society would have been harder to achieve—as well as much less immediately palatable—than some lofty concept of a single Arab world.

After the death of Stalin in 1953, the Soviet Union began to adopt new attitudes towards what it now regarded as potentially friendly or neutral regimes. In the Middle East, this signified the beginning of a period of superpower tension and rivalry, but it also gave a certain amount of freedom of manoeuvre to various Arab leaders who could now sometimes play the superpowers off against each other. Determined to get the best deal possible for Egypt, Nasser moved to take advantage of this new situation. In 1954 Britain and the United States, with whom Nasser was still on reasonably cordial terms, had offered Egypt a substantial development loan and the promise of further finance for the construction of the Aswan dam. However, the price was Egyptian involvement in the collective security arrangement known as the Baghdad Pact. This Nasser was not prepared to entertain. After a particularly audacious raid on Egypt by Israeli forces early in 1955, Nasser, using Czechoslovakia as an intermediary, entered arms negotiations with the Soviet Union. In September the 'Czech arms deal' was concluded. The United States and Britain refused further aid. Relations deteriorated. In July 1956, Nasser played his trump card: he nationalised and closed the Suez Canal. In response, Britain and France, with the covert assistance of Israel, invaded Egypt. Isolated diplomatically–the adventure incurred particular disapproval from the United States–and able to make only marginal military gains, France and Britain were forced to withdraw almost at once. For Britain in particular, it was a profoundly humiliating exercise.

Along with most of the 'revolutionary states' in their turn, Nasser's Egypt eventually became almost completely dependent on the Soviet Union for arms supplies and for certain other forms of aid. Through one of the peculiar paradoxes of Middle East politics, however cordial Nasser's relations with the Soviet Union, communists continued to be persecuted. Much the same was true for Iraq and, to a lesser extent, for Syria throughout the 1960s and 1970s. In addition, political and military ties with the Soviet Union did not rule out substantial trading relations with the United States and other Western countries.

Palestine, Israel and the Arab–Israeli conflict

The presence of Israel, and its implications for its neighbours and the Palestinians, is probably the single most intractable problem of the Middle East in the 20th century. The notion of a Jewish state dates from the late 19th century, a time of emergent nationalism in Europe generally, and which coincided with the increasing persecution of Eastern European Jews. Migration to Palestine had begun in the late 19th century, and by 1914 the Jewish population of Palestine was about 75,000 out of a total population of 750,000 to 800,000. The Arab population were mostly peasant cultivators, although the small cities of Jerusalem, Nablus, Hebron, Jaffa and Acre probably accounted for about a quarter of the total population.

Zionist lobbying in Britain and the friendship between the head of the Zionist organisation, Chaim Weizmann, and the politician A. J. Balfour were largely responsible for the issue of the Balfour Declaration in 1917. The Declaration was of course incompatible with the various promises made to the Arabs, and the smooth implementation of the Palestine mandate, which came into force in 1923, proved impossible. In the late 1920s there was some hope that the problem might disappear: in 1927 more Jews left Palestine than entered it, but Hitler's rise to power in the early 1930s encouraged an enormous exodus of Jews from Eastern and Central Europe, many of whom made for Palestine. Between 1917 and 1948, when Britain finally left Palestine, there was little hope for a peaceful solution. The Arabs saw the Balfour Declaration as a monstrous imposition, fearing the effect of the incursion of hundreds of thousands of Europeans into their country, and also resented the land acquisitions of the Jewish Agency, although virtually all the land was purchased from absentee Arab landlords over the heads of the cultivators. For their part, the Jewish population of Palestine in the pre-holocaust period attempted to cooperate as far as possible with Britain while vigorously pressing for the right to unlimited immigration. The Arabs, meanwhile, refused any cooperation that might imply any legality for the British presence.

The climax came in 1947–48, when elements of the Jewish population, impatient at Britain's procrastination, attempted to force the issue by launching attacks on British troops and Arab and British civilians. In November 1947 the United Nations resolved on the partition of Palestine into Arab and Jewish areas; Britain announced that she would evacuate by 15 May 1948. In the early months of 1948 Jewish guerrilla forces began terrorist attacks on Arab communities, driving the Arab population from the area, a policy which, together with the war which followed, resulted in some 900,000 Palestinian refugees outside the state of Israel by 1949. As the evacuation date drew nearer, more fighting broke out. On 14 May an Arab army, composed of Egyptian, Iraqi, Jordanian, and Syrian forces moved in to defend Palestine against the Zionist army. Though superior in numbers, the Arabs were badly equipped, poorly co-ordinated and poorly led. The war ended with half of Jerusalem in Israeli hands, and an Israeli state rather larger that the original mandated territory of Palestine.

For reasons similar to those preventing an amicable settlement before the end of the mandate, no comprehensive peace agreement has been reached over the four decades since 1948. Apart from Egypt, which recognised Israel in 1978, no Arab state accepted Israel's right to exist as a political entity until the Palestinian National Council's acceptance of UN Resolution 242 (see below) in November 1988. The Arab states always feared that one of their number would do what Egypt in fact did, that is, split Arab ranks and make a separate peace. For its part Israel refused to discuss the problem of the refugees or compensation for them or to acknowledge the existence of the Palestinians as a political entity until

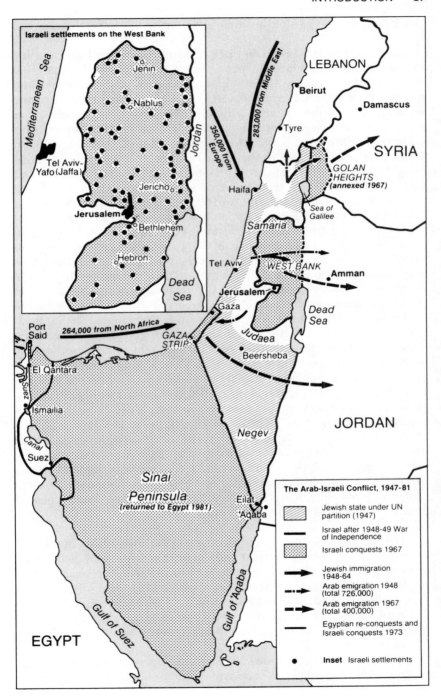

Israeli settlements on the West Bank

Mediterranean Sea

Jenin

Nablus

Tel Aviv-Yafo (Jaffa)

Jericho

Jerusalem

Bethlehem

Hebron

Jordan

Dead Sea

LEBANON

Beirut

Damascus

283,000 from Middle East

350,000 from Europe

Tyre

SYRIA

Haifa

GOLAN HEIGHTS (annexed 1967)

Sea of Galilee

Samaria

WEST BANK

Amman

Tel Aviv

Jerusalem

Dead Sea

Gaza

Judaea

Port Said

264,000 from North Africa

GAZA STRIP

Beersheba

El Qantara

Ismailia

Suez Canal

Suez

Negev

JORDAN

Sinai Peninsula (returned to Egypt 1981)

Eilat
Aqaba

Gulf of Suez

Gulf of Aqaba

EGYPT

The Arab-Israeli Conflict, 1947-81

Jewish state under UN partition (1947)

Israel after 1948-49 War of Independence

Israeli conquests 1967

Jewish immigration 1948-64

Arab emigration 1948 (total 726,000)

Arab emigration 1967 (total 400,000)

Egyptian re-conquests and Israeli conquests 1973

● **Inset** Israeli settlements

Israel itself was recognised as a sovereign state by its neighbours and belligerents.

Thus three wars have taken place since 1948 between Israel and the various Arab states. In 1956, Egypt refused passage through the Suez canal and the Gulf of 'Aqaba to Israeli shipping and ships bound for Israel, and when Nasser nationalised the canal, Israel took part in the tripartite invasion. In the spring of 1967, with a particularly radical government in power in Syria, Nasser came under increasing pressure to demonstrate his leadership of the Arab world. He closed the Gulf of 'Aqaba again, and asked for the withdrawal of the United Nations peace-keeping force in Sinai. On 5 June Israel launched a pre-emptive strike on Egypt, Syria and Jordan. Most of the Egyptian air force was destroyed on the ground, and Israel took possession of the Golan Heights, Sinai, the Gaza Strip, and Jordanian territory west of the Jordan River, including Arab Jerusalem.

This crushing defeat had a devastating effect upon the Arab world. In particular, it gave new impetus to the Palestinians, many of whom interpreted it as a clear indication that their salvation lay in their own hands rather than in the hands of the leaders of the Arab states. In 1968 the Palestine Liberation Organisation (PLO), founded under Nasser's aegis in 1964, was taken over by al-Fatah, the largest of its members, under the leadership of Yasir Arafat. The PLO began to launch guerrilla raids on Israel from camps in Lebanon and Jordan, acting very much as a state within a state, and through their political and military activities, greatly alarming the host countries. The Palestinians, in general highly politicised, posed a major threat to the stability of the right-wing and pro-Western regimes in Lebanon and Jordan in particular. One consequence was the expulsion of the PLO from Jordan in 1970; another was that the Palestinian presence in Lebanon was to be a major factor in the Lebanese civil war.

A further consequence of the 1967 war was the decision on the part of the richer Arab countries to subsidise the 'front-line' states, namely Jordan, Egypt and Syria. At the Khartoum conference in September 1967 Saudi Arabia and Kuwait agreed to pay £540 million annually to these states. In November 1967 the United Nations Security Council passed Resolution 242, which ended the conflict:

'The Security Council . . . Emphasising the inadmissibility of the acquisition of territory by war and the need to work for a just and lasting peace in which every state in the area can live in security . . . Affirms that the fulfilment of Charter principles requires the establishment of a just and lasting peace in the Middle East which should include the application of the following principles.
(1) Withdrawal of Israeli armed forces from territories occupied in the recent conflict;
(2) Termination of all claims or states of belligerency and respect for and acknowledgement of the sovereignty, territorial integrity and

political independence of every state in the area and their right to live in peace within secure and recognised boundaries free from threats of acts of force . . .'

As a result of the Six Day War, Israel greatly increased its territories, and secured very substantial military assistance from the United States over the next decades. It also acquired an extra one-and-a-half million Arab population, and began to build Jewish settlements on the West Bank, mostly on confiscated land, to the intense fury and frustration of its inhabitants. However, 1967 was not followed by negotiations, nor by peace, and tensions continued. On 6 October 1973, the myth of Israeli invincibility was successfully if not decisively challenged when Egypt and Syria unexpectedly attacked Israel. The Arab states were not victorious (in the sense that they were not able to force a settlement upon Israel), but more aid was forthcoming to the front-line states, and a new bargaining counter, the threat to withdraw or decrease oil supplies, made its first appearance. By 22 October the United Nations had organised a cease-fire, which was accepted by Israel, Egypt and Syria; Security Council Resolution 338 set up a peace conference at which the belligerents along with Jordan, the United States and the Soviet Union–but not the PLO–were to be represented. The conference met once, at Geneva on 21 December.

In the course of the 1970s there were important but generally inconclusive developments in the conflict. In October 1974, the PLO was recognised at Rabat as the 'sole legitimate representative of the Palestinian people', which gave Arafat the right to negotiate on the Palestinians' behalf wherever such negotiations might take place, although this function was not recognised as such either by Israel or any Western state. After the 1973 war, President Sadat of Egypt began a process of step-by-step negotiations with Israel through the medium of Henry Kissinger, the United States secretary of state, who was virtually negotiating on Israel's behalf. As a result of his efforts the Geneva Conference was adjourned indefinitely, and the Soviet Union excluded from the peace process. Although President Carter expressed initial willingness to include the Palestinians in any Middle East settlement, his efforts were stalled, first by the election of a right-wing Israeli government under Menachim Begin in May 1977, subsequently in November 1977 when Sadat flew to Jerusalem to deal directly with Israel. This was followed by the Camp David Agreement in 1978 and the Egyptian–Israeli peace treaty of March 1979, which removed Egypt from the Arab–Israeli conflict without securing any concessions from Israel on the future status of the populations of the West Bank, Gaza and East Jerusalem.

One major consequence of Egypt's withdrawal (which was visible from the time of the disengagement agreements in 1974–75) was that the already unequal balance of forces between Israel and the Arabs became further distorted. In addition, a variety of other factors combined to initiate a civil war in Lebanon, where the PLO had made its headquarters after its expulsion from Jordan in 1970–71 (*see* Chapter 6, Jordan, and Chapter 7, Lebanon). Israel took the Syrian invasion and occupation of parts of Lebanon in the summer of 1976 as a pretext to extend its own influence in south Lebanon (from where the PLO had been launching raids and rocket attacks into Israel), and consolidated its position there with a proxy army in the south after a full-scale invasion of the area in March 1978. In the summer of 1982, Israel invaded Lebanon again, advancing as far as Beirut in an attempt to destroy the PLO completely and to install a government which would do its bidding. These objectives were only partially realised, as the PLO was able to withdraw its surviving forces to new headquarters in Tunis, and Bashir Jumayyil, the Israelis' candidate for the Lebanese presidency, turned out to be less pliable than they had anticipated. Jumayyil's assassination was followed by the massacre of thousands of unarmed Palestinians in the Sabra and Chatila refugee camps. Israel withdrew formally from Lebanon in September 1983, while maintaining its 'South Lebanese Army' under a former Lebanese army general.

By 1986, United States' aid to Israel was running at $3.7 billion annually, while Egypt received $2.7 billion. In addition, in spite of various alliances, treaties of friendship and other agreements between the Soviet Union and several Arab states since the mid-1950s, and however much the Soviet Union might rail against the United States, it had been clear at least as early as 1973 that the Soviet Union would not, ultimately, assist the Arab states to defeat Israel or even encourage any state or combination of states to inflict very serious damage on Israel.

Throughout the 1980s various peace plans were put forward, most of which were frustrated by Israeli unwillingness to recognise or negotiate with the PLO and by the preoccupations of Arab leaders both with maintaining themselves in power and the ramifications first of the Iranian revolution and then of the Iran–Iraq War. No sustained pressure could be put on Israel; Syria remained belligerent but ineffectual and a long-standing personal hostility between Asad and Arafat resulted in the departure of the PLO from the camps in Tripoli, its last stronghold in Lebanon, in 1984. By 1985 Jordan and the PLO appeared to be coming to a settlement of their differences and considering a joint approach to Israel that might isolate Syria further. The latter eventuality was averted by Syrian pressure, but Palestinian and Jordanian relations with Syria remained strained. In July 1988 it was announced that Jordan was planning to cut all legal and administrative ties with the West Bank, highlighting the PLO's independent status.

In December 1987 the movement known as the *intifada* or uprising began in the Gaza Strip. Broadly speaking, this took the form of a campaign of unarmed civil disobedience, including strikes, shop closures, and the resignation of police, civil servants and others employed by the Israeli administration in the Occupied Territories. It has also involved violence, on the part of children and adolescents throwing stones at Israeli soldiers, and about 980 Palestinians killed by Israeli security forces since it began. It has certainly galvanised and given new momentum to the Palestinians in the Occupied Territories, but by the time of the invasion of Kuwait in the summer of 1990 it seemed to be running out of steam, in the sense that the Israelis had learned how to control it and seemed more or less impervious to the international criticism which their repressive tactics were provoking. In addition, Israel had not responded positively to the Palestine National Council's acceptance of UN Resolution 242 in November 1988, a decision which included the recognition of Israel and the renunciation of terrorism. At the time of writing (March 1992) it is at least possible that the beginnings of a solution may be in sight. All the belligerents, together with representatives of the Palestinians, have met together several times, if inconclusively, in Madrid, Washington and Moscow, while the collapse of the Soviet Union as a superpower has meant that there is no longer advantage to be gained by American and Soviet proxies scoring points in the region on each other's behalf. Perhaps it is not too optimistic to discern some faint glimmering of light at the end of this particular long dark tunnel.

Islamic Revival

The spread of literacy, increasingly wider access to education and the growth of modern communications networks had a swift and dynamic impact on Middle Eastern society in the first half of the 20th century. Traditional pathways to power were modified or blocked, and new ones came into being. In the inter-war and immediately post-1945 periods, the Arab world and Iran experienced great ferment; new classes and new political institutions came into existence, and there were growing pressures for an end to foreign rule, and for wider and more meaningful political participation. Several political movements emerged: leftist/communist; Arab nationalist; nationalist (in the sense of movements expressing 'Iraq for the Iraqis' or 'Egypt for the Egyptians'); quasi-fascist; and religious. In broad terms, apart from the Muslim Brotherhood, most political movements were avowedly secular, although 'secularism' has manifested itself rather differently in the Islamic Middle East than it has in Europe.

The 1950s in particular were years of hope for the future. The rise of Nasser and the triumph of his early years—his rejection of the West, his embrace of neutrality and his championship of a united Arab world—seemed to herald a new era. Furthermore, the potential of 'socialism', or state-sponsored economic development, together with the friendship of the Soviet Union and the possibilities held out by increasing oil revenues, gave new confidence. The reality, above in the shape of the crushing defeat in the Six Day War, was infinitely less inspiring. Faced by a dispiriting combination of determined opposition by Israel and the United States and opportunism, ineptitude and increasing despotism of their rulers, the peoples of the region gradually discovered that rhetoric was no substitute for the less glamorous struggle against poverty and human degradation.

Between the early 1960s and the mid-1970s, Arab rulers tried a variety of expedients, ranging from the nationalisation of key sectors of the economy to the reintroduction of *laissez-faire* economics, all with the goal of 'development'. Arab nationalism, pan-Arabism, Arab socialism and even Islamic socialism were the labels for a host of piecemeal solutions that had little effect on the region's most intractable social problems; urban drift, rural decline, the Palestine problem, the Lebanese civil war, the weakening of moral and religious values in the face of an almost mindless consumerism, a sense of bewilderment and deracination.

Politically, this was accompanied by the rapid growth of military forces, with poor states spending large proportions of their GNP on armaments, and of unrepresentative governments propped up by ruthless security establishments. Such democracy as there had been in the region had largely disappeared by the end of the 1950s. Most Middle Eastern states were ruled either by family oligarchies or forms of populist dictatorship. The result was a gradual alienation of the mass of the populations from their government, the sense that government was beyond the control of ordinary individuals, above all that it was frequently corrupt, arbitrary and oppressive. In addition, the absolute power of the state, reinforced either by indigenous oil wealth or aid from oil-rich neighbours, prevented the growth of authentic political movements; the political arena was appropriated by the state, with the result that political activity was either opportunistic, in the service of the state, or, if in opposition to it, extremely dangerous.

In this atmosphere of resignation, 'Islam' seemed to offer another way. The various ideologies seemed to have failed either because they were imported, and thus had no local resonance, or, particularly in the context of communism or socialism, because they were atheist or propounded by atheists. One answer was to reject the seductions of the West (or the communist East) and to return to 'true Islam', which was familiar, part of the social fabric and, because of its moral framework, informs the values of practically all the inhabitants of the region. In addition, many of those who embraced secular ideologies retained their Islamic beliefs: the (Christian) founder of Ba'thism, Michel 'Aflaq, wrote that Arab nationalism and religion are not incompatible since both 'spring from the heart and are issued by the will of God.' Finally, for all that they claimed to be guided by secular values, none of the regimes in the region except Turkey is explicitly secular: with the exception of Lebanon (which is also not a secular state) all state constitutions, however otherwise disregarded, contain clauses to the effect that Islam is the religion of the state and that the president must be a Muslim. Although the various Middle Eastern regimes were both worried by and attempted to control manifestations of Islamic sentiment when 'political Islam' became a major force in the 1970s, it is almost inconceivable that they would have banned or otherwise restricted such activities as public worship in mosques.

Given the immensity of the problems, it is hardly surprising that those who advocate an 'Islamic solution' do not themselves have ready answers to them. Here it is worth attempting to correct, or at least to mention some important misconceptions. In the first place, although Islam has rightly been characterised as being 'both religion and state', the 'state' in this context means the universal Islamic state rather than the national states of our own time, which the first Muslims neither knew nor could have anticipated. Secondly, there is very little in the way of 'political theory' within the traditional Islamic canon; neither the prophet nor his near contemporaries had much to say about government as such. For good or ill, the tradition is virtually silent on such matters as statecraft, diplomacy, the mutual obligations of ruler and ruled, lawful resistance to injustice and oppression and other ethical-political topics. In consequence, Islamic fundamentalist activists (such as those who assassinated President Sadat of Egypt in 1981) do not generally have a detailed blueprint for the kind of society that they would like to substitute for, say, contemporary Egyptian society, however eloquent they may be in their condemnation of 'present ills.' Of much practical significance is Islamic law, an exhaustive guide to life and conduct, and the means through which man's relations both with God and with his fellow men are regulated. In the words of one noted commentator, the role of the 'Islamic state' is the 'collective enforcement of public morals'.

Iran and the Iranian revolution

Although the Iranian revolution can obviously be attributed to many of the causes mentioned above, certain features unique to Iran and Shiism make it unlikely that it will be the pattern for similar events elsewhere. In the Sunni Muslim world in modern times, the 'clergy' have generally acted both as the exponents of Islamic orthodoxy and as the mouthpiece of governments. In contrast, the Shia clergy have always enjoyed a much more independent and critical role. Nonetheless, the perceived legitimacy of the state and its actions requires, to a greater or lesser extent, the consent or validation of the clergy. By implication, the capacity to confer legitimacy on the clergy's part includes the right to withdraw it, and the right to criticise the state. In addition, and strengthening further the independence of the clergy, it is a matter of some importance that the leading shrines of Shia Islam are in Iraq, and thus outside the political control of the rulers of Iran.

In the late 19th and early 20th centuries, when the British and the Russians were vying for influence over the Iranian Qajar shahs, the clergy were in the forefront of the opposition, both to the state's cravenness in giving in to the foreigners, and in attempting to limit the shah's absolutism. Thus in 1891–92 the clergy joined with merchants to organise a successful ban on the sale of tobacco, in protest against a monopoly granted to an Englishman. They were also prominent in the Constitutional Revolution of 1905–6, which resulted in the grant of a parliamentary assembly by the shah.

In the chaos that followed the end of the First World War, Reza Khan, the leader of the Cossack brigade, the only organised military force in the country, seized power. After crushing tribal opposition and deposing the last of the Qajars, in 1925 he had himself proclaimed shah. Reza Shah faced daunting obstacles, since Iran had not undergone a period of reform comparable with that in the Ottoman Empire. The authority of the central government was not universally recognised, and there was no standing army or universal system of taxation. Like his contemporary Atatürk, Reza Shah was a dictator; he, too, tried to impose secularism, though generally with less success. He was succeeded in 1941 by his son Mohammed Reza, then aged 21. The next decade saw a flowering of political activity in which leftists and nationalists allied again with religious leaders against the monarchy, although the national movement was checked by the overthrow of the popular prime minister, Mohammed Mosaddeq, in a coup engineered by the CIA in 1953. For the next 26 years, Mohammed Reza Shah presided over a highly unstable dictatorship, enjoying close relations with Israel and with the United States. In the late 1950s and early 1960s the shah introduced a land reform and female suffrage. Both outraged religious conservatives, who were led by Ayatollah Khomeini. In 1963 Khomeini was arrested; the following year he was deported.

During the rest of his reign, and particularly after the increase in oil prices after 1973, the shah attempted to modernise Iran at great speed, but although living standards rose inflation soared, and rapid rural to urban migration severely disrupted both agriculture and urban life. Large numbers of Europeans, Americans and Japanese came to work on contracts in Iran, and the influx of Western habits and consumer goods in a country that had only recently been exposed to Western penetration on such a scale produced severe dislocations. In addition, the shah's pivotal role as one of the United States' principal allies in the Middle East made him highly unpopular. Once more, criticism of the government came from the clergy, including Khomeini, who spent the years between 1964 and October 1978 in the Iraqi shrine city of Najaf. The storm of protest grew in the latter part of the 1970s, particularly after Jimmy Carter, who became president of the United States in 1976, took public exception to Iran's dismal human rights record.

Matters came to a head in 1978, when demonstrators in Qom and other cities were fired on by armed police and many thousands were killed. The opposition began to call for the overthrow of the shah and the return of Khomeini, now exiled in France. On 16 January 1979 the shah went into exile; on 1 February, Khomeini returned to Tehran. Over the next few months Khomeini and his supporters maintained the initiative they had seized in the last months of the shah's reign, and set up the Islamic

Republic of Iran by a referendum on 1 April 1979, in the face of opposition both from more moderate members of the religious establishment and from liberals and leftists. Although Khomeini did not take personal charge, he became *vali-i faqih*, or trustee of religious law. He held that in the absence of the Twelfth Imam—the mahdi or redeemer—the clergy must establish a system for the implementation of Islamic law. This was a major innovation: no previous Islamic regime had insisted that the clergy them-selves should rule the state. In Khomeini's view, according to one authority, 'a just and learned jurisconsult with administrative abilities has the same authority as the Prophet Mohammed in administering society.'

As the Islamic Republic began to establish itself, a campaign against those associated with the former regime was mounted. Figures vary, but the most conservative sources estimate that by 1985 at least 4,000 had been executed and 20,000 imprisoned. At the same time, many of the govern-ment's supporters were killed by its opponents. There were also struggles for power within the government, symbolised by the disagreements over the seizure of the United States' Embassy in Tehran on 4 November 1979. The (relatively) liberal cabinet was then forced to give up its power to an Islamic Revolutionary Council. In retaliation, over $10 billion of Iran's assets in the United States were seized and economic sanctions were declared. Also under prompting from the United States, Iran's diplomatic standing was severely damaged. The regime's radicalism united Western opinion forces against it, and created an atmosphere in which few protests were made when Iraq invaded south-west Iran in September 1980. By then, in the eyes of many Arab states as well as to the West, the Iranian revolution had developed into a 'menace to the security of the region'. Iraq was regarded as performing a valuable service by keeping it in check.

To an important extent, the eight-year Iran–Iraq War eventually united the various factions within the country, although serious differences of principle continued. Khomeini's authority was challenged by the more moderate President Bani Sadr, who was supported by the Mojahedin-e Khalq, a Muslim guerrilla organisation founded to fight the shah in the early 1960s. In the course of 1981, many senior members of the Islamic Republican party were killed in bomb attacks attributed to, if not always carried out by, the Mojahedin. However, by the middle 1980s the Islamic Republic was more securely established; repression continued, but on a greatly diminished scale. In addition, a measure of continuity has been preserved at the top in that four key figures, the president, Ayatollah Khamenei'i, the prime minister, Husain Musavi, the speaker of the *majlis* (parliament), Hojjat al-Islam Rafsanjani, and the foreign minister, Ali Akbar Velayati, have held these or other senior offices from 1981 until the time of writing.

The war continued until 18 July 1988, when Iran accepted UN Resolu-tion 598, which had called for an immediate cease-fire. Khomeini himself died a year later. Well before his death, however, there were signs that the extremism and radicalism of the post-revolutionary period had been modified in favour of a less ideological approach. Apart from its influence among Lebanese Shias, fears that the revolution would find an echo in other Muslim states, particularly Iraq, had proved largely groundless, partly because of the Iran–Iraq War, partly because of the very specific quality of Iranian Shiism and partly because of its Iranian nationalist colouration.

In addition, the government of the Islamic Republic found it increasingly difficult to find 'Islamic solutions' to economic and social problems. Attempts at land reform, for example, foundered on divisions between those who stressed a more egalitarian society and those who stressed the sanctity of property in Islam. Again, calls from Islamic radicals for Iran to side with Iraq against the coalition forces after Iraq's invasion of Kuwait in August 1990 fell largely on deaf ears; the Iranian regime understood that it was closely dependent on the good will and cooperation of the West to secure the economic recovery desperately needed after the upheavals of the previous decade.

The Iran–Iraq War

The war between Iran and Iraq was one of the most costly and futile conflicts of the 20th century. It is difficult to arrive at a reliable estimate of casualties. Perhaps as many as 400,000 people were killed and 750,000 injured. The war stemmed from two fundamental miscalculations on Saddam Husain's part. In the first place, he evidently feared the potential encouragement the Iranian revolution might give to Iraq's Shia population. Secondly, it was widely believed that the Iranian armed forces had been reduced to such a state of disarray by the revolution that Iraq would have no difficulty in gaining an easy victory. Underpinning these pragmatic considerations was Saddam Husain's overweening ambition to make himself leader of the Arab world, and, if less explicitly, the West's gendarme in the Gulf.

In the event, although Iran was eventually forced to concede defeat, Iraq's victory was largely technical, and was in any case virtually nullified by the consequences of its invasion of Kuwait two years later. In fact, the longer the war dragged out, the more it favoured Iran. Iraq's 'triumph' came as a result of a combination of French weaponry, United States' naval and military assistance and support from the Soviet Union, all of which became decisive between early 1986 (when Iraq appeared very likely to lose) and the end of the war. Iran has more than three times the population of Iraq; the two countries share a common frontier over 800-miles long, and, apart from the oil fields, most major targets within Iran are a considerable distance from the frontier.

The war began in September 1980 when Saddam Husain announced the abrogation of the Algiers Agreement, which he had signed with the shah in 1975, thereby implicitly claiming the disputed Shatt al-'Arab waterway. Iraqi forces invaded Iran and remained on Iranian territory until they were forced out in the summer of 1982. The war then shifted to Iraq, where all the fighting took place until August 1986. For the Iranians, the war was represented as the struggle of Islam against unbelief, the great Satan in Baghdad; for Iraq, its troops were fighting the Iranian threat to the Arab nation, the Arabian Gulf, the Arabian peninsula, and, somewhat more incongruously, Zionism and its Iranian collaborators.

Immense damage was caused to the infrastructure in both countries. It is difficult to gauge the extent of domestic opposition to it, particularly in Iraq, where the personality cult around Saddam Husain and the repressive tactics of the regime both greatly increased. By August 1983 Iraq's foreign-exchange reserves had almost disappeared, and it became dependent on handouts from Saudi Arabia, Kuwait, and the other Gulf states. Although there were efforts at external mediation, one somewhat Machiavellian factor should not be overlooked: in a world where oil prices were falling dramatically, it was scarcely a matter of urgency to the other oil exporters or to the major companies that production in two of the region's main producing states should be restored to pre-1980 levels.

Although the war ended officially in July 1988, no settlement had been reached by August 1990. A few days after the invasion of Kuwait, Saddam Husain offered Iran a full settlement based on the implementation of Resolution 598 and the restoration of the Algiers Agreement of March 1975, which Iran accepted, although, apart from exchanges of prisoners, there has been little in the way of concrete progress since. On the other hand the removal of the military threat to Iran is probably sufficient to calm Iranian apprehensions for the time being; in addition, Iran has shown no signs of being in a hurry to return to their rightful owners the Iraqi military aircraft flown to Iranian air bases at the beginning of the Gulf War.

Once the threat of 'exporting Islamic revolution' had begun to recede, the war between Iran and Iraq generally ceased to engage the active attention of most of the other states in the region. Indeed, many neighbouring states, while deploring the conflict, either (in the case of the oil states) regarded bankrolling Iraq as a price they would grudgingly be prepared to pay or (in the case of many of the others) were evidently not averse to profiting from it. Thus Turkey's agricultural exports to both sides increased considerably; the Jordanian economy was also boosted by sales of agricultural produce, but even more so by transit dues from the port of 'Aqaba. There was also substantial road construction to facilitate the transport of Iraqi goods. Egypt, still ostracised in the Arab world because of Camp David, edged its way back to respectability under Mubarak, exporting several hundred-thousand workers to Iraq to take the place of the men at the front and providing Iraq with much-needed spare parts for its Soviet-made weaponry.

Syria alone of the Arab states maintained a passive alliance with Iran (in the sense of siding with Iran without taking an active part against Iraq), played host to various factions of the Iraqi opposition, and generally consolidated its own position in Lebanon. However, a major and damaging consequence of the Iran–Iraq War as far as the Palestinians and Lebanon was concerned was its effect in distracting attention from the Arab–Israeli conflict; although other factors were also at work, this preoccupation partly explains the lack of response from the Arab states to the Israeli invasion of Beirut in 1982, and the relegation of the Palestinian question to the back-burner for much of the 1980s.

The invasion of Kuwait and its aftermath

The invasion of Kuwait can be seen as emanating from the folly and the ambition of Saddam Husain, but it also both highlighted and reflected the decline of the Soviet Union as a world power. It is a measure of Saddam Husain's isolation and lack of judgment that he did not immediately realise that such excesses as the annexation of an oil state would not be tolerated by the major consumers of oil, and that his neighbours would not willingly condone such an infringement of territorial sovereignty. Indeed he himself had declared in an interview in Fez–actually on the question of the Iraqi–Kuwaiti border–on 8 September 1982 that

'Arab unity can only take place after a clear demarcation of borders between all countries . . . The Arab reality is that the Arabs are now 22 states and we have to behave accordingly. Therefore, unity must not be imposed, but must be achieved through common mutual opinion.'

It may be that he was sufficiently out of touch with reality to believe that his military might was sufficient to ward off any possible challenge. In any case, no Arab government threw itself wholeheartedly behind Iraq while some joined the United States-led coalition ranged against it.

The result of the fighting was a foregone conclusion, although it must be underlined that there was no sense in which the war itself was inevitable; Saddam Husain could have withdrawn from Kuwait at any time, and the war could have been averted. However cynical some of the real intentions of the West may have been, a stream of high-level politicians from all over the world paid visits to Baghdad in an attempt to avert what they saw as a certain catastrophe. The invasion was not a popular cause in Iraq, its population exhausted after eight years of fighting Iran. However, the aftermath of the Gulf War demonstrated either the gullibility, the indecision or the criminal irresponsibility of the coalition, whose troops were not prepared or permitted to come to the aid of those popular uprisings in Kurdistan and the south of Iraq which were savagely put down by Saddam Husain's Popular Army. Apparently fearful of 'chaos' or the dismemberment of Iraq, they seem to prefer the maintenance of a weakened Saddam Husain in power to the establishment of a representative or at least potentially democratic regime in Iraq.

The Future

Clearly, it is much safer to analyse the past than to predict the future. However, it may not be inappropriate to suggest ways in which the Middle East might develop in the aftermath of the Gulf War, and to set out the main determinants for the future peace and stability of the region. In the first place, the evident helplessness of the governments of Saudi Arabia and the Gulf states in the face of the invasion, and the extent of their dependence upon the United States, raise questions about the legitimacy of even the most apparently stable among them in the eyes of many of their own citizens. Elsewhere in the Arab world, the hesitant and unco-ordinated response of most regimes aroused displays of anger from their populations. The knee-jerk reaction of some of the 'Arab masses' was to demonstrate broad support for the Iraqi invasion, less perhaps out of conviction of the justice of the cause than as an expression of frustration at the moral and political bankruptcy of their own governments and the unequal distribution of wealth and political power in the Arab world as a whole. For the more reflective, the need for the introduction of more responsible and accountable governments through the region became even more acute.

The invasion of Kuwait had other important consequences for the Middle East. In the first place, although the legitimacy of the regimes in Kuwait and Saudi Arabia was called into question—and will continue to be called into question as long as the ruling oligarchies retain all power in their own hands—Saudi Arabia's position within the region and as an American ally was greatly strengthened. It doubled its oil production and exports in response to the stoppage of exports from Iraq and Kuwait, thus averting an energy crisis by keeping oil prices down and at the same time ensuring its continuing control over OPEC (the Organisation of Petroleum Exporting Countries), at least in the short run. Secondly, the United States became more firmly embedded in the Arab world than before, albeit nominally under the aegis of the United Nations.

Furthermore, although there is no direct causal relationship, the crisis served to highlight the region's most deep-seated problems. Perhaps the most immediate is the steep decline in living standards and employment, to the accompaniment of soaring inflation, since the early 1980s. This has brought about a profound sense that there is 'no future' for much of the population of the region, a striking percentage of which is under 15. In addition, the pressing need to solve the Palestinian problem—a problem exacerbated by the intransigence of Israel—has cast its long shadow over the Middle East for many years. Finally, there is the paramount need to promote democracy and the rule of law. Their absence is among the most depressingly conspicuous features of the region.

Western policy generally is coming under close scrutiny by Middle Easterners of a variety of political persuasions. Suspicion of and support for the West has become even more deeply entrenched than before. Has 'all this' simply been to ensure Western hegemony in the region, to ensure Western control of the price of oil? Or is the West—above all, is the United States—committed to the implementation of the rule of law in Iraq and other countries? The perceived inadequacy of American policy in the latter respect has tended to give currency to the opinion in the Arab world that the United States is not serious about political reform in the Middle East, in marked contrast to its sustained pressure in that direction on the states of Eastern Europe in the 1980s. Without such a commitment, there can be no lasting peace or security in the Middle East.

Peter Sluglett and Marion Farouk-Sluglett

1 EGYPT

During the 19th century Egypt was virtually an autonomous state, ruled by the Mohammed Ali dynasty, although in strictly legal terms Mohammed Ali and his successors were merely viceroys of the Ottoman sultan in Istanbul. The British military occupation of Egypt in 1882 placed Great Britain in de facto control of the country, but did not alter Egypt's legal status. Only in 1914, after the outbreak of war, did Great Britain declare Egypt a British protectorate, thereby ending four centuries of Ottoman sovereignty. After the end of the war, Egyptian nationalists pressed Great Britain to grant Egypt independence and formed a delegation ('wafd' in Arabic) to present their case at the Paris peace conference. The scale and force of the Wafd's agitation throughout Egypt during the following years obliged Great Britain in 1922 to grant Egypt formal independence as a sovereign state under King Fuad of the Mohammed Ali dynasty. There were, however, severe limitations on this sovereignty. Among other things, the British reserved for themselves alone the right to organise the defence of Egypt and to ensure the security of 'imperial communications', which meant the continuation of British military occupation.

Consequently, one of the major preoccupations of Egyptian politicians during the following decades was the negotiation of a complete British military withdrawal from the country. At the same time, the royal family was locked in competition with the Wafd, as the former tried to assert the royal prerogative and the latter tried to realise the principle of popular sovereignty laid down in the constitution of 1923. Both factions resented the continued British presence, but both sought to enlist British support in their struggles. The treaty of 1936 signalled a formal end to the British military occupation; Great Britain agreed to withdraw its forces to the Canal Zone and Egypt became a fully independent member of the League of Nations. In reality, British influence remained predominant and was reinforced by the outbreak of war in 1939, when Egypt became central to British strategy. Only after the end of the Second World War did Great Britain begin to disengage from the shaping of Egyptian politics.

By that stage, however, new forces were emerging in Egypt, impatient with the record of the dominant political and economic order. Both the king and the Wafd were accused of having failed to win complete independence for Egypt and of having collaborated with the British. The formal existence of a parliamentary system of government derived from the constitution of 1923 had not prevented the frequent suspension of parliament, rule by decree and rigged elections. Nor had it allowed much progress on social or economic issues, since the parliament was dominated throughout the period by large landowners and other economically powerful figures who regularly placed their own interests above those of the national community. The indictment of the regime was not confined merely to one part of the political spectrum. The nationalists of the Young Egypt party, the socialists and the communists, the Islamic activists of the Muslim Brotherhood—all were vocal in their denunciation of the established order and were listened to by an increasing number of Egyptians.

In the midst of this period of disorder and protest came the military disaster of the 1948 Palestine war, in which the Egyptian armed forces were defeated by the forces of the newly established state of Israel. The general political discontent and the humiliation of the defeat found a focus in the Egyptian officer corps. A group calling itself the Free Officers was formed by Gamal Abdel Nasser and his associates. Although they differed in their ideological sympathies, all were united by their belief that something radical needed to be done to change the status quo in Egypt and by their conviction that, as officers of the Egyptian army, they had both the right and the means to bring about that change. In July 1952 they carried out a coup d'état. King Farouk was forced to abdicate in favour of his infant son, a land reform law was brought in which eliminated the economic power of the great landowners, the constitution of 1923 was annulled and the political parties associated with the old regime were banned. In June 1953 the Republic of Egypt was proclaimed.

Egypt under Nasser

Nasser rapidly emerged as the dominant figure among the Free Officers and formalised this position by becoming president of the republic in 1954. His personal authority, and skilful use of the administrative and coercive apparatus of the state made his position virtually unassailable. In addition, his ability to appeal to the aspirations of large numbers of Egyptians, stressing themes of social equality and national independence, gave him an authority and a mass following on a remarkable scale. However, it rapidly became clear that he could neither tolerate opposition, nor bear to be beholden, ideologically or otherwise, to any other group or faction in Egyptian politics.

Concentration of power allowed Nasser to chart his own course and to become the eponymous originator of 'Nasserism'. This mixture of ideas was to have considerable appeal throughout the Middle East, especially after the defiant stance adopted by Nasser during the Suez crisis of 1956. Nasserism came to symbolise anti-imperialism, non-alignment, pan-Arabism, republicanism, social justice and, increasingly, state socialism. It was an exciting mixture for the times and seemed to hold out the promise of a radically reshaped Arab world, united in purpose, and offering the possibility of a better life for its inhabitants. The reality was rather different.

Official name	Arab Republic of Egypt
Area	1,002,000 sq. km (386,900 sq. miles) (cultivated and settled area = 35,580 sq. km)
Population	50.74 million (1989)
Capital	Cairo
Language	Arabic
Religion	Muslim (90%, mainly Sunni), Coptic Christian (7%), with Roman Catholic, Protestant, Greek Orthodox and Jewish minorities
Currency	Egyptian pound

Nasserism created enemies as well as enthusiasts, not least because many saw it simply as a vehicle for Egyptian domination over the Arab world. The ill-fated union between Egypt and Syria—the United Arab Republic—(1958–61) seemed to confirm this impression. Even within Egypt, it was difficult for many to see consistency in the Nasserist ideal as Nasser's ideological eclecticism became more pronounced during the 1960s.

The decade began with a spate of nationalisations in which the principal sectors of the Egyptian economy were taken under state control. At the same time, even more stringent land-reform measures were taken, seeming to herald a far-reaching change in social and economic relations in the Egyptian countryside. However, within a few years, Nasser was having second thoughts: the nationalisations were not producing the surplus required to fund the provisions of the welfare state, and the expectations of radical change in the countryside seemed to threaten his own vision of political order. The only consistent feature was Nasser's determination to retain absolute control of the whole process through the subservient sole political party, the Arab Socialist Union (ASU), through state control of the media and of industry, and through the use of the intelligence services to suppress dissent.

Egypt's military defeat by Israel in the 1967 Six Day War shook Nasser's rule to its foundations. He continued in office, but his authority and his system of power were now openly questioned. Increasingly, calls were heard for the accountability of government, for an end to the police state, and for greater freedom in political and economic life. Nasser, however, was preoccupied with rebuilding Egypt's shattered military strength, with the economic consequences of a failing state socialist experiment, and with the effects of the loss of Sinai and the closure of the Suez Canal. In 1970 Nasser died, having solved none of these questions, and leaving them, in consequence, as the legacy with which his successor was obliged to cope.

Egypt under Sadat

Anwar Sadat, Nasser's vice-president and a fellow Free Officer, succeeded to the presidency on Nasser's death. He began immediately to consolidate his own position. Initially, this involved moving against those on the left within the ASU, their allies in the military and the bureaucracy. In their place, Sadat encouraged the advocates of greater economic liberalisation, as well as the adherents of the Muslim Brotherhood, whom he released from the prisons where they had been incarcerated for much of Nasser's rule. At the same time, he expelled the 15,000 Soviet military advisers stationed in Egypt. This not only secured the support of the Egyptian military, it greatly enhanced Sadat's authority in the country at large and in much of the political apparatus. Egyptians saw in him the hope for change and above all the chance to escape the economic, political and diplomatic burdens of Nasser's legacy.

In this atmosphere Sadat launched the October War against Israel in

1973. The initial successes of the operation, regardless of the military reversals at the end of the campaign, restored the confidence of the Egyptians in themselves and boosted Sadat's authority. He had intended the war not simply to efface the shame of the 1967 defeat, but to break the diplomatic deadlock of the situation of 'no war, no peace' with Israel. This, in turn, he believed would allow him to open the country up to much-needed capital investment from abroad.

However, the disengagement talks with Israel during 1974/75, the policies of the *Infitah* or 'economic opening' and the very marked alignment with the West and the United States in particular which followed produced more limited results than Sadat had expected. The military debt to the Soviet Union remained large, foreign investors were wary of placing funds in Egypt, the expected aid from the oil-rich Arab states were not forthcoming and yet the massive subsidies on basic food and consumer items still needed to be maintained. The widespread and violent riots of January 1977 demonstrated the political risks which the government ran in trying to cut back on this aspect of the welfare state in Egypt. Faced with this impasse and the threats of disorder produced by underlying frustration, Sadat made another of the dramatic moves for which his presidency became famous. In November 1977 he flew to Jerusalem to address the Israeli Knesset.

This was the first in a series of moves which led to the American-brokered negotiations between Israel and Egypt and to the signing of a formal peace treaty between Egypt and Israel in March 1979. Under it, Israel agreed to withdraw from all of Sinai within three years and Egypt to let Israeli ships pass through the Suez Canal. In addition, full diplomatic and trade relations were established. The United States was the guarantor of the treaty, supervising the Israeli withdrawal from Sinai and its subsequent demilitarisation, whilst simultaneously pledging equal amounts of substantial military and economic aid to both Egypt and Israel. The issue of Palestinian autonomy was put aside, supposedly to be addressed once moves to establish bilateral relations and trust had been completed.

These developments provoked consternation among most of the other Arab states, and in 1979 Egypt was expelled from the Arab League. Within Egypt itself the opposition to the treaty with Israel came chiefly from the remnants of the Nasserist left and from the growing Islamic trend. They were disconcerted by moves apparently so much at odds with the course charted in the Arab world by Egypt over the previous 40 or so years. Nevertheless, Sadat was able to rely on the support of a political class which tended to share his views of Egypt's national interests. In addition, a mixture of Egyptian nationalism and the belief that these moves heralded a new and more prosperous future for Egypt created considerable initial popular enthusiasm.

Once again, however, the almost instantaneous prosperity which Sadat had promised his countrymen failed to materialise for the majority of

Egyptians. Unrealistic as this may have been in any case, it was noticeable that some sectors of Egyptian society began to reap considerable profits from opportunities offered by the encouragement of private-sector activity. Inequalities of wealth, never absent from Egyptian society, became more marked as new forms of consumption became available to the rich. Inevitably, criticism arose, not only on the left but from the Islamic wing. When linked to condemnation by these same groups of Egypt's increasing reliance on the United States and the apparently bilateral peace process with Israel, these became the foundation for wide-ranging criticisms of the regime, criticisms to which Sadat was extremely sensitive.

Mistrustful of the Nasserist tendencies of the ASU and aware of the need to allow greater freedom of expression in Egypt, Sadat had begun the process of establishing a more plural party system. Cautiously at first, with increasing speed in 1977, the ASU was broken up into three separate parties which Sadat believed would provide him with a platform of support and a semblance of opposition. Genuine opposition was harder for him to tolerate. The short-lived revival of the New Wafd in 1978 and the increasing difficulties faced by the Nasserist/Marxist National Progressive Unionist party showed that there were limits to Sadat's idea of liberalisation. Although he had encouraged the re-emergence of a more open political debate and a relaxation of the government's tight grip on all aspects of life, Sadat found it difficult to accept the consequences of this when it led to criticism of his own policies. Nor did he believe that he should be systematically answerable to those over whom he ruled, since he was convinced that he knew better than they where their true interests lay.

Like his predecessor Nasser, Sadat relied increasingly on his control of the state administration and the security services to enforce conformity with his views. Those who dissented, he regarded at best as guilty of folly, at worst as subversive of the whole political and social order. In the late summer of 1981 he arrested virtually every prominent critic of his regime, regardless of their political affiliations. However, while much of his attention was focused on his public critics, there were more dangerous enemies in the shadows.

During the 1970s small groups of Islamic radicals had protested publicly and often violently against what they regarded as an impious and unjust social order. Clashes with the security forces and between Copts and Muslims had marked the emergence of these groups. Possibly disillusioned with the relative quietism of the legally sanctioned Muslim Brotherhood, these groups advocated violence as the only means of destroying the existing corrupt state. Their vision was of an Islamic order governed by the sharia arising from the ruins of the old order. In 1981 the mass arrests seem to have galvanised one of these groups, *al-Jihad*, into action. Its members were told that the killing of the president was a duty incumbent upon them as devout Muslims and might, furthermore, bring closer the moment when a truly Islamic order could be established in Egypt. In

October 1981, at the military parade commemorating the war of 1973, they carried out their plan and assassinated Sadat.

Egypt under Mubarak

Although there were associated incidents of violence in Asyut, there was no more general attempt to overthrow the government of Egypt. The political order remained intact, since the state establishment and the armed forces rallied round the surviving leadership, headed by Husni Mubarak, the vice-president, who succeeded Sadat as president. Whatever misgivings some may have had about the increasingly autocratic course taken by Sadat, there was little disagreement within the political elite over the priorities he had set for the country.

Mubarak was able, therefore, to capitalise on support both from the political establishment and from the public opposition. The nature of this support was ambiguous, however. On the one hand, there were those who saw Mubarak as a guarantor of stability and order, and thus a figure of continuity with the previous regime, on the other hand, there were many who believed that the change of president in such a highly centralised system of power held out great hopes for progress in the fields of political as well as economic liberalisation. Seeking to appeal to both constituencies simultaneously has been the mark of Mubarak's presidency.

The resulting ambiguity or contradictions have been noticeable features of his rule. Mubarak himself seems to have a largely authoritarian vision of political power. He is a former air-force general and the inheritor of a political order which bases its claim to legitimacy on a revolution carried out by the officer corps of the armed forces. Consequently, Mubarak is sympathetic to arguments that suggest that the armed forces are not simply the defenders of the country's borders but are the ultimate guarantors of order. This seemed to be borne out graphically for him by the decisive part played by the armed forces in suppressing the violent Central Security Forces mutinies in early 1986.

Nevertheless, his summary dismissal in 1989 of the long-serving minister of defence, Field Marshal Abu Ghazzala, proved that Mubarak did not want to become beholden to any particular military officer, however influential or powerful. His replacement, General Abu Talib, was himself replaced in May 1991, when the president appointed General Tantawi minister of defence. These moves stemmed partly from considerations appropriate to the specific times they were made, partly from the president's determination to assert political control of the armed forces. The latter form an important element in the dominant structure of order, just as their senior officers are generally influential figures in the political elite. However, the clear message is that the armed forces should be at the disposal of the president and his political establishment, rather than vice versa.

As far as the realm of civil politics is concerned, Mubarak's vision of acceptable political behaviour allows for criticism and organised opposition, but up to a certain point and in certain spheres of policy. The condition of its existence seems to be that it should neither disrupt nor challenge his political and economic preoccupations as president. Nevertheless, a gradual opening up of political life has taken place: new parties have been allowed to form and to organise; they have been allowed a greater, although scarcely threatening, degree of representation in the People's Assembly; and freedom of the press has been enormously enhanced, with a greater variety of opinions represented than at any time since the revolution of 1952.

Welcome as these developments have been for those who wish to see the greater liberalisation of Egyptian politics, there is still an uneasy feeling that all these manifestations of political freedom exist only on government sufferance. Behind the apparent willingness to encourage the emergence of a plural political order, an unreconstructed apparatus and set of authoritarian prejudices endure. This has been evident in the security of the Ministry of Interior, in the prominence accorded to the armed forces in national life, and in the convention that the president himself is somehow 'above politics'—and thus above criticism—when, in fact, he is supremely powerful. Mubarak's presidency has, therefore, been characterised by a series of gradual, incremental and occasionally reluctant steps to greater freedom of political expression and activity. The fact that a number of these steps have been forced upon the government by an increasingly active and independently minded, if not wholly independent, judiciary, has been one of the more noteworthy aspects of this process.

The judiciary's activity can be seen as a determination on the part of many in the legal profession never to allow the arbitrariness of Nasser's dictatorship to re-emerge. They have thus taken the president seriously when he proclaims himself committed to the 'rule of law' and the 'state of institutions'. A series of court decisions in 1983 and 1984 obliged the government to accept the legal existence of the New Wafd party and allowed the surviving pre-revolutionary leaders of the party to play an active role in public life once more. A further series of court rulings in 1986 and 1987 found the electoral law of 1983 unconstitutional. This forced the government both to amend the law and to call for new elections, since the legality of the existing People's Assembly had been called into question. There were some who were still dissatisfied with the amended electoral law and, in May 1990, the litigation arising from this dissatisfaction came to fruition. Once again, the Supreme Constitutional Court ruled that the electoral law, as amended in 1986, was unconstitutional and that, as a consequence, the People's Assembly elections of 1987 were invalid. This obliged the president once again to dissolve the assembly and to call for new elections in November 1990.

The 1990 elections

The circumstances surrounding the general election of 1990 demonstrate the limits to the gradual dismantling of the authoritarian political order in Egypt. In the elections of 1984 and 1987, some of the opposition parties had succeeded in winning representation in the People's Assembly. However, the overwhelming majority of the President's National Democratic party (NDP) was never in question (in 1984 it had won 390 out of the 448 seats; in 1987, 346). Quite apart from the proven problems of the electoral law, the opposition parties had alleged in both years—and with considerable justification—that the elections could not be regarded as free. The NDP, through the president and the government, had an overwhelming advantage, in the form of state patronage and control of broadcasting. More seriously, the opposition asserted that it was difficult to conduct any form of free election under the State of Emergency legislation, which had been in force since the assassination of President Sadat in 1981. In particular cases, there were charges that local security forces had intimidated opposition candidates and prevented opposition supporters from gaining access to polling booths. On a more general level, the Ministry of the Interior was accused of ensuring that in each case, and by whatever means thought necessary, the majority returned for the NDP was sufficiently overwhelming not simply to give the government a free hand in the People's Assembly but to reinforce the impression of near-unanimous acquiescence in the authority of President Mubarak.

As a result, the main opposition parties (the Wafd, the Liberals, the Socialist Labour party and the Muslim Brotherhood—the latter not strictly or legally a party, but very much a contestant) declared that they would boycott the 1990 elections unless the State of Emergency was lifted and the conduct of the elections was transferred from the Ministry of the Interior to the judiciary. The government refused and the elections went ahead, contested by the ruling NDP, the NPUP, a large number of Independents and some smaller parties (Young Egypt, the Green party, the Unionist party and the Umma party). In all, 3,000 candidates contested the 444 seats (two seats for each of the 222 constituencies). The result was, of course, an overwhelming majority for the NDP which won 348 seats, while 83 went to Independents and 6 to the NPUP.

Government and opposition

The system of government in Egypt remains centred on the presidency. Consequently, parliamentary elections have little to do with the actual or possible transfer of power. They are more important for gauging the willingness of the president to give dissent a voice. Mubarak evidently sees some utility in this exercise. At the same time, there are those within the state administration who have a more restrictive view of politics and find it difficult to distinguish dissent from treason or subversion. President Mubarak has consistently appointed such people and charged them with maintaining public order. This is as crucial for the maintenance of his authority among the elite as are any pretensions to liberalisation.

Between 1986 and 1990, this tendency was personified by the notorious minister of the interior, Zaki Badr, who represented the unreconstructed and repressive side of the regime. When this became too obvious and an embarrassment to the president both in Egypt and abroad, Badr was dismissed. His successor, General Abd al-Halim Musa, has come up by the familiar route of police service and the governorship of troublesome provinces. He is less outspoken than his predecessor in his attitude to the legal opposition. However, the forces under his command have been no less ruthless in dealing with disruptive expressions of opposition, such as street demonstrations, factory sit-ins, or the activities of underground organisations.

Since the early 1980s, such organisations have carried out sporadic acts of violence. Although most espouse a radical Islamic ideology of protest, others have also been involved, such as the Nasserist-nationalists of the group 'Egypt's Revolution'. The incidents have generally taken the form of attacks on figures of authority, ranging from ministers to local police officers. Sometimes there have been attacks on people believed to symbolise some aspect of Egyptian government policy of which the perpetrators disapprove–such as Israelis and Americans. Some of the more extreme Islamic protest groups have attacked fellow Muslims whom they regard as having deviated from the strict interpretation of Islamic dress or behaviour which they wish to impose. Others have attacked Copts and Coptic property and churches, especially in Upper Egypt, in the towns of Asyut and El Minya.

Devastating as this violence has been for those who have been directly involved, it has not claimed many victims, nor has it been widespread, let alone sufficiently sustained seriously to threaten the political order. Nevertheless, these incidents and the existence of the small groups which are responsible for them have been used by the government to justify the slow pace of liberalisation. It is frequently suggested by the president and his ministers that only the firm hand of the government prevents latent anarchy from erupting and engulfing Egyptian society, threatening to bring to an abrupt end the relative political stability which Egypt has witnessed during the past forty years. This has been the rationale for the State of Emergency, in force since 1981 and renewed for a further three years in May 1991. These regulations allow the security forces wide powers of arrest, detention and interrogation. Paradoxically, Egyptian political life has become more open and free under these regulations than at any time since the 1952 revolution. Nevertheless, the apparent reluctance of the government to abandon the emergency laws is a disturbing indicator of the degree to which authoritarian ideas of governance persist among the ruling elite.

The activities of the Islamic protest groups alone cannot be held to justify the retention of this legislation. Appealing in the main to relatively small numbers of urban and educated young people and junior officials, the seriously conspiratorial groups, such as *al-Jihad* or *al-Najun min al-Nar* (now dissolved), do not constitute serious threats to the political order. Although they have caught public and press attention through some of their activities, the chief representative of those who want to see a more identifiably Islamic order instituted in Egypt is still the Muslim Brotherhood. Led by Hamid Abu'l-Nasr since 1986, the Muslim Brotherhood has explicitly renounced violence and works within the existing laws of the state, seeing its tasks chiefly as education, propaganda and the advancement of the sharia as the sole foundation for public life in Egypt. Although it has been denied legal recognition as a political party, it is allowed to organise, publish its journals and put up candidates in parliamentary elections, as long as they are sponsored by one of the legal political parties. This led to an alliance with the Wafd in 1984 and with the SLP and the Liberals in 1987. In the 1990 elections a substantial number of Muslim Brotherhood sympathisers were elected as Independents.

Nevertheless, the centre of gravity of the Egyptian political system remains the presidency. Much Egyptian political life is spent speculating on the next moves of the president, interpreting his words and deeds, as well as manoeuvering to catch his eye. It is an institution which has demonstrated its resilience, in the important sense that the unexpected deaths of the two previous incumbents did not destabilise the system as a whole. Nevertheless, the personality and the vision of the president is important in shaping not only the direction of government policy, but the dimensions of national political debate. Neither as conspiratorial nor as insecure as his predecessors, President Mubarak has shown himself able to tolerate a degree of transparency and of criticism which has allowed political life to revive. Nevertheless, his determination to oversee the whole process remains strong. Mubarak's vision of Egypt's future may not be as grandiose as those of Nasser or Sadat, but from his perspective even the more modest goals of economic solvency and public order require a close and controlling presidential hand.

Economic problems

Since November 1986 Dr Atif Sidqi has held the office of prime minister. The fact that he is a trained economist underlines the nature of the task with which the president has entrusted him. On the one hand, he is responsible for the conduct of negotiations with Egypt's external creditors, both bilaterally and through the IMF; on the other, he is in charge of the gradual reduction of state control of the economy, in both the industrial and service sectors. The scale of the task facing him in all these areas is visible from even the most cursory glance at Egypt's economic situation.

By 1990, the country's total external, non-military debt amounted to nearly $50 billion. This was greater than Egypt's annual GNP and required over $2 billion annually in debt service payments. The trade balance is continually in the red, amounting to about $8 billion in 1989/90. Agricultural imports to feed Egypt's relentlessly growing population (an estimated increase of one million every 10 months) account for nearly half the deficit. To meet these requirements, Egypt has four chief earners of foreign currency–oil, tourism, Suez Canal dues and the remittances of the estimated three-and-a-half million Egyptians working abroad. During 1989/90 these brought in roughly $7 billion in foreign exchange. However, since 1990 all have been shown to be vulnerable to developments over which the Egyptian government has no control. Prior to the Gulf War, the oil revenues suffered from the collapse in the oil price. Thereafter, the uncertainties of the crisis and war led to a sharp drop in tourism, a return of many Egyptian workers from the region and a fall in the volume of shipping using the Suez Canal.

Domestically, the government is seeking to privatise some of the many sectors of the economy brought under state control during the Nasser era. The public sector still accounts for roughly 70% of the country's GDP and includes all the major industrial and service sectors of the Egyptian economy. However, there have been cautious experiments in privatisation in certain governorates. Some small-scale industrial concerns have been sold off and the management structure of a number of state enterprises overhauled. The relative success of these efforts has led to more ambitious plans to sell off hotels, public sector interests in joint-venture enterprises and state-run factories producing consumer goods and foodstuffs. Nevertheless, the principal industries, such as textiles, iron and steel and consumer durables, are likely to remain state-run concerns for the foreseeable future.

Egypt's military structures

Another economic sphere in which the state is dominant is that of military production. During the 1980s there was considerable investment in, and development of, the Egyptian arms industry, partly in conjunction with foreign military suppliers, partly as an indigenous development, due to the Egyptian government's determination to become self-sufficient in the production of ammunition, spare parts and basic items of military equipment. As well as being thought necessary for national security, this was also seen as a means of reducing the growth of the military debt, estimated in 1989 at around $10 billion. At the same time, closer relations with Iraq during the war with Iran led to an increasingly lucrative export market for Egyptian manufactured arms. During the last three years of that war, from 1985 to 1988, it was estimated that Iraq was importing $800 million–$1 billion worth of Egyptian military supplies each year. Precise figures on the growth of this sector are understandably impossible to obtain. However, it is clear that considerable resources have been dedicated to the military industries and, further, that the organisation of this state-run sector of the economy has been one of the most successful examples of industrial enterprise. It is perhaps not surprising that this should be the case, given the importance attached to re-armament and the favoured place in the political hierarchy enjoyed by the military in Egypt.

Nevertheless, the great bulk of Egypt's armament comes from abroad, obliging the Egyptian government to incur considerable foreign military debts. In 1987 the government succeeded in coming to an agreement with the Soviet Union on Egypt's military debt of $3 billion. Generous re-scheduling terms were granted, largely because the Soviet Union was anxious to improve the state of its rather cool relations with Egypt. Unable to raise the capital required to repay those loans, Egypt was instead trading on its importance for outside powers as a key Middle Eastern state.

This asset was particularly in evidence during the Gulf crisis. The Arab creditors of Egypt (chiefly Saudi Arabia and Kuwait) cancelled the $6.5 billion owed to them by Egypt and, in addition, made an outright grant to Egypt of $2 billion. The United States cancelled the whole of Egypt's military debt of $7 billion. During the preceding ten years the question of the military debt burden had been an irritant in US–Egyptian relations. Not only did the Egyptian government take exception to the way in which the loan had been structured, it also clearly resented the fact that it was being forced to accept terms far less generous than those offered to Israel. The military debt to the United States thus became both an addition to the overall economic burden of the government and a symbolic issue on which the opposition could focus its criticism of the meagre rewards of the alliance with the United States. The cancellation of the debt was, therefore, a highly effective way for the United States to reward the Egyptian government for the active part it played in the allied coalition formed to eject Iraq from Kuwait.

Debt, reform and subsidies

As far as the Egyptian government is concerned, the political significance of its overall debt burden is twofold. First, there is the restriction it places on Egypt's independence of action. Not only does it restrict the options open to the government, it places the Egyptian government in the rather humiliating position of a petitioner, constantly having to plead its case before such organisations as the Club of Rome, the Paris Club, the IMF and the World Bank. There is a perennial concern that this humiliating posture undermines the authority of the government and provides ammunition to those who claim the government is incompetent in its protection of Egypt's interests. Secondly, as the series of negotiations with the IMF and others have demonstrated, the Egyptian government fears the domestic political consequences of some of the stringent reform measures demanded by its creditors as a condition of rescheduling Egypt's debt.

In particular, these proposals invariably include demands that the government remove or reduce the extensive subsidy system operating in Egypt, which makes a range of items available to the population at well below their true economic cost. These include not simply subsidised seed, fertiliser and energy for the agricultural and industrial sectors, but a range of basic foodstuffs for the population as a whole. For Egypt's creditors the reduction and eventual removal of these subsidies is thought imperative if the Egyptian economy—and thus its ability to generate the surplus required to repay the debts incurred—is to be established on a sound footing. However, the Egyptian government is clearly anxious about the impact of the removal of subsidies on the mass of the urban poor who depend upon them in fundamental ways. The protests and disorder which are thought likely to follow any dramatic move on this front have been a strong deterrent to action.

Nevertheless, the government has recognised the economic arguments for reform and is equally aware that the subsidy system has been greatly abused. Under the present prime minister, some reforms have been attempted and there have also been cautious, phased moves aimed at reducing the overall cost of the subsidies to the government. This received added impetus in 1991 when the leading industrial states of the Paris Club offered to wipe out roughly one-third of Egypt's debt (between $5 billion and $10 billion) on condition that Egypt accept the reform package proposed by the IMF. This included the usual package of exchange rate reform, effective devaluation of the Egyptian pound, the freeing of interest rates, the reduction of state subsidies, especially on energy and basic foodstuffs, and the imposition of a sales tax. In April 1991 the Egyptian government reached an agreement on these terms with the IMF, having already set up a social fund, financed largely by the World Bank, which was intended to protect the poor from the worst effects of the inevitable price rises. In return, one-third of Egypt's debt was cancelled and the remainder was rescheduled, making debt repayment far less onerous.

The issue of subsidies, however, is not only affected by fears of public reaction and possible disorder in the streets: it is intimately bound up with the structure and impulses of elite politics in Egypt. In the final analysis, it goes back to the basic question of the interests which the government is expected or intended to serve. As in the case of political liberalisation, so with the attempted economic deregulation, the Egyptian government finds itself subject to conflicting pressures from different sectors of the elite. On the one hand, there are those entrenched in the massive structures of the state bureaucracy. They argue that without the protection afforded by state control of industrial and economic interests, free competition, operating through private enterprise and foreign capital, will lead to the running down of Egyptian industry and a loss of independence. Given the social and corporate structure of the elite, these people are in a position to make their voices heard. Their appeal to the principles of economic nationalism strikes a sympathetic and popular chord with many in Egypt. It is a theme which President Mubarak has often taken up in his occasional denunciations of 'cowardly capital' and in his often-expressed frustration that private enterprise does not always act in the public interest.

On the other hand, there are many who believe that this bureaucracy stifles initiative and who, therefore, hold it responsible for the poor performance of the Egyptian economy, with all the loss of independence which that implies. After all, they argue, a $50 billion external debt and periodic debt rescheduling agreements are not ideal conditions in which to assert economic independence. This faction has advocated a much faster pace of privatisation, which they believe will afford them greater economic opportunities and, in the process, strengthen the competitiveness of Egyptian agriculture and industry. The negative social consequences of this they see as either necessary or temporary, or both. Confusingly for outside observers, the groups of people who hold these conflicting views do not constitute identifiably separate elites. On the contrary, they are generally closely linked to each other by ties of marriage, kinship, education and background. Equally, their contrasting views are represented in the government and are stressed by the president at different times, depending upon which audience he happens to be addressing.

As in the case of political liberalisation, Mubarak seems to have forged, if not a consensus, an agreement on fundamentals that allows members of the same administration to hold rather different views on how those fundamentals might best be protected. The appearance of consensus may also, in part, be a symptom of inertia. Considerable interests have built up over the years in the structure and maintenance of the state-run economy. Ideologies and rationales to justify these interests are also widely held both among the elite and in society in general. Radical reform will clearly have social costs, as the comfortable, if inefficient and costly, apparatus of state subsidies is dismantled. Nor is there any guarantee that the reforms will work as intended. Consequently, the desire to avoid fundamental conflicts prevails and the search focuses on the pursuit of some 'middle way', which may not hold out much hope of dramatic economic improvement but at least prevents serious dissent among the elite. In such an environment, the priority is clearly the preservation of the political order and the achievement of as great a degree of national independence as possible.

Foreign policy

A similar kind of minimal consensus exists in the field of foreign policy. Though there may be differences in the interpretation of the exact ingredients of Egyptian national interests, as well as in the best ways of securing them, there is general agreement that the independence, security and prosperity of the national community of Egyptians should take precedence over all else. This relative unanimity about national identity and interests makes Egypt noteworthy among the Arab states of the Middle East. It has also given its leaders considerable latitude in formulating foreign policy, as well as a secure base from which to take foreign policy initiatives. This helps to explain not only why Sadat was able to sign a peace treaty with Israel in 1979, but also why Mubarak has been able to abide by the terms of that treaty. During his presidency Egypt has maintained correct, if not necessarily cordial, relations with successive Israeli governments. The same feature also explains the confidence with which the Egyptian government was able to oppose the Iraqi annexation of Kuwait, to rally the Arab members of the international coalition against Iraq and to participate actively by sending 35,000 troops to join the coalition forces.

In the aftermath of the assassination of President Sadat, one of the priorities of the Egyptian government was to reassure Israel that Egypt would abide by the treaty. This reassurance was successful and the final phase of the Israeli withdrawal from Sinai was completed in April 1982. The Israeli invasion of Lebanon which came soon thereafter led to a 'freezing' of the relationship but did not cause any fundamental breach. It did, however, frustrate any idea the Egyptian government might have entertained to press for the implementation of the second part of the Camp David Agreement on the central question of the future of the Palestinians and the Occupied Territories. Nevertheless, it was evident by the mid-1980s that Egypt had succeeded in repairing its relations with the Palestine Liberation Organisation (PLO) and that, increasingly, the latter saw Egypt as a possible advocate of its cause in any attempt to arrange negotiations between Israel and the Palestinians. During 1989/90 the Egyptian government became deeply involved in helping to put into effect the so-called Baker Plan, which had precisely such an end in view. As always in such attempts, the plan could not overcome the basic obstacle caused by Israel's refusal to recognise the right of the PLO to play a part in such negotiations. Yet neither Egypt, nor of course the PLO itself, could accept any other form of Palestinian representation. Equally, in April and May 1991, the Egyptian government encouraged Baker's shuttle diplomacy, but was powerless at the time to bring the Israeli, Syrian and Palestinian positions close enough to allow negotiations to begin.

On the purely bilateral level of Egyptian–Israeli relations, once these had thawed sufficiently in the aftermath of the Lebanon episode, the issue of the Taba enclave in Sinai came to the fore. This dispute concerned a small area of the coast which both sides claimed and from which Israel had refused to withdraw in April 1982. It was a considerable achievement of Mubarak's government to persuade Israel to submit the case to international arbitration. In 1989 the Egyptian handling of the issue was vindicated when the arbitration commission ruled in Egypt's favour and Israel agreed to withdraw. The reassuring aspect of this case, as far as Egyptian foreign policy was concerned, lay not simply in the fact that Egypt had won its argument, but that the issue itself—border demarcation between two sovereign states—and the method of its resolution—

peaceful arbitration—symbolised the very real normality of the relationship between Egypt and Israel which had developed since 1979. The peace
treaty may not have lived up to the utopian expectations of some in Israel
and Egypt, but it had introduced an element of stability and non-
contentious normality in the relationship between the two states.

This was particularly necessary at a time when passions among many
in Egypt were running high as a result of the continuing Palestinian
intifada, or uprising, and Israeli efforts to suppress it. In fact, such passions
had been evident at a number of times during the years since the signing of
the treaty. They had occasionally erupted into isolated acts of violence
against individual Israelis by Egyptians who found it difficult to reconcile
themselves to the implications of peaceful coexistence. More generally,
however, they were evident in the repeated charge by most of the
opposition parties that the Egyptian government was being too passive in
its response to Israeli behaviour in the Occupied Territories and too
cautious in advancing the cause of the Palestinians.

The fact that the opposition press could voice openly what many felt,
even among the supporters of the government, made the government
sensitive to such criticism. Yet beyond formal indications of diplomatic
displeasure, which might in any case have been considered counterproductive at a time when Egypt was trying to promote negotiations
between Israel and the Palestinians, there was not a great deal that Egypt
could do. A complete rupture in relations and the abrogation of the treaty
would have had immediate and severe consequences for Egypt's national
security. Nor did the Egyptian government ever consider it. Interestingly,
only those on the extreme fringes of the opposition ever advocated such a
dramatic reversal of Egyptian foreign policy. The rest of the opposition
seemed prepared to accept it as a pillar of Egyptian security, or, at the very
least, as a fact of life.

A similar attitude seems to have emerged among the Arab states that
had initially ostracised Egypt for signing a peace treaty with Israel. This
was encouraged by the Egyptian government as it sought to repair its
relations with the rest of the Arab world. Mubarak made plain at the
outset, however, that this reconciliation would take place on Egypt's
terms. That is, Egypt's treaty with Israel would remain in place and the
other Arab states would have to accept it. The confusion and the dilemmas
afflicting much of the rest of the Arab world during the 1980s considerably
strengthened the Egyptian argument that the isolation of the most populous and significant of the Arab states made little sense and could only
harm Arab interests.

By the late 1980s, therefore, as a result of the growing involvement of
Egypt in the search for a settlement of the Palestine question, relations
with the PLO and with Jordan were restored. At the same time, a close
relationship, founded mainly on military sales and advice, was built up
between Egypt and Iraq. These improvements in Egypt's relations with the

Arab states were finalised with the readmission of Egypt to the Arab League in May 1989 and the restoration of diplomatic relations even with those Arab states, such as Syria, which had been the fiercest critics of the Egyptian–Israeli treaty.

Egypt and the Gulf crisis

Ironically, the restoration of Egyptian relations with the Arab states occurred not long before the Arab League was faced with its gravest challenge. The Egyptian government had been concerned for some time by the prospect of Iraq's ambitions and the dangers of its leader's frustrations in the wake of the Iran–Iraq War in 1988. As part of a strategy of reassurance and as a means of moderating the thrust of Iraqi ambition, Egypt helped to found the Arab Cooperation Council (ACC) in February 1989. This brought together Egypt, Iraq, Jordan and Yemen in an arrangement of formal cooperation, ostensibly dedicated to economic goals, but in reality to establish a form of consultation whereby Egypt might act as a moderating influence on Iraq. Set against the insecurities and ruthlessness of Saddam Husain, this had little chance of success. When Iraq invaded and annexed Kuwait in August 1990, the ACC virtually ceased to exist, the Arab League was split and Egypt aligned itself with the Gulf states and Syria in vehement condemnation of Iraq's action. Subsequently, Egypt became an active member of the coalition of states which sent forces to Saudi Arabia, first to protect the kingdom and then to drive Iraq from Kuwait by military means, under the terms of the UN resolutions.

Although many in Egypt were disconcerted by a chain of events which led to Arab being pitted in battle against Arab, and which saw the armed forces of Egypt, Syria and Saudi Arabia cooperating with the United States and other Western powers to inflict military defeat on another Arab state, there was little public reaction in Egypt against the policy pursued by the government. On the contrary, the return to Egypt of nearly one million Egyptians who had been working in Iraq added to public resentment of that country's regime, largely of the humiliating and brutal treatment which they had received. Equally, the claims made by Saddam Husain that he was acting in the name of Arabism and of Islam fell largely on deaf ears in Egypt. Few were willing to concede that the actions of his armed forces furthered the cause of Arab nationalism. As far as the Islamic groups in Egypt were concerned, the followers of the Muslim Brotherhood were split between their dislike for Saddam Husain, their links with Saudi Arabia and their unease at witnessing the rapid and massive Western military build-up in the region. The only protest demonstrations in Egypt took place after the war had begun in January 1991. Even then, they were limited either to small opposition parties or to the campuses of universities. The violence which erupted during these demonstrations appears to have been due as much to the overreaction of the security forces, as to the vehemence shown by the demonstrators.

In the aftermath of the liberation of Kuwait, the centrality of Egypt in the Arab world was publicly acknowledged once again. The headquarters of the Arab League returned to Cairo and Egypt's former minister of foreign affairs, Ismat Abd al-Magid, was elected secretary-general of the organisation. However, this does not signify a reassertion of Egyptian ascendancy in the manner of the 1950s or 1960s. Neither Egypt nor the Arab world itself are in the same situation as they were then and, if anything, state sovereignty is even more jealously guarded by Arab governments. The recent Egyptian decision to bring all its forces back from Saudi Arabia was a result of the inability of Egypt to sustain the cost of such a deployment single-handed, as well as of the usual difficulty of agreeing with the Gulf states about the nature of their future security needs. The bold declaration in Damascus in March 1991 that Egypt, together with Syria, would constitute one of the pillars of a future regional security order in the Gulf has since been tempered by Egyptian unilateralism, founded on an enduring perception of Egypt's national interests. This remains a fundamental characteristic of Egyptian policy and Mubarak can be confident that it will continue to form a common concern both of the political elite and of the Egyptian public. It is here that a truly national consensus can be discerned in Egyptian politics.

Egypt's future

The maintenance of such a consensus, on both domestic and external issues, is one of the major preoccupations of the Egyptian government. The concern of the president is that there are forces at work that may exert sufficient pressure to cause it to fly apart and fragment. This would not only make his position and that of the dominant order less secure, but would reduce his capacity to formulate policy and exercise leadership. Some of these pressures are visible in the effects of the perennial economic crises and in the activities of those who hold out a radically different, but seductive, alternative with the slogan 'Islam is the solution'. Less visible are the pressures at work within the structures of the state itself. There are conflicts of economic interest between the state administrators and the would-be economic liberalisers when it comes to crucial questions of the distribution of economic power. Similarly, the demand for more open forms of political expression and activity is a challenge to the imagination, as well as to the interests of those who cling to the short-term reassurances of an authoritarian state.

Clearly, President Mubarak and his government are an integral part of this system. The question which arises, therefore, concerns their abilities in dealing with the more insidious forms of resistance to a more open political order. The president has succeeded in maintaining the impression that he is no less desirous than some of his principal critics for the establishment of a plural political system. Within limits, this is probably the case. The crucial question, however, is whether the limits on representation, openness and answerability envisaged by the president correspond to the beliefs of those within the political class who are asking for more. Equally, the effect of economic insecurity on the government's confidence in handling the issue of political liberalisation is of central importance. Much will depend on its capacity to extricate the Egyptian economy from its perennial crisis. These are not easy tasks. However, the fact that President Mubarak has managed to foster a measure of consensus within quite flexible limits gives grounds for optimism that a political system is being created which can handle debate, dissent and controversy without throwing its own existence into question.

Charles Tripp

2 THE KURDS

Kurdistan is the name given to a geographical area on the borders of Iran, Iraq, Syria, and Turkey, the homeland of the Kurds, a pastoral nomadic people of Indo-European origin. In the words of one authority, the Kurdish people have the 'unfortunate distinction of being probably the only community of over 15-million persons which has not achieved some form of national statehood, despite a struggle extending back over several decades'. Kurdish is an Indo-European language, so that of the other languages in the area it is most closely related to Persian. There is no structural relationship between Arabic and Kurdish or between Turkish and Kurdish. Partly because of the isolation of the mountain regions in which they live, and partly because of the wide geographical distribution of the Kurdish community, there is no 'standard Kurdish'. There are several different dialects in addition to the three main divisions, Sorani (or Kurdi), spoken in Iran and southern Iraq (around Sulaimaniyya), which is recognised officially and taught in schools in Iraq; Kurmanji, spoken in northern Iraq and much of eastern Turkey; and Zaza, spoken in parts of central Turkey. These dialects are not mutually intelligible (although an individual might know more than one dialect); Zaza speakers might well only be able to communicate with Sorani speakers through the medium of another language.

The majority of Kurds are officially Sunni Muslims. Many belong to the Qadiriyya and Naqshbandiyya religious brotherhoods, both manifestations of 'popular' Islam, which gained adherents in the area in the mid-19th century. Many Kurds in south Iranian Kurdistan and in south and south-east Iraqi Kurdistan are Shias, although most of the latter, the Failis, were expelled to Iran in the 1970s. There are also three other heterodox Muslim groups to which some Kurds adhere: Alevi Shiism, Ahl-i Haqq; and Yazidism. In addition, there are a number of Assyrian and Syrian Orthodox Christians and a handful of Jews in the region. This variety of sects reflects both the plurality, and generally, unless incited otherwise by governments or other external forces, the tolerance, of the peoples of the area.

In broad terms, most Kurds probably no longer aspire to a 'Grand Kurdistan' extending over eastern Turkey, western Iran and northern and north-eastern Iraq. Rather, they aspire more realistically to some form of self-government or local autonomy within the borders of the state in which they live. For most of the period since the First World War, the Kurds' main problem has been persuading the governments of the newly created national states in which they have found themselves that local autonomy would not imply the derogation of sovereignty which the states themselves purport to fear.

Estimating the Kurdish population is fraught with difficulty, largely because ethnic affiliation is not usually recorded in the censuses of the countries concerned. Nevertheless, in 1980, the Minority Rights Groups estimated that Kurds formed 19% of the population of Turkey, 23% of Iraq, 10% of Iran and 8% of Syria, with smaller communities in Lebanon and the Soviet Union. If this is applied to the latest census figures for each country, it would produce a Kurdish population of between 20 and 21 million. Most Kurds can trace their origins to particular tribes, although increasing urban migration (and, in the case of the Turkish Kurds, to Western Europe) has tended to weaken tribal bonds. Furthermore, the passage of time and the political constraints on cross-frontier transhumance have combined to increase sedentarisation. An additional focus of loyalty, and often of political power, has been provided by the leaders of the various religious orders; thus, in Iraq, Sheik Mahmud of Sulaimaniyya, Mullah Mustafa Barzani and Jalal Talabani have derived at least part of their authority from their sheik backgrounds. In Turkey, according to one authority, 'Even since 1970, when leftish movements . . . started to make real inroads into Kurdish society, the unpoliticised have still voted for candidates who are [tribal] chiefs or [religious] sheiks, or possess these connections. Loyalty will persist even in an exploitative situation for a long time.'

History

Until the end of the First World War, the Kurdish populations as a whole were generally subject, at least nominally, to either the shah of Iran or the Ottoman sultan, with a few small communities in the Russian Caucasus. The boundary between Iran and the Ottoman Empire was not finally charted until 1913, which meant that attempts on the part of both governments to assert their authority in the Kurdish areas could be kept in check by reinforcement from the 'other side'. Ottoman efforts to consolidate authority over the Kurds caused major risings in 1837–52 and 1880–81, but by the end of the century the Ottomans had managed to recruit many Kurdish tribesmen into the Hamidiyya cavalry, named after Sultan 'Abd al-Hamid, which was used to put down Armenian risings in Eastern Anatolia in the 1890s. Nonetheless, it is clear that government authority had not been universally accepted in either the Iranian or Ottoman Kurdish areas by the First World War.

In common with the other non-Turkish peoples of the Ottoman Empire, the Kurds were affected by the currents of nationalism in Europe and Asia in the second part of the 19th century. Kurdish intellectuals began to form secret societies aiming either at some form of decentralised

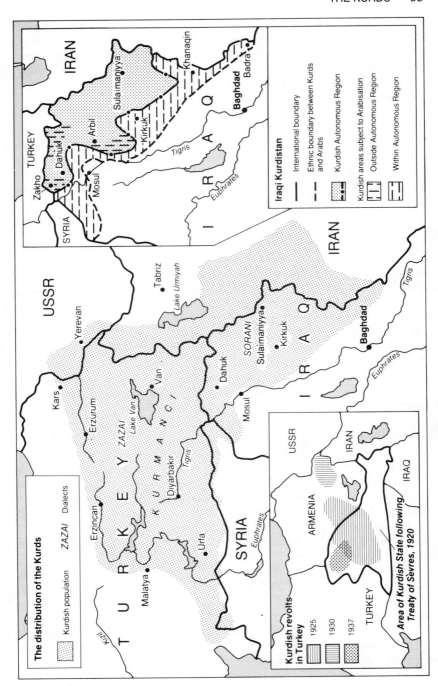

Iraqi Kurdistan

International boundary
Ethnic boundary between Kurds and Arabs
Kurdish Autonomous Region
Kurdish areas subject to Arabisation
Outside Autonomous Region
Within Autonomous Region

The distribution of the Kurds

Kurdish population
ZAZAI Dialects

Kurdish revolts in Turkey

1925
1930
1937

Area of Kurdish State following Treaty of Sèvres, 1920

administration of the Kurdish provinces, or (more rarely) for complete independence from the Ottoman government. In an essentially rural and tribal society, however, such activities were to have little effect unless accompanied by the support of powerful tribes and their leaders, who alone could produce the weapons and the men necessary to effect political change.

During the First World War, the Turks and the Russians were on opposite sides, while Iran remained neutral. However, Russian troops had been stationed in Iran since 1909 (when they had intervened on the shah's side in the Constitutional Revolution), and Turkish troops actually captured Tabriz from the Russians for ten days early in 1915. After the Treaty of Brest-Litovsk in December 1917, when Russia withdrew from the war, there was a power vacuum in eastern Turkey until well into 1919 and in western Iran until Reza Khan's seizure of power in 1921. In general, the absence of centralised authority permitted widespread disorder and the massacre or expulsion of most of the Assyrian and some of the Armenian populations, who, as Christians, had tended to take the Russian side. Farther south, Mosul town was occupied a little after the Treaty of Mudros (October 1918), and the area of British occupation was soon afterwards held to extend over the whole of Mosul province. Kurdish nationalists in exile outside Turkey, and local tribal leaders in ex-Ottoman Kurdistan, saw the defeat of the Ottomans and the occupation of Mosul as a golden opportunity for pressing their claims. In this, they were encouraged by President Woodrow Wilson's '14 Points' (8 January 1918), the twelfth of which states that 'the nationalities now under Turkish rule should [in the event of an Allied victory] be assured an undoubted security of life and an absolutely unmolested opportunity of autonomous development'.

At this time the two southern Iraqi provinces were under direct British administration, but because of the circumstance of the occupation of Mosul province, and because of its mountainous terrain, it could not be occupied in the same way. In fact, the whole question of the future of Mosul, and whether it was to be 'returned' to Turkey or be part of the new state of Iraq, was not to be settled until 1925. In mid-November 1918, it was British policy to encourage the appointment of suitable local figures to administer the area with British political advisors. The most prominent of these notables was Sheik Mahmud Barzinji, who was installed as governor of Sulaimaniyya.

A variety of factors combined to ensure that this was not to be the prelude to the creation of an independent or quasi-independent Kurdish state. In the first place, the British government gradually became committed to the establishment of an Arab state under British auspices in Iraq, and to the inclusion of the oil-bearing province of Mosul within that state. Secondly, the defeat of the Ottomans was followed by the rise of a national resistance movement in Anatolia in the spring of 1919, the prelude to the war of independence, which ended with Atatürk and his forces victorious and the withdrawal of the British and Greek occupying armies from Anatolia by October 1922. In these changing circumstances the Kurds both north and south of the present Turco-Iraqi frontier naturally hesitated over whether to throw in their lot with Britain or with Turkey, since Britain's *locus standi* in the area was by no means clear. Finally, and of great significance for the future, the concept of an 'independent Kurdistan' or 'self-determination of the Kurds' required consensus on the part of the Kurds themselves as to suitable representatives. At this stage, the desire for Kurdish autonomy did not, because of traditional clan and tribal rivalries, produce any coherent movement towards Kurdish unity: Sheik Mahmud, for example, was removed by the British in May 1919 largely because his support base was so inadequate that he could not control areas less than 20 miles from Sulaimaniyya.

Throughout 1919 and for most of 1920, there were constant risings in northern Iraq. Some were attempts to drive British forces out of the Mosul area, but some were the normal Kurdish expression of distaste at the imposition of outside authority. In the summer of 1920, a few months after the award of the mandates for Palestine and Iraq to Britain and Syria and Lebanon to France, the Istanbul government accepted the Treaty of Sèvres, against the wish of the Grand National Assembly convened by Atatürk and his supporters in Ankara. The treaty amounted to the dismemberment of what was left of Turkey and its partition between Italy and Greece, with 'independent states' in Armenia and Kurdistan. Although the rise of Atatürk ensured that Sèvres was never ratified, it marked an important turning point in the evolution of the Kurdish movement, as the first formal declaration of intent to set up a separate, specifically Kurdish, political entity.

Turkey and Iran in the inter-war period

By the early 1920s, therefore, the political geography of the Kurdish areas had begun to assume much of the shape that it does today, with the Kurds divided between Turkey, Iraq, Iran and Syria. In general terms, Turkish governments until the end of the 1980s pursued consistently repressive policies towards the Kurdish population, which amounted to a virtual denial of the separate ethnic and linguistic identity of the Kurds. Drastic reprisals, involving executions, massacres and mass deportations, were taken against any attempts to assert Kurdish nationalism or independence. The risings led by Sheik Sa'id (1925), the Khoybun revolt (1929–30) and the Dersim rebellion (1937) were all put down with great ferocity.

In Iran, the early 1920s were filled with uncertainty. The Iranian Kurds were told firmly by the British to respect the rule of the Iranian government, and to expect no assistance from Britain in setting up a Kurdish political entity. However, the Russian Revolution had removed the Iranian monarchy's main support, which meant that there was anarchy throughout most of the country. In the Kurdish area, Simko Agha, the chief of the

Shakkak tribe, seized power shortly after the end of the war. Although checked by the Cossack brigade, he managed to gain the support of several Kurdish tribes in the Mahabad region, and began to talk of creating a Kurdish state, taking the towns of Mahabad and Khoi in the autumn of 1921. By July 1922, however, the Iranian army had been reorganised sufficiently to defeat Simko and his allies, and he was forced to flee to Iraq. Throughout the inter-war period, Reza Shah extended his centralising policies to the Kurdish areas, confiscating the land of recalcitrants and often moving tribes to other parts of the country.

Iraqi Kurdish politics, 1920—46

In Iraq, the situation of the Kurds was more complex. In 1922 the British mandatory authorities had promised the Kurds a form of autonomy in northern Iraq, but by this time Sheik Mahmud Barzinji, whom the British had reinstated, *faute de mieux*, in Sulaimaniyya, seems to have decided against accepting any form of Iraqi suzerainty. Eventually his attempts at rebellion were crushed, at least temporarily, and Rowanduz, Koi Sanjak and Sulaimaniyya were occupied by British troops in 1924. By this time, the League of Nations had decided to send a special commission to decide whether the Mosul *vilayet* should be part of Iraq or Turkey. After several months' deliberations, the commissioners decided that Mosul should be part of Iraq, a recommendation which generally found favour in the region. Early in 1926, the prime minister of Iraq declared that civil servants in the Kurdish area should be Kurds, that Kurdish and Arabic should be the official languages of the area, and that Kurdish children should be educated in Kurdish. Although these provisions were only half-heartedly carried out, it is fair to say that the Kurds' separate ethnic identity has generally been recognised to a greater or lesser extent by all Iraqi govern-ments since then, and token Kurds served as ministers in virtually all the governments under the monarchy.

However, much of the Kurds' enthusiasm for the state of Iraq derived from their belief that their status would in some sense be underwritten by the British presence. Britain's announcement in 1932 that she would support Iraq's application for independence consequently caused serious misgivings, especially when it became known that the treaty contained no minority guarantees. After serious rioting in Sulaimaniyya in September 1930, Sheik Mahmud indicated that he was once more prepared to go on the offensive, and fighting broke out in the spring of 1931. The revolt was decisively defeated, but almost simultaneously a new and generally more effective nucleus of Kurdish opposition was developing, in the Barzani tribal lands in the subdistrict of Baradost. Mullah Mustafa Barzani, the younger brother of the Barzani religious and tribal leader Sheik Ahmad, emerged in the early 1930s as the principal figure in Iraqi Kurdish politics, a position he was to retain until his death in exile in 1979.

After organising a series of revolts against the Iraq government in the

Barzan area, the Barzani brothers were finally forced to surrender and, from 1936, to live under a loose form of house arrest in Sulaimaniyya. Here Barzani came into contact with Kurdish political writers and thinkers, some of whom joined together to form the clandestine Hewa (Hope) party in 1939, which included individuals from both the left and the right; that is, on the one hand, those who believed that social reforms were an essential prerequisite for the Kurds to achieve their national rights, and on the other, those who felt that the key to obtaining Kurdish rights lay in Britain's hands, and that some form of alliance with Britain was necessary. Barzani himself was inclined to favour some sort of accommodation with Britain.

After the reoccupation of Iraq by British forces in April 1941, the Iraqi government was preoccupied with events in the south and left the north more or less to its own devices. In 1943 Barzani escaped from Sulaimaniyya and proceeded to make overtures to the British authorities in an attempt to gain British support for a formal recognition of Kurdish autonomy, although this eventually came to nothing. By the summer of 1945 the Iraqi government evidently felt sufficiently confident to launch a campaign to restore its authority in the north. 14,000 troops were dispatched, and this army succeeded in chasing Barzani out of Iraq and into Iran in October 1945.

The Republic of Mahabad

In June 1941, Nazi Germany invaded the Soviet Union, which immediately joined the Allied side. In order to supply the Soviet Union, the Allies needed to use the land routes across Iran, and when Reza Shah attempted to resist this he was deposed and exiled. With the collapse of the Iranian army the Kurdish tribes were once more virtually autonomous in their own areas, a situation reminiscent of the hiatus between the end of the First World War and the assumption of power by Reza Khan in 1921. By May 1943 the authority of the Iranian government in north-west Iran had collapsed altogether and Soviet officials from across the border had begun to make approaches to influential Kurdish figures in the area. The political centre of the region west of Azerbaijan was the small town of Mahabad, south of Lake Urmia, which had a population of some 16,000 inhabitants in 1945. In 1942 a Kurdish nationalist association, the Komala, had been formed in the region and had developed links to with Hewa in Iraq. In October 1944 the leading citizen and judge of Mahabad, Qadi Mohammed, was asked to become a member of the Komala.

At the same time, Soviet officials were encouraging a separatist movement in the eastern province of Azerbaijan. Both the Kurds and the Azeris regarded the Soviets as natural partners, since they were encouraging the autonomous movements in both areas. In the autumn of 1945, after a meeting with Soviet officials in Nakhichevan, just across the frontier, Qadi Mohammed and a number of prominent citizens of Mahabad founded the

Kurdistan Democratic party (KDP). At almost exactly the same time Mullah Mustafa Barzani and his supporters were preparing to enter Iran from Iraq.

The arrival of Barzani meant the addition of 3,000 fighting men pledged to the Kurdish cause. Accordingly, the Iranian Kurds proclaimed an autonomous Republic of Mahabad, which was inaugurated by Qadi Mohammed on 22 January 1946. However, with the onset of the Cold War in 1946, knowing that the Soviet Union was anxious to obtain an oil concession in north-west Iran, the British and American governments began to press for the withdrawal of all foreign troops from Iran, a move which implied the eventual restoration of the authority of the Iranian government over all parts of the country. The effects of this took some time to be felt in Mahabad, where the republic was building up a defence force, composed largely of Barzani's tribal irregulars. The Soviet government provided military equipment, but also promised the Iranian government that it would withdraw its own troops some time in May 1946.

Like many other Kurdish politicians after him, Qadi Mohammed did not want total independence, but, in his case, some kind of federal association with the government in Tehran that would not involve the entry of Iranian troops into the territory of the republic. In addition, he wanted education to be conducted in Kurdish, a locally based administration and a locally controlled military force. Although the presence of Soviet troops in the neighbouring area had been essential for the republic's initial foundation, Mahabad itself had never been occupied by the Red Army but had enjoyed a degree of de facto independence for some five years. None of its citizens' aspirations was to be achieved: on 16 December 1946 the Iranian army entered Mahabad, and on 31 March 1947 Qadi Mohammed and two of his close relatives and political allies were hanged in the main square.

For his part, Barzani now sought some kind of accommodation with the Iranian government through the good offices of the British Embassy in Tehran, but in vain. He was eventually forced out of Iran into Iraq, and in mid-May 1947 he and 600 of his followers undertook a daring journey to the Soviet Union across Turkey and Iran, crossing the Aras River between 15 and 18 June and covering 220 miles over mountainous country in about a fortnight. They stayed in the Soviet Union until 1958.

The Kurds in Turkey, 1920—80

As has already been described, the policies of most modern Turkish governments towards the Kurds since the 1920s have generally aimed to repress and to deny separate Kurdish ethnic and linguistic identity. Although most Kurds had fought first for the Ottoman Empire and then for Atatürk, they did not support Atatürk's 'Turkism' or his secular policies. When the caliphate was abolished in 1924, all Kurdish associations, schools and publications were closed. This provoked revolts against the central government in the Kurdish areas, often led by religious leaders, who were represented as obscurantist enemies of progress by the new government in Ankara. The 'pacification' of the area was brutal. Perhaps a quarter-of-a-million Kurds were killed and over a million deported to other parts of Turkey. Simultaneously, large numbers of Turks moved into the area from outside. Much of Turkish Kurdistan remained under martial law for several decades.

The situation eased somewhat in 1950, when a non-Kemalist party was elected to power. Although they could not identify themselves as such, Kurds became members of parliament and ministers, and efforts were made to develop the Kurdish areas economically. Especially after the Iraqi revolution of 1958, Turkish Kurds became aware of the activities of Kurdish political organisations in Iraq. In addition, the hundreds of thousands of displaced Kurds in the cities of western Turkey became increasingly conscious of their national status, and a separatist Turkish KDP was founded in 1965. The paradox of Turkish political life in the 1950s, '60s and '70s was that, although most of the members of parliament for eastern Turkey were Kurds, they could not organise as such. As late as 1979 a prominent ex-minister was sentenced to two years' imprisonment for a speech in which he stated that there were both Kurds and Turks in Turkey.

In the late 1960s various left-wing parties and organisations were founded in the area, and there were mass anti-government demonstrations in Sivas and Diyarbakir in 1967. The 1970s saw great instability throughout Turkey generally, with Kurdish urban and rural guerrilla groups especially active. A radical organisation, the Workers' Party of Kurdistan (PKK), emerged in the late 1970s and proclaimed armed struggle against the government in the Kurdish area, denouncing, and sometimes killing, local leaders and members of opposing political organisations as 'collaborators'. Its activities resulted in increasing government repression in the area.

A major difficulty for the forging of a unified Kurdish movement in Turkey (as elsewhere) has been the cleavage between (generally pro-Barzani) nationalist groups on the one hand, and leftists, attached either to mainstream left-wing Turkish parties or groups such as the PKK, on the other. Both sides are often as vehemently opposed to each other as to the Turkish government. After the military coup in 1980 the official government view became that the Kurds were actually Turks who had somehow lost their way and their language over the centuries. About half the Turkish army was permanently stationed in the Kurdish area, ostensibly because of its proximity to the Soviet Union and Iran, but also to be able to act quickly to suppress any risings there.

Iraqi Kurdish politics after 1947

With the fall of Mahabad and the departure of Barzani, Kurdish politics remained virtually in limbo until the overthrow of the Iraqi monarchy. In Iran the KDP was proscribed; it reappeared briefly in support of the government of Mohammed Mosaddeq in 1951–53, but suffered in the reprisals against the left that followed Mosaddeq's fall. In 1956, still underground, it published a draft programme calling for Kurdish autonomy. Broadly speaking, the principal events in the history of the Kurdish movement since 1947 relate to its activities in Iraq. This is because, in spite of the unwillingness of successive Iraqi governments to render more than lip service to the principle, the Iraqi Kurds enjoyed certain basic freedoms denied to their fellows in Iran and Turkey, perhaps most significantly the recognition, tacit and grudging though it may often have been, of their separate ethnic status. In Turkey, and to a lesser extent in Iran, Kurds were persecuted as Kurds; in Iraq, provided that they did not actually engage in activities against the central government, the Kurds were generally no more—and no less—deprived of civil liberties than their Arab fellow citizens. This attitude only changed significantly with the bombing of Halabja with chemical weapons in 1988, and of course with the failure of the Kurdish rising against Saddam Husain in the spring of 1991.

Perhaps the most important development in Kurdish politics between Mahabad and 1958 was the foundation and rise to maturity of the Iraqi KDP. At first an Iraqi branch of the Iranian KDP had been founded in Mahabad in 1946 by Barzani and his close associate Hamza 'Abdullah, who was charged with organising the party in Iraq, but his mission ended in the creation of a separate Iraqi KDP. This had the effect of formalising a permanent administrative separation in terms of Kurdish politics between Iraqi and Iranian Kurdistan. Thus in August 1946 the Iraqi KDP was formally inaugurated, with 'Abdullah as secretary general and Mullah Mustafa, then still in Mahabad, as president. At the same time there was a branch of the Iranian KDP in Iraqi Kurdistan, based at Sulaimaniyya, under the leadership of Ibrahim Ahmad (a long-standing rival of Barzani), who denounced the new Iraqi KDP as a potentially dangerous derogation of the authority of Qadi Mohammed and the Mahabad republic. After the fall of Mahabad, Ahmad reluctantly joined the Iraqi KDP, becoming its secretary-general in 1951, taking advantage of Barzani's absence in the Soviet Union to push the party to the left. The KDP now worked mainly among students and intellectuals and had little support in the countryside, which continued to be dominated by tribal leaders and landlords.

When the Free Officers seized power in 1958, Ahmad, then under house arrest in Kirkuk, immediately telegraphed a message of congratulation. For the time being at least, the auguries seemed favourable. The new constitution stated that 'Arabs and Kurds are partners in the Iraqi homeland, and their national rights are recognised within the Iraqi state'. On

6 October 1958 Barzani returned from exile to a rapturous welcome from his Kurdish supporters and what seemed to be expressions of genuine cordiality from the new leader, 'Abd al-Karim Qasim. A new era in Arab–Kurdish relations appeared to have begun.

The Free Officers had no special commitment to the Kurdish question—none was Kurdish—but their attitude towards the Kurds was positive. A distinguished Kurdish civil servant and former army officer, Khalid al-Naqshabandi, was made a member of the three-man ceremonial 'sovereignty council'. In the conflict that ensued in 1958–59 over whether Iraq should join the United Arab Republic, the Kurds' attitude was generally negative: the pan-Arab-inspired UAR was a most unlikely vehicle for the furthering of their aspirations, however defined. As Qasim himself was also opposed to unity with Egypt, relations between the central government and the KDP, which had now been taken over by Mullah Mustafa Barzani, continued to be amicable. However, the prospect of the extension of the new land reform to Kurdistan caused alarm among Barzani and his circle, especially as such policies would have widespread popularity. This was a further manifestation of the contradiction between 'social reform' and 'national aspirations' which has acted as a major brake on the effectiveness of the Kurdish movement over the past quarter century.

In January 1960 the KDP was legalised; in the course of the same year Ibrahim Ahmad and his son-in-law, Jalal Talabani, managed to find their way back into Barzani's favour so that by October 1960 Ahmad had been 're-elected' secretary-general of the party. Gradually, however, it became clear that many of the more conservative Free Officers were opposed to any real concessions to the Kurds, and also that Qasim's own commitment was limited. For his part, Barzani's basic instincts and sentiments were those of a tribal leader. Though interested in gaining the support of Kurdish intellectuals and urban dwellers, his real power base lay in his own tribe, and his force of some 2,000 fighting men. Hence the wording of the party manifesto was not as important to him as to 'the politicals', who saw the party as a means of political and ideological mobilisation. For their part, the 'politicals' were often obliged, against their better judgment, to defer to Barzani precisely because he was the only Kurdish figure with sufficient magnetism, tribal following and military experience to be able to carry the day in Kurdistan.

Eventually it became clear that Qasim was not willing to grant real autonomy to the Kurds; by the beginning of 1961 he began to turn against Barzani. He began to favour the leaders of tribes opposed to him (especially the Herki and Zibari) and banned Kurdish newspapers and magazines. For a while, Barzani was content to bide his time in the north, and let Qasim arrest or harass the urban leadership. Thus Ahmad and another member of the politbureau, 'Umar Mustafa, were arrested in March 1961 and the KDP was refused permission to hold its annual congress in July.

Nevertheless, by September 1961 fighting had broken out in earnest, and this continued intermittently until 1975.

By May 1962, Barzani had gained control of the road between Rowanduz and the Iranian border; the Iraqi army was only able to return to this area after the collapse of the Kurdish movement in 1975. When the Ba'th-nationalist alliance eventually overthrew Qasim in February 1963, the coup leaders had obtained assurances from both Barzani and the KDP leaders that if they were successful the Kurds would announce a cease-fire, which duly materialised. Talabani and Salah al-Yusufi were dispatched to Baghdad a few days after the coup to negotiate with the new regime. As could easily have been foreseen, these negotiations proved futile and fighting broke out again in June 1963.

The Kurds since 1963

For the next few years the conflict was generally three-cornered: between the government, the KDP, and Barzani. Sometimes the KDP could co-operate with the government, sometimes with Barzani, and sometimes, though rather more rarely, Barzani and the government would join forces to attack the KDP. Thus in August 1964 Barzani chased Ahmad and Talabani out of Iraq across the Iranian border in revenge for the KDP's attack on his truce with 'Arif (February 1964 to April 1965). In July Barzani had set up his 'own' KDP from which all supporters of the Ahmad-Talabani group had been purged. This rupture between Barzani and the 'politicals' had the effect of handing over the day-to-day control of much of the Kurdish movement on the ground to Barzani; while his military talents were unquestioned, his political acumen was sufficiently limited as to put the Kurdish cause at a grave disadvantage.

When fighting broke out again in April 1965 virtually the whole Iraqi army was dispatched to the north, but Barzani, who was receiving large quantities of arms from Iran, inflicted a crushing defeat on the Iraqi army in mid-May 1966. The government began to negotiate seriously with him, and a 'third interlude' began, which lasted until January 1969. On 26 June 1966 the Iraqi prime minister put forward a peace plan for Kurdistan, which, although honoured largely in the breach over the following years, has generally formed the basis for most subsequent peace initiatives for the area.

In July 1968 the 'Arif government was overthrown and Ba'th came to power with the tacit support of the Ahmad-Talabani faction of the KDP, some of whom were briefly appointed to the cabinet. However, attempts to reach a more durable agreement between Barzani and the Ba'th failed and fighting broke out once more. The government replied by sending four divisions to Kurdistan, and the fighting continued for most of that year. In August 1969, a major offensive was launched by the government, once more without any visible success, in spite of atrocities designed to terrorise the inhabitants into submission. At this stage the Ba'th regime was not yet sufficiently firmly established to continue the campaign indefinitely. It therefore approached Barzani with a view to opening negotiations. These lasted from mid-December 1969 until March 1970 and ended with the publication of an agreement, the 'March Manifesto'. This recognised 'the legitimacy of the Kurdish nationality,' and promised Kurdish linguistic rights, Kurdish participation in government, Kurdish administrators for the Kurdish area, and a new province based on Dahuk. It also envisaged the implementation of the Agrarian Reform Law in the north, and, perhaps most controversially, as future events were to show, stated that 'necessary steps shall be taken . . . to unify the governorates and administrative units populated by a Kurdish majority as shown by the official census to be carried out . . .'. The most contentious area here was that of the town of Kirkuk and the oil wells which surrounded it.

The manifesto had two important drawbacks for the Ba'th. First it was specifically concluded with Barzani himself, which meant that, at least by implication, it gave recognition to Barzani and the KDP as the sole political (and, by extension, administrative) authority in an area extending from Zakho to Halabja. Secondly, this recognition had the effect of undermining 'the writ of the Iraqi state in the Kurdish areas'. As events were to show the manifesto was essentially a device by the Ba'th to gain time to recast its Kurdish policy to its own advantage. One consequence of the agreement was that the Ahmad-Talabani faction of 'pro-government Kurds' became redundant, and in fact dissolved itself in the course of 1970, to reappear, in a somewhat different guise, as the Patriotic Union of Kurdistan in 1976.

The government's bad faith became apparent soon after the publication of the manifesto. Large numbers of families were forcibly removed from their homes to change the ethnic balance of particular areas, especially Kirkuk, which the Kurdish leadership had insisted should form part of the Kurdish area and which the government wanted to retain within 'Iraq proper'. Again, in September 1971 some 40,000 Faili (Shia) Kurds were expelled to Iran from the border area near Khanaqin on the absurd grounds that they were not really Iraqis. In these and other measures the Ba'th showed that they were intent on limiting the extent of Kurdistan as far as possible. In September 1971 the Ba'th attempted unsuccessfully to assassinate Barzani; similar attacks on him and his sons took place during 1972 and 1973. Tensions grew and clashes occurred between government forces and the Kurds in Sulaimaniyya and in Jabal Sinjar, where several thousand Yazidis were forced to leave their homes in February and March 1973.

Although a major breakdown seemed inevitable, negotiations between the parties continued throughout the end of 1973 and the beginning of 1974. A few members of the KDP (notably Barzani's eldest son, Ubaidallah) broke with Barzani and joined the Ba'th dominated NF. But most Kurds stood solidly behind Barzani and the KDP. In April 1974 fighting broke out again, with the Iraqi air force bombing Qala Diza, Halabja and Galala, killing 193 civilians. A mass exodus of refugees took place to Iran, where there were over 110,000 in the autumn and about 275,000 by the spring of 1975. For a few months, the Kurds had the upper hand; in spite of their numerical superiority, the government forces had as usual become seriously bogged down, and no end seemed in sight.

At this point, help arrived from an unexpected quarter. Iraqi concern to get the better of the Kurds coincided with the shah of Iran's desire to end frontier disputes and other hostilities with Iraq which had inflamed relations between the two countries over the previous decade. In March 1975, in the course of the OPEC (Organisation of Petroleum Exporting Countries) conference at Algiers, Saddam Husain and the shah came to an agreement, which, on the Iraqi side, effectively abrogated the Sa'dabad Pact of 1937, gave the Iranians free rights of navigation in the Shatt al-'Arab, and, on the Iranian side, closed the Iran–Iraq frontier in the north, thus preventing aid from reaching the Kurds and equally preventing the Kurds themselves from regrouping and rearming in and from Iran. The Iranian artillery, which had supported the Kurds, withdrew within 24 hours and the Kurdish resistance collapsed almost immediately. Barzani left for Iran, dying in the United States in 1979.

In the months that followed, most of the refugees trickled back to Iraq under a series of amnesties. In the meantime the government continued to Arabise the area forcibly. The inhabitants of the more remote areas were removed from their homes and 'resettled' in new concrete villages on the sides of roads where surveillance would be easier. Kurdish was no longer taught at schools and Kurdish teachers and administrators were sent to work in southern Iraq and replaced in the Kurdish areas by Arabs. By 1979 an estimated 200,000 Kurds had been deported from the frontier area and some 700 villages burnt down as part of a scorched-earth policy which aimed to clear a strip along the border with Iran and Turkey some 12 miles wide and 500 miles long.

The Iranian revolution

After the fall of Mahabad, the Iranian Kurdish movement went underground, surfacing in 1958 in the hope of taking indirect advantage of Barzani's return to Iraq from the Soviet Union. However, the Iranian government continued to harass and suppress Kurdish activists, and also had a complex relationship with Barzani, whom, as has been mentioned, it armed from time to time against the government in Baghdad. As far as Barzani was concerned, his intermittent dependence on the shah meant that he was unable or unwilling to assist the Kurdish movement in Iran, even going so far as to hand over to SAVAK (the Iranian secret service) a number of Iranian Kurdish refugees who had fled to Iraq. During the Ba'th/ Kurdish honeymoon period (1970–74) Iranian Kurdish activity moved to Baghdad, although it was clear that the shah was continuing to support Barzani. Between 1973 and 1989 (when he was assassinated in Vienna) Abd al-Rahman Qasimlu, a former professor at the Sorbonne, was the leader of the Iranian KDP. It generally lacked the tribal base of the Iraqi KDP, but has probably been more intensely politicised as a result.

The Iranian revolution was naturally greeted with great excitement in Iranian Kurdistan, since the possibility of autonomy had appeared once more–and, as one authority points out, the prospects seemed better than at the time of Mahabad as no Great Power interest was involved. However, as the Islamic Republic established itself, it became clear that it would not support Kurdish separatist demands since it was ideologically opposed to the notion of any ethnic or other divisions within the Islamic community, recognising only the canonically sanctioned religious minorities (Christians, Jews and Zoroastrians). On the other hand, the situation was so unstable and the control exercised by the centre over the provinces so precarious, that 'creeping autonomy' seemed to be coming in any case. Unfortunately for the Iranian Kurds, the regime in Tehran attracted the support of both Mas'ud Barzani and Jalal Talabani, so that the Iraqi KDP and the Patriotic Union of Kurdistan (PUK) sided with Tehran against the Iranian KDP and its leftist allies (a step which caused severe convulsions within the Iraqi KDP itself). Sharp clashes took place in the spring and summer of 1979, but by August the Kurds had lost all the towns they had captured to the Iranian army. As Kurdish forces continued to control much of the countryside, an uneasy stalemate persisted until the outbreak of the Iran–Iraq War in September 1980.

The effects of the Iran–Iraq War

Again, internal disagreements within the Kurdish movement inside Iran and Iraq, and between the Kurdish movements of the two countries, resulted in the loss, or the frittering away, of yet another promising opportunity. In the first place, the government of the Islamic Republic recruited the Barzanis and the Iraqi KDP to fight against the Iranian KDP. Partly as a result, partly because of the Iranian army's recovery, the Iranian KDP gradually lost control of the areas it dominated in north-west Iran. In Iraq, Talabani's PUK made several attempts to negotiate some sort of settlement with Baghdad (Iran was supporting the Iraqi KDP at the time), which was itself uneasy at the large number of Kurdish deserters from the army. In addition, the PUK was uncertain as to what an Iranian victory might bring. On 10 December 1983 Talabani reached an agreement with Baghdad, ostensibly because of the latter's willingness to admit some of the PUK's demands, but in fact to release Iraqi troops for more effective deployment in the war zone.

As could easily have been predicted, this agreement did not last long. A few months later 24 Kurds were executed in Sulaimaniyya. It was clear that Baghdad was not going to give up its claim to control the area. Such incidents, and what was widely regarded as opportunism on the part of the PUK, lost it much credibility and support in the Kurdish areas. By 1987, however, all the main Kurdish groups had formed an alliance against

Baghdad, and stated that they would press for autonomy within Iraq. Simultaneously, the PUK dropped its opposition to cooperation with Iranian forces, and by the spring of 1987 Iranian and PUK forces were fighting side by side inside Iraqi Kurdistan. KDP and PUK forces now controlled the area between the Great Zab and the Diyala, Rowanduz, and much of the area between Zakho and Agra. All this took place against a background of the most terrible brutality on the part of the Iraqi government, 8,000 members of the Barzani clan were arrested in 1983 and have not been seen since. A further 2,000 hamlets were stripped of their population, and as many as half-a-million Kurds were deported to lowland Kurdistan or southern Iraq.

In March 1988 Iranian troops captured Halabja. The following day, the town was attacked with chemical weapons, and over 6,000 civilians, including large numbers of women and children, were killed. This policy was continued after the cease-fire on 20 August. In the face of further gas attacks, some 60,000 Kurdish civilians fled to Turkey and a similar number to Iran. As a result, armed Kurdish opposition virtually ceased. The refugee problem inside Iran and Turkey was considerable, with over 150,000 in camps in Iran and a further 70,000 in Turkey. For its part, Turkey, concerned about the effect on its 'own' Kurds, refused to allow the Iraqi Kurds to be described as refugees, insisting that all aid be distributed through the Turkish Red Crescent and generally playing down allegations that some of the refugees had been the victims of gas attacks. At the same time the PKK was apparently gaining support in south-east Turkey, and Kurdish deputies, knowing that human rights issues were an important item on the agenda of Turkey's relations with the EC, made use of the situation to push for further concessions from Ankara.

The Kurds in the aftermath of the Gulf War

As the PKK became increasingly active in Turkey in the late 1980s, popular hostility to the security forces' activities grew. Curfews were declared in the south-east, and new decrees forbade press reporting and permitted forcible resettlement. Local support grew steadily throughout 1990 and 1991, compounded with resentment at the government's generally insensitive handling of the Iraqi Kurdish refugees. At the same time the prime minister, Turgut Özal, pressed for changes to lift some restrictions on the use of the Kurdish language. In general the Gulf War and its aftermath aroused great concern on the part of the Turkish government, which feared that successful moves towards separatism or autonomy on the part of the Iraqi Kurds might have a 'domino effect' within Turkey. The problem seemed as acute as ever, but the establishment seemed incapable of producing a new or original policy to cope with it.

In Iran the outlook for a Kurdish settlement became far more uncertain with the assassination of Abd al-Rahman Qasimlu in Vienna in July 1989, probably, though not certainly, at the hands of the Iranian government, with which he was engaged in negotiations at the time. The only hope for Kurdish autonomy lay in the generally more pragmatic policies of the post-Khomeini regime in Tehran, and the possibility that some relaxation of the grip of the central government might take place.

By far the most spectacular and terrible developments in Kurdish politics over the last few years have taken place in Iraq. Kurdish organisations admitted in 1989 that they had been wrong to let the Iranians take Halabja in 1988, and that they had greatly overestimated the chances of Saddam Husain's regime falling. Neither the PUK nor the KDP was any longer capable of taking the Iraqi army on. The invasion of Kuwait in August 1990 caused a considerable dilemma to the Kurdish leadership, some believing that they should force concessions out of Saddam Husain while he was weak, others not wishing to side too openly with external forces against him. In December 1990 most of the Kurdish organisations joined the rest of the opposition in declaring their hostility to the Ba'th government, calling for an end to human rights abuses and for the introduction of democracy and the rule of law; for their part, the other opposition groups all accepted the notion of Kurdish autonomy.

After the defeat of the Iraqi ground forces in February 1991 two spontaneous and uncoordinated risings broke out in Iraq, one in the south and the other in the Kurdish area. For two weeks it appeared that the opposition was decisively in command, and then the table turned. Kurdish guerrilla forces were driven out of the northern cities, and by the beginning of April massive numbers of Kurdish refugees were camped out on the Iranian and Turkish borders. This human tragedy, which unfolded daily in front of millions of television viewers throughout the world, brought the desperate plight of the Kurds to world attention for the first time. A rapid relief operation was mounted to assist an estimated one-and-a-half million people. By mid-April, Jalal Talabani and Mas'ud Barzani of the PUK and KDP were back in Baghdad, engaged in another round of the futile negotiations in which both had been so often engaged in the past, extracting superficial concessions from Baghdad which were most unlikely to be translated into reality. Again, although perhaps more urgently this time, the negotiations had the effect of giving Saddam Husain time to regroup his resources, confirming not just his survival but his determination to remain in power.

Peter Sluglett and Marion Farouk-Sluglett

3 IRAN

Iran (formerly Persia) is an ancient country that has formed several empires in the past two-and-a-half millennia. In the 7th century AD the Muslim Conquest broke up the Sassanian Empire and brought Islam to Iran. Later, the loosening of the caliphate in Baghdad led to the creation of a number of autonomous kingdoms, followed by the formation of various Turkic and Mongol empires by invaders from central and east Asia. In the 16th century the country was once again reunited through the creation of the Safavid Empire, which established Shia Islam as Iran's official religion. The fall of the Safavid Empire early in the 18th century led to turmoil and disintegration which—except for a brief period under the Zand dynasty— continued until the end of the century when the Qajar state was established. In the 19th century, the rise of industry and empire in Europe exposed Iran's weaknesses vis-à-vis the European powers. It led to loss of territory to Russia and the growing domination of the country by European powers in general, Russia and Britain in particular. Attempts at partial reforms within the traditional framework having failed, attention was increasingly drawn to the possibility of drastic action for political and economic development. This led to the Constitutional Revolution at the beginning of the 20th century.

The Constitutional Revolution

The Constitutional Revolution of 1905–11 was a product of many factors. The rise of industry and empire in 19th-century Europe had provided a mirror against which Iranian political and economic backwardness could be critically examined. At the same time, it had supplied a model for political modernisation and economic progress. The revolution had had a successful prelude in the Tobacco Rebellion of 1891–92 when, for the first time in Iranian history, an organised popular campaign forced an arbitrary monarch to retract an important state decision.

The central aim and objective of the revolutionary movement was the abolition of arbitrary rule (*estabdad*), and the establishment of the rule of law. Inevitably, however, this led to further demands for the granting of a written constitution to limit the powers of the monarch and lead to a form of parliamentary government. Almost all urban social classes were represented in the revolution, including merchants, religious leaders and preachers, urban-dwelling absentee landlords, notables of the bureaucracy, and intellectuals, with landlords and notables emerging

Official name	The Islamic Republic of Iran
Area	1,648,000 sq. km (627,000 sq. miles)
Population	58 million (1991)
Capital	Tehran
Language	Persian, Kurdish, Arabic, Azeri, Luri, Baluchi
Religion	majority is Twelver Shia Muslim, with several million Sunni Muslims, also mystic dervishes, Zoroastrians, Christians, Jews and others
Currency	Iranian rial

as the main beneficiaries of its successful outcome. Nationalist, modernist and liberal ideas were represented by the intellectuals, but these remained strictly on the sidelines, until later developments led to their emergence and domination of Iranian politics for decades to come. The constitution (together with its supplementary articles) was an essentially secular document modelled mainly on the Belgian constitution, although it declared Shia Islam the state religion and provided a mechanism for the vetting of parliamentary legislation by the religious authorities.

The First World War

The revolution ended traditional arbitrary rule, thus strengthening private property in land and merchant capital; but it achieved little else. The country was still poor and backward, its politicians were far from united, and foreign imperial influence was still strong. In 1911, a Russian ultimatum forced the government to dissolve parliament, which was resisting a Russian demand for the dismissal of the American financial adviser, Morgan Shuster.

The First World War brought greater chaos and political disintegration. While the central government remained neutral, some of the more radical democratic and nationalist politicians were in favour of siding with the Central Powers. This eventually led to the formation of Nezam al-Saltaneh's provisional government in Kermanshah, which existed side by side with the central government in Tehran, but declared war on the Allies. Meanwhile, various northern, western and southern provinces were occupied by Russian, Turkish and British forces, and German agents intensified their activities especially among the central and southern nomadic tribes. At the same time, a group of younger constitutionalists, led by Kuchik Khan, began a guerrilla campaign in the Caspian province of Gilan with the aim of achieving full independence and democratic government for the whole of Iran.

After the war

The Russian Revolution and the end of the First World War introduced new factors to an already complex socio-political situation. The Bolsheviks renounced Tsarist concessions and ambitions in Iran, but at the same time encouraged dissent among Iranian socialists and nationalists, especially in the northern provinces. Britain emerged as the sole foreign power in Iran, appearing to democrats and nationalists as a domineering imperialist power, to conservatives as the country's potential saviour from domestic chaos and the threat of Bolshevism. There were British (or British-led) forces in the provinces of Fars, Khorasan and Gilan. The forces in Khorasan and Gilan were initially intended to contain possible German and Turkish drives southwards, but those in Gilan later brushed with the Bolsheviks and was then concentrated in Qazvin as a deterrent against a thrust by Kuchik Khan who had reluctantly entered an alliance with

(Russian-backed) Iranian Bolsheviks in the Soviet Socialist Republic of Gilan. The situation demanded a strong government and, in 1918, Vusuq al-Dowleh became prime minister.

In August 1919, Vusuq's cabinet entered an agreement with Britain. This provided for the reform and reorganisation of the Iranian army, administration, finance, etc. under the supervision of British advisers—employed and paid by the Iranian government—against a British loan of £2 million, to be repaid over 20 years at a 7% annual rate of interest. The agreement (the brain-child of Lord Curzon, the British foreign secretary) was given an almost completely hostile reception by the Iranian political public. It was viewed as no less than an attempt by Britain to turn Iran into its protectorate, a sentiment that was intensified when it became known that the ministers who had negotiated it had received a certain sum from Britain for which no public account was available. It was decided to submit the agreement to parliament for ratification after the general election. But Vusuq's cabinet fell in July 1920, and the agreement was already a dead letter when it was abrogated by Sayyed Zia's government early in 1921.

The 1921 coup

On 21 February 1921 the Iran Cossack force stationed near Qazvin occupied Tehran, arrested a number of politicians of all colours and persuasions, and declared martial law. The coup was jointly led by Sayyed Zia al-Din Tabataba'i and Brigadier Reza Khan. Sayyed Zia, who became prime minister, was an ambitious journalist with well-known ties with the British legation in Tehran. Reza Khan, now commander of the Cossack Division, was an officer from humble origins who had risen from the ranks. The British Foreign Office had no knowledge of the coup before the event, though some British military and diplomatic officers in Iran had a hand in encouraging and/or organising it. This was the beginning of a new era in Iranian politics, for all that it took a few years for the full implications of the event to be assimilated.

Sayyed Zia's government proved impermanent, though during its short life Reza Khan played an increasingly important role in it, first as minister of war then as prime minister. He managed to divide the opposition of old-school politicians, attract sufficient support from nationalists and modernists, and suggest himself to both Britain and the Soviet Union as Iran's only effective leader. The military forces were expanded, reorganised and turned into a uniform body. Regional political, ethnic and nomadic unrest was largely subdued. Sheik Khazal's semi-autonomous role in Khuzistan was ended. Meanwhile, press freedom began to be curbed, the military tended to dominate political life, especially in the provinces, and the parliamentary majority swung behind Reza Khan for both genuine and opportunistic reasons. The parliamentary opposition, was led by Sayyed Hasan Modarres, supported by a number of independent deputies, the most significant among whom was Mohammed Mosaddeq.

Having become prime minister as well as commander-in-chief of the armed forces, Reza Khan decided to depose the ruling Qajar dynasty and place himself permanently at the helm. At first, his military and civilian supporters led a campaign for the declaration of a republic. The attempt failed: many feared the rise of a dictatorship while the religious establishment was anxious that Reza Khan planned a wholly secular state. Having allayed the fears of the religious authorities, Reza Khan and his supporters then moved to bring down the Qajars and establish the Pahlavi dynasty. This was done, in October 1925, by a vote in parliament, which was ratified, early in 1926, by a special constituent assembly.

Iran under Reza Shah

The outlook and objectives of Reza Shah and his lieutenants was to centralise and modernise Iran along West European models. Legal and administrative reforms were effected, roads and railways constructed, cities modernised, education expanded and industrial plants purchased and installed. However, three fundamental issues were ignored in the process: the need to reconcile modern values with Iranian culture and civilisation; the necessity of land reform to avoid the creation of an increasingly dualistic society; and the importance of political development for social and economic progress. Indeed, in the realms of politics there was retrogression, with the shah increasingly assuming dictatorial and, later, arbitrary powers, ridding himself of his advisers and creating an over-centralised state which tended to suppress regional and ethnic differences. The compulsory wearing of European hats by men, for example, and the ban on veils for women—which led to revolt and bloodshed in the holy city of Mashad—were twin instances of Reza Shah's dictatorial embrace of Western values. While imposing himself in this idiosyncratically modernising manner, Reza Shah, whatever his insistence on absolute probity in public life, neglected few opportunities to raid the public purse or to appropriate private property, in the process amassing a huge fortune and alienating his unfortunate people still further.

Oil exports from Iran began in earnest during the First World War and rapidly became an important factor in politics. From the 1920s there were disagreements with the Anglo-Persian (later Anglo-Iranian) Oil Company over the terms of the 1901 D'Arcy oil concession. Protracted negotiations failed to resolve the problem, until 1932 when the shah ordered the unilateral abrogation of the concession. The British government, which owned 51% of the company's shares, took the dispute to the League of Nations, but the conflict was later resolved with the conclusion of the ill-fated 1933 Oil Agreement, which extended the concessionary period by a further 30 years. This led to charges of 'treason' in the 1940s when the agreement's ex-officio signatory, Sayyed Hasan Taqizadeh, publicly declared that he had signed it under duress.

With the rise of Nazi Germany, Reza Shah began to develop and extend

Iran's economic and political relations with that country. Germany was viewed as an important countervailing power to both Britain and the Soviet Union. Further, Nazi propaganda about the superiority of the Aryan race found an enthusiastic audience in (Aryan) Iran. Germany enjoyed the additional advantage of having never attempted to impose itself imperially in Iran, unlike both Britain and the Soviet Union. In consequence, though Iran remained neutral in the Second World War, its sympathy for Germany was clear.

War and after

In August 1941, the Anglo-Soviet allies invaded Iran from the north and west. For some time they had been warning Iran against the activities of 'German agents' in the country. But the invasion is more likely to have been due to a fear of a possible German drive through the Caucasus, the need to protect Britain's oil supplies, and the importance of the trans-Iranian railways in sending supplies to the Soviet Union. The shah first ordered military resistance to the invasion, but called it off quickly and agreed to cooperate with the Allies. However, it soon became apparent that there could be no settlement so long as he remained on the throne. Reza Shah abdicated in favour of his son, Mohammed Reza, and was taken to Mauritius. He later went to Johannesburg where he died in 1944.

The Allies did not take over the administration of the country and agreed to withdraw their troops when the war ended, although it was clear that their needs were not open to negotiation with the new Iranian government. The devaluation of the rial, coupled with Allied demands for Iranian goods and services and administrative ineptitude, led to high inflation, shortage of basic goods and the threat of famine. Meanwhile, parliamentary government was restored, press censorship was lifted, and organised political activity once again became possible. The Tudeh party was formed by a combination of Marxists and (old as well as new) democrats and socialists, although its leadership and activists were dominated by Marxist elements. Its original programme was the promotion of parliamentary government, social reform and redistribution of income. By 1950, however (after the split in its ranks of 1948 and its official banning in 1949), it had become a fully fledged communist party.

The decade 1941–51 was marked by instability and disorder. Cabinets were short-lived; nomadic power had been largely restored; centrifugal ethnic and regional forces were rekindled. The parliament tended to enjoy excessive powers relative to the executive. It was dominated by landlords and provincial magistrates, but it lacked a mechanism (such as large and lasting parliamentary parties) that would result in durable parliamentary alliances, and hence durable governments. Press freedom was at times excessive, resulting in licentious behaviour. It was the product of lack of political development at a time when the authority of an all-powerful state had been lifted.

In September 1944, while Soviet troops were still in Iran, the Soviet Union formally demanded a concession for the exploration and exploitation of northern Iran's oil. Neither the government of Mohammed Sa'ed nor the conservative parliamentary majority were in favour of granting such a concession, though they were concerned about the consequences of its outright rejection. Yet though the Tudeh party and its parliamentary deputies were caught in a dilemma they eventually threw their weight behind the Soviet demand. Mohammed Mosaddeq seized the opportunity, and as a popular and non-partisan deputy with a firm reputation for opposing dictatorship as well as foreign dependence, he launched a campaign against the granting of the proposed concession. He put forward his policy of 'passive balance', which proposed both that Iran should not give new concession's to foreign powers and that it should attempt to remove existing ones. This was to become the theoretical basis for the nationalisation of Iran's oil six years later. Mosaddeq further managed to pass a parliamentary bill that laid down that the government could not give any concession to foreigners without the approval of parliament. This act enabled the following parliament to reject Ahmad Qavan's oil concession to the Soviet Union, granted as a part of his policy to resolve the Azerbaijan crisis.

Late in 1945 the Democratic party of Azerbaijan, led by Sayyed Ja'far Pishevari—an old-style communist—seized power in that province and declared autonomy. The people of Azerbaijan had many grievances against the central government's attitude and policy towards them under Reza Shah. Reza Shah's abdication made it possible for the province to begin to air its grievances. But the movement quickly fell into the hands of the Democratic party of Azerbaijan, itself being manipulated by the Soviet authorities whose ultimate aim was the integration of the Iranian province into the Azerbaijan Soviet Republic. The province was still under Soviet occupation, and the successive governments of Mohsen Sadr and Ebrahim Hakimi were unable to cope with the situation.

In January 1946 Ahmad Qavan became prime minister, with Soviet backing, in the hope of resolving the crisis. He brought the Tudeh party (who backed the Azerbaijan movement) into his cabinet for a short but crucial period, paid a visit to Moscow where he negotiated with the Soviet government, and tried to enlist the United Nations to persuade Russia to withdraw its troops from Iran. Whether or not the American government delivered a secret ultimatum to the Soviet Union is a matter for historical disagreement, but Qavan's negotiations with the Soviet ambassador in Tehran finally led to an agreement which effectively exchanged the Soviet withdrawal from Azerbaijan for the promise of north Iran's oil concession to the Soviet Union, a promise later rejected by parliament. The Iranian army was then sent to Azerbaijan. The Democrats were defeated, and the Kurdish republic of Mahabad, which had meanwhile been set up in the neighbouring province of Kurdistan, was also overthrown.

Oil nationalisation

With successive waves of labour unrest in the southern Iranian oil fields, growing public attention was drawn to Iranian grievances against the Anglo-Iranian Oil Company (AIOC), and the 1933 Oil Agreement. Early in 1949, negotiations between the Iranian government and the AIOC management led to the Gass-Golsha'iyan (Supplemental) Agreement, which proposed a number of amendments to the existing (1933) agreement. This was regarded as inadequate, and was met with a small but vociferous opposition in parliament, led by Mozaffar Baqa'i and Hosain Makki, who began to attract widespread popular support outside the Assembly. This was towards the end of the parliamentary session, and the campaign for the next general election began soon afterwards.

Mossadeq emerged as leader of the popular movement and stood as a candidate for Tehran. In the following months the National Front (NF), a coalition of democratic and nationalist parties and personalities, was formed, and it managed to send eight deputies to parliament. Mosaddeq became leader of the opposition, and the Front demanded the nationalisation of Iranian oil. The government of General Ali Razmara—a gifted and ambitious soldier politician—wished to pass the Gass-Golsha'iyan Agreement through parliament, but then parliament set up an oil committee, chaired by Mosaddeq, to report on the proposed agreement. In March 1951, Razmara was assassinated by a member of the Feda'iyan'e Islam, although there is a strong belief that the royal court was also implicated. This event was quickly followed by the parliamentary approval of Mosaddeq's oil nationalisation bill, and in April 1951 (following a short-term caretaker government) Mosaddeq was elected prime minister.

It is now clear why agreement between Mosaddeq and AIOC would have been impossible as long as both parties remained committed to their basic aims, as they in fact did. Mosaddeq was prepared to compensate the AIOC, but he was determined not to grant a new concession to it or any other foreign company. The AIOC, on the other hand, would not consider any compensation short of a new agreement that would once again enable it to produce and market Iran's oil. That is why from the very beginning Britain's effort was directed towards the removal of Mosaddeq's government. At first, Mosaddeq enjoyed a certain sympathy from President Truman's government. But later, under Eisenhower, British and American attitudes began to converge, and this eventually led to the coup d'état of August 1953. Early in 1952, Mosaddeq made the mistake of turning down the World Bank's offer of mediation in the oil dispute, primarily for fear of appearing to substantiate Tudah party accusations that he was an American puppet.

The export and sale of Iran's oil having been boycotted by the world's major oil companies, Mosaddeq faced a difficult economic problem. He obtained delegated powers from parliament that enabled him to enact important laws to run for six months before being submitted to parliament.

Later, the period was extended by another year, although not without some vocal opposition. Britain took the oil dispute first to the UN Security Council, then to the International Court at The Hague. On both occasions Iran's argument that the matter was in the jurisdiction of Iranian courts carried the day.

At first the Tudeh party labelled Mosaddeq as an American agent who wished to replace the AIOC with American oil companies. This attitude was somewhat modified later, but the party remained in opposition throughout Mosaddeq's government. Both the shah and the conservative opposition were unhappy about Mosaddeq's oil policy as well as his attitude to domestic political relations. The shah was especially offended by Mosaddeq's slogan that 'in a democracy, the Shah must reign, not rule'. In July 1952, Mosaddeq suggested to the shah that the latter should not appoint the minister of defence but should let the ministry be 'supervised' by Mosaddeq himself. The shah disagreed, and Mosaddeq resigned. Ahmad Qavan became prime minister, but his threats against political unrest in a radio broadcast angered the public. There was a general strike, which led to bloodshed. Qavan resigned and Mosaddeq returned to office.

Further developments led to a split in the leadership of the Popular Movement (PM). The disagreements—led by Ayatollah Kashani and Mozaffar Baqa'i—were the result more of personality problems than policy differences. They were nevertheless damaging to Mosaddeq both at home and abroad. Meanwhile, Mosaddeq's policy of cuts in defence expenditure, and his retirement of some top army officers on charges of corruption or disloyalty, alienated an organised minority within the army. The stability of Mosaddeq's government was severely tested by riots on 28 February 1953, and the kidnap and murder of the police chief the following April. In July, fearing a vote of no confidence in parliament, Mosaddeq held a referendum to dissolve the chamber and hold new elections. On 16 August, an attempted coup was aborted, and the shah, who had dismissed Mosaddeq and named General Fazlollah Zahedi as the new prime minister, suddenly left the country. This led to anti-shah demonstrations, followed by another, and this time successful, coup on 19 August. The plot to overthrow Mosaddeq had been planned and financed by American and British intelligence, but it enjoyed the support and cooperation of the conservative politicians, some leading ayatollahs as well as sections of the army in Iran itself.

After the coup

Both Zahedi's government and the parliament elected during his premiership reflected the coalition of domestic forces which had supported the coup against Mosaddeq. The elections were not free, but the deputies were not simply hand-picked by the shah and his entourage, as became the practice later in the 1960s and 1970s. Mosaddeq and other NF leaders and activists were interned and put on military trial. The NF and other PM forces, though not formally suppressed, were effectively banned from political activity. The campaign against the Tudeh party was savage and effective. Many of the party's leaders had already left Iran for Eastern Europe before the coup. A few more managed to do likewise. Most of the remaining activists and many ordinary members were arrested and jailed, with or without trial. The party's extensive military network was un-covered and destroyed. Within a couple of years, little of the party's considerable apparatus was left intact.

Zahedi's government restored diplomatic relations within Britain and, in 1954, concluded the (Amini-Page) Consortium Oil Agreement, with 40% of the shares going to British Petroleum, another 40% to American oil companies, 14% to Royal Dutch Shell, and 6% to the French Oil Company. Iran's royalties were to be 50% of the net proceeds, and the concessionary period was to run for 25 years. Meanwhile, the American government provided financial aid, enabling Zahedi to deal with pressing economic problems while oil royalties were still, temporarily, at a low ebb. In addition, the Soviet Union entered an agreement with Zahedi to repay its war debts in Iran, although the actual payment was made to his successor.

Zahedi's government was replaced by that of Hosain Ala in 1955, which itself gave way to the government of Dr Eqbal the following year. This rapid turnabout marked a tendency for the shah to begin concentrating power in his own hands, and reduce the influence of independent, though loyal, politicians in his administration. In 1955, Iran joined the Baghdad Pact which included Turkey, Iraq and Pakistan as well as Britain and the United States, and was changed into the Central Treaty Organisation (CENTO) after 1958, in the wake of Iraq's departure from it. Soviet–Iranian relations began to warm despite these developments, and, in 1959, the two countries were about to enter a non-aggression pact when Iran made a mutual defence pact with the United States instead. This event greatly soured relations between Iran and the Soviet Union until a *rapprochement* in 1963.

In 1949, an ad hoc planning body had been set up which drafted a statement of state investment projects, the Seven-Year plan (1949–56). The plan allocated a quarter of its proposed expenditures to agriculture, 32% to social and public services, and 24% to industrial and mining projects. However, since much of the required funds were expected to come from oil revenues and World Bank loans, the Anglo-Iranian oil dispute meant that only a small proportion of planned investments could be carried out. In 1955, the plan organisation was turned into a permanent and extensive body with special powers, and was charged with the preparation and execution of the Second Plan (1955–62).

The funds earmarked for the Second Plan were much larger than for the first, comprising 75% of the annual oil revenues. In practice, only 54% of the revenues were spent, the rest being diverted to the current military and civilian budget. This, together with related problems, gave rise to growing frictions between the plan organisation's strong managing-director, Abolhasan Ebtahaj, on the one hand, and the shah and the prime minister on the other. In 1959, Ebtahaj resigned, and the plan organisation lost the autonomy which it had briefly enjoyed. Meanwhile, over 70 billion rials were spent on a variety of projects for the development of the infrastructure, agriculture, and industries and mines.

Late in 1957 an attempted coup by General Vali Qarani, head of the army intelligence, was foiled. This was a sign of growing alienation of a wider public from the shah and the government. It was followed by the dismissal of Ali Amini, Iran's ambassador to the United States, who was fast emerging as the leader of the regime's reformist wing. Meanwhile, the government policy of creating a middle-class consumer boom, together with a liberal importing policy, led to rising inflation and a balance of payments deficit that was to become acute towards the end of the 1950s.

The crisis of 1960–63

The parliamentary session having ended in 1960, new elections provided an opportunity for the expression of public dissent. The economic crisis added to domestic unrest and foreign criticism led to the dismissal of Dr Eqbal and his replacement by Ja'far Sharif-Emami. At the same time, the second National Front was formed by Mosaddeq's former associates, and Ali Amini declared his programme for a land reform. The new parliament met early in 1961, but the wave of unrest continued unabated, and a teachers' strike for higher pay resulted in street clashes with the police.

In April 1961 the shah reluctantly appointed Ali Amini premier. Amini asked him to dissolve the landlord-dominated parliament so that he could implement his land-reform policy. The shah had already begun to distribute his own agricultural lands against payment by the government, but these were the lands that had been appropriated by Reza Shah, and the proceeds of the sales were diverted to the Pahlavi Foundation, whose operations involved much financial irregularity. Amini's Land Reform Law of 1962, subsequently known as the First Stage, eventually affected about 20% of the peasantry. Although it was later modified to temper the opposition of the landlords, it was still more progressive than the following three stages of land reform, which were carried out under the shah's direct leadership.

Amini's government fell in June 1962 following his disagreement with the shah over the size of the military budget. His downfall was inevitable because the shah, the landlords, as well as the NF were opposed to his government, and hence there was little logic for the American support he had initially enjoyed. He was replaced by Asadollah Alam, a close friend of the shah. The shah decided to take over the land reform and turn it into his own 'White Revolution'. The programme of the White Revolution initially contained six points of principle: distribution of arable land; nationalisation of woods and forests; electoral reform, including the right for women to vote and be elected to parliament; denationalisation of some state monopolies to finance the land r~form; company profit-sharing for industrial workers; and the creation of a 'literacy corps' to campaign against illiteracy in rural areas. This was put to a referendum in January 1963, and was predictably endorsed by a large vote.

Yet the opposition to the shah was growing daily. The landlords were opposed to land reform and the consequent loss of political power. Religious leaders were becoming restless for a variety of reasons, including the land reform, women's suffrage and the shah's assumption of dictatorial powers. The NF still demanded free elections and constitutional government. The movement reached its climax during a three-day uprising in June 1963, which was crushed by the army. It was led by landlords and religious leaders, but it included the bazaar, university students and the urban crowd. It was a dress-rehearsal for the revolution of 1977–79.

Oil and the state: 1963–72

The general elections that followed led to a 'classless' parliament, because the government now had the total power to decide who would enter parliament, a pattern which persisted until the revolution. A new cabinet, consisting mainly of young technocrats, and headed by Hasan Ali Mansur, was installed. However, Mansur was soon to be assassinated after he had granted judicial immunity to American advisers in Iran, a decision vehemently denounced by Ayatollah Khomeini, leader of the uprising of June 1963. The ayatollah was banished to Turkey, whence he went to Iraq until his return, via Paris, early in 1979. Meanwhile Amir Abbas Hovaida was made prime minister, and was to remain in office until August 1978, when increasing political unrest compelled the shah to replace him.

These political developments coupled with steadily rising oil revenues greatly strengthened the state, and made possible a strategy of high growth and economic modernisation, although this was not pursued in a realistic manner, especially (though not exclusively) after the quadrupling of the oil prices late in 1973. Economic development was based on an import substitution strategy, yet it resulted in fast-growing imports which were met by the use of oil revenues. Manufacturing expanded, but the highest growth was experienced by public and private services as well as construction. Modern education also expanded rapidly at primary, secondary and tertiary levels. The third stage of land reform, the creation of farm corporations each comprising a number of villages, led to disenchantment among small farmers, and tended to concentrate ownership in the villages affected. The fourth stage went much further and turned huge tracts of agricultural land into bureaucratic agro-business industries. Agriculture grew at a much slower rate than other economic sectors, the gaps between the urban and rural sectors increased rapidly, and there was massive rural-urban migration. The high rate of population growth added force to these tendencies in creating urban unemployment, housing short-ages, pressures on public services, etc. While the general standard of living was rising fast, the distribution of income and wealth was becoming increasingly uneven. Widespread public and private corruption fuelled social discontent.

With the power of the state increasing and the demise of the old social classes, it became almost impossible to air any opinion, however moderately, criticising the shah and the state. Parliament was reduced to no more than a legislative instrument, which passed government bills with hardly any debate and disagreement. Later, it even became difficult for ministers and high officials to disagree with the shah on routine matters of social and economic policy. SAVAK, the civilian secret service, was founded in 1957, expanded rapidly in the 1960s and 1970s, and extended its operations to every sphere of political, social and economic life. It tried to stifle any expression of dissent by means of arrest, imprisonment and torture. Open public opposition became impossible, with the inevitable result that dissent was forced underground and became progressively more willing to embrace guerrilla warfare.

The quadrupling of the oil prices late in 1973 led to an intensification of all the existing political and economic problems, and paved the way for the revolution. The unprecedented increase in the oil revenues led to an immediate doubling of planned public expenditures. But the economic and social capacity, already strained, could not absorb such a sudden influx of cash into the economy. Ports, roads and other infrastructural facilities were congested, there was labour shortage in such sectors as education and construction, the supply of some goods and services fell short of the demand for them, and inflation became rampant. The sense of insecurity which the politico-economic situation created led to a rapid flight of capital out of the country; by 1976–77 Iran had a deficit on its capital account.

In 1974, the shah launched his one-party state by creating the National Resurgence party (NRP). The existing official political parties—Iran'-e Novin and Mardom—were dissolved, and it became all but compulsory for members of the public to join the new party. Meanwhile, political discontent was spreading fast, and the Feda'iyan-e Khalq (Marxist-Leninist), and Mojahedin'e Khalq (Islamic-Marxist) groups were con-tinuing their guerrilla campaigns in towns and cities. The Islamic parties had also been secretly active since the early 1960s, although they did not resort to guerrilla tactics.

The revolution

Early in 1977 a combination of increasing economic and social dissociation at home, and pressures for human rights reforms from abroad, led to a loosening of the tight political grip that had been hitherto maintained on public criticism. Some political prisoners were released, the use of torture was officially banned, and limited freedom of expression was tolerated. This resulted in a growing expression of political dissent that spread rapidly. In August 1977, Hovaida resigned and was replaced by Jamshid Amuzegar, the interior minister as well as oil spokesman.

In January 1978, a personal attack on Ayatollah Khomeini, published in a leading daily on instructions from the court, resulted in riots and bloodshed in the holy city of Qom. The demonstrations soon spread to Tabriz, Tehran and other town and cities. Late in August 1978, the burning of a cinema in Abadan resulted in 400 deaths, and was widely believed to have been the work of the SAVAK. This, together with the spread of public disorder, led to the resignation of Amuzegar's cabinet and its replacement by Ja'far Sharif-Emami's. The latter adopted a liberal stance and promised rapid political and economic reforms, but the revolutionary movement continued unabated.

On 8 September, following a declaration of martial law, soldiers fired on a large crowd of unarmed demonstrators in central Tehran. Huge numbers were killed, though precise figures have never been established. In the meantime Ayatollah Khomeini had been calling for the overthrow of the Pahlavi regime from his exile in Iraq. Iran's pressure on the Iraqi government to restrict the ayatollah's activities forced him to leave Iraq. Kuwait being unwilling to play host, the ayatollah flew to Paris, and continued his campaign amid a glare of Western publicity. The revolutionary movement was thus united behind the leadership of the ayatollah and his call for the downfall of the shah's regime.

The shah turned to Gholamhosain Sadiqi, a highly respected former associate of Mosaddeq. Sadiqi agreed to act on the condition that the shah gave up all executive power, and moved to the Iranian island of Kish in the Gulf. The shah refused and turned to Shahpur Bakhtiyar, the NF's effective deputy leader. Bakhtiyar accepted on condition that the shah left Iran for an unspecified period. This he agreed to do, taking advantage of a state visit to Egypt to depart with at least a semblance of dignity rather than face the humiliation of formal abdication. Bakhtiyar introduced further measures of political liberalisation and declared his opposition to Islamic government. But his government failed to stem the tide of the revolution, and he himself was expelled from the NF. On 11 February 1979, following armed clashes between revolutionaries and the royal guards, the army declared itself neutral and withdrew the troops to their barracks. Bakhtiyar's government fell. The revolution succeeded. Ayatollah Khomeini, who had returned to Tehran ten days earlier to a tumultuous welcome, named Mehdi Bazargan—a devout Muslim and former associate of Mosaddeq—prime minister.

The Islamic Republic

Shortly after the revolution a referendum was held which abolished the monarchy and established an Islamic government. But Bazargan's

Provisional Government was short lived. It had to face the combined opposition of leftist and Islamist parties, which enjoyed large popular support and which demanded more drastic action at home and in foreign relations than the Provisional Government was prepared to take. A constituent assembly was elected, and it drafted a constitution with which the government disagreed. The main bone of contention was the provision of the office of *velayat-e faqih* (or the Guardianship of Jurisconsult) as the ultimate arbiter of state decisions. The constitution also provided for a National (later renamed Islamic) Assembly, an elected president, and an executive cabinet, led by a prime minister. A constitutional reform later in the 1980s abolished the office of prime minister, and placed the president at the head of the cabinet. The constitution also created a Council of Guardians, made up of senior Islamic jurists, to vet parliamentary legislation on the basis of Islamic law and the principles of the constitution. Two further bodies later came into being: an Assembly of Experts, for the interpretation of the constitution, and a Council of Determining the Expediency of the Islamic Republic, charged with approval of legislative and executive decisions.

In November 1979, the Provisional Government resigned in the wake of the hostage-taking of American diplomats in Tehran. This was an important turning-point in the post-revolutionary period and resulted in a radical shift in domestic policy as well as international relations. Meanwhile, elections were held both for the National Assembly and for the presidency, and Abolhasan Banisadr—a committed Muslim and former Mosaddeq supporter—was elected president with Ayatollah Khomeini's blessings. However, the power struggles were to intensify until the opposition to Banisadr, led by Ayatollah Beheshti (president of the Supreme Court), won the day. Banisadr was impeached by the National Assembly, and left Iran for Paris in August 1981. This provoked an uprising by the Mojahedin and other leftist parties, which was comprehensively crushed. For a few years afterwards terror and counter-terror was to continue until the country achieved a relative measure of stability.

The Iran–Iraq War

In September 1980, Iraq attacked Iran. The Iraqis had hoped for a quick victory in the face of Iran's revolutionary turmoil, which had weakened army morale and greatly diminished its effectiveness. In fact, the war was to continue for almost eight years at great human and material cost. The Iraqis received military supplies from the Soviet Union, France, and a number of other Western countries. But in view of its international isolation, Iran had to resort to costly informal markets for military equipment. This was compensated for by a mobilisation of large numbers of young volunteers (called *Basij*) who were used in massive infantry attacks. In turn, the Iraqis resorted to the use of chemical weapons.

Apart from its human and social costs, the Iran–Iraq War had a devastating effect on the Iranian economy. With declining oil prices as well as diminishing world demand for crude oil, much of the oil revenue had to be diverted to the war effort, starving industry of funds for investment and curtailing non-military imports. The restriction on consumer goods imports, coupled with the expansion of military-related domestic goods and services, led to a shortage of many basic goods. The government introduced rationing, which is still partially in operation. Its effect was, at least partly, to encourage a thriving black market.

The cease-fire in 1988 was followed by a new policy to end Iran's diplomatic isolation and improve the economy. This was temporarily disrupted by the Salman Rushdie incident early in 1989, which saw the West united in condemnation of Iran's fundamentalist extremism, but the trend has been continuing, especially since 1990. Iran remained neutral following Iraq's invasion of Kuwait in August 1990, though its tacit opposition to Iraq did much to help restore diplomatic relations with a number of Western and Middle East governments afterwards. To help restore the economy and meet the requirements of a rapidly increasing population, an economic plan was approved to be implemented at two consecutive five-year stages. The most important macro-economic bottlenecks are shortages of foreign exchange and of skilled labour. The government has recently tried to encourage the return of those Iranian investors and specialists who had emigrated to escape the revolutionary turmoil and war.

The future

The Islamic Republic's future peace and stability is dependent largely (though not exclusively) on its success in a steady improvement of its economy. Living standards have fallen relatively to the pre-revolutionary period, and there is high inflation and unemployment. Regarding both economic and political questions, two trends of thought may be distinguished which are often described as 'moderate' and 'radical'. President Rafsanjani's government, supported by Ayatollah Khamenei'i (appointed Iran's spiritual leader after the death of Ayatollah Khomeini in June 1989), represents the former tendency. It favours improved foreign relations, economic development, and a less restricted social environment. Apart from the restoration of diplomatic links with some countries, it proposes to abolish subsidies on a number of goods and services, privatise some state monopolies and increase freedom of expression, although there is still much restriction on organised political activity outside the official framework. On the other hand, the 'radical' trend, led by Hojjat al-Islam Ali Akbar Mohtashemi (a former interior minister), favours a more isolationist diplomatic policy, greater state participation in the economy and a more fundamentalist approach to politics and society. Perhaps the outcome of the forthcoming general election for the Islamic Assembly will help determine more clearly the trend of events for the next few years.

Homa Katouzian

4 IRAQ

The modern state of Iraq was created in 1920, as part of the peace settlement after the First World War. The victorious Allies divided the Arab provinces of the former Ottoman Empire between them; Britain, which had been in occupation of the provinces of Basra and Baghdad for most of the war, and Mosul by the end of the war, was appointed mandatory power under the new system of international trusteeship established by the League of Nations.

Although parts of the country had been united under a single government at various times in the past, the entity which emerged in 1920 had had no previous independent existence as a nation state. Britain imported a king, Faisal, the son of Sharif Husain of Mecca, and endowed Iraq with a constitution and a bicameral legislature. The mandate, a form of indirect rule where Arab ministers and officials were closely supervised by British advisers whose advice had to be taken, came to an end in 1932, when Iraq was admitted to the League of Nations as an independent state. By this time Britain had secured Iraq's present northern boundary, had made sure that the concession for oil exploration and exploitation was given to the Iraq Petroleum Company, a conglomerate of British, Dutch, French and United States oil interests, and had created a social base for the monarchy by confirming 'suitable' tribal leaders in full possession of what had previously been the customary holdings of 'their' tribes. In addition, Britain retained military bases in Iraq and continued to exercise strong political and economic influence.

In 1941, a group of Iraqi officers led a short-lived resistance movement against Britain which resulted in a second British occupation until the end of the war. Between 1945 and 1958 the country was governed by a succession of 24 cabinets, most of which contained combinations of the same handful of individuals, often headed by the veteran pro-British politician Nuri al-Sa'id. Genuine opposition parties were banned for most of this period, which meant that there was little room for the development of a democratic tradition. Many Iraqis believed that the country's most urgent need was national independence, which would be followed by economic development and social reforms, both of which were being blocked or denied by the monarchy and its British sponsors. At the same time the state was almost universally seen as the 'natural' vehicle to carry out these reforms and to implement the development so urgently needed. This kind of thinking, usually but not always associated with 'socialism',

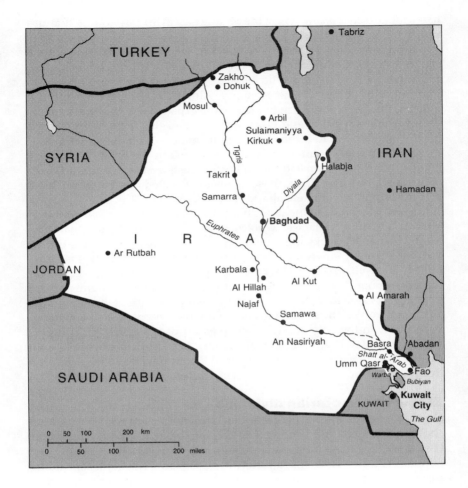

Official name	Republic of Iraq
Area	434,924 sq. km (167,925 sq. miles)
Population	17,064,000 (1988)
Capital	Baghdad
Language	Arabic, Kurdish, Turcoman, Armenian and Persian languages
Religion	Sunni and Shia Muslim (95%), Christian (3.6%), Yazidi (1.4%)
Currency	Iraqui dinar

had wide currency elsewhere in the Middle East in the post-war period and was by no means unique to Iraq.

During and after the Second World War, members of the rising middle classes were expanding their investments in manufacture, commerce and real estate, a process which accelerated in the 1950s when oil began to make a major impact on the economy. Although oil revenues were still modest, they were sufficient to finance the expansion of the bureaucracy, the educational system and other services, and this increase in government expenditure had a generally stimulating effect on the economy.

Private capital continued to be concentrated in the hands of some 25 families, many of whom had controlling interests in several different kinds of business. Between them, these families controlled more than half of all private corporate commercial and industrial wealth. Far below them in status and wealth were medium-to-small property-owners, religious dignitaries and local notables, wholesale and retail merchants, manufacturers, owners of workshops and repair shops, petty traders and so on, as well as the newly emerging intelligentsia of professionals, lawyers, army officers and civil servants. This latter group, together with large sections of the urban poor, felt acutely aware of the exclusive nature of the political system and came to form the core of the independence movement in the 1940s and 1950s. The beginnings of a working class were also emerging, particularly in the large foreign-owned enterprises such as the railways, Basra port and the Iraq Petroleum Company. Because of its close links with the independence movement, organised labour developed into an effective political force in the years preceding the revolution.

Ethnic and sectarian divisions

On another level, in spite of the far-reaching effects of these changes, Iraqi society contained, and continues to contain, elements which had never been combined in an independent and separate polity. Then as now, the population was divided into a variety of overlapping categories, including social and ethnic origin, religious sect, occupation, and regional and tribal background. Apart from the Christian (3.6%), Sabaean and Yazidi (1.4%) communities, some 95% of Iraqis are Muslims. About a quarter of the Muslims are Kurds, who are mostly Sunni Muslims; the remaining three-quarters are Arabs. The Arab Muslims are divided into Sunnis and Twelver Shias, the latter forming the largest single religious community in the country.

Iraqi censuses do not provide details of sectarian affiliation, but as the two sects (Sunni and Shia) live in distinct parts of the country (apart from Baghdad and Basra, which are mixed) it is possible to make some broad generalisations. The Shias form 52% of the total Muslim population, and, perhaps more significantly, 70% of the Arab Muslim population. Southern Iraq is predominantly Shia, while the centre, west and north of the country are mainly Sunni. The main shrines of Twelver Shiism (also the 'state religion' of Iraq's neighbour Iran) are located in Iraq, at Najaf, Karbala, Samarra, and Kadhimain, a district of Baghdad. These shrines are major centres of religious learning as well as the traditional residences of the spiritual leaders of the worldwide Twelver Shia community.

As the Ottoman Empire was a Sunni institution, what state educational facilities existed in Iraq were mainly for Sunnis; in addition, Shias were both disinclined to enter, and not recruited into, government service. Furthermore, before the First World War most Shias were concentrated either in the countryside away from the centres of government or in the shrine towns, which had a fairly independent existence. Hence, when the new state was created in 1920, very few Shias entered government service, a situation which changed only with the rapid expansion of (secular) education in the 1940s, 1950s and 1960s. In consequence, the Shias 'started off' by being under-represented politically. This tendency has continued, and has been compounded by other factors such as an increasingly repressive state, which reinforces communal identity, the exclusive nature of the regime since 1968, and the continuous deterioration in Iraq's relations with Iran. In the latter context, however, it should be said that although Iraqi and Iranian Shias are members of the same sect, Iraqi Shias feel themselves to be Arab Iraqis, and Iranian Shias feel themselves to be Iranians. While there is a certain affinity between Shias relations have not always been cordial, and there is also a degree of rivalry between the religious establishments at Qom and Mashhad and those at Karbala and Najaf.

The population is also divided along ethnic lines. About 72% are Arabs, 23% are Kurds—there are also Kurdish communities in Iran, Syria and Turkey—while the remaining 5% consist of Turcomans, Assyrians, Armenians and other smaller ethnic groups. The Kurds form a compact majority of the population in the north and north-west of the country. Most Kurds were originally members of semi-nomadic tribes, but constraints on cross-frontier movements and other economic factors have encouraged seden-tarisation and wider educational provision, urban migration and various political developments have tended to reduce tribal ties. In general, both the sectarian and ethnic divisions were becoming less important in the decades preceding the 1958 revolution, as the national independence movement acted as a crucial unifying factor and helped to transcend them.

Political parties before the revolution

For a variety of reasons, no liberal democratic party was able to muster anything like mass support or to build up an effective machinery under the mandate and monarchy (1920–58). Such parties as existed tended to be loose organisations centred around prominent personalities. After the mid-1920s most of the leading Iraqi participants in the Arab Revolt, in company with Faisal himself, made their peace with the mandatory power (unlike their Syrian counterparts; see Chapter 13, Syria) and had become dependent on Britain for the maintenance of the status quo and their own positions within it. As long as they remained in control it was virtually impossible for an effective pluralistic democratic system to emerge, and no genuine opposition party could gain power through the ballot box. As a result, constitutional democracy had become widely discredited by the end of the 1950s and the military came to be regarded as an acceptable vehicle for initiating change.

It is a peculiarity of Iraqi politics that the independence movement functioned almost exclusively underground, and that many of its members came under the influence of the Communist party (founded in 1934), which organised almost all the mass demonstrations and strikes of the 1940s and early 1950s. After Nasser's rise to power in Egypt in 1952, the pan-Arab nationalists and the Ba'thists also began to gain influence, especially among the Sunni population. Before Nasser, partly because of Iraq's ethnic and communal heterogeneity, pan-Arabism had made little headway; Iraqi nationalism had a far wider appeal. Even in the late 1950s there was no Nasserist party as such, and the Ba'th, founded in Syria and brought to Iraq by Syrian school-teachers in the early 1950s, had only 300 members in 1955, the year when Saddam Husain joined.

The Iraqi republic

On 14 July 1958 a group of military officers seized power, overthrew the monarchy and abolished the old political order. The new government was headed by self-styled Free Officers, under Brigadier 'Abd al-Karim Qasim, and cabinets consisted of a combination of military and civilian members. The feebleness of the parliamentary tradition and the limited commitment to parliamentary democracy became particularly obvious when the Free Officers began making overtures to 'moderate' civilian politicians to whom they might hand over after a period of consolidation. Although some, notably Mohammed Hadid, Kamil Chadirchi, and Mahdi Kubba, were well known and respected, none had a properly functioning political party at his disposal, nor any experience in government.

In addition, there seems to have been an unspoken agreement among these politicians and the Free Officers that it was important to block communist participation in government. Probably overestimating the proportion of the electorate that would vote for the communists, Qasim preferred to stall the democratic process. An ironic consequence was that the main pressure to hold elections came from the communists, who organised huge demonstrations (1959 and 1960) in favour of free elections and the legalisation of the Communist party. Since no elections were ever held, the extent of communist support can only be conjectured. Nevertheless, as elsewhere in the Middle East, the spectre of communism continued to dominate the political scene, which became polarised between the pan-Arab nationalists and their supporters, and the communists and theirs.

In the autumn of 1958 the immediate point of contention became the question of whether Iraq should join the United Arab Republic (UAR) of Egypt and Syria, which had been formed the previous February (*see* Chapter 13, Syria). The nationalists and Ba'thists wanted to join the UAR, partly out of conviction, partly as a means of controlling the communists, since Nasser had made political parties illegal. The communists opposed it, again partly out of conviction and partly because they understood its implications for their own political future. For his part, Qasim had no desire to defer to Nasser and thus quite fortuitously found himself on the same side as the communists, whose political views he did not share. In an attempt to distance himself from the communists, Qasim began to clamp down on the left and to dismiss individuals suspected of communist sympathies from the army and other key positions. In doing so he undermined his own political base (since he had irretrievably alienated himself from the pan-Arabists in the early 1960s) and thus fell prey to a coup engineered by nationalist and Ba'thist officers in February 1963.

The atrocities of February 1963 marked the most savage repression yet perpetrated by any Middle Eastern government against its population. Qasim was killed and the Ba'thist-Arab nationalist junta, which seized power under the leadership of 'Abd al-Salam 'Arif, established a reign of terror against their communist adversaries. The most notorious of those involved in this bloodshed, particularly 'Ali Salih al-Sa'di, were Ba'thists. Nine months later the Ba'thists fell out with the Nasserists and with 'Arif, who sent most of their leaders into exile in Franco's Spain, and the intensity of political persecution diminished. 'Arif's presidency was mainly taken up with fighting a fruitless and expensive war in Kurdistan and with keeping himself in power. After his death in a helicopter accident in 1966 his brother 'Abd al-Rahman 'Arif took over as president, but was ousted by another Ba'th coup in July 1968.

Political groups in post-revolutionary Iraq

The main groupings in Iraqi politics after 1958 were the communists, the Kurds and the pan-Arab nationalists, both Nasserist and Ba'thist. With their roots in the shanty-towns, the emerging labour movement and the professional middle classes, the communists continued as a significant political force in the country in the years immediately after the revolution, but their position was ambivalent. They supported President Qasim, partly because of his welfare state measures and his attempts to negotiate with the Iraq Petroleum Company—his Law 80 of 1961 was the first major restriction on activities of foreign oil companies in any Arab country— partly because the communist leadership did not support the idea of a military takeover by the party. Although this issue remained highly contentious within party circles for many years, the possibility of such a coup had definitely passed by 1961, since most of the party's supporters in the army had been dismissed.

The second political force, the Kurdish national movement, was divided into a number of factions, the most important of which was the Kurdistan Democratic party (KDP), led by Mullah Mustafa Barzani. Most Iraqi Kurdish politicans and parties have sought some form of regional or local autonomy within the Iraqi state and Kurdish organisations and political groupings have been in armed conflict with the authorities in Baghdad for much of the period since 1920, largely because of the authorities' refusal to countenance such aspirations.

The party that has achieved the greatest long-term success in post-revolutionary Iraq is the Ba'th, which is still in power at the time of writing. The basic tenets of Ba'thism, 'one Arab Nation with an Eternal Mission' expressed in the slogan 'Unity, Freedom and Socialism', were first developed in Syria by Michel 'Aflaq and Salah al-Din al-Bitar in the 1940s and early 1950s. 'Unity' is the unity of the Arab nation, 'Freedom' is freedom from imperialism and Zionism, and 'Socialism' expresses a general aspiration towards state-directed economic development supported by a mixed economy. Ba'thism is a variety of pan-Arab nationalism, based on the general premise that there is a single Arab nation, which has been divided artificially, first by the Ottomans, subsequently by European and American imperialism and Zionism. Once the Arabs are liberated and united, it is believed, social conflicts within particular states (or 'regions of the Arab nation') will subside.

Ba'thism first came to Iraq in 1951 but was slow to take root, partly because pan-Arab nationalism was not particularly attractive to Shias or Kurds, partly because the political scene was dominated by the communists. Nevertheless, the Iraqi Ba'th party, which had 300 members in 1955, joined a National Front with the communists and other parties in 1957, and welcomed the revolution of 1958. Though the Ba'thists never attracted mass support, they eventually succeeded in taking power and maintaining it in their hands by a combination of skilful organisation, ruthlessness and an alliance with key military officers.

The second Ba'th coup

On 17 July 1968 a group of Ba'th officers led by Ahmad Hasan al-Bakr (who had been prime minister in 1963–64) organised another Ba'th coup, taking over the government in a second coup two weeks later. Both al-Bakr, who became president, and his deputy and successor Saddam Husain, came from Takrit, a small town about 100 miles north of Baghdad. The Ba'th had few roots in Iraq and was primarily remembered for its reign of terror in 1963. At various times over the next few years it attempted to convince the communists and the KDP to join in a national government in which the Ba'th would play the leading role, while simultaneously attacking, and sometimes killing, members of both parties. At the same time, it attempted to increase its popularity by advocating wide-ranging social and economic reforms and pursuing apparently 'progressive' and 'anti-imperialist' foreign policies, stridently attacking Zionism and imperialism and supporting 'the left' in the rest of the Arab world.

In this general spirit, in 1972 Iraq signed a 15-year treaty with the Soviet Union. Thus fortified, in the same year it nationalised the Iraqi Petroleum Company. Largely because of their espousal of such policies, the Ba'thists finally convinced the communists to join them in a National Progressive Front (NPF), although the KDP refused to participate. The regime's confidence and economic power was boosted further by the massive rise in oil prices which followed the Arab–Israeli war of October 1973; between 1972 and 1974, oil revenues increased tenfold, from $575 million to $5,700 million.

The Ba'th and the Kurds

Although the KDP refused to join the NPF, other overtures on the part of the Ba'th appeared to be bearing fruit. In March 1970 an agreement was reached between the government and Mullah Mustafa Barzani which envisaged the inauguration of an autonomous Kurdish area four years later. However, it soon became clear that the March Manifesto was nothing but a ruse on the part of the Ba'th, which wanted to gain time until it was in a position to recast its Kurdish policy to its own advantage. One of most crucial stumbling blocks in the subsequent negotiations—which continued until 1974—was whether Kirkuk, where one-third of Iraq's oil is produced, should be included in the autonomous area. The KDP insisted that Kirkuk, with a Kurdish majority population, was part of Kurdistan. The Iraqi government denied this but also refused to carry out the census which the Kurdish side requested. With the ending of the Gulf War in 1991, Kirkuk has once more become a bone of contention between Saddam Husain and the Kurdish leaders.

When it became clear that the Ba'th's promises on Kurdish autonomy would not be fulfilled, a major conflict between the armed forces and the Kurds broke out in the spring of 1974. The Kurds were supported by the shah of Iran, who took the Ba'th's radical and leftist rhetoric seriously and was worried about Soviet influence in the region. Barzani's access to sophisticated weapons made the KDP a formidable foe, to the extent, indeed, that it was impossible for the Iraqi government to defeat it. The Ba'th, supported by the communists, made capital out of the shah's support for the Kurds, and presented itself as the victim of an 'imperialist conspiracy' masterminded by the West and 'its agents'.

By the end of 1974 a familiar stalemate had set in, though the Ba'th leadership, preoccupied with internal intrigues and power struggles, was keen to 'solve' the Kurdish problem. In October 1974 King Husain of Jordan arranged preliminary meetings between representatives of Iraq and Iran, which paved the way for the Algiers Agreement between the two countries in March 1975. Within hours of the agreement Iran withdrew its heavy artillery and closed the border so that the Kurds could not regroup or attack from Iran. The Kurdish resistance collapsed; Barzani himself went into exile, dying in the United States in 1979. Relations between Iraq and Iran now became extremely cordial and continued to be so until the Iranian revolution of 1979. In the autumn of 1978, after a request from the shah, Baghdad obligingly expelled Ayatollah Khomeini from Najaf, where he had been in exile for the previous 15 years.

The Algiers Agreement saw the settlement of the Kurdish question on the Ba'th's terms, as well as the resolution of the frontier dispute which had bedevilled relations between Iran and Iraq since the 1930s. Briefly, the Algiers Agreement restored the boundary between the two countries along the Shatt al-'Arab waterway, effectively dividing the waterway. By contrast, the previous arrangement imposed by the Iraqis had insisted that Iraqi territory extended to the Iranian side of the Shatt, thus making Iranian use of the waterway dependent on Iraqi good will. The agreement had been masterminded by Saddam Husain, the real power behind the al-Bakr regime, and was to mark the beginning of an important U-turn in the Ba'th's internal and regional policies.

The Ba'th took the most ruthless measures to prevent a revival of Kurdish resistance. The strip of territory parallel to the borders with Iran and Turkey was turned into a *cordon sanitaire*; the villages in the area were destroyed and their inhabitants rounded up in trucks and taken to southern Iraq or resettled in specially constructed villages surrounded by barbed wire and fortified posts. Although now more divided internally following the creation of the Patriotic Union of Kurdistan (PUK) under Jalal Talabani in 1975 (roughly speaking, the KDP's membership is from northern, and the PUK's from southern Kurdistan), the Kurds had regrouped sufficiently by the beginning of 1977 to mount guerrilla operations in the area. Other opposition forces, including the communists, began to join in these activities in 1979.

The emergence of Saddam Husain

By the late 1970s the dividing lines between the Ba'th leadership and the state had almost disappeared. At the same time, the spectacular rise in oil revenues during the 1970s meant a parallel increase in the economic muscle of the leadership. In addition, having 'solved' the Kurdish question, the Ba'th were no longer in need of the communists, and accordingly turned against them once more. In May 1976, 12 communists were executed, allegedly for political activities in the army, while in July 1978 the Ba'th enacted a blanket decree making any non-Ba'thist political activity illegal and membership of any other political party punishable by death for all members and former members of the armed forces. Given Iraq's universal conscription, the decree applied to all adult males. The NPF gradually lost all significance, and, although never officially dissolved, was no longer meeting by 1979. Over the next few years, hundreds of thousands opposed to the Ba'th were imprisoned, murdered or forced into exile.

Between 1975 and 1979 Iraq gradually returned into the general orbit of the West on a global level and towards the moderate Arab states on a regional level. Real power moved away from the Ba'th party and the RCC and became concentrated almost exclusively in the hands of Saddam Husain and a few trusted subordinates. The party itself was transformed into an instrument of the state and gradually assumed the characteristics of a national rally, in which adulation of the party and its leaders came to take the place of whatever political discourse may once have existed. By 1979 it was clear that it was only a matter of time before Saddam Husain would take over full control of the state. President Ahmad Hasan al-Bakr, whose contacts with senior army officers had been crucial in the first few years, had handed over the Ministry of Defence to his son-in-law (and Saddam Husain's brother-in-law) 'Adnan Khairullah Tulfah in October 1977. In addition, a number of rival security services, all reporting directly to Saddam Husain, had been assiduously built up. It came as no surprise when al-Bakr appeared on television on 16 July 1979 and announced his resignation and the succession of Saddam Husain.

Potential internal Ba'th opposition to these developments was pre-empted 12 days later, after the 'discovery' of a plot to overthrow the regime, allegedly masterminded by Syria. A special party court was set up under Na'im Haddad; five RCC members and 17 other party members were sentenced to death. These 'democratic executions', as Na'im Haddad called them, were carried out personally by Saddam Husain and the remaining members of the Ba'th leadership. The victims included 'Abd al-Khaliq al-Samarra'i, a prominent Ba'th figure, who had been in prison since July 1973, 'Adnan Hamdani, one of Saddam Husain's most intimate friends, and other key members of the leadership. The fact that even those who had been closest to the leader could fall so suddenly showed that no opposition, whether inside or outside the party, would be tolerated.

The impact of oil wealth

The spectacular rise of oil prices in the 1970s meant an equally spectacular rise in Iraq's revenues and expenditures. Huge sums were spent on welfare and building projects, while higher wages, together with the employment opportunities generated by an expanding economy, helped bring about substantial improvements in living standards. In addition, as the Ba'th leadership had full control over these revenues—and was not accountable as to how they were spent—increases in receipts from oil automatically increased the independence of the state from society.

The combination of the new oil money and the successful elimination or subordination of most of the opposition gave Saddam Husain a major boost of confidence. He promoted a spectacular personality cult, with massive portraits and statues of the benevolent leader visible everywhere, and towns, suburbs, public buildings and streets renamed in his honour. He also expanded his own personal presidential force, the Republican

Guard, an elite corps founded in November 1963. The guard had played a crucial role in the Ba'th coup of 1968, when it had been commanded by Colonel Ibrahim al-Da'ud, who subsequently served as prime minister for two weeks, after which he was ousted and went into exile in Saudi Arabia. The guard itself was gradually transformed into Saddam Husain's personal instrument, officered and manned almost exclusively by Takritis, and given the most up-to-date weaponry. It was further expanded and its military capacities enhanced during the war with Iran.

The country's oil wealth also permitted Saddam Husain to equip the various parallel security services with the most up-to-date means of surveillance and riot control imported from both East and West. Together with a greatly expanded communication system, they made the state machinery more efficient than ever. During the 1980s security was further refined with the construction of huge underground complexes, most designed and built by British firms, to serve as emergency headquarters in the event of attacks upon the regime. These were to be put to use with considerable effect when Iraq was attacked by the coalition forces early in 1991. In this way the regime became both more distanced from the population and more apparently invulnerable.

The Shia opposition

The existence of a Shia political movement in Iraq dates back to the late 1950s. Disconcerted by the extent of support for the communists among the Shia community, in the autumn of 1958 a number of religious leaders (ulama) in Najaf, led by Ayatollah Mohammed Baqir al-Sadr, formed a political organisation, the Association of Najafi ulama. Its aim was to raise the consciousness of the Muslim community as a whole and to arrest the spread of communism and atheism. In their publications the ulama refuted Marxism and criticised Western economic and social thought and philosophy.

By the late 1960s, the ulama's main concern was no longer communism but the Ba'th party itself. The ulama formed themselves into a political party called al-Da'wa al-Islamiyya (The Islamic Call). The foundation of al-Da'wa, as it became known, was partly a reaction against the secularism of the Ba'thist state, but more particularly against the state's new-found determination to interfere directly in the affairs of the Shia clerical hierarchy, a sensitive area from which all previous Iraqi governments (including the Ottomans) had tended to keep their distance. The Ba'th responded in familiar fashion. In 1974 five ulama were executed without trial; in February 1977 numerous arrests were made in the Holy Cities during the Muharram ceremonies, after which eight members of the clergy were executed and 15 sentenced to life imprisonment. In 1979, encouraged by the Iranian revolution, al-Da'wa began to engage the government in open conflict, attacking Ba'th party offices and police posts and openly declaring its support for the new government in Iran.

The Ba'th in turn intensified its campaign against *al-Da'wa*, making membership of the party punishable by death. In April 1980 Ayatollah Mohammed Baqir al-Sadr and his sister Bint Huda were executed. When a few months later, Iraq invaded Iran the regime was then able to assert that Shia opposition was an attack on Iraq and Arabism and thus tantamount to treason. It is difficult to gauge how strong the appeal of *al-Da'wa* was, but, although the majority of Iraqi conscripts (like the majority of Iraqis) were Shias, there was no mass desertion or any other manifestation of widespread feelings of common cause between Iraqi and Iranian Shias. Nevertheless, the fact that the Shia community was the principal target of the Iraqi government's domestic repression throughout the war meant that its sectarian loyalties were heightened. Hence, although repression effectively pre-empted the revival of *al-Da'wa*, it made many Shias more aware of their Shiism than ever before.

The Iranian revolution and the Iran–Iraq War

The Iranian revolution of 1978–79 had momentous significance for Iraq, signalling the end of the friendly relations between the two countries that had existed since 1975. In particular, the fall of the shah meant the de facto abrogation of the Algiers Agreement and the resurrection of the Kurdish question. In addition, the establishment of a populist Shia government in Iran was a matter of grave concern in Iraq, where, as elsewhere in the Arab world, populist Islam was beginning to fill the void created by the ideological bankruptcy of Arab nationalism and socialism.

Underestimating the enthusiasm engendered by the revolution, misjudging the nature of its impact on the morale and efficiency of the Iranian armed forces, and overestimating his own economic and military strength, Saddam Husain resurrected the old disagreements over the Shatt al-'Arab and the status of the south-west Iranian province of Khuzistan/Arabistan. On 22 September 1980, he took the frequent cross-border incidents as a pretext for war. In Saddam Husain's calculations, a quick defeat of the new Islamic republican regime in Iran would have made him undisputed master of the Gulf and Iraq a major regional power, ambitions given a considerable boost by Western and Saudi fears of the consequences of an anti-Western form of Islam for the region as a whole.

However, although Iraq met with initial success, Iranian forces were more resilient than expected. An impasse, which lasted until the spring of 1982, developed. Iran then began to advance and expelled Iraqi troops from Iranian territory. A further stalemate developed until Iran took Fao in 1986 and advanced to within 40 miles of Basra. In the meantime, KDP forces under Barzani's son Mas'ud had re-formed and had gained control over much of the Kurdish mountains. By the middle of 1986, the tremendous losses sustained by both Iran and Iraq had resulted in a stalemate where both contenders were bogged down in entrenched positions with no end in sight. In addition, the burden of having to support Iraq financially was beginning to cause strains on the economies of Kuwait and Saudi Arabia. As the OPEC (Organisation of Petroleum Exporting Countries) conference in October 1985 had failed to reach a satisfactory agreement on export quotas, Saudi Arabia decided to increase its own oil exports and thereby to drive the price of oil down in an attempt to cripple the Iranian economy. Saudi exports increased from an average of 2 million barrels per day to an average of 4.5 million barrels per day, and the price of oil dropped from $27 per barrel in 1985 to £15 per barrel in early 1986.

By 1987 the cumulative effect of these developments had led to a major shift in the war. Iran and Iraq began to make serious attempts to destroy each other's oil export facilities, and Iraq made sustained if generally unsuccessful attacks on tankers carrying Iranian oil in the spring and summer of 1987. Ironically, worried about the wider repercussions in the region of an Iraqi collapse, Iraq's Arab neighbours now committed themselves unequivocally to its support, especially after the Iranian offensive against Basra in January/February 1987, and the 'War of the Cities' which accompanied it. In this way Saddam Husain achieved his objective of regionalising the war and of drawing Saudi Arabia, Kuwait and their Western allies more seriously into it.

Kuwait's attitude to the war had been deeply affected by Iran's successful Fao offensive in 1986, which Kuwait had felt to be too close to home for comfort. It put its forces on full alert and began to take a more publicly pro-Iraqi stance. In return, following Iraqi raids on Iranian oil-terminals in August 1986, Iran began to step up its attacks on Kuwaiti tankers. As a result, Kuwait approached both the Soviet Union and the United States with requests for naval protection. Although the Soviet Union's involvement remained marginal (it leased a few tankers to Kuwait), even the hint of Soviet participation was enough for the Reagan administration to be able to mobilise a suitable American response. America was now firmly behind Iraq, a development which was eventually to prove decisive in Iran's final defeat. Over the same period, the Soviet Union also backed Iraq, in the process dramatically stepping up its trade links.

On 20 July 1987, after considerable international pressure, the UN Security Council passed Resolution 598. This called for an end to the war and promised a commission of enquiry to determine which of the parties was the aggressor. Iraq accepted the resolution; Iran did not. Furthermore, although greatly weakened, Iran retained the capacity both to inflict serious damage on Iraq and to occupy Iraqi territory. In the spring of 1988 Iran launched an offensive in northern Iraq with the assistance of the two most prominent Iraqi Kurdish organisations, the PUK and the KDP, capturing the city of Halabja on 15 March. The next day the Iraqi air force bombed Halabja with poison gas, causing 5,000 deaths among the civilian population. In April and June Iraqi forces again used chemical weapons to recapture Fao and Mehran.

By now, Iranian resistance was clearly crumbling, with the government in Tehran further demoralised by the shooting down of an Iranian airliner by an American warship at the beginning of July. By the middle of the month Iran had suffered a further series of military reverses, losing almost all the Iraqi territory it had captured. On 18 July Khomeini announced that the Iranian government would accept Resolution 598 without conditions. The Iraqis then drove Iranian forces out of central and southern Iraq, and by 20 August a cease-fire had come into effect.

The costs of the Iran—Iraq war

The human and economic costs of the war were staggering. According to Western sources there were nearly 400,000 dead, roughly a quarter of whom were Iraqi and three-quarters Iranian, and perhaps 750,000 wounded. One commentator has estimated that the total costs of the war were $452.6 billion for Iraq and $644.3 billion for Iran. The combined total exceeds by $678.5 billion the entire oil revenue received by Iran and Iraq since they started to sell their oil in the world market in 1919 and 1931 respectively.

After the cease-fire of August 1988 Iraq dragged its feet in the peace negotiations, largely because of Saddam Husain's desire to be seen to have gained a meaningful victory, partly because the implementation of Clause 6 of Resolution 598 ('inquiring into the responsibility for the conflict') would have indicated that Iraq had started the war. Iraq rejected a Soviet offer to chair (and thus presumably to speed up) face-to-face negotiations early in 1989, and this inconclusive state of affairs continued until the invasion of Kuwait in August 1990. In a dramatic volte-face a few days after the invasion, Saddam Husain offered Iran a settlement based on the full implementation of Resolution 598 and the restoration of the Algiers Agreement of March 1975, which he had ceremoniously torn up on Iraqi television ten years earlier. In effect, it was a public admission that the war had achieved nothing.

The economic impact of the war on Iraq

In addition to the human loss and suffering, the war had greatly distorted the Iraqi economy. As well as infrastructural damage, Iraq had amassed foreign debts estimated at between $60 and $80 billion. In the early years of the war, the Ba'th had tried to insulate Iraqi society from it as much as possible, continuing its lavish development programmes and putting no restrictions on imports. In consequence, Iraq's foreign reserves of some $35 billion had declined rapidly, while the effects of Iranian attacks on the southern oilfields and on Basra, and Syria's closure of the pipeline to Baniyas in 1982, caused oil revenue to fall dramatically, from $29 billion in 1980 to $7 billion in 1983.

Iraq's greatest debts were to Saudi Arabia and Kuwait, which sold 'war relief crude' worth between $18 and $20 billion. If these figures are added to the direct aid given to Iraq by Kuwait and Saudi Arabia, these two countries alone provided Baghdad with between $50 and $60 billion. Iraq also owed substantial amounts to the Organisation of Economic Cooperation and Development, around £24 billion by the end of 1987. A further $10 billion was owed to the Soviet Union. By the end of the war Iraq was also importing around $30-billion worth of food, principally from the United States and Turkey, while inflation was running at between 40 and 50%. The only consolation for Iraq was that its Arab creditors, force-fed on Husain's endlessly repeated claim to have fought the war on behalf of 'the Arab nation', had no effective means of enforcing payment of the huge amounts owed them.

The aftermath of the Iran–Iraq War

It is a curious paradox that though chronically indebted and with much of its infrastructure in ruins, Iraq emerged from the war a far more substantial military power than in 1980. In 1979/80 the Iraqi army numbered 190,000; by 1987/88 it had more than quintupled, to around one million, with comparable increases in military hardware. In addition, there was now an important armaments industry whose products included a surface-to-surface missile based on the Soviet Scud and developed with Egyptian and Argentine assistance. The Ministry of Industry and Military Industrialisation, headed by Husain Kamil Majid, Saddam Husain's son-in-law, had been created to oversee these activities in July 1988. By 1989–90 the scale of military production was beginning to give rise to serious international concern. It became widely known that Iraq was manufacturing chemical weapons and sophisticated missiles and was making repeated efforts to produce nuclear weapons. The essential components of all of these were being provided by firms in Western Europe and the United States.

Although he had frequently appeared in field-marshal's uniform before the outbreak of the war, Saddam Husain had no military training, and only honorific military rank. As the war progressed, and no immediate end appeared, the officer corps grew in importance, and there was always the possibility that a rival to the president might appear from within its ranks. In order to guard against this Saddam Husain exerted as much control as possible over the army and its commanders, in the process seriously hampering the conduct of the war. Not only was it difficult for commanders to make independent decisions, they were constantly aware that they were likely to be punished if they made mistakes or were defeated; several officers were reportedly executed after the rout at Fao in the spring of 1986. A similar fate awaited anyone suspected of 'disloyalty'. Paradoxically, military success was equally dangerous, and successful commanders were removed or transferred if it was felt that their exploits might turn them into heroes.

The immense military build-up served ultimately to ensure Saddam Husain's consolidation of power. After the war he made use of his 'victory' over Iran to make explicit claims to the leadership of the Arab world, which he and the 'noble people of Iraq' had so assiduously defended for eight years. Nevertheless, his power base within the country consisted almost entirely of members of his own extended family and those who had, so to speak, been incorporated into it by long association with him. Thus his son 'Udayy was married to the daughter of the vice-president, 'Izzat al-Duri; Husain Kamil Majid, the minister for industry and military industrialisation, himself a distant cousin of Saddam Husain, was married to Saddam Husain's daughter Raghad, and his brother, Saddam Kamil, a colonel in the missile brigade, to another daughter, Rima'. Until his untimely death in a helicopter accident in a sandstorm near Basra in April 1989, 'Adnan Khairullah Tulfah, brother of Husain's wife, Sajida, was minister of defence; 'Adnan's wife was the daughter of the former-president, Ahmad Hasan al-Bakr; and 'Adnan and Sajida's father, Khairullah Tulfah, a former primary-school teacher, was for some years mayor of Baghdad, during which he became a wealthy businessman. Qusayy, Saddam Husain's youngest son, was married to the daughter of General Mahir 'Abd al-Rashid, though apparently separated from her when her father fell out of favour in the autumn of 1988. Saddam Husain's two other closest colleagues, Tariq 'Aziz, a Christian from Mosul and Taha Yasin Ramadhan, from the Jazirah (north-western Iraq), were not related by blood or marriage, but were already closely associated with him before the Ba'th takeover in 1968.

Infitah

The Ba'th's increased development expenditures had not only stimulated the economy but had made the state—with its substantial oil revenues—into the principal generator of opportunities for private business. Although most major capital-intensive schemes were carried out by international companies or corporations, local firms profited enormously, especially in areas such as urban real estate, construction, transport, communications, services and agriculture. In addition, many local businessmen acted as contractors or middlemen for foreign firms, a particularly lucrative activity. Nevertheless, although Ba'th rule provided extraordinary opportunities for personal enrichment, the economic might of the state remained dominant, as reflected in the country's continuing dependence on oil, which accounted for over 90% of foreign exchange. Hence, after the war with Iran, Iraq's capacity to muddle through depended crucially on its OPEC quota and its ability to defer or reschedule its debts to its international creditors.

In the early years of the war the regime had attempted to encourage private capital to diversify away from real estate, contracting, commerce and services towards light and medium manufacturing. Some measures of privatisation were introduced, particularly in agriculture, in an attempt to reduce food imports, to promote better quality and more regular supplies, and to broaden support for the regime among the burgeoning entrepreneurial middle classes. However, as the war progressed the economic situation steadily deteriorated and a more drastic economic reappraisal became necessary. Claiming to have been a long-time closet supporter of the market economy, Saddam Husain took the opportunity to give private enterprise a more prominent role. He made a series of declarations and policy statements, known collectively as the 'administrative revolution' whose intention was to reduce the powers of the bureaucracy. This also implied a reduction in the influence of the Ba'th party, as party officials controlled the key positions in the civil service.

This combination of deregulation and relaxation of bureaucratic controls in the state economic sector and the declining emphasis on Ba'th ideology was symptomatic of the regime's efforts to build up new constituencies among the middle classes and the military establishment. The president and his circle continued to base their powers almost exclusively on the various instruments of coercion (the police and the internal intelligence services) and on the burgeoning military. All this was accompanied by an intensification of the already relentless cult of personality and the erection of a plethora of 'victory' monuments. According to Iraqi exiles all key positions in these services and the military are occupied by around 700 Takritis who constitute the core of the elite and have a vested interest in the maintenance of the regime.

The much-vaunted economic initiatives, heralding a return to, or an advance towards, greater liberalisation, were also accompanied by declarations of intent to move towards greater political liberty. Elections to the National Assembly, a parliamentary body provided for in the provisional constitution, were first held in 1980. A second election was announced for 1 April 1989 against a background of further promises of privatisation and somewhat vaguer assurances that opposition political parties would be licensed at some time in the future. Of course, were such parties ever to be permitted (there was no sign of this in 1991) they would naturally have to work at a safe distance from, and in support of, the real centre of power, and would have no chance of survival if they overstepped certain unwritten but definite limits. In fact none of these measures had any long-term effect on relieving the economic crisis in which Iraq was floundering in 1989 and 1990. This was largely because the kind of economic reform which Saddam Husain thought would set Iraq on the road to reconstruction could not be achieved without a radical transformation of the political system and the establishment of the rule of law. He found himself trapped between his desire to expand his personal dictatorship and the basic requirements of a market economy.

The background to the invasion of Kuwait

Although Iraq's economic situation after the Iran–Iraq War was precarious, it could not be described as desperate, given the country's substantial oil reserves. Prudent house-keeping would have brought about a gradual economic recovery, provided that there was no disastrous collapse in the price of oil. However, such policies were not adopted. A clear indication of Husain's priorities was the decision to allocate $5 billion per year between 1988 and 1992 to rearmament projects. Over the same period, $2.5 billion was earmarked for reconstruction projects that included 'victory' monuments and a new presidential palace.

At the same time, the various efforts to restructure the economy led to high inflation and steep rises in the cost of living. As might have been expected, private capital had responded to the privatisation measures by speculative or 'quick' rather than sustained investment, with the result that the rich got richer and the middle and lower classes got poorer. The tension that resulted after eight years of increasing wartime austerity, though held vigorously in check by the security forces, could not be ignored indefinitely.

Nonetheless, for his part, Saddam Husain saw himself as a triumphant leader who had brought his country to a great victory and who was now entitled to take his rightful place in the counsels of the Arab world, although his Arab counterparts began to regard these pretensions with increasing alarm. When Iraq was not immediately pressed to join the Gulf Cooperation Council (GCC) at the end of the war, Husain founded his own regional association, the Arab Cooperation Council, which included Jordan, North Yemen and Egypt. In addition to this belief that his 'defence of the Arab nation' entitled him to a major role within it, other major events in the world were beginning to influence his actions.

Two interconnected points should be made here. In the first place, in spite of the fact that Iraq had and has one of the most, if not the most, vicious and tyrannical regimes in the Middle East, Saddam Husain had always attracted a certain following both within Iraq and in the rest of the Arab world. Some of this was opportunistic, in the sense that the support was bought, but, where it was not bought directly, his strident anti-imperialist and anti-Israeli rhetoric found an echo on the streets and in the refugee camps, especially in Jordan, the West Bank, and Gaza. There was also the sense that, however wicked and ruthless Saddam Husain might be, he 'got things done', somewhat in the spirit of Mussolini. Again, although he would have lost the war with Iran had it not been for Western support, the folk memory in the region was sufficiently selective for it to be widely believed that, unlike most of the other rulers in the area, he was not afraid to stand up to the West. Saddam Husain always had his finger on the pulse of certain sentiments in the Arab world, and knew well how to exploit them.

At the same time, Husain was well aware that the increasing pace of reform in the Soviet Union and Eastern Europe must in the longer term hold some threat to him. Though it had been clear since the October War of 1973 that the Soviet Union was not prepared to jeopardise its relationship with the United States by supporting decisively the Arab states in their opposition to Israel, Soviet support for Iraq among other Arab states nonetheless provided some counterbalance to the influence of the United States in the region. Almost all Iraq's basic weaponry came from the Soviet Union, for example, and, as long as superpower considerations determined Soviet policies, Iraq could count on Soviet support if it was ever to fall out seriously with the West. The warning of Soviet muscle worldwide and its simultaneous improvement of relations with the West in the late 1980s, however, meant that even this qualified support was unlikely to remain for long. The events of 1989 were particularly chilling: the fall of Honecker; the destruction of the Berlin Wall; the takeover of Czechoslovakia and Poland by democratic movements; and, perhaps most frightening of all, the overthrow and execution of Ceausescu, were all the results of popular revolts against more or less severe forms of dictatorship. A familiar world was in disarray.

When the report of the US-based Human Rights Watch on Iraq was the subject of questions in Congress in February 1990, Saddam Husain understood full well that the West was going to turn against him. Taking the view that the best form of defence is attack, he launched a virulent campaign against the United States, whom he accused of preparing to establish its hegemony in the region.

These sentiments were summarised in a speech to the members of the ACC in Amman on 24 February 1990. He laid out the possible consequences for the Arab world of the decline of the Soviet Union as a world power and the affirmation of American superiority which this implied: the Gulf would become an American lake, and the United States would use its naval power to control the price of oil. To pre-empt the permanent establishment of American hegemony, the Arabs should agree to build themselves into a regional power capable of setting the agenda on a more equal basis. This was clearly an attempt to present himself as the Bismarck around whom lesser leaders should rally.

Over the next few months the discourse became more strident. Several more incidents enabled Saddam Husain to present himself as 'embattled', the victim of conspiracies forged by Zionism, imperialism and the agents of imperialism in the region. A few weeks after the Human Rights Watch report came the 'trial' and execution of the British journalist Farzad Bazoft, which occasioned widespread verbal condemnation of Iraq in the West; in April, a scandal erupted over the so-called Iraq supergun and over the discovery of essential parts for nuclear weapons in the baggage of Iraqi travellers passing through Heathrow. These incidents were represented as evidence of machinations against Iraq and the 'Arab nation', and had a considerable echo around the Arab world.

Iraq's Arab neighbours were also accused of betraying Iraq and/or the interests of the Arab nation. There were major differences of opinion on oil-pricing policy within OPEC; Kuwait and the UAE were apparently flouting their oil export quotas while Iraq, which was producing well within its capacity, was keen to press for a price increase. Early in 1990 Iraqi officials lobbied the Gulf rulers to lower their production and to push the price up from $18 to $20 per barrel. At the same time Saddam Husain became determined to provide Iraq with access to a deep-water anchorage on the Gulf, probably to accommodate the new frigates and corvettes which he had ordered from Italy. The Kuwaiti islands of Bubiyan and Warbah would provide ideal alternative anchorages. In the spring of 1990 he raised the stakes further, demanding access to the islands and reviving Iraq's claim to that part of the Rumaila oilfield that ran from Iraq into northern Kuwait. He also castigated Kuwait for allegedly having had the temerity to demand repayment of some of Iraq's debts. In July, Iraqi army units were sent to the Kuwaiti border. On 2 August, when Kuwait refused to give in to Saddam Husain's demands, Iraq invaded Kuwait.

The Gulf war

Reaction to the invasion was swift. In broad terms, no state supported Iraq, but some Arab states, notably Jordan, hesitated to condemn the action outright, seeking to maintain a position from which they might mediate. On a broader international level, the UN Security Council passed a series of resolutions condemning Iraq. Resolution 660 of 2 August called for the immediate withdrawal of Iraqi troops. Britain, France and the United States froze all Iraqi assets the same day, with Germany and Japan following suit a day later. On 3 August Iraq moved troops to the Iraqi/Saudi border; on 4 August the American secretary of state and the Soviet foreign minister issued a joint declaration suspending arms deliveries to Iraq. UN Resolution 661 on 6 August declared a commercial, financial and military boycott of Iraq. On 7 August President Bush ordered an immediate airlift of American troops to Saudi Arabia. On 8 August Iraq proclaimed that Kuwait was an integral part of Iraq (it was to become Iraq's 19th province on 28 August). Resolution 662 on 9 August declared the annexation of Kuwait illegal. The Iraqi pipelines across Turkey and Saudi Arabia were closed. Arab and Asian workers began to pour out of Kuwait across Iraq towards the Jordanian border, where they were crossing at the rate of 10–15,000 a day during August and September. Within a few days it became clear that Western contract workers and visitors to Iraq were not going to be allowed to leave; Saddam Husain announced this explicitly on 18 August. Western embassies in Kuwait were closed and their staffs were sent to Baghdad.

Over the following months Iraqi troops killed large numbers of Kuwaitis indiscriminately. They also rounded up all Iraqis in Kuwait and took them into custody. At the same time, several thousand Kuwaitis were arrested; many have not been seen since. Hospitals and other public buildings were stripped of their equipment, and looting of property and attacks on civilians became commonplace. With neither Kuwait nor Iraq exporting oil, the price rose steadily, from about $20 per barrel before the crisis began to above $40 by mid-September.

Various attempts at mediation were made. On 12 August Saddam Husain first began to talk in terms of 'linkage' with the Palestinian issue, offering to withdraw from Kuwait if Israel withdrew from the Occupied Territories. More joint US/Soviet declarations were made condemning Iraq's actions, although the Soviet Union made it clear that it would not join in any military campaign against Iraq. On 15 August Iraq accepted Iran's peace terms unconditionally, restoring the *status quo ante* in the Shatt al-'Arab to what it had been under the Algiers Agreement of March 1975.

In some parts of the Arab world—Jordan, the Occupied Territories, the towns of North Africa—there was widespread support for Saddam Husain, for many of the reasons that have already been mentioned. The PLO and Jordan—the former with some decisiveness, the latter with a good deal more equivocation—also supported Iraq, a reflection above all of the traditionally cool relations between Palestinians and the Gulf states. Ever alert to any weapon to turn to his advantage, Husain made what capital he could from their protestations on his behalf and called for a *jihad* or holy war against the enemies of Islam. The aged Ayatollah 'Abd al-Qasim al-Khu'i issued a *fatwa* on 17 August, condemning any alliance of Muslims entered into with unbelievers against other Muslims. Saddam Husain continued this line of attack over the next few months, condemning the stationing of non-Muslim troops on the sacred soil of Arabia. However transparent his manoeuvering his defiance of the United States nonetheless gained him some support in the Arab and Muslim world.

Why did Saddam Husain persist when he could not conceivably prevail? Nasser's seizure of the Suez Canal in 1956 was often mentioned, but Nasser was taking over a waterway which ran through his country, and his cause was widely regarded as just. In contrast, Saddam Husain had not only invaded the territory of a small and defenceless neighbour which had spent much of the previous decade paying his debts, his forces had killed and imprisoned many of its inhabitants, laid the country waste and carried its portable assets off to Baghdad. There also was no sense in which Kuwait was engraved on every Iraqi's heart. The invasion may have been a morale booster for the Palestinians, but most Iraqis were heartily sick of military adventures and had little enthusiasm for fighting after eight years of senseless war with Iran.

In the five months between the invasion of Kuwait and the beginning of the Gulf War in January 1991, an impressive array of forces from Saudi Arabia, Egypt, Syria, Morocco, Britain, France, Pakistan and Bangladesh, spearheaded by 500,000 troops from the United States, mustered in Saudi Arabia, backed by the moral support of the EC countries, Japan, and all the states of the then Warsaw pact. No state gave military assistance to Iraq; most Arab states, even those relatively well disposed to Iraq, were unequivocal in their condemnation of the invasion. Algeria, Jordan, Libya,

Sudan, Tunisia, Yemen and the PLO gave varying degrees of moral support to Iraq when the extent of the United States' determination to force it to withdraw from Kuwait became clear.

At the end of November, the United Nations, under pressure from the United States, issued Resolution 678. It authorised member states to use all means necessary to force Iraq to withdraw from Kuwait if it had not done so by 15 January 1991. Over the next few weeks various mediation efforts were made, but Saddam Husain remained adamant; the only progress made was in the freeing of the Western hostages, all of whom were released by 17 December. On 17 January 1991, the coalition forces unleashed an awesome aerial bombardment of Iraq, causing countless civilian deaths and great damage to the country's infrastructure. Iraq retaliated by launching Scud missiles at targets in Israel and Saudi Arabia; about 15 Israelis died in Tel Aviv from causes attributable to the missile attacks; Israel did not retaliate. After five weeks of bombing, a ground offensive was launched on 23 February. It ended with the rout and destruction of much of the regular Iraqi Army on 27 February.

The aftermath of the Gulf war

According to one account, the invasion and war resulted in at least 100,000 deaths and 300,000 wounded. Damage estimated at $170 billion was caused in Iraq; excluding the as-yet unknown costs to Kuwait's oil industry, the damage in Kuwait may total $60 billion. Furthermore, 200,000 Palestinians and 150,000 Egyptians were forced to leave Kuwait, as well as 600,000 Asians. A further 350,000 Egyptians left Iraq when Egypt joined the coalition.

The effect on the economies of the Middle East and South Asia was catastrophic; Jordan lost about $400 million per annum in remittances, Egypt about $500 million. Bangladeshis in Kuwait lost some $1.4 billion worth of deposits and assets. In addition, Jordan lost its transit fees for Iraqi goods, its cheap oil from Iraq, about $500 million in grants from Kuwait and Saudi Arabia and its export market in Saudi Arabia. Similarly, 700,000 Yemenis were expelled from Saudi Arabia between September and December 1990. Extended curfews in the West Bank and Gaza (especially after the Temple Mount killings on 8 October) meant few workers who commuted daily to Israel were able to get to their jobs, thus losing income estimated at around $2 million daily.

A few days after the war ended, popular insurrections broke out in southern Iraq and in Kurdistan; by 4 March Kurdish forces had taken Sulaimaniyya, and by 24 March were in control of most of Kurdistan, including the towns of Arbil and Kirkuk. Although the 'rebels' gained control of large areas between the end of February and the beginning of March, units of the Republican Guard responded with exceptional brutality, and were able to gain the upper hand fairly quickly in Basra, Najaf and Karbala. The terms of the cease-fire had not included an embargo on the Iraqis' use of helicopters; in fact, just before Iraqi troops re-captured Samawa on 26 March, the United States explicitly announced that it would not shoot down Iraqi helicopters. In the southern cities, the insurgents had captured and killed local Ba'thist officials, members of the security services and their families, venting their hatred for the regime upon them. When the Republican Guard regained control of the southern cities they carried out indiscriminate executions. Many tanks were painted with the slogan 'No Shias [will survive] after today' and there was widespread destruction of Shia shrines and other mosques in the Holy Cities. The devastation of the south was almost entirely the work of the regime itself after the end of February.

In the last week in March, Iraqi helicopters and troops launched raids on Kirkuk and other Kurdish cities. Kirkuk was recaptured after a massive bombardment on 28 March, and Sulaimaniyya on 3 April. A mass exodus of Kurds to the Iraqi/Turkish and Iraqi/Iranian borders began; by the end of April there were about 2.5 million refugees, both Kurds and southerners. The Kurds fled largely because they feared a repetition of the regime's bombing of Halabja with chemical weapons, which had killed more than 5,000 people. Figures for casualties in these uprisings are difficult to estimate, and several thousands more died of exhaustion and exposure on the borders of Iran and Turkey. The problem continued to be acute throughout the spring and summer of 1991, and, although some Kurds have returned to Kirkuk, Dahuk and Zakho at the time of writing, hundreds of thousands have not.

The American and British troops who came to northern Iraq in April and May to encourage the Kurds to return and to protect them when they did departed in the course of the summer and were replaced by a small United Nations force. The leaders of PUK and KDP spent several months in Baghdad apparently negotiating Kurdish autonomy with Saddam Husain. The Iraqi population, Kurds, Shias and Sunnis, were left at the mercy of that 'pariah president' whom John Major urged them to overthrow on 28 February. Such calls to action naturally raise questions about the 'real' war aims of the allies, which may never become completely clear. The attitude of the United States administration was incoherent and constantly shift-ing, giving an overall sense of confusion and lack of direction. However, as the military build-up increased in the late autumn and winter, and Saddam Husain remained intransigent, the crisis developed its own momentum. Two clear-cut and consistent, if undeclared, objectives emerged. First, it was vital that the Gulf area, which contains 62% of the world's oil reserves, should not fall under the control of interests hostile to the United States. Secondly, Iraq's military capacity would somehow have to be cut down to size.

On the surface it was all rather different. Initially, the declared aim was the expulsion of Iraq from Kuwait and the restoration of the rule of the Sabah family. As the autumn wore on, and as the hostage crisis intensified and accounts of Iraqi atrocities in Kuwait seeped through to the media, the focus shifted to Iraq's appalling human rights record. During the war the notion increasingly gained ground that the removal of Saddam Husain would not be unwelcome, and indeed that things might change dramatically if he were to be overthrown. On 2 April, however, a State Department spokeswoman announced that the United States 'never, ever stated as either a military or a political goal of the coalition, or the international community, the removal of Saddam Husain'.

Maybe not. But broad hints were being dropped in January and February 1991—until, that is, the implications of Saddam Husain's overthrow were analysed by Middle Eastern experts in Washington. Iraq would become 'Lebanonised'; the Kurds would join forces with other Kurds in Turkey and Iran; the Iranians would help the clerics in southern Iraq to create an 'Islamic Republic of Iraq'; the Saudis would be extremely concerned if militant Shias took over the south; many of the regimes in the region would be at risk if some sort of quasi-democratic replacement for Saddam Husain emerged. Most of these assumptions are inaccurate, to say the least. Nevertheless, an emasculated Saddam Husain seemed, at least for the time being, the easiest scenario to control.

Peter Sluglett and Marion Farouk-Sluglett

5 ISRAEL

Israel is a state born in war, a standing challenge to those Arab states who refuse to accept its very existence. Some go so far as to argue that the question of Israel lies at the heart of the seemingly endemic instability of the Middle East. It's a view not all share. None, however, denies that conflict has been, and continues to be, at the core of Israel's story.

Israel has been embroiled in war six times in its brief history: in 1948–49 (the War of Independence); in 1956 (the Sinai Campaign); in 1967 (the Six Day War); in 1973 (the Yom Kippur, or October War); in 1982 (in Lebanon, 'Operation Peace for Galilee'); and in 1991, albeit only indirectly (the Gulf War).

The Israeli War of Independence brought to a head the struggle between the Jewish and Arab populations of Palestine, which had raged throughout the years of the British occupation and mandate (1917–48). It pitted a Palestinian Arab population of one million, supported by five varyingly effective Arab armies from the surrounding states, against 650,000 Jews intent on forming a Jewish state. The Jewish forces consisted of the Haganah and Palmach (the regular forces) and guerrilla groups such as the Irgun and the Stern gang (Lehi). These irregulars, whose methods were frequently extreme, were forcibly incorporated into the regular forces by David Ben-Gurion, Israel's wartime commander and first prime minister.

Though relatively few in number and lightly armed, the Jews were highly motivated. Arab attacks began the moment the state of Israel was declared by Ben-Gurion in May 1948. After bitter fighting and two UN-imposed truces, armistices were signed in 1949. They left Israel in control of the coastal plain, the Negev and Galilee. Jordan, whose British-officered Arab Legion was by far the best of the Arab armies, took over the West Bank of the River Jordan (which it annexed formally in April 1950). Jerusalem was divided between Israel and Jordan. The war left hundreds of thousands of Palestinian Arabs as refugees, with Israel claiming—as it still claims—that the refugee problem was perpetuated deliberately by the Arab states who had no intention of ever reconciling themselves to Israel.

The Jewish victory led to major upheavals in the Arab world, including the assassination of King Abdullah of Jordan in July 1951, accused of 'collusion' with Israel, and the overthrow of the Egyptian monarchy in 1952. In late 1955, President Nasser of Egypt announced that he would block Israeli navigation in the Straits of Tiran on the Red Sea and formed

Official name	State of Israel
Area	20,770 sq. km (8,017 sq. miles)
Population	4,822,000 (1990)
Capital	Jerusalem
Language	Hebrew, Arabic
Religion	Jewish (3,659,000), Muslim (634,600), Christian (105,000), Druze and others (78,100) (1988)
Currency	shekel

a joint command with Syria. The following year, Egypt nationalised the Suez Canal, in which Britain and France had the majority shares. There followed the 1956 Anglo-French-Israeli war against Egypt, which ended with humiliating reversals for France and Britain and considerable military successes for Israel. The fighting was ended by a UN cease-fire in November 1956. Israel was obliged to withdraw from the lands it had occupied, including Gaza and Sinai, during fierce fighting.

After 1956 the Israeli-Egyptian border stayed quiet. But there were increased attacks on Israel from Syria, which shelled Israeli settlements from the Golan Heights, and from Jordan, including raids by the Palestine Liberation Organisation (PLO). In 1967 Nasser again mobilised Egyptian forces, and Yitzak Rabin, the Israeli chief of staff, warned Damascus that Israel would not tolerate further 'provocations'. Faced by 250,000 Arab troops, 2,000 tanks and 700 fighters, and urged on by Moshe Dayan, Israel's defence minister, Israel launched a pre-emptive strike. On 5 June 1967, Israel destroyed the Egyptian air force on the ground; those of Jordan and Syria were similarly devastated. Israel was left with the whole of the West Bank, including Jersualem and the Golan Heights. For the Arabs defeat was in many ways more traumatic than in 1948.

Israel had thrown off the image of the European ghetto Jew and had stunned the world with its military prowess. Perhaps in partial consequence, it was lulled into a false sense of security. On 6 October 1973— Yom Kippur, the Jewish Day of Atonement, when Israel was at prayer— Syria and Egypt struck again. Caught unawares, Israel suffered serious reverses as Egypt launched a remarkable crossing of the Suez Canal. Once installed in Sinai, however, the Egyptian forces did not consolidate their gains. Israel fought back and re-took both the Suez Canal and the Golan Heights. Sadat was forced to appeal to his Soviet backers for a cease-fire.

Though the victory was Israel's, the Arabs nonetheless felt they had regained their honour. Ironically it was this new pride, in the Israeli analysis, which enabled President Sadat of Egypt to seek peace with Israel in 1977. There followed the Camp David Agreement, negotiated by President Sadat of Egypt, the Israeli prime minister, Menachem Begin, and the American president, Jimmy Carter, and the Israeli-Egyptian peace treaty of 1979. Whatever hopes exist in the summer of 1991 for peace, it remains the case that Egypt is still the only Arab country to have made peace with Israel, for all that the provisions of the Camp David Agreement relating to a political statement of the Palestinian question remain unfulfilled.

If the October War dented Israel's image as the military superpower of the Middle East, the 1982 Lebanon campaign went far toward undermining its moral reputation. The campaign, launched in June 1982 with an invasion across the Litani River, pitted Israeli forces against both Syria and the PLO in an all-out drive to force the PLO from its strongholds in Lebanon. Israel's 'hidden agenda' was the installation of a pro-Israeli

Christian Phalangist regime in Beirut. Israeli hopes suffered a substantial setback when Bashir Gemayel, Israel's preferred presidential candidate, was murdered in September. A further blow came when Phalangists entered Palestinian refugee camps at Sabra and Chatila, with the evident blessing of the Israeli forces, and massacred the residents. Combined with the Israeli shelling of West Beirut, it was an event that sharply polarised Israeli public opinion. In 1985, Israel withdrew from Lebanon, though retained a 'security zone'in south Lebanon, which it patrols with the Israeli-financed South Lebanese Army, led by the former Lebanese army officer, General Antoine Lahd.

In 1987 Israeli attention turned to the *intifada*, the 'internal war' waged against Israel by Palestinians in the Occupied Territories with such determination that some count it as a sixth war. After 20 years of occupation, untrained Palestinians of all ages and classes rose up to force Israeli troops out (*intifada* means 'shaking off' or 'eruption' in Arabic). The image of Israel took a further blow as television audiences worldwide saw Israeli soldiers shooting and beating Palestinians armed only with stones.

By 1990–91, with the *intifada* losing momentum, Israel found itself drawn into the Gulf War when Iraq launched conventionally armed Scud missiles at Israeli cities. In a transparent ruse to divert Arab attention from its invasion of Kuwait, Iraq claimed that the invasion had been carried out in the name of the 'Arab nation' as part of the struggle against imperialism and Zionism. The tactic generally failed to gain support, however, except in Jordan with its substantial Palestinian population. Instead, a number of Arab regimes, including those of Egypt and Syria, turned against Baghdad. The Arab world suffered its most serious split, and the creation of the American-led coalition, under UN auspices, gave rise to the extraordinary situation in which Israel found itself on the same side (though not in formal alliance with) several of the Arab states with which it was technically still at war. Israel meanwhile, armed with hurriedly deployed American Patriot anti-missile missiles, and despite Iraq's calculated provocation, allowed itself to be persuaded not to retaliate, a policy that did much to restore its reputation in the wider world.

The geopolitical shifts set off by Iraq's invasion of, and subsequent expulsion from, Kuwait, are still taking place. Palestinians and many other Arabs feel the West will have to address their grievances with greater urgency in the aftermath of the Gulf War to ensure regional stability and a 'new Middle East order'. In contrast, many Israelis argue that it is their position that has been strengthened and that the Palestinian cause has been reversed by the PLO's historic error in siding with Baghdad. Nonetheless it seems clear that the realignment brought about by the Gulf War has improved the prospects for peace significantly. The announcement in August 1991 that Israel was prepared to join the peace talks so tenaciously pursued by the American secretary of state, James Baker, may, as some believe, genuinely mark the end of more than 40 years of conflict. Though the status of Jerusalem, claimed by Jews and Palestinians alike as their 'eternal' capital, and the question of who should represent the Palestinians may yet prove insurmountable, optimism, however guarded, seems justified. Nonetheless, as even the most cursory review of the agonisingly complex and consistently unsuccessful attempts to bring peace to the Middle East shows, nothing should be taken for granted.

The search for peace

Recent attempts to resolve the Arab-Israeli dispute have taken as their starting point the Six Day War of 1967, the aim being, in effect, to restore the 1947 UN partition plan. However permanent Israel's presence in the Occupied Territories may in practice be, in theory at least the West Bank and Gaza, unlike Jerusalem and the Golan Heights, have never been annexed by Israel. Instead, in Israeli terminology, they have been 'administered', on the assumption that their final status is subject to negotiation. UN Resolution 242 of November 1967 requires the withdrawal of Israeli forces 'from territories of recent conflict' and the guaranteed peaceful existence of 'every state in the area . . . within secure and recognised boundaries'. The Palestinians, using first terrorism, then diplomacy, have sought to persuade the international community to make Israel 'give back' the West Bank and Gaza. For its part, Israel insists that it cannot deal with 'extremist' Palestinian leaders whose real aim, in Israel's view, is not compromise but the destruction of the Israeli state. While some Palestinians want a return to pre-1948 Palestine, with Arab and Jewish communities, most are prepared to settle for a reduced homeland. However, many Israelis allege that even moderate Palestinians would merely use a 'mini-PLO' state from which to undermine Israel. Equally, many Palestinians suspect Israel will never relinquish its grip on the Occupied Territories. Nonetheless, the West, notably under America's President Bush and Secretary of State Baker, have sought to exploit what chance of compromise exists to bring the two sides together, though there are clear limits to the extent to which the United States can bring pressure to bear on Israel and there is little more the Palestinians, having recognised Israel, can meaningfully concede.

These issues continue to dog progress towards a settlement, much as they effectively sabotaged the plan put forward by Yitzak Shamir, Israel prime minister, in April 1989. Of perhaps equal significance has been the absence of consensus within Israel. The Israeli 'national unity' coalition government of 1988 to 1990, the product as much as anything of Israel's complex system of proportional representation, was permanently unable to agree a concerted policy towards Shamir's proposals, effectively making further progress impossible. The swing to the right in Israel, a trend evident since the formation of the first Likud government under Begin in 1977, is a further stumbling block. The present right-wing Israeli government, formed in June 1990 under the continuing leadership of Shamir, seems highly unlikely to concede anything of substance to the Palestinians, as witness its absolute refusal to negotiate with the PLO.

Israeli society today

The shift to the right in Israel and the rise of the ultra-Orthodox groups underline the fact that in many ways the prevailing image of Israel in the West is outdated. Europeans and Americans still tend to think in terms of pioneering post-1948 Israel, with Zionist volunteers working in shorts on kibbutzim (cooperative farms) 'making the desert bloom'. It is also widely believed that Israeli political culture is still dominated by the European-born left-wingers who formed the backbone of Mapai, the Labour party, which did indeed dominate Israeli life until 1977.

The rugged ideal of Israel was further reinforced by the Six Day War. But profound changes have since taken place, with Israel increasingly influenced by Sephardic Jews, mostly of North African and Middle Eastern origin, rather than Ashkenazi (European) Jews of the kind who shaped the state and led it in its early years. Although not all Sephardic Jews are conservative in outlook, many are, and their conservatism is reinforced by Orthodox Jewish groups.

It must be stressed, however, that the principal figures within the Likud party—Shamir, Begin, Arens and Sharon, for example—are of European origin, as are many Likud supporters, Spiralling political violence, the downturn in the economy, suspicion of US and European intentions, the massive influx of Soviet Jews and the deterioration of Arab-Jewish relations have reinforced a general move to the right.

The image of the army—the Israel Defence Forces (IDF)—has been adversely affected by the experience of putting down the *intifada*, a genuinely popular uprising, since late 1987. Two-thirds of the IDF is made up of reservists rather than full-time professionals, making it a true 'army of the people'. These divisions—right versus left, secular versus religious—have always been present. But their accentuation has made Israel a society less at ease with itself and more unsure of the future. There is consensus on the need for Israel's guaranteed security, but no consensus on how to achieve it.

The rise of the religious right-wing has helped to create an impression of religious intolerance in Israel not dissimilar to the spread of Islamic fundamentalism in the Arab world and Iran, even though in reality the great majority of the population is secular in outlook. The problems of the Israeli economy, much of it still state-managed, make Israel part Western, part Third World. In general, there is a paradoxical sense in which Israel is gradually merging with its Middle Eastern surroundings, a process which creates confusion in the West, not least among Jewish supporters of Israel in the United States.

Yet Israel remains committed to the democratic values of its founders, and is still, with Turkey, the only functioning democracy in the region. To a degree, democracy was also inherited from the laws and institutions of the British mandate, as were the various emergency regulations, which remain the basis of Israeli actions in the Occupied Territories. Israel's democracy is vividly expressed in the parliament, the Knesset, with its multitude of parties, noisy debates and complex procedures. The chaotic parliamentary scenes, and the disproportionate influence wielded by the ultra-Orthodox, have led to demands for electoral reform (see below).

Israel is also the only Middle Eastern country to enjoy a virtually free press (subject to censorship on security matters), an independent judiciary and freedom of assembly, although the Israeli Arabs (those living within the frontiers of pre-1945 Israel) both feel and are treated as second-class citizens. Israelis love to argue and do so fully and freely, with endless debates in homes, in cafés and on television. The spiritual and ideological roots of the country lie firmly in Judaism, with even secular Jews observing rituals such as circumcision and bar mitzvah. Israel remains an outdoor society, with a strong emphasis on healthy living, hiking, and hard work. Alcohol, apart from beer, is rare: young and old alike drink fruit juice or soft drinks. Drug abuse, although on the rise, is rare by outside standards. Finally—and this is perhaps the very basis of society—all Israelis are bound together by the memory of the horror of the Nazi holocaust, and by the certainty that Israel must serve as a refuge for Jews and as a vigilant guardian against anti-Semitism.

At the same time recent Israeli films such as *One of Ours*, which depicts an elite army unit murdering an Arab terrorist it has taken prisoner, illustrates the mood of self-questioning into which Israel has fallen. Some of this is due to the *intifada*: opinion polls suggest that while 60% of Israelis favour even tougher measures to put down the revolt, 40% regard this as a betrayal of the ideals on which Israel was founded. Another view is that having survived over 40 years in the face of Arab hostility and often international disapproval, Israel has somewhat lost its way and is unsure of its purpose.

This is felt most strongly on the left, whose declining fortunes have been dealt a further blow by the support given by the Palestinians to Saddam Husain. In the eyes of many Israelis this makes the policy of talking to the PLO—epitomised by the Peace Now Organisation—unacceptable. But Labour was declining even before the Gulf War, partly for demographic reasons, as the Sephardic Jews, who form an increasingly larger proportion of the population, gradually turn to Likud. The 1977 elections marked the end of a 30-year period in which the Israeli establishment was synonymous with Labour, led by such dominant figures as David Ben-Gurion and Golda Meir. Rabin and Peres, despite participation in the Likud-Labour coalition government of 1988–90, have been unable to maintain Labour's grip. The Rabin administration of 1974–76 was damaged by financial scandals. But in any case Labour was losing popularity, and has suffered from the global swing toward conservatism rather than socialism. One young Labour leader, Yossi Bailin, has proposed dropping such socialist symbols as the Red Flag and May Day, partly to court the voters of Soviet newcomers, who tend to be right-wing and could decide the next election.

Kibbutz left versus settler right

The crisis in the kibbutz movement is clearly related to the problems of the left. Kibbutzim still thrive, and will remain a feature of Israeli life, with their stress on thrift and the communal life. There are still some 270 kibbutzim, with 126,000 members. But many are deeply in debt, and although admired for their role in the creation of Israel, they no longer automatically produce the country's political and military elite. Some kibbutzim supplement their farm income with light industry. But a new middle class has grown up in areas like Tel Aviv, with nouveaux riches Israelis addicted to consumers goods, yachts and cars. The ideal of an egalitarian society, which motivated the pioneers fleeing from ghettoes and persecution, no longer has the same appeal. Most kibbutzim have long ago abandoned the concept of communal child care and are altogether less collectivist.

Right-wingers, by contrast, some of them recent immigrants from the United States, have gained ground. In its most militant form the right embraces such groups as Kach, which follows the overtly racist precepts of Rabbi Meir Kahane (murdered in New York in November 1990), and the shadowy Sicarii, a small group of fanatics who take their name from the Jewish Zealots who defied the Roman occupation. Such militants trace their modern origin to the Jewish Underground, formed from radical Jewish settlers on the West Bank who in the early 1980s committed acts of violence against Palestinian leaders, including attempting to assassinate several pro-PLO West Bank Arab mayors.

The Jewish Underground was broken up by Israeli police and its ringleaders arrested. But its spirit lives on, not least among members of the settler movement Gush Emunim (Bloc of the Faithful) led by the extremist Rabbi Moshe Levinger. When the last three Jewish Underground members still in prison were released in December 1990, after serving only seven years of their life sentences for murder, they warned that unless the Shamir government took tougher action against the *intifada*, Jewish militants would continue to take the law into their own hands. On both right and left the concept of Arab-Jewish coexistence has given way to the assumption that the two communities should be kept apart as far as possible. 'If people cannot live together decently, let them live in separate cages' was the comment of the liberal writer Amos Oz.

Ashkenazi, Sephardic, Orthodox and secular

The swing to the right in Israel can be partly explained in terms of an important trend in Zionist thinking, and partly in line of the balance between the Ashkenazi and Sephardic communities. To some extent the two have intermingled: 20% of Israeli marriages are 'mixed' marriages. But the Jews who arrived en masse from North Africa, Yemen and Iraq in the late 1940s and early 1950s still have a separate identity, and have progressed from being a poor and backward minority, an Israeli underclass, to being a force to be reckoned with. David Levy, the foreign minister, embodies this development: a man at the pinnacle of the Israeli system, and a potential prime minister, he is of humble Moroccan origin and speaks no English.

A poll by the Smith Institute published in *Davar* in December 1990 showed that 63% of Sephardic Jews support Likud and its right-wing allies, while only 19% vote for Labour and the left. This is mirrored by the Ashkenazi side: only 28% of Israelis of European origin vote for Likud, while 50% support Labour. This is a marked change from the 1960s and 1970s when half the Sephardic community were Labour voters. The change began in 1977 when Likud, having successfully courted Sephardic votes, formed the first non-Labour-led government. The trend has continued, leading to what *Davar* described as 'tremendous ethnic polarisation'.

The same poll showed that support for Labour is drawn largely from Israel's secular population. The increasingly influential ultra-Orthodox Jews of Israel, a familiar part of the scene in their black hats and ringlets, support either Likud or religious parties such as the National Religious party (NRP), Degel, Hatorah and Shas (the latter drawing on Sephardic Jews). Because of Israel's proportional representation system and the proliferation of parties, the religious groups hold the balance of power in the Knesset and receive generous state funding for religious seminaries (yeshivas). This in turn has exacerbated tensions between secular Israelis, who observe Sabbath rituals lightly if at all and want Israel to be a haven for Jews of all kinds, and ultra-Orthodox Jews who want stricter religious laws and a life devoted to study of the Torah.

Secular Jews especially resent the fact that yeshiva students are exempt from national service. Orthodox Jews often study religious texts while their wives go out to work. Israel is far from being a theocracy but Orthodox groups wield great power, not least in Jerusalem, and have succeeded in banning sales of pork and 'sexually enticing' public advertisements. El Al, the national airline, loses tourist revenue by not being able to fly from Friday evening to Saturday evening, the Jewish Sabbath. Religious courts decide matters of marriage and divorce, and streets in Orthodox areas are closed off on Saturdays with residents often stoning any cars which appear.

Paradoxically, many Orthodox or *haredin* (meaning 'God-fearing') Jews regard the creation of the state of Israel as premature, since, strictly speaking, such a theocratic state could only come into existence after the Messiah makes himself known on earth. For the same reason Orthodox groups oppose the Temple Mount Faithful, a tiny group of zealots who want to destroy the Islamic mosques on Temple Mount and restore the Jewish temples. This has not however prevented the religious parties from taking part in politics, and indeed manipulating coalitions to great effect. The Orthodox parties are pressing for stricter criteria for the Law of Return, which allows Jews to settle in Israel. The question of 'Who is a Jew' has become highly charged: The Law of Return defines a Jew as someone who was either born of a Jewish mother or has converted to Judaism. But Orthodox groups do not recognise the validity of conversions conducted by conservative or reform Rabbis who do not acknowledge *Halacha*, the religious law as narrowly interpreted by the *haredin*.

Pressures for electoral reform

It would be wrong to conclude that secular/Ashkenazi Jews are all on the left, while Orthodox/Sephardic Jews are all on the right. The picture is more complex: a secular Israeli of Polish origin might support Likud (Shamir himself is Polish-born) while a Jew of Yemeni parents demonstrates for Peace Now. But the general trend is for Oriental and Orthodox Jews to back 'hawkish' policies over Israel's control of the West Bank and the building of Jewish settlements in the Occupied Territories. Some rabbis oppose the occupation, on the grounds that Jewish soldiers' and settlers' lives are put at risk unjustifiably. But most argue that the West Bank is Jewish land by right.

Secular, left-wing Israelis resent this influence, and are increasingly vocal in their demands for electoral reform, so that the religious parties can be reduced to their 'proper status'. Indeed, Israelis on both the left and the right have joined the movement for electoral reform, with voters of all shades of opinion finding the process of coalition-haggling which follows any election distasteful and demeaning. Reformers opposed to unstable coalitions and the excessive power of the Orthodox groups have been able to mobilise tens of thousands of supporters on the streets of Jersualem and Tel Aviv, with direct elections for the post of prime minister as one of their aims. There have been hunger strikes and petitions to the Knesset, with President Chaim Herzog joining the ranks of the reformers and describing the present system as a 'mockery of democracy'. However, so powerful are the vested interests involved that neither Labour nor Likud appears willing to risk upheaval by forcing the necessary changes through the Knesset.

Meanwhile the right-wing continues to reinforce its hold, and the left continues to seek a return to its former dominance. Rehavam Zeevi, a 63-year-old former general who now heads the Moledet party, claims that over 50% of Israelis favour the once outlandish concept of 'transfer' of the

Palestinian population to Jordan to make way for a 'Greater Israel'. 'The only solution for the Palestinians is separation from the Jews' Zeevi said. 'Each people has to return to the land of its forefathers. We Jews have returned, but the Palestinians' forefathers came here from Saudi Arabia, from Sudan, from Libya.' Israel, in this view, should either persuade the Arab states to accept the one-and-three-quarter million Arabs of the West Bank and Gaza or force the Palestinians out by shutting down industries and universities until they leave of their own accord. This growing Jewish militancy is matched on the Palestinian side by a growing self-confidence and increasing determination to obtain a national homeland, the direct result of the *intifada*.

The Israeli economy

In the early years of the Jewish state, economic progress was remarkable. In agriculture, kibbutz pioneers used new irrigation techniques and sheer hard work to 'make the desert bloom'. In industry, growth rates averaged 9% in real terms between 1960 and 1973, with inflation kept down to single figures. Trees were planted, swamps drained, roads built, and an advanced defence industry took shape to give Israel military self-sufficiency. A modern banking system developed. The burden of high defence spending was largely borne by the United States, through loans and aid.

But underlying strains in the economy came to the fore after the 1973 Yom Kippur War and the impact of the OPEC (Organisation of Petroleum Exporting Countries) oil embargo the same year. Israel suffers from Arab attempts to impose an economic boycott of the Jewish state. But above all it suffers from an antiquated state-dominated economic structure in which a huge concern like Koor, owned by the Histadrut, the trade union organisation, can control a large proportion of Israeli manufacturing and retailing. This tradition of state interventionism, coupled with a bureaucracy which is one of the world's most complex and Byzantine, creates severe obstacles to initiative and growth. Israel has launched a privatisation programme, with one eye on the competitive trade conditions likely to follow the completion of the Single European Market in 1992. But entrenched attitudes are proving hard to shift, and foreign investors are often alienated by Israeli statism.

The tradition of state intervention and control has its origins in the pioneering days of the state and the socialist ethic which Israel's European-born elite brought with it as part of its vision of Zionism. This however has tended to frustrate efforts to move the Israeli economy toward a more modern, liberalised model. By 1985, the faults in Israel's economy had become obvious, with inflation running at around 400% and foreign reserves dangerously low. Under Shimon Peres, the then Labour prime minister, and with American help, the Israeli leadership succeeded in imposing an austerity programme and brought inflation down to levels below 20%. Some state subsidies, for example in transport, were phased out, and expensive projects such as the Lavi fighter aircraft were cancelled. Budget deficits dropped from 15% of GNP to under 2%.

Nonetheless the essential problem of turning a bureaucratised, monopolistic system into a Western-orientated free market system remained. Foreign debt and defence expenditure together account for a staggering 60% of the Israeli budget. Twenty years ago, according to the Israeli Centre for Social and Economic Progress, one in five Israelis were employed by the government: today the figure is one in three. Taxation is high, and an ability to manufacture and market high-quality technology, from biomedicine to communications, goes hand in hand with an economy which in some respects is of Third World standard. Food packaging is often primitive and standardised. Nearly a third of all business activity, according to Israeli economists, is controlled by cartels and monopolies, and competition in agricultural products such as fruit and vegetables is strictly regulated by a state marketing board. Protectionism abounds in all commercial sectors. The building industry is also inhibited by the rarity and high cost of land—nearly all land is leased by the Israel Land Authority— and by a complex and stifling system of planning permission and licensing. In 1990 workers at *moshavim*—cooperative farms which combine agriculture with light industry—in the north of Israel staged *intifada*-style strikes, claiming they were owed £2 million in subsidies. The Israeli annual trade deficit is approximately £3 billion ($5 billion).

Some economists propose, as a drastic measure, that annual American economic aid to Israel—currently $3 billion—should be reduced or even eliminated. This, radical economists suggest, would force Israel to face harsh economic realities and introduce market reforms faster. Others put their faith in the privatisation programme, under which a number of state-owned companies such as the Israel Electrical Corporation and Maman Cargo Handling have been sold off. The state airline, El Al, now emerging from receivership after becoming bankrupt, is to be offered to private investors. On the other hand, investors often find that privatisation contracts are hedged about with conditions which allow for a degree of continued state control, especially if the company concerned has some strategic value or is considered crucial to the national interest. Such conditions have so far deterred potential investors from taking over Israel Chemicals, a profitable company based on the exploitation of Dead Sea minerals.

For some Israeli officials, the most disturbing factor is the failure of many Israeli manufacturers and traders to realise the significance of 1992. Israel has traditionally looked to Europe as well as the United States, and has a free trade agreement with the EC. But Israeli officials are aware that Israel could find itself excluded from lucrative EC markets after 1992 and are seeking special concessions equivalent to the privileged trading arrangements enjoyed by the EFTA (European Free Trade Association) nations with the twelve EC members. Some Israelis would even like to see Israel applying for EC membership, or at least associate status. This is highly unlikely, however, given that several other countries with undoubted European credentials are ahead in the queue for EC membership, and that Brussels has no intention of considering membership applications until the 1992 process is fully completed and running smoothly. Israel, moreover, has a diminishing claim to a European identity (apart from its participation in the Eurovision Song Contest) and in the long run is more likely to find a new trading status in a Middle Eastern context—if there is a political and diplomatic settlement of the Arab-Israeli dispute. The Bank of Israel has calculated that the Palestinian *intifada* has cost the Israeli economy, in terms of lost output and tourist revenues, about 2% of GNP per year since 1988.

Soviet Jewish immigration

Strains in the already overburdened Israeli economy have been increased by the massive influx of Soviet Jews into Israel which began in late 1989 and gathered momentum in 1990 and 1991, partly because of the freedoms opened up by Gorbachov and partly because of rising anti-Semitism, itself a product of the political loosening-up in Russia. On the other hand, Israeli leaders, and for that matter ordinary Israelis, have welcomed Soviet Jewish immigration on a huge scale as a 'miracle', a fresh infusion of blood into the Jewish state which can only strengthen Israel and give it new vigour and economic growth. Palestinians take a less sanguine view, fearing that new Russian arrivals will settle in the West Bank and Gaza, altering the demographic character of these areas and displacing Arabs by competing for scarce jobs and housing.

According to the Jewish Agency, which together with the Ministry of Absorption and Immigration deals with immigration matters, 200,000 Soviet Jews arrived in Israel in the course of 1990. The projected figure for 1991 is 600,000, with a million expected by 1992. Of the 200,000 who arrived in 1990, a quarter came from the Ukraine, some 40,000 from European Russia and 25,000 from Central Asia. About half had received higher education and professional qualifications: 20,000 were classed as 'engineers', and there were some 5,000 doctors among the new immigrants, not to mention teachers, musicians and technicians. On the other hand, experience has shown that Soviet qualifications in fields such as medicine and science are below the Western standards to which Israel adheres, so that retraining or 'top-up' programmes have had to be organised. The description 'engineer' moreover does not necessarily imply the kind of engineering qualifications common in the West.

A further difficulty has simply been finding jobs for Soviet immigrants in a country which already has an unemployment rate of 9%. Soviet doctors, for example, have gone to development towns like Beersheba, which boasts an excellent hospital and medical school, only to find that there is a surfeit of medically qualified personnel and that the only way to make a living—at least for the time being—is to undertake manual work or even (in some documented cases) sweep the streets.

The Shamir government's response has been to appoint an immigration ministerial task force headed by Ariel Sharon, the forceful former general who became minister of housing in the government formed in June 1990. Sharon's handling of immigration has been harshly criticised in the Israeli press, partly because of expensive projects such as the mass purchase of temporary housing and caravans from overseas rather than domestic firms, and partly because of Sharon's incessant political in-fighting with Rabbi Yitzham Peretz, the immigration and absorption minister, who controls the immigration process.

The government's hope is that the long-term benefits of mass immigration will eventually come to outweigh the short-term strains on jobs and housing. Partly because of the new manpower, official forecasts suggest growth in the economy of between 8% and 10% 'in the near future'. This is based on the assumption that 600,000 new jobs can be generated through private enterprise. The economic plan presented to the cabinet by Yitzhak Modai, the finance minister, and Michael Bruno, governor of the Bank of Israel, in September 1990 called for far-reaching liberalisation of financial markets, a restructuring of the labour market, reductions in import barriers and further privatisation to generate growth and help absorb the new-comers and make use of their talents. Several factors remain unclear, however, including whether Russian Jews brought up in a system of complete state control can adapt to a free market climate requiring individual initiative and effort, and whether the projected $40 billion worth of investment—domestic and foreign—can be generated as planned over the next five years. Economists foresee an inevitable rise in Israel's foreign debt, which already accounts for 35% of GNP.

Exports will have to show an annual average gain of 13%, which in turn requires close cooperation between the government and the Histadrut, the trade union confederation, over wage levels. Russian immigrants, however, tend to be wary of the Histadrut precisely because its socialist tradition offers an uncomfortable reminder of the state socialism from which they have escaped. Many Soviet immigrants are also disillusioned by the complex and wearisome bureaucratic procedures they encounter in Israel as they cope with banks, schools, social insurance and the Immigration Ministry itself. On the other hand, many take the view that such obstacles are a small price to pay for the privilege of leaving Russia for the 'Promised Land'.

What alarms Western governments, and of course the Palestinian Arabs, is that some Russian immigrants may come to share the Likud view that the 'Promised Land' includes the West Bank as much as Israel proper. Such anxieties were fuelled in January 1990 when Shamir observed that 'a big immigration requires a big Israel', and again later in the year when he remarked that mass *aliyah* (immigration in Hebrew) invoked the Likud vision of a Greater Israel stretching 'from the Jordan River to the Mediterranean Sea'. In both cases Shamir was addressing the Likud party faithful, and aides were at pains to point out that the vision of Greater Israel was just that—a vision, not a policy. But when the Israeli consulate in Moscow was formally reopened in January 1991, the Soviet authorities made clear that further improvements in Israeli-Soviet relations, notably the full restoration of flights between Moscow and Tel Aviv, were dependent on assurances from the government of Israel that new immigrants were not being settled in the Occupied Territories.

The Israeli response to such demands has been to assert that the government has no policy of directing immigrants to live in the West Bank, but that new arrivals have the right to live wherever they wish. In practice, despite the efforts of settler groups such as Gush Emunim to attract Soviet *olim*, less than 1% have chosen to go to the West Bank or Gaza. Ariel, near Nablus, the most successful settlement in attracting Russians, has some 1,200 Soviet immigrants living in suburban-style conditions. But few Russians find the idea of living a pioneer life on a rural settlement surrounded by hostile Arabs an attractive proposition, and most tend naturally to settle in areas such as Tel Aviv and Haifa where friends and relatives from earlier waves of Soviet immigration already live. On the other hand, government forecasts estimate that the settler population of the West Bank, currently over 80,000 (the settlers themselves claim a figure closer to 100,000), will rise to 250,000 by the year 2010, and some of the new settlers are bound to be Russian immigrants. Some 10% of the Soviet arrivals, moreover, choose to live in newly built Jewish suburbs of East Jerusalem, which has been annexed by Israel as part of its 'united and eternal capital' (see below) but which the international community regards as occupied land whose final status has yet to be negotiated.

Many Soviet immigrants appear unaware of the fact that East Jerusalem is held to be occupied territory in international law. Many, for that matter, arrive with limited knowledge of Israel, and have to learn Hebrew, accustom themselves to the practices of Judaism, and even—in very many cases—undergo circumcision. Their 'Jewishness', long suppressed in the Soviet Union, is rediscovered.

The issue of demography and settlement remains an explosive one, and has caused strains in relations between Israel and the United States (see below). Many of the Russian Jews arriving in Israel—a quantifiable figure is not available—would almost certainly have preferred to emigrate to the United States. The huge wave of Soviet emigration to Israel which began in late 1989 was in part due to new immigration restrictions in America. The Israelis, for their part, have turned to America, and above all to American Jewish groups, for financial aid in raising the $2 billion needed to absorb immigrants to Israel over the next three years.

US officials, and to a degree US Jewish groups, are wary of giving money which may be used to aggravate the Israeli-Palestinian problem.

America has demanded guarantees from the Israeli government that US housing loans will not be used beyond the Green Line (the pre-1967 border between Israel and the West Bank), but Shamir, Levy and Sharon have not gone beyond the standard Israeli undertaking not to 'direct' immigrants to the West Bank.

Meanwhile, 10% of the new arrivals live temporarily in run-down, often squalid 'absorption centres' while they try to find their feet in Israeli society. Some experts, such as Julia Mirsky, a Hebrew University psychologist who helps newcomers to adjust, complain that many of the new arrivals are not committed Zionists in the manner of earlier refusenik immigrants such as Natan Sharansky, but rather refugees from the privations and pressures of Gorbachov's Russia. After the killing of 18 Arabs on Temple Mount in October 1990 and the revenge stabbings of Jews by Arabs which followed, some Israeli employers began laying off Arab labourers and hiring Soviet immigrants instead. But as Sharansky, who runs the Soviet Jewish Zionist Forum in Jerusalem, has observed, 'many of the immigrants are physicians, engineers, musicians and other professionals. They are not looking for jobs on building sites'. According to Soviet consular officials in Israel, quoted in the Israeli press, several thousand new immigrants have become so disenchanted they have indicated a desire to return to the Soviet Union (the newspaper *Hadashot* put the figure at 18,000). The Jewish Agency and government bodies have denied that the numbers of those wishing to leave Israel so soon after arriving are anything like so high. But using the 'miracle' of massive immigration to strengthen Israel, creating new jobs and housing for the Russian arrivals, moulding them into Israelis and perhaps Zionists, all while avoiding further aggravation of the Palestinian issue or further strains in US-Israeli relations, all presents perhaps the greatest challenge the state of Israel has faced (apart from war) since its inception.

US-Israeli Relations

It is widely assumed in the Arab world that Israel is a 'client state' of America, and that American policy in turn is influenced if not shaped by the American Jewish lobby. The US is indeed Israel's most loyal supporter in the international community, and its main financial benefactor. The influence of the Jewish lobby in Washington is not to be underestimated. On the other hand, stresses have grown in relations between the United States and Israel, with the American Jewish lobby often expressing concern over Israeli policies in the Occupied Territories. Such strains reflect a degree of alienation between America and Israel. This has recently taken the form of United States' support for resolutions in the United Nations Security Council critical of Israel, and Israeli alarm over the priority given by Washington to maintaining and nurturing its alliance with Arab States. US arms sales to Saudi Arabia and the American concept of a post-Gulf crisis 'new strategic order' in the Middle East cause deep anxiety in

Jerusalem. On the other hand, Israel's remarkable self-restraint when subjected to Iraqi missile attacks in the 1991 Gulf War has given it a great deal of future credit, and the right to a say in the post-war Middle East settlement. The US-Israeli relationship—apart from ties derived from the American-Jewish connection—is based in formal terms on a strategic cooperation agreement. In financial terms, relations revolve around US aid to Israel of £3 billion a year, annually renewed, of which $1.75 billion is earmarked as military aid to help Israel defend itself against Arab states bent on its destruction. The rest is economic aid to support Israel's troubled economy.

The refusal of the Shamir government to accede to the Baker proposals for Israeli-Palestinian talks in 1990 caused a strained atmosphere between Washington and Jerusualem, or in personal terms, between Bush and Shamir. American disapproval of Likud policies toward the Occupied Territories, and in particular the continued expansion of Jewish West Bank settlements—which the United States regards as a serious obstacle to a future peace—have led the Bush administration to withhold aid programmes and even military equipment. The failure of the Americans to supply Israel with the advanced Patriot anti-missile system in time to prevent Iraq's Scud missile attacks on Tel Aviv in January 1991 caused particular bitterness in Israel, all the more so since the Patriot system was used to great effect against Iraqi missile attacks on Saudi Arabia. On the other hand, American officials say it was Israel itself which held up the deployments until the eleventh hour.

Such tensions came against the background of growing American public dismay over Israel's handling of the *intifada* from December 1987 onwards. Even some American Jewish groups and supporters of Israel in the US Congress voiced concern over television images of Israeli troops behaving with brutality toward Arab protesters. The images did not convey the other side of the story: Israeli troops were often provoked by stone throwing, and stones can cause serious injury. Nonetheless, Israel's heavy-handed actions severely dented its image and did much to undermine American sympathy for Israel which had developed during and after the 1967 Six Day War.

The Bush administration, moreover, is perceived as far less sympathetic toward Israel than the Reagan administration had been. One flashpoint came after the Temple Mount killings on 8 October 1990 (see below), when Shamir resisted American efforts to persuade Israel to cooperate with a proposed UN investigation into the incident. 'So long as the Palestinian problem is unsolved, so long as Shamir believes time is on his side, Israel will be at odds with the US', *Hadashot* wrote in November 1990. The ending of the Cold War and the Soviet-American *rapprochement* of 1990 have also affected the Israeli-US relationship. While still providing Israel's underpinning, the United States no longer needs Israel to the same extent as 'a low cost land-based aircraft carrier' to represent Western interests in a regional East-West confrontation. The 1991 Gulf War also illustrated this, with America forging a new alliance with Saudi Arabia, Egypt and Syria to wage war on Saddam Husain, attempting to leave Israel on the sidelines. While rejecting the 'linkage' Saddam Husain had created between Kuwait and Palestine, the United States was clearly obliged by its new coalition with anti-Iraq Arab states to engage in harsher criticism of Israel at the UN and demonstrate a firm commitment to a resolution of the Palestinian question. At the same time, the United States distanced itself from the PLO by breaking off the US-PLO dialogue following Arafat's failure to condemn Palestinian terrorist acts in sufficiently clear and precise terms. Israel was also pleased by Bush's decision in January 1991 to go to war with Iraq in order to force Iraq out of Kuwait and also to destroy Saddam Husain's nuclear, chemical and biological warfare capacity.

Equally, American financial support for Israel shows no sign of diminishing, despite calls from some American politicians such as Senator Robert Dole for a 5% reduction. In November 1990 Congress voted to cancel Egypt's $6.7 billion military debt to the United States without cancelling Israel's. On the other hand, the Senate overwhelmingly approved the annual $3 billion aid package for Israel and added $700 million worth of military equipment.

The support of American Jews for Israel as the Jewish state is axiomatic. But some Israelis resent attempts by American Jews, who do not share the burdens of Israeli life, to interfere in Israeli affairs. Conversely, American Jewish support is not unqualified. One opinion poll in the *New York Times* in 1990 showed that the number of those who believed the American administration should be more sympathetic to the plight of the Palestinians had risen from 26% in 1988 to 38%. Similarly, the number of those favouring an increase in aid to Israel had fallen from 72% to 61%.

Israel's remarkable agreement to refrain from retaliation against Iraqi Scud attacks in the early stages of the Gulf War against Iraq was swiftly rewarded with the supply to Israel of American-made Patriot anti-missile systems, with American crews. This one incident has helped to forge a new understanding between Washington and Jerusalem. But this has not ended the Bush administration's insistence that Israel under Shamir should be more flexible over the Palestinian issue, nor has it reduced United States' support for the idea of an international peace conference, a proposal Israel vehemently opposes in case such a conference involves the PLO and attempts to impose a solution on Israel. In April 1991 Israel agreed to a Baker proposal for a 'regional' peace conference leading to bilateral Arab-Israeli talks, but the Arab states accused Israel of using a device to avoid a fully fledged international conference with UN involvement. American irritation on the issue had already surfaced in mid-1990 when Baker told the Israeli government publicly: 'Our telephone number is 456-1414. When you're serious about peace, call us.' Lobbies such as AIPAC (the American-Israel Public Affairs Committee) can influence politicians by encouraging or discouraging election campaign contributors, but even AIPAC has occasionally voiced criticism: when militant Jewish settlers, with official finance, took over a Christian hostel in Jerusalem's Old City in 1990, AIPAC described the move as 'insensitive and provocative'. The question of Jerusalem, the Occupied Territories and the settlements on the West Bank remain at the heart of US-Israeli tensions.

The question of Jerusalem

Since 1967 all Jerusalem has been in the hands of Israel which asserts that the city has never been an Arabic capital. Nonetheless, Palestinians still regard Jerusalem as their capital. This struggle for a city at once holy to Muslims, Jews and Christians, is one of the most intractable of Arab–Israeli issues.

The 1947 UN partition plan saw a Jerusalem under international control (as a *corpus separatum*). Israel now sees this solution as irrelevant, and is determined to control the whole city. The 140,000 Palestinians living in East Jerusalem carry Israeli papers as residents of an annexed area. Faisal Husaini, the leading Palestinian in Jerusalem and a descendant of the city's former mufti, proposed to Teddy Kollek, the veteran mayor, in January 1991, that there should be 'one city but two municipalities, one Arab and one Jewish'. Kollek, noted for his tolerance and attempts to ensure equal rights in the city for Arabs and Jews, rejected this.

For Arabs and Jews alike, the emotive focus is the Old City, where the Muslim shrines of al-Aqsa and the Golden Dome stand on the destroyed Jewish Temple. In theory Israel allows Muslims free access to the site, but Muslim worshippers have been banned at times of tension. The most serious such incident occurred on 8 October 1990 when 18 Arabs were killed by Israeli border police. Israel accused Arabs of starting the riot by throwing large stones down on Jewish worshippers at the Wailing Wall below as part of a PLO conspiracy to foment unrest and help the cause of Iraq in the Gulf crisis. The Arabs said the deaths were due to unprovoked Israeli police brutality, and that the large Arab presence on the Mount was to prevent an attempt by a small group of Jewish zealots (the Temple Mount Faithful) from trying to lay the foundation stone of a new Temple. A persistent Arab fear is that such zealots will blow up Muslim shrines. Israeli police said they had guaranteed that the Faithful would be banned from the Mount – as they were – but Palestinians said they had no faith in Israeli assurances. An Israeli inquiry referred to 'indiscriminate shooting' by border police but blamed the Palestinians for the riots.

The Temple Mount killings reinforced and even increased mutual suspicion. Kollek has repeatedly invited Palestinian residents to take part in municipal elections, but the Arabs argue that this would be to acquiesce in the annexation. In July 1991 a judicial enquiry concluded that police incompetence lay behind the Temple Mount tragedy, but said there was no reason to prosecute individual policemen.

Future prospects

Jerusalem and the question of Palestinian representation remained the chief obstacles to peace in 1991 as the United States persevered with its post-Gulf Middle East diplomacy and vigorously pursued the regional peace conference proposed by Baker, setting October as the date. After his initial post-war diplomacy Baker made four further regional tours in the spring and summer of 1991, noting that the 'window of opportunity' had again opened but would not last forever. On 1 June President Bush wrote to presidents Asad and Shamir offering a compromise formula over UN involvement in peace talks: given that Syria wanted full UN participation and Israel wanted none, Bush suggested a one-day opening meeting at which the UN would preside but not take part.

In July, Asad agreed, accepting at the G7 Western economic summit in London. Jordan also said it would attend, with Palestinians forming part of its delegation. In August Shamir – who had initially rejected Bush's approach – also agreed, but again on condition that the PLO would be excluded and East Jerusalem Arabs would not form part of any Palestinian delegation. The Israeli cabinet approved this by 16 to 3. Palestinian activists denounced the Baker initiative as a Zionist plot, but the Palestinian National Council agreed to discuss it in Algiers in September. Ultimately, the influence of the United States prevailed, and a series of talks attended by parties to the Arab–Israeli conflict began in October.

The coalition government of Yitzhak Shamir fell in January, after the right-wing Tehiya and Moledet parties withdrew their support for Likud in protest at the government's apparent readiness to discuss autonomy for the Palestinians. A large proportion of the Israeli people (74 per cent according to a poll conducted the previous November) appear prepared to give up land in exchange for peace. Before the Madrid talks, only 42 per cent of the population were in favour of giving up occupied land. This fact, and the replacement of Labour leader Shimon Peres by Yitzhak Rabin, a potential prime minister favoured by the United States for his professed willingness to continue dialogue with the Arabs, brought renewed hopes for peace.

The peace talks continued intermittently in Washington and Moscow until the time of writing (March 1992), despite the killing by Palestinian guerillas in February of three Israeli soldiers in Northern Israel. The Israelis retaliated with air raids on Palestinian refugee camps at Ain el-Hilweh and Rashidiyeh, and by killing the most senior Hezbollah leader, Sheikh Abbas Moussawi, in a helicopter gunship attack on his motorcade in Lebanon.

The danger now is that delays caused by the forthcoming Israeli elections, Israel's continued building in the Occupied Territories, and random incidents by extremists from both sides may undermine the progress towards peace made over the preceding year.

Richard Owen

6 JORDAN

More, perhaps, than any other Middle East state outside the Arabian peninsula, the Hashemite Kingdom of Jordan has revolved around the fortunes of a single family. It is scarcely an exaggeration to say that Jordan owed its establishment in 1921 to the coincidence of Britain's interest in establishing some sort of political authority under its own aegis on the east bank of the Jordan with Abdullah ibn Husain's presence in the area at the time. Nor is it an overstatement to say that modern Jordan is almost entirely the creation and creature of his grandson, Husain.

Under the Treaty of San Remo of April 1920, Britain had been given the mandate for Palestine and Iraq, and France the mandate for Syria. A month earlier, the General Syrian Congress, a gathering of Arab nationalists and notables, had elected Faisal, son of Sharif Husain of Mecca, king of Syria, and his older brother Abdullah king of Iraq. Faisal had, formerly, been king of the Arab kingdom of Syria since October 1918. However, the French had other plans for Syria in which the Hashemites, thought to be too close to Britain for France's comfort, did not feature. Forced out of Syria in July 1920. Faisal was invited by the British to become king of Iraq and was eventually crowned in Baghdad in August 1921.

Although rather less dashing, Abdullah was no less ambitious than his brother. While Faisal's dreams had long been fixed on 'Syria' (in the sense of the area to the north and north-west of the Hijaz), Abdullah's gaze had been directed south and east, towards Yemen and central Arabia. While Faisal was heading northwards in June 1916, Abdullah stayed in the Hijaz, and, after the surrender of the Turkish garrisons of Mecca, Jedda and Ta'if in the autumn, embarked upon the siege of Medina, whose garrison held out until February 1919. A few months later, on 21 May 1919, Abdullah's ambitions to dominate the peninsula were brought to an abrupt and violent conclusion; his forces were routed at Turabah, 80 miles east of Mecca, by the man who was rapidly emerging as the principal power in Arabia, Ibn Saud.

Turabah was decisive in the history of the modern Middle East. For a while, Sharif Husain clung to what he had in the Hijaz, but as Ibn Saud's star waxed the Hashemites' waned. The sharif was eventually deposed by Ibn Saud early in 1926, and his territories were absorbed into what is now Saudi Arabia. For his part Abdullah stayed in the Hijaz for over a year after Turabah, his suspicions of Faisal allayed after Faisal's forced removal from Syria in 1920 but revived when he saw Britain preparing him for the throne

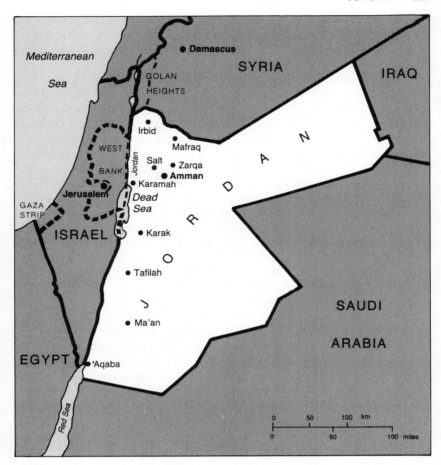

Official name	Hashemite Kingdom of Jordan
Area	89,206 sq. km (34,443 sq. miles)
Population	3,165,000 (1989)
Capital	Amman
Language	Arabic
Religion	Sunni Muslim (about 80%), Christian and Shia Muslim minorities
Currency	Jordan dinar

of Iraq. At the end of September 1920 he headed northwards out of the Hijaz, settling with a considerable entourage at Ma'an in the south of what is now Jordan. Ostensibly, he was on his way to wrest Syria from the French and restore it to the Arabs.

Extraordinary as it may seem in the 1990s, it was the case that in 1920 the status of Transjordan, the 'East Bank', had not yet been decided—or, to put it another way, that it had not occurred either to the British or the French at San Remo to delimit the southern boundary of 'Syria'. Ottoman administrative maps of the period are imprecise as to the Syrian interior; the province of 'Syria' simply peters out in the vicinity of 'Aqaba, a vagueness that would prove a fruitful source of irritation between Ibn Saud and Abdullah when the borders between Transjordan and Saudi Arabia came to be drawn up. In 1920–21, however, Britain, as mandatory for Palestine, was concerned to keep the French as far away from the Suez Canal as possible. It was accordingly decided in London in August 1920 that Transjordan should have some loose form of administrative attachment to Palestine. A few British political officers, but no British troops, were despatched from Palestine a couple of months before Abdullah arrived with his followers at Ma'an.

In the autumn of 1920, as his brother was being offered the throne of Iraq, Abdullah held court in southern Transjordan. By February 1921 it had been decided in London that Transjordan should be administered separately from Palestine, that the clauses in the Palestine mandate referring to Zionist settlement should not apply to the area, and that it should have an Arab ruler, Abdullah. In March 1921 Winston Churchill invited Abdullah to Jerusalem for talks, at the end of which Abdullah agreed to govern Transjordan for an initial period of six months. The Emirate of Transjordan, subsequently the Kingdom of Jordan, came into being.

Jordan under Abdullah, 1921–51

Both the emirate and its emir were British creations, and the relationship with, and dependence upon, Britain remained central to Transjordanian politics well beyond Abdullah's assassination in 1951. The transparency and the closeness of the connection were to prove awkward for Abdullah, who felt cramped within the borders of his small state. The mainspring of almost all his actions seems to have been his ambition to play a wider regional role, for which he needed a more substantial political base. He succeeded in consolidating his position in Transjordan in the 1920s and 1930s, checking tribal raids from the east and south, and having the boundaries of the state (with Syria and Saudi Arabia) recognised internationally. Nonetheless, he seems to have regarded Transjordan principally as a stepping stone to greater things. For most of his life he directed his attention towards the throne of Syria, and, increasingly, towards the creation of a greater Jordan, which would include the Arab parts of Palestine. Almost as remarkable as his persistence in these two objectives was the extent to which he was prepared to ignore his isolation in pursuit of them. No more than a handful of Palestinians or Syrians gave him their support in either endeavour, but this did not deter him. In addition, he does not seem to have taken any particular pains to conceal his double dealing. His negotiations with the Zionists, and the subsidies he received from them for most of the 1930s, for example, were public knowledge. Similarly, he and other Transjordanian landlords sold options on leases of their land to the Jewish Agency in 1932, and these were renewed annually in the face of routine denials from the royal palace. His support of schemes for the partition of Palestine between Arabs and Zionists both before and after the Second World War, which greatly assisted the Zionists, was so blatant as to form the principal motive for his assassination.

The area which Abdullah took over in 1921 had a population of about 225,000, less than half of whom were nomadic tribesmen. Amman, the present capital, had a mere 2,400 inhabitants in 1921. By 1946, when the emirate gained its independence from Britain and became the Hashemite Kingdom, and just before the creation of the state of Israel, the population had risen to 435,000, about 100,000 of whom were nomads. After the creation of Israel, in 1948, the population doubled, with the influx of 450,000 Palestinian refugees. In April 1950, Jordan annexed the West Bank (against the wishes of most of the other Arab countries as well as of most of the population of the West Bank), which it had held under military occupation since May 1948. This brought the total under Hashemite rule to around one-and-a-half million, two-thirds of whom were Palestinians and who regarded Abdullah as being at least partially responsible for their plight.

Left to their own devices, the Palestinians would hardly have chosen Abdullah as their ruler, but economic and political realities after 1948 left them with little choice. Some, no doubt, consoled themselves, in April 1950, with the belief, or perhaps the hope, that the unification of the West Bank with Transjordan was merely an expedient pending a full settlement of the dispute between Israel and the Arabs. It is a wry tribute to Abdullah's geopolitical prescience, if not to his sense of self-preservation, that his creation has so long survived his death.

Husain, the early years

Abdullah was assassinated on 20 July 1951 while on his way to pray at the al-Aqsa mosque in Jerusalem, probably by supporters of the mufti of Jerusalem, Hajj Amin al-Husaini, the unofficial leader of the Palestinians. He was succeeded by his eldest son, Talal, who had a history of mental instability, and was removed a year later in favour of Abdullah's grandson, Husain, who attained his majority and became king of Jordan in May 1953.

Husain's reputation as a survivor is well deserved, given the extraordinary tensions both within and around Jordan since the early 1950s, not least the different political aims of the original [Trans]Jordanians and the Palestinians. The immense upheavals of the period brought entirely new population strata into Jordan changing its character almost as much as the loss of the West Bank would in 1967. Although sharing a common Arab/Islamic culture, many of the Palestinian incomers had little in common with their new compatriots. They were generally better educated and more dynamic than the East Bankers, to whom they in any case considered themselves superior.

Their alienation from the Jordanian government gradually increased with Nasser's championing of pan-Arabism in the 1950s and 1960s, and with the rise of the Palestine Liberation Organisation (PLO). Whatever its limitations—not least the vagueness of goals—pan-Arabism was as attractive to the Palestinians as it was to the dispossessed of the Arab Middle East in general. Husain, educated at Harrow and Sandhurst, seemed to represent an entirely different strand of political thought, reactionary and backward-looking. Indeed, in the eyes of his opponents he was little more than a 'lackey of imperialism'. In 1955, for example, he seemed to bow to British pressure to join the pro-Western and anti-Soviet Baghdad Pact; similarly, until March 1956, when the king dismissed him, the Jordanian army was commanded by an Englishman, Glubb Pasha.

In October 1956 parliamentary elections were called in an atmosphere of rising tension. Nasser had nationalised the Suez Canal a few weeks before; anti-Western feeling was running high across the Middle East. The results reflected the situation, as the nationalist, leftist and Islamic parties between them gained a majority of the seats, and the leader of the largest party. Sulaiman Nabulsi of the National Socialists became prime Minister. Anti-Western feeling increased after the Anglo-French invasion of Egypt in October–November. In March 1957 Nabulsi negotiated the termination of the Anglo-Jordanian Treaty, and with it the annual subsidy Jordan received from Britain. To make good the shortfall, Husain appealed to the United States. Thus began the close relationship with the United States which, though not without its vicissitudes, has endured to the present day.

Husain's new relationship with the United States was not at all to the government's liking. Nabulsi, assisted by the commander of the army, launched a coup against the king. Decisive action on Husain's part saw the coup repulsed, and the king secured complete control of the army. Political parties and trade unions were banned, and, until 1989, all parliamentary elections were tightly controlled. There were further upheavals in 1958, both after Husain's adhesion in February to a 'fertile Crescent Union' between Jordan and Iraq—to counter the Arab nationalist-inspired United Arab Republic of Egypt and Syria—and after the overthrow of the Iraqi monarchy in mid-July. In the same month, the United States sent marines to Lebanon, and Britain sent troops to Jordan.

In spite of apparent differences in political alignment between Jordan and most of her neighbours, opposition to Husain became less strident as time passed, and a modus vivendi with the other Arab states was gradually established. This came about for a number of reasons. First, as we have seen, a certain stability developed from the maintenance of the relationship with the United States. Secondly, Husain moved closer towards his family's former foes, the Saudis, partly because of a shared hostility to Arab nationalism and 'communism', at a time when the Saudis were increasingly able to assist him financially. Thirdly, Husain, however reluctantly, gave his approval to the creation of a separate political organisation to represent the Palestinians, the PLO, founded under Nasser's aegis in 1964. In addition, he greatly increased his authority within the state by his control of all crucial appointments in an army which expanded from 6,000 in 1948 to 55,000 in 1967.

The Six Day War and the PLO

Husain further increased his credibility, both domestically and externally, by casting his lot with Egypt and Syria on 30 May 1967, when it was clear that war with Israel was about to break out. Whatever the boost to his popularity, however, in all other respects the move was disastrous. By 10 June, Israel was in occupation of the Sinai peninsula, the Golan Heights, East Jerusalem and the West Bank. Jordan lost a third of its population and its prime agricultural land. Of some eventual benefit to Jordan, on the other hand, was that Israel's obduracy in the face of UN Resolution 242, which called for it to leave the West Bank, was sufficiently irritating to the United States to encourage it to give Husain a considerable part of the wherewithal to rebuild his armed forces. In addition, Jordan began to receive substantial financial aid from other Arab states. A considerable part of this went to the West Bank, where Jordan continued to pay the salaries of public employees and maintained schools, hospitals and other public service institutions until it gave up its claim to the area in July 1988.

The enormity of the defeat brought about a sea change in the attitude of the Palestinians, large numbers of whom now became convinced that the Arab regimes were either unable or unwilling (or perhaps both) to liberate Palestine. The PLO's new tactics, formulated in response to the defeat in 1967, began to pose a severe threat to the continuation of the Jordanian monarchy; Palestinian guerrillas, based in Jordan, began to raid into Israel, occasioning severe Israeli reprisals. As the PLO's confidence increased, its presence within Jordan became increasingly disruptive and its relations with the Jordanian authorities increasingly strained. In mid-June 1970 the Jordanian army entered Amman to assert its authority over the guerrillas. It was the start of a conflict that lasted over a year, in the course of which 3,000 Palestinians were killed, and a number of the refugee camps in Jordan virtually razed to the ground. Driven out of Jordan, Yasir Arafat and the remaining armed guerrillas moved to Lebanon where history was to repeat itself, after a fashion, over the next decade and a half.

Jordan as peace broker

Over the next few years the Jordanian government gradually reasserted its authority over the country, and a highly efficient security service and surveillance system was developed to check and deter dissidence. There was no elected parliament, a state of affairs which continued until 1984. Jordan did not participate in the October War of 1973, though the hoped-for boost to Jordan from a grateful United States this reticence might have been expected to generate largely failed to materialise. A further blow came at the Rabat Summit in October 1974 when Husain, along with his fellow Arab leaders, was obliged to recognise the PLO as the 'sole legiti-mate representative of the Palestinian people', a move that inevitably diminished both his authority and much of what was left of his appeal on the West Bank.

Presumably in an attempt to regain some of his standing as an inter-locutor for the Palestinians, Husain held secret negotiations with Israel in 1975 and 1976. They came to little in the end, however, with Israel refusing to return more than 70% of the West Bank. In the late 1970s a new dimension was added to Arab/Israeli relations with the sequence of events beginning with President Sadat's visit to Jerusalem in November 1977 and ending with the Camp David Agreement in September 1978. Jordan was neither consulted nor asked to participate in the process; in addition to his misgivings about the negotiations in general Husain naturally resented the fact that Camp David provided for 'autonomy' for the West Bank rather than its eventual reabsorption into Jordan. In addition, the terms and tenor of the agreements were such that Husain could not have accepted them without gravely weakening his position both domestically and in the Arab world.

In consequence, Jordanian/PLO relationships improved, at least on a formal level. Arafat and Husain were reconciled (they had had no official contact since 1971) in Amman. Throughout the early 1980s amity between the two prevailed, much to the alarm of Syria. The United States put forward the Reagan Plan involving a confederation between the West Bank and Jordan, and in the course of 1982 and 1983 Husain almost succeeded in persuading Arafat to allow him to negotiate with Israel jointly on behalf of both Jordan and the Palestinians. In November 1984 Husain told the 17th Palestine National Council, which he had invited to Amman, that Jordan and the PLO should make a settlement with Israel on the basis of 'land for peace'. In February 1985 an accord between Husain and Arafat appeared to give Husain a mandate to open peace negotiations with Israel under UN auspices. Fearing complete isolation in the region, Syria eventually forced Husain to abandon the tactic, partly by a series of assassinations of Jordanian diplomats abroad, partly by arranging a joint command between Abu Nidal's terrorist organisation and Abu Musa, Arafat's main rival, to attack the accord. At the end of 1985 Asad and Husain issued a joint statement rejecting any direct negotiations with Israel, and the two rulers exchanged visits to each other's capitals, in Asad's case the first for nine years.

Israel's response, at least while Peres took his turn as prime minister between September 1984 and September 1986 (when he became foreign minister, changing places with Shamir), was to strike hard at the PLO, Asad and Qadhafi (in such incidents as the bombing of PLO headquarters in Tunis in October 1985 and of Libya in April 1986). Israel's strategy was to draw Husain away from the more militant Arab leaders and into direct talks. By February 1987 this had succeeded to the extent that Peres had convinced Husain to enter into bilateral negotiatons, although the talks were eventually blocked by Shamir, leader of the right-wing Likud party, whose ideological commitment to the West Bank as part of 'greater' Israel made the probability of negotiations with Husain unlikely. Shamir acted, too, in the knowledge that the Reagan administration was neither prepared to put pressure on Shamir nor to give Husain satisfactory pledges of support if he were to 'go it alone'. The peace process was stalled, and was to remain so until the new initiatives launched in the summer of 1991.

Jordan and Iraq

On a regional level, Jordan enjoyed fairly cordial relations with most of its neighbours in the late 1980s after the reconciliation with Damascus in 1985. Jordan re-established relations with Egypt in 1983, and King Husain used his good offices generally on Egypt's behalf; at the Amman summit in November 1987 those Arab states who had not so far done so were persuaded to restore diplomatic relations with Egypt. Relations with Saudi Arabia, cordial for much of King Husain's reign, remained close until their near rupture as a result of Husain's equivocation over Iraq's invasion of Kuwait in August 1990.

However, although its outward political orientation might seem to have precluded such an alignment, Amman's closest political and economic ties for most of the last two decades have been with Baghdad. Before the invasion of Kuwait, given Iraq's perennially poor relations with Syria, it was important that Iraq's relations with Jordan should be, if not always cordial, at least always correct, which is more or less what they have been since the Iraqi Ba'th came to power in the summer of 1968. It is only a slight exaggeration to say that King Husain owes his continued occupation of the Jordanian throne to the fact that neither Iraqi nor Syrian troops intervened in support of the PLO guerrillas in the fighting in Jordan in September 1970. On 9 September 1970 Baghdad radio announced, with its customary militancy: 'Revolutionary Iraq, which declared to the world that its forces were at the disposal of the Resistance forces [the PLO], reaffirms to the masses that it will not remain idle in the face of current events in Jordan.' In fact, Iraqi troops played no part in the fighting, substantially facilitating the victory of the Jordanian army.

This mixture of noisy radicalism and quiet opportunism characterised

Iraq's policy towards Jordan for most of the 1970s. King Husain's policies towards the West and the Palestinians were regularly attacked as reactionary and pro-imperialist in the Iraqi media, while economic exchanges between the two states were increasing and Iraq was financing improvements at the port of 'Aqaba and the development of the Jordanian road-system, which were soon to stand it in good stead. More cordial official relations were inaugurated after the Baghdad Summit of November 1978, at which Jordan was given promises of $1.25 billion annually for not participating in Camp David. Jordan's support for Iraq in the war with Iran was unswerving, and, at least initially, the Jordanian economy benefited greatly as 'Aqaba became the main port of entry for goods bound for Iraq. By 1988, however, after Iraq's deregulation of foreign trade after the end of the war, its oustanding debt to Jordan had so far exceeded the quota agreed between the two countries that the Jordanian Central Bank suspended export financing, thus causing a major flight from the Jordanian dinar. Iraq's enthusiasm for post-war reconstruction tended to exceed its immediate capacity or willingness to pay for what it wanted, and of all Iraq's, creditors the Jordanians were beginning to find the strain particularly difficult to bear.

In the latter part of the 1980s King Husain made a number of unsuccessful attempts to reconcile Hafiz al-Asad and Saddam Husain, although the two met secretly on Jordanian territory in April 1987. As we have seen, relations between Syria and Jordan were erratic in the late 1970s and early 1980s partly because of Syria's fears that Jordan would do a separate deal with Israel and partly because Damascus believed, not without some justification, that Jordan was financing or otherwise assisting the Muslim Brotherhood in its campaign against the government in Damascus. Again, Asad was not pleased at King Husain's immediate pledge of support for Saddam Husain when Iraq invaded Iran in September 1980. However, by 1985, relations began to improve. The two governments continued to disagree over Jordan's relations with Iraq and Egypt, but were united by their distrust and dislike of the PLO. It was largely at King Husain's initiative that Syria was persuaded to take part in the Amman Summit in November 1987, at which the Arab states signed a joint statement condemning Iran for occupying Iraqi territory and for failing to implement UN Security Council Resolution 598. At the same summit, the English text of the adopted resolutions pointedly omitted the standard reference to the PLO as the 'sole legitimate representative of the Palestinian people.'

Jordan and the *intifada*
In the course of the 1970s and 1980s the PLO consolidated its influence on the West Bank and among Palestinians outside Jordan. In spite of all attempts to reinforce it, Jordanian influence on the West Bank gradually diminished as the idea of a Palestinian state began to take more significant shape. Whatever support Jordan retained on the West Bank was further

marginalised at the end of 1987 by the uprisings in the Occupied Territories, the *intifada*, which did not even pay lipservice to Jordanian sovereignty, and, at least initially, greatly enhanced the role of the PLO. At the same time, the government was seriously concerned that unrest, or at least demonstrations of solidarity, would break out in Jordan itself. After eight months of the *intifada* Husain took the momentous decision to cut his ties with the West Bank for good: on 31 July 1988 he announced formal Jordanian disengagement from the Occupied Territories. The move had important economic as well as political implications, since Jordan would no longer fund the social, educational, health and other services in the Territories.

A few months later on 15 November 1988, the PLO took the equally historic step at the Palestine National Council in Algiers of announcing the inauguration of a Palestinian state in the Occupied Territories with its capital at Jerusalem. At the same time, the PLO voted to accept UN Resolutions 242 and 338, thus, by implication, recognising the state of Israel within its pre-1967 frontiers. After further negotiations, the PLO specifically recognised the existence of two states in Palestine, one Jewish, one Arab, in the Stockholm Declaration of 7 December. This opened the way to informal United States-Palestinian discussions in Tunis in the first months of 1989.

These events naturally had serious repercussions in Jordan. The ending of the link with the West Bank caused the value of the dinar to fall sharply, and money-changing activities were severely restricted in 1988 and 1989. Austerity measures, including sharp rises in import taxes, and rises in charges for work permits and exit visas, were announced in November, and in April 1989 there were increases in the prices of fuel, drinks and cigarettes and a new austerity programme, as the result of negotiations with the World Bank to reschedule Jordan's $6.6 billion external debt. In the middle of May there were mass demonstrations in the towns of Ma'an, and Karak, areas traditionally steadfast in their support for the regime, in which eight people were killed and 83 injured. Ten of the country's 11 professional and trade union associations called for the resignation of the government and the formation of a government of national unity. King Husain cut short a visit to Britain, returning to Jordan to take personal charge of the situation. He dismissed the prime minister, Zaid Rifa'i (who had been in office since April 1985), replacing him with his cousin, General Zaid ibn Shakir. Large numbers were arrested, but most were released in the course of May and June. On 29 May the governor of the Central Bank announced that Jordan had lost a third of its gold reserves over the previous six months.

In July it was announced that parliamentary elections would be held in the autumn. These were the first general elections since 1967, and a new electoral law was promulgated, dividing the country into 80 constituencies. This time there were, of course, to be no representatives from the Occupied Territories. Political parties, banned since 1957, were to be permitted in the future, though not immediately. Jordan's foreign debts were further rescheduled by its major creditors; in August the six states of the Gulf Cooperation Council deposited $400 million in the Central Bank in an attempt to relieve Jordan's most pressing financial difficulties. Only 52% of those eligible voted in the elections, held in November; abstention was particularly high among Jordanians of Palestinian origin. The results cannot have been particularly welcome to Husain; 34 out of the 80 seats went to 'Islamic' candidates and 18 to 'leftists'. Further steps in the direction of democratisation, including the release of prisoners of conscience and the recruitment of a number of former teachers dismissed for political reasons, were taken early in 1990.

The crisis of 1990

In spite of these and other major concessions, it was becoming apparent in the period immediately before the Iraqi invasion of Kuwait that the political system was under immense strain, and that the stability and even the integrity of the country were under grave threat. On the economic front, it was estimated in April 1990 that the dinar had lost two-thirds of its value in less than two years, and that 20% of the economically active population was officially unemployed. Every few months the king and other prominent personalities were obliged to tour Arab capitals with begging bowls simply to keep the country from imminent bankruptcy. No end to this bleak prospect seemed in sight.

In addition, the peace process had reached that point in its depressingly familiar cycle where progress seemed as far away as ever. Levy, Arens, Sharon and Eytan had gained portfolios in a particularly intransigent Israeli cabinet formed after several weeks of negotiations with extreme right-wing parties between late April and mid-June 1990. Ever more settlements were being constructed on the West Bank, partly as a consequence of the huge influx of Jews from the Soviet Union, perhaps the largest single wave of immigrants since the early 1950s. The *intifada* seemed to have become almost routinised and was not making any tangible impact. In the disturbances following the killing of seven Palestinians by an apparently mentally deranged young Israeli at Rishon-le-Zion on 20 May a further eight Palestinians were killed and 650 wounded in the Occupied Territories, now under almost permanent curfew. Finally, President Bush officially terminated the Palestinian-US dialogue on 30 May. This followed Arafat's refusal to dismiss Abu'l-Abbas of the Palestine Liberation Front from the executive committee of the PLO following a raid on the Israeli coast carried out by the Front.

On 14 May 20,000 people marched towards the Allenby Bridge, threatening to cross it to 'return' to the Occupied Territories. At a press conference on 10 June Husain delivered his sombre judgement that Jordan was going through the most difficult period in its history, and made an impassioned, if all familiar, appeal for Arab aid. On 15 July, the Muslim Brotherhood demanded that the government should arm the citizens to protect them against the threat of Israel. In such circumstances Husain's room for manoeuvre seemed to be shrinking by the minute; his former interlocutors in Israel were by and large out of power, he had no money, and his own inaction was seen as proof of his deference to Israel and the United States. Hence, although the Kuwait crisis added enormously to his difficulties, the fact that the new problems were of a different nature, and that they replaced more directly threatening concerns, combined with Husain's adroitness in handling them, provided an unexpected and, as events were to show, highly opportune breathing space. Politically, Husain has emerged from the crisis with his position substantially enhanced; this, coupled with other recent developments which place the onus for any progress towards a settlement more squarely than ever before at Israel's own door, most probably means that whatever the strains on the Jordanian economy, the sword of Damocles no longer hangs over the Jordanian policy as it did in the summer of 1990.

The economy

An important, though short-lived, positive development for Jordan in the 1970s and early 1980s was an annual growth rate of some 10%. This was made possible by a combination of foreign aid and labour remittances; these were the years of the oil boom in the Gulf, and during this period some 350,000 Jordanians (including Palestinians) were working abroad. Two other factors assisted Jordan's prosperity: the devastation wrought upon Beirut caused many of its financial and other services to be transferred to Amman; and the Iran-Iraq War and the closure of the Shatt al-'Arab transformed 'Aqaba, and the transit route across Jordan, into a vital supply line for Iraq.

However, although the country undoubtedly enjoyed a considerable increase in prosperity, this did not rest upon solid foundations. Apart from a small but lively agricultural sector, and some phosphates, Jordan has little in the way of natural resources. Thus in 1988, agriculture, mining and manufacture *together* contributed only 22.5% to GDP (compared with 27.4% for Syrian agriculture alone), which means that the economy is dominated by services, and thus extremely vulnerable to events entirely outside its control. Remittances, which far outstripped export earnings between 1975 and 1985, began to fall drastically when oil prices halved in 1985–86, and many Jordanians (along with other expatriates) were obliged to leave the oil-rich states. Economically, the invasion of Kuwait was a catastrophe for Jordan, as almost all its aid, as well as its transit earnings as an entrepôt for Iraq, together with most of its agricultural and manufacturing export earnings (also largely from Iraq) were suddenly cut off. It is difficult to regard Jordan's economic prospects, whether in the short or the long term, with optimism.

Peter Sluglett and Marion Farouk-Sluglett

7 LEBANON

It is extraordinary that as recently as the late 1960s Lebanon was held up by political scientists as a model of political stability and good neighbour-liness. Even now, some political scientists think of Lebanon as emblematic of the 'mosaic' pattern which they regard as endemic to Middle Eastern politics.

In fact Lebanese politics are unique in Middle Eastern terms and largely reflect the failure to create a political system, or even a polity, that is either viable or enduring. A great part of the responsibility for the failure of the system must be laid at the door of the Lebanese themselves in that it seems to have been in the interest of many groupings or factions to maintain a weak central state structure. But it is also the case that a number of external forces have done their best to see to it that Lebanon either does not survive or does so in a highly fragmented manner. In that sense the struggles and clashes within Lebanon since the early 1970s mirror the conflicts taking place in other parts of the Middle East.

Although most Lebanese support the concept of a Lebanese state there is no consensus as to the institutional form it should take, except, gener-ally, that it should encroach as little as possible on them. 'The state', in the Lebanese historian Kamal Salibi's words, 'has long ceased to exercise sovereign control over its own national territory. There remains an ad-ministrative bureaucracy which continues to provide a cover of legitimacy to public and private transactions as well as a minimum of public services of steadily deteriorating quality.'

The last years of Ottoman Lebanon

Lebanon as it exists today is a considerable enlargement of a much smaller original entity. The *mutasarrifiyya*, or governorate of Lebanon, an auto-nomous province within the Ottoman Empire, was created by the Otto-man authorities in 1861 after a major outbreak of violence the previous year. This was partly a sectarian clash between Maronite Christians and Druzes, partly a struggle between peasants and landlords, in which some 11,000 people, mostly Christians, lost their lives. Before the creation of the *mutasarrifiyya*, although nominally part of the Ottoman province of Sidon, the area was more or less independent under a series of mainly Christian dynasties, which ruled from the mid-16th century until 1840.

The population of the *mutasarrifiyya* was roughly fourth-fifths Christian and one-fifth Muslim. It is a fundamental precept of Islam that the

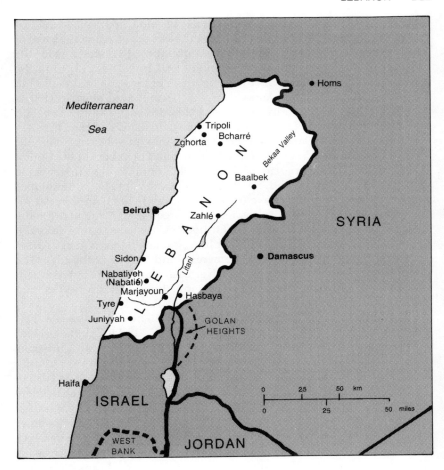

Official name	Republic of Lebanon
Area	10,452 sq. km (4,036 sq. miles)
Population	2.8 million (1989)
Capital	Beirut
Language	Arabic
Religion	Shia and Sunni Muslim (62%), Christian (38%) (including 22% Maronite)
Currency	Lebanese pound

'peoples of the book', as the Koran terms Jews and Christians, should be free to practise their religion in return for the payment of a capitation fee, or head tax on adult males, to the Muslim authorities. This accounts for the survival of fairly substantial communities of Christians and, until the creation of the state of Israel, of Jews, in much of the Arab Middle East to the present day. The mountainous areas of Greater Syria always acted as places of refuge for minority groups or heterodox sects. Mount Lebanon was the home of two of these, the Maronite Christians and the Druzes.

Christians in Lebanon can be divided into members of Catholic churches in communion with Rome (Uniate), and members of the Orthodox churches. The patriarchs of the Catholic communities are generally cardinals in the Vatican; and, apart from the Armenians, the communities are mostly Arab, but they have their own liturgical languages, Syriac for the Maronites and Syrian Catholics, and Greek and Armenian for the Greek and Armenian Catholics. All Orthodox Christians share a common set of beliefs, and also have different liturgical languages (Greek, Armenian and Syriac for the Greek, Armenian and Syrian Orthodox). The communities are autocephalous, which is to say that they are independent of each other and do not recognise any over-arching authority beyond that of their own patriarchs. There is no 'Orthodox Pope'.

The Orthodox, or 'Eastern Christians', have tended to associate their political destinies with that of the Sunni Muslims, and to see themselves very much as Arabs. Many individual Greek-Orthodox Arab Christians were pioneers of the early Arab nationalist movement; more recently, leaders of nationalist and leftist political organisations, such as Michel 'Aflaq of the Ba'th party and George Habash and Na'if Hawatmeh, leaders of two influential factions within the Palestine Liberation Organisation (PLO), are also Orthodox. The Catholics and other Uniates, on the other hand, have tended both to be identified with, and identify themselves with, European, particularly French, culture, often, though by no means always, regarding 'Arab' identity as inferior to their own. In any discussion of Lebanon, the notion of a strict Muslim/Christian divide is misleading; there are important divisions *within* the two principal religious communities as well.

In the course of the 18th and 19th centuries, when the Great Powers began to take a closer interest in the political and economic affairs of the Ottoman Empire, Russia, as the major Orthodox power, emerged as the protector of the Orthodox Christians while France emerged as the protector of the Catholics. Apart from the Maronites, who had accepted papal supremacy since the 12th century, many Middle Eastern Catholics were converts from Orthodoxy—a step many had taken partly because they regarded the protection of France as more secure than the protection of Russia—so there was often little love lost between them and the Orthodox communities from which they had come. The Druzes were a heterodox sect which had broken away from another sect of Shia Islam in the 12th century; other important Muslim groupings in Lebanon are the Sunni Muslims, whose coreligionists form the majority (about 90%) of all Muslims in the world, and the Shia Muslims, mainly from the south and east of Lebanon, now generally acknowledged to be the most numerous single sect in the country.

On the whole, this multi-sectarian population lived in reasonable harmony before the explosion of communal violence in Mount Lebanon in 1860. The civil war of 1860 was brought on partly by interference by the Great Powers, France supporting the Maronites while Britain supported the Druzes, and partly by economic and social factors related to the way in which entry into the world market had affected Lebanon, whose principal cash crop in the 19th century was silk. As a result of the violence, and to forestall further intervention on the part of the Powers (the French immediately sent an expeditionary force), the Ottomans agreed to an arrangement whereby a committee of the Powers would assemble at Istanbul and elect a governor of Lebanon, who was to be an Ottoman Christian, usually from some other part of the empire.

Between 1861 and 1914 the *mutasarrifiyya* was an autonomous province and became prosperous from the silk industry, whose products went mostly to Marseilles. Like other ports in the eastern Mediterranean, Beirut (itself an administrative enclave separate from the authority of the *mutasarrifiyya* and thus under direct Ottoman control) expanded considerably throughout the rest of the 19th century. The French invested heavily in the port itself, and formed the companies that provided the city with its electricity and tramways. The *mutasarrifiyya* had a total population of 285,000, of whom about 156,000 were Maronites, 59,000 other Christians, and 73,000 Muslims, about half of whom were Druze. Thus, on the eve of the First World War, as well as being the largest single sect, the Maronites formed an absolute majority of the population as a whole.

The creation of modern Lebanon

After the First World War the Ottoman Empire was dissolved and the Arab Middle East divided into the states that exist today. In this share-out, France was awarded Syria, and Britain Iraq, Palestine and Transjordan. In Syria, France created two separate political entities, Lebanon and Syria, partly in an attempt to contain the Arab nationalist movement within the Syrian interior, and partly because the Maronites of Lebanon, with whom the French had had links since the 16th century, were the only community in the area on whom they could rely entirely. The new state of Lebanon, created in August 1920, was almost twice the size of the Ottoman *mutasarrifiyya*. It included the town of Tripoli and the 'Akkar plain in the north, the Bekaa valley in the east, and the districts of Rachaiya, Hasbaiya and Jabal 'Amil in the south, as well as the coastal cities of Tyre, Sidon, and Beirut.

For a long time, many non-Maronite 'Lebanese' considered the formation of a separate and greatly enlarged Lebanon both as a French imperial stratagem *and* a temporary expedient. It took some time for them to get used to the idea, let alone accept it. There were many grounds for these objections, the most basic that many Arabs had wanted—and indeed some of them had fought for—an independent united Arab state, rather than a set of smaller entities under the tutelage of one or other of the victorious powers. In addition, 'Greater Syria' as a geo-political entity had been divided into Lebanon, Palestine, Syria and Transjordan, not to mention the various smaller quasi-autonomous statelets for the Druzes and the Alawites in what is now Syria. All these divisions rankled, but in the case of Lebanon what rankled particularly was that territories which had traditionally been part of a larger entity thought of as 'Syria' were now detached from it and given to this new state, Lebanon, 'Grand Liban'. Grand Liban may have been more viable economically than its predecessor, but large numbers of its inhabitants always regarded themselves as Syrians, and long continued to do so.

Only the Maronites were satisfied with this new arrangement. Many thought of themselves as the 'real' Lebanese, the descendants of the Phoenicians, forming an island of Christendom and 'civilisation' in a sea of Muslim barbarism. They believed themselves culturally superior and were in fact generally better off than the rest of the population around them. Furthermore, many prominent Maronites had actively lobbied for a separate state under French protection. Less satisfactory for the Maronites was that the 'added areas' were largely non-Maronite. The smaller entity had 285,000 inhabitants; the areas added brought another 318,000. Of these only 43,000 were Maronites; 160,000 were Sunni Muslims and 85,000 were Shia Muslims.

Thus, although the Christians formed 55% of the population, and the Maronites were still the largest single community, they no longer formed an absolute majority. In the census of 1932, the Maronites formed 29% of the population, the Sunnis 22.5% and the Shias 20%. Not only were the Maronites reduced from an absolute majority, the new state had virtual parity between its Muslim and Christian populations. It is significant that the 1932 census was the last taken in Lebanon. Subsequent governments have consistently refused to repeat the exercise, since any new census would almost certainly reveal that the Maronites had ceased to be the largest single element in the state.

Lebanon under French mandate, 1920—46

Although the Maronites had lost their numerical preponderance, they saw to it that they did not lose their supremacy. In this they were greatly assisted by the virtual boycott of the new state throughout the 1920s and most of the 1930s by almost all the Sunni Muslims, the only other community which could seriously have challenged them politically. As well as being the principal losers by the separation from Syria, the Sunnis resented their demotion from the status they had exercised under the

Ottomans (since the Ottomans themselves were Sunnis) and their sub-jugation to the Maronites. In consequence they boycotted the 1922 elections, the first to be held on a sectarian, or 'confessional', basis. When the Lebanese republic was officially proclaimed in 1926 it had a Greek Ortho-dox president and a Sunni speaker of the chamber of deputies, but all the other posts, and eventually the presidency as well, were held by Maronites. In time, however, it became clear to what was to become the dominant faction among Maronite politicians that the survival and pros-perity of the new state would only be possible if the Muslims, particularly the Sunnis, could be induced to accept it.

In general, the Maronites' pre-eminence meant that their community continued to do best out of the new arrangements. The main beneficiaries of the penetration of European capital after 1860 had been the Maronites of Beirut and Mount Lebanon, although a significant stratum of Sunni merchants from Tripoli and Beirut had also participated in the process. At a humbler social level, many of the Maronites of Mount Lebanon in the 1920s were smallholders, while the majority of the Sunni and Shia cultivators on the periphery—the Bekaa, Jabal Amil, the 'Akkar—were sharecroppers on the great feudal estates. The Maronites' head start was also reinforced by their earlier access to modern European-style education; through most of the period of the mandate (1920–46) education was predominantly in the domain of foreign missions, and thus directed particularly towards the Christian population. As late as 1968, 62% of all school-children attended private, that is, mostly Christian, schools. In addition, although the Maronite community was not monolithic, and there were regional and other rivalries among its leaders, being centred on Lebanon gave Lebanese Maronitism a particularly strong sense of cohesion.

In contrast, among the Sunni Muslims—the rise of the Shias to their present level of political muscle is relatively recent—this sense of cohesion developed in a different way. Since 90% of the population of the Arab world (and 70% of the population of Syria) is Sunni Muslim, the Sunnis did not have the Maronites' sense of being embattled, and were aware of their membership of a wider Muslim world outside the boundaries of Lebanon, which, in fact, they spent a considerable part of the early years of the Lebanese state trying to join. It was only in 1936, when the French indicated that they were prepared to consider a Franco-Syrian and a Franco-Lebanese treaty, that most Sunnis (in Syria as well as in Lebanon) finally accepted that insisting on reuniting Lebanon with Syria might jeopardise any hopes of obtaining independence for both countries, and reluctantly gave up their virtual boycott of the Lebanese state.

This change in outlook also required a recognition on the part of the Maronite leaders that the prosperity of the new entity would require a partnership of a kind between the sects, particularly, in the 1940s and 1950s, between themselves and the Sunnis. The 'historic compromise' was enshrined in the unwritten National Pact of 1943 between the Maronite president, Bishara al-Khuri, and the Sunni prime minister, Riyadh al-Sulh. Essentially, Lebanon was to be independent, neither part of Syria nor a French protectorate; as such it became one of the founder members of the Arab League in 1945. The National Pact continued the political arrangements of the republic but in rather more detail, essentially enshrining the principle of confessionalism (that is, the distribution of posts on a religious-sectarian basis to ensure an adequate or 'just' representation of each community) in all spheres of public life and the armed forces.

On the (arguable) basis that the Maronites were the largest single community, they were given the key posts of the presidency and the commander-in-chief of the armed forces. The Sunnis were given the premiership, and the Shias the post of speaker of the chamber of deputies. Notables from the smaller communities were also given appropriate functions in the scheme of things. The Christian–Muslim balance in offices and in the chamber of deputies was maintained by requiring a fixed ratio of six Christians to every five Muslims. It was the existence of these apparently satisfactory arrangements that encouraged the view that Lebanon was a byword for order, stability and tolerance in the 1940s and 1950s.

The 'traditional structures' of Lebanese politics

One important effect of the way in which the Lebanese political system was organised was that political activity took place along vertical rather than horizontal lines, that is, within confessional boundaries rather than within social classes. As important, it also promoted an acute sense of an individual's confessional affiliation, *and* of the confessional affiliation of anyone with whom he or she might come into contact. This sense of sectarian identification was, understandably, particularly strong at times of political crisis, when the state authority tended to break down.

In consequence, when ideological parties did begin to emerge, the constraints of the system were such that they often found it difficult to transcend sectarian affiliations. Though some managed to recruit across confessional boundaries, most continued to be identified with a particular sect. Thus the Communist party when it began to take shape was basically Greek Orthodox and Shia; the Nasserists/Arab nationalists were Sunni Muslims almost to a man; the Syrian Social National party (SSNP)—which advocated greater Syrian nationalism or national socialism—was largely Greek Orthodox; the Progressive Socialist party (PSP) consisted mainly of Druzes, members of the sect of its founder, Kamal Jumblatt; and the Kata'ib, or Phalanges Libanaises were Maronite populists gathered around their founder, Pierre Jumayyil, the father of two presidents of Lebanon.

What emerged as the dominant form in political and public life was a network of horizontal alliances between the leaders of the various communities which gave them the wherewithal to distribute patronage vertically to their clients, who could be coreligionists, political allies or dependents, or all three. This arrangement inevitably perpetuated the divisions between the communities except at the top, where the power-sharing and most of the power-broking actually took place. An important ingredient, and consequence, was an essentially fragile state structure. The state provided only a minimum of essential services and promoted a climate of extreme *laissez faire*: low taxes, flexible banking regulations, minimal customs and excise dues, and minimal social services.

The patronage system, through which these arrangements were mediated, was managed at the lower level by strong-arm men or *qabadays*, petty gangsters and quarter bosses who were the essential link between patrons and clients. Again, the range and nature of their activities implied by-passing whatever rudimentary machinery the state itself possessed. It all worked after a fashion, with a slight hiccup in the civil war of 1958, until the civil war of 1975–76. The leading notables of the various communities were linked with one another in a complex system of bargaining, whose main objective was to ensure their dominance within their communities, and, as a class, within the system as a whole. They were able to maintain their position because of their monopoly of patronage in the fields of political favours, the direction of contracts, employment, education and so forth and by means of the ingrained shared ideology which, in addition to stressing the primacy of the sectarian ties already mentioned, emphasised those of family, clan, and locality.

In a certain sense, the Christian, and in particular the Maronite, political leader had an easier task than his Muslim counterpart in the 1950s, when the Arab world was experiencing major political upheaval and change. The system, with its built-in Maronite/Christian superiority, was relatively easy to maintain among a Maronite clientele, which, as a group, had no alternative political arena or external groupings or forces around which its members might rally. Of course, it would be simplistic to suggest that the Maronite community itself was or indeed has always remained entirely monolithic; for example, the Maronites in the north and those in the centre shared in the economic and, to a lesser extent, political rivalry between Tripoli and Beirut, those in the north being more prepared to cooperate with their Sunni fellow townsmen and with Syria than the Beirutis. However, while the system also suited most of the Sunni political leadership, its beneficial effects were less apparent to the rank and file. A similar process was to take place among the Shias, when another external factor, the Iranian revolution, galvanised them into new forms of political awareness.

Lebanese politics before 1975

But this is to anticipate; the first signs of a challenge to the status quo came in the 1950s, with Nasser's successful seizure of power in Egypt. This coincided with the beginnings of the oil boom in the Arabian peninsula, whose general effect was to increase the self-confidence and economic power of the Sunni bourgeoisie, whose links with the Arab hinterland had always remained strong. Here we can see the tensions beginning within the Sunni community; the leaders were consolidating their wealth from their position of advantage within the Lebanese economy, while many of the rank and file were eagerly following Nasser's progress and hoping that a closer integration of Lebanon with the rest of the Arab world, or at least its closer identification with the 'revolutionary' populist aspirations of much of the rest of the Arab world, might result.

Eventually—and the similarities with what was to happen to the Shias later on is almost uncanny—the greater radicalism of ordinary Sunnis forced at least the appearance of a change of attitude onto the political leadership. Many Sunnis came increasingly to identify themselves with Arabism and Nasser; there were mass demonstrations against the Baghdad Pact, in support of the nationalisation of the Suez Canal, and against the Anglo-French invasion of Egypt in 1956. When President Camille Chamoun refused to break off diplomatic relations with Britain and France in November 1956, the two serving Sunni cabinet members were virtually forced to resign. The only way for such leaders to retain credibility among their coreligionists and stay in power was to compete for identification with Nasser.

Such splits, intensified after the creation of the United Arab Republic of Egypt and Syria in February 1958 and reflecting larger divisions between progressive and the conservative elements in society, led to a brief civil war in June/July 1958. This was brought to an end by the landing of United States troops, and at the end of July the army commander, General Shihab, was elected president of the republic. The period that followed, that is, between 1958 and 1970, was perhaps the only time in recent or contemporary Lebanese history in which the state became a major actor. Between 1958 and 1970, Shihab and his associate and successor Charles Hilu (Lebanese presidents have six-year terms of office) were determined to introduce a more reformist style of government, and were particularly keen both to develop the more remote regions of the country and to curb the powers of the political bosses of all sects, whose 'Byzantine and internecine factionalism', as one commentator has called it, had been an important factor in the clashes of 1958. Shihab also came to a tacit understanding with President Nasser, a sort of second national pact, under which he undertook to follow a generally pro-Egyptian foreign policy in return for Egyptian approval of his containment of pro-Nasser movements within Lebanon–a task which was considerably eased after the collapse of the United Arab Republic in 1961.

Shihab used the intelligence service he had inherited, the notorious *deuxième bureau*, both to curb the Nasserist movement and to restrict the activities of the political bosses. This in its turn caused the leaders themselves to cooperate more fully with each other to ward off the increasingly unwelcome encroachments of the state. Almost all Shihab's predecessors as president had been members of the class of political leadership for whom the original spoils system had been designed, so that the office of president had been seen as one of the principal channels through which patronage was distributed; Shihab himself, although a senior member of the Maronite aristocracy, refused to play by what the others had come to consider the rules.

It is possible that Shihabism, as it became known, might have become the norm of Lebanese politics had it not been for events beyond the frontiers of Lebanon. The growth of populist politics across much of the Arab Middle East, the exigencies of the Arab–Israeli conflict and the presence of large numbers of armed Palestinians in Lebanon (most of whom had arrived after the expulsion of the PLO from Jordan in 1970–71) combined with galloping inflation to deal the system an almost mortal blow.

The roots of the crisis

Between the early 1950s and the late 1960s the Lebanese economy was transformed from being based substantially on agriculture to being based mostly on services. In 1970 there were 80 banks in Lebanon, only 15 of which were controlled by Lebanese majority interests: the equivalent of between 50 and 60% of GDP left the country annually through the banking and financial system, while local investment was both minimal and went largely into the non-productive part of the economy. Industrial firms and agrobusinesses were run by a handful of rich families (about 17 Christian families and eight Muslim families). While 50% of the economically active population were employed on the land in 1959, only 18.9% were in 1970. In addition, the oil price rises of the 1970s encouraged continuously accelerating inflation throughout the Middle East, particularly in non-producing countries such as Lebanon. In consequence, many smallholders on Mount Lebanon were forced to sell up to become wage labourers, swelling the ranks of Pierre Jumayyil's Kata'ib, the Maronite populist movement. Elsewhere, the sharecroppers on the periphery, mostly Sunnis and Shias, were driven off the land by increased mechanisation. By 1974, half the families of Lebanon lived in greater Beirut.

The effects on the labour market can easily be imagined. An enormous sub-proletariat came into existence, participating occasionally at the lower end of the service sector. When Lebanon became the battleground for so many of the other conflicting forces in the Arab world, partly, but by no means entirely because of the presence of some 300,000 Palestinians (about 12% of the population) on Lebanese territory, there were in addition large numbers of under- and unemployed Palestinians and Lebanese ready to be recruited into the various militias, which gave them a more or less regular salary as well as the status derived from the ability to sport a sub-machine-gun. It was a state of affairs that the Lebanese state strikingly lacked the wherewithal to resist. Furthermore, contributions from the oil-rich states of the Gulf have ensured sufficient means to finance the rival militias ever since.

The Palestinians and the more politically conscious Lebanese had a radicalising effect upon each other, and the attitudes of individual Lebanese or groups of Lebanese towards the Palestinians became effectively the touchstone for a whole set of political ideas and attitudes. Thus there arose the pressing question of the norms that should govern the Palestinians' relations to the Lebanese authorities—especially the Lebanese armed forces. Which was more important: that the Palestinians should not violate Lebanese sovereignty, or that they should be able to pursue the struggle against Zionism and imperialism from Lebanese soil? Naturally, this raised a variety of acute questions about the nature of the Lebanese state and the legitimacy of its activities.

In the late 1960s and early 1970s, therefore, many of the more radical Palestinians began to join forces, ideologically, and eventually militarily, with the more left-leaning Lebanese to press for the creation of a secular democratic state that would abolish the confessional political system and all that this stood for. Various radical and leftist groupings had joined together to form the Lebanese National Movement (LNM), a coalition eventually comprising 18 groups and organised by the Druze Kamal Jumblatt. Apart from the Druzes, the LNM was composed primarily, though by no means exclusively, of Sunni and Shia Muslims disillusioned with the inadequacy of their own traditional leaderships. Palestinian raids on Israel were attracting severe reprisals from Israel, and the different resentments felt by the various segments of Lebanese society found expression in clashes between the Lebanese army and the Palestinian militias which came to a head in November 1969.

Egyptian mediation calmed things for a while, but economic and political pressures within and outside the country built up throughout the early 1970s. By the beginning of 1975 various Maronite organisations, most prominently Pierre Jumayyil's populist Kata'ib, had become dissatisfied with the state's incapacity to control or contain the guerrillas (or the forces of the left), and had built up militias of their own to a point where they felt ready to take them on. The crisis came on 13 April 1975, after an incident at a church in Ain Rummaneh, where one of Pierre Jumayyil's bodyguards was killed by a passing gunmen. The Kata'ib fired back, and the fighting began.

The Lebanese civil war

Over the next few months there were various attempts to patch up a case-fire, but by the autumn of 1975 the fighting had become more intense. Dialogue proved impossible, as the PLO and the LNM insisted on political and constitutional reform, while the Kata'ib insisted that the army (which was under Maronite control and influence) should first restore order–in other words, should disarm the PLO and the LNM. By the beginning of 1976 the Kata'ib, together with other Maronite militias, attacked Palestinian refugee camps in East Beirut, provoking severe retaliation from LNM and PLO forces. At the same time, the increasing intensity of the crisis provoked alarm in Syria, soon to emerge, with Israel, as the principal arbiter of Lebanon's future.

For reasons connected both with its own survival and what it thought might be the Israel response, the Syrian government could neither afford to let the PLO and LNM gain an outright victory nor (though this turned out to be a secondary consideration) let the Maronites set up their own Maronite mini-state in Lebanon. Thus Syrian forces, together with contingents of pro-Syrian Palestinians, were despatched to Lebanon early in June 1976. This turned the tide in the Maronites' favour, and enabled them to expel the remaining Palestinian and Shia population from East Beirut after the siege of the Palestinian camp at Tall Za'tar. The first stage of the civil war was brought to an end after the Riyadh Summit in October 1976, at which an Arab Deterrent Force (ADF) was created, which consisted primarily of the Syrian forces already in Lebanon. The casualties between April 1975 and October 1976 were estimated at 30,000 killed, while at least a third of the population of three-and-a-quarter million had been forced to leave their homes, either to move to less affected parts of the country or to go abroad. The infrastructure was in ruins.

The main gainers were the Israelis, who supported and encouraged their Maronite allies' desire for partition (to the extent of giving $100 million of aid to the Maronites). The crisis also weakened the PLO, allowed Israel to enter Lebanese territory, and diverted Syria's attention from Israel. A few weeks after the Syrian incursion, Israel made it clear that it would prevent any resumption of PLO activity in south Lebanon, and, in association with Major Haddad of the Lebanese army, began its open-border policy for the inhabitants of the frontier area. The official Lebanese administration was not readmitted to this area after the war ended.

By this time the conflict had created a de facto partitioning of the country. This was most marked in the Maronite-controlled areas in East Beirut and Mount Lebanon, where the Lebanese Front, a rather fractious alliance of Maronite groups, set up what amounted to a parallel administration, with its United Forces under the command of Bashir Jumayyil, the son of the Kata'ib leader, Pierre Jumayyil. However, the end of the first stage of the fighting brought about important changes in attitudes on all sides. In the first place, many Shias, who were numerically important in the LNM, were becoming increasingly disillusioned with the activities of the PLO in south Lebanon, where they bore the brunt of Israeli retaliation against the PLO's activities. Some 300,000 Shias had become refugees (mostly in the suburbs of Beirut) by the autumn of 1977. Secondly, the presence of the Syrian ADF proved an increasing irritant to both Muslims and Maronites. Thirdly, the LNM was thrown into considerable disarray with the assassination of its charismatic leader, Kamal Jumblatt, in March 1977. Finally, there was a perceptible hardening of sectarianism, visible both within the LNM itself and with the return to prominence of some of the old sectarian leaders, and, though these were still early days, with the beginnings of the claim of the Shia organisation Amal (founded in 1975) to be the sole legitimate focus and representative of Shia social and political aspirations, a claim which was to gain added momentum with the Iranian revolution of 1979–80.

The Israeli invasions of 1978 and 1982

An uneasy state of tension and expectation persisted throughout 1977. The tension reflected obvious uncertainties about the likely activities of Israel and Syria, even if a degree of optimism had been engendered in some quarters by President Carter's apparent willingness at least to recognise that the PLO and the Palestinians had a legitimate interest in any settlement of the Arab–Israeli conflict. There were signs that this cautious American goodwill was beginning to rub off on to the more extreme Palestinian groups, and that the PLO was prepared to enter negotiations. On 1 October 1977 the United States and the Soviet Union jointly declared their readiness to call a peace conference at Geneva.

The high hopes invested in this encouraging development were soon to be dashed. On 9 November President Sadat of Egypt, partly in response to the deepening economic crisis at home, which he considered could be solved only by total commitment to the West, announced his intention to travel to Jerusalem to initiate direct peace negotiations with Israel. For the Lebanese and the PLO, this had three principal effects. In the first place, Sadat's action effectively removed the only major military opposition to Israel from the scene. Secondly, the Palestinians were effectively excluded from any decisions about their future, which was to be decided by Egypt and Israel, and possibly Jordan. Thirdly, Israel was now free to take whatever action it liked in Lebanon, since the threat of Syrian retaliation did not constitute a decisive deterrent. Sadat himself remarked in the course of an interview in November 1977 that 'blood will flow in Lebanon and Syria'.

Israel was not slow to capitalise on the new situation, invading south Lebanon (as far north as the Litani River) on 14 March 1978, nominally in response to a PLO attack on a bus in Israel in which 34 Israelis were killed and 78 injured. As a result of the invasion 2,000 Lebanese and Palestinians were killed, and 250,000 new refugees created; Israel was now in occupation of about one-tenth of all Lebanese territory. A UN force, UNIFIL, was given an international mandate to police the area, and various UN resolutions prevailed on the Israelis to withdraw. They did so, but on 12 June 1978 handed over a strategic part of the area to their surrogate, Major Haddad and his South Lebanese Army (SLA), which Israel financed and equipped, thus creating a 'South Lebanon security belt' as a permanent buffer zone under their control.

As a result, Lebanese politics became polarised once more. On the one hand, there were those (generally the LNM, the PLO, pro-Syrian groups and some older Sunni politicians, including Rashid Karami) who saw the main priority as fighting Israel's territorial aims in Lebanon. On the other hand, there were those who considered that Israel's invasion was entirely due to sins of commission on the part of the PLO, the obvious corollary being that Israel withdrawal—and thus eventually Syrian withdrawal—required prior PLO withdrawal. This was the view of the Maronite right, and of some more 'traditional' Shia leaders, who were beginning to regain their former constituency among the southern Lebanese. It was eventually to bring about a split in Maronite ranks, between those who were steadfastly anti-Syrian—mostly from south and central Lebanon—and those who generally favoured closer relations with Syria—mostly from the Maronite enclave in the north, around Tripoli and its hinterland, the most notable representatives of the latter tendency being ex-President Sulaiman Franjiyya (1970–76) and his supporters. The breach was formalised by the assassination by Kata'ib militiamen—under Bashir Jumayyil and Samir Ja'ja' (Geagea)—of Franjiyya's son, Tony, and other members of his family, in June 1978.

Over the next four years the conflict continued on a variety of levels. Israel continued to bombard south Lebanon, and, partly as a result, relations between the Shias and the PLO steadily deteriorated. Having silenced his Maronite rivals in the north, Bashir Jumayyil turned on the militia of his father's rival, Camille Chamoun, in Beirut in July 1980. Having subjugated them, he emerged as the de facto ruler of the Maronite enclave centred on East Beirut; all the Maronite militias, now styled the Lebanese Forces, were under his command. Early in 1981 he attempted to expel the Syrians from east Lebanon, besieging Zahlé (on one of the main roads to Damascus) for two months. Syria made it unmistakably clear that any attempt on Jumayyil's part to extend his authority beyond the 'traditional Maronite enclave' would be challenged: SAM missiles were deployed in the Bekaa, and there was heavy fighting between Jumayyil's forces and the Syrian army in Beirut, evidently coordinated with the shelling of Tyre by Haddad and the Israeli-backed SLA.

In July 1981, after a heavy PLO bombardment of northern Israel, an indirect cease-fire between Israel and the PLO was negotiated. This held until the Israeli invasion of Beirut in June 1982. The pretext for this second and far more massive Israeli invasion was the attempted assassination of the Israeli ambassador to London, Shlomo Argov, by Iraqi agents (who had no direct connection with the PLO); in conformity with the July 1981 cease-fire, the PLO itself had not attacked across the Lebanese–Israeli border for over a year. The objects of the invasion were to set up a pro-Israel regime (under the Kata'ib) in Lebanon, to crush the PLO in Lebanon once and for all, and, by this means, to end Palestinian resistance to the settlement, and perhaps eventually to the annexation, by Israel, of the

Occupied West Bank and Gaza. The Israelis were welcomed by the Maronites, and by some of the Shia population of the south. Altogether 20,000 people, the great majority non-combatants, were killed in the fighting. The Israelis apparently thought they would take West Beirut within a week, but, quite remarkably, given the small number of the city's defenders (perhaps 15,000 altogether) and the relentless savagery of Israeli bombardment and siege, it took more than three months. Even then, the fact that the PLO fighters were evacuated under safe conduct meant that the Israeli triumph was somewhat less than total.

The evacuation took place at the end of August, with various marine detachments from the United States and EC countries to supervise it, and, in theory, to protect the remaining Palestinian civilian population. The massacres of Sabra and Chatila are a terrible testimonial to the lack of seriousness with which this part of the assignment was taken. On 23 August, Bashir Jumayyil had been elected president of Lebanon; 22 days later, the day after the departure of the marines, he was assassinated, either by the Syrians or by the Israelis, concerned that he might not prove as docile in office as they had expected. The Israeli Defence Forces promptly surrounded Sabra and Chatila camps, and its commanders, together with the Maronite leaders of the Lebanese Forces, planned to search out and destroy the 'terrorists' supposedly still in the camps who were held to be responsible for Jumayyil's murder. According to the Israeli journalist Amnon Kapeliouk, between 3,000 and 3,500 people were killed in Sabra and Chatila a few hundred metres from detachments of the Israeli Defence Forces. Israel subsequently appointed a commission of investigation but it did not go to Lebanon nor interview any Lebanese or Palestinian witnesses. Nevertheless, it did make the point that 'all forces operating inside the camps were under the authority of the Israeli Defence Force and acting according to its directives'.

Partition, 1982—88

A week after his brother Bashir's assassination, Amin Jumayyil was elected to the presidency. He found it impossible to set up a cabinet of politicians, and proceeded to rule by decree. He also appointed Kata'ib militia commanders to senior posts in the Lebanese army, which was now being supplied with arms and advisers by the United States on the grounds that this was a necessary precondition for national reconstruction (though as was obvious to any observer, given that the army had become little more than an auxiliary of the Maronite militias, 'national reconstruction' was most unlikely to result). Jumayyil controlled only West Beirut, about 1% of the country's land area, while the Lebanese Forces controlled a further 10%, including East Beirut and the coast to the north. His government now attempted to do what the Israelis had been unable to do: to expel all remaining Palestinians from Lebanon. European doctors working in Palestinian hospitals were harassed and some were eventually deported;

Palestinians in south Beirut and in Sidon were evicted from the area, and many were killed on their way to and from their homes in the refugee camps in south Lebanon.

At the same time, the Israelis began to convert south Lebanon into a market for Israeli products, dumping fruits at prices with which local producers could not compete, while raising the costs of chemical fertilisers and other essentials landed at Sidon. Israeli sales soon reached $5 million a month, and, according to an International Monetary Fund (IMF) study in 1985, much of the agricultural land of the south had been put out of production in 1984 as a result of the deliberate destruction of orchards and meadows. Early in 1984, Israel closed the sole direct crossing point between north and south Lebanon, the Awwali Bridge, diverting traffic through the Chouf mountains, thus virtually cutting the two parts of the country off from each other. By the middle 1980s, according to a Lebanese economist, Lebanon was beginning to lack 'all the elements essential for economic activity'; the Lebanese pound had been devalued by 40% (although far worse was to come); the public debt had risen to a point at which debt service outstripped national income; industry was working at about a quarter of capacity; there was 60% unemployment; exports had almost ceased. Nearly a quarter of the population had either lost their homes or moved between 1975 and 1984.

In May 1983 Israel negotiated an agreement with Jumayyil to withdraw from Lebanon on draconian terms, including the creation of a buffer zone extending almost 30 miles into south Lebanon. However, as it had made the agreement without involving Syria, it was effectively rendered void almost immediately. This sparked off another furious round of fighting between the LNM and the Lebanese Forces. This time the LNM had been reconstituted as the National Salvation Front (NSF), a grouping loosely allied with Syria and consisting principally of the Druze leader Walid Jumblatt (whose militia formed the nucleus of the fighting forces), the Sunni politician Rashid Karami, and, until his defection in 1984, ex-President Sulaiman Franjiyyah. In addition, the Amal leader, Nabih Berri, who repeatedly declared that his movement had no sectarian goals, had an informal alliance with Jumblatt, albeit outside the NSF. At this stage the Shias (organised along both 'secular' and 'religious' lines) had re-emerged as a vital element on the political scene, much feared by the Maronites, who realised the implications of their numerical supremacy within the population.

As Israel withdrew from the Chouf and the Lebanese Forces attempted to take its place, Jumblatt's Druze forces, with Syrian assistance, fought effectively against the Lebanese Forces. At the same time, Amal initiated a campaign of resistance against the Israelis in south Lebanon, where, apart from Major Haddad and his successor, Antoine Lahd, Israel had found it impossible to maintain credible collaborators. By the end of September 1983 the cease-fire left the Druze forces in control of the Chouf, and brought the Druzes' Syrian allies back into negotiations. At the beginning of 1984 Amin Jumayyil had been obliged to rescind the May 1983 agreement, and Syrian forces remained in the Bekaa, demonstrating clearly that no settlement could be imposed on Lebanon without Syrian consent. American involvement in Lebanese affairs was dealt a severe blow in October 1983; a few days after the apparently gratuitous Israeli disruption of the Shia *ashura* procession in Nabatié, some 240 American marines were killed when a commando drove a truck of explosives into their barracks. By 1984, Amal was in virtual control of West Beirut.

In spite of American attempts to paint the Syrians as Soviet puppets, and thus to legitimise and underpin their own support of Israel and its Lebanese allies, the next few years saw a gradual strengthening of anti-Israeli forces in Lebanon, to the extent that Israel was forced to withdraw from the south by the summer of 1985. However, the PLO, some of whose fighters were slowly infiltrating back into Lebanon, also suffered great losses during this period, especially after Abu Musa's 'defection' to Damascus, Arafat's break with Asad in June 1983 (at a time when Asad feared that Arafat and King Husain were about to enter Palestinian/Jordanian negotiations with Israel under the aegis of the 1982 Reagan Plan), and the intra-Palestinian fighting around Tripoli in the autumn of 1983. At the end of 1985 some sort of settlement seemed in the offing, partly because of the apparent end of the PLO's role as a serious contender for power (or as a key ally of the various contenders for power) in Lebanon. The leader of the Lebanese Forces, Hubaiqa, had negotiated this agreement, the Damascus Accord, in Damascus with Berri and Jumblatt; if implemented, it would have abolished the confessional system over a three-year period, given equal Muslim and Christian representation in parliament, and enhanced the powers of the prime minister at the expense of the president, all within the framework of fairly close involvement with Syria. However, Amin Jumayyil and another powerful militia leader, Samir Ja'ja' (who had previously split the Lebanese Forces from the Kata'ib), managed to unite their forces against Hubaiqa and expel his forces from Beirut in January 1986, wrecking the arrangement.

A further dimension to the Lebanese conflict in the early and middle 1980s was the growing influence of Islamic fundamentalist groups, whose rise in the 1970s had been boosted by the Iranian revolution, as well as the moral and practical failings of declaredly secular progressive political movements in Lebanon and elsewhere in the Arab world. The fundamentalist campaign in Syria, and the terrible events of Hama in February 1982 (*see* Chapter 13, Syria), meant that many members of the (Sunni) Muslim Brotherhood fled to Tripoli. Others gathered in Sidon, while, among the Shias, an 'Islamic Amal' was founded in Baalbek, and a Hezbollah movement was established in 1982 in Beirut and the Bekaa (although a similar organisation had been founded in 1978). In spite of her support of Iran in the war with Iraq, the existence of more extreme Shia groups was anathema to Syria, which assisted Amal but not Hezbollah. Such groups were fiercely opposed to political movements on the left, as was shown by the massacres of communists by Sunni fundamentalists in Tripoli in 1983.

The rise of fundamentalism was another reason for the 'return of sectarianism' in the middle 1980s, but also, in another context, could be, and was, presented by the United States, Israel and their Lebanese Christian allies as irrational 'Islamic terrorism' against which virtually unlimited force could be directed. Hezbollah became the principal channel through which the Islamic Republic of Iran attempted to influence events in Lebanon, not always to Syria's liking.

The gradual increase in the military power of Amal brought great tensions throughout 1985–87, with fierce fighting between Shia and Druze militias, though this represented a struggle for territorial conquest and supremacy rather than a clash of ideologies. As always, Syria was concerned to prevent any individual party to the conflict reaching a position where it could not be checked by a combination of Syrian and other forces ranged against it; in this case the imbalance in the numbers of the Shia and Druze 'constituencies' (respectively perhaps 35% and 7% of the population) made it likely that Amal's forces would ultimately prevail. Thus the Syrian army was despatched to occupy West Beirut in March 1987 to put an end to the fighting between Syria's main allies. This period was also one of fierce fighting between Shias and the reconstituted Palestinian movement, partly with Syrian encouragement, as well as between pro- and anti-Syrian factions in the Maronite militias, all indications of the folly of trying to identify the various parties in this apparently endless conflict according to neat ideological or sectarian categories.

Nevertheless, although almost mortally wounded, the Lebanese state managed to survive, and the question of the succession to the presidency when Jumayyil's term of office expired in September 1988 was vigorously discussed, indicating that most parties and factions in Lebanon were fundamentally opposed to partition and wanted the existing system to continue. The names of several prominent personalities, including Dany Chamoun, Ja'ja', the army commander Michel Aoun, and even the Maronite patriarch, as well as the incumbent, Amin Jumayyil, were ventilated as possible candidates. Though constitutionally excluded from standing again, Jumayyil clearly had ambitions in that direction.

Both the largest communities continued to be torn by internal dissent; Jumayyil was at loggerheads with the Lebanese Forces' commander, Ja'ja', and Amal was fighting both Hezbollah and the PLO. The cabinet did not meet at all in the course of 1987, but the chamber of deputies, which had been elected in 1972, formally abrogated both the Cairo Accord of 1969 (which formalised the PLO presence in Lebanon) and the May 1983 agreement with Israel. Although the Damascus Accord of December 1985 had proved a dead letter, it was clear that some sort of arrangement on these lines would be necessary if any permanent settlement were to be reached. Jumayyil himself certainly understood this, and tried, unsuccessfully, to mend his fences with Asad throughout 1987.

A major disadvantage for Jumayyil was the highly circumscribed nature of his authority and his inability to exercise control over events on the ground in Lebanon. Attempted and successful assassinations, killings of prominent personalities and kidnappings had become nightmarishly routine; the list of murders and attempted murders in 1987 included individuals from all sides of the political spectrum, including the prime minister, Rashid Karami, closely identified with Damascus, on 1 June. By July 1987, 130,000 people had been killed in Lebanon since April 1975, and 14,000 kidnapped, of whom 10,000 were subsequently murdered. On 20 January the Archbishop of Canterbury's envoy, Terry Waite, was abducted by Hezbollah; 25 other Europeans were being held by various militia groups at the same time.

Partition: 1988—90

The presidential elections of 1988 provoked a new political crisis, as the Lebanese parliament (which elects the president) failed to elect a successor to Jumayyil. Just before his presidential mandate expired. Jumayyil himself nominated the commander of the Lebanese army, General Aoun, as prime minister, in contravention of the National Pact, under which this office always goes to a Sunni; the incumbent Sunni prime minister, Salim al-Huss, supported by Syria, refused to give up his post. This development, which came shortly after the end of the Iran–Iraq War, signified the reappearance of Iraq as a major actor in Lebanese politics. Iraq wanted to undermine its bitter enemy Syria through Lebanon, and had been supplying Aoun with weapons for this purpose since the summer of 1988; for reasons connected with his own hostility to Syria (and his increasingly close relations with Iraq), Yasir Arafat also gave his tacit support to Aoun. The general also gained tentative recognition from France and the United States because of his hostility to Syria, then seen as the West and Israel's principal foe in the region.

Aoun gained a certain popularity in the course of 1988 and 1989 for his apparent ability to control the Maronite militias, notably the Lebanese Forces under Ja'ja', whom his forces managed to subdue early in 1989. This meant that the Lebanese Forces' control of (and thus income from) the port of Jounié and part of the port of Beirut was assumed by 'the state', in so far as Aoun could be said to represent it. Such activities brought a swift response from Syria, and the fighting in and around Beirut between Aoun and his supporters, and the Syrians and theirs, reached new levels of intensity, to the extent that all those inhabitants of Beirut who could leave the city tried to do so. On 30 June 1989, the UN Disaster Relief Organisation announced that in the preceding 16 weeks in Beirut, 438 people had been killed, 2,300 wounded, and 500,000 had left the city. The struggle continued until the end of September 1989, when Aoun was obliged to give up, at least for the time being, after his Iraqi suppliers had been persuaded to stop delivering arms to him.

The lull brought new efforts to find a solution on the part of the Arab League, Syria and Saudi Arabia. The surviving members of the (1972) Lebanese parliament were flown to Ta'if in Saudi Arabia, where a modest political agreement (the Ta'if Accord) was hammered out in the course of October. In brief, the powers of the president of the republic were to be reduced, and those of the prime minister enhanced; Muslims and Christians were to have parity (54 seats each) in a new parliament, replacing the former 6:5 ratio in favour of the Christians. Syrian troops would be withdrawn two years after the adoption of 'constitutional reforms.' Reaction in Lebanon itself was not particularly favourable; Jumblatt, Berri, Hezbollah and the Iranians disapproved, largely because the accord seemed too generous to the Maronites, and, as far as the Shias were concerned, did not provide them with sufficient additional representation, although Syria's commitment to the accord meant that Amal gradually came to accept it. On 4 November 1989 parliament met again in Beirut and elected the Maronite deputy Rene Mu'awwad president; 18 days later he was assassinated, and succeeded by Ilyas Harawi, who declared himself in favour of 'good and solid relations with Syria'.

For his part, Aoun declared himself president on 7 November. Throughout late November and early December there were demonstrations in his favour, largely because of his anti-Syrian stance. He continued to hold out against the Ta'if Accord in his virtually separate state in East Beirut well into 1990, and his forces (units of the Lebanese army) were involved in bitter fighting with the Lebanese Forces under Ja'ja', who declared himself ready to participate in any government formed by Harawi. However, Syria was also anxious to ensure that Ja'ja' and the Lebanese Forces were not in a position to defeat Aoun outright, since this would put the latter in too powerful a position in Lebanon. Syria was anxious that the two factions should exhaust themselves rather than that the one should triumph over the other. The economic effect of this was that the dollar exchange-rate fell from some 45 Lebanese pounds (LL) in late 1985 to 650 LL in May 1990, and to 1,040 LL in October 1990.

It is impossible to estimate how long Aoun could have held out had Iraq not invaded Kuwait and thus ceased to be able to supply him. Syrian ground attacks and aerial bombardment of his headquarters eventually forced him to take refuge in the French Embassy on 13 October. In the course of the next few weeks, the Druze, Hezbollah and Amal militias gradually withdrew from Beirut; on 24–25 October the capital was formally reunited; on 19 December a cabinet uniting most shades of political opinion was formed. Syrian orchestration of these arrangements could not have been carried out without American approval, given in a number of high-level visits to Damascus and underlined by a cordial meeting between

Hafiz al-Asad and George Bush at Geneva on 22 November. While certainly consolidating Syrian influence within Lebanon, these new measures produced a state of affairs closely approximating to peace in most parts of the country, and the Lebanese army, now about 30,000 strong, and firmly under the control of a relatively representative government, substantially outnumbering the militias.

Of course the major constitutional changes necessary to make a permanent settlement still have not taken place. The Maronites still fear for their political survival; many Muslims remain relatively deprived, both economically and politically; and it remains to be seen how Israel will react to these changed circumstances if little or no obvious progress is made on a Middle East peace settlement. Nevertheless, the change in atmosphere is palpable, and, on the whole, welcome to most sections of Lebanese society after nearly two decades of continuous murder and destruction.

In September 1991, the Lebanese army, with the help of the Syrians, ordered the disbanding of all private militias in Lebanon, in accordance with the Ta'if Agreement on Lebanon of 1989. Despite the opposition of Palestine and indeed some Christian and Muslim militias, the move had considerable success. Also in September, General Aoun left the French Embassy annex, where he had taken refuge since his defeat the previous October and sought asylum in France.

Coupled with moves towards a resolution of the hostage crisis such developments have done a great deal to restore a measure of stability to Beirut. By the end of 1991 almost all the foreign hostages held in Lebanon had been freed, and the government announced in September 1991 that foreign businessmen and tourists could visit Lebanon without fear, adding that their safety could be guaranteed in a Lebanon in which Muslims and Christians were cooperating. On the other hand, the infrastructure of Beirut remains in disarray, with frequent power cuts (many Beirutis have private generators), and with local residents still avoiding slum areas in which kidnappers may still lurk. Beirut landlords have raised rents in the hope of restoring their pre-1975 prosperity; water supplies are unreliable, as is the telecommunications system. But the government is making a determined effort to revive commercial life and to make Beirut once again the centre of Middle Eastern commercial and banking activity.

Peter Sluglett and Marion Farouk-Sluglett

8 LIBYA

When Libya was granted independence by the United Nations in 1951, it faced a bleak future. With Libya essentially a desert state, many of its problems were geographical. Only 1.2% of its land area is arable, while only a further 4% can be used for pastoralism. The rest forms part of the Sahara desert, stretching west to east across the country, except for the Gefara plain and the Jabal al-Akhdar regions, and actually reaching the Mediterranean in Sirtica, at the base of the Gulf of Sirte.

Water was the major problem facing the new state, however. Rainfall rarely reaches eight inches per annum and then only in the northern coastal areas of the Gefara plain and the Jabal al-Akhdar. Limited underground water reserves were really all that were available for drinking and for agriculture. There seemed to be nothing left for industrial use. Not surprisingly, therefore, the new country was one of the poorest states in Africa and its 1.1 million-strong population seemed to have little prospect of escaping its chronic poverty.

The situation had been worsened, however, by what had happened to Libya during the first half of the 20th century. Between 1911 and 1927, the country had been ravaged by war, as Italy tried to impose colonial rule. Italy had then created a settler colony in Libya, bringing in 110,000 Italians to add to the 800,000 Libyans who had survived the war. Although the Fascist administration had created a basic infrastructure, its main concern had been the settlers and native Libyans had suffered in consequence.

Despite modest British and French aid when they jointly administered Libya after 1943, Libya's essentially subsistence economy at independence was still trying to recover from the three decades of Italian Fascist colonisation and the damage caused by three years of warfare during the Second World War. Its export potential, according to a World Bank report issued three years after independence, was limited. It lay in the traditional export of esparto grass (for high-grade paper manufacture) and in metal scrap from the battlefields which had ranged along Libya's Mediterranean littoral.

Within ten years, however, the economic picture had completely changed, as Libya entered the oil era at the start of the 1960s. The political situation was also transformed at the end of the decade, when the Idrisid monarchy, which had ruled the country since independence, was suddenly overthrown by an army coup—the 'Great September Revolution'. Its authors turned out to be junior army officers, powerfully affected by the

Arab nationalist ideology of Egypt's president, Gamal Abdel Nasser, and under the leadership of a communications officer, Mu'ammar Qadhafi.

Colonel Qadhafi has since created one of the world's most idiosyncratic political systems and, aided by the country's oil wealth, has also attempted to carve out an international role for Libya in the modern world. Yet even if Libya's economic status has been transformed, its international reputation has been clouded by the Qadhafi regime's notorious involvement in international terrorism—although the media image tends to be far more impressive than the reality in this respect. The policies and means that the Libyan leader has chosen to achieve these objectives, however, reflect as much Libya's own past as they do the diplomatic and political freedom of manoeuvre bequeathed by oil or the inspiration generated by an ideological imperative.

Libya before the colonial era

The name 'Libya'—first applied to the modern state in 1934 when the Italians created a single administration for their colony of 'Libya'—derives from the name 'Lebu' or 'Rebu' given by the Egyptians of the Old Kingdom in 2700–2200 BC to marauding Berber tribes that penetrated from Cyrenaica into the Nile Delta. Even then, pressure on the scanty resources of a marginal environment forced the population of Libya to migrate. The modern form of the name, however, was first applied to the coastal regions by Greek and Roman settlers in Classical times, when Tripolitania and Cyrenaica formed part, first, of the Carthaginian empire in Tunisia and Tripolitania, together with Greek colonies in the east, and, later, of the Roman Empire.

The reality of political control up to the Italian occupation in 1911, however, highlighted the fact that population settlement concentrated on four separate and separated locations. These were the Jabal al-Akhdar region of Cyrenaica; the Gefara plain of Tripolitania; the oasis complexes of the Fezzan; and, to a much lesser extent, the oases of Kufrah, al-Jawf, Sarir and Tazirbu. Around these settled regions were nomadic hinterlands that stretched down towards the desert and that controlled the trade routes across the Sahara towards the Sahel, Egypt and the Maghrib (*see* Chapter 9, The Maghrib).

The Islamisation of Libya, which began in the late 7th century, initially touched only the Christianised and Judaised coastal Berber populations. Thereafter, the country tended to be polarised politically, with Cyrenaica falling under the control of Islamic dynasties based in Egypt and Tripolitania being part of Ifriqiya, the Islamic political entity created in modern Tunisia. The Sahara desert fell under the control—direct or indirect—of central African empires, such as the Zaghawa and the Safawa in Kanem-Bornu. It was only in the 11th century that Islam penetrated into the hinterland and Libya became an essentially Arab-speaking region, as a result of the invasions of the Banu Hilal and the Banu Sulaim—tribal

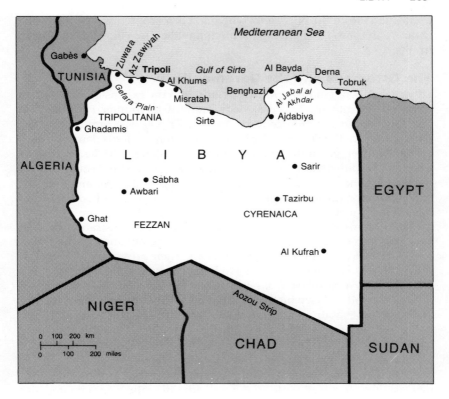

Official name	Great Socialist People's Libyan Arab Republic
Area	1,759,540 sq. km (679,358 sq. miles)
Population	4 million (1990)
Capital	Tripoli
Language	Arabic
Religion	Sunni Muslim (97%)
Currency	Libyan dinar

populations from the Nile Delta who had been ordered westward by the Fatimids in Cairo in an attempt to discipline their rebellious governors in Ifriqiya.

The Ottomans and the Qaramanlis

Libya's independent history really begins with the expansion of Ottoman naval power into the western Mediterranean to counter Hapsburg influence there in the 16th century. In 1551 Tripoli was captured by the Ottomans from the Order of the Knights of St John of Jerusalem who had, originally, been given the city, along with the island of Malta, in 1530 by Charles V. Charles had wished to reduce the burden on Spain of defending the North African coastal cities which the states of the Iberian peninsula had conquered during the previous century. Tripoli itself had been conquered in 1510 but was too exposed for effective defence.

The Ottomans soon established an effective administration of their new province of Tarablus Al-Gharb (Western Tripoli) and, by the 1580s, had extended their control into the Fezzan. Their presence in Cyrenaica, however, was nominal and limited to Benghazi, while the hinterland was intermittently controlled from Egypt. At the same time, the focus of diplomatic and military interest shifted away from the southern interior and from neighbouring states to the east and the west. Instead, Tripoli became a significant Mediterranean base for the *corso*—the corsairing tradition that pitted Islam and Christendom against each other in a form of naval warfare that masqueraded as legalised piracy.

Ottoman control from Istanbul was rarely more than formal and power increasingly devolved onto the local administration, dominated—as elsewhere in the Ottoman world—by the janissaries. Ottoman Turks also intermarried with the local population, producing a warrior-caste known as the *kulughlis*. In 1711, a popular *kulughli* leader, Ahmad Qaramanli, seized power and extracted formal recognition as pasha from Istanbul. His successors formed the Qaramanli dynasty, which ruled over the Regency of Tripoli—one of the three Barbary states familiar to European history from the 17th to the 19th centuries because of their role in the *corso*—until 1835, when the Sublime Porte in Istanbul seized power in Tripoli once again. During their rule, the Qaramanlis asserted effective control over Cyrenaica for the first time, while extending their power in the Sahara and making the Regency of Tripoli into a leading corsairing state.

The second Ottoman occupation

The Ottoman reoccupation in 1835 came hard on the heels of France's occupation of Algiers in 1830. It resulted from a rebellion in Tripoli that pitted factions of the Qaramanli family against each other in which each enjoyed the support of France or Britain. The regency itself had been bankrupted by a combination of over-ambitious plans to conquer the declining Sahelian empire of Bornu and the collapse of corsairing. The last

Qaramanli ruler, Yusuf Pasha, had begun the fatal process of contracting foreign loans from the two major European powers of the day in order to overcome his financial difficulties but had merely sunk deeper into debt.

In this situation, Istanbul feared a European colonial takeover as a result of the dynastic rebellion and acted to forestall such an event. The Ottomans found themselves in charge of an unruly country and without the proper resources to control it. Nonetheless, tribal rebellions in the Gefara plain were suppressed, small garrisons were left in the Fezzan oases and a rudimentary administration was set up in the coastal towns.

The Sanusiya

In Cyrenaica, however, the Ottomans came up against a new problem. Two years after they took over the regency, a new Islamic religious order, the Sanusiya, was founded at Mecca in Saudi Arabia by an Algerian scholar, Mohammed bin Ali al-Sanusi. The purpose of the order was, first, to revive Islamic values in the face of the growing European cultural and technological onslaught and, second, to resist European occupation of the Muslim world—particularly in North Africa.

In 1843, the first *zawiya*, or 'lodge', of the new order was set up in Cyrenaica, at al-Bayda. The order rapidly gained support amongst the Cyrenaican tribes and in 1859, to avoid conflict with the Ottoman authorities along the coast, its headquarters were established at the desert oasis of al-Jaghbub. In 1895, as the order's influence spread into Egypt and Sudan, the headquarters were moved down to al-Kufrah and, in 1902, to Gourou in northern Chad. By then, there were 146 *zawiyas* in Libya (mainly in Cyrenaica), western Egypt, northern Sudan, northern Chad and Saudi Arabia.

The order's success in garnering universal tribal support lay not just in its ideological and religious message but in its unique organisational abilities. *Zawiyas* were set up at the boundaries of tribal territories, at local markets, and on the major trade routes. In addition to providing shelter, education and religious guidance, they also provided a neutral arena for the settlement of tribal disputes and, thereby, a focus for administrative authority. Eventually they also became the focus of indigenous resistance to European occupation, particularly in Chad. In short, the order provided an informal but cohesive alternative administration with which the Ottomans, given their own weakness as their empire began to disintegrate elsewhere, had to collaborate.

Colonialism and independence

By the start of the 20th century, the decline of Ottoman authority made the conversion of Ottoman Libya into a colony only a matter of time. Although France had appeared a likely contender, its occupation of Tunisia in 1881 and its campaign of pacification of central Africa from the start of the century onwards distracted Paris from ambitions farther east in North

Africa itself. In any case, in an agreement between France and Italy in December 1902, the French government made it clear that it was prepared to allow Italy to satisfy its own colonial ambitions in Libya. Paris had come to this decision in order to avoid further difficulties over French and Italian borders in Europe or over Italian claims to Tunisia—where Italians had long formed the majority of the European community.

Italy was a latecomer to the colonial scene, largely because of its own belated development in 1861 as a modern nation-state. Nonetheless, Italian politicians as far back as Mazzini in 1838 had cast eyes on North Africa as a strategic key to the central Mediterranean and as a means of recovering the Classical grandeur of Imperial Rome. More pragmatically, Italy coveted control of trans-Saharan trade and saw in Libya an empty land to absorb its poverty-stricken peasantry in the dispossessed south, the *mezzogiorno*. As a result—and even though trans-Saharan trade was being rapidly undermined by the construction of railways in west and central Africa—a press campaign popularised Italy's claims on Libya. Italian economic penetration into Tripolitania also proceeded apace.

The Italo–Sanusi wars

In 1911 a crisis with Tripoli was engineered by Rome and war erupted. However, the rapid Italian invasion of the coastal towns soon bogged down and, although Ottoman Turkey abandoned the struggle in October 1912 when, through the Treaty of Ouchy, the sultan renounced all territorial claims on Cyrenaica and Tripolitania, the Sanusiya maintained a vigorous resistance, particularly in Cyrenaica. Ottoman Turkey maintained clandestine support for the Sanusiya struggle during the First World War, until, as a result of British pressure from Egypt, a truce was arranged in 1917.

The Sanusi leader, Idris al-Sanusi, was recognised as Emir of Cyrenaica. A separate group of Tripolitanian nationalists in Misratah also attempted to persuade Italy to recognise an independent republic, as did the Berber community of the Jabal Nafusa. In 1922, however, all these initiatives collapsed and the disparate groups attempted instead to rally behind Idris al-Sanusi as the Emir of both Cyrenaica and Tripolitania.

Italian hostility to this development coincided with the creation of a more efficient military command in Libya itself under Count Giuseppe Volpe and the arrival of the Fascists to power in Rome. The second Italo–Sanusi War, which began in 1923, was to prove to be a much more serious affair. The principal theatre of operations was to be Cyrenaica and, although Emir Idris soon fled to Egypt, where he was to stay for 25 years under British protection, the leadership of the struggle devolved onto a Sanusi sheik, Umar al-Mukhtar, one of the greatest figures of the anti-colonial struggle in the Islamic world.

Eventually, the methodical and calculated brutality of the local Italian field commander, Rudolfo Graziani—which involved herding the population of Cyrenaica into concentration camps, introducing a scorched-earth policy throughout Cyrenaica and building fortifications for 200 miles inland from the Mediterranean along Libya's border with Egypt—brought the struggle to an end in 1932. In September 1931, Umar al-Mukhtar was captured and hanged before 20,000 unwilling Arab spectators. The final resistance collapsed a few months later.

Italian Fascist colonialism

The following decade of Fascist colonisation of Libya saw a determined attempt to realise the dream of converting Libya into Italy's 'Quarta Sponda' (Fourth Shore). By 1942, there were 110,000 Italians living there, of whom 40,000 were directly involved in agriculture. The creation of a modern infrastructure and the settling of the colonial arrivals had cost Italy 1.8 billion lira, in what appeared to be only the beginning of a constant drain on the finances of metropolitan Italy. In part, the magnitude of the costs involved arose from the Fascist policy of 'demographic colonisation'. This involved the settlement of individual family farm units through state-sponsored schemes.

Libyans played little part in these grandiose plans. Instead, they were to become 'economic collaborators' and 'coparticipants' without the benefit of state aid. After 1937, when Italy sought to become the 'Protector of Islam', in Mussolini's words, Libyans were to become Muslim Italians. In fact, they continued to survive in considerable poverty, as land was alienated for colonisation, as a modern Italian-dominated economic sector was created and as the economy of Libya overall was integrated into that of Italy. Nonetheless, the Italian colonial experience did, for the first time, create the administrative structures and the infrastructure for a unitary Libyan state.

Italian colonialism also established internationally recognised borders for its African colony. These were delimited between Italy and its two colonial neighbours, France (in Tunisia, Algeria, French West Africa—Niger—and French Equatorial Africa—Chad) and Britain (in Egypt and the Sudan). The borders were even rectified, with the Sarra Triangle's being ceded from the Anglo-Egyptian Sudan to Libya and the secession of the 500-mile-long and 60-mile-deep Aozou Strip by French Equatorial Africa to Libya being proposed in 1935.

The secession of the Aozou Strip was a French response to Italian irredentist demands for border rectification in Europe and to other demands over the Italian colony in Tunisia, as well as being an attempt to avoid formal treaty links developing between Fascist Italy and Nazi Germany. Although the transfer was negotiated and codified in the Mussolini-Laval Treaty, which was ratified by both countries, the instruments of ratification were never exchanged and, by 1938, Italy–by then in the Axis (the Pact of Steel) with Nazi Germany–no longer had any interest in what was being offered. Nonetheless, the modified border was internationally accepted for the next two decades, until Libya obtained independence and signed a border treaty with France in 1956, in which, under duress, it tacitly tolerated border revision. The Aozou Strip dispute, together with similar disputes with Algeria, have continued to bedevil Libya's relations with its neighbours ever since.

The run-up to independence

Italy's colonial presence in Libya was destroyed by the Second World War. British forces occupied Cyrenaica and the Tripolitanian littoral, while Free French forces from Chad occupied the Fezzan in early 1943. Separate British military administrations were set up in Cyrenaica and Tripolitania, while France created an indirect system of administration based on the Sayf al-Nasr clan—the traditional tribal notability of the Ait Sulayman, the dominant tribe in Fezzan. Although the administration was designed to operate on a 'care-and-maintenance' basis, as required by international law, British administrators also began to create a Libyan civil service, while France integrated parts of Fezzan into its Algerian colony.

In 1947, Italy renounced its colonies and Libya became the protégé of the newly founded United Nations, although both Britain and France maintained administrative trusteeship. A search for a permanent solution then began. Several countries expressed interest in a United Nations mandate for Libya before full independence was granted, although popular pressure inside Libya was for immediate independence. To forestall Soviet interest in a mandate, Great Britain and Italy proposed the Bevin-Sforza Plan in 1949, under which Britain would take a ten-year mandate over Cyrenaica, Italy a similar mandate over Tripolitania and France would retain control over Fezzan for the same period. Independence would then be granted. There was massive hostility to the plan in Libya. In consequence, the United Nations General Assembly failed to adopt it.

Instead, it was decided that a single independent state should be created; a Dutch diplomat, Adrian Pelt, was appointed to determine what sort of political structure should be established for it. Idris al-Sanusi had returned to Cyrenaica in 1947 and, under British pressure, had unilaterally proclaimed himself Emir of Cyrenaica once again in 1949. Although there was a strong nationalist movement in Tripolitania that sought a unitary republican state for independent Libya, it was eventually persuaded to accept a federal solution under a Sanusi monarchy, with Idris as king. Independence was proclaimed in Libya on 24 December 1951.

Independence under the monarchy

The newly independent state started with a series of handicaps over and above its harsh geographic environment and poor resource base. The political system bequeathed to it proved extremely difficult to operate, not least because local and provincial loyalties continued to be stronger than loyalties to the new state itself. In Tripolitania, resentment at a Cyrenaica- and Sanusi-dominated government intensified and, after elections in mid-February 1952, all political parties were abolished. In addition, there were problems within the monarchy over the succession question which led to a crisis in 1954.

Popular dislike of the Sanusi monarchy continued to strengthen during the 1950s and 1960s, particularly in Tripolitania and Fezzan. Growing anger over corruption in the administration and government and with intensifying Cyrenaica influence crystallised around the monarchy's decision to build a new capital at al-Bayda, the site of the original Sanusi *zawiya*. These sentiments were fed by popular sympathy for the Arab nationalist Nasserism of neighbouring Egypt. This was also fostered by the large number of Egyptian teachers who had been brought in to bolster Libya's educational system and by the inflammatory broadcasts of Radio Cairo.

Egyptian antagonism towards the Sanusi monarchy was, in turn, intensified by the pro-Western option adopted by King Idris's government. Britain and the United States maintained large military bases in the country, while France's military presence in the Fezzan was ended only in 1956. Libya depended heavily on foreign aid, particularly from the Anglo-Saxon world, and correspondingly tried to avoid being dragged into the complex and increasingly anti-Western politics of the Middle East and the Arab–Israeli dispute, a stance which in turn increased governmental unpopularity at home.

In 1959 the discovery of oil dramatically altered the options open to Libya's government. Oil came on stream in 1961; almost overnight, Libya began to be transformed by oil revenues. Concomitantly, it also began to play a more assertive role in regional affairs, not least because of domestic pressure for a more pro-Arab and less pro-Western attitude. This came to a head with the 1967 Six Day War, when rioting in Libya forced the government to take a more active role in support of the Arab cause. In a foretaste of the future, Libya even proposed to its fellow oil producers collective Arab action to increase oil prices, although, in the end, nothing was done. Increasing domestic repression in response to popular unrest led to disaffection in the army and, eventually, to the junior officer coup on 1 September 1969.

The coup took everybody by surprise. It had been evident for some time that the monarchy faced serious problems of credibility and an army-based coup had been long anticipated. However, the senior officer corps was expected to organise it and, apparently, even had a degree of tacit support from Libya's main Western allies. Although there was plenty of evidence of discontent amongst junior officers and the government had taken some desultory steps to curb it, nobody was aware of the degree of organisation that had taken place in secret and that had ensured success.

For some time after the coup itself, those involved remained anonymous, nor were their objectives and ideological preferences immediately evident. Although the organisers of the coup appeared to have Nasserist sympathies, Egyptian leaders had no contact with them and were unaware of the movement that had masterminded the actual coup attempt. Thus the Union of Free Officers was headed by a 12-man directorate, which, after the coup, reconstituted itself as the Revolutionary Command Council (RCC) and became the new Libyan government.

Mu'ammar Qadhafi

It gradually became clear that the dominant influence in the new government was a 27-year-old Signals captain—soon to be appointed colonel—Mu'ammar Qadhafi. He had been born in 1941 into the transhumant Qadhadhfa tribe, located along the Gulf of Sirte, where his father had been a client of a local notable from the Sayf al-Nasr family. After a mosque-based primary education, the future Libyan leader attended secondary school in the Fezzanese centre of Sabha, as the family followed their patron who had been appointed to a high administrative position there. His secondary-school career was relatively short-lived; Qadhafi soon became a political activist, publicly espousing the Arab nationalism of Gamal Abdel Nasser.

His expulsion from secondary school was followed by recruitment into the military academy in Benghazi in 1961. With his military education completed in 1966, he was transferred away from elite army units, such as the Cyrenaican Defence Force, into the communications branch in the mistaken belief that his political radicalism could be safely contained there. Instead, it provided him with an excellent cover for the creation of the Free Officers Movement and, eventually, with the means necessary to launch a successful coup d'état while King Idris was on holiday in Turkey.

By early 1970 it had become clear that the new Libyan regime was dominated by the personality of Colonel Qadhafi. Although the new government promised to be a typical army-backed radical Arab nationalist regime—it dramatically expanded the armed forces, arrested and sentenced its predecessors for corruption, insisted on an immediate end to British and American military bases and soon forced the remaining 13,000 Italians out of Libya—it also quickly developed characteristics typical of its leader and his background. In imitation of its Egyptian mentor, the new regime founded a mass movement to provide popular backing for the role of the army within the regime—the Arab Socialist Union (ASU)—and dedicated itself to radicalism in inter-Arab affairs, to confrontation with Israel and to Arab unity, as well as to state-directed economic development, Libya was to undergo a unique ideological evolution over the next decade.

That evolution mirrored the experiences, attitudes and beliefs of its leader. Mu'ammar Qadhafi had grown up in the strongly Islamic, egalitarian and communal environment of tribal Libya. His political views had been profoundly influenced by this experience and by the wider currents of Nasserism. They also reflected, however, a series of

resentments; resentments of the tribal groups of Sirtica against the dominant tribes of Cyrenaica; resentments of rural Libya against the merchant
communities of Tripoli and Benghazi; and resentments of many Libyans
over the arrogance of many in the Middle East and North Africa towards
them because of supposed Libyan backwardness and primitiveness. It has
been a combination of these three factors of personal background, Arab
nationalism and national sensitivities that has formed the idiosyncratic
ideology of Colonel Qadhafi's revolution, as enshrined in the doctrines of
the Third Universal Theory and as described in the colonel's *Green Book*.

Domestic politics

Up to the publication of the *Green Book* in 1976, Libya's domestic politics
were largely a question of experiment and a quest for stability as the regime
grappled with the twin problems of discrediting its predecessors and of
finding a viable political structure for the new state. It quickly had to face a
serious challenge, with arrests of its new defence and interior ministers,
Adam al-Hawwaz and Musa Ahmad, for plotting its overthrow in December 1969. A tribal-based coup in Fezzan, allegedly masterminded by
members of the Sanusi family and the Sayf al-Nasr clan, was uncovered in
July 1970. Then, in 1975, after major disagreements within the RCC over
economic management, Major Umar Mihaishi, an RCC member and
minister of planning, suddenly fled abroad after trying to organise an
abortive coup of his own. He had tried to recruit other RCC members to
support him and had also expected support from his home town of
Misratah in order to force Colonel Qadhafi to resign.

The three atttempted coups made clear the alienation of the new regime
from important groups within Libyan society. The December 1969 coup
marked the breach between the RCC—all basically junior officers—and
their military superiors, still tied to the policies of the monarchy. The July
1970 coup marked a final breach between the Sanusi movement and
traditional tribal elites, such as the Sayf al-Nasr, which had been the
backbone of the monarchy, and the RCC. The Mihaishi coup in August
1975 marked the collapse of consensus within the RCC and the reduction
of the regime's geographic and social power-base, as the Misratah region
became disaffected by its loss of access to influence with the disgrace of
Umar Mihaishi himself.

However, these polarisations in Libya's political life did not matter
provided they only involved groups already discredited by their association with the monarchy. When they involved the core of the regime itself—
the RCC—the situation was far more serious. In part, this development
was an inevitable reflection of the regime's attempts to create an authentic
base of radical popular support. During the previous five years, it had
attempted to supplement the effectiveness of the Nasserist ASU, which it
had created in 1971. It had done this by appealing to traditions of popular
consensus inherent in Libya's Islamic heritage, appeals supplemented by

laws repeating the ban on political parties and limiting the freedom of trade unions and the press. Tribalism and regionalism were also attacked and an attempt was made to replace the role of traditional elites in the administration—the so-called 'movement of modernising administrators', whereby young civil servants with no personal following in specific areas were foisted on rural and urban areas.

By 1973, however, it was clear that none of these measures had worked. Tensions inside the RCC, furthermore, had intensified and, after a threat to resign from his positions of RCC chairman, head-of-state and commander-in-chief, Colonel Qadhafi suddenly radicalised the government by bringing in Major Abd as-Salam Jallud, his closest collaborator in the RCC, as premier and then announced a 'cultural revolution'. In April, in a speech at the coastal town of Zuwarah, the colonel warned that the Libyan revolution was threatened and proposed a five-point programme to revive it. These included the suspension of the legal system, arming the population to protect the revolution, purging the country of the 'politically sick', the destruction of the bureaucracy and the bourgeoisie, and the destruction of all aspects of culture contrary to the Koran. In place of the existing institutions of government there were to be popularly elected committees, which would become responsible for administration, while a purified Islamic culture would determine Libya's cultural environment.

In the event, although over 2,000 popular committees were formed and up to 400 'opponents of the regime'—communists, Ba'thists and members of Islamic fundamentalist organisations—were arrested, while a whole echelon of senior managers and administrators were dismissed (thereby destroying a group which had been as opposed to the monarchy as it had to the RCC), the 'cultural revolution' had petered out by August 1973, with the collapse of a proposed union agreement with Egypt. However, it had set the stage for the next radical shake-up of the political system in March 1976.

The *jamahiriyah*

A year after the 'cultural revolution', Colonel Qadhafi resigned his position in the RCC and devoted himself to preparing for the final stage in the evolution of Libya's new political system—the creation of the *jamahiriyah*, 'the state of the masses'. Its proclamation was foreshadowed by the publication of the colonel's Third Universal Theory in late 1973, whereby he argued that Islam represented the source of the only viable political philosophy for the Third World, superior to both capitalism and communism. Its proposed structures were described in instalments of the colonel's *Green Book*, which were published in the official newspaper *Al-Fajr al-Jadid* (although most commentators doubt whether the colonel was the sole author of this three-volume political textbook).

The *Green Book* proposed a political system based on direct popular consensual democracy, with popular control of the means of production, and limited private ownership set within the context of an austere collective social structure. It was a vision that owed much to Islamic legal and moral precursors and the collective social order of traditional rural life. Despite oft-repeated claims that its inspiration was Rousseauian, there is no evidence to show that Colonel Qadhafi had or had felt the need to have any familiarity with European political philosophy. Instead, his own Islamic and rural upbringing, together with the influence of modernist North African Islamic polemicists, was sufficient.

The new political system was installed in March 1977, after the 'people's authority' (popular sovereignty) had been proclaimed in Sabha at the final meeting of the now defunct ASU which, thereby, transformed itself into the new embodiment of popular sovereignty, the General People's Congress (GPC). The new system was based on a series of Basic Popular Congresses (BPC) to which all Libyans belonged. The 187 BPCs (enlarged to 2,150 in 1984) were structured in terms of population location, and their elected chairmen, secretaries and assistant secretaries became delegates to the GPC. The GPC also included an equal number of delegates designated by trade unions, and by trade, social and professional organisations. The GPC thus represented all shades of opinion, both by population location and by economic activity. Delegates were mandated by their nominating organisations to express only the organisation's view over all matters of policy, whether local, regional, national or international—thus ensuring that the ultimate political decision should reflect the direct democratic views of the population at large.

Daily administration was to be carried out by a series of popular committees which, at least in theory, were elected by those who were to be administered—the organisations which provided delegates to the GPC, whether BPC or another occupational organisation. The popular committees were under the ultimate control of the General People's Committee, itself elected by the GPC and answerable to the General Secretariat of the GPC, which maintained continuity in GPC policy between its biannual sessions. The General People's Committee was, in short, the equivalent of a cabinet and its secretaries the equivalent of ministers. The GPC General Secretariat was the key body, as far as the regime was concerned, for its members were the five remaining members of the original RCC which had organised the 1969 overthrow of the monarchy—with Colonel Qadhafi at its head and with Major Abd as-Salam Jallud, Colonel Abu Bakr Yunis Jabr, Major Mustafa Kharrubi and Major Khuwaildi Hamidi as its other members. They have since been joined by Khalifa Khanash, a cousin of Colonel Qadhafi. Their presence ensured political continuity, for, as the 'people's authority' was declared, they abandoned all other formal positions of power.

This political system has been formally in operation in Libya since 1977. However, it has several inherent shortcomings. First, despite its claim to provide for direct popular democracy, it still involves massive delegation of authority. Secondly, it demands a degree of mass political commitment that is simply unrealistic. Thirdly, by excluding any form of political party or current it excludes wide sections of Libyan society who might legitimately disagree with the general tenor of political life and whose disagreement becomes a form of treachery to the established political order.

These problems rapidly became apparent. Within a year of the establishment of the *jamahiriyah*, the Qadhafi regime found it necessary to modify the basic structure. During 1978 revolutionary committees began to appear, apparently spontaneously, in reality under central direction by the small group of former RCC members around Colonel Qadhafi. Their function was to radicalise the BPC and popular committee system and to 'guarantee the revolution'—in short, to ensure that the system worked and that dissent was excluded. Their membership was clandestine and under the direct control of Colonel Qadhafi and Major Jallud. By February 1980, the revolutionary committee system had spread throughout the political structure, paralleling it at every level, and with its own annual congress. At the congress in February 1980, Colonel Qadhafi gave the movement an additional function, that of eliminating what he called 'the stray dogs of the revolution', those Libyans who rejected the *jamahiriyah*, both inside Libya and abroad.

The revolutionary committee system, as it developed during the 1980s, also betrayed another sign of the Qadhafi regime's failure to establish genuine popular support. Its members, by definition, had to be people committed to the regime, either by political persuasion or by personal interest. Many of them, it is true, were young enthusiasts, such as those drawn from the student movement inside Libya that had been responsible for suppressing anti-regime student riots at Garyounis University in Benghazi in April 1976. The most important elements of the revolutionary committee movement—those who took over responsibility for eliminating the 'stray dogs of the revolution'—also had another mode of identity with the regime: they were members of tribal groups that were themselves linked to leading members of the regime around the colonel himself.

In fact, the irony was that the Qadhafi regime, in seeking a popular mandate, had alienated such large sections of Libyan society that it had to fall back on its most basic element, the tribe. It was a notable fact that most of those who held real power inside the regime were linked to the major tribes of Sirtica—the Qadhadhfa, the Maghara and the Warfalla. Others were linked to the Fezzan. It was striking that few were linked either to the traditional urban communities of Tripolitania or to the traditional repository of Sanusi support, Cyrenaica. They include relatives of Colonel Qadhafi, such as Said Qadhaf Adhm (the military commander of Sirtica) and Ahmad Qadhaf Adhm (seen as Qadhafi's heir apparent), Abd al-Hafid Massa'ud (commander of the southern military region) and Abd al-Hafid Yunis (commander of the eastern military region). They had also included Hassan Ishkal, who was executed after an abortive coup in December 1987.

Others include Musa Kursa, the former diplomatic chief in London until his expulsion in 1980, and Abdullah al-Sanusi and Said Rashid of the Maghara, which is Major Jallud's own power-base.

This process of 'retribalisation' of Libya through the revolutionary committee movement has effectively created a third level of political control, which, although informal in nature, is the real repository of political power. It extends into every key area of society and the economy and, by this process of fragmentation of Libyan political, social and economic structures into a series of personalised fiefs, ensures that the core of the Qadhafi regime maintains effective personal control. The five close collaborators of the colonel control the oil industry (Major Jallud); the army, which is now also penetrated by revolutionary committees and is threatened with replacement by a popular militia movement (Abu Bakr Yunis Jabr); the security services (Khalifa Khanash); the popular militia movement (Mustafa Kharrubi); and the police system (Khawaildi Hamidi).

It is largely because ultimate control depends on this informal system that the Qadhafi regime has been able to survive the vicissitudes of the 1980s, including the United States bombing of Tripoli and Benghazi in April 1986 and the catastrophic defeat of the Libyan army in Chad in March 1987. It is typified by the colonel's decision, in late 1987, to decentralise the administration away from Tripoli and to create a new capital on the Gulf of Sirte under the direct control of the Qadhadhfa.

Opposition to the regime

This system has also generated a massive popular discontent, both inside Libya and abroad. It has resulted in at least seven major exile dissident organisations, of which the best-known is probably the National Salvation Front for Libya, organised in 1980 by the former Libyan ambassador to India, Muhammad al-Mughariaff. It has also engendered a growing anti-regime Islamist movement, against which the authorities have reacted savagely.

Much of the basis for the discontent has been engendered by the campaigns waged by the regime against what it considered disaffected elements of Libyan society during the 1970s. Royalists left, of course, in 1969. They were followed in 1973 by the bulk of Libya's intellectuals, who took warning from the Zuwarah speech and the 'cultural revolution'. In 1977 they were followed, in turn, by much of Libya's business class, who took fright at the implications for the economy of the political changes introduced under the *jamahiri* system. In essence, these required enterprises to be taken over by workers' popular committees; domestic trade was centralised progressively under state control, as was foreign trade. Wage employment was formally banned; instead, employees became the owners of the means of production. Private ownership and personal property were limited by decree. In effect, although Libya was supposed to be a 'stateless state', it was the state that took over control of the economy.

Islamist opposition to the Qadhafi regime has, strangely enough, been engendered by the regime's own assumption of an Islamic mantle. In 1977, the religious leadership in Libya had the temerity to question the religious orthodoxy of the *Green Book*. There was also a quarrel between the regime and the religious authorities over control of *waqf* property. Colonel Qadhafi reacted by claiming that true Islam required no mediation between Allah and man and that, therefore, the religious authorities had no function. He went on to claim that Islamic law was valid only insofar as it was a restatement of the principles of the Koran and had no intrinsic validity because of its status as authoritative interpretation of Islamic doctrine. He finally concluded that each Muslim had an equal capacity to interpret the Koran in the light of modern conditions. The colonel rammed home his convictions by altering the starting date of the Islamic calender from the date of Mohammed's migration to Medina to the date of the prophet's death.

All these actions were construed to be heterodox and attracted the antagonism of the orthodox Muslim community. Radical Islamists were further antagonised by the colonel's view of the major Islamic fundamentalist orders and movements as political parties designed to split Muslim unity, rather than seeing them as valid reinterpretations of Islamic doctrine. The result has been growing Islamic opposition to his regime. The colonel's individualistic attitudes towards Islam, however, are exactly paralleled by his attitude towards foreign affairs.

Foreign affairs

Foreign policy under the Qadhafi regime has been influenced by the principles of radical Arab unity, a Libyan conviction of its primordial role within the Third World and an opportunistic determination to maximise benefits to the Libyan state. Arab nationalism has bequeathed to Libya a profoundly confrontational attitude towards Israel over the Arab–Israeli dispute and the Palestinian problem, as well as justifying Libya's constant search for partners for projects of political and economic unity within the Middle East and North Africa. Libyan perceptions of its anti-imperialist role, as the embodiment of the principles of the Third Universal Theory, has led to confrontation with the West and a concomitant attempt to ensure security by an alliance since 1973 with the Soviet Union. Opportunism has forced the Qadhafi regime into a series of irresponsible actions towards its neighbours, not least its intervention during the 1980s in Chad.

Libyan attempts at achieving unity reflect both ideological and practical preoccupations. The original attempts in 1970 and 1973 to create such agreements with Egypt and Sudan and then with Egypt alone were both rational attempts to match Egypt's population or Sudan's agricultural potential with Libyan oil wealth as much as they were ideological imperatives. Indeed, Egypt under both Nasser and Sadat had an acute interest in unity with Libya because of Libya's potential to offer strategic depth to

Egypt's armed forces in any confrontation with Israel. Once Egypt had embarked on a search for peace with Israel, Libya ceased to offer any attractions in this respect.

For Libya, however, unity with neighbouring states also offered a means of guaranteeing the security of a state that otherwise had little means of ensuring its own security. Despite massive spending on armaments–$14 billion with the Soviet Union alone during the 1980s–Libya's armed forces have not acquitted themselves well in any of the major armed clashes in which they have been involved: in Chad in 1987; in Uganda in the mid-1980s; or in the border war with Egypt in 1977. In fact, Libya has had to use states such as Algeria to ensure its territorial integrity; it was Algeria, after all, that prevented Egypt from prosecuting the 1977 conflict.

It is this concern over regional security that explains Libya's constant search for allies within North Africa. It did so unsuccessfully with Algeria, Tunisia and Mauritania in 1983; temporarily with Morocco in the Arab–African Union between 1984 and 1986; and now it is part of the Arab–Maghrib Union with all four countries since February 1989. It is also this concern that has now led Colonel Qadhafi to seek, once again, close links with the Mubarak regime in Egypt, as much as any lingering ideological preference that reflects the remnants of the Nasserist vision.

Unity can, however, follow ideological prejudice as well. It was undoubtedly because of Syria's and Libya's common opposition to Egypt's acceptance of the Camp David Agreement with Israel in 1978 that the two states, which had formed part of the Confrontation Front along with Algeria and Iraq, actually declared formal unity in 1980. This decision also brought Libya into the pro-Iranian camp during the Iran–Iraq War, a move which earned considerable hostility for the Qadhafi regime in the rest of the Arab world. Libya gained little benefit from this move, not least because its support for the Islamic revolution in Iran was also the cause of intensifying hostility between Tripoli and Washington during the Reagan administration of the 1980s.

The other main cause of American hostility was the growing perception in Western capitals that Libya was heavily involved in promoting international terrorism. Statements by leading Libyan politicians only encouraged this belief. Libya's insistence on its role as an anti-imperialist leader, its support for national liberation movements, particularly in the Middle East and Africa, above all its attitude towards Libyan political dissidents abroad, all encouraged this attitude. In 1980, 1982 and again in 1984, Libyans connected with the diplomatic service or with the Foreign Security Bureau, which was run by a former policeman, Yunis Beljasim, and staffed by revolutionary committee members such as Umar Sudani, Musa Kursa and Ahmad Zadma, were involved in assassinations and assassination attempts in London, Athens, Rome and Vienna and in the United States.

The terrorist crisis culminated in April 1984 in the murder of a police-woman, Yvonne Fletcher, in London during an attempt to machine-gun anti-Qadhafi Libyan demonstrators from the Libyan People's Bureau (embassy) in St James' Square. British diplomatic relations with Libya were severed and American hostility towards Libya, which had already resulted in a military confrontation in the Gulf of Sirte in August 1981, was racked up a notch. Typically, the Qadhafi regime, rather than taking warning from the London incident, extended its clandestine activities. Two years later, Washington accused Libya of being involved in terrorist attacks on United States servicemen in Berlin and in March 1986, attacked military installations in the Gulf of Sirte. One month later came the bombing attack on Tripoli and Benghazi.

Ironically, the American attack on Libya had precisely the opposite effect from that intended. Instead of rallying against the Qadhafi regime, Libyans, outraged that they should have been made personally re-sponsible for the vagaries of a leadership they could not control, rallied behind it. Although Colonel Qadhafi himself prudently took a back seat for some months, Libya's involvement in explicitly anti-Western terrorist acts—which had not been clearly demonstrated before the attacks—now came into the open. There were 14 Libyan-organised terrorist attacks immediately after the bombings, including the murders of Britons at Libyan instigation in Lebanon.

Most strikingly, Libya renewed massive aid to the IRA in Northern Ireland in revenge for the role played by Britain in the bombings. Libya had supplied limited aid to the IRA between 1973 and 1975, in the mistaken belief, so officials in Tripoli later claimed, that it was a genuine movement of national liberation. Now Libya's support was without any ideological coloration, and, until it ended in 1988, Tripoli is believed to have supplied five shiploads of weapons and explosives to the IRA.

American hostility towards Libya also touched on another area of Libyan foreign policy: that concerned specifically with Libya's own oppor-tunistic advantage. Libya's claim to northern Chad had never been aban-doned, despite the 1956 treaty with France, which was ostensibly meant to rectify the border situation. Indeed, the monarchy had even given cautious support to a national liberation movement in Chad that developed from a tribal rebellion in 1965, FROLINAT. The Qadhafi regime maintained the policies of its predecessor and, in 1972, taking advantage of the weakness of the Tombalbaye regime in N'Djamena, moved troops and an admin-istration into the disputed Aozou Strip region around the mountain massif of Tibesti.

By 1980, the Chadian civil war had degenerated into a struggle between two northern factions, one of which headed the provisional government placed in N'Djamena by the Organisation of African Unity (OAU) in 1979. In June 1980, Libya responded to an appeal from this group, headed by Goukouni Queddai; by December of that year, Libyan troops were present in the Chadian capital. Although the leader of the opposing faction, Hissan Habré, was forced to flee, he returned triumphantly to Chad two years later, now with Egyptian, French and American support. Libya continued to support the defeated Queddai faction in the hope of making its presence in the Aozou Strip permanent, until its forces were forced out with massive losses—$1.4 billion-worth of equipment were abandoned and thousands of Libyans killed in early 1987.

The Habré regime's success was due in no small part to French and United States perceptions of the need to humiliate the Qadhafi regime in Libya. Libya, however, had its revenge. Three years later Tripoli was to finance a successful overthrow of the Habré regime and to see a more sympathetic government installed in its place. At the same time, under Algerian urging, Libya decided to place its claim to the Aozou Strip before the International Court of Justice at The Hague. Libya has twice successfully placed disputes over its maritime borders with Tunisia and Malta before the court, and no doubt expects a similarly happy outcome on this occasion.

The economic dimension

One crucial reason why Libya has been able to engage in its domestic political experiments and its risky foreign policy has been its access to substantial oil income during the past three decades. In 1985, 41% of Libya's GDP was derived from oil production. Despite the fall in international oil prices over the intervening years, 27% of GDP was still attributable to oil in 1989. If manufacturing industry, which is largely petrochemical in nature, is included, the proportion of GDP attributable to the oil sector rises to 45% and 35% respectively.

Oil also generates 99% of Libya's export revenues, with oil production currently running at around one-million barrels per day, compared with a maximum of two-million barrels per day in 1979. The actual level of oil revenues has varied greatly, however, depending on the level of international oil prices, from a maximum of $22 billion in 1979 to as little as $5.8 billion in 1986. Revenues are currently estimated to be around $8–9 billion and Libya's oil reserves, although shrinking, are expected to last for 60 years.

Interestingly enough, Libya's oil industry has, in theory, been preserved from the ravages of the *jamahiri* system. This is not only because of its strategic importance for the Libyan economy and for the regime's freedom of action; it is also because Libya is almost unique amongst OPEC members in that its oil industry has always involved joint ventures with foreign companies. Currently, only the UAE has a similar system, although some OPEC members are beginning to reconsider their position in this respect.

This pragmatic approach towards oil exploitation and exploration is all the more surprising since Libya played the key role in the radicalisation of

OPEC at the start of the 1970s. It was a Libyan decision unilaterally to force up prices in 1971 that eventually destroyed the international oil companies' control of world oil prices and their control of national oil industries in the Middle East. Colonel Qadhafi took a straightforward approach to the oil companies operating in Libya, most of them 'independents' and therefore without access to worldwide crude that would have allowed them to face Libya down. He pointed out that Libyans had done without oil revenues for 5,000 years and could, therefore, do so again if need be.

Oil revenues have funded Libya's massive arms purchases. One analyst has calculated that these and other hidden expenditures over the past 25 years have cost Libya between 32 and 67% of its total oil revenues of around $150 billion. Nonetheless, sufficient has been left over to pay for development of an elaborate infrastructure and for industrial and agricultural development, including a petrochemical industry and a steel industry at Misratah. Oil revenues have also financed Libya's sizeable foreign labour force, made up mainly of Egyptians and Tunisians and providing up to 60% of the total labour force. It has also paid for Libya's chronic food deficit: over 65% of all the food required by Libya's 3.6-million-strong population, now growing at a rate of around 2.8% annually, has to be imported.

Most strikingly, oil has provided Libya with the hope that it could achieve food self-sufficiency by irrigating the desert. Since 1968, Libya has been engaged in a series of experiments using fossil underground water to grow wheat and alfalfa at al-Kufrah oasis and at Maknussa. Since the mid-1980s, Libya has also tried to overcome its inadequate water supply to coastal cities—now saline through over-use—by constructing a massive water pipeline from al-Kufrah and Sarir oases in the east and from the Fezzan in the west to supply the Gefara plain and Jabal al-Akhdar areas. This, the Great Manmade River Project, is ultimately expected to cost between $18 and $21 billion. Water from the scheme is also to be supplied to Sirte, in the hope of creating an agricultural base there. Expert opinion varies as to the utility of the scheme, but few doubt that urban and industrial demand for water will soon vitiate the objective of food self-sufficiency.

Libya is, in short, an oil-rich state with a high absorptive capacity which is becoming ever more oil dependent. Its ambitions of economic self-sufficiency are, no doubt, delusions, and Libyan planners are looking more and more towards the Kuwaiti example of foreign investment and downstream integration of their oil industry with expansion of marketing networks into Europe. The Libyan Arab Foreign Bank, Libya's major foreign investment arm, has invested in many European and African countries. Libya now owns a refining and distribution network in Italy. Its economic hopes, however, have been tarnished by its reputation as an unreliable international partner with an unsavoury reputation for terrorism—a reputation that the Qadhafi regime is trying to alter.

Recent events

Since its defeat in Chad in 1987, the Qadhafi regime has attempted to moderate its domestic and international reputations. Within Libya, the rigours of the *jamahiri* system have been significantly eased. Private enterprise has been permitted in agriculture, retail trade and small-scale manufacture. Barriers to foreign travel and to private importing from abroad have been abolished. Borders have been opened and Libyan political prisoners have been freed. Most important of all, virtually all Libyan exiles have been permitted to visit Libya and even to return if they wish.

In international affairs, Libya has gone out of its way to demonstrate that it is a responsible international partner. It has sought to improve links with Europe, its major trading partner, particularly with Italy, France and Germany. It has also attempted, unsuccessfully, to improve relations with Britain and the United States. It has, successfully, integrated itself into North African regional political and economic structures. It has also moderated its attitude towards inter-Arab affairs, although it still cannot accept the idea of an end to the Arab–Israeli dispute that would leave Israel benefiting from the 1967 war.

The most striking example of this new atmosphere of moderation occurred during the recent conflict between the UN-authorised and US-led coalition in the Gulf to force Iraq out of Kuwait in early 1991. Despite widescale popular antagonism to the Western intervention, the Qadhafi regime condemned Iraq's invasion as 'injurious to the Arab world' and even offered to supply troops to the coalition. It is believed that Colonel Qadhafi heeded Egyptian advice of the consequences if he backed Iraq and that, opportunistically, the Libyan leader perceived advantages for Libya in backing the West.

Whatever the reason, Mu'ammar Qadhafi's decision underlined his essential pragmatism over international affairs. He had realised from 1986 that the Soviet Union would prove to be an insubstantial partner for Libya in its difficulties with Western states. As a result, he has been prepared to abandon his long-standing eastward diplomatic links which, in any case, never mirrored his political convictions.

Yet Libyans view this conversion with suspicion. Many believe that, once the opportunity is right, Colonel Qadhafi will revert to his preferred persona as a radical political visionary and that the full rigours of the *jamahiri* system will be reimposed. Indeed, his diplomatic atavism is never far below the surface: at the start of the Gulf crisis, he toyed for several days with the idea of supporting Iraq in a gesture of radical solidarity. Iraqi indifference and the threat of renewed American hostility changed his mind. But the gesture was there and could always be repeated in different circumstances.

George Joffé

9 THE MAGHRIB

The three states of the Maghrib—Algeria, Morocco and Tunisia—form, in some respects, a neglected and isolated corner of the Arab world. Despite their rapid integration into the religious culture and society created by Islam shortly after the Prophet Mohammed's death in AD 632, all three states long resisted a concomitant integration into the linguistic universe of Arabic. Even today, substantial minorities in the Maghrib speak languages other than Arabic—basically one of the Berber group of languages, such as Tarifit, Tamazight and Tashilhit in Morocco and Taqbilt, Mzabi and Tamarshak (a Touareg language) in Algeria—as their mother tongue. The Maghrib's geographical location, furthermore, excluded it from the great events that shaped the Mashriq—the Middle East. It was indeed, as the Arabic version of the name given to the region today suggests, the 'Far West' of the Arab world. At the same time, however, the Maghrib forms a significant demographic component of that world; with total populations of 58.632 million (mid-1990 estimate), it provides 27.7% of the total population of the Arab world, as defined by the members of the Arab League.

Even in religious and cultural terms, the Maghrib differs significantly from the Mashriq. In place of the religious confusion of the Mashriq, where Islam's dominant position is split between Sunni and Shia and exists alongside significant Christian and Jewish minorities, the Maghrib's religious character is predominantly Sunni Islam. Colonialism, too, has left a different mark on each region: while France and Britain vied for influence in the Middle East, the Maghrib was the preserve of France and today French is almost as important a language as Arabic or Berber. Nor did the Maghrib have to deal with the divisive effects of the creation of the state of Israel, just as the era of independence was beginning to dawn.

Yet, from another point of view, isolated though it may be from the Middle East by the deserts of Libya and by distinct cultural differences, the Maghrib also forms a vital part of two other worlds. Traditionally, the states of the Maghrib have seen themselves, and have been seen, as an integral part of Africa, for the vast Sahara desert, now seen as a barrier to communication, used to be viewed as the equivalent of an inland sea, crisscrossed from time immemorial by trade routes. At the same time, the confrontation between Islam and Christianity in the Mediterranean since the Spanish Reconquista in the 15th century has made them into Mediterranean states. That northward dimension of their historical and cultural experience has been profoundly intensified in modern times as a result of colonialism.

The colonial experience differed considerably between the three modern states, however. Algeria, for example, which had not had a sovereign existence as a state before the colonial period, was occupied by France from 1844 and was administratively integrated into France for much of its subsequent colonial period. There was also massive European settlement in Algeria, with the result that independence was only gained in 1962 after eight years of intense warfare which cost up to one million lives. Indeed, independence was granted as much because of changes in metropolitan perceptions in Paris of the utility of colonial empires as because of the Algerian success in military conflict.

In Tunisia and Morocco, by contrast, the basic structures of unitary states existed before the colonial period. Indeed, in the case of Morocco, the state can claim an unbroken 1,000-year-old tradition of independent government. The two countries were colonised in 1881 and 1912 respectively, however. Having learnt from its experience in Algeria, France created 'protectorates', in both countries, whereby the French presence was supposed to assist indigenous authority in modernising the administration and the economy, while France took over responsibility for external affairs. In reality, French colonial interests dominated. Nonetheless, far more of the innate fabric of indigenous society was preserved than was the case in Algeria.

Yet, at independence, which came to Morocco and Tunisia six years before it was granted to Algeria, all three states were endowed with the structures of a modern European-style nation-state. They had modern-style administrations, defined territorial borders and the rudiments of a modern economy, created by European settlers during the colonial period. They also had comprehensive links with the economy of metropolitan France, for which they had served during the colonial period as sources of cheap raw materials and food. Those distortions in commercial links have persisted since independence, today reflecting the preferential position occupied by Europe in the Maghrib's economic horizons.

In short, it is the Mediterranean dimension of the Maghrib which is of most immediate importance to it today. All three states are acutely dependent on Europe for trade and for economic survival. In 1989, 53% of the Maghrib's total trade was with the countries of the EC. Algeria is a major hydrocarbon supplier; Morocco and Tunisia sell agricultural goods; Morocco is also Europe's major source of phosphate. The EC, in turn, supplies most of the region's consumer goods and much of its grain. More importantly, perhaps, Europe has traditionally absorbed excess labour from the Maghrib. Now, with Europe facing the challenge of the collapse of communism in Eastern Europe and the Soviet Union and the certainty of greater economic unity after 1992, the Maghrib is anxious about the consequences of these momentous changes for its own future. The resolution of this dilemma, however, will be as much a consequence of history as it will be of economic, social and diplomatic change.

In fact, given their pre-colonial experiences, the political divides between Maghribi states ran across an underlying sociological reality which emphasised a common historical and cultural experience. Indeed, until the 16th century, few Maghribis would have noticed a significant difference in society and culture anywhere in the region. It was only with the penetration of Ottoman power into modern Tunisia and Algeria in response to European attempts to dominate the Mediterranean—Morocco was never part of the Ottoman Empire—that specific cultural distinctions began to emerge. Even then, they were essentially limited to the Maghrib's Mediterranean littoral. Inland, society continued to follow its region-wide norms.

The imposition of colonialism

The 19th century was a period of gradual disillusionment for the Maghrib, as its rulers came to understand the implications of European dominance. In the immediate aftermath of the Napoleonic wars, however, European interest appeared to have been diverted away from the region. Apart from lingering irritation over commercial misbehaviour, particularly in Algiers, where deliveries of cereals to the Napoleonic armies had never been paid for, the Maghrib seemed to have relapsed into the somnambulism of the pre-Napoleonic period.

The picture was to change dramatically in 1830 when, in ostensible revenge for an insult offered to the French consul by the Bey of Algiers in 1827, France decided to occupy the beylik. In reality, the decision represented a desperate attempt by the government of the Bourbon monarch of France, Charles X, to avoid a military coup against him. The Algerian adventure was supposed to distract the army; it failed to do so and the Bourbon monarchy soon disappeared into oblivion.

France, however, having neglected to formulate a plan of occupation, was dragged into the political vacuum it had created in destroying the bey's administration. By the end of the decade, French troops were forced to suppress the beyliks of the interior and to create a countrywide administration to replace them. In western Algeria, the French army soon found itself confronting a tribal federation under the leadership of the Emir Abd al-Qadir. It was only when a ruthless scorched-earth policy was instituted that resistance was broken.

As France was sucked into its first territorial acquisition in the Maghrib, so it had to manufacture a system of administration and determine what it would do with the territory it now administered. Colonial settlement was encouraged as land was confiscated from the rural tribes. After initial hesitation, the new colony was integrated into the metropolitan administration of France. Algerians, however, were merely colonial subjects in their own land, denied virtually all rights, their culture marginalised.

By 1870, as the Second Empire was being destroyed by Prussia, eastern

Algeria burst into rebellion. It was to be the last such outburst until independence almost a century later. The rebellion was suppressed with great brutality, and European control, particularly by the local settler population—the *colons*—was powerfully reinforced. Thereafter, it would be colonial Algiers, with its one-million *colons*—the *pieds noirs*—which would call the tune that Paris would have to follow, whatever the official nature of the relationship. It was to be a relationship that would, eventually, lead to the destruction of France's North African empire.

In Tunisia, the Husainid beylik had taken note of what had happened in Algiers. Ahmad Bey had also realised, like Mohammed Ali in Egypt some years before, that European success was based on an efficient military machine supported by an effective industrial base. He tried to modernise Tunisia on a similar pattern, both to create a powerful modern state and to counter the growing privileges extracted from his government by the European consuls in Tunis.

Tunisia, however, was still an Islamic state, in which the basic tax structure could not sustain the costs of modernisation. To counter the financial weakness of the state, the government began the disastrous policy of borrowing from European powers and mortgaging its tax revenues in repayment. Soon Europeans took over control of the state finances and government power weakened. In 1859, the bey was forced, in imitation of European practice, to concede a formal constitution—the Destour—the first to be granted in the Arab world. The following year he was obliged to permit European land and property ownership in Tunisia. Attempts to restructure the government were thwarted by European pressure. Finally, in 1881, on the ostensible grounds of incursions into eastern Algeria by a Tunisian border tribe, the Khrumir, but in reality to prevent other European powers from intervening, France invaded the beylik.

Under the treaties of Bardo and La Marsa, France instituted a novel form of control. It did not wish to repeat the expensive mistake of direct rule on the Algerian model. Instead, it created a structure of indirect rule, in which France was supposed to 'aid' and 'modernise' the administration of the beylik alongside the existing authorities. France would also take over responsibility for security and foreign affairs. This 'protection' system, in effect, became a cover for the slow assimiliation of the Tunisian economy into that of metropolitan France, while a significant 100,000-strong, mainly Italian, settler colony was introduced.

The process of colonial assimilation of Morocco was to take a further 30-odd years. Although Morocco had been rudely shocked by its defeat in the Battle of Isly in 1844 and the sultanate's authority had been threatened by a series of tribal rebellions in consequence, France was not anxious to exploit its weakness, though pressures from Britain made it unlikely that it could have done so anyway. Nonetheless, Morocco was forced to grant economic privileges to both countries and to introduce a variant of the 'Capitulations system'—the protégé system—to protect foreign nationals.

It was only in 1860 that the process of colonisation began to lumber into action. The spark that set it off was provided by tribal unrest along the borders of two Spanish coastal enclaves, Ceuta and Melilla. War broke out, which Spain easily won, demanding, in consequence, a massive indemnity. The payment of this, in turn, led to the disastrous process of Moroccan borrowings from Europe—first from Britain, later from France—and to the opening of Morocco to European commercial exploitation. By 1906, under the terms of the Treaty of Algeciras, Morocco had lost control of its taxation system to a European debt commission and Europeans administered its customs system in order to pay off its accumulated debts. France took over control of the state financial system.

Although Britain had entertained ambitions for colonial control in Morocco, these were abandoned in the Entente Cordiale of 1904, when France offered, instead, a free hand in the eastern Mediterranean and in Egypt. Despite German objections France continued to expand its presence in Morocco, with military encroachments from Algeria and from the coastal port of Anfa, later, as Casablanca, Morocco's economic centre and port. Tribal anger at constant European encroachment sapped the sultanate, which in turn encouraged ever-deeper European penetration.

Finally, in 1912, under the provisions of the Treaty of Fez, France imposed a protectorate system on Morocco, similar to that imposed on Tunisia 30 years before. Eventually, 500,000 European settlers moved in. The protectorate was shared with Spain which took over control of northern Morocco and the province of Tarfaya in the south. Spain also instituted a separate colony over the Western Sahara, which it had begun to create after 1884.

It was, however, to take a further 22 years before the country was brought under French control. The complex process of pacification was also to cost Spain massive losses in the Rif War. That, in turn, led directly to the Spanish civil war and, following his victory, to Franco's Fascist government. It was a political system which, ironically, ended only in 1975, as Spain abandoned its last colony in Africa in the Western Sahara.

The nationalist response

The French colonial experience was to alter profoundly the physical appearance and the social structure of the Maghrib. Widespread agricultural settlement—settlers took over two-million acres in Tunisia, six-and-a-half million acres in Algeria and around two-and-a-half million acres in Morocco—created a modern cash-crop agricultural system. This was encapsulated within a traditional subsistence farming and pastoral system that had to support rapidly growing rural populations. Despite massive and accelerating rural drift, particularly after the Great Depression of the early 1930s, urban populations remained a minority overall. At the same time, a modern industrial sector grew up in urban centres, particularly along the coast, under European ownership and management. The French administrations, in addition to pacifying even the most remote corners of the countryside and the desert, created modern communications and infrastructural systems.

Even though indigenous populations were excluded from the benefits of modernisation, life expectancies and population growth increased significantly. Nonetheless, the overall balance of the colonial experience for Tunisians, Algerians and Moroccans must be negative, not least because it was marked by massive population dislocation and famine as the countries of the Maghrib were, first, integrated into centralised monetary economies and, second, linked into the European regional economy.

Tunisians, Algerians and Moroccans were also well aware of what was being done to their societies and they developed their own responses to it. These fell into two categories and were, at first, the prerogative of the elite groups that dominated national society, although the movements they initiated were later to win much wider support. Initially, however, the elites both wished to participate in and benefit from the innovations introduced by France, while at the same time reaffirming the Maghrib's Islamic and historical heritage. They desired, in short, to adapt and adopt European modernism within the indigenous cultural and sociological framework and sought cooperation with Europe, not exclusion from it.

In this respect, the initial movements of proto-nationalist protest were similar to the Young Ottoman and Young Turk movements which, from the 1880s onwards, had done so much to reform and, eventually, to replace, the sultanate in Ottoman Turkey. The Young Tunisian, Young Algerian and Young Moroccan movements were also inspired by the revivalist movements sweeping the Middle East, particularly by the Salafiyya movement, and they began to reaffirm also the Maghrib's conscious political and cultural identification with the Mashriq.

The early nationalists were optimistic about the French response to their demands. During the First World War, for example, all three countries generously provided manpower and resources to France's war effort. Indeed, the tradition of labour migration into Europe actually began as a result of French calls on Maghribi labour to make up for the shortfalls caused by conscription. Nationalists assumed—and were persuaded by French propaganda—that France would reward the Maghrib after the hostilities were over by encouraging political and economic participation.

The hopes, however, were disappointed, for during the 1920s nothing changed. Admittedly, this would have been difficult in Morocco, where, between 1921 and 1926, France was engaged with Spain in crushing the Riffian tribes of the northern Mediterranean littoral. In reality, however, the French administrations were deaf to indigenous protest. By 1930, furthermore, the Great Depression caused vast economic damage to settler societies and indigenous communities alike, so that France was even less disposed to consider political reform as economic hardship engendered growing popular anger and protest. Towards the end of the decade, the nationalist movements in Tunisia and Morocco began to widen their popular support through their leadership of such protest. In consequence, colonial repression intensified.

In any case, indigenous protest did not speak with a single voice. The *assimilationistes* argued that North Africans should integrate fully into French political life on a basis of formal equality. Others, the *associationistes*, argued that integration was to be avoided in favour of parallel development so that Maghribi society could preserve its identity while taking from Europe what it required for the purposes of modernisation.

In Tunisia and Algeria, these different points of view convulsed the nationalist movement. In Tunisia, the Young Tunisian movement in the Destour party, founded in 1920, had called for the restoration of the 1859 *destour* (constitution). Such a move by the bey would have forced the French administration to accept political partnership. However, the party's failure forced it to concede the leadership of the nationalist movement in 1934, at the Ksar Hellel conference. Habib Bourguiba, a young French-trained lawyer, thereafter successfully created a far more activist political movement, the Néo-Destour, which was eventually to lead the struggle for independence after the Second World War.

In Algeria, the *assimilationistes*, led by Ferhat Abbas and Ben Djelloul, confronted the *associationistes*, dominated by the moderate Islamist movement of the Algerian *ulama* and led by Ibn Badis. The French administration ignored them. Real nationalist sentiment, however, was gathering steam amongst Algeria's migrant populations in France, where the Etoile Nord-Africain group, led by Messali Hadj, demanded complete independence. It was only after the Second World War, however, that an effective nationalist movement, the Front de Libération Nationale (FLN), developed, demanding full independence from France for which it was prepared to fight.

In Morocco, the nascent nationalist movement of the 1920s had realised that the country's political and cultural traditions would not allow a fully secularist option. Under the leadership of Allal al-Fassi, in 1930 the movement fought a successful campaign to prevent the French administration from limiting the role of Islamic religious law in Berber areas and, thereby, splitting the nascent Moroccan body politic. After the French authorities rejected a plan for Moroccan participation, the movement rallied itself behind the political legitimacy of the sultanate. After the exiling of its leaders at the end of the decade, the movement reformed in 1944 and, under the banner of 'Istiqlal' (Independence), demanded the ending of the protectorate and the restoration of Morocco's sovereignty under Sultan Mohammed V.

In fact, the Second World War was a crucial turning point in the nationalist struggle. France's defeat by Nazi Germany and the installation of pro-Nazi Vichy administrations throughout the Maghrib, together with continuing conflict with Free French sympathisers, shattered the myth of

French omnipotence. Nazi propaganda also persuaded some nationalists that colonialism was not an immutable fact. However, probably the most profound experience was the extension of fighting into the region and the Torch landings in the Maghrib in late 1942, which brought United States and British servicemen into the region. Despite Free French attempts to reassert colonial control, United States leaders made it clear that they had no wish to see the French colonial presence prolonged.

The struggle for independence

Immediately after the war, France moved to suppress nationalist aspirations throughout North Africa. In Tunisia and Morocco, steps were taken to modify the protectorate system—which left sovereignty fully in indigenous hands—by a new concept of 'co-sovereignty' in which France and the country concerned would share full sovereign rights. Such a development would have made the removal of France legally impossible and the proposal was powerfully resisted. The French authorities imposed new governmental structures in both countries at the start of the 1950s, expelling Neo-Destourians from power in Tunisia in 1952 and exiling the sultan of Morocco to Madagascar in 1953.

The result was an immediate outbreak of violence in Morocco and Tunisia. By 1955, the French government had come to realise that compromise was essential. French politicians decided that the colonial presence in Morocco and Tunisia could be abandoned in order to safeguard France's colonial control of Algeria. Morocco was offered negotiations in 1955 and independence was granted on 2 March 1956. Tunisia was offered autonomy in 1955, which Habib Bourguiba, as leader of the Neo-Destour, accepted. This was converted into full independence in 1956, while at the same time the beylik was abolished and the new independent government transformed Tunisia into a republic.

The French hold on Algeria remained, however. Both the nature of French rule there, which was manipulated by the leaders of the *colon* community, and the metropolitan reluctance to abandon control after the debacle in Vietnam made it impossible for Paris to repeat what it had done in Morocco and Tunisia. In addition, the discovery of oil in the Sahara and French ambitions for nuclear weapons—for which the Sahara made an ideal testing ground—intensified French determination. However, against France was ranged a new kind of clandestine resistance movement in the FLN, led by individuals from modest rural or urban petit bourgeois backgrounds, with familiarity with nationalist aspirations from their pre-war connections with the Messalist movement and with experience of military action from the war.

They formed the FLN in October 1954 and, on 1 November 1954, initiated a guerrilla campaign. Although the FLN was not initially a mass movement, it moved rapidly and ruthlessly against all other Algerian nationalist groups, forcing them into line behind its own policy of armed struggle. It capitalised on the destruction of Algerian traditional society to impose its own structures and paid special attention to the massive Algerian migrant community in France. The result was that by 1956 it had become a genuine mass movement and the authentic voice of Algerian nationalist aspirations. Its leadership also realised that armed struggle alone could not win independence and, as a result, the movement sought to win international support for its demands.

In fact, by the end of the decade, it had become evident that military victory was impossible. New recruits to the FLN's military bases in Tunisia and Morocco were kept out of Algeria by elaborate border defences—the 'Ligne Challe'—and the exhausted guerrillas inside were hunted down by an ever-more efficient and brutal French army, while millions of Algerian peasants were uprooted from their villages to improve military control. At the same time, however, the continuing guerrilla campaign in the cities and *colon* suspicion of the commitment of successive French governments to the struggle led to a political collapse in France.

In 1958, a combined *colon*-army revolt in Algiers led to the return to power of General Charles de Gaulle in Paris. The French Algerian population anticipated that the general would safeguard it in Algeria by maintaining the French presence there: the general quickly realised that this would be impossible. However, he moved cautiously, seeking out Algerian 'moderates' with whom to negotiate and attempting to isolate the FLN while prosecuting the military campaign to the full. His policy was frustrated, however, by *colon* hostility to compromise and by the FLN's complete control over the nationalist movement itself.

By 1961, de Gaulle had accepted that the FLN would have to be the partner for negotiations and, after obtaining a popular mandate by referendum in January 1961, negotiations began. Their course was disturbed, however, by a revolt amongst France's leading generals—the 'generals' revolt'—and by the outbreak of violent guerrilla actions against the government by a clandestine military organisation within the French army in Algeria, the OAS. The negotiations continued, however, and France eventually recognised full Algerian independence, despite its anxieties over access to Algerian oil and over its Saharan nuclear-testing sites. With the signing of the Evian Accords on 18 March 1962, the war was over—at the cost of over one million killed and apparently unbridgeable hostility between *colon* and Algerian. Within six months, virtually all the *colon* community had fled Algeria, leaving the country to start its independent existence with no specialist experience to manage agriculture or industry.

INDEPENDENCE—Tunisia

Independence presented the new Tunisia leader, Habib Bourguiba, with a dual problem, that of asserting his control over both party and state. The Neo-Destour, the political vehicle through which independence had been achieved, was to become Tunisia's single political party, now renamed as

Official name	Republic of Tunisia
Area	164,150 sq. km (63,378 sq. miles)
Population	7,745,500
Capital	Tunis
Language	Arabic, Berber
Religion	Sunni Muslim
Currency	Tunisian dinar

the Destourian Socialist party (DSP). At the same time, all other state-wide organisations in effect became subordinated to it. The DSP also acquired a parallel position within the institutions of the state, so that the bureaucracy also acted as a party machine.

Other factors of political organisation—such as Islam—were coerced into acquiescence or by-passed. In 1961, for example, President Bourguiba outraged religious opinion by proclaiming a legal end to the month-long annual Ramadan fast, on the grounds that fasting was excused during *jihad*, or holy war, and that economic development was a form of *jihad*. Although public opinion forced the government to moderate its position, the incident showed just how far the president was prepared to go in trying to create a secularist, pro-Western regime through his own charisma. He was, for example, the first Arab statesman to call for peace for Israel in the mid-1960s, a time when such a statement was unthinkable for any Arab statesman who wished to remain in power.

It also underlines the peculiarly personal nature of Bourguiba's rule in Tunisia. As a result, his period of office, which lasted until he was deposed (although in theory he was president-for-life) in November 1987, was marked both by his personal capriciousness and his skill in weathering political crises. Furthermore, the crises have also been peculiarly personal in nature, for they have reflected popular and party perception of the role that Habib Bourguiba played in government. Each has involved potential rivalry from a ministerial colleague.

The first crisis, in fact, even pre-dated the full achievement of independence. The autonomy agreements negotiated by Bourguiba allowed Paris to control foreign affairs and security matters, as well as leaving French civil servants in key positions. Both the Neo-Destour secretary-general, Salih Ben Youssef, and the head of the UGTT, the powerful trade union organisation, Ahmed Ben Salih, objected to the agreement. Ben Salih eventually acquiesced, but Ben Youssef denounced it and was expelled from the party. He fled abroad and tried to organise armed resistance from Cairo. In 1961, he was assassinated in Frankfurt.

Ben Salih, however, was rewarded by being given the planning portfolio in the new government in 1961, just after France had agreed to abandon its last military base in Tunisia at Bizerta. The Bizerta crisis had developed as a result of French bombing of a Tunisian border village, Saqiat Sidi Youssef, because of Tunisian support for the Algerian independence struggle. Armed incidents between French military and Tunisian volunteers outside the Bizerta base eventually led to an agreement for a French evacuation by 1963. At the same time, French capital in Tunisia began to be withdrawn and, in 1964, Tunisia retaliated by nationalising all French-held land there.

The crisis forced a radical approach to Tunisia's economic problems. The Bourguiba administration wanted to counter the loss of French investment by encouraging popular participation in industry and agriculture through the creation of cooperatives. These were also expected to enhance output and improve efficiency, and Ben Salih was put in charge of the cooperative experiment. Fishing, crafts and construction cooperatives were set up in 1960, agricultural cooperatives in 1962 and expanded onto former French and now state land in 1965. By 1968, however, it was clear that popular resistance had caused the experiment to fail; despite massive state investment, output was stationary and there were widespread anti-government demonstrations. By September 1969 Bourguiba had accepted that the experiment was a failure; when Ben Salih protested, he was removed from his post, and, later, arrested.

Tunisia now radically altered its economic course and, under Hedi Nouira as premier, introduced liberal policies. Political control, however, remained firmly in the president's hands. The next decade was marked by two significant developments; heightened tension with the new radical Qadhafi regime in Libya and the growth of Islamic fundamentalism in Tunisia itself in response to growing urban poverty, particularly in the south, and to the DSP's domination of the political scene.

The crisis with Libya revolved around Colonel Qadhafi's anxiety for political unity with neighbouring states. Although Bourguiba rejected such advances in 1971, in 1974, in a surprise move, he signed a unity agreement with Libya. The president's decision had been strongly influenced by Tunisia's Arab nationalist foreign minister, Mohammed Masmoudi. Once news of the decision reached the premier, however, it was swiftly overturned. The union treaty was, as a result, still-born, much to the Libyan leader's irritation. Tensions between Tunisia and Libya intensified, and Libya began to support Tunisian dissidents.

Among those dissidents were young Tunisian fundamentalists who sought the violent overthrow of the Bourguiba regime. Moderate forms of Islamic fundamentalism had appeared in Tunisia in the early 1970s, as economic disparities increased as a result of Hedi Nouira's liberal policies. Foreign investment, particularly from Germany, sought to exploit cheap Tunisian labour, while the 1973 explosion in oil prices caused rapid inflation. Agriculture continued to stagnate and Tunisian labour sought opportunities for employment abroad—not in Europe, where the barriers had already begun to descend, but in the Middle East, particularly in Libya. In Tunisia itself, demonstrations began in January 1978 and were violently suppressed, a process that began to estrange labour leaders from the Bourguiba regime.

Quite apart from the looming economic crisis, the Arab defeat in the Six Day War in 1967 by Israel had both discredited Arab nationalism and had estranged many from the West, now apparently committed to Israel's preservation as a Western strategic bastion. Islamic fundamentalism appeared the obvious alternative. These two developments came to a head in January 1980, with an abortive Islamic rebellion in the southern town of Gafsa. In the middle of the crisis, the Tunisian government was suddenly incapacitated when the prime minister suffered a disabling stroke.

A new political moderate was appointed as premier, Mohammed Mzali, a former school teacher who had made a name for himself as an ideologue of Bourguibism. However, the president's growing interference rendered Mzali virtually impotent. In November 1981, the regime's intention of holding on to power was made clear in the legislative elections in which officially tolerated opposition parties failed to win a single seat, largely because of electoral irregularities.

The 1981 elections marked the beginning of a slow dissolution of the Bourguiba regime. It had already forfeited labour support after the January 1978 riots. Now a prolonged confrontation between the UGTT and the government began, which, in 1985, resulted in a lengthy prison sentence for the veteran labour leader, Habib Achour, on trumped-up charges, and his replacement at the head of the UGTT by an DSP party hack. Economic policy provided the next arena for discord, when the respected planning minister, Mohammed Moalla, and the finance minister, Abdelaziz Lazram, resigned in a row over proposed consumer subsidy cuts. Basic food prices rose at the start of 1984 when all subsidies on flour and bread were removed—to the accompaniment of countrywide riots.

Although the president annulled the price rises, his premier's authority was virtually destroyed by the crisis. Mzali's remaining credibility was undermined by an attempt to blame the minister of interior, Driss Guiga, for the riots. Although the hapless minister fled abroad, Mzali had, by his action, managed to offend the president's powerful wife, Wassila Bourguiba, who had been patron of both of them. The consequent crisis forced the president to take control of the government and to replace the cabinet by a cabal around the president as the major executive arm of government. Within two years, Mzali himself had fled abroad.

The latter period of Mzali's period of office had seen a new crisis with Libya, when 30,000 Tunisian migrant workers were suddenly expelled in August 1985, and political tensions rose In large measure this was because of Libya's disappointment at being excluded from a new 20-year treaty of fraternity and concord signed between Tunis and Algiers in March 1983. Tunisia had continued to play a moderating role in Arab affairs. In 1980, it became the home for the Arab League after the pan-Arab organisation had moved from Cairo in the wake of Egypt's peace treaty with Israel. In 1982, Tunisia also agreed to accept the PLO leadership after its expulsion from Lebanon but, in October 1985, Tunisia suddenly found itself the victim of an Israeli bombing raid against the Palestinian organisation, an experience was repeated in 1988 when an Israeli commando assassinated a leading PLO official in Tunis.

Bourguiba himself began to behave increasingly irrationally. Rapid changes in government personnel were accompanied by the sudden disgrace of his wife. He also clearly felt that Tunisia's growing fundamentalist movement—itself a consequence of his government's economic failure—was a major threat to stability. As result, government actions

against the major Islamist movement, the Mouvement de Tendence Islamique (MTI), were intensified and its leaders were either arrested or fled
abroad.

By now, however, other members of the government had come to the
conclusion that it was the president himself who was the major threat to
stability. Under the leadership of Premier Ben Ali, Bourguiba was deposed
on 7 November 1987 on the grounds that he was incapable of discharging
his official functions and the prime minister stepped into his shoes. The
changeover in government came in the midst of a major economic crisis, as
Tunisia, in return for IMF support, began finally to remove consumer
subsidies and to restructure its economy.

The new president sought a new political consensus. He liberalised the
political system and tried to persuade political leaders to rally around a
national political charter. He was unable, however, to accept that the
fundamentalist movement should be allowed to join the formal political
arena, even though it reorganised itself as the Nahda party, in accordance
with the government regulations that forbade political parties to adopt
openly religious platforms. The result has been that, although Tunisia has
begun to address its economic problems successfully, the political scene is
almost as stagnant as ever.

Indeed, President Ben Ali has had to rely once again on Tunisia's
sclerotic single political party, now renamed the Democratic Constitutional Grouping (DCG). In recent legislative elections, other opposition
parties were unable, or were prevented by electoral irregularities, to gain
representation and the president is, once again, turning increasingly to his
personal advisers for solutions to the domestic political stagnation. The
danger is, however, that he will himself become isolated from the population and that the mistakes of the latter part of the Bourguiba era will be
repeated.

Algeria

The signing of the Evian Accords on 18 March 1962 marked the end of the
Algerian war of independence but not the beginning of a smooth transition
to independence. Not only did the European *colon* population virtually
disappear over the next six months, while a vicious secret war was fought
out in Algeria and France by the OAS, but the FLN itself was in disarray.
Nonetheless, an economic programme was drawn up in May 1962 during
FLN discussions in Tripoli. The Tripoli Charter, as it was called, proposed
a socialist economic future for independent Algeria and attacked the
wartime provisional government for 'feudalism' a clear reference on the
moderate policies of its leader, Ferhat Abbas.

The political problems of the FLN were more severe, however, for its
membership fell into four distinct factions, which now lined up to contest
the leadership of the victorious movement. In addition to the moderate
provisional government, there were the *vilayet* guerrilla groups inside

Algeria, which had borne the brunt of the war against the French army and felt, thereby, that they were the legitimate FLN leadership, and the leadership of the Armée de Liberation Nationale (ALN), a military force created in Morocco and Tunisia which had not participated in the military struggle because of the French army's successful border campaign to keep it out. Its leadership under Houari Boumedienne now represented a formidable military force. Finally, there was a group of five of the nine *chefs historiques*, the nine original organisers of the FLN. They had been imprisoned in France early in the war but were released to participate in the negotiations over independence.

In the aftermath of the Evian Accords, battle over the leadership was joined. Ben Bella, leader of the *chefs historiques*, obtained the support of Houari Boumedienne and the ALN. The new allies turned, first, against the *vilayet* leaders, whose forces were crushed by the ALN. Then Ben Bella dealt with the provisional government; Ferhat Abbas was forced out of office but Mohammed Khider, the FLN's secretary-general, had an independent power-base. He eventually resigned his post in April 1963 while Ahmed Ben Bella became president of the newly independent state.

Finally, the new Ben Bella–Boumedienne coalition turned on the dissident *chefs historiques*, led by Hoceine Ait Ahmed, Krim Belkacem, Mohammed Boudiaf and Mohand ou el-Hadj. Under the leadership of Ait Ahmed, a native of the Berber stronghold of Kabylia, a rebellion against the central government was organised in 1963. By 1964, however, resistance had been eradicated and the dissident leaders had either been arrested or had fled abroad. A separate rebellion in the Sahara under Colonel Chaabani was also suppressed.

Ahmed Ben Bella was not to enjoy presidential power for long, however, for he was overthrown by an army coup on 19 June 1965 and replaced by his former ally, Houari Boumedienne. One major reason for the coup was the apparent chaos and economic disarray of his period in office. The other was that army leaders suspected that Ben Bella was about to move against them to cut the army's political power. In fact, the chaos in Algerian affairs under Ben Bella merely reflected the condition the country had been left in after eight years of war and the subsequent departure of virtually all its technocratic elite.

The short-term response was workers' self-management. The workforce of the enterprises in agriculture and industry abandoned by their French managers and owners took over control of operations. The movement was initially spontaneous, but the government soon saw its utility and began to take it over. Central control was slowly imposed both to rationalise economic activity and to crush a dangerously anarchic development in the revolution. The price paid, however, was a halt in growth.

Ben Bella's move against the army began when, in late 1964, Mohammed Medeghri, the army-backed minister of the interior, was stripped of his powers over provincial administration. The government that began to

Official name	The Democratic and Popular Republic of Algeria
Area	2,381,741 sq. km (919,595 sq. miles)
Population	25,360,000 (1990)
Capital	Algiers
Language	Arabic and Berber
Religion	Sunni Muslim
Currency	Algerian dinar

seek support from the trade union movement and from the clandestine Algerian communist party (PAGS, or Parti de l'Avant-Garde Socialiste), which, although formally banned, was well represented within the FLN. Other ministers backed by the army were then sacked or demoted. Inevitably, Boumedienne reacted by removing Ben Bella from power with support from the army and from the security services. Ahmed Ben Bella was confined to prison for the next 15 years.

Houari Boumedienne came to power on the promise of the restoration of order and of progress after the sacrifices of the war and the chaos of the Ben Bella period. The new regime soon made its priorities clear: domestic conformity and order, and national social and economic development. In return, Algerians were to obtain basic social services and education, while international respect was to be achieved from a neutralist foreign policy. Oil revenues were to pay for this and for a programme of industrialisation that would lay the foundations for Algeria's future prosperity. The state would direct development through state companies, which would develop the basic sectors of the economy, with heavy industry receiving priority.

The austere future proposed by the Boumedienne regime did little to improve its popularity initially. It was only after the Six Day War, in which the regime took an uncompromising pro-Arab stance, and after French oil interests in Algeria were nationalised in 1971, that a degree of popular support was achieved. The oil and gas nationalisation programme was, needless to say, extremely unpopular in France and clouded relations between the two countries until the latter half of the decade. Algeria justified the move, however, by claiming that it needed complete control of these resources to finance its development plans. Its actions anticipated similar decisions by OPEC in 1973 and ensured that Algeria captured all of the benefits of international energy price rises of 1973–74 and in 1979–80. Boumedienne also increased Algeria's international reputation by his speech to the UN in 1974, in which he called for a new economic relationship between the developed and the developing worlds.

The regime then moved to consolidate its support and to counter growing factionalism in political life. It sought to do this by providing greater democracy in the workplace; limited participation in government; and improved access to land in agriculture. The last objective was to be achieved by an agrarian reform programme which began in 1971. Large landowners had their holdings restricted and land was distributed to the peasantry. The programme, however, turned out to be a failure, largely because of inadequate financing and a failure to reform distribution systems. The result was that urban drift continued unabated and that Algeria continued to import up to 65% of its food.

The political reforms were intended to revive the FLN which, as a result of the factional struggles of the first decade of independence, had become moribund. They were also intended to create a hierarchy of representative assemblies, culminating in an elective National Assembly. Before this was instituted, however, a new political compact between government and populations had to be forged. This was done in 1976 by the promulgation of a National Charter, in which the principles for the next stage of national development were laid down. After extensive public debate, the document was approved by referendum, and National Assembly elections were subsequently held in February 1977.

Within a year, however, the Algerian president died from an unexpected illness and, since the constitutional changes envisaged by the National Charter debate were not fully implemented, the army again became the arbiter of Algeria's political future. Despite a challenge from within the FLN by the incumbent secretary-general, Mohammed Salah Yahyaoui, and from the liberal foreign minister, Abdelaziz Bouteflika, the army imposed its choice as successor, the commander of the Oran military region, Chadli Ben Jedid. His selection was confirmed by a national election in February 1979 and he has since been re-elected in January 1984 and in December 1988.

The new president confronted a complex set of problems. The Algerian economy was riven by inefficiency, particularly in the state sector, which accounted for 70% of the economy. Despite the National Charter, the Algerian population was increasingly disaffected with the austere regimen still in force. New generations had come to maturity who were no longer prepared to delay the benefits of independence and who were not prepared to accept the strict Islamic and Arab cultural character that the regime had defined for Algeria.

The initial official response was to liberalise the economy, particularly in the agricultural sector. In April 1980, however, the government had to face a major crisis when rioting occurred in the Berber stronghold of Kabylia. This, sparked by a clumsy administrative decision to ban cultural events involving Berber languages, spread into a general attack on the regime's cultural and religious policies. The regime's policy of Arabisation—whereby French was to be reduced in favour of Arabic—came under attack because it excluded Algeria's indigenous languages, such as Berber and *darija* (Algerian dialectic Arabic). The official support of Islam was also attacked, as an aspect of the regime's attempt to enforce conformity and because of the implied official support for the growth of Islamic fundamentalism.

By 1984, the regime had to deal with a growing popular disaffection. Cautious political liberalisation—which did not touch the formal institutions of government, however—was partnered by a growing pragmatism in economic affairs. The 90-odd massive state sector companies were split into over 300 autonomous institutions and freed from direct state control. In 1985 the National Charter was revised and liberalised in a further attempt to win popular support.

In foreign affairs, the Chadli Ben Jedid regime tried to follow the example of its predecessor and sought to play a role as an international mediator. It did this successfully in 1981, when it helped end the siege of the American Embassy in Tehran. It also sought, less successfully, to play a mediating role in the Gulf War. Algeria also improved relations with the United States, after the president made the first official visit by an Algerian leader to Washington in May 1985.

In regional affairs, Algeria had to moderate its support for the Polisario Front, engaged in war with Morocco for control of the Western Sahara, seeking a solution through diplomatic means rather than by armed conflict. In fact, Algeria's growing economic weakness has imposed a self-denying ordinance on Algiers in this respect. At the same time, the Chadli Ben Jedid regime attempted to improve its regional role by signing a mutual support treaty with Tunisia in March 1983, which Mauritania joined in the following December. In the past five years, however, Algeria's diplomatic freedom has been severely hampered by its growing economic weakness.

As a result of declining oil prices after 1980, Algeria found increasing difficulty in maintaining its ambitious development plans. Even though natural gas has played an increasingly important part in its export revenues over the past decade, heavy investment in uneconomic gas liquefaction technology, together with too sanguine a view of international gas prices, continued to hamper its ability to maximise revenues. The consequence of this was that, since the government was not prepared to abandon its plans, nor to service its growing foreign debt, which had risen from $14 billion in 1984 to $23 billion in 1989, domestic consumer imports were severely cut back.

In 1986, however, Saudi Arabia's decision to increase production, and thereby to allow oil prices to fall, coupled with a rapid decline in the dollar, produced an 80% shortfall in Algeria's oil revenues—equivalent to around half of its total export revenues. The Algerian government set its face against increasing its foreign debt and, instead, compressed imports. Although its economic management seemed to be successful, social tension was rising dangerously. In October 1988, a wave of strikes exploded into a frenzy of countryside riots and the army had to be brought in to restore control.

Chadli Ben Jedid, shaken by the strength of popular feeling, promised widespread political liberalisation (while also exploiting the situation to remove his opponents within government). The major benefactors of the riots, although they had not been involved in their initial organisation, turned out to be Algeria's growing Islamic fundamentalist movement, the Front Islamique de Salut (FIS). Almost overnight, Algeria was transformed into the most liberal of Arab states and the original single political party, the FLN, lost its privileged status. In addition to the fundamentalists, Berberist groups began to appear and former political exiles returned to the country as constitutional reforms guaranteed a multiparty system in future. Eventually over 40 political parties were recognised by government.

In June 1990, municipal elections were held under the new conditions. Most of the new parties abstained, on the grounds that insufficient time had been provided to prepare for elections. The result was a sweeping victory for the FIS. The FLN was humiliatingly beaten into second place, retaining its hold only in the south and in rural regions. The way appeared to have been cleared for national elections in 1991, but the Hamrouche government, determined to prevent a FIS victory, tried to gerrymander constituency boundaries.

By spring 1991, the FIS had begun to protest, its leaders fearing government attempts to prevent a potential FIS victory in the planned national elections. The protests turned into a trial of strength. The Hamrouche government was forced from office, but the new Ghozali regime had FIS leaders Abbasi Madani and Ali Bel Hadj arrested in June. The army moved into the streets and the FIS was effectively disbanded, although its leadership reformed in time for the legislative elections in December 1991.

In the first round of the electoral process, the FIS won 188 of 430 seats in the National Assembly. Fearing an overall FIS win and the threat of an Islamic republic undermining the secular state created over eight bloody years of warfare, the authorities cancelled the second round. Ben Jedid resigned and a five-man Council of State took control. Some 5000 Islamic fundamentalists were arrested and a state of emergency declared on 10 February, with the leader of the new presidential council, Muhammad Boudiaf, justifying the cancellation of elections because the FIS 'did not seek national unity'.

Morocco

The advent of independence in Morocco was characterised by the fact that the ultimate victor had been given the sultanate. Because it had been supported as a symbol of national legitimacy by the nationalist movement, Istiqlal, it stood at independence as the sole guarantor of the victory that had been achieved. In addition to support from Istiqlal, the sultanate could also call on the loyalty of the traditionalist countryside and much of the population of Morocco's newly expanding cities. Sultan Mohammed V (to become King Mohammed V in 1957 when dynastic succession was based on primogeniture) was determined, however, that there should be no competitors for power in the future and that Istiqlal—which believed that it, too, had a claim to power—should be reminded of its real place in the monarchical scheme of things.

In addition to its new-found legitimacy and potential monopoly of power, the monarchy had several other advantages, which stemmed directly from the changes made during the colonial period. Most importantly, it possessed a modern administration. It also possessed defined territorial boundaries which, since they excluded territory in Algeria that had been traditionally part of Morocco, as well as the Western Sahara that Morocco claimed as part of its pre-colonial territories, could always serve as a rallying call when popular support was required. Indeed, in 1963, Morocco and Algeria fought a six-month border war over their common frontier and there is still a dispute over the Western Sahara. Although the Algerian–Moroccan border was delineated by treaty in 1972, the actual treaty was not ratified until 1989.

The monarchy also had considerable economic power at its disposal. Large sections of the Moroccan economy, as a result of French colonial administration, were in the hands of the state, including the crucial phosphate industry. The independent state would also be interventionist, despite the monarchy's preference for liberal economic theory. The problems it faced were too large for it to take any other course.

Demography was the greatest problem, then as now. The Moroccan population was exploding at 2.7% annually, with the urban population growing even faster. From 15% of the population in 1912, it had grown to be 35% in 1956 and over 45% 30 years later. New cities, such as Casablanca which had hardly existed in 1912, had been created. Casablanca itself, then the second-largest city in Africa, was the new economic capital of Morocco and typified the way in which colonialism had reoriented the country's economy from integration inside the Maghrib towards Europe.

Immediately after independence, the monarchy chose to collaborate with Istiqlal. It was only biding its time, however, and, in 1959, Mohammed V seized on splits within the movement to end its hegemonic control over government. The radicals in Istiqlal, under Mehdi Ben Barka, broke away to form a new party, the Union Nationale des Forces Populaires (UNFP). The palace invited both parties to participate in government, but with the UNFP being given the major governmental posts. At the same time, its radical wing was disciplined by arrests. A year later, the UNFP-dominated government was dismissed.

The new government was dominated by the royal family, with Crown Prince Hassan the new premier. He had long been groomed for government and, in addition to sharing his father's exile in 1953, had been educated in France, at the University of Bordeaux. At independence he had taken over Morocco's armed forces and had played a leading role in suppressing a rebellion in the Rif. He succeeded unexpectedly to government in 1961 when his father died during a minor operation.

King Hassan II made clear that he was anxious to introduce a limited democratic system under royal tutelage through a constitutional monarchy and a limited multiparty political system. The experiment was a failure, however. Parliamentary politicians exploited their positions for personal gain, and the extremist positions adopted by the political parties prevented parliament from carrying out its obligations under the constitution. In November 1963, the UNFP was accused of plotting against the

Official name	Kingdom of Morocco
Area	458,730 sq. km (177,115 sq. miles)
Population	24,500,000
Capital	Rabat
Language	Arabic, Berber
Religion	Sunni Muslim
Currency	dirham

monarchy with help from Algeria and its leaders, including Mehdi Ben Barka, were arrested or fled.

Royal attempts to form a government of national union were frustrated by the refusal of left-wing parties to cooperate and, when riots occurred in Rabat, Fez and Casablanca in March 1965, the king seized the opportunity to suspend the constitution and declare a state of emergency. Over the next five years, government was directly controlled by the palace, aided by a non-political cabinet of ministers. A new constitution was planned and elections were held under it in 1970. The new parliament was one with which the palace could work, for the centre-right parties and independents—in effect, supporters of the monarchy—marginalised the left. However, within ten months this constitutional experiment also collapsed.

The cause was a coup attempt, mounted from within the army, on the summer palace at Skhirat, just outside Rabat, on 10 July 1971, the king's birthday. It was partnered by a simultaneous army attempt to take over government centres in Rabat itself. The coup, which had been masterminded by General Medboh in response to growing evidence of widespread corruption in government, collapsed when the general himself was killed and Hassan was able to restore control over the army. Ten senior officers were executed for their involvement in the plot and many other soldiers were imprisoned (some are still held, according to Amnesty International). The composition of the officer corps, which had been based on Berber groups, was also gradually changed, so that members of the Fassi urban elite, with a stronger tradition of loyalty to the palace, replaced them.

There were also claims that the UNFP had been involved, and party members were put on trial in Marrakesh. The new constitution was again suspended. A non-partisan government was brought in and a new constitution was drafted. Care was taken on this occasion to address the growing social and economic inequalities inside Moroccan society. Once again, however, the process was disrupted by another attempted coup. On 16 August 1972, King Hassan's personal aircraft was attacked by Moroccan air-force fighters. The attempt failed largely because the king persuaded the attacking aircraft by radio that he had been killed in the initial attack.

Once order had been restored, it was discovered that the defence minister and *éminence grise* of the regime, General Oufkir, had organised the attempt, in order, he claimed, to forestall a left-wing coup from within the army. According to official sources, he committed suicide; 11 other officers were later executed. Government sources also claimed that Libya had been involved. A violent war of words subsequently developed between the two countries.

In March 1973 there was new evidence of public disaffection with the Hassan regime. UNFP militants, trained, according to the Moroccan government, by a veteran Ba'thist opponent of the government, 'Fqih' Mohammed Basri, who had fled to Algeria in 1969, infiltrated Morocco and attempted to start a guerrilla campaign. Bombings in Oujda, Nador and

Casablanca were followed by a small revolt at Tinehrir and Goulmima, in the southern High Atlas mountains. The government lost no time in decimating the UNFP by arrests; 13 people were condemned to death for involvement in the plot.

In the wake of the government's wave of repression, the UNFP split, with the new splinter group, led by Abderrahim Bouabid, taking the name Union Socialiste des Forces Populaires (USFP). It has since replaced its predecessor in popular support and the UNFP has dwindled into insignificance. Student protest now appeared and a clandestine pro-Marxist-Leninist opposition formed. Known as the Front Progressiste (FP), it brought together three left-wing groups: the March 23 Movement; al-Alam; and al-Mutaqatilun. Government repression soon dismantled the groups and leading intellectuals began to populate Morocco s prisons.

The trials of the FP coincided with a new development in Morocco's already complicated political scene. This was the government's decision, in 1974, to make the integration of the Western Sahara into Morocco a national priority. The government's claim to the Western Sahara, then still under Spanish control, was based on arguments that it had been part of the pre-colonial Moroccan state and thus could be recovered legally without a referendum over self-determination. Spain had been most reluctant to accept this, even though the Franco government had been under considerable pressure to abandon its last African colony.

In mid-1974, Spain announced that it was prepared to put the issue of decolonisation to a referendum in the Western Sahara, largely as a result of military pressure from the newly founded national liberation movement, the Polisario Front. Morocco, in turn, insisted that the matter be placed before the International Court of Justice at The Hague. The court's judgment, handed down in October 1975, satisfied no-one. It accepted that there had been links with Morocco in pre-colonial days, but decided that these did not amount to sovereignty. Morocco, nonetheless, occupied the region; Spain, by then gripped by the succession crisis as Franco lay dying, acquiesced under protest.

By early November 1975, Morocco was tied into a major military commitment, as the Polisario Front shepherded thousands of Western Saharans into refugee camps around the Algerian border town of Tindouf and then began a widespread guerrilla campaign, with Algerian and Libyan support, to force Morocco out. Mauritania, which had occupied the southern part of the territory, was forced out in 1979, whereupon Morocco took over the former Mauritanian claim. Nonetheless, until 1980, Morocco was seriously disadvantaged by Polisario guerrilla activity. Thereafter, however, a new strategy of fixed defences enabled the Moroccan army, by then 180,000-strong, of which two-thirds were deployed in the Sahara, to re-assert control over 80% of the territory.

Morocco has suffered in diplomatic and economic terms from the conflict. In 1982, it precipitately withdrew from the Organisation of African

Unity, when that organisation recognised the Polisario Front as a national liberation movement. The Moroccan boycott lasted until 1986, when it finally accepted the principle of a referendum for self-determination in the disputed territory. At the same time, King Hassan knows that neither the Moroccan army nor the population of Morocco would tolerate any abandoning of the territory and it is therefore likely that a referendum will only be held when Morocco is certain of success.

The Western Saharan operation has also been an expensive undertaking, with the war costing an estimated $1 million a day. Much of the cost has, however, been borne by friendly Gulf states. Morocco has, nevertheless, had to spend heavily on arms, around $250 million annually. Considerable sums have also been expended on improving the infrastructure of the Sahara, an operation estimated in 1988 at $1 billion. There has also been significant migration into the region, which depends entirely on southern Morocco for essential supplies. Of the 170,000-strong population, up to 90,000 are believed to have come from Morocco itself. There are also around 170,000 refugees in the camps around Tindouf, although many of them are believed to come from other parts of the Sahara.

The Western Sahara issue did create a degree of consensus within Morocco in support for the monarchy, not least because the political parties were bought off by a promise of renewed democratic activity. Indeed, since 1976, there have been elections every six years and the Chamber of Representatives has been allowed a limited executive role. It cannot question basic economic policy, the role of the palace in government, or the basic policy towards the Western Sahara issue. Yet, outside these limits and as a result of parallel measures to decentralise the administration, Morocco has enjoyed relative political calm.

The result has been that since the mid-1980s there have been no further attempts to overthrow Hassan. Morocco has still had to weather severe problems, however. Many of these are economic in origin, for, in 1975, Morocco attempted to exploit its quasi-monopoly over world phosphate exports to quadruple international phosphate prices. The enlarged revenues were to pay for ambitious development plans. Unfortunately, Florida phosphate producers increased output dramatically, forcing prices down to their previous levels. Since then, phosphate prices have been stagnant.

The Moroccan government, faced by the collapse of its export revenues, gambled. It did not cut its development plans but instead borrowed the required funds, on the assumption that, by the time the loans had to be repaid, improved output as a result of development would enable the additional revenue to be raised. By 1983, it was clear that the experiment had failed and Morocco was forced to reschedule its $11 billion-worth of foreign debt in September of that year. The Moroccan government then gambled again, agreeing to accept IMF and World Bank requirements for economic restructuring and reform: the removal of consumer price subsidies, export-oriented growth, trade regime liberalisation, and the reduction of public sector expenditure through privatisation.

Although Morocco's debt has continued to rise and is now around $22 billion, the economic restructuring is considered by international organisations to have been a success. The privatisation programme is in full swing and Morocco benefits from the provisions for debt relief in the Brady Plan. The reforms have not been without economic cost, however. In January 1984, as consumer subsidies were cut, there were country-wide riots involving over 100 deaths. The riots were not as intense as riots in Casablanca in June 1981 over economic hardship, which developed out of a political confrontation between two trade union organisations and led to over 630 deaths in a single afternoon. Nonetheless, they were a salutary warning to the government of the limits of popular tolerance; the subsidies were partly restored in consequence. Tensions still run high, however, and new rioting occurred in Fez in December 1990.

Despite these tensions, however, Morocco has been spared the kind of intense Islamic fundamentalism which has characterised Tunisia and Algeria. In part, this is because the king himself, through his claim to direct descent from the Prophet Mohammed, monopolises the sphere of religious legitimacy. It is also the case, however, that the Moroccan government has been skilful at diffusing socio-political tension through effective security monitoring and judicious use of the courts to stamp out religious protest. Nonetheless, there is a growing public fundamentalist movement, partnered by a violent clandestine wing, and observers fear that this may become a serious problem.

In foreign affairs, Morocco has astutely ensured the support of the West throughout the 1980s. It has been prepared to provide facilities for United States strategic military planners concerned over rapid deployment facilities to the Gulf. Furthermore, King Hassan has been only the second Arab leader after the late President Sadat formally to meet Israeli leaders. In summer 1986, the then Israeli premier, Shimon Peres, visited Morocco and was received by King Hassan. Nothing came of the visit, because of Israeli reluctance to compromise over the Palestinian issue. Nonetheless, the king's willingness to break ranks caused considerable anxiety elsewhere in the Arab world.

Nowhere was that anxiety greater than in Libya, where Colonel Qadhafi seized on the news of the king's initiative to attack Morocco for the first time in two years. His attack allowed King Hassan to break off a formal relationship with Libya which had become an embarrassment. In 1984, Morocco and Libya, in a riposte to the Algerian–Tunisian treaty of concord and fraternity signed the previous year, proclaimed their own 'African–Arab Union'. The arrangement quickly served Morocco's purpose of detaching Libya from its support for the Polisario Front in the Western Sahara dispute and of demonstrating to Algeria that Morocco was still its most potent adversary in the Maghrib. The Libyan condemnation in 1986 provided the ideal opportunity to break off a relationship which had served its purpose.

The Maghrib today

The general tendency towards relative political stability has been intensified in recent years by the creation of the Arab Maghrib Union, better known under its French acronym as the UMA. This is a customs union, with objectives of political and economic integration, created in February 1989. The agreement has already enabled trade between Morocco and Algeria to increase dramatically and has helped to diffuse remaining tensions over the Western Sahara issue.

The real objective of the UMA, in the short term at least, has been to provide a forum for unifying policy towards Europe and the EC. North African states are acutely anxious over the implications of the Single European Market in 1993 and over growing European antagonism towards labour migration. They also fear that the full integration of Spain and Portugal into the EC in 1995 will have a devastating effect on Tunisian and Moroccan agriculture. The UMA, therefore, is both an attempt to find an indigenous solution to the region's economic problems and a structure designed to provide a unified platform for negotiations with the EC in the future.

The Maghrib continues to be worried by recent political developments in the European arena. The collapse of communism in Eastern Europe and the Soviet Union, while good news to all—except, perhaps, Algeria—also carries worrying undertones. The Maghrib fears that it will be the great loser in these events. European investment is already travelling eastward, European labour will in future be satisfied by Eastern Europe and European agricultural needs—where they are not already satisfied by Spain and Portugal—will now be satisfied from the East.

These anxieties have been heightened by the realisation that the region is now of marginal strategic interest to the West. The success of the US-led coalition against Iraq's occupation of Kuwait in 1990–91 made little use of North African strategic military facilities. Furthermore, with the departure of the Soviet Union from its former role as a balancing superpower, North Africa no longer has a wider strategic role either.

In any case, Western attention has been drawn away from the region because of what is seen in Western governmental circles as an adverse series of reactions towards the conflict in the Gulf. It is a fact that Maghribi populations were virtually unanimous in their opposition to military action against Iraq. Although government attitudes varied, from initial Moroccan enthusiasm for the proposed coalition's intervention (later toned down when the Moroccan government appreciated the tenor of Moroccan public opinion) to chilly Algerian neutrality and Tunisian protest, popular local reaction was greeted with outraged disbelief by the Arab Gulf states and the West. It will take the Maghrib some considerable time to restore the trust that has been lost.

George Joffé

10 THE PALESTINIANS

There are over four million Palestinians living around and outside the Arab world. Less than half live on the land to which they lay claim, and they live under Israeli rule. More than two million live in the Arab world or beyond. Many of these exiles are stateless, carrying only refugee papers, while others carry passports from their host countries. Their plight has been a major source of conflict in the Middle East since 1948, although the problem has its roots in the 19th century. However politically and physically divided they may be, most Palestinians today feel a common sense of identity based on dispossession.

The immediate result of Israel's victory in 1949 for the Palestinians was exile. Though some members of the educated middle and upper classes managed to establish themselves in cities like Beirut and Amman, for the vast majority of mainly impoverished refugees, life in refugee camps run by the United Nations Relief and Works Agency (UNRWA) was bleak. With little or no access to land, there were few opportunities for employment for the majority, who had been peasants. UNRWA did, however, provide primary education for registered refugees, and over the generations this has laid the basis for a relatively well-educated population.

The conditions of exile for the Palestinians varied. The Arab host countries were generally poor, and unprepared economically and politically for the influx, which seemed likely to threaten the often fragile stability of their regimes. In Syria, which has the smallest number of refugees, they were not granted citizenship, though they were accorded many of the same rights to social benefits and employment as nationals, while being kept under tight political control. Jordan, with the largest concentration of refugees, gave passports and citizenship to the refugees but social assistance was limited and, after the early 1950s, political restrictions were imposed. In the Gaza Strip, Palestinians under Egyptian rule had no citizenship or political rights, and employment opportunities were very limited. In Lebanon, refugees' efforts to find employment were frustrated by the difficulty of obtaining work permits and by travel restrictions. Furthermore, until the PLO effectively took over control of the camps in the early 1970s, the Lebanese security services maintained strict surveillance over the camp dwellers, severely restricting their political activities. By the 1960s, the demand for labour and skills in the newly oil-rich states of the Gulf drew many Palestinians to Kuwait, Saudi Arabia and Iraq. Some prospered, eventually becoming professionals, civil servants or wealthy businessmen, but they have generally remained without the security of citizens' rights and cannot even own property.

The revival of Palestinian nationalism

Despite the variety of the Palestinians' experiences, all have suffered the profound insecurity of a people without a national identity. In the early years after 'the Catastrophe' many Palestinians hoped that the international community would come to their aid and restore their national and natural rights. However, the most that they were offered were a variety of resettlement schemes, which they strenuously resisted, preferring to remain refugees than to give up all claim to their homes. Their only other hope was that the Arab states would resolve the problem, whether by force or diplomacy. In the prevailing climate of Arab nationalism of the 1950s and 1960s, the liberation of Palestine became a rhetorical touchstone of Arab unity for both Nasserists and Ba'thists—yet it brought the Palestinians no closer to a solution to their problems. Individual Arab states, while remaining hostile to Israel, were suspicious of any signs of independent political activity on the part of the Palestinians in their midst.

Eventually, the educated younger generation of Palestinians in exile began to take a more active role in resolving their future. Opinions were divided on what strategy to follow. In the early 1960s, many still believed in the Arab nationalist ideal and saw the restoration of their homeland taking place within the broader framework of the unification of the Arab world, chiefly under the leadership of Egypt's President Nasser, who, after the immeasurable boost provided to his own position and to the self-confidence of the Arabs in general by the bungled efforts of Britain and France to retake the newly nationalised Suez Canal in 1956, pledged himself to sweep all traces of Zionism, imperialism and the forces of reaction from the region. Others, seeing the increasingly diverse interests of the Arab states took the view that Palestinians, too, should focus on their own specific national interests. It was in this context that the PLO emerged.

The development of the PLO embodies contradictory political and ideological pressures: the different strategies advocated by Palestinians themselves and the desire of the various Arab states to exercise control over the stateless Palestinians and their organisations. The PLO was initially established in 1964 under the auspices of the Arab League by a decision taken at the first Arab summit conference in Cairo. It was essentially Nasser's creation, an organisation through which he could control the Palestinians.

The PLO was not the first Palestinian grouping, however. In 1959 another Palestinian organisation, Fatah, had been founded by a group of Palestinians in Kuwait. These included Yasir Arafat, Khalid al-Hasan, Salah Khalaf, Khalil al-Wazir and Faruq Qaddumi (all of whom would later become senior figures in the PLO). They espoused a more specifically

Palestinian brand of nationalism, which stressed the need for Palestinians to struggle for the liberation of their country themselves, without necessarily giving priority to the goal of Arab unity. Influenced by the struggles of the Front de Libération Nationale (FLN) against French colonial rule in Algeria, and by other anti-colonial nationalist struggles, Fatah advocated the principle of armed resistance while at the same time arguing for non-interference in the internal politics of the Arab states in which it was based.

The adherents of Fatah distanced themselves from the 'official' PLO and its chairman Ahmed Shuqairi, and in 1965 Fatah's military wing, al-Asifa, began to launch guerrilla attacks against Israel. For the most part the attacks had limited military success, but the raids added to the already tense situation on Israel's border with Syria. In 1965 and 1966, Fatah's activities, supported by Syria in order to counterbalance Egypt's support for the official PLO, contributed to an escalation of border incidents, leading up to the Six Day War.

Though the scale of the Arab defeat in the war shocked the Arab world, it was necessarily a particularly heavy blow to the Palestinians, with over a million more Palestinians—in the West Bank, the Gaza Strip and East Jerusalem—coming under Israeli rule. The swiftness of the defeat and its emphatic demonstration of Israeli military superiority also undermined the widely held Arab nationalist view that the liberation of Palestine would be achieved by military victory. In consequence, Fatah began to step up its armed struggle against Israel from its bases in Jordan. In the immediate aftermath of the war, it was hoped that internal resistance in the Occupied Territories would escalate the armed struggle on Palestinian soil. But when Arafat entered the West Bank clandestinely in late 1967 he found little support for armed action, largely because the inhabitants of the West Bank still assumed that international pressure would force the Israelis to withdraw. Furthermore, when the nationalist forces did begin to regroup, the Israelis used captured Jordanian security service files to identify and jail or deport many leading nationalist figures. Only in the Gaza Strip did the Israelis meet sustained resistance, and this was harshly suppressed by the end of 1970.

Between 1968 and 1970 both Fatah and other Palestinian groups, including the Popular Front for the Liberation of Palestine (PFLP, formed in 1967) led by George Habash, and Na'if Hawatmeh's Popular Democratic Front for the Liberation of Palestine (PDFLP, later the DFLP, formed in 1969) based their operations in the Jordanian capital, Amman. In contrast to Fatah, these groups had emerged from the pan-Arabist movement and were Marxist in outlook. The liberation of Palestine, they maintained, could occur only when reactionary Arab regimes elsewhere in the region had been overthrown.

Support for all the groups, particularly Fatah, grew rapidly. Volunteers flocked to the cause, especially from among the refugee camp populations, who saw armed struggle as the only means by which the humiliating defeat of 1967 could be redeemed and Israeli gains reversed. The armed groups increasingly gained influence at the expense of the ineffectual and now largely discredited 'official' PLO. After Shuqairi's resignation in 1968, Fatah became the dominant group within the PLO, and at the Fifth Palestine National Council meeting in 1969 Yasir Arafat became PLO chairman as well as leader of Fatah.

The structure of PLO decision-making

The Palestine National Council (PNC), the Palestinian parliament in exile, is a hybrid organisation, reflecting ambiguities and constraints inherent in the Palestinians' overall situation. Cumbersome to assemble, it has met only 20 times since the founding of the PLO. It takes major policy decisions but has little influence on the day-to-day conduct of PLO affairs, which are controlled mainly by the central committee. The PNC reflects the wide range of opinion within the Palestinian community, and includes representatives from all the Palestinian political and military organisations (except where a group has temporarily withdrawn because of disagreements with the mainstream): the 'mass' organisations (for example, trade unions and women's organizations, which generally owe allegiance to one of the political groups); refugee camp populations; and so-called 'independents' from Palestinian communities in the Arab world and beyond. Least well represented are the 'occupied lands'—the West Bank, the Gaza Strip and Palestinians who are Israeli citizens. They are not included in the PNC quorum since Israeli restrictions rarely make it possible for their representatives to attend, unless they have already been deported from Israel. Each group is allocated a fixed quota of members and votes. Although there is frequent dissent, Fatah and its allies have usually managed to carry the day. Similarly, Fatah carries the most weight in the central committee, though has at times had to compromise with other groups.

Both the strength and weakness of the PLO, and of Fatah as its dominant element, have stemmed from its flexibility and its pragmatic approach to ideological questions, characteristics its opponents claim as deliberate obscurantism and opportunism, but which, equally, have prevented lasting splits from developing. Until the end of the 1980s, no other Palestinian grouping successfully challenged the hegemony of the PLO, or of Fatah within it, and only a few groups have permanently disassociated themselves from it—the dissident Abu Nidal faction being perhaps the prime example. Since the 1970s, the majority of Palestinians have regarded the PLO as their legitimate representative, whatever their criticisms of its leadership, of its internal politics, and of particular groups within it.

The PLO has survived a large number of crises and disasters since its inception: the Six Day War; the bloody expulsion from Jordan (Black September); the civil war in Lebanon; the Israeli invasion of Lebanon; the expulsion from Lebanon and the consequent split in Fatah's ranks; and the Israeli bombing of the PLO's Tunis headquarters. The full consequence of the PLO's controversial decision to support Saddam Husain in the Gulf War has yet to become clear, though it seems reasonable to suppose that this, too, will in due course add to the organisation's difficulties. But it has enjoyed a number of triumphs, too, carrying off some significant diplomatic coups: for example, Arafat's address to the UN in 1974, and the announcement in 1988 of a Palestinian state 'in exile' and the recognition of Israel.

Nevertheless, while it has achieved recognition in the Arab world and the UN as the 'sole legitimate representative of the Palestinian people', the PLO has never entirely enjoyed the support of the West. The 'terrorist' label, regularly applied to it by Israelis, has been generally accepted in Europe and the United States, at least until the mid-1980s. Certainly the 'armed struggle' has at times been little more than an excuse for generally futile attacks on civilians. The widening of targets from the direct enemy—Israel—to Israeli and United States-linked targets worldwide, entailing bombings, hijackings and shootings, often in countries not connected with the conflict, has done little to help the Palestine cause in the wider world. Though the majority of these actions have been carried out by the small radical splinter factions—Abu Nidal notoriously—often in collaboration with other Arab intelligence services, all Palestinian groups have used these tactics at some time. However, the mainstream of the PLO has increasingly come to see terrorism as counterproductive, and indeed in 1988 publicly renounced its use. In 1987 the uprising or *intifada* in the Occupied Territories presented a new model of civil resistance, one which has favourably altered the image of Palestinian resistance in the eyes of the world.

Relations with the Arab states

With no secure territorial base, to a considerable extent the nature of the PLO's confrontation with Israel has been determined by its relations with the rest of the Arab world, whether as financial backers or as hosts to the PLO and Palestinian communities. It is a relationship that has been fraught with difficulties. As an organisation the PLO has needed funds and a base for its political and military operations. At the same time, the mass of the Palestinians in exile have naturally needed at least some degree of stability in their daily lives: some assurance of basic civil rights and the opportunity to make a living. These goals have not always proved compatible. Though the PLO and its constituent organisations have received funds and arms from a number of sources, including at various times the Soviet Union and China, the bulk of its finances has been provided by Arab states. However, the particular states from which the funds have come, and the particular groups to which the funds have been channelled, have depended on the state of relations with the PLO at the time. Syria and Saudi Arabia have been major backers, Syria funding both Fatah and the more radical groups, Saudi Arabia, at least until 1990, when the PLO declared its support for

Saddam Husain, supporting Fatah. Similarly, until 1990 the Kuwait government collected a tax amounting to 5% of resident Palestinians' salaries
and channelled it to the PLO. Libya has generally funded 'Rejection Front'
groups rather than Fatah, while Iraq has funded both dissident groups and
Fatah. In all cases, however, the provision of funds was made with the
specific intention of controlling the policies of the various Palestinian
organisations. However much individual Arab states may proclaim their
support for the Palestinian cause, the presence on their soil of substantial
armed Palestinian groups—in effect, miniature armies answerable not to
them but to the PLO—has necessarily been a cause of some anxiety to
them. The need to control them has therefore been paramount.

The resulting tension between the PLO and its backers has about it an
air of inevitability. These difficulties have been increased by the disparate
nature of the PLO. For example, while Fatah has taken the view that the
PLO should not involve itself with the internal politics of its host states,
other elements of the organisation, notably the DFLP and the PFLP, have
taken an entirely different line. As revolutionary movements, they have
argued not just for the overthrow of Israel but of the governments of many
Arab states, too, including those in which they are based, on the grounds
of what they see as their conservative pro-Western stances. Furthermore,
the presence of armed Palestinian groups, particularly in Lebanon and
Jordan, has inevitably invited Israeli military retaliation, often on a massive
scale, in which the local population has suffered almost as much as the
Palestinians. This, too, is a development not best calculated to endear
either those directly affected or their governments to the PLO.

Confrontation in Jordan and Lebanon

The contentious nature of this relationship first became clear in Jordan
between 1967 and 1971. With Palestinian guerrilla organisations sniping at
Israel from bases in Jordan, Jordan found itself being sucked into further
conflict with Israel. At the same time, the growing strength and autonomy
of the Palestinian movement began to present a challenge to the Jordanian
regime. The more radical Palestinian groups made the challenge quite
explicit, demanding the overthrow of King Husain. In September 1970,
'Black September' to the Palestinians, a full-scale conflict broke out between the Jordanian army and the Palestinian armed organisations and
their supporters. As the Palestinian fighters were driven northwards out of
Amman, Syrian tanks crossed the border into Jordan, apparently in
support of the Palestinians. However, with no air cover, they were
helpless to challenge the Jordanian forces. Iraqi units, still stationed in
Jordan after the Six Day War, made no move to help the Palestinians.

After 1970, the focus of PLO military and political activity accordingly
shifted to Lebanon. Lebanese relations with the PLO organisations had
been regulated by the 1969 Cairo agreements, which confined the PLO's
military activities to an area close to the Israeli border. However, the

weakness of the Lebanese army, and indeed of the Lebanese state generally, left the PLO considerable latitude. Its forces were based in and around
the refugee camps on the outskirts of Beirut and in Tripoli in the north, as
well as along the Israeli border in the south. The role of the PLO became
threefold: first, to bring the refugee camps under its protection and
control; second, to operate as a political and military organisation in the
Lebanese area; third, to mount attacks on Israel across the Lebanese
border.

The PLO was able to do much to help those in the refugee camps,
ending the restrictions imposed by the Lebanese security services, providing social services and financial support and strengthening the refugees'
sense of national and cultural identity. At the same time, as a political and
military force, it incurred the hostility of influential and important sections
of Lebanese society, especially among the politically dominant Maronites,
who argued that the Palestinians were creating 'a state within a state' and
were undermining Lebanese sovereignty as well as exposing Lebanese
civilians in the south to Israeli retaliatory actions. At the same time, the
presence of the PLO tended to exacerbate the already fragmented nature of
Lebanon. The more disadvantaged elements of Lebanese society quickly
came to regard the PLO as potential allies against the Maronites. When the
tensions that had long existed in Lebanon erupted into a full-scale civil war
in 1975, the PLO was rapidly drawn into the conflict on the side of the
Lebanese National Movement (LNM), a coalition of largely Muslim and
leftist forces, against the Maronite-dominated Lebanese Forces. The PLO
survived both the 1975–76 fighting and the Syrian intervention against the
LNM in 1976. In fact, despite defeat by the Syrians, the PLO's power in the
region south of Beirut increased, with its armed forces exercising virtual
hegemony in some areas. Nonetheless, many contend that the period
between 1976 and 1982 gave rise to miscalculations, mistakes and insensitivity on the part of the PLO leadership, the results of which were
deteriorating relations with its allies, particularly those in the Shia movement, Amal, and with the Lebanese civilian population. What seems less
contentious is that the Lebanese period also saw the Palestinian organisations transformed from the groups of *fida'i* (guerrilla fighters) of the 1960s
to an army, or at any rate a series of armies, defending fixed positions
around the refugee camps. Parallel developments saw the Palestine National Fund, established in 1964, evolve into something akin to a centralised treasury, and the setting up of health and social services by a
variety of PLO organisations. The PLO and its offshoots, in other words,
were becoming more and more like a modern state government, though
with no accepted or secure territorial base. The result, paradoxically, was
to make both its military and civilian components more cumbersome and
vulnerable to attack.

During the late 1970s the PLO's confrontation with Israel also intensified, with cross-border PLO attacks answered by frequent Israeli air-raids

on southern Lebanon. In 1978 the first Israeli invasion of southern Lebanon resulted in the establishment of the Israeli-backed South Lebanese Army (SLA) in a buffer zone north of the Israeli border. A UN force was later stationed north of the SLA in an effort to maintain the subsequent cease-fire. The cease-fire itself produced splits in the PLO, with Fatah agreeing to it, and more hard-line elements opposing it, the dissidents going so far as to launch a campaign of assassinations of Fatah officials in Europe. In 1980–81 the Israelis intensified their attacks on the PLO in Lebanon and in 1981 clashed with the Syrians when the latter moved SAM missiles to the Bekaa valley. A further cease-fire, negotiated by the United States, was agreed and was to last, with only relatively minor breaches, until the full-scale Israeli invasion of Lebanon in June 1982.

The Israelis' goal in 1982 was to destroy the PLO, both politically and militarily, and to drive its remnants out of Lebanon, in the process, they hoped, undermining political resistance among the Palestinians in the Occupied Territories. Besieged by the Israelis, the PLO duly found itself with little option but to withdraw. This they did under terms negotiated with Philip Habib, American special presidential envoy. Their safe departure and the subsequent safety of the Palestinian civilian population, which had necessarily remained in Beirut, was guaranteed by a multinational peace-keeping force. In fact, after the PLO left Beirut, the peace-keeping force also withdrew. In its wake, and using the assassination of Maronite President Bashir Gemayel as a pretext, Israeli forces then entered West Beirut. While they controlled the city, militias associated with the Lebanese Forces and other Christian groups entered the refugee camps at Sabra and Chatila, and in the course of two days massacred some 1,000 civilians, mostly Palestinians.

The impact of these events on the Palestinians was profound. For one thing, the PLO leadership in its war headquarters in Tunis was sundered from its own communities. These in turn, especially those still in Lebanon, were left vulnerable and undefended. As important, a major split developed within the ranks of Fatah, upon which the Syrians, increasingly estranged from Yasir Arafat and the Fatah mainstream, rapidly capitalised. This led to fierce inter-Palestinian fighting in 1983 in the northern Lebanese city of Tripoli, where a handful of the PLO remained, and the final expulsion of Palestinian fighters from Lebanon. The rift seriously damaged the movement throughout the 1980s, compounding a power struggle with Syria with genuine popular discontents and grievances against the PLO leadership. Though the PLO leadership has never returned to Lebanon, many PLO fighters nonetheless returned to their old bases in the Lebanese camps where they duly became involved in bitter internecine struggles between the Syrian-backed dissidents and the mainstream PLO forces for control of the camps. The Palestinians joined forces to fight off their former allies, Amal. Again, fearful of resurgent PLO influence in Lebanon, the Syrians backed Amal.

In 1985–86, in the face of continuing Syrian hostility, Arafat turned back to Jordan as an ally in an attempt to open up a dialogue with the United States. The PLO re-established its political presence in Amman, but after two years attempts to start negotiations with Israel on the basis of a joint Palestinian–Jordanian delegation foundered on splits within both the Israeli government and the PLO.

The nature of Palestinian demands

Behind all these events lies the question as to how the 'Palestine question' can be solved. Clearly this cannot be fully answered without also examining the Israeli viewpoint. However, even for the Palestinian nationalist movement there have been significant difficulties in defining goals. Palestinians often point out, for example, that while the Israelis have a Law of Return which allows every Jew the right to live in Israel, no such provision is open to them. Even if it was, however, many questions remain. What should be the nature of any return? Should the Palestinians be able to return to the towns and villages they lived in before 1948 and long since taken over by Israelis? Or should they have as a goal only a general return to Palestine? In either case, what would happen to the Israelis—whether long-standing inhabitants or recent immigrants? How could the 'Jewish State' be transformed into one in which both Jews *and* Palestinian Arabs, whether Christian or Muslim, could live as political equals?

In the years since the foundation of the state of Israel in 1948, the answers to these questions have necessarily evolved to accommodate changing political and military realities. In the 1950s and early 1960s, for example, there was little thought of coexistence with the inhabitants of Israel. It was widely assumed that Arab military powers would prove irresistible and that the liberation of Palestine would automatically follow the Nasser-inspired drive for Arab unity. The Jews would be 'driven into the sea'. In the mid-1960s, after the establishment of the PLO, the goal was a 'return to all of Palestine'. The Palestine National Charter, the founding document of the PLO, embodied this view and asserted that 'Jews who are of Palestinian origin will be considered Palestinians if they undertake to live loyally and peacefully in Palestine'. This was amended in 1968 to 'Jews who were living permanently in Palestine until the beginning of the Zionist invasion will be considered Palestinians', i.e. only those Jews resident *before* the British Mandate period, which, by 1968, meant a mere and extremely elderly fraction of the total population of Israelis.

As others have pointed out, the whole debate about relations in a future Palestinian state between Arab Palestinians and the present citizens of Israel is in any case complicated by the fact that no clear definition can exist in advance of the nature and character of a Palestinian state. Defining who should qualify for citizenship in a hypothetical state is necessarily difficult. This ambiguity became more evident with the proposal at the end of the 1960s for a non-sectarian and democratic state in the whole of Palestine.

Though the existing Jewish population would be accommodated in this putative state, whether there should be a two-tier system of citizenship determined by religion (Jews and non-Jews) or on some other definition of 'nationality' remained unclear.

All such niceties were rendered academic with the Israeli occupation of the West Bank and Gaza Strip in 1967; hopes of an imminent return to 'all of Palestine' perished almost overnight. Instead, the notion of a 'mini-state' on some part of Palestinian land, most likely the territories occupied in 1967, emerged, an idea particularly favoured by Palestinians living in the Occupied Territories. UN Resolution 242, passed after the Six Day War, called for Israeli withdrawal from 'territories occupied in the recent conflict' and for the acknowledgement of the right of all states in the region to live in peace and security. The Israeli accepted the resolution without acknowledging that it required them to withdraw from all territories occupied. The PLO, meanwhile, rejected it out of hand because it did not acknowledge the Palestinians' right to a homeland but called only for a 'just settlement of the refugee problem'. Furthermore, acceptance of the resolution was taken as tantamount to recognition of Israel. After the 1973 October War had failed to dislodge the Israelis from the Occupied Territories, this position was adopted officially by Fatah and the DFLP. Implying a willingness to engage in political negotiations with Israel, however, it was opposed by the PFLP and other radical groups—the so-called Rejection Front—who argued instead for a continuation of the armed struggle and no political negotiations based on territorial concessions.

In the early 1970s, the UN recognised the 'inalienable right' of the Palestinians to a homeland and accepted the PLO as 'the sole legitimate representative of the Palestinian people'. In 1974 Arafat addressed the UN. His speech proclaimed a double-edged strategy, 'the gun and the olive branch'. The door was to be left ajar for negotiations on a Palestinian homeland, but the armed struggle would remain an option.

Plans for peace

The Camp David Agreement, negotiated by President Sadat of Egypt and Prime Minister Begin of Israel in 1978, and proposing only 'autonomy' for the Palestinians in the Occupied Territories, united the Palestinians in opposition to them, indeed turned Egypt, historically the most important supporter of the Palestinians, into an enemy scarcely less vilified than Israel. The rejection was all the more unanimous because the autonomy plan, as interpreted by the Begin government, allowed the growing number of Jewish settlers to remain in the Occupied Territories; autonomy was to be restricted to 'people and not land'; it was scarcely equivalent to local self-government.

The peace plans put forward during the 1980s were based either on the idea of a mini-state or of autonomy. In the view of the Palestine National Council (PNC), that proposed by the Fez Summit in 1982 and recognising the Palestinians' right to a homeland represented the minimum basis for 'political moves by the Arab states'. In fact the PNC continued to suggest that military action was still required 'to adjust the balance in favour of Palestinian and Arab rights'. The Reagan Plan, put forward in the same period, was based on the possible confederation with Jordan. The idea of confederation was raised again during the mainstream PLO's brief reconciliation with Jordan in the mid-1980s.

Although some research has been done on the question of the economic viability of a Palestinian state in the West Bank and Gaza Strip, a solution has never been near enough at hand to warrant either close consideration of how it would work, or how many and which Palestinians might return to live in such a state. Indeed, the social and political nature of any future Palestinian state has been little addressed. On this as on other issues Fatah has remained ambiguous, partly to allow consensus, partly because, on the whole, the leadership has tended to favour existing social structures and to emphasise 'traditional values', which it sees as especially important in maintaining the Palestinian identity in exile. Generally speaking, the PLO employs a mixture of secular political language and religious rhetoric to evoke notions of national struggle and renewal. The term *thawra* (revolution) refers generally to a national rather than to a social revolution.

A more immediate question, interwoven with debates on the nature of a future 'Palestine' and relations with the Israeli population, has been the issue of mutual recognition. In the 1970s, the Israelis still refused to accept that a 'Palestinian people' separate from other Arabs existed. Since that time the existence of the Palestinians has been fairly widely acknowledged by Israel, though successive governments have consistently refused to recognise the PLO. Generally speaking, both the United States and Israel have conceived of peace negotiations with Arab governments taking place on a bilateral basis. This was the goal of Kissinger's 'step-by-step' diplomacy of the 1970s and was still the underlying principle of the 1991 Baker initiative. In the mid-1980s, the increasing political significance of the Occupied Territories led to unsuccessful attempts by the United States and Israel to find 'representative' Palestinians from the territories to form part of a joint Palestinian–Jordanian delegation in which the PLO had no acknowledged role. Even despite the unprecedented spirit of compromise engineered by the United States in mid-1991, the prospect for peace remain jeopardised by Israel's continuing refusal to deal with the PLO, or indeed to admit them as representatives of the Palestinians at all.

In the 1970s and 1980s, Jordan was regarded as an important player in any peace negotiations. Israeli Labour politicians had long favoured a settlement with Jordan in which the Palestinians of the West Bank were returned to Jordanian tutelage, with some redrawing of territorial boundaries to accommodate Israeli security needs. On the Israeli right wing the old idea was mooted once more that Jordan (in other words, the East Bank) *was* the Palestinian state. The most radical version of this view implied that

Palestinians within 'Greater Israel', including those living in the West Bank, should be removed to Jordan. Since 1988, Jordan's decision to withdraw from involvement in the affairs of the West Bank in the wake of the *intifada*, and the impact of the Gulf War (see below), have tended to diminish the Jordanian role. Since 1982 the lack of consensus within Israeli governments has further complicated the question of a peace settlement, since the various Likud–Labour coalitions and the fragile Likud-dominated coalition of the early 1990s have been consistently unable to agree a consensus among themselves as to what strategy to follow over possible terms for peace.

On the Palestinian side, the recognition of Israel's right to exist was in some ways implicit once the possibility of a two-state solution was accepted. However, formal recognition was considered a bargaining counter not to be given up until concessions had been made by the Israelis in turn, specifically withdrawal from the territories occupied in 1967, as envisaged in Resolution 242. Naturally enough, the prospect of a deal with Israel, however tentative, provoked—and provokes—bitter objections on the part of more hard-line elements of the PLO in precisely the same way that hard-line elements within Israel have strenuously resisted the prospect of a deal with the Palestinians.

The PLO's decision in 1988, after years of impasse, to give explicit recognition to Israel, while at the same time declaring a Palestinian state in exile, was a calculated risk. It stemmed not just from a recognition that the PLO was in no position to strike a hard bargain but from the hope that, by making concessions themselves, the United States would in turn put pressure on Israel to compromise. Although these overtures were endorsed by the 19th Palestine National Council, some members still clearly doubted the wisdom of it. But the most important consideration was the new dynamic created by the *intifada* in the Occupied Territories, which began in December 1987. This signalled a new form of resistance and shifted the balance of influence in the Palestinian movement from the 'outside' to the 'inside'.

Palestinians in Israel

The experience of Palestinians living within the pre-1967 borders of Israel, as Israeli citizens, is very different from that of Palestinians in exile, and different again from that of those living in the occupied West Bank and Gaza Strip.

Since military rule ended in 1966, the 'Israeli' Palestinians have become integrated into the labour force, mainly in jobs with relatively low levels of skills, but remain socially and politically marginal to Israeli society. The majority still live outside the major cities—though have lost most of their land—and form a rural-based, migrant proletariat. While some 'Israeli' Palestinians have become successful businessmen and professionals, the majority remain among the least privileged sections of society. They can vote and stand for the Knesset (parliament), but political parties expressing Palestinian nationalist aspirations, rather than demands for civil rights, are not able to operate freely. Palestinians do not serve in the Israeli army and are thus also ineligible for a range of social benefits available only to army leavers. Furthermore, many jobs, especially in industry, are not open to them because they rarely receive the relevant security clearances. Palestinians are educated in separate Arab-language schools, which are poorly funded and whose curricula until recently clearly reflected Israeli concern to prevent the emergence of a strong Palestinian identity.

Despite these handicaps, the younger generation of 'Israeli' Palestinians has proved increasingly unwilling to accept the restrictions imposed upon them, and are more willing to assert a Palestinian identity, whether of a secular nationalist or Islamic fundamentalist kind. Since the beginning of the *intifada*, many 'Israeli' Palestinians have been sympathetic to its goals, though no widespread insurrectionary action has taken place within Israel.

Political activism in the Occupied Territories

The nature of Palestinian political activity in the West Bank and Gaza Strip has changed considerably since the Israeli occupation began in 1967. The pro-PLO Palestinian National Front was founded in 1972. It signalled the revival of nationalist forces and backed the nationalist mayors who came to power in the municipal elections in the West Bank in 1976, the last election permitted by the Israelis. In 1978, these mayors formed the nucleus of the National Guidance Committee, which attempted to coordinate nationalist political action. This was banned by the Israelis in 1982, and two of the mayors, Bassam Shaka'a of Nablus and Karim Khalaf of Ramallah, were victims of car bombs planted by right-wing Israelis. The remaining mayors were ousted, in some cases exiled, and Israeli military officers were appointed in their places. These were later replaced by Israeli civilians or new Palestinian mayors appointed by the Israelis.

The background to these developments was the high-profile settlement programme in the Occupied Territories begun by the Begin government in the late 1970s. This added further to the area of occupied land under the direct control of the Israeli military and of civilian settlers during previous Labour administrations. The settlements signalled the Israeli intention not only to hold on to the Occupied Territories but substantially to increase the Jewish population there, in the process dispossessing the Palestinians even of these lands. It was a development made easier for the Israelis by increased Palestinian emigration from the Occupied Territories, the result of both their worsening economic position and of the political instability.

The Camp David Agreement between Israel and Egypt, and the autonomy plan for the territories, seemed to confirm this prospect of long-term occupation and dispossession and led to the 1978 Arab Summit resolution

to provide funds for 'steadfastness on the land'. These funds were administered through the Occupied Territories and the Jordanian government.

In the 1980s, however, the nature of Palestinian political organisation
began to change. All the main groups in the PLO are represented in the
Occupied Territories, with the addition of the Palestine Communist party
(PCP), although its existence and activities are illegal under Israeli military
rule and its activists are subject to constant harassment. The main radical
groups—the DFLP, DFLP and the PCP—developed a strategy of 'institution building' in place of the previous high-profile political leadership
'committee structures'. These new committee organisations focused on
social and economic problems rather than on specifically political issues,
hoping thereby to involve a wider cross-section of Palestinians in their
activity. Though dogged by frequent factional in-fighting, the influence of
the new 'committee' movements was considerable.

The *intifada*, which began in the Gaza Strip in December 1987, was a
wholly different kind of political phenomenon from armed resistance in
exile. The people concerned still live on their land, although they are
progressively being deprived of control over it, while the PLO externally
has clearly played a part in sustaining the *intifada*. The uprising's origins
were firmly rooted in the Occupied Territories, while the nature of its
leadership was quite new. Being no longer dependent on key individuals
in the leadership, the momentum of the *intifada* has been able to survive
Israeli arrests of members of the leadership. But it, too, has been unable to
escape the factionalism endemic to the PLO, and has had to cope in
addition with class and regional differences among the Palestinians.
Nonetheless, these hurdles were negotiated with sufficient flexibility to
allow the uprising to sustain itself over more than three years.

The principal source of disunity in the Palestinian ranks during the
intifada was the activities of the Islamist group Hamas, which, in contrast to
Islamic Jihad in the Gaza Strip, has refused to cooperate with the leadership. Hamas represents an Islamist current which ran against the predominantly non-sectarian nationalist movement throughout the 1980s,
both in the West Bank and the Gaza Strip, and has demonstrated some
strength among the student community.

Participation in the *intifada* has been much wider than in previous
periods of unrest, notably in 1982. The initial uprising was centred in the
refugee camps, particularly those with a history of confrontation with the
Israelis. It then spread to merchants and shopkeepers, who staged strikes
and shop closures, along with townspeople, students, teachers and university staff. However, the key new element was the wide-scale involvement of rural communities, where many young people commute daily to
work in Israel, and the erosion of the older, more pliant village leaderships.

The most visible signs of the *intifada* were confrontations with the
Israeli security forces and strikes. However, the major achievements have

mainly been forms of civil disobedience—the resignation of police, civil servants and tax collectors employed by the Israeli administration in the territories, the boycott of the civil administration, and the refusal to pay taxes. Punitive measures by the Israelis have limited these actions but nonetheless a major disengagement between Israel and the Occupied Territories has taken place. This has also occurred in economic relations, where the territories have been most subordinated to Israeli priorities. Forms of economic disengagement have included commercial strikes, campaigns to boycott Israeli goods, and the withdrawal of Palestinian migrant labour from the Israel economy. These have been intensified by Israel's punitive measures, particularly curfews, which prevent people from working in Israel, limit commercial activity and hamper the harvesting and distribution of crops.

The Gulf War and beyond

In the aftermath of the Gulf War, the position of the Palestinians has deteriorated further. The PLO's precipitate and rash support for Iraq has done much to weaken its position. Among much else, it made Kuwaiti reprisals against Palestinian in Kuwait that much easier to justify. It is estimated that the Palestinian community in Kuwait has shrunk from up to 400,000 in 1990 to a little over 100,000 in August 1991. Most of those who left have gone to Jordan, itself in the grip of a severe economic crisis, or have attempted to return to the Occupied Territories.

In the Occupied Territories the situation is hardly more favourable. The comprehensive curfew measures taken by the Israelis during the war, when movement was halted for many days at a time, has been subsequently systematised to cut off population centres from each other in a random and unpredictable fashion. This has severely hampered the movement of goods and workers, intensifying an economy already under great stress as a result of the *intifada*. The economic situation has been further worsened by the cutting off of remittances from the Gulf since the beginning of the war. At the same time, the post-war period has seen an intensification of Israel's settlement activity in the Occupied Territories, ostensibly to house Soviet Jewish immigrants, in reality designed to create further 'facts' in the territories in advance of any negotiations over a peace settlement.

From the Palestinian point of view, the question of whether to participate in the American-brokered peace talks posed a severe dilemma. First, while the Israelis have provisionally agreed to participate, they have done so stressing 'peace' with Arab neighbours, and show little inclination to discuss territorial concessions in the Occupied Territories.

Secondly, whatever its real views, the United States government agreed to comply with Israel's insistence that no Palestinian from annexed East Jerusalem attend the talks. This effectively withdraws the issue of Jerusalem's future status from the agenda. In the circumstances, there seemed little hope of the Palestinians' being able to agree to the conference. In the event, at the end of September 1991 the Palestine National Council voted to attend the Conference, hosted in Madrid. However hopeful the very fact that Jew and Arab were talking at all, for the Palestinians, as much as for the Israelis, the outcome of the talks remains shrouded in doubt.

Sarah Graham-Brown

11 SAUDI ARABIA AND THE GULF STATES

At the beginning of the 20th century the Arabian peninsula excluding Yemen was partly under distant and weak Ottoman influence (al-Hasa, Najd, Hijaz) and partly under British protection in various forms (Muscat and Oman, Bahrain, Qatar and the Trucial States). In so far as these would be described as states, they were small entities based on the domination of one family over small tribes spread out over large areas. The determinants of power were the enforcement of Islamic law and the defence of the group's economic interests against potential raiders. The economy relied on fishing and pearl diving at sea, the latter controlled by merchants, on nomadic herding and trade caravans in the desert, and on date palm and subsistence crop agriculture in the oases. None of this provided any opportunities for considerable wealth or the extraction of much surplus value by the tribal leaders.

In the first decades of the 20th century, as pearl diving declined and motor transport took over from camels, the political leaders and ruling families of the smaller states relied increasingly on subsidies from the 'protecting' power, Britain, to maintain and strengthen their control over their people. After Britain's subsidies came to an end in the 1920s the ruling family of Saudi Arabia was almost totally dependent on income from the annual pilgrimage to Mecca, the *hajj*, that all Muslims were obliged to undertake. The situation changed dramatically with the discovery and exploitation of oil.

The discovery of oil helped the rulers to consolidate their power, as they suddenly found themselves the recipients of regular and substantial amounts of royalties, which were transferred from the international oil companies directly to the local rulers, thus strengthening their position disproportionately at the expense of potential internal challengers. Initially no differentiation was made between the rulers' private purse and the state treasury, and indeed, even today these rulers treat oil revenues like private income, and use them as they see fit. They consider using oil revenues for the welfare of their people as an indication of their traditional generosity and their concern for their subjects, not as a duty incumbent upon them.

Saudi Arabia

In 1902 Abd al-Aziz ibn Saud took Riyadh from the Rashid family and over the next decades gradually built himself up as the ruler of the interior of the

Official name	State of Bahrain
Area	687.75 sq. km (265.5 sq. miles)
Population	486,000 (1990)
Capital	Manama
Language	Arabic
Religion	Muslim, also Christian, Jewish, Bahai, Hindu and Parsee minorities
Currency	Bahraini dinar
Official name	State of Kuwait
Area	17,819 sq. km (6,880 sq. miles)
Population	2,040,000 (1990)
Capital	Kuwait
Language	Arabic
Religion	Sunni Muslim (78%), Shia Muslim (14%), Christian (6%), other (2%)
Currency	Kuwaiti dinar
Official name	Sultanate of Oman
Area	300,000 sq. km (105,000 sq. miles)
Population	2 million (1990)
Capital	Muscat
Language	Arabic
Religion	Ibadi Muslim (75%), Sunni Muslim (25%)
Currency	Rial Omani
Official name	State of Qatar
Area	11,437 sq. km (4,415 sq. miles)
Population	371,863 (1987; only about 25% are Qatari, most others from Pakistan and India)
Capital	Doha
Language	Arabic
Religion	almost entirely Muslim (fundamentalist Wahabi)
Currency	Qatari riyal

Official name	Kingdom of Saudi Arabia
Area	2,200,000 sq. km (849,400 sq. miles)
Population	12 million (1988)
Capital	Riyadh
Language	Arabic
Religion	Sunni Muslim (92%), Shia (8%)
Currency	rial

Official name	United Arab Emirates
Area	83,657 sq. km (32,300 sq. miles)
Population	1,600,000 (1988)
Capital	Abu Dhabi
Language	Arabic
Religion	Sunni Muslim
Currency	UAE dirham

Arabian peninsula. In 1915 he signed a Treaty of Protection with Britain, which gave him internal control over the areas in the peninsula he had conquered and British management of his foreign affairs, as well as a small subsidy. By 1927 he had expanded out of Najd into the Hijaz and a new treaty was signed at Jedda which gave him full independence in return for his recognition of British suzerainty over the Gulf sheikdoms; Qatar, Bahrain, the Trucial States (now the UAE) and Oman. In 1932 he named his state the Kingdom of Saudi Arabia.

The first oil concession was granted in 1933 though oil was not discovered in commercial quantities until 1938. Since then it has been under the control of American companies, who retain this position of supremacy today despite the minor participation of Japanese and other oil companies. King Abd al-Aziz presided over the consolidation of his state, surviving first on the modest revenues from the pilgrimage (£800,000 in 1938) and later from oil royalties. He died in 1953 and was succeeded by his eldest surviving son, Saud, who reigned officially until 1964, though in practice he lost power in 1958 after the exposure of a scandal involving his attempt to fund the assassination of President Nasser. Overall his period in power was marked by oscillations between Arab nationalist tendencies and autocratic authoritarian rule. He was replaced by his brother, Crown Prince Faisal, who was formally named king in 1964.

Faisal was in charge of the Saudi state intermittently between 1958 and 1964, and continuously from 1964 until his assassination in 1975. Internally, he concentrated on the development of a modern physical and social infrastructure, carefully negotiating his way around the strictures of Wahabism when it suited him, while bowing to pressure from the Islamic establishment on other issues such as those relating to women's work and the enforcement of religious observance. He opposed any form of political liberalisation and firmly repressed all opposition; during his reign even ministers had almost no power, and reformers were treated like enemies of the state.

Internationally, his rule marked a transition from weakness to strength. In the early years Saudi weakness was shown by its inability to influence the outcome of the civil war in Yemen (1962–68), the perseverance of internal opposition groups, and the ideological domination of Nasserist nationalism throughout the Arab world. The 1967 Six Day War marked a watershed; thereafter Saudi Arabia's growing financial power enabled it to dictate to its erstwhile rivals, in particular to Egypt where Nasser and Nasserism were seriously weakened. Saudi Arabia's contributions to the budgets of Egypt, Jordan and Syria allowed it to influence their policies and thus gave it a significant political role. In the 1970s, having achieved a position of dominance in Arab politics after the end of the Yemeni civil war, Faisal gave sufficient support to the 1973 oil embargo to demonstrate his commitment to the Arab cause but not so much as to harm his position as a guarantor of Western interests in the region.

In 1975 Faisal was assassinated by a nephew; although there were fears of a conspiracy, the motives seem to have been personal rather than political. He was succeeded by Crown Prince Khalid, who ruled until 1982, when he died a natural death. Khalid's period on the throne witnessed the first public manifestation of large-scale political unrest. After the severe repression of reformist groups under Faisal, and given his absolute autocracy, expectations of unrest had focused on the Westernised, democratising and liberal middle classes, who increasingly resented the unparalleled social conservatism enforced by the government in matters of dress, alcohol, cinema, photography etc., let alone freedom of speech and democracy. In fact the outburst on the first day of the 15th Islamic century (November 1979) came from Muslim fundamentalists, themselves Wahabis, followers of the official ideology of the state. This is probably why the revolt was not identified prior to the explosion, which took place in Mecca in the Ka'ba, Islam's holiest shrine. The armed revolt was suppressed after two weeks of fighting in the city, with the death of hundreds of insurgents. Dissatisfaction with the regime can be gauged by the fact that the revolt encouraged the Shias, who form a majority of the population in the eastern oil-producing region, to start their own uprising, which was also severely repressed. A further Shia revolt took place the following year.

No political liberalisation took place during Khalid's reign and his early promises to introduce an advisory council were soon abandoned. Otherwise his period in power was marked by the boom in oil revenues, further vast expenditure on 'development' projects, and increased flexibility in international relations. In addition to taking a leading role in the foundation of the Gulf Cooperation Council (GCC) this included recognition of the People's Democratic Republic of Yemen, which Faisal had opposed as an atheist communist state; Khalid believed it was more sensible to buy off his enemies than to fight them. This was paralleled by unprecedented expenditure on sophisticated arms of all sorts, purchased primarily from the United States. The military programme had three main objectives: to spend some of the vast oil revenues; to recycle this income back to the country's main sponsor, the United States; and to underline the country's dominant position in the region, though despite the huge expenditure Saudi Arabia's military muscle in some ways remains more apparent than real, as witness its evident inability to repel the threatened Iraqi invasion following Iraq's successful invasion of Kuwait in 1990.

In 1982 Khalid was succeeded by Fahd, who named Abdullah as crown prince on accession to the throne. Fahd, who is still in power at the time of writing, has had a completely different situation to deal with. With the Iran–Iraq War and other international developments in the early 1980s, oil revenues started to decline seriously and Fahd presided over a variety of attempts at austerity, ranging from delayed payments to national and international contractors to attempts at introducing income tax for foreign workers, which he was forced to withdraw within days of its announcement in 1988.

Internationally, Fahd's fear of Shia fundamentalism led him on the one hand to support Iraq financially and politically during its war with Iran, and on the other to try to strengthen his own Muslim legitimacy by asserting his position of Guardian of the Shrines of Mecca and Medina in 1986. This latter became particularly urgent after the armed conflict during the *hajj* in 1987 when Iranian Shia pilgrims fought members of the Saudi Arabian security forces. The end of the Iran–Iraq War was followed by a non-aggression pact with Baghdad in 1989, at a time when Saudi Arabia and other Gulf states started to fear Iraqi political ambitions. Despite its political closeness to the United States, Saudi Arabia had refused consistently to allow American military bases on its territory since the early 1950s, primarily because of the political repercussions this might cause at home and throughout the Arab and Muslim worlds. The policy disappeared overnight when Iraq invaded Kuwait in August 1990.

Kuwait

A British protectorate from 1899 to 1961, Kuwait was a small city-state living primarily off pearl diving, trading and port activities until the discovery of oil in 1938. Ruled by the al-Sabahs since the 18th century, the family worked out a variety of alliances, first under the Ottoman Empire as part of Basra province, and then under British protection. In 1961 Kuwait became independent and immediately had to deal with a challenge to its sovereignty from Iraq. This was resolved with the intervention of British and, later, Arab troops and Kuwait remained independent until August 1990 thanks to a variety of alliances and to skilful use of its financial power to provide development assistance to states which might otherwise have posed a threat to its sovereignty, including Iraq. Kuwait was a founding member of the GCC in 1981.

Sheik Ahmad al-Jabir al-Sabah ruled from 1921 to 1950 and thus presided over the first years of oil production and the early transformation of Kuwait City from a traditional Gulf port into a modern city. His successor, Abdullah al-Salim, became the first emir of independent Kuwait and was active in starting up the health and education facilities for Kuwaiti nationals, which have since become a hallmark of the regime's paternalistic approach. He also weathered the storms that surrounded the independence of Kuwait, particularly Iraq's initial challenge to its right to exist as a separate state. It was also during his rule that the constitution was drawn up by a Constituent Assembly, which included 20 elected members, a move unprecedented in the Arabian peninsula at the time. Under this 1962 constitution, a National Assembly of 50 members was elected in January 1963, albeit by a restricted number of (male) Kuwaitis only, the sole group allowed to vote. Sheik Abdullah died in 1965 and was succeeded by Sabah, who gave support to the Arab cause during the Six

Day War, and later in the 1973 oil embargo. 1971 saw the end of the British presence in the Gulf, and with its the termination of its defence arrangements with Kuwait. The National Assembly developed into a vigorous forum, in which there was much criticism of corruption, inefficiency and other aspects of Kuwaiti government practice. Its activities increasingly displeased the rulers, who, not uncharacteristically, suspended it for four years in 1976. Sheik Sabah died in 1977 and was succeeded by Jabir al-Ahmad who is still the ruling emir in 1991; the crown prince is Saad al-Abdullah.

In 1981 a restricted franchise was introduced for new assembly elections and its powers were reduced. Moreover the composition of the new assembly did not include the radicals. Despite this, continued confrontations took place between it and the government, in a decade when the strains of Kuwaiti political life were increasing with a number of terrorist attacks sponsored by groups supporting the Iranian and Iraqi regimes in attempts by both sides to force Kuwait to change its position on the conflict. Pressure for the reintroduction of the elected assembly grew, particularly after the end of the Iran–Iraq War, and a new assembly was elected in June 1990. During the Iraqi occupation of Kuwait there were a number of meetings and assemblies of Kuwaiti rulers and democrats in exile, but it is difficult to predict what position the reinstated Sabah family will take on this issue in the long run, despite widespread popular demands for democracy among Kuwaitis.

Kuwait's social development has been impressive in terms of the quantity and quality of social services it has provided for its citizens. In addition, its long-term policy of investment of oil surpluses in a fund for the future has proved wise, even if much of this is likely to be spent in the massive reconstruction effort after the war. These policies emphasise the ruling family's paternalistic concern for its citizens. It is important to remember that Kuwaiti nationals formed only about 30% of the emirate's total population in 1990, the rest being immigrants, some of them very long-standing residents who had no rights, and could not obtain Kuwaiti citizenship. These immigrants, many of whom were from the poorer Arab states including some 400,000 Palestinians, worked both in the private and the public sectors, though all positions of power were reserved for Kuwaitis. Internal stability has also suffered after the collapse of the Suq al-Manakh stock exchange in the 1980s.

Internationally, Kuwait maintained a high profile in working to mediate in a variety of inter-Arab conflicts, such as those which opposed the Yemen Arab Republic and the People's Democratic Republic of Yemen in 1979. Its geography and history meant that it would be involved in the Iran–Iraq conflict regardless of its intentions, and, despite its efforts to mediate and resolve the crisis, it was compelled to support Iraq financially, though simultaneously managing to retain relations with Iran.

Bahrain

A group of small islands off the north and eastern Saudi coast, Bahrain has been attached to Saudi Arabia by a causeway since 1986. Bahrain differs from other Gulf states in many ways, among them the fact that its national population is in the majority and immigrants form only a minority and that Shias are more numerous than Sunnis, although the ruling family is Sunni. Oil production started in 1932, earlier than in the other states, but it has always been modest and reserves are almost exhausted. The population is relatively highly educated and the country has been able to develop a sophisticated industrial base as well as becoming a good location for offshore financial service industries in the late 1970s and early 1980s after many such institutions found it necessary to relocate from Beirut.

Having achieved full independence from Britain in 1971, Bahrain's ruling family toyed briefly with democracy, but the elected assembly only lasted a year and a half before being dissolved by the ruling family. However, Bahrain has seen more serious and fundamental challenges to its ruling regime than any of the other small Gulf states, including opposition from the Shias, and trade union demands, which have often been severely repressed. In the 1980s the opposition movement, which had previously been mainly nationalist became more closely related to the revolution in Iran, with unrest in 1979, 1981, 1984 and 1985. A number of people were arrested and sentenced to lengthy terms of imprisonment.

Qatar

Qatar is the only state apart from Saudi Arabia whose population subscribes to the fundamentalist Wahabi form of Islam. Ruled by the al-Thani family since the departure of the Ottomans in 1915, Qatar was extremely poor until oil exploitation started in 1949, ten years after its initial discovery. Oil revenues have been used to create a modern social and physical infrastructure for the emirate. After independence from Britain in 1971, these revenues increased substantially with the 1973–74 oil rises. Sheik Khalifa has ruled since 1972 with the assistance of an advisory council of 20 members, who were selected from representatives elected on a selective suffrage in 1975; no elections of any kind have been held since.

Closely allied with Saudi Arabia and active in the GCC, Qatar has limited foreign policy concerns of its own; its only land border is with Saudi Arabia and its size precludes an active international role. However, it has a long-standing dispute with Bahrain, which still occasionally flares up despite their both being members of the GCC, most recently in 1986. This revolves over the sovereignty of the Fasht al-Dibal and Hawar islands and a piece of mainland Qatar known as Kubara. None of these has been solved, though occasional discussions on the subjects are held in the GCC.

The United Arab Emirates

Formerly known as the Trucial States because of their treaties with Britain, the United Arab Emirates (UAE) became a state in 1971 after the departure of the British. They had previously been separate independent sheikdoms though reliant on Britain for their external affairs. A collection of minute statelets, some little more than fishing villages in the 19th century, they attracted British attention thanks to the sea power of Ras al-Khaimah in particular, whose ships had occasionally attacked British and other shipping heading for India. As a result Britain intervened to force a treaty to suppress piracy and the slave trade; this was imposed on the main sheiks of the coast. In addition to the 'perpetual maritime truce' of 1853, the sheiks had previously agreed to prohibit the transport of slaves on their vessels. The end of the 19th century saw additional individual treaties between the sheiks and Britain, which were standard protectorate treaties, in which the rulers agreed not to cede any parts of their territories to any state except Britain without prior British agreement, nor to develop any relations with any government other than Britain's without British consent. These agreements arose primarily from British fears that France and Germany might impinge on their area of influence. The last such treaties were signed in 1952 with Sharjah and Fujairah. It was then that the seven emirates took the shape they still retain today: they are Abu Dhabi, Dubai, Sharjah, Ras al-Khaimah, Umm al-Qaiwain, Ajman—all on the northern coast of the Gulf—and Fujairah, which is on the Indian Ocean coast and sandwiched between parts of Oman.

In the 1950s Britain's involvement increased, first to settle state boundaries, particularly the conflict with Oman, Saudi Arabia and Abu Dhabi over sovereignty in the Buraimi oasis. A Trucial Council was established, in which all seven rulers met once a year under British chairmanship, and started to create some joint administrative bodies with a view to future closer cooperation. A small armed force known as the Trucial Oman Scouts was also established, under British officers, with many of its troops from nomadic backgrounds or migrant workers from Oman and the Yemen. Some embryonic educational and health development also started in this period.

Abu Dhabi was the first to see oil production, in 1962, and is an oil producer in a totally different class from its fellows. This is clearly illustrated by estimated oil reserves in 1988, which were 92.2 billion barrels for Abu Dhabi compared to four billion barrels for Dubai, while Sharjah's long-term potential is mainly in gas and its oil reserves are about one billion barrels. The other emirates' reserves are negligible, and they are basically dependent on handouts from Abu Dhabi's ruler for survival and development.

Given the absence of any other primary resources, oil has been instrumental in determining the politics of the area. Soon after oil exploitation started in 1962, the al-Nahayan rulers of Abu Dhabi found that the conservatism and traditionalism of Sheik Shakhbut, ruler since 1928, prevented them from enjoying the benefits of oil. In 1966 they forcibly retired him and replaced him with Sheik Zayd, today the president of the UAE and the single most important individual in Abu Dhabi and the UAE.

The UAE's political structure clearly reveals the tensions that remain between the emirates. The federal constitution is still provisional, as the rulers cannot agree on a permanent version, which would necessarily reduce the formal independence and autonomy of each individual emirate. The rulers together form the Supreme Council of the Federation. The latter's president is the ruler of Abu Dhabi and the vice-president and prime minister the ruler of the second most important state, Dubai. The supreme council is advised by a 40-member Federal National Council. Even after independence, internal territorial disputes have not been settled. Saudi Arabia has only accepted with difficulty that Buraimi should remain within the UAE, and only recognised the UAE in 1974 after a settlement over the Liwa oasis. Ras al-Khaimah only joined in 1972 when it found that no one would pursue its claim against Iran after the latter occupied the Tunb islands (see below).

Efforts at centralisation and unification have had mixed receptions. On the one hand all the smaller emirates resent the domination of Abu Dhabi; on the other, they all want Abu Dhabi's financial support. The major input into the federal budget comes from Abu Dhabi, with Dubai contributing a significant amount, while the other emirates are entirely dependent either on this budget or individual handouts from the ruler of Abu Dhabi. Long-standing rivalry between the emirates has been affected by their relative financial situations; only Dubai is in a position to challenge decisions from Abu Dhabi. In the first two decades of the UAE there was continuous rivalry between the President Sheik Zayd of Abu Dhabi and the Prime Minister Sheik Rashid of Dubai. This diminished as the latter's age and health reduced his abilities. He died in 1990 and was succeeded by his son, Maktum, who formed a new government.

The principal institutional form of 'national unity' is the Federal Army, and there have been serious tensions throughout the 1970s, with Dubai acting independently on some occasions. Sharjah has also suffered some instability, with two attempted coups against its ruler (expressions of family rivalry) since independence, in 1972 and 1987.

The main characteristics of the UAE are that in little more than a decade it has undergone a transformation that has taken several generations elsewhere in the peninsula. With the production of oil and under the influence of Western advisors, the UAE implemented a development policy, which consisted primarily in the building of a modern glass- and concrete-city of skyscrapers linked by ultra-modern roads and functioning thanks to constant airconditioning. Stated simply, in 1962, when oil was first discovered, living conditions and social structure were those of a tribal subsistence economy; by 1980 the UAE had one of the highest per capita incomes in the world. Among much else, its financial clout has attracted a

huge number of immigrants; indeed its indigenous population now numbers less than 25% of the UAE's total population.

Oman

Oman is much larger than the UAE, with, moreover, a substantial indigenous population. Its history in the 20th century has been marked by a
long period of isolation and poverty followed by a sudden and rapid transition to a consumer oil economy.

Ruled by the Al Bu Said dynasty since 1749, Oman used to be known as
the Sultanate of Muscat and Oman and, from the island of Zanzibar,
exerted considerable influence over East Africa and its slave trade. The
country's links with Britain never included a formal protectorate treaty,
but relations were nonetheless close: Treaties of Friendship, Commerce
and Navigation were signed in 1891, 1939 and 1951. Sultan Said ibn Taimur
ruled from 1932 to 1970 and kept his country as isolated as he could,
forbidding all the trappings of modern life in the belief that such contacts
would jeopardise his own absolute rule. He was assisted by British
advisors and troops, and dealt with two major revolts, first in the northern
hinterland of Oman, which claimed autonomy, even independence, under the Ibadi Imam Ghalib ibn Ali. This culminated in an armed rebellion in
the 1950s, which was repressed with the assistance of British forces.

Less than a decade later, Dhofar, in the south-west, became the focus of
a new struggle against the sultan's rule. Opposed to the ruler's backwardness, some workers who had experienced life abroad in the oil fields and
elsewhere rebelled. Emboldened by early successes, the rebels, turning
increasingly to communism (and in receipt of considerable aid from
China), posed a growing threat to the stability of the region. Realising that
the aging sultan was unlikely to prevail, Britain threw its weight behind his
son, Qabus. In 1970 he overthrew his father, and, with substantial military
backing from Britain, Jordan and Iran, launched a renewed campaign
against the rebel forces. By 1975 he had gained a decisive victory.

The new policies of Sultan Qabus were financed by oil revenues, which
had been discovered in modest quantities in 1967 and which was the
financial basis for the new Oman, as the sultanate was renamed immediately after his accession to power. As well as suppressing the armed
struggle the government pushed forward rapid development policies in
the 1970s and 1980s comparable to those which took place in the UAE.
Politically, there were no signs of liberalisation, though exiled rebels were
encouraged to return, particularly those with skills. The country has no
democratic institutions. In 1981 a 45-member Consultative Assembly was
created, and its membership expanded to 55 in 1983, but all candidates are
nominated by the sultan and 19 of them are members of the sultan's
government.

At the social and economic level there has been a considerable expansion of services and the creation of a modern infrastructure, including

some items of conspicuous consumption (which the country can ill afford given its quite modest oil revenues). It has obtained assistance from richer oil states and suffers less than they do from the social disruption brought about by a massive influx of immigrants as the latter are only a small minority in the country.

In the 1980s, having successfully achieved control over the whole country, the regime found itself able to play a wider regional role. Its long-standing dispute with Saudi Arabia over Buraimi and other borders was effectively terminated with the creation of the GCC, which agreed to shelve territorial conflicts. Oman continued to have excellent relations with Iran, only slightly marred by the Iran–Iraq War. In 1982, Oman and the People's Democratic Republic of Yemen established diplomatic relations after a long period of hostility, which had occasionally flared up into border skirmishes. Oman also became the first Gulf state after Kuwait to open diplomatic relations with the Soviet Union, despite its close links with the United States.

International relations

The main feature of the foreign relations of the peninsula states during this century has been the shift from British to American supremacy. While all the states started the century with some degree of 'protectorate' relationship with Britain, American dominance of their oil industries has led inevitably to its pre-eminent influence over the region. Britain nonetheless retained its political supremacy in the smaller states until the 1980s.

The Soviet Union has never been able to penetrate the Gulf. While it enjoyed good relations with some of the surrounding states—Iraq, Syria and the People's Democratic Republic of Yemen—Kuwait was the sole Gulf state to have diplomatic relations with it, opened in the early 1960s, until, in the 1980s, the minor Gulf states began gradually to formalise their relations with the Soviet Union. Bahrain and Saudi Arabia were the last of the Gulf states to establish formal diplomatic links, in 1990, once the decline of the Soviet Union had removed any threat it might once have been seen to pose.

Relations with Iran have been erratic. During the shah's rule, Iran's commercial relations with the UAE were excellent while Oman had an extremely close political and military relationship, inviting thousands of Iranian troops to assist the sultan to overcome the uprisings in Dhofar (1968–75). This caused serious concern in Saudi Arabia, which had been in competition with Iran for domination over the area, and whose relations with Oman were tense despite their common opposition to the rebels. Iran also had a long-standing claim of sovereignty over Bahrain, resolved in 1970 when a UN mission found that the population wanted independence, a conclusion Iran accepted. The islands of Greater and Lesser Tunb and Abu Musa in the mouth of the Gulf were not so lucky: Sharjah relinquished its claim on Abu Musa but as Ras al-Khaimah was unwilling to do the same for the Tunbs, Iran simply invaded them and took them by force just as Britain was withdrawing from the area.

The situation changed considerably after the Iranian revolution in 1979. Relations with Saudi Arabia rapidly worsened and remained hostile throughout the 1980s, the result principally of their rival claims to be the true homeland of Islam. Saudi hostility to Shia fundamentalism was particularly virulent given the Saudi claim to incarnate Sunni Islam in its most fundamentalist form. Hence Saudi Arabia was firmly committed to Iraq in the Iran–Iraq War. In the course of the 1987 *hajj* there were serious riots in which hundreds of Iranian pilgrims were killed. Iranian–Kuwaiti relations were also tense despite the presence of may Kuwaitis of Iranian origin in the emirate. Similarly in Bahrain the Shia allegiance of the poor majority was encouraged by Iran, which sponsored and supported some of the unrest which took place in the 1980s. In contrast, the UAE and Oman retained good relations with Iran throughout the period, informally when it was not expedient to do so formally. The Iraq invasion of Kuwait in 1990 brought Iran back into the Gulf fold; a GCC meeting in February 1991 held that Iran should be included in any future security arrangement for the region. How this might materialise in practice, given the substantial American military presence in the area, remains to be seen.

The apparent threat of the Iranian revolution 1979 and the beginning of the Iran–Iraq War in 1980 prompted Bahrain, Kuwait, Qatar, Oman, Saudi Arabia and the UAE to form an alliance, the Gulf Cooperation Council, in 1981. The determination to exclude Iran is clear from its official title, Cooperation Council for the Arab States of the Gulf. The name also helps explain the absence of Yemen: in the early 1980s there was speculation that the Yemen Arab Republic might join, but its poverty, its size, its hostility to Saudi Arabia and its status as a republic prevented it from being invited. In fact, the GCC is an alliance of oil-rich Gulf states who are ruled autocratically by hereditary dynasties. The member states are under considerable Saudi pressure to follow its policies, although Saudi leadership has been resisted in varying degrees by Kuwait, the UAE and Oman, all of which have long-standing territorial and boundary disagreements with the Saudis. The GCC is a joint defence and security organisation with a high degree of coordination and exchange of information between members. It is also an economic alliance, with an internal free-trade zone and attempts the coordination of industrial and agricultural development policies.

Conclusion

Except for Yemen, the Arabian peninsula states are all ruled by families whose power and dynastic potential has been strengthened by oil revenues. While political power in the pre-oil era could be removed from one family and given to another by tribal councils, British protection and, subsequently, oil income meant that the ruling families have consolidated their dynastic status and their power, principally as a result of their control over their respective states' income.

That colonialism did not really penetrate the Gulf states delayed their exposure to the modern world. In consequence, when the oil revenues started to flow they experienced a uniquely rapid transformation—from a pre-capitalist nomadic/agricultural society to the ultimate in late 20th-century consumerism within a few decades. What is important is not the nature of the transformation, but its speed, which has had profound social consequences. Within a generation the traditional economy was destroyed.

Yet though for the most part immensely wealthy, they are far from being economically self-sufficient, having little more than oil to support their economies. Efforts to diversify and to broaden their economic bases have mostly yielded little. Similarly, with generally small populations the Gulf states are largely dependent on immigrant labour, with the result that tensions in the social fabric are an unmistakable reality. It is a situation exaggerated by the highly stratified and deeply traditional nature of society, as resistant to social change as, in many instances, it is eager to enjoy the fruits of their new-found riches.

Helen Lackner

12 THE SUDAN

The modern Sudan, bordering eight other states, may be divided geographically into three broad zones. The northern third is mainly desert, the central band mainly semi-desert and savannah, the southern third savannah and forest. The dominant feature, crucial to the economic and political history of the Sudan, is the Nile and its tributaries. Rising in the Great Lakes of Africa, the White Nile, having been joined by the Bahr el-Ghazal, the Sabat, and other feeders, itself joins the swifter, silt-laden Blue Nile at Khartoum to form the main Nile, the lifeline of the northern Sudan and Egypt. It was the Nile system that presented motives and avenues for the Turco-Egyptian conquest of the Sudanese lands in the 19th century. Lured by the promise of slaves and gold, the armies of Mohammed Ali Pasha and his successors easily subdued the decrepit states and tribal confederacies of the northern Sudan and pushed gradually south, west and east until, by the mid-1870s, Egypt had extended its nominal control even beyond today's Sudanese borders. In doing so, the Turco-Egyptian regime imposed itself on a wide variety of peoples in greatly varying stages of development: the northern riverain Sudanese, who mostly resembled (and some were akin to) the Nubians of Upper Egypt; the Arabs of Kordofan and the Bayuda, largely camel and cattle nomads who chafed at outside control; and the enormously variegated African peoples of the south, who in language, culture and political and economic development differed widely not only from their Turco-Egyptian conquerors and northern neighbours, but also from each other. No less than the European creations elsewhere in the Middle East and Africa, the Sudan's borders are the result of imperialism, albeit in this case mainly Ottoman-Egyptian rather than Western European.

The Mahdiyya: reaction and reformation

Ironically, the Middle East's most determined and successful resistance to imperialism occurred in the Sudan. That this assumed a religious—indeed messianic—form should not obscure its social and political natures, nor the foreign innovations and intrusions against which it reacted. In 1881, significantly at a time when the Egyptian government at home was in the throes of a nationalist movement that would end in British occupation, Mohammed Ahmad Abdullah, a Dunqalawi sufi, proclaimed himself mahdi—the Expected Deliverer of the Muslims. Gradually gaining strength over several years, his movement scored stupendous successes against the poorly led and demoralised Egyptian forces at Shaykan in 1883 and, famously, at Khartoum in January 1885. Viewing the Sudan as a waste of money that Egypt, in bankruptcy, could ill afford, its new ruler, Sir Evelyn Baring (later Lord Cromer), agent and consul-general from 1883 to 1907, argued successfully for a purely defensive policy. The death of the mahdi in June 1885, and the destruction of the Mahdist invasion force at Tushki in 1889 punctuated a period of watchfulness on the Sudan–Egypt border where, however, no serious Mahdist threat again appeared. Indeed, it was the changing fortunes of the European Powers that dictated Britain's adoption of a more aggressive policy in 1895–96. An Anglo-Egyptian force first took Dongola in 1896, then, with massive technological superiority, pushed southwards in a campaign that ended in the rout of the Sudanese at Karari in September 1898. Two weeks later Kitchener, the Anglo-Egyptian commander, confronted the less well-armed but yet more dangerous Major Marchand at Fashoda. Though the British now understandably viewed Mahdism as an 'exploded cult', it survived: in the sect itself, which formed the nucleus of a powerful political movement, and, less obviously, in its unifying, 'nation-building' effects—the mahdi has come to be called Abu 'l-Istiqlal, the Father of Independence.

The Anglo-Egyptian condominium

The formula devised to salvage French honour at Fashoda was to dominate the political development of the Sudan throughout the age of European imperialism. Rather than claim the upper Nile for Britain, Kitchener claimed it for Britain's ward, Egypt, thus allowing the French to defer to the unenforceable claims of the khedive rather than to dispute the fire-power of the Royal Navy. Likewise Lord Cromer, having been hampered in Egypt by the Capitulations, Mixed Courts, and other machinery of internationalism, devised a 'hybrid form of government' for the Sudan, by which Egypt and Britain would in theory be joint rulers. The so-called Condominium Agreement(s) of 1899 enshrined this principle; in fact, until 1956 Britain was the dominant partner. Great power was invested in a single individual, the governor-general of the Sudan, who was always British, while the Sudan's budget and development debts were assumed by an Egyptian government fearful of total exclusion. Thus a regime was created that was unique in the Middle East, indeed nearly so in the world. The interplay of the co-domini with each other, and with the various Sudanese interest groups, complicated the Sudan's political development, with results all too apparent today.

The Sudan was under direct colonial rule longer than any other Middle Eastern state. Although the device of condominium deeply affected the character of the regime and acted as a brake on the British, it did not result in economic, social or religious policies very different from those pursued in other British dependencies. Thus to conciliate Muslim opinion direct taxes were kept low, the concurrence of the *ulama* (religious experts) was

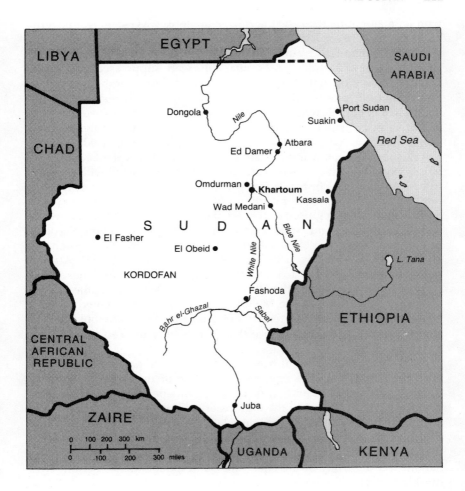

Official name	Republic of Sudan
Area	2,505,813 sq. km (967,500 sq. miles)
Population	25,560,000 (1987)
Capital	Khartoum
Language	Arabic and local languages
Religion	Muslim (about 73%), majority of the Southern provinces are animist (18%) or Christian (9%)
Currency	Sudanese pound

won for major initiatives, the pilgrimage to Mecca was facilitated, government funds were earmarked for mosque construction and repair, slavery was not prohibited (and, although the slave trade itself was banned, it, too, continued), new 'Mahdist' and similar cults were suppressed, and Christian proselytisation in the northern Sudan was virtually prohibited. While Sufi *turuq* (religious brotherhoods) were at first deeply suspected—the mahdi had begun his religious career as a sufi, and Sudanese sufism was, in British eyes, 'fanatical' and therefore unpredictable—individual sufi sheiks who proved amenable were cultivated and supported. Notable among them were the Mirghani family, hereditary sheiks of the Khatmiyya *tariqa*, who had opposed the mahdi and now openly sided with the new rulers. As correct as British policy was towards Islam, however, it could not reorient the loyalties of northern Sudanese towards orthodoxy: the *ulama* were soon recognised as respected but not widely influential, while sufi sheiks retained and expanded their hold on popular opinion. Recognition of this came most obviously during the First World War, when not only sufi sheiks, but even the son of the late mahdi, Sayyid Abd al-Rahman, were recruited to exhibit publicly among the Sudanese their support for Britain against the Ottoman sultan and self-proclaimed caliph of Islam. Conciliation of the Mahdists, however, was resented by both *ulama* and sufi sheiks, and resulted in a polarisation that would match, among the ruled, the divergence that increasingly marked their Anglo-Egyptian rulers.

That divergence, present from the start, grew to breaking point after the First World War. The Egyptian revolution of 1919 led inexorably to Britain's unilateral declaration of Egyptian independence in 1922, after which the Sudan, as one of the four 'reserved points', came to dominate, even to symbolise, Anglo-Egyptian relations. As Britain withdrew direct control from Egypt, so control in the Sudan (and, through the Nile, therefore indirectly still of Egypt) assumed greater importance; to Egyptian nationalists the Unity of the Nile Valley and independence became irreducible aspects of Egyptian sovereignty, negotiable only in so far as negotiations might lead to their unequivocal acceptance. In 1924 the dispute turned violent. The British governor-general of the Sudan (who was still, anomalously, also commander-in-chief of the Egyptian army) was assassinated in Cairo. The British reacted by demanding evacuation of the Egyptian army from the Sudan, and this was taken in hand. Some Sudanese troops, suffering from divided loyalties, were engaged by British forces in a shoot-out in Khartoum, with heavy casualties. The Egyptian units were evicted, as were many Egyptian civilian officials, and a new Sudan Defence Force (SDF), responsible to the governor-general alone, was set up. That the Egyptians went quietly was not lost on Sudanese public opinion which, however, was now preoccupied with a reactionary British policy that sought to combat the danger of Sudanese nationalism by curtailing modern advance.

Thus during the 1920s and early 1930s education stagnated, and administrative functions were increasingly assigned by the British to conservative tribal leaders rather than to the 'class' of educated Sudanese that had been created to assume subordinate posts in the government. This policy of indirect rule or 'native administration' had its origins and echoes as far afield as Nigeria and Iraq; in the Sudan it was proclaimed with particular emphasis but not in fact seriously implemented because it proved impracticable. The return of Egyptian troops in 1937, symbolic of the relations restored in the Anglo-Egyptian Treaty of 1936 (itself the result of complex British and Egyptian regional and international interests), marked the resumption of rivalry between the co-domini for sole dominion in the Sudan.

From the late 1930s that rivalry was heightened and complicated by direct Sudanese involvement. In 1938 the Graduates' General Congress was established as an ostensibly social but obviously political organisation to represent the interests of the small, Western-educated northern Sudanese elite. The British welcomed, even encouraged, this development in the hope that it would foster a Sudanese nationalism distinct from the Unity of the Nile Valley. In fact what emerged was a dichotomy in the nascent nationalist movement mirroring the split between the co-domini. One Sudanese faction eventually sided with Egypt, and proclaimed its unalterable (though never clearly defined) demand for union, while the other upheld the goal of the Sudan for the Sudanese, if necessary in temporary cooperation with Britain to combat Egyptian pretensions. The continuing resilience of traditional tribal and religious authority and the numerical insignificance of the nationalists meant, however, that they had to ally with sectarian forces in order to win mass support. Thus, by the end of the Second World War, two opposing lines were discernible. On the one hand was a pro-independence group, dominated by Sayyid Abd al-Rahman al-Mahdi and deriving its mass support from his followers, the Ansar, in loose tactical alliance with the British. On the other hand were the unionists, in alliance with Egypt and supported, though much less openly, by Sayyid Ali al-Mirghani of the Khatmiyya, the long-standing rival of the Mahdists. Although this dichotomy greatly complicated political development, it both helped and hindered the British in retaining effective control. Significantly, however, it led to a debasing of those parliamentary institutions that were created in the post-war decade, as each side saw these in terms of its sectarian advantage rather than of consequence to the national good.

The 'southern problem'

That we come only now to consider developments in the southern Sudan is itself a reflection of the peripheral nature of the region during the 19th- and 20th-century colonial periods. The Turco-Egyptian regime had seen the south as a source of slave labour and natural resources, notably ivory. Such administration as existed was designed to facilitate extraction of those commodities, and was often indistinguishable from mere raiding. The period of the Mahdiyya was if anything even more disastrous, as the rudimentary Turco-Egyptian administration was destroyed but not replaced: the region degenerated into a chaos from which recovery would be slow and fitful. This was in turn because the next wave of foreign conquerors, the Anglo-Egyptians, again saw the south in largely negative terms, as territory that had to be occupied in order to safeguard the Nile basin. Thus again only very basic administration was set up, largely military in character and personnel, and with limited goals. Indeed, so loose was the control that the period from 1898 to 1929 was punctuated by a depressing series of local 'risings' and 'punitive expeditions' launched to assert government authority.

Whereas in the northern riverain Sudan some government resources had been invested in social services, little was spared for the south. In the north, for example, primary and elementary schools were established, albeit on a limited scale, and the Gordon Memorial College in Khartoum provided secondary education in order to supply the government with subordinate officials. In the south, however, education was left entirely in the hands of foreign Christian missionaries who, while long-suffering and admirable in their dedication, necessarily enhanced the separateness of the region and provided education to a lower standard. Again, whereas in the north medical care was increasingly available, especially in the towns but even in important rural areas like the Gezira, in the south health was a matter for missionaries or the army. Indeed, in the whole wide field of social and economic development, the first three decades of the condominium witnessed in the north such massive (if problematic) projects as the Gezira Scheme, the Sudan Railways, and the construction of Port Sudan; in the south no such investment was made. The result was a widening gap that was recognised, indeed formalised, in the famous Southern Policy of 1930.

The Southern Policy was designed to allow a breathing space during which the south would be allowed to develop free from the dangerous influences of the more advanced north, while indigenous political institutions were strengthened and modern education extended, so that the peoples of the region could stand on their own. In practice, however, the prescribed educational advances were not made, but the reactionary, exclusionary aspects of the policy were ham-fistedly enforced. The result, of course, was that by the end of the Second World War, when the northern Sudanese embarked on the road to self-government and self-determination, the south was still mired—indeed arguably more deeply—in backwardness. The British decision, taken in 1946 that the south should remain part of a unitary Sudanese polity (rather than, as had from time to time been mooted, being attached to Britain's East African dependencies) was itself never matched by real attention to the urgent social and economic advances that successful implementation of that decision required. By 1946 northern Sudanese politicians saw British concern for the south as cynical foot-dragging rather than belated paternalism, and this coloured their views on the constitutional disputes ahead.

Independence

Decisions taken in 1946 hardly took into account the prospect of self-government in 1953, still less of full independence in 1956. That such rapid advance took place was the result of the interplay of Sudanese politics and Anglo-Egyptian relations, which in turn were affected by Western interests in the Middle East. An Advisory Council of the Northern Sudan, established in 1944, was superseded in 1948 by a Legislative Assembly representing the whole country. Its powers were limited, and its efficacy further damaged by the refusal of the unionists to take part in it. Indeed, it is a telling comment on the politics of the period that the main constitutional bodies had little to do with major political advances. Thus continuing Anglo-Egyptian negotiations, concentrating on the Sudan and the Suez Canal Base, were mirrored in the Sudan by heightening rivalry between the independents and unionists which was, in turn, only the 'modern' face of the old sectarian rivalry of the Mahdists and Khatmiyya. The hollowness of political discourse—for the only 'issue' of moment remained union or independence—in fact suited the British and continued until the overthrow of the Egyptian monarchy in 1952. The successor regime called the British bluff: abandoning the old Egyptian claim to sovereignty in the Sudan, the government of General Najib publicly recognised the Sudanese right to self-determination, confident that the eventual decision would favour union. The promise of immediate self-determination was one around which all Sudanese parties could unite, for against it the British policy of eventual independence paled even for the Mahdists.

Events moved quickly. An Anglo-Egyptian Agreement enshrined the main points of separate deals made by Egypt and the Sudanese political parties. That agreement called for a period of self-government during which prescribed steps would be taken towards self-determination. Elections to a Sudanese parliament were held in late 1953. To the shock and dismay of the British, these were swept by the unionists; the close association of the Mahdist Umma party with the British, and even more its obvious subordination to the dynastic ambitions of Sayyid Abd al-Rahman al-Mahdi, had turned public opinion towards a unionism that really meant the disappearance of the British rather than their replacement by the Egyptians. Indeed, 'union' was still a vague concept susceptible of interpretations ranging from a complete absorption to mere consultation of independent states. Thus the first Sudanese government, formed in early 1954 by the unionist leader Ismail al-Azhari, was more anti-British than pro-Egyptian: its ultimate ambitions had yet to be decided.

A number of factors and developments led eventually to independence rather than union. In 1954 the Mahdists made clear, through violent demonstrations, their absolute opposition to union—even unto civil war. The eclipse in Egypt of General Najib, personally popular in the Sudan, by Nasser was achieved at a cost of Sudanese support. This was made worse by the suppression of both the Egyptian communists and Muslim Brotherhood, raising further fears among the Sudanese. Finally the true views of al-Azhari and his sometime patron, Sayyid Ali al-Mirghani, were crucial. Sayyid Ali had never favoured union, but had backed the unionists in order to oppose his rival, Sayyid Abd al-Rahman; with the Mahdists now in unaccustomed parliamentary opposition and considerable disarray, Sayyid Ali could turn against Egypt's Sudanese allies. And among those allies, including especially al-Azhari himself, unionism had evidently been a strategy, not an end in itself. He now moved adroitly to preside over Sudanese independence, which was achieved with British enthusiasm and Egyptian acquiescence on 1 January 1956.

Parliamentary and military regimes, 1956—69

Although the end of the condominium and creation of a republic appears as a clear demarcation in the political history of the Sudan, in fact the more important dividing lines are in 1953, when the Anglo-Egyptian Agreement sealed the demise of the condominium, and 1958, when the regime established under that agreement was overthrown by the Sudanese army. The period from 1953 to 1958 was in fact largely out of continuity, during which the Sudanese government assumed the attributes of sovereignty but failed to achieve a depth of legitimacy sufficient to withstand the winds of change in the Muslim Middle East.

Faced with a deteriorating economy, growing disaffection in the southern Sudan, and the probable combination of his parliamentary enemies, Abdullah Khalil, the Umma politician who had succeeded al-Azhari in 1956, handed power to the army in 1958. Intended as a manoeuvre to win temporary respite from mounting difficulties, this flouting of the (still provisional) constitution opened the door not only to a six-year military regime but to all the coup-makers who followed. The demonstrable frailty of parliamentary government in turn has been a major difficulty in settling the Sudan's north–south problem, because formal arrangements inspire little public confidence. In any event, the military regime of General Ibrahim Abboud failed ultimately in the major tests it faced, economic and political, and was itself overthrown. In what has become a peculiarly Sudanese phenomenon, he and his generals were driven from power in 1964 by a wave of popular disaffection, fed by economic malaise and, importantly, by the inability of the military to defeat rebellion in the south.

That rebellion, as we have seen, had its roots in the colonial period and even earlier. In 1955, on the eve of independence, the insensitivity of northern politicians—and the intrigues of Egypt—led to a mutiny of southern units of the Sudan Defence Force (SDF). This spread quickly across Equatoria and resulted in some 300 deaths, mostly of northern civilians. Although the rising was suppressed, its warning was never heeded in Khartoum, and disaffection merely simmered thereafter. Southern support for independence had been won by the promise of northern parliamentarians to consider a federal system of government; that promise was shelved as soon as independence was won, and southerners saw themselves at the mercy of northern politicians. The Abboud regime was even more misguided than its civilian predecessor. It pursued an unabashed policy of Islamisation, thus fomenting the opposition—indeed helping to create the separate southern identity—its ostensibly 'nation-building' measures were supposed to combat. By 1964 open civil war was under way, and the generals were disastrously exposed as no more effective in the military sphere than in the civilian.

The transitional government that administered the Sudan from October 1964 until elections in 1965 was one of unfulfilled promise, still wistfully recalled to this day. The broad coalition of trade unions, professional groups, and illegal politicial parties that brought down the Abboud regime was dominated by progressives who wished to avoid a return to the sterile politics of the old parties. In this they were foiled by their own disunity and the strength of the parties' sectarian bases. The Sudanese Communist party, for instance, although instrumental in the movement against the military regime, and prominent in the transitional government, had only a tiny following in the country; its hopes depended on a long transition period rather than on early elections. A promising Round Table Conference held to help settle the civil war fell victim, too, to the jockeying of the old parties, none of which would make concessions to African southerners on the eve of parliamentary elections. Thus the war continued, elections returned a government dominated by the Mahdist Umma party, and the structural changes envisaged by the 'New Forces' were either still-born or rescinded.

If the fall of military governments is a theme of post-independence Sudanese politics, so is the failure of their parliamentary predecessors and successors to learn from their own mistakes. The second parliamentary regime (1965–69) witnessed heightened in-fighting between the sectarian parties, constant manoeuvring within them for personal advantage, splits over issues of little substance, and a partly consequent decline in the country's economic and social life. The war in the south worsened, as Khartoum politicians, now prisoners of their own rhetoric, dared make no concessions to the rebels. It proved impossible, too, to devise a permanent constitution, as such knotty problems as the nature of the state—secular or Islamic—took precedence over the practical concerns of the mass of the people. It was with relief, even satisfaction, that public opinion welcomed the military coup that overthrew the regime in May 1969.

The 'May regime'

The young officers who took power in 1969 saw themselves as successors not of Abboud and the old-style soldiers of 1958–64, but of the visionaries of the transitional government of 1964–65. The May Regime, as it came to be called, was thus consciously reformist, even radical, in its ideology, which it derived in part from that of Nasser in Egypt and progressive regimes elsewhere in the non-aligned world. Although it would survive longer than any government in the Sudan's independent history, it, too, failed to fulfil its initial promise, and by the time that it, too, was overthrown, the Sudan was set on a downward spiral from which it has yet to recover.

The new government acted quickly to assert itself in a potentially hostile political environment. In 1970 the open opposition of the Mahdists was suppressed violently: thousands died, including the leader of the Ansar, the Imam al-Hadi al-Mahdi, killed while trying to escape; his nephew, the former prime minister, Sadiq al-Mahdi, went into exile. In this suppression of the religious right wing, the fledgling government was helped by the active support of the left; now the regime turned on them. Increasingly emboldened, the leader of the junta, Jafar Mohammed Nimayri, made bitter public attacks on the Communist party and removed its sympathisers from the government; the party itself was split over whether to subsume itself in a new one-party organisation the regime was planning, or to maintain its independence. In the event, a disastrous miscalculation played into Nimayri's hands. In July 1971 leftist junior officers led by Hashim al-Ata staged a coup, arrested Nimayri, and occupied key installations. Their announcement of socialist goals preceded their consolidation of power: Nimayri escaped, and with Egyptian and Libyan help rallied to defeat the rebels. A violent purge ensued, and the May Regime, destined to last another 14 years, turned its back on the left. Foreign and domestic policies were adjusted accordingly, as Nimayri acted to solidify his personal position through alliances with the West and by conciliating both the religious right-wing and the southern rebels.

The Addis Ababa Agreement of 1972 ended the war in the south. Although the May Regime had developed from the outset a new attitude towards the south, it had failed to achieve a settlement and indeed had turned towards military means. But the nearly successful coup of 1971 and, more importantly, the new unity of the Southern Sudan Liberation Movement (SSLM) under Joseph Lagu allowed both Khartoum and the rebels to approach peace talks with considerable momentum. Secret meetings led to formal talks, and in March 1972 agreement was reached by which the war would end, the south would be granted a degree of autonomy, and the rebel forces would be integrated into the national army. Although some elements of the rebel movement never accepted it, and its terms were soon dishonoured, the Addis Ababa Agreement brought the war to an end, allowed the start of an experiment in southern autonomy, and shored up Nimayri's personal position both at home and abroad.

The abandonment of the May Regime's self-proclaimed socialism was accelerated in the 1970s by Nimayri's renewed need to placate the religious right-wing. Coup attempts punctuated his presidency (which was formalised by a spurious plebiscite in 1972). In July 1976 Mahdists almost succeeded in bringing down the regime; hundreds were killed, and Nimayri himself escaped only by luck. He resolved therefore to conciliate and thus de-fang the Mahdists, and after secret talks with Sadiq al-Mahdi he announced a policy of 'national reconciliation', by which Sadiq would be allowed to return to the Sudan and re-enter public life; in return he would recognise the institutions of the May Regime. Thus the opposition to Nimayri was again split, as Sadiq al-Mahdi returned, the promised reforms were slow in coming, and Nimayri successfully played a masterly role in exploiting his opponents' weaknesses. Yet lip-service on 'Islamic' issues was paid at a cost in southern and other secularist support, and in any case could not itself suffice indefinitely. By the early 1980s Nimayri's measures to protect his personal position rekindled southern opposition, and this led to a new civil war and the eventual downfall of the regime itself.

The revolt of the south and the fall of Nimayri

The autonomy enjoyed by the southern Sudanese between 1972 and 1983 was vitiated by the ineptness and corruption of southern politicians and by the manoeuvres of Nimayri and his government in Khartoum. Cynical exploitation of the perquisites of power in the south played into Nimayri's hands, and allowed many of the practical benefits of autonomy—especially rapid social and economic development—to be postponed indefinitely. Nimayri's national reconciliation, promising, for instance, country-wide implementation of the sharia, or Muslim law, could not be so long postponed, and by the early 1980s southern disaffection had been recharged. The final straw came when, in 1983, Nimayri proclaimed the 'redivision' of the south into three separate 'regions' corresponding to the old southern provinces of colonial days and, a few months later, the implementation of the sharia. In fact the spark of southern revolt had already been applied to the tinder in May, when units of the army rebelled and took to the bush.

In allowing this Nimayri reckoned without important changes in the southern radical leadership. The new rebellion was spearheaded by the Sudan People's Liberation Movement and Army (SPLM/SPLA), an organisation with a tightly knit political-military command (in contrast to the disunity that bedevilled earlier movements) and with the vehemently asserted goal not of secession but of bringing down the Khartoum regime and replacing it with a new democratic and socialist one. After suppressing rival movements supported by Khartoum, the SPLM/SPLA quickly emerged as a formidable political-military adversary, and won adherents even among secularist northern Sudanese.

Civil war was a decisive factor, but hardly the only one, in bringing down Nimayri in April 1985. A disastrous economic collapse, attended by a series of catastrophes of almost biblical proportions—drought, famine, pestilence—brought the Sudan to bankruptcy and the verge of collapse. The black humour of the Sudanese expressed itself in the view that a coup was unlikely because there was no longer anything worth taking over, but this belied the continuing failure of the opposition to unite against a discredited regime. The SPLM/SPLA, despite its protests to the contrary, was tellingly seen even by most northern intellectuals as a southern movement, and thus perhaps as an ally but never as the object of their primary personal or factional support. The old parties, having successively collaborated with Nimayri, were reduced to their core support of 'holy families' and their economic dependents. The communists had not re-covered from 1971. Indeed, the most coherent political grouping left in the northern Sudan was the Muslim Brotherhood, and it was to them that Nimayri turned in the early 1980s. They were glad to cooperate with a weakened president who was willing to implement some of their own programme; Hasan al-Turabi, the brilliant leader of the Muslim Brother-hood, occupied important posts in the government. When, however, in late 1984 Nimayri tried to curb their power, he was left with only the army to support him. In April 1985, as mass protests escalated and Nimayri haughtily went on a foreign tour, the army leadership acted to save itself and deposed him.

It is important to note that the Transitional Military Council that ruled until the spring of 1986 was essentially a continuation of the Nimayri regime without Nimayri. No radical departures were taken by the generals or by the weak civilian cabinet they appointed. The infamous September Laws, whereby Nimayri had made the sharia the law of the land, went largely unenforced but were not repealed. The war therefore continued: absurd rumours that the SPLM/SPLA leader, Dr John Garang de Mabior, would lay down his arms or even join the new government showed the depth of misunderstanding of both that movement and the disaffection it had tapped. Hopes among northern secularists, trade unionists, members of professional associations, and other progressives, that a lengthy transi-tion period might be used to prepare thoughtfully for a new, democratic political system, were dashed. Just as they had in 1965, so in 1985–86 the old sectarian parties re-emerged to retake power. Elections were held as early as possible and, as predicted, the Umma party formed a government under Sadiq al-Mahdi. Yet even this sequence of events, coming as it did after the debacle of the May Regime, seemed to promise a new start.

Despite 20 years out of power, during which he had endured exile, prison, impoverishment, the enormous strain of coup and counter-coup, Sadiq al-Mahdi returned to the premiership with no clear policy. Perhaps more than any other Sudanese he had by virtue of intellect and traditional sanction the means to forge a truly national programme, one that might end the war, win over northern Sudanese to a secularist constitution, and resume by slower processes the very nation-building that stubborn northern chauvinism had prevented. Yet he did not exploit the opportunity. Instead he presided over a series of weak coalitions, the survival of which seemed always to depend on lip-service to the sharia, an Islamic constitution, the defeat of rebels (rather than the conciliation of fellow opponents of Nimayri), and other discredited policies. As the country's economic situation worsened, the war was effectively lost in the south (but continued to drain the treasury), and the government frittered away the goodwill that had attended a return to parliamentary rule. By the spring of 1989 the army, in an unprecedented move, publicly warned the government to break the impasse in the south or face overthrow. Sadiq finally acted but, characteristically, too late: just as an important preliminary agreement was about to be signed, which promised real progress towards a peaceful settlement of the war, elements of the army stepped in and overthrew the regime in June 1989.

The Sudan since 1989

The composition and aims of the group of officers who took power in 1989 were not immediately clear. At first it was thought that the army, having publicly warned the prime minister, had simply fulfilled its promise. It gradually became evident, however, that the coup had been staged by junior officers against the army leadership and in full but secret support of the Muslim Brotherhood. By the time this orientation was evident, the new junta had consolidated its hold on power and, with the tightly knit organisation of the Muslim Brotherhood behind it, had set out to implement radical changes of its own. The timing of the takeover was based on the need to subvert the arrangements for a cease-fire, not to guarantee them.

Since the June 1989 coup the political and economic situation has further deteriorated. Shocking human-rights abuses have been fully documented, at times with dire results for their Sudanese expositors. The junta's willingness to prosecute the war by any means, including mass starvation of civilians in the south, to the point of genocide, has been made clear. The harassment of international aid agencies has threatened large numbers of people in the western and eastern Sudan as well. Purges of the army, the bureaucracy, the judiciary, the universities, and other institutions have been extensive and debilitating. Price inflation, a rampant black market, virtual worthlessness of the currency, the drying-up of foreign credit and other aid (not least because of the junta's self-defeating support of Iraq in the Gulf War) have left an economic shambles. Huge numbers of refugees have crowded into neighbouring countries. The SPLM/SPLA has occupied virtually the entire southern Sudan, leaving only two or three major garrison-towns in the hands of the junta. The question of how bad conditions can become before this regime, too, is overthrown is a familiar one: ominously, there is consensus only about the degree of violence that is likely to accompany its downfall.

The outlook for the Sudan is bleak. The country shares with others in the region the lack of a unifying principle under which its many ethnic, religious, and social differences might be reconciled. Like Ethiopia and Somalia, the Sudan may face imminent break-up. While Iraq, Iran, Lebanon, and other middle Eastern states—to say nothing of Yugoslavia, India, even Canada and indeed Ireland—face intractable problems of ethnic and religious diversity, the dismissive 'tribal' explanation of the Sudan's woes ignores more appropriate analytical tools. But in the aftermath of the Cold War, the Sudan's stability matters less to the world beyond its neighbours, one of which, Egypt, is, however, eternally vigilant of events along the Nile lifeline; Khartoum's excesses may, as before, be contained by fear of Egyptian intervention. The prospect of a separate southern Sudanese state, in fact if not in law, grows apace. The capital demands of Eastern Europe, Asia, and elsewhere make a new era of intense foreign interest in a bankrupt economy even less likely. The spectacle of millions of unfed Sudanese written off by their own nominal government exhausts the patience of all but the most dedicated. As so often since independence, another change of government is awaited, and another fresh start, in a system in which, however, the legacy of failure grows increasingly heavy.

The apparent role as laboratory for Afro-Arab coexistence and Muslim toleration should not mask the grim reality of conflict in the Sudan between a small urban elite and the neglected rural masses. In this, as in other aspects of its colonial and post-colonial history, the Sudan differs from other Middle Eastern states mainly in degree.

Martin Daly

13 SYRIA

At the end of September 1918, with Damascus surrounded by Australian and British Indian troops, the Northern Arab Army under Faisal ibn Husain was allowed to enter the city and take control. Faisal subsequently proclaimed 'an absolutely independent government embracing all Syria'. This was the beginning of the 'Arab Kingdom of Syria', which lasted from October 1918 until 25 July 1920, when Faisal and his supporters were expelled from Syria by the French and the mandate administration installed.

By the end of October 1918, the British had penetrated as far north as Aleppo. The whole of Greater Syria had been detached from the Ottoman Empire and was now under British military control. The area was divided into three zones under the Occupied Enemy Territory Administration (OETA): south, west, and east—corresponding to Palestine, the Syrian coast, and the Syrian interior—the whole under the command of General Allenby. Of crucial importance was that, in spite of France's well-publicised territorial ambitions in the area, there were only a few small detachments of French troops in Greater Syria and only one senior diplomat. This was François Georges-Picot, former consul-general in Beirut.

Much of the confusion of the next few years, and the fact that the ultimate 'disposal' of Syria took place in circumstances of rancour and bloodshed, can be ascribed to intense French suspicions as to the intentions of Britain and its Hashemite protégés. The British foreign secretary, Sir Edward Grey, had declared to the French ambassador in London in December 1912 that Britain had no territorial designs on Syria. The Sykes-Picot agreement (*see* Introduction) of February 1916 had effectively assigned the Syrian coast, as well as 'influence' over the potentially Arab-administered Syrian interior, to France. However, the situation on the ground in Syria at the end of 1918 seemed to threaten the security of these guarantees. It was in what is now Syria that the latent contradictions between the aspirations of the Arabs and the French surfaced with the greatest violence. Faisal, relying on his interpretation of Britain's promises to his father, Sharif Husain, insisted on his claim to rule Syria, while the French demanded the fulfilment of the agreements they had made with the British.

Since Anglo-French cooperation was essential in other areas of the post-war settlement, the French government eventually got its way, in the face of strenuous objections by Faisal. After the announcement that British troops would be evacuated from 'Syria and Cilicia' in November 1919, Faisal rushed to Europe in a desperate effort to have the decision reversed. When he realised he would not make any headway he tried to come to an accommodation with the French before returning to Syria at the beginning of 1920.

Syria was then in ferment, with contradictory rumours claiming both that liberation and a great struggle with the French were imminent. It gradually became clear that the latter was the reality. In February, Faisal announced that independence would be won 'by the sword', and on 8 March the Arab National Congress proclaimed him king of all Syria. This galvanised the British and French into action. On 25 April the mandates for Mesopotamia, Palestine and Syria, and the approximate boundaries of these states, were decided upon at San Remo. At this, Faisal's supporters took the law into their own hands, and launched a series of raids into the French-controlled area on the Syrian coast. In early July, following a Franco-Turkish armistice under which the Turks finally withdrew from northern Syria, the French commander, General Gouraud, delivered an ultimatum. Faisal had little option but to accept it. As a final act of quixotic defiance, a few of his supporters attacked the French column at Khan Maisalun, on the road between Beirut and Damascus. They were defeated, and Faisal sent into exile.

Syria under French mandate, 1920–46

Although Faisal's rule had not been universally popular, the provocative and frequently brutal nature of the French mandatory regime was vigorously opposed by wide sections of the population for much of the mandate. In the first place, Lebanon, considerably enlarged by the addition of areas traditionally considered parts of Syria, was constituted by the French as a separate state (see Chapter 7, Lebanon). What remained of Syria was then further divided into smaller administrative units: one including the four main cities of Aleppo, Hama, Homs and Damascus; one for each of the 'compact' minorities, the Druzes and the 'Alawites; and one for the sanjak of Alexandretta (which the French ceded to Turkey (in violation of the terms of the mandate) in 1939). The thinking behind the divisions was that the religious minorities, living mostly in the rural areas, would be bound to France for having been saved from domination by the Sunni majority, who were considered to be infected by the virus of Arab nationalism. The extent to which this failed can be gauged from the fact that the Druze area in particular was the source of some of the most vigorous opposition to the French during the mandate period, and that the rural minorities regularly sided with the people of the cities against those whom they regarded as their colonisers and occupiers.

The first major revolt of the period actually began in the Druze area in 1925, under the leadership of the Druze notable Sultan al-Atrash.

Official name	Syrian Arab Republic
Area	185,800 sq. km (71,498 sq. miles)
Population	11,338,000 (1988)
Capital	Damascus
Language	Arabic (89%), Kurdish (6%), Armenian (3%), other languages (2%)
Religion	Sunni Muslim (68%), 'Alawite (12%), Christian (15%), remainder Isma'ilis, Druzes and Yazidis
Currency	Syrian pound

Beginning as a tribal revolt against the French administration in the Jabal Druze, it became a national rising when al-Atrash was joined by a number of Damascene notables centred around 'Abd al-Rahman al-Shahbandar and his People's Party, who called for national independence. Although the uprising was defeated in 1926, it led eventually to some relaxation in French policy in that the French showed themselves prepared to countenance a constitution and the gradual withdrawal of French troops. Negotiations continued well into 1928, and the nationalists were successful to the extent that a national assembly was elected and asked to draw up a constitution for Syria.

Although the assembly was dominated by 'moderate' rural and tribal notables and other pro-French elements, the constitutional committee itself was outnumbered by the more educated and generally more enlightened representatives of the urban elites. The draft constitution that emerged recommended the transfer of all powers to the (non-existent) polity of Greater Syria (that is, an entity which was to include Lebanon, Palestine, Syria and Transjordan), reflecting the widely felt anger at what was seen as the arbitrary division of 'Syria' by Britain and France. The draft was rejected and France introduced its own constitution by decree under which Syria was declared a constitutional republic. Negotiations for a Franco-Syrian treaty on the lines of the Anglo-Iraqi Treaty of 1930, which provided for an independent Iraq under strong British influence, continued until stalemate was reached in 1933. Negotiations were then resumed in the spring of 1936, mainly as the result of a seven-week general strike in Aleppo and Damascus. The election of the Popular Front government in France later in the year seemed to presage a more favourable atmosphere for the talks.

Unlike in Iraq, where the nationalists had generally been in partnership with Britain and the Iraqi monarchy, most Syrian nationalists continued to oppose the French mandate. They did not constitute a unified body, however, but continued to be divided into regional factions centred around the urban-based absentee landowning families of the great cities, especially Damascus, Aleppo, Hama and Homs, where they maintained their political base and social networks. Nonetheless, although rivalries persisted, they came together in 1931 to form the National Bloc, an independence movement rather than a political party, which was to dominate Syrian politics until independence in 1946.

Although the Bloc had not instigated the general strike in 1936, and many of its members began to be alarmed when it seemed to get out of control, its potential ability to contain the strike became an important asset. When it managed to assume leadership and take control of the strike, the French showed their preparedness to negotiate and invited its representatives to Paris. The leader of the Syrian delegation was Jamil Mardam Bey, a moderate inclined to accommodate French interests. In September 1936 a draft treaty was initialled, which provided for a form of qualified Syrian independence while guaranteeing French hegemony. The 'Alawite and Druze regions were integrated into the Syrian state but retained a degree of autonomy, as did the *sanjak* of Alexandretta. By 1939, however, the new French government had not yet signed the treaty; autonomy had been restored to both the minority regions; and the Jazirah, in the north-east of the country, recently settled mostly by Christians and Kurds, had been put under the direct rule of the high commissioner. Parliament was dissolved, martial law declared, and Syria fell once again under direct French rule. In June 1939 Alexandretta was annexed by Turkey, with tremendous loss of prestige to the nationalists and great economic damage to the city of Aleppo.

By the Second World War the efforts of the Syrian nationalists to free themselves from the French had thus come to nothing. In the end, it was only with British support that independence was achieved. British and Free French troops invaded Syria and Lebanon in 1940 in a successful attempt to prevent Axis forces from gaining a foothold in the Middle East. Although the constitution was restored and the minority areas integrated into the Syrian state, the Free French seemed in no more of a hurry to grant independence than their predecessors. The nationalists, however, now under the leadership of Shukri al-Quwwatli, continued to push for uncon-ditional independence. In the clashes between the Syrian leaders and their French opponents, Britain began to back the leaders of the National Bloc, particularly al-Quwwatli.

In the course of the mandate, the French High Commission and its representatives in the administrative subdistricts took all major decisions and controlled the country's principal sources of revenue. The Syrian lira was linked to the franc, which, given the precarious state of the French economy in the interwar period, meant that the currency was highly unstable. The French also controlled the bank of note issue, the Banque de Syrie et du Grand Liban, whose gold reserves were kept in Paris.

No national Syrian army was created during the French mandate. The French controlled Syria by means of the Armée du Levant—mainly colonial troops from Africa and Madagascar—and the Troupes Speciales du Levant (TSL), who were mostly recruited from the minority commu-nities in Syria and Lebanon, as were many of the rural gendarmerie. (The preponderance of minorities in the TSL was to give them a dispropor-tionate influence in the Syrian army after independence; few of the majority Sunni community opted for military careers.)

Independent Syria, 1946—63

When independence was finally gained in 1946, those who came to power were the old urban absentee landowning notables who had dominated the National Bloc. Although generally more progressive than the rural and tribal notables who had been the mainstay of French rule, the new political leaders were mostly too short-sighted to realise that things could not simply continue as before. The country desperately needed major reforms to solve its most outstanding social and economic problems. Competition and personal rivalries weakened the new government; the political situation continued to be precarious; and in 1949 Syria experienced three military coups. The first was led by Husni al-Za'im, the second by Mohammed Sami al-Hinnawi and the third by Adib al-Shishakli, who managed to cling to power until he was brought down by provincial revolts in 1954.

The old nationalist leaders who came back to power after Shishakli was ousted in 1954 gained a landslide victory in the famously free elections held in the same year. However, they were too divided and too set in their ways to be able to take up the new challenges and expectations of change both in Syria and in the Arab world. In addition, preoccupied with the threat of communism and the rise of the left, they did not appreciate the threat to their own interests posed by the military. But if the old elite was generally incapable, some of its leading figures, notably Khalid al-'Azm, did make serious attempts to lead the country towards social reform and the creation of a democratic pluralist political system. However, although Khalid al-'Azm came from one of Syria's wealthiest and oldest families and had no intention of establishing any kind of communist state, the mere fact that he had good relations with both the Soviet Union and the Communist party, and was attempting to introduce a number of social democratic reforms, laid him open to charges of 'communism' from his Pan-Arab rivals.

The presidential elections of 1955 brought Shukri al-Quwwatli back to power. However, the government fell in 1956 and a 'government of national unity' was formed under the leadership of Sabri al-'Asali. This included representatives of most of the existing political parties, including Khalid al-'Azm's Democratic Bloc and the Ba'th party. Early in 1958, when al-'Azm, who was already minister of defence and of finance, became deputy prime minister, his political rivals began to regard the growth of his power and personal popularity as a serious threat to their own ambitions.

The United Arab Republic

Accordingly, fearing al-'Azm might win a landslide victory in the impending parliamentary elections, Salah al-Din al-Bitar, co-founder of the Ba'th party, hit on the expedient of a United Arab Republic (UAR) of Egypt and Syria. This had the double advantage of satisfying the Pan-Arab aspirations of many Syrians and of advancing the prospects of al-Bitar and his Ba'th colleagues as authors of this grand gesture. Furthermore, unification would effectively check the perceived threat of communism, though, in the absence of free elections, no accurate measure of communist support at the time is possible.

The 14-man military delegation that left for Cairo on 12 January 1958 had no clear authority from the civil government, indeed their action was in effect a coup d'état. Nevertheless, on 1 February 1958 al-Quwwatli and Nasser proclaimed the creation of the United Arab Republic of Egypt and Syria. As a political entity, 'Syria' disappeared temporarily from the scene. Though the union with Egypt created an atmosphere of euphoria in Syria and other parts of the Arab world, the enthusiasm proved temporary, and the UAR 'experiment' lasted only three years. Frustrated by Egyptian domination, many former advocates of unity became disillusioned and came to favour secession; in the autumn of 1961 a military coup in Syria put an end to the UAR. Civilian rule was restored and elections held, bringing back the old elite of the pre-1958 period. Apart from Akram Hawrani's wing, which had opposed union with Egypt and was able to gain 15 seats, the Ba'th did badly. Independents gained the highest number of seats (62) and Ma'ruf Dawalibi and Nazim al-Qudsi, both from the old elite, became respectively premier and president of the republic.

Over the next two years, members of the old notability, particularly al-'Azm and Dawalibi, pressed for the restoration of democratic liberties and the creation of a mixed economy. A fierce jockeying for power behind the scenes ensued, expressed in three minor military coups in Damascus, Homs and Aleppo in 1962. Nonetheless, the civilian leadership survived, and in September 1962 the National Assembly asked Khalid al-'Azm to form a National Union cabinet, in which the Ba'th refused to serve.

An important consequence of the UAR episode was a lowering of the standing of the Ba'thists and pan-Arab nationalists for having taken Syria into the Union. Their poor showing in the elections clearly indicated that they could only regain power through a military coup. Al-'Azm's efforts to establish a functioning democratic parliamentary system and to keep the army at bay therefore constituted a direct challenge to the ambitions of the pan-Arab nationalists and their allies in the army.

Economic trends after independence

Although it does not possess the extensive natural resources of its richer neighbours, Syria was able to sustain one of the most integrated and productive economies in the region for several decades after the Second World War. Perhaps the lack of such resources was not entirely unfortunate, in that the country was forced to make prudent use of what it had. Despite increasing urban migration and population growth from the mid-1960s, both of which placed some strains on the Syrian economy, the country prospered, benefiting significantly from its well-established and expanding middle class and a skilled labour force. Only after the October War of 1973 did Syria begin to rely heavily on aid, principally from the oil-rich Arab states.

During and immediately after the Second World War both industry and agriculture prospered and textiles experienced a boom. Industrial and agricultural development were left to private initiative, while the state concentrated on infrastructural projects, including building new roads, the port of Latakia and the Homs oil refinery, the latter with the help of a Soviet loan. Syria produced a range of light consumer goods such as textiles (based on local cotton), processed food, soap, glass and cement. In 1960 industry accounted for 15% of GDP and employed 12% of the labour force, agriculture employing 60%.

The rise of the Ba'th

In spite of al-'Azm's serious illness the government stood firm when tensions mounted in the spring of 1963. Radio Cairo intensified its campaign against 'reactionary and secessionist [i.e. from the UAR] elements'; socialist and Muslim Brotherhood ministers continued to quarrel; the military command continued to squabble over proposals to promote or dismiss various officers. Although the Ba'th-Nasserist coup in Iraq in February 1963 had been directed by the CIA, as King Husain of Jordan later confirmed, it was hailed as 'progressive' by both the pan-Arab nationalists and the Ba'thists. Clearly encouraged by events in Iraq, a group of Ba'thist and Nasserist officers engineered its own military coup on 8 March 1963 and asked the Ba'th to take over. The Ba'th agreed and integrated the officers into the party structure. Salah al-Bitar, whose party had failed miserably in the 1961 elections, was asked to form the government.

Real power remained with the armed forces, and it was within the military that the struggle for key positions and control, which characterised the period until 1970, took place. Although a few Sunnis maintained their positions, all key posts in the armed forces were gradually taken up by members of the non-Sunni minorities, the 'Alawites, Druzes and Isma'ilis, all of whom came mainly from the rural areas. The Ba'th, which had only about 400 members in March 1963, substantially increased its membership, especially among these same communities. In the relentless infighting which ensued between the various Ba'th factions, political actors began increasingly to seek support among their own immediate kin and within their own communities.

The 'Alawites, who constitute 11% of the Syrian population, came originally from the mountainous north-west of the country where they worked as peasants or sharecroppers on the land of 'Alawi landowners or on the plains, where the landowners were either Sunni or Greek Orthodox. They did not form a uniform entity but consisted of a number of loosely tribal confederations and included several smaller religious sects. Thus Hafiz al-Asad, president of Syria since 1970, originates from the Matawira tribe from the village of Qardaha and belonged to the Qamariyya sect. One of the attractions of Ba'thism for the Syrian minorities was that a secular state would diminish the importance of sectarian affiliation and enable them to be integrated into the state of Syria as citizens rather than as members of a particular sect.

During the second half of the 1960s control over the state was increasingly concentrated within the 'Alawite community, although some of its most severe critics came from its ranks. However, instead of diminishing its sectarian identity. Ba'th rule became almost exclusively identified with 'Alawite rule. On 23 February 1966 a military coup ended the long struggle for dominance between the old Ba'thists, notably Amin al-Hafiz and Salah al-Din al-Bitar, and the 'Neo-Ba'th', mostly from the provinces and centred around Salah al-Jadid and Hafiz al-Asad, in favour of the latter. Although both the new president and the new prime minister were Sunnis, real power lay in the hands of Jadid and Asad. Subsequently the two began to compete with each other for control of the key positions within the state. Jadid tried to do this by controlling the party machine, while Asad built up his network within the army and the air force and, in November 1970, managed to oust Jadid.

The Ba'th's economic policies

The Ba'th takeover led to a complete transformation. Both the land reform, inaugurated under the UAR and subsequently carried out more thoroughly throughout the 1960s and 1970s, and the wholesale nationalisation of the same period, substantially weakened the political and economic power of the established elites. They found themselves compelled either to leave the country, with as much of their capital as they could take with them, or to cooperate with, or at least acquiesce in, the new structures of power. As a result, the success or failure of particular businesses became increasingly dependent on the degree to which those running them managed to accommodate themselves with the state.

Nonetheless, after Asad came to power in 1970 there was a degree of economic liberalisation. Restrictions were relaxed and exchange and trade regulations freed. The repatriation of Syrian capital from abroad that followed, together with increased aid Syria as a front-line state began to receive from other Arab states after 1973, led to an economic boom that lasted until the late 1970s. At the same time, the state began to launch some of its most ambitious industrial development schemes, earmarking almost half of total investment for industry. As most required investment far beyond the capacity of local private capital to provide, all major industries soon became state owned.

Private manufacture benefited indirectly from the infrastructural improvements and from the general rise in living standards. Most private manufacturing enterprises—around 85,000—are small, employing less than ten people, often family members; only a small proportion—some 2,000—employ more than ten workers. The most profitable businesses are in construction and in contracting, in which private individuals act as middlemen between private companies—both foreign and domestic—and the government.

In order to make Syria more self-sufficient in food, the Ba'th began to promote agriculture more systematically. Increased investment in agriculture was begun, while price controls for vegetables and fruit were lifted. In spite of the land reform, 70% of land is still worked privately. In order to stimulate agricultural investment further during the 1980s the government began to support new mixed public/private-sector ventures, many of which were concerned with vegetable growing and poultry farms. This has resulted in improved supplies of fresh vegetables, fruit, eggs and chicken markets but has also meant substantial price rises. Farms employing wage labour, utilising modern machinery and production methods, coexist with small traditionally run family farms. Another lucrative business is live-stock raising, which is entirely in private hands; the value of animal produce constitutes almost a third of total agricultural output.

Political developments since the 1970s

The most striking political development of the 1970s was the transformation of the state in favour of the presidency. The president, elected every seven years, is supreme army commander and determines the overall outlines of government policies; he appoints and dismisses ministers and cabinets and makes the key appointments in the judiciary. Hafiz al-Asad was elected in 1971 and re-elected in 1978 and 1986, always with over 99% of the vote. Real power continues to lie with the army, the various security services and a group of trusted men who report directly to the president. These include 'Ali Duba (head of military intelligence), Mohammed al-Khuli (head of air-force intelligence), Fu'ad 'Abri (head of civilian intelligence) and Mohammed Nasif (head of political police). Individual ministers generally carry little political weight and are there to carry out executive decisions. Parliament consists of a single-chamber People's Council, which has a Ba'th majority but also includes members of other parties and a number of independents. The Ba'th party reputedly has almost a million members (out of a population of 13 million). It also controls a number of affiliated political organisations. In 1972 the Ba'th coopted a number of rival political parties (including the communists) into a National Progressive Front (NPF), thus ensuring a minimal degree of pluralism.

Hafiz al-Asad became ruler of Syria at a time of mounting tensions in the Middle East. An important consequence of the Six Day War of 1967 for Syria, when it lost the Golan Heights, was that its role in the Arab–Israeli conflict was greatly enhanced. Indeed the conflict came increasingly to dominate both Syria's domestic and foreign policy. Syria's role in the Arab–Israeli conflict is, almost inevitably it seems, ambiguous. On the one hand, the leadership is probably genuinely committed to the Arab cause. On the other, more mundane and immediate considerations of *realpolitik* have caused it to act in ways motivated more perhaps by self-interest than by the best interests of 'the Arabs'. In addition, as a result of its role as a front-line state, since 1973 Syria has received substantial quantities of aid from the oil-rich Gulf states. These have enabled it to expand its armed forces, mainly through purchases of arms from the Soviet Union.

Syria and Lebanon

In 1973, Syria took part in the October War against Israel alongside Egypt. Egyptian Prime Minister Sadat's failure to provide adequate logistical support exposed the Syrian forces to a dangerous extent. In consequence, relations between the two states deteriorated sharply, especially when it became clear in the latter part of the 1970s that Egypt was prepared to enter separate negotiations with Israel. A further important consequence of the Arab–Israeli wars was the rise of the Palestine Liberation Organisation (PLO) as a political and military force able to challenge national armies and national governments, as it did in Jordan and Lebanon. In 1974, at the Rabat Summit, the PLO was recognised as the sole legitimate representative of the Palestinian people, which enhanced its own political role and altered the position of other actors in the region, especially King Husain of Jordan.

Early in 1976 the Lebanese National Movement (LNM), led by Kamal Jumblatt in close cooperation with the PLO, was beginning to gain the upper hand in the Lebanese civil war. At this point a fortuitous community of interest developed between Syria and the United States, both of which were alarmed, for their own reasons, at the prospect of a radical leftist government transforming the balance of power in Lebanon.

America was particularly concerned about Soviet influence in Lebanon increasing on the back of LNM and PLO success. It thus intimated to Syria that neither it nor Israel would oppose Syrian intervention. Thus reassured, Syria sent a detachment of its forces, as well as troops from Sa'iqa, a Syrian-financed Palestinian militia, into Lebanon in June 1976. The intervention was crucial in turning the tide against the PLO and its Lebanese allies, enabling Maronite forces to attack Palestinian and LNM areas in East Beirut, with fearful consequences, notably at Tall Za'tar, where 3,000 civilians were massacred.

The Syrian incursion had taken place without consultation with the Soviet Union, Syria's principal arms supplier. In spite of the conventional wisdom, and in spite of the Syrian/Soviet Treaty of 1980, Syria was never a 'true' Soviet satellite: throughout the relationship, Syria insisted on maintaining its political autonomy. Though the Soviet Union then reduced the supply of arms to Syria, by March 1978 they were returned to the previous level following Syrian concern that the Israeli invasion of south Lebanon was the prelude to an Israeli attack on Syria.

Years of political turmoil

The late 1970s and early 1980s were years of great turmoil in Syria. The apparently endless involvement in Lebanon continued, causing a huge drain on the economy, especially after the Israeli invasion of Beirut in 1982. Relations with Iraq, which had been less than cordial since the late 1960s, deteriorated steadily after Saddam Husain's assumption of power, to the extent that Syria, alone of all Arab countries, supported Iran in the Iran–

Iraq War. The improvement in Jordanian/PLO relations and the possibility that King Husain might obtain a mandate to negotiate with Israel on behalf of the PLO similarly caused anxiety in Damascus, which feared that such a *démarche* would leave Syria isolated. In addition, violent events within Syria, which external forces, particularly Jordan and Israel, were widely suspected of attempting to orchestrate, caused a major crisis of confidence in the Asad government.

Ba'thism is a form of secular pan-Arabism with strong statist, or, in Ba'thist terminology, 'socialist', connotations. Although the government attempted to incorporate the Sunni population (as long as control of the power centres remained in its own hands), resentment at what could easily be labelled secular and minority rule grew, and found expression in the activities of the Muslim Brotherhood, with whom some members of the majority Sunni community began to identify. Political opposition to the status quo was expressed in sectarian rather than political terms. In June 1979 some 60 'Alawite officer cadets were killed at the Aleppo artillery school, the first of a series of sectarian attacks over the next three years. These culminated in a major rising, instigated by Islamic militants, in the city of Hama in February 1982. It was brutally put down by government forces over a period of three weeks, in the course of which the city was shelled repeatedly and many thousands of its inhabitants killed.

Though the massacre effectively ended the 'Islamic' threat to Asad's government, its situation remained precarious, especially when Asad himself became seriously ill in the autumn of 1983. At this point his younger brother Rif'at, the flamboyant commander of the well-armed 55,00-strong 'Defence Brigades', began to think of himself as a suitable candidate for the presidency, for which he received some support among senior military officers. Once Asad began to recover, support for Rif'at evaporated, but the latter's continuing ambitions brought him into conflict with the heads of other paramilitary units. Eventually Rif'at was sent on a semi-official visit to Moscow at the end of May 1985, after which, although returning to Syria from time to time, he lived mostly in France and Spain.

Political and economic crisis in the 1980s

During the second half of the 1980s Hafiz al-Asad's health improved and he was able to re-establish his position. This was a time of economic and social crisis, aggravated by Syria's continuing involvement in Lebanon. In addition, Asad had to steer a delicate course when most of his Arab neighbours began to rally behind Iraq in the Iran–Iraq War. As one of the only Arab supporters of Iran, Syria was left somewhat on the margin of regional politics. Nevertheless, Asad was able simultaneously to maintain friendly relations with Iran, and to reintegrate himself into the mainstream of Arab politics. This found its expression in a number of meetings with various Arab leaders (including a secret meeting with Saddam Husain in Jordan in 1987), a more conciliatory Syrian line towards Egypt (with whom diplomatic relations were eventually resumed in December 1989), and participation in various Islamic and Arab summits.

As far as Lebanon was concerned, Syria had kept a low profile during the mid-1980s, while PLO forces had gradually infiltrated back into the country. Sensing that the Amal militia was gaining the upper hand, Syrian forces reoccupied West Beirut in February 1987 (*see* Chapter 7, Lebanon). When the Iran–Iraq War ended in July 1988, Iraq sought to destabilise Syria by supporting its enemies in Lebanon, sending arms to the commander of the Lebanese army, General Michel Aoun, who was subsequently nominated prime minister of Lebanon by the outgoing president, Amin Jumayyil. Syria's regional standing was further weakened by the PLO's acceptance of UN resolution 242 (and thus its de facto recognition of Israel) in December 1988.

In spite of the heavy military opposition which it engendered, Aoun's defiance of Syria and his claim to represent 'Lebanon' against 'Syria' gained him considerable popularity in Lebanon, popularity that extended well beyond the Maronite community. However, in the spring of 1989 the main pro-Syrian factions and militias joined forces with the Syrians to dislodge Aoun, imposing a virtual blockade on the area he controlled between July and September. This was lifted only after pressure had been brought to bear on both Aoun and Iraq by the United States. The ending of this round of fighting enabled Syria and Saudi Arabia to arrange an interim settlement, the Ta'if Accord, in October. Members of the Lebanese parliament were taken to Ta'if in Saudi Arabia where they elected a new president, Rene Mu'awwad.

Mu'awwad was assassinated shortly afterwards, but his successor, Ilyas Harawi, was also staunchly pro-Syrian and undertook to maintain the Ta'if process. Aoun continued to hold out in his stronghold in East Beirut, denouncing Ta'if and its supporters as Syrian lackeys. This confrontation persisted more or less unabated until October 1990, by which point Iraq's preoccupations elsewhere meant that it was no longer capable of supplying Aoun. On 13 October, the general fled to the safety of the French Embassy. Syria then proceeded to impose a *pax Syriana* on Lebanon. Whatever its shortcomings, this at least introduced a period of tranquillity unknown since the late 1960s.

Although small, with few raw materials and substantially dependent on foreign aid, Syria has generally managed to maintain a degree of political autonomy. In spite of what often appeared as virtually insurmountable obstacles (mainly the result of its being identified by the West as a supporter of international terrorism, and because of its friendship with Iran and hostility to the West's major ally, Iraq), Syria managed to sustain its position successfully throughout the latter 1980s, restoring full diplomatic relations with the US and all EC countries except Britain (broken over the Hindawi affair in 1986) during 1987. At the same time, Syria managed to overcome some of the ambiguities of its relations with

Moscow and to ensure Moscow's continued support within the newly emerging framework of international and regional alliances. During Asad's visit to Moscow in 1987 a Syrian/Soviet communiqué was signed calling for an international peace conference under the auspices of the UN and the establishment of an independent Palestinian state, though significantly it made no mention of the PLO, with which Syria was not on good terms. The Soviet Union also reiterated its commitment to maintain Syria's defensive capacity.

One consequence of perestroika and glasnost in the Soviet Union was that trade relations with friendly states were to be based more on commercial criteria than before and thus, in Syria's case, on its ability to pay rather than simply on the Soviet Union's geopolitical interests. Soviet sources estimated Syria's debts to the Soviet Union in 1990 to be in the region of $9 billion. An indication of the continued importance of the Soviet Union to Syria was the fact that it was the destination for over a third of its exports in the same year. Nevertheless, the Soviet Union made it clear that Syria would have to abandon the idea of matching Israeli's military capacity and instead pursue defensive rearmament in a way which would restrain Israel. The Soviet Union was currently engaged in talks with Israel in order to re-establish diplomatic relations (broken off in 1967), and by 1990 the emigration of thousands of Soviet Jews to Israel could be seen on Syrian television, watched with awe and amazement by the audience.

One by-product of Syria's 'outsider' role during the 1980s was a drastic decline in Arab aid, which, together with the costs of its activities in Lebanon and the reduction in remittances resulting from the falling price of oil, brought about a major economic crisis, aggravated by widely believed rumours of large-scale corruption in high places. Nonetheless, with Syria stepping up its oil production, its economic future seems likely to improve. The country has no reserves comparable to those of the Gulf states, but it is at least self-sufficient in oil and, following fresh oil strikes, will almost certainly be able to increase its oil exports. Income from oil in 1990, for example, amounted to $1.5 billion, almost double the figure for 1989.

The invasion of Kuwait

The indirect effects of the Iraqi invasion of Kuwait were of great benefit to the Syrian government. On the negative side, there was an immediate decline in remittances caused by the forced return of thousands of Syrians from Kuwait; in addition, the government's decision to condemn the invasion and subsequently to send forces to Saudi Arabia did not meet with universal approval, especially from Syria's substantial Palestinian community. But on the positive side, Syria was able to stabilise the situation in Lebanon to its own advantage, at least for the time being, and to profit from the rise in oil prices. On the wider political front, the decision to support the coalition forces brought immediate and substantial financial rewards, in the form of large injections of aid and credits from Saudi Arabia, the Gulf states, the United States, the EC and Japan, all of which acted as a great boost to the economy and to the Asad regime itself.

Although Syrian forces played a relatively insignificant role in the Gulf War Syria's anti-Iraqi line was of major political significance and resulted in the re-emergence of Asad as a crucial player in the politics of the region. His enhanced standing became clear when he met George Bush in Geneva in November 1990 and was given the green light to move into Lebanon. After the end of hostilities on 28 February 1991, the Syrian and Egyptian foreign ministers met representatives of the Gulf Cooperation Council in Damascus to work out the establishment of a new regional security framework. In July 1991 the Syrian government indicated its preparedness to accept the United States' proposals for an international peace conference to establish a lasting settlement of the Arab–Israeli conflict, thus putting Israel into a position where it was difficult for it to refuse to do the same.

Peter Sluglett and Marion Farouk-Sluglett

14 TURKEY

Within the Middle East, Turkey has a distinctive but sometimes ambiguous status. The Ottoman Empire, from which the modern Turkish state evolved, was one of the superpowers of Renaissance Europe, embracing a huge territory running as far as Hungary in the north-west to the Red Sea and the Persian Gulf in the south. Within this vast empire, ethnic Turks formed the ruling class, but proportionately they were only a small minority in a patchwork of diverse nationalities. The empire collapsed during the 19th and early 20th centuries, leaving modern Turkey a relatively compact and ethnically homogeneous unit in the Turkish heartlands of the old empire. In the 1920s, under Kemal Atatürk, a concerted effort was made to redefine its political identity as a nation-state on the European model, committed to secular political values, and institutional and economic modernisation. As a result, most modern Turks tend to see their country as being more a part of Europe than of the Middle East, or else as being balanced between the two, both culturally and politically.

Turkish culture is also distinctive. Turkish tribes, who were only recent converts to Islam, moved into Anatolia from central Asia during the 10th to 13th centuries. Their language and religion gradually supplanted those of the Byzantines, while absorbing elements from the ancient past of the region. As Muslims, the Turks added a large number of Arabic and Persian words to their language, but its basic structure and vocabulary remains distinct: linguistically, the Turks are closer to the Turkic people of central Asia than to the other nations of the Middle East. Ethnically, there is a high degree of homogeneity; following the deportations and massacres of the Armenians during the First World War, and an exchange of minority populations with Greece in the 1920s, the Kurds (who, according to an estimate by the Minority Rights Group in 1980, probably account for around 19% of the total population) remain the only important ethnic minority in Turkey.

Turks are sometimes apt to exaggerate their national unity. Turkish society is divided, like those of the other Middle Eastern states, between a Westernised and urban middle class and the millions of villagers who mix Western and traditional values in their social and cultural life. Urban workers and artisans lie culturally between the two. Economically, the relatively prosperous and industrialised regions of western Anatolia are a world apart from the poor and neglected regions of the east. The division between the Sunni Muslim majority, and the minority of Alevi Shias (probably around 15 to 20% of the total) is also an important social cleavage

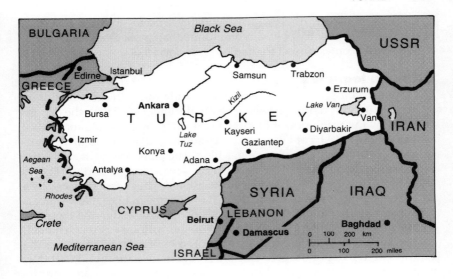

Official name	Republic of Turkey
Area	779,452 sq. km (300,947 sq. miles)
Population	50,664,458 (1985)
Capital	Ankara
Language	Turkish, Kurdish
Religion	Sunni Muslim (90%) and Alevi Shia (10%)
Currency	Turkish lira

in rural society. Nevertheless, it is probably true to say that Turkey is nearer to being a unitary political community than most other states in the region, and it comes closest to the European model of a nation-state.

Ottoman legacies

The Ottoman Empire reached its apogee during the 16th century, but by the end of the 18th century it was clearly in decline. Faced with the danger of defeat by the rising power of Russia and, later, by their nominal vassal Mohammed Ali Pasha of Egypt, a succession of sultans began to modernise their army and administrative machine. The janissary regiments—the professional core of the old Ottoman army—were suppressed in 1826 by Mahmud II, the greatest of the reformist sultans. They were replaced by a new model army, organised and trained on European lines. New schools to train army officers and civil servants were opened, and in the 1860s the administrative system was reconstructed on the centralised French model.

The sultans' intentions were that the process of reform (known as the *Tanzimat* or 'regulation') would stop short at their own thrones. What they wanted was a sharper sword in their own hands, without altering the distribution of political power, two aims which proved impossible to reconcile. On the one hand, the states of Western Europe pressed for the concession of political and legal rights, especially to the Christian minorities; on the other, the new educational institutions opened the eyes of the elite to the idea of constitutional, rather than just military or administrative reform. These two forces came together in 1876 when the government was faced with bankruptcy, a major revolt in the Balkans, the imminent prospect of war with Russia, and renewed pressure from the Western powers, who wished to prevent a Russian takeover in south-east Europe. The army and navy intervened to depose the incompetent Sultan Abdul Aziz, replacing him first with his nephew Murad, who suffered a mental breakdown, and then, in September 1876, with another nephew, Abdul Hamid. The reformers wanted the sultan to introduce a constitution. This, it was hoped, would give all the peoples of the empire political representation, staving off partition, and place the guardianship of the state in more reliable hands. As the price for the throne, Abdul Hamid agreed. Amid booming guns, the constitution was duly proclaimed on 23 December 1876, and the empire's first (indirectly) elected assembly was convened the following March.

The constitutional experiment of 1876 turned out to be a false start. The threatened war with Russia began in April 1877; the Ottoman armies suffered defeats in the Balkans, but the temporary survival of the empire was secured by the Congress of Berlin of June–July 1878. Meanwhile, Abdul Hamid seized the opportunity to suspend the assembly indefinitely in February 1878. Without formally abolishing the constitution, he ruled as an absolute monarch for the following 30 years. Like his predecessors, he refused to concede political powers to his subjects, but continued the modernisation of the education system and the state's military and administrative machine. Nevertheless, the conflict between modernisation and autocracy eventually re-emerged. In the army and outside, the so-called 'Young Turks' (more specifically the 'Committee of Union and Progress') demanded the reactivation of the constitution.

The Young Turk Revolution began in July 1908, when the army in the Balkans rose in revolt. Hoping to gain time, the sultan gave ground by promising to reconvene the assembly. This was duly elected at the end of 1908, and a new era of liberalism seemed to have dawned. It was challenged in April 1909, when conservative elements of the army in Istanbul mutinied. Under the command of Mahmud Shevket Pasha, pro-constitutionalist army units from the Balkans marched to Istanbul, overcame the mutineers, and deposed Abdul Hamid. His brother Reshad took the throne as Mehmet V, but with the constitution altered to reduce the royal powers. In this way, Mehmet V became the first sultan who, constitutionally, merely reigned rather than ruled.

Unfortunately, the events of 1909 did not lead to the establishment of a stable and liberal regime. By this time, the Young Turks were divided into a pro-liberal group, and the 'unionists', who put greater emphasis on the revival of a powerful state, and who stressed the 'Turkishness' of what was left of the empire. The result was a period of instability and struggle. In the meantime, in 1912–13, Bulgaria, Serbia and Greece launched yet another war against their former Turkish overlords which finally ended Ottoman rule in the Balkans. Within the empire, the internal power struggle ended in January 1914 when Enver Pasha, one of the leaders of the original revolt of 1908, became minister of war. He imposed himself as the head of a three-man junta, consisting of himself, Ahmed Jemal (the minister of the navy) and Mehmet Talat (minister of the interior). The sultan and grand vizier were reduced to insignificance. This triumvirate dragged the empire into its final defeat, by entering the First World War on the German side. In the ensuing struggle, the Turkish army put up a far stiffer resistance than many outsiders had expected. Nevertheless, by the autumn of 1918 the empire was in ruins. Its existence as an imperial entity was ended by an armistice with the Entente powers, signed on 30 October 1918.

The new republic: 1919—38

It can be argued that the Young Turks failed because they attempted an impossible task—to preserve and at the same time to liberalise a multi-national empire in an age in which ethnic nationalism was gradually becoming the dominant ideology. For their successors, the problem was solved by the fortunes of war. The Balkan Wars of 1912–13 removed most of its Christian subjects from the empire's control. Similarly, the loss of the Arab provinces in the First World War ended the political link between Turks and Arabs, as well as the old Ottoman claim to hegemony over the whole Muslim world. Henceforward, supra-nationalism and pan-Islamism both became unrealistic as legitimising ideologies for the Turkish state. Reduced as it was to the Turkish heartland of Anatolia, it became possible to reconstruct the state according to the principles of secular nationalism.

This outcome was only achieved by yet another war. After their victory, the Entente powers put together a complex and at points vague partition plan to divide Anatolia into Greek, Italian and French zones, with international control of the straits of the Bosporus and Dardanelles, and reducing Turkey to a rump of territory in northern and central Anatolia. This scheme, formalised as the Treaty of Sèvres, was officially accepted by the government of the last sultan, Vahdettin (Mehmet VI) in August 1920. However, it was decisively rejected by a movement of national resistance, led by Mustafa Kemal (later Atatürk), which effectively set up a rival government in Ankara. Greece was the only Entente power prepared to back her claim to territory in western Anatolia by force of arms. Moving eastwards from its base at Izmir, the Greek army reached the River Sakarya, 50 miles west of Ankara, in August–September 1921. This marked the limit of its advance. In the summer of 1922 the Turkish forces counter-attacked, driving the Greeks out of Anatolia by October 1922. The verdict of the battlefield was confirmed by the Treaty of Lausanne of July 1923, which established Turkey within what are virtually her present frontiers (the only subsequent frontier change occurred in 1939, when the province of Hatay, or Alexandretta, was transferred from Syria to Turkey).

The victory of 1922 swept Atatürk into a position of virtually un-challangeable national authority. He used it to effect a sweeping recon-struction of the state, and to mount a determined campaign of cultural reorientation and economic development. Vahdettin was deposed, and the sultanate abolished in November 1922: just under a year later, Turkey was declared a republic, with Ankara as its capital, and Atatürk elected president. The office of the caliphate previously occupied by the sultans, which had been the principal constitutional link between the state and the Muslim religion, was abolished in March 1924. Simultaneously, the Minis-try of Education took over control of the formerly separate Muslim educa-tional establishments. The Islamic legal system was swept aside in 1926, and replaced by secular criminal, civil and commercial codes copied from Western Europe. Even the fez—the symbol of attachment of male Turks to Islam—was banned, in 1925, while in 1928 the Arabic script was replaced with a version of the Latin alphabet. The change in the script was part of a determined attempt to nationalise culture—to promote the principle that the Turks were culturally and historically separate from the rest of the Muslim world. Among the rural masses, the campaign was never entirely successful, but it had a significant effect on the educated elite and, as time went on, among non-elite groups as well.

Atatürk's regime was culturally progressive but politically authori-tarian. But for two brief experiments with a multi-party system, in 1924–25 and 1930. Turkey was ruled as a single-party state under the Republican People's party (RPP) and organised dissent was outlawed. At the same time, the government made determined moves to develop the national economy, and enhance its own role within it. Under the first five-year industrialisation plan, implemented between 1934 and 1938 and introduced as part of the official policy of étatism, Turkey began to acquire a range of basic industries (textiles, sugar, steel, chemicals, paper and coal) most of which were dominated by state enterprises, competing in some sectors with private firms.

Challenge and change: 1938–60

Kemal Atatürk died in November 1938, to be succeeded by his principal and faithful lieutenant, Ismet Inönü. The new president carefully steered Turkey through a difficult path of neutrality during the Second World War, maintaining–indeed, tightening–the single party regime. In November 1945, however, he took the momentous step of announcing that he favoured the formation of an opposition party. The resultant Democrat party was set up in January 1946 by dissidents from the RPP, notably Adnan Menderes, scion of a wealthy landowning family in the Aegean region, and Celal Bayar, who had served under Atatürk as minister of economy and as prime minister between 1937 and 1939. The Democrats emerged as the major opposition party in Turkey's first post-war elections, held in July 1946, and then swept to power with a massive majority in the following elections of May 1950. A new era had begun, as commitment to a liberal, multi-party system was added to the Atatürkist ideological legacy of secular nationalism and modernisation.

Besides the need to create a safety valve for domestic discontent after years of heavy-handed rule by the RPP, foreign policy considerations contributed to Inönü's dramatic change of course. In 1945–46 Stalin launched a diplomatic campaign for revision of the Montreux Convention of 1936, with the aim of establishing Soviet-controlled military bases at the Straits. The defeat of fascism in the Second World War, allied to the need to strengthen Turkey's moral claim for Western assistance against the Soviet Union, helped to create the climate for internal political liberalisation. It also laid the basis for Turkey's overriding foreign policy alignments since then, signalled by its admission to NATO in 1952. For Turkey, NATO membership has been the vital element in its national security: for NATO, Turkey's adherence to the alliance is regarded as essential to Western security in the eastern Mediterranean.

The election of 1950 brought about a fundamental shift in political power. Resting on the votes of millions of peasant farmers, a new elite of businessmen, landowners and professionals took over power from the state-centred metropolitan elite that had held the dominant position under the RPP. As prime minister, Adnan Menderes fully realised his debt to the peasants, and repaid it by putting new emphasis on agricultural development, granting easy loans and subsidised crop prices to farmers. In industry, greater emphasis was put on private investment. In response to the sentiments of a conservative rural electorate, there was also some relaxation of secularist policies, but no attempt was made to alter the basis of the secular political system laid down by Atatürk. During the first half of the 1950s, these policies paid handsome dividends, as both agricultural and industrial output grew fast. During the second half of the decade, however, the economy deteriorated: the growth of national income slowed to a crawl, inflation rose, and a large foreign trade deficit developed. Menderes responded with a return to heavy-handed political tactics, by rigging the elections in some constituencies in 1957, and restricting oppositional political activity.

The growing political crisis came to a head in the spring of 1960, when the government voted to establish a special commission, with arbitrary powers of search and arrest, 'to investigate the activities of the Republican People's Party'. The result was widespread disturbance in Ankara and Istanbul, with fierce fighting between students and police, and the imposition of martial law in the two cities. Hitherto, the army had abided by Atatürk's principle that it should stay out of politics. However, the declaration of martial law forced it back into the political arena for the first time since the Young Turk period. Within the army, there was a group of relatively junior officers who had long planned to overthrow Menderes. The crisis enabled them to win sufficient generals to their side. In a virtually bloodless coup, launched and completed in the early morning of 27 May 1960, the government was overthrown, and Turkey's first post-war military regime was installed. The titular leader of the coup, General Cemal Gürsel, became Turkey's temporary head of state, at the head of a 38-man junta, known as the National Unity Committee (NUC).

Generals and politicians: 1960—80

Like their predecessors of 1908, those responsible for the coup of 27 May had divided aims. Among the junior officers, there were many who had never really accepted the introduction of the multi-party system and who wished to establish a long-term military regime that would supposedly implement further 'Atatürkist' reforms. On the other hand, the senior members of the NUC wanted to keep the army's political involvement to a minimum. Hence they were anxious to abide by Gürsel's promise, made on the morning of the coup, to hold free and fair elections as soon as possible. The contest between the two factions reached crisis point in November 1960 when 14 of the radicals were expelled from the NUC. This cleared the way for the preparation of a new constitution, providing a wider definition of civil liberties, and a two-chamber parliament consisting of a House of Representatives and Senate. Elections were held in October 1961, and civilian government restored. In the meantime, Menderes and two of his cabinet colleagues were tried and eventually executed for having violated the previous constitution. It was a move that would create a legacy of bitterness over the following three decades.

The process of military disengagement was complicated by subsequent instability in parliament. Thanks in part to the system of proportional representation introduced in 1961, the RPP failed to win an overall majority. In the new parliament, it was challenged by the Justice party (JP), which effectively established itself as the unofficial successor to the Democrats. Under strong pressure from the army, the two parties formed a coalition government, with Inönü as prime minister and Gürsel as president. It was an uncomfortable arrangement for both sides, and it collapsed in June 1962. It was followed by two further coalitions under Inönü, the second of which fell in February 1965. In the meantime, the radicals within the army, led by Colonel Talet Aydemir, tried to reverse the decisions of November 1961, by launching two failed coup attempts, in February 1962 and May 1963. It was not until 1964–65 that an accommodation between the army and the JP became possible. In 1964 a newcomer to politics, Süleyman Demirel, took over the leadership of the JP, and worked hard to bury the hatchet between the army and the old Democrats. Under his leadership, the JP won an overall majority in elections held in October 1965, and increased it in the following elections, held four years later. Turkey thus came to enjoy an interval of stable government, and *rapprochement* between the generals and the politicians.

The accommodation of 1964–65 fell apart in 1971. At the end of the 1960s, Turkey began to be wracked by a wave of urban terrorism conducted by extremists of both left and right. In response, the commanders of the armed forces began to demand stronger government. On 12 March 1971, they issued a 'memorandum', which forced Demirel to resign, and, without closing parliament or the parties, called for the formation of a 'powerful and credible government' appointed by parliament in a 'non-partisan spirit'. The result was two coalition governments headed by Nihat Erim, who resigned from the RPP for the purpose. However, the Erim governments were anything but powerful and credible, and effectively followed the offstage directions of the military chiefs. By the spring of 1973, the generals had been forced to the realisation that the 'half-way coup' of March 1971 was unworkable. Since they were unwilling to take over openly, they decided to return to their barracks, allowing free general elections and a return to full civilian government in October 1973.

With the return to an elected regime, much depended on whether one of the parties could win an overall majority and provide a reasonably stable government. The proportional representation system made this difficult. In May 1972, Bülent Ecevit captured the leadership of the RPP from Inönü, and redirected the party towards a centre-left position, modelled on that of the social democratic parties of Western Europe (Inönü, who was by now 89 years old, died on 25 December 1973). Under Ecevit, the RPP recaptured some of its old popularity, but just failed to win an absolute majority in the

1973 elections. After months of bargaining, a coalition was patched to-gether between the RPP and the populist-Islamic National Salvation party (NSP), led by Necmettin Erbakan, a new entrant to the party fray. Ecevit enhanced his image as a national leader when the Turkish army invaded northern Cyprus in July 1974, following a botched attempt by the colonels' junta in Greece to take over the island. However, his coalition with Erbakan was rickety from the start, and duly fell apart in September 1974. It was followed by a caretaker government, under an Independent senator, Sadi Irmak, which lasted until the end of March 1975. By this stage, Demirel had succeeded in putting together a 'Nationalist Front' coalition, including the JP, the NSP, and two smaller right-wing parties.

In a bid to end the need for further coalitions, Ecevit and Demirel agreed to hold general elections in June 1977, four months ahead of the date required under the constitution. Both were disappointed, with the elections resulting in another hung parliament. After a month's interval, Demirel reconstructed the Nationalist Front, but it was faced with constant feuding between the constituent parties. The government's majority was sapped by backbench defections, and it was forced to resign at the end of December 1977. By incorporating no less than ten defectors from the JP in his cabinet, Ecevit then put together an RPP-led government, but this only survived by the thinnest of margins. After a severe defeat in the partial Senate elections held in October 1979, Ecevit stepped down, allowing Demirel to form yet another government—this time as a minority JP administration with outside support from the NSP and other small right-wing parties.

Thanks to these constant turns of the political whirligig, between 1973 and 1980 Turkey had no less than eight governments, and long periods of hiatus with no effective government at all. The state rapidly collapsed into a downward spiral of political anarchy and economic crisis. Political terrorism re-emerged on an increasingly horrendous scale. In spite of the declaration of martial law in more and more provinces, successive govern-ments seemed incapable of stemming the tide of violence. Almost 900 people were killed during the first nine months of 1979; over the following 12 months, the total rose to above 2,800. Economically, Turkey was badly hit by the oil price rises of 1973–74, which pushed up both inflation and the balance of payments deficit. Unwilling to court electoral unpopularity by taking harsh deflationary measures, governments allowed inflation to surge upwards, to reach three-digit levels by the end of the decade. By 1979–80, many Turks had lost confidence in the ability of elected civilian governments to prevent a Lebanese-style slide into civil war and economic collapse.

Generals and politicians: 1980–83

In these circumstances, another military intervention was only a matter of time. At the beginning of 1980 the chief of the general staff, General Kenan Evren, and his fellow commanders, acting through the president, tried to persuade Demirel and Ecevit to form a national unity government. When these efforts failed, they decided that there was no alternative to a full military takeover. Accordingly, on 12 December, they deposed Demirel's administration and dissolved the parliament, promising to introduce a new constitution and electoral laws and to return power to an elected government at an unspecified date. Evren became temporary head of state, and chairman of the ruling National Security Council (NSC), which included the commanders of each of the armed forces. Day-to-day responsibility for government was born by a cabinet of technocrats headed by a retired admiral, Bülent Ulusu.

The NSC ruled Turkey for just under 39 months, until 6 December 1983. During this period, Evren and his fellow commanders were careful to keep both political power and military command in their own hands, preventing the split and threats of a counter-coup that had plagued their predecessors in 1960–61. Their first task was to restore law and order. This was achieved with impressive swiftness. Mass arrests, allied to far tighter control by the security forces, saw civil order re-established by early 1981. The regime also made a determined and generally successful effort to tackle the country's economic problems–a task in which the leading part was played by Turgut Özal, the deputy prime minister, and main economic policy-maker. Through the classic methods of devaluation, restriction of state expenditure and market pricing in the public sector, by 1982–83 inflation had been brought under control, exports had grown impressively, and economic growth had been restored.

Their political task—establishing a democratic and stable successor regime—caused most problems for the generals. A new constitution was prepared, which abolished the Senate, gave increased powers to the president, and narrowed civil liberties. It was accepted by an overwhelming majority in a referendum in November 1982, in which Evren was also elected unopposed as president. Provisional articles added to the constitution by the NSC banned Demirel, Ecevit and other previous party leaders from participation in politics for ten years. A new electoral law, enacted in 1983, aimed to prevent the proliferation of small parties by requiring parties to win at least 10% of the vote in future elections to qualify for any seats, and by reducing the size of constituencies. To compete in the first elections, which were scheduled for November 1983, the NSC encouraged the formation of a centre-right party, the Nationalist Democracy party (NDP) and a centre-left competitor, the Populist party (PP). The race was also joined by Turgut Özal, who had left the Ulusu cabinet in July 1982, and established the Motherland party (MP) as an alternative party of the centre-right. Meanwhile, Demirel circumvented the bans included in the constitution by having close colleagues set up what was in effect his own party, the True Path party (TPP). Similarly, previous members of the RPP established a Social Democracy party (Sodep) headed by Erdal Inönü, the son of the former president, Ismet Inönü.

The Özal era: 1983–89

The emergence of the TPP and Sodep faced the NSC with a dilemma, since they were popularly identified as reincarnations of the RPP and JP, which had officially been dissolved. In consequence, they were prevented from taking part in the elections by a legal loophole. But if the exclusion of the two parties undermined the democratic legitimacy of the elections, this was offset by the fact that the NDP, the party most favoured by the military, was roundly defeated, winning only 71 of the 400 seats in the new assembly, against 117 for the PP and 211 for the MP. Although Evren had indirectly attacked Özal in a televised speech just before polling day, he seems to have recognised his mistake, accepting Özal's victory with good grace. Turgut Özal was thus able to take office as the new prime minister with both a comfortable parliamentary majority and presidential support. His position was confirmed by local elections held in March 1984: although both Sodep and the TPP were allowed to compete, the MP emerged a clear winner, giving it a broad control over both central and local government.

As prime minister, Özal buttressed his success over the following years. His free market policies continued to bring growth to the Turkish economy, as well as a dramatic improvement in the balance of foreign trade. The 1980s also saw a steady withdrawal of the military from the political scene. The process of military disengagement was aided by President Evren, who stuck strictly to a neutral role as president. Özal's position was also crucial: as a moderate leader of the centre-right, he was acceptable to the military, but sufficiently distanced from them to retain credibility as an independent actor in the eyes of the public.

The strength of Özal's government was reinforced by the simultaneous division of the opposition. An artificial creation from the start, the NDP withered away and was formally dissolved in 1986. Meanwhile the PP avoided the same fate by merging with Sodep to form the Social Democrat Populist party (SDPP) in November 1985, under Erdal Inönü's leadership. Its position as the standard bearer of the centre-left was challenged by Bülent Ecevit, who soldiered on at the head of his own Democratic Left party (DLP) which was nominally led by his wife Rahşan. Besides Demirel's TPP, Necmettin Erbakan sponsored the Welfare party (WP), as a virtual recreation of the NSP. Turkey thus had no less than four discordant opposition parties, and no credible alternative government.

By 1987 it had become clear that the ban on the pre-1980 party leaders was both undemocratic and, since it had not prevented them from setting up front parties under the nominal leadership of close colleagues or relatives, unworkable. Accordingly, a referendum to decide whether to remove the bans was held in September 1987. The motion in favour was carried by the hairsbreadth margin of 50.2 to 49.8%. Buoyed up by this result, Özal decided to call a snap general election, on 7 November. His gamble paid off handsomely: the MP won only 36% of the vote (compared with 45% in 1983) but changes in the electoral system, besides the split of the opposition vote, enabled it to retain power with 292 of the 450 assembly seats. The SDPP finished in second place, with 99 seats, followed by the TPP with 59 seats. Since they failed to clear the 10% barrier, the DLP and the WP were left with no clear parliamentary representation.

The victory reinforced Özal's position in parliament, but created problems in his relationship with his own party. Increasing resentment was voiced from MP ranks, on the grounds that Özal was abusing his power, by turning the party into a one-man band, and promoting his own relatives to top positions. The party's internal problems were increased by rivalries between its two main ideological elements: a secular liberal majority; and a minority which favours more conservative Islamic attitudes. Resentments at Özal's personal role became acute in November 1989, when Kenan Evren's term as president expired. An important sign of the times was that Evren was not succeeded by a retired military commander, as all presidents had been since 1961. However, by deciding to run for the presidency himself, Özal further strengthened his personal position, while creating some serious constitutional problems. Like its predecessors, the present constitution provides that the president should be elected by an absolute majority in parliament. Thanks to the MP's large majority, Özal was easily able to win the election, and took office on 9 November 1989. He immediately appointed the relatively unknown Yıldırım Akbulut, previously speaker of the assembly, as his successor as prime minister.

Current political developments

Turgut Özal's election to the presidency in 1989 effectively reversed the constitutional tradition, established since 1961, that policy was decided by the prime minister. Although Özal was constitutionally obliged to sever official links with the MP on assuming the presidency, he continued to act as prime minister in all but name. Özal's personal dominance was enhanced by international events, in particular, the Gulf crisis of 1990–91. Crisis management in an age of telephone (and even television) diplomacy put a premium on personal contacts and instant decisions. Thanks to his position as the head of government for the previous seven years. Özal was virtually the only politician in Ankara with the range of experience and acquaintance with other world leaders that was needed. Inevitably, by putting the prime minister and cabinet in the shade, this opened up institutional opposition to Özal.

Yıldırım Akbulut was chosen as prime minister primarily because, as a comparatively little-known and neutral figure, he would be unlikely to challenge the new president, and would not exacerbate the tensions within the MP. However, his evident weakness and lack of experience of government have clearly been a liability, and have led to growing calls for his replacement. These are intensified by the fact that the government's failure to control inflation has severely eroded its popularity. In local elections, held in March 1989, the MP scored only 22% of the vote, compared with 28% for the SDPP and 26% for the TPP. Since general elections must be held by November 1992 at the latest, there is a real possibility that the MP will lose power unless the government can present a more successful record. On the same showing, there is also the risk that the elections will result in a hung parliament, and that a coalition government will be necessary. Granted the long-standing personal rivalry between Ozal and Demirel, as well as the fairly deep policy differences between the SDPP and the two other main parties, it is hard to see how a stable coalition could be achieved. Meanwhile, Özal has been considering the possibility of constitutional amendments to end the rule that presidential candidates may not compete as members of parties, and to provide for direct election of the president by popular vote. In other respects, the powers and functions of the president and prime minister would be similar to those in France. If such amendments are enacted, they would probably prolong Özal's tenure of power, as well as give constitutional legitimacy to a situation that has existed de facto ever since his election to the presidency.

Kurds, Islam and human rights

Apart from the state of the economy and the relationship between the cabinet and president, the two main issues in Turkish politics in recent years have been the problem of the Kurdish minority, and the questions of political secularism and human rights. Of these, the first is currently the most acute. The position of Turkey's Kurds differs from that in neighbouring countries, in that the operation of a relatively liberal political system gives their traditional leaders a role in parliament, and hence in government. On the other hand, until recently the Kurdish question has been treated virtually as a taboo subject in Turkey: any use of the Kurdish language was banned, and the economic neglect of the south-east, combined with poor communications and geographical remoteness, has meant that levels of income, education and general welfare are far lower in the Kurdish region than in other parts of Turkey.

The main Kurdish guerrilla organisation in Turkey is the PKK, or Kurdistan Workers' party, which receives most of its financial and logistic support from Syria. Its aim of establishing an independent Kurdistan is not widely supported, but its terrorist attacks on the Turkish security forces and on Kurdish villagers who side with the government continue to take a heavy toll. Faced with criticism on this issue from abroad, as well as pressure from MPs from the south-eastern provinces, the government withdrew the ban on the Kurdish language in April 1991. However, it is as yet unclear whether this will apply to written publications or broadcasting, while it is virtually certain that any likely future government will vigorously oppose any sort of regional autonomy for the Kurds in Turkey. Politically, the future evolution of the problem is likely to be strongly influenced by events in neighbouring countries, especially Iraq. In the meantime, reducing the economic disparities between the Kurdish region and the rest of the country, and countering raids by the PKK, will remain a major problem for the government.

The contest between political secularism and Islamic conservatism has been simmering for many years. Although officially a secular state, a significant body of support for a reassertion of Islam in public life exists, a trend the MP has been successful in exploiting. It has initiated a massive increase in religious education and in the construction of mosques. This programme is strongly opposed by a still substantial body of secularist opinion, most of it to the left of centre.

On the other hand, Islamic radicalism appears a far weaker political force in Turkey than in other Middle Eastern states. In a poll conducted by the Istanbul daily *Milliyet* in 1986, only 7% of respondents said they favoured the reintroduction of the Islamic sharia as the law of the land. Similarly, the WP—the sole party with a clearly Islamic image—won only just over 7% of the vote in the 1987 elections. Two reasons for this comparative weakness can be suggested. One is that, in a relatively open political system, economic and social discontent is dissipated in a wide variety of ideological channels, socialist and nationalist as well as Islamic. Hence, Muslim fundamentalism finds it hard to establish itself as the leading oppositional element. The second is that the government's policy of an official reassertion of Muslim piety has coopted Islam, turning it into a pre-status quo force, and effectively marginalising the radical fundamentalists.

The question of civil rights probably receives more attention in foreign reporting on Turkey than in Turkey itself, where economic, social and cultural issues normally dominate the domestic political agenda. However, it is of considerable importance, especially for intellectuals, journalists and trade unionists. In April 1991, together with the lifting of the ban on the Kurdish language, the government withdrew Articles 141, 142 and 163 of the penal code. The first two had been widely criticised, since they authorised the prosecution of anyone deemed guilty of what the authorities could characterise as 'communist' activities, and has been the basis of most previous political trials in Turkey. Article 163 had made it illegal to set up a society aiming to base the state on religious principles. The liberalisation is not complete, since articles of the Political Parties Law continue similar restrictions on political parties. Moreover, laws on the press and trade unions are still a good deal more restrictive than in Western Europe. Nevertheless, the signs are that gradual liberalisation will be continued. It also has to be remembered that, even if civil rights in Turkey do not meet the standards of the EC, to which Turkey aspires, Turkey has a far more open and liberal regime than those found in most other Middle Eastern states, and has made a far more sustained effort to make multi-party politics work.

The economy: changes and prospects

Since the 1930s, the economy has moved away from its traditional dependence on primary production and has steadily built up the industrial base. Although 40 to 50% of the workforce is still employed in agriculture, mainly on small peasant-owned farms, farming only accounts for about 18% of GNP, compared with 35% for industry (including construction) and 47% for services. This pattern is repeated in foreign trade, in which industrial products (in particular textiles, clothing, and iron and steel) now account for 80% of exports, with traditional agricultural products (tobacco, dried fruit and nuts) providing only around 20%. Per capita GNP in 1990 stood at around $1,680 at current exchange rates. At purchasing power parities, which reflect differentials in costs of living, per capita GNP is around $4,350. This is well below the levels of Western Europe, but compares favourably with those of most other Middle Eastern countries, except for the oil-rich states of the Gulf. This economic growth is reflected in social changes. Almost 60% of the population now live in towns and cities: primary-school enrolment is virtually universal, and the literacy rate is probably around 70%. There is also some evidence that urbanisation and better education are reducing the birth rate: the net annual population growth rate has fallen from a high point of 2.8% in 1955–60 to 2.1% in 1985–90.

After becoming prime minister, Özal put the reorientation and development of the economy at the top of his agenda, attempting to liberalise the domestic market and to move away from protectionism towards export-oriented growth. These policies have had mixed results. After the severe slowdown of the late 1970s, economic growth was restored, giving an annual average growth of GNP of 5.3% for 1981–90: however, this is about the same level as that recorded for the Turkish economy before the crisis of 1978–80. Despite the MP's Thatcherite rhetoric, the state still plays a major role in the economy, with the public sector accounting for about 45% of total investment and 35% of non-agricultural employment. The promised privatisation of state enterprises has proceeded slowly and haltingly, notwithstanding the spectacular growth of the Istanbul stock market in recent years.

The main success of the Özal programme has been in foreign trade. Thanks to the introduction of a realistic exchange rate, and regular devaluations, exports have grown from $2.9 billion in 1980 to $12.9 billion in 1990. This, together with sharply increased earnings from tourism, transit trade and emigrants' remittances, has allowed annual imports to grow from $7.9 billion to $22.3 billion in the same period. Although this improvement suffered a setback in 1990 (partly due to the Gulf crisis), Turkey has been able to pay its way internationally, and to service and refinance its foreign debt of around $42 billion.

For the vast majority of Turks, the greatest failure of the MP has been its inability (or reluctance) to bring down inflation. Through severe policies, the military regime reduced the inflation rate from over 100% in 1980 to around 30% in 1983. Since then, however, the annual average has surged back up to around 53%, with a high point of 75.4% in 1988. The reasons for recent inflation are primarily over-spending in the public sector, most of which is accounted for by subsidies to loss-making state enterprises, and the payment of artificially high prices for farm products. On the revenue side, the government, like its pre-1980 predecessors, has allowed wealthy farmers and businessmen to go almost tax-free, while imposing high direct taxes on wage earners.

Özal's policies may also have had damaging effects on income distribution. During the first half of the 1980s there was a sharp fall in real wages, mainly due to the restrictions on the power of trade unions introduced by the military regime. There has been some recovery since then, so that real wages in the private sector were about 55% higher in 1990 than they had been in 1980. On the other hand, real wages in the public sector fell by around 20% in the same period. While recent and reliable figures on overall income distribution are not available, the evidence is that the rich have almost certainly gained wealth faster than the poor. These social inequalities are paralleled by disparities between regions, in particular between the relatively prosperous western areas and the backward south-east.

Foreign policy trends

For most of the period since the Second World War, foreign policy has not been a major subject of political debate in Turkey. The election manifestos of the five main parties in the 1987 election, for example, devoted less than 5% of their space to foreign policy and defence. The tendency has been to regard these as technical subjects best left to professional diplomats and soldiers, an attitude strengthened by a generally stable external environment and a broad national consensus on foreign policy questions. Since 1952, only the extreme left has seriously questioned Turkey's membership of NATO, or the main lines of policy towards Cyprus. Similarly, support for membership of the EC is virtually universal, except among a small minority of pan-Islamicists and unreconstructed Marxists. In relations with the other Middle Eastern states there has been general support for the idea of closer economic ties, while avoiding any serious military or political commitments. Of the main parties, only the WP would like to associate Turkey with some sort of Islamic political community.

The picture has begun to alter in recent years, however, mainly due to changes in the external environment. The ending of the Cold War has had important effects or Turkey, since its role in NATO, and its overall defence policy, were based on a threat which no longer exists. In the economic sphere, the Özal administration was quick to seize the opportunity to improve relations with the Soviet Union, notably through the construction of a pipeline to carry Soviet natural gas to the main cities of Turkey.

Contacts have also been developed with Azerbaijan and the other Turkic republics of the Soviet Union. Nevertheless, the government has been careful to avoid siding with Azerbaijan in its conflict with Armenia, since overt interference could damage the vital relationships with Moscow, though the collapse of the Soviet Union since August 1991 must inevitably lead to a reformulation of Turkish policy in this direction. As important, Ankara does not seem to have developed any broad policy towards the reconstruction of NATO, or the evolution of a new role for Turkey within it. If concrete plans are put forward by the other allies, the Turks will have to decide whether, or how, they can fit into them.

The Gulf crisis of 1990–91 also upset previous foreign policy assumptions, mainly because its unpredictability made it hard to adhere to established positions. Turkey's main actions during the crisis were, first, to apply the UN economic sanctions campaign against Iraq in full, by closing the Kirkuk–Yumurtalik pipeline, which normally carries about half Iraq's oil exports, and (at serious cost to itself) by ending all exports to Iraq. Secondly, army units along the border with Iraq were strengthened, pinning down about ten Iraqi divisions in the north of the country. Thirdly, permission was given to the United States to use NATO air bases on Turkish soil for offensive missions against targets in northern Iraq.

With the war over, Özal could reasonably claim that his policy had been a success: Turkey had got through the crisis without firing a shot in anger, and had increased its international credit, especially in Washington. It was noticeable, however, that for the first time for many years, the government did not have cross-party support. Unlike their fellow Muslims in some other countries, such as Jordan and Palestine, few Turks actively supported Saddam. On the other hand, there was reluctance to allow Turkey to be seen as the servant of the United States, or to send Turkish troops to fight for the liberation of Kuwait. When the government tried to obtain full war powers from parliament on 12 August 1990 it was defeated. Parliament changed its mind on 5 September, but only reluctantly. Prior to the start of the air war in January 1991, both Demirel and Inönü strongly attacked Özal's policies. Though Demirel later changed tack, Inönü kept up his opposition. After the war, the crisis caused by the flood of Kurdish refugees created further contentious problems for Turkey, as well as the danger that events in Iraq could inflame Turkey's own Kurdish problem. All these developments threatened to make Turkey's relations with the other Middle Eastern countries far more problematic than they had previously been.

The three other problems in Turkish foreign policy are old stagers, and seem unlikely to alter substantially in the near future. The longstanding dispute with Greece over offshore oil rights and territorial waters in the Aegean seems set to continue, unless there is a dramatic change of attitudes on both sides. On the Cyprus question, Turkey continues to support the principle of inter-communal negotiations, under UN auspices, for the eventual establishment of a federation of the two communities. Equally, Turkey's relations with the EC are currently in the doldrums. In December 1989 Brussels responded to the Turkish application for full membership of the Community (submitted in 1987) by saying that no negotiations could begin until 1993 at the earliest. This did not extinguish Turkish hopes for eventual admission, but delayed any serious consideration of the problems involved for the next few years. The possibility that Turkey might join the Community by the end of the century cannot be ruled out, but the number and complexity of the obstacles it faces, besides the uncertain future of the Community's relations with the rest of eastern Europe, leave the shape of this process in doubt.

William Hale

15 YEMEN

On 22 May 1990, the most populous state of the Arabian peninsula, the Republic of Yemen, was born. This major event in Yemeni history was the culmination of years of intermittent conflict and dialogue between the two Yemeni states, the Yemen Arab Republic and the People's Democratic Republic of Yemen.

Yemen before the revolution

At the end of the 19th century, the Ottomans ruled the coastal plain of the Arabian peninsula along the Red Sea and the highlands. In 1904, Yahya Mohammed Hamid al Din succeeded his father as imam of the Zaydis, a branch of the Shia in the northern highlands, and raised support from the Zaydi tribes in an uprising that forced the Ottoman Turks to recognise his control over the highlands, though the Ottomans retained control of the coast and the southern uplands. With the defeat of the Ottomans in the First World War and the disintegration of their empire, Imam Yahya imposed his rule throughout what later became the Yemen Arab Republic.

The southern border of the imamate was agreed with Britain in 1934. However, this did not prevent clashes between Britain and the imamate, largely on the grounds that where Britain interpreted the frontier as absolute, the Yemenis saw it more as marking only an area over which ownership must necessarily be vague. There were disputes, too, with Britain over the Aden protectorate, which the Yemenis similarly claimed. Yemeni support for anti-British uprisings in Aden was consistent. The northern border of Yemen, with Saudi Arabia, was also determined in 1934, though again not to Yemen's advantage. Following defeat by the Saudi forces, Yemen was forced to accept Saudia Arabia's terms, as encapsulated in the Treaty of Ta'if. These entailed handing to Saudi Arabia the province of 'Asir and the oasis of Najran.

Imam Yahya was assassinated in 1948 in a coup aimed at modernising Yemen. The coup failed, however, largely as a result of the ruthlessness of Crown Prince Ahmad in countering it. Ahmad, now imam himself, then oversaw the execution of many of the more prominent leaders of the coup and the imprisonment of others. Ahmad ruled until 1962, dying in his bed, having overcome a series of attempted coups and assassination attempts. Though his son and successor, Mohammed al-Badr, had been close to the would-be reformers, he found himself swept away by events. With Yemen strongly influenced by the rhetoric of Arab nationalism expounded by

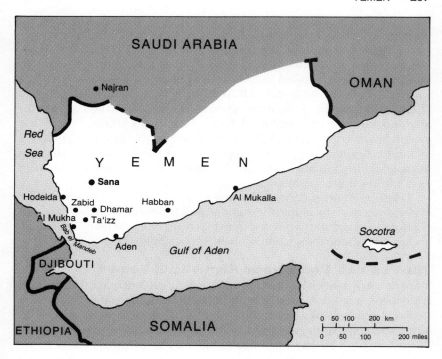

Official name	Republic of Yemen
Area	531,000 sq. km (205,020 sq. miles)
Population	12 million (1990)
Capital	Sana (commercial capital, Aden)
Language	Arabic
Religion	Sunni and Zaidi, Shia Muslim
Currency	northern riyal and southern dinar coexist for transitional period following unification

Nasser in Egypt, the new king was overthrown in a revolution which erupted on 26 September 1962.

From the revolution, the Yemen Arab Republic (YAR) emerged. Having failed to capture the imam in the course of the revolution, however, its leaders found themselves engaged in a protracted civil war with him. From his base in Saudi Arabia, the imam launched a series of offensives against the YAR, itself now largely reliant on Nasser's Egypt for men and arms. Egypt's crushing defeat by Israel in the Six Day War of 1967 meant, however, that, from 1967, it was no longer able to support the YAR militarily. Egyptian support was replaced the following year by aid from the neighbouring Republic of South Yemen (RSY). This proved decisive in ensuring the defeat of the imam.

The support of the RSY was in no sense unconditional, indeed the RSY itself was as riven by political in-fighting and factionalism as the YAR, and relations between the two states were to remain bitter for many years. The background to the foundation of the RSY is complex.

The Peoples' Democratic Republic of Yemen

Since the early 1960s it had become increasingly evident that Britain, which had ruled Aden and, more loosely, the surrounding statelets since the mid-19th century, was looking for ways to divest itself of its colony. Not only had Aden's strategic significance as a guarantee of imperial communications become all but non-existent, demands for independence, frequently accompanied by rioting, had made the region a financial and political liability. But British attempts to create a new and independent state—to be known as the Federation of South Arabia—had foundered on the rival ambitions of the traditional tribal leaders of the colony. In consequence, and much as in Palestine after the Second World War, Britain, having realised it could not hope to control the destiny of the putative state, accordingly determined simply to leave with whatever dignity it could muster and let the tribal leaders fight it out among themselves.

The establishment of the YAR in 1962 provided one model for Aden's future, and in fact republican forces from the YAR were active in promoting similar movements within Aden. The chief beneficiary was the National Liberation Front (NLF), founded in 1963 and allied closely with republican groups in the YAR, where indeed it held its first congresses. Its principal rival was the Front for the Liberation of Occupied South Yemen (FLOSY), founded in 1965. United only by their desire to see Britain leave as early as possible, the NLF and FLOSY engaged in a violent struggle for supremacy, despite Egyptian pressure to force them to merge. Matters came to a head in 1967 when Britain announced that it had brought forward its departure and would pull out of Aden at the end of November that year. In the event, it was the by-now pro-Soviet NLF that gained the upper hand. On 30 November, it declared the People's Democratic Republic of South Yemen.

As events unfolded in Aden, so in the YAR the republican movement consolidated its position. As it did so, it shifted perceptibly to the right. Tension between the left-leaning People's Republic and the YAR was inevitable. In early 1969 bitter words were exchanged between the two capitals, as Sana accused Aden of having 'separatist' tendencies because it had become independent rather than merge into the (much larger) YAR to form a united Yemen when the British left. In the following years the rulers in Sana supported FLOSY and others who opposed the regime in Aden, including some of the former rulers, and there were many armed clashes on the borders. In 1969 a 'Corrective Move' took place in Aden, which marked a distinct additional shift to the left and the country was renamed the People's Democratic Republic of Yemen (PDRY). Even this title added to the tension with Sana, implying that the Aden regime saw itself the legitimate ruler of all Yemen.

This socialist regime lasted throughout the life of the PDRY. During the 1970s and 1980s there were a number of policy changes affecting internal politics and the economy, revolving around the extent of state control proposed for the different economic sectors. In practice, the PDRY retained a substantial private sector in agriculture and small-scale industry alongside the cooperative and state sectors. Other issues under debate were political organisation and the role of the single party, as well as local democracy. In foreign policy, relations deepened with the Soviet Union and weakened with China, while support for liberation movements in the Third World continued. Relations with Western countries such as Germany and France gradually improved while those with the United States were only re-established on the eve of unification. The period was marked by a series of major crises: the overthrow and execution of President Salim Rubay'i Ali in 1978; the exile of President Abd al-Fattah Ismail in 1980; and the 'events' of 1986 which led to the exile of President Ali Nasir Mohammed.

Rivalries and conflicts

Meanwhile in Sana the first president, Abdullah al-Sallal, hitherto closely identified with Egypt, lost power soon after the Egyptian withdrawal in 1967. He was succeeded by a three-man presidential council, chaired by Qadi Abd al-Rahman al-Iryani. Having survived the imamist siege of Sana in early 1968, the republican regime consolidated itself mainly through the absorption of the majority of the imam's supporters, thus removing them from the latter's influence. With the rival states marching so decisively to the left and right respectively, the resulting tension led in September 1972 to the outbreak of full-scale war. A cease-fire was soon arranged, and was closely followed by the first Unity Agreement, signed in Cairo in October, followed by a summit held in Tripoli in November. Unification committees started to meet.

In June 1974 the civilian government in Sana was overthrown by a group of army officers and the constitution suspended. The new regime was headed by Ibrahim al-Hamdi, an army officer, who introduced a modernising regime and turned out not to be the Saudi stooge he had first been assumed to be. He encouraged the creation of local development associations in the rural areas, and continued to develop relations with Aden. He was due to come on the first official visit by a YAR president to Aden in October 1977 when he was assassinated. There were rumours at the time that he and Salim Rubay'i Ali were about to sign a full unification agreement during the visit and that he was assassinated to prevent this from being reached. He was briefly succeeded by another army officer, Ahmad al-Ghashmi, who stalled on relations with the south and left little positive mark of his period in office. In turn, he was assassinated, in June 1978, supposedly by a bomb sent by Salim Rubay'i Ali. This led to an outburst of political conflict within the party in Aden, which brought about Salim Rubay'i Ali's execution two days later.

In June 1978, when Ali Abdullah Salih became president of the YAR after the assassination of his short-serving predecessor, he was considered too politically inexperienced to retain power for long in the face of well-known tribal leaders, who had years of practice at the complex politics of the country. His personal history and modest tribal origins were further factors to suggest that his position was precarious. Contrary to all expectations, he proved to be the longest-serving Yemeni president; moreover, he has ensured his place in history by achieving Yemeni unity.

President Ali Abdullah Salih has proved to be a skilful politician. Initially he survived the 1979 border war with Aden, which marked the exacerbation of conflict after the 1978 assassinations. In the early years of his leadership he was able to play off the rival demands of the Saudi-supported northern tribes, by moving closer to the PDRY, and the southern-supported National Democratic Front (NDF). In 1982 he successfully negotiated with Aden to reduce its support for the NDF and then defeated it militarily. It was to prove a significant development. In 1980–81 the NDF had expanded well beyond its traditional area of influence, southeast of the main Taiz–Sana road to become a serious challenge to central government rule.

Although his power was based on the army, having proved his ability to control both the northern tribal leaders and the Saudis, as well as to withstand pressure from Aden, he was in a position to strengthen the basis for his popular support in the 1980s. He also made considerable efforts to strengthen central government by involving some of the tribal leaders, as well as representatives of all local forces, in the parliament. In addition, he introduced direct elections. Despite increasingly difficult economic circumstances due to stagnation in agricultural production and a serious drop in remittances from Yemenis in the oil-rich states, and a hefty drop in oil prices just at the time when his country became a small-scale oil producer, he managed to keep the country afloat and somehow balance people's increased expectations (particularly after the discovery of oil) against the reality of a recession.

The situation was much more turbulent in the PDRY, where a political crisis dealt a severe blow to the regime. Ten days of fighting in Aden in January 1986 destroyed infrastructure valued at the equivalent of many years of investment, while the loss of life shattered faith in the government. The government's credibility suffered enormously from the widespread belief that the crisis had been nothing more than a power struggle stemming almost entirely from personal rivalries and ambitions. 5,000 soldiers and civilians were killed, having been sucked into the conflict, most on tribal rather than ideological grounds. The killings came at a time when the regime was in serious economic difficulties. The low resource-base of the country was unable to sustain the level of investment which the regime was trying to maintain. Investment in small and medium processing industries by emigrants had never reached the levels hoped by the government, and foreign aid was not commensurate with the regime's ambitions or expectations. In addition, devastating floods in 1989 destroyed much of the rural infrastructure built over the previous decade. Against this background, the huge expense run up by the lavish social services the regime provided came to seem a particularly ironic burden.

A further weakening of the regime stemmed from developments in the Soviet Union after the mid-1980s. As the Soviet Union, itself on the verge of economic collapse, began to make clear its intention to end the Cold War, so the strategic importance to it of its Third World allies such as the PDRY began to lessen. Not only was the PDRY increasingly politically isolated, it was clearly unable to bank on sustained economic aid from the Soviet Union.

Unity

Thus at the end of the 1980s both the Aden and the Sana regimes were seriously weakened politically; both were suffering economically from dramatically reduced remittances, the fall in oil prices and the effects of recession throughout the world. Moves toward unity began to take on a new urgency. Unity committees met increasingly regularly, especially after the 1986 and 1987 crises, which almost led to a renewed border conflict over oil rights. The work of the committees was eventually to build up a momentum which, by the end of the decade, was decisive.

Though the announcement of unity on 22 May 1990 was greeted with enthusiasm, the reality of unification has proved significantly more difficult than had been predicted. One of Ali Abdullah Salih's objectives in pushing for unity had been to enable the YAR to benefit from the administrative skills that the PDRY had developed over the years, themselves largely an inheritance from Britain's colonial administration. This administrative sophistication contrasted sharply with the system prevailing in the YAR, where tribal influence, and even at times armed tribal pressure, were exerted to determine administrative decisions in all fields. But there were also pressing economic arguments in favour of unification, not the least being economies of scale. The population of united Yemen is sufficiently large, at 12 million, to justify certain types of medium- to large-scale industrial investment in processing and manufacturing which neither the YAR nor the PDRY could attempt on their own. In addition, oil exploration, production and export had been major factors in pushing for unity. While the YAR had discovered oil in commercial quantities in 1984, this only happened in the PDRY in 1987. While the former's potential is estimated at about 300,000 barrels per day, the latter's is estimated at twice that for a population five times smaller. Nonetheless, while the population has great hopes for the country's future as an oil producer, these hopes are in many ways misguided, based as they are on migrants' experience of Saudi Arabia and the Gulf states in the boom period of the late 1970s and early 1980s, and bear no relation to the reality which oil can bring to their country. A more realistic comparison would be with Algeria or Nigeria, but neither of these countries is within the experience of ordinary Yemenis who simply see the apparently fabulous wealth of Saudi Arabia. They think they can, and should, have the same. These dreams also ignore the fundamental facts of life in a world oil market where the price of oil has now dropped to less, in real terms, than before price rises of 1973–74. At best, Yemini oil could assist the state in funding many of its own agricultural and industrial development projects, and help it towards achieving more balanced economic development. But it is not a bonanza which can, or will, provide a life of leisure.

While unity can help create a more viable economic entity in Yemen, and in the long run encourage better economic planning and improvements in agriculture and fisheries as well as industry, these are long-term hopes that will depend on the establishment of effective development policies, planning strategies and good management. In the short term, there is no way that unity can solve instantly the urgent economic crisis which both parts of Yemen have been suffering in the second half of the 1980s.

Yemen's attitude to Iraq's invasion of Kuwait in August 1990 has also hindered its economic prospects. Though Yemen issued ritual denunciations of Iraq's aggression, it also vigorously refused to support the US-led coalition that subsequently opposed Iraq on the grounds that the problem could and should be resolved by the Arabs. Saudi Arabia promptly seized on Yemen's pronouncement as an excuse to harass Yemeni citizens resident in Saudi Arabia.

Yemenis in Saudi Arabia had enjoyed favourable status for many years. Unlike nationals from other countries, for example, Yemenis were exempt from the burdensome and expensive immigration and sponsorship regulations affecting other foreign workers. In September 1990 the Saudi authorities changed the regulations and gave Yemenis a month to obtain visas and sponsors. As a result, about one million of the one-and-a-half million Yemenis in Saudi Arabia were forced to leave the kingdom by the end of 1990, leaving behind much of their property or having to sell it at give-away prices. Their return to Yemen has caused further difficulties. First, there has been a loss of $2 billion in remittances which would otherwise have been received by families in Yemen; second, the new arrivals are joining a labour market where there is already considerable unemployment. At the same time, Saudi Arabia has also stopped all aid payments to Yemen. Kuwait, the United States and some other Western countries have followed Saudi Arabia in reducing or suspending aid to Yemen.

None of these difficulties should overshadow the achievement of Yemen in achieving unity. Nor should they be allowed to detract from the welcome process of political reform and the extension of liberty. There are about 40 political parties in formal existence representing all shades of opinion, from the Muslim fundamentalists to socialists. The expanded National Assembly has 301 members—the elected members of the YAR and PDRY's former assemblies, as well as 31 new members nominated to represent the NDF and other former opponents of one or the other regime. The Assembly is actively involved in discussing new laws and establishing a unified legislature. The transition period to the completion of institutional and political unification was set at 30 months and there is no current expectation of change in this respect. The new government includes officials from both parts in senior posts, and the same goes throughout the administration with every senior person having a deputy from the other part, thus establishing the basis for balance and for gradual merging of all institutions.

Helen Lackner

16 OIL IN THE MIDDLE EAST

The development of the Middle East's oil reserves since the 1940s and 1950s has brought great wealth to many countries in the region. Only Cyprus, Israel, Lebanon, Morocco, Jordan, the Sudan and Turkey have little or no crude oil production. However, all the Arab states are linked economically or politically through joint-venture investments in oil-related activities and through organisations such as the Arab League, the Gulf Cooperation Council (GCC), the Organisation of Arab Petroleum Exporting Countries (OAPEC) and the Organisation of Petroleum Exporting Countries (OPEC).

According to some estimates, the Middle East (excluding North Africa) holds 667 billion barrels of proven oil reserves, around 67% of the total discovered in the world. Ninety-nine per cent of these reserves are located in the countries surrounding the Persian Gulf; the remaining 1% is in Egypt. North African reserves were estimated at 32 billion barrels in 1990. The industrialised world is consequently highly dependent for its oil supplies on these Persian Gulf states. Likewise, the Middle East's economies rely heavily on income derived from either crude oil and oil-derived product exports and from economic links, such as trade, remittances of migrants and aid, with oil-rich countries.

Despite a high-level of concern since the early 1970s over the political implications of Western dependence on oil from the Persian Gulf, petroleum liquids still accounted for around 44% and 39% of the primary energy needs of Europe and North America respectively in 1990. The political concerns of the West were demonstrated by the adoption of policies designed to safeguard supplies, such as the development of alternative energy sources and conservation and efficiency measures. At the same time, a growing awareness of the interdependence of the world's economies will help both oil consumers and producers to realise the merits of cooperation.

History

Exploration for oil in the Middle East began in the 19th century, with the first wells drilled in Iran in 1884 by Hots and Co. of Bushire. However, it was not until the early years of the 20th century that oil was struck in commercial quantities. The search for oil in Iran was conducted by William Knox D'Arcy, who secured a concession from the shah in May 1901. The concession included mineral exploitation rights throughout Iran with the exception of five northern provinces awarded to the Russo-Persia Naphtha Company in 1896. The financial terms of the concession required the payment of £40,000 upon the establishment of a company to manage operations within the concession and 16% of the future net profits of that company. On 26 May 1908, almost seven years to the day after the signing of the concession agreement, the Concession Syndicate Company, owned by Burmah Oil Company, but with D'Arcy as director, struck oil at Masjid-i-Suleiman. In Egypt, the first commercial discovery, known as the Gemsa oilfield, was made by the Egyptian Oil Trust in March 1909.

1909 proved a significant year. In it, the first cargo of Middle Eastern oil, transported first by pipeline from the Masjid-i-Suleiman oilfield, was loaded at Abadan on the Shatt al-'Arab waterway. However, the development of oil production and markets was slow and at the outbreak of the First World War Persia was producing only two million barrels annually, less than half a per cent of total world production. In the same year the Concession Syndicate Company was re-formed as the Anglo-Persian Oil Company, which later acquired and took on the name of a small distribution company in England, British Petroleum.

During the First World War production from the Masjid-i-Suleiman oilfield more than doubled from 2.9 to 8.6 million barrels. This production was transported to the Abadan refinery, completed in 1912, which supplied the growing fuel-oil demand of the Royal Navy and also exported kerosene as heating oil.

The outbreak of the First World War had set back complex negotiations relating to oil exploitation rights in Iraq, then a part of the Ottoman Empire, between Turkey, Germany and Great Britain. The reconciliation of the three countries' interests through the formation of the jointly owned Turkish Petroleum Company (TPC) in 1912 was short lived. After the defeat of Germany and the Ottoman Empire, new players, namely France and the United States, expressed their wish to be included in any agreement authorising exploration in Iraq.

Negotiations over shares in TPC and its Iraqi concession were concluded in July 1928 with the signing of the Red Line Agreement between Royal/Dutch Shell, Anglo-Persian, Compagnie Française des Petroles, Gulbenkian (who had founded the original TPC in 1912) and the Near East Development Company, a consortium of American oil companies. This famous agreement represented a truce between the Americans and the British interests in the area. Within this 'red line' area, which included the Arabian Peninsula, Iraq, Lebanon, Palestine, Syria and Transjordan, no member of the TPC (now the IPC) could act without the other. This was to prove a great advantage for other oil companies operating within the area and who were not constrained by this agreement, such as Standard Oil of California (Socal). The conclusion of negotiations had been hastened by the discovery of the huge Kirkuk oilfield in October 1927 and the consequent desire on the part of all participants to realise the potential of this oil-bearing region.

The status of Iraq as an oil producer was greatly enhanced in the 1930s by the Iraq Petroleum Company's construction of a 267-mile pipeline, with a capacity of around four million tons per year, linking the Kirkuk field to terminals at the ports of Haifa and Tripoli in Palestine and Lebanon respectively.

The shock discovery of the Awali oilfield in Bahrain in October 1931 by a newcomer to the Middle East, Socal (now Chevron), began a scramble on the part of the oil companies in the Persian Gulf to secure concessions over neighbouring states. In the 1930s the search spread to Bahrain, Kuwait, Qatar and Saudi Arabia. With the help of Harry St John B. Philby, explorer and diplomat as well as friend of the Saudi king, Socal secured the mineral exploitation rights over the whole of Saudi Arabia on 29 May 1933. This concession has since proved the richest in the world. Its proven oil reserves were estimated at 258 billion barrels in 1990, 26% of all known reserves.

The Second World War had an ambiguous effect on the pace of oil development in the Middle East. For countries with established oil production and export infrastructures, namely Bahrain, Egypt, Iran, Iraq and Saudi Arabia, the period was one of rapid expansion. However, 78 billion barrels of Kuwaiti oil reserves located in the late 1930s, out of a total 94 billion barrels, were left undeveloped for the duration.

Post-1945

The post-war period saw the meteoric rise of Saudi Arabia and Kuwait as oil producers. The development of Iran by Anglo-Persian and the development of Iraq by the IPC foundered in the 1950s as a result of political instability in those countries and with their respective neighbours. Meanwhile, the extraordinary efforts of two new companies, the Kuwait Oil Company, owned by Anglo-Iranian (formerly Anglo-Persian) and Gulf Oil, and the Arabian American Oil Company (Aramco) owned by Socal, Socony-Vacuum Oil Company (now Mobil), Standard Oil of New Jersey (now Exxon) and Texaco, raised the oil production of Kuwait and Saudi Arabia from nought and 58,000 barrels per day in 1945 to 1.24 million and 1.62 million barrels per day in 1960 respectively. The 1950s was also the most significant decade for the Middle East—specifically the Gulf—in terms of oil exploration: 157 billion barrels of recoverable oil were discovered. 1951 saw the discovery of the two largest oilfields yet known, both Saudi Arabian: the Ghawar and the (offshore) Safinaya oilfields.

While the Kuwait Oil Company was primarily concerned with the infrastructure and output of oil in Kuwait, Aramco was beginning to show growing maturity toward the management of its oil operations and in consolidating its position in world oil markets. On 2 December 1950 the 1,070-mile pipeline linking the oilfields in eastern Saudi Arabia with the port of Sidon in Lebanon became fully operational. The pipeline reduced the distance between the oilfields on the Persian Gulf to the major centre of oil demand in Europe by some 3,500 miles. At the same time, diversification of outlets helped Gulf oil producers to avoid interruption to their oil exports from political turmoil near their borders or along established shipping routes. Aramco's management of its oil operations was furthered in the 1950s with oilfield programmes designed to optimise recovery through the use of water and gas injection. In addition, as well as expanding the crude capacity of the Ras Tannurah refinery, built in 1945, Aramco began to add more complex processes to increase the quality and diversity of its oil product exports.

Middle East oil production and exports increased four-fold between 1960 and the early 1970s. At the same time, world demand for oil tripled. However, despite this apparent stability, the conditions for a revolution in the world oil market were being established. The growing confidence of the oil producers, underlined, for example, by their foundation of the Organisation of Petroleum Exporting Countries (OPEC) in 1960, was placing increasing stress on their relations with oil companies and the major oil-consuming countries.

By the late 1960s, the combination of government fiscal incentives and desire on the part of oil companies to diversify their sources of oil income had led to a surge of exploration in the higher-cost oil provinces outside the OPEC region, of which the Middle East is the most important part. Before the first oil price shock in October 1973, production had begun in the large oil provinces of western Siberia, north-east China, offshore Malaysia and offshore Australia, while the development of the North Sea, Alaska and the Reforma province of Mexico was at an irreversible stage. Certain Middle East countries which had remained outside OPEC, such as Egypt and Oman, gained from this reorientation of investment, their combined oil production increasing from 61,000 barrels per day in 1960 (Omani production did not begin until 1967) to 730,000 barrels per day in 1970.

On its own, the increase in the supply of non-OPEC oil would not have altered the balance of power in the world oil market. However, the impact on world oil markets of the price shocks of 1973 and 1979–80 was both to reduce the growth of the industrialised world's demand for oil and to encourage the pace of oil development outside OPEC. The result was that, in order to maintain the high oil price introduced in 1973, OPEC was forced to take on the role of residual supplier and to cut oil production and exports. From its 1976 peak of around 21.6 million barrels per day, Persian Gulf oil production fell to around 10.2 million barrels per day in 1985.

During the 1970s and 1980s those Middle Eastern countries with large surplus of oil production for export had two concerns. The first was how to invest their new-found wealth; the second, how to retain their market share without adversely affecting the oil price. Investment in oil-related industry was seen by these countries as a partial solution to both concerns.

Since 1970, therefore, oil investment in Middle Eastern countries has

been redirected from the 'upstream' sector—namely, crude oil exploration, production and export capacity—to the 'downstream' sector—
namely, refining, petrochemical and energy-intensive industries.

Oil and politics in the Middle East

From the perspective of the West the importance of the Middle East lies,
simply, in its oil resources. All the political crises in the Middle East,
namely the Iranian nationalisation of 1951, the Suez Crisis of 1956, the
Arab–Israeli wars in 1967 and 1973, the Iranian revolution and subsequent
Iran–Iraq War of 1979–88 and the invasion of Kuwait by Iraq in August
1990, have involved the interruption of, or threat to, oil supplies, often
triggering intervention by Western powers.

The Middle Eastern countries have never been slow to realise the
equation of oil and politics. The political history of oil in the Middle East
can be divided into two periods. In the first, from 1932 to 1974, governments of the oil-exporting countries vied with the oil companies for control
over their natural resources. Having succeeded in gaining control over the
crucial instruments of policy—oil production and price—the oil-exporting
countries, alone or in concert, have sought a balance between economic
and political objectives. For instance, an economic decision taken by one
oil-exporter to raise oil production in order to maximise revenues may have
the effect of lowering prices across world markets. This may, in turn,
irreversibly lower the revenues for other oil exporters producing at the
upper limit of their capacity. The initial economic decision must therefore
take into account its associated effect on political relations in the region. A
similar argument may be viewed in reverse in relation to the economic
well-being of the oil-consuming countries.

1932 to 1974

The history of nationalisation dates back to the 1930s. The first full-scale
nationalisation of oil resources and operations was engineered by President Cardenas of Mexico in 1938. However, even earlier, in 1932, Reza
Shah of Iran, annulled the oil concession rights awarded to Anglo-Persian
in 1901. Three over-lapping motives lay behind the appropriation and
were to resurface time after time during this contest of political wills
between government and company. The first related to the shah's lack of
control over oil production and pricing, and then control over a major part
of the country's revenue. This concern was prompted by the drastic fall in
Iranian oil revenues in 1917. The second related to the contradiction
between the fundamental principles of concessions and of national
sovereignty. The third was the shah's intention to use his sovereign power
as a bargaining tool in his negotiations with the British government, who
had purchased 51% of Anglo-Persian in 1914. Nonetheless, having
renegotiated the terms of the concession Reza Shah gave it back in
1933.

Oil production in the Gulf area 1945-90 (in millions of tonnes per year)

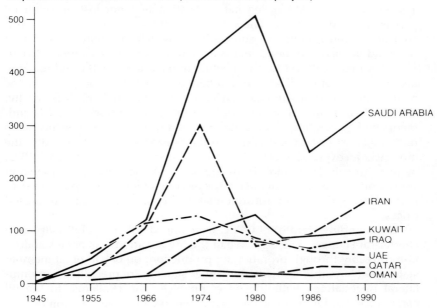

The assertion of oil producers' aspirations were fated to fail again as a result of the dismissal of Iranian Prime Minister Mosaddeq in August 1953. On 1 May 1951, Mosaddeq succeeded in forcing the new shah, Mohammed Reza Pahlavi, to sign a law nationalising the country's oil resources. Mosaddeq's move followed the failure of Anglo-Iranian to agree terms of renewal for the original oil concession granted in 1901 and revised in 1933. Mosaddeq was in a strong position. Aramco had recently agreed to an unprecedented increase in the Saudi government's take to 50% of profits less the exploration, development and production costs. In addition, the outbreak of the Korean War had made the West more dependent on petroleum product supplies from the Middle East to fuel the military effort in the Far East as well as more keen to maintain good diplomatic relations with Iran to prevent the incursion of Soviet influence. However, Mosaddeq was no mere lone opportunist: he had tapped strong nationalist and anti-British sentiment in Iran and, even if he had wanted to, was constrained in his negotiations by these popular feelings. In the end, Mosaddeq failed because he had acted in isolation, without the cooperation of other oil-exporting countries. The embargo of Iranian oil engineered by the West was successful in harming the Iranian economy and turning public opinion against him.

The role of OPEC

The lesson of the Mosaddeq nationalisation was not lost on other oil producers in the region. The third attempt by governments to wrest control over indigenous oil resources began with the formation of OPEC in Baghdad in 1960. All the elements evident in 1932 were again apparent. First, the initial catalyst for the meeting in Baghdad was the sudden 15% fall in governments' oil revenues in between 1959 and 1960. This was the result of oil companies' unilateral decisions to cut posted prices. Secondly, Middle Eastern and, more especially, Arab oil exporters' national senti-ments had grown hugely in confidence as a result of Nasser's successful moves against Britain and France in the Suez crisis of 1956. Thirdly, the move was an expression of the bargaining power of the founders of OPEC, namely Kuwait, Iran, Iraq, Saudi Arabia and Venezuela (Qatar joined in 1961), and had the effect of forcing the oil companies to raise posted prices and deterring them from future unilateral actions with regard to posted prices.

The founding statutes of OPEC were not so much revolutionary as 'a charter for change'. The objective of the organization was price stabilisa-tion, possibly through prorationing production, on behalf of all member states, meaning that individual member states were precluded from uni-lateral negotiations with the oil companies. The challenge to the oil companies that OPEC presented led inevitably to a deterioration of rela-tions between the oil companies and OPEC during the 1960s. The slack oil market conditions of the 1960s led to resentment over the fall in oil prices (in real terms) and suspected bias in the allocation of production increases between oil-exporting countries. Positive hostility to the West as a whole was furthered by the Six Day War in June 1967.

Following the war and Israel's crushing victory, in June 1967, OPEC issued the 'Declaratory Statement of Petroleum Policy in Member Countries'. The statement called for member countries to develop their oil reserves directly and that only where state-owned technology was insuffi-cient should overseas companies be allowed to share ownership of re-serves. Further, it called for government participation in all current oil operations and direct control over the posted, or tax-reference, price.

The upturn in the oil market in the late 1960s and early 1970s enabled OPEC to realise its ambitions. The catalyst to that realisation was provided by the October War between Israel and the Arab world in 1973. At a meeting of the six OPEC Gulf producers—Iran, Iraq, Kuwait, Qatar, Saudi Arabia and the UAE—in Kuwait on 16 October 1973, it was resolved that OPEC should 'establish and announce the posted prices of crudes in the Gulf'. The following day nine Arab member states of the Organisation of Arab Petroleum Exporting Countries resolved to cut production by a minimum of 5%. In just two days the Middle Eastern states had taken control of the two crucial instruments for their economic and political independence: the control of oil production and pricing.

1974 to the present

Four areas of political and strategic concern may be discerned in the formulation of oil exporters' production and pricing policies: regional stability; the Arabic-speaking world; the Third World; and the world economy. These represent different priorities for each according to political circumstance and the individual resource endowment of the oil exporter.

From the advent of the first oil price shocks in October and December 1973 to December 1985, OPEC remained loyal to its first objective: price stabilisation at an agreed level. In the tight oil market conditions up to 1982 the OPEC countries were able to control price with only implicit reference to production prorationing through the use of Arabian Light as the 'marker' crude.

However, with the Persian Gulf states increasingly pursuing different political objectives, it was no surprise that this unanimity proved impossible to sustain. Both in December 1976, at the OPEC conference in Doha and, more significantly for the oil market, between 1979 and 1981 in the wake of the second oil price shock, a two-tier price system emerged. Saudi Arabia, concerned by the possible implications of a high oil price for the world economy and, so, future oil demand, exercised its sovereign right to sell its oil at a lower price. Saudi Arabia has always taken a longer-term view on the oil market because its revenue needs are low relative to its potential oil income. Other countries without surplus revenues or oil-producing capacity, such as Iran and Iraq, must face the more immediate problems of revenue maximisation.

The fall in world oil demand and concurrent rise in non-OPEC production over the early 1980s made it impossible for OPEC to achieve its price objectives without a significant sacrifice of oil production. In 1982 it was agreed that this sacrifice should be shared on the basis of a production prorationing scheme. However, Saudi Arabia was to be excluded on the basis that it had to be free to adjust its output of Arabian Light, the marker crude, to fine-tune the impact on the price of the production cuts.

In December 1985, after three years of accusation and counter-accusations relating to production quota violations, the fixed-price system was finally laid to rest by the decision 'to secure and defend for OPEC a fair share of the world oil market'. The result was the price collapse of 1986, when the price of a barrel of Brent fell from over $30 (in August 1985) to under $10 (in June 1986). The collapse meant that a new price objective had to be agreed by the Persian Gulf states. The probability of agreement was remote, however, with relations strained by increasing mutual suspicion over quota 'cheats' and by the continuing threat to regional stability posed by the Iran–Iraq War.

It was in reaction to the increasing political instability around the Gulf that Bahrain, Kuwait, Qatar, Oman, Saudi Arabia and the UAE formed the Gulf Cooperation Council (GCC) on 25 May 1981. A major concern during the 1980s was the threat of Iranian fundamentalism to the traditional regimes of the GCC States. The GCC States were concerned both militarily (in the case of Iraq's being defeated Iran would threaten their borders) and internally, as a result of Shia terrorist bombings and assassination attempts.

The adoption of the low oil price objective of $18 per barrel by the GCC States and Iraq, in spite of Iran's wishes, cannot be viewed in isolation of this political context. Whether intentional or not, the low oil prices of 1986 to 1988 were instrumental in the economic attrition of Iran and, so, in ending the war. Iraq was able to support the low oil price objective without suffering a drastic fall in oil revenues due to the supply of 'war-relief' crude from the Neutral Zone.

The ending of the Iran–Iraq War led to further divisions in the price objectives of the Persian Gulf states, despite the continuing adoption of the $18 reference price. Iran still called for higher prices but was effectively marginalised. The UAE continued to refuse to support any increase in price until its long-term grievance against its allocated quota was settled within OPEC. The primary concern of Saudi Arabia and Qatar, meanwhile, continued to be the maintenance of regional stability. However, after 1988 Kuwait and Iraq began to adopt strongly opposing positions on the price issue. Iraq, increasingly confident that the military threat from Iran had been curtailed, no longer had any interest in a low oil price and its inability to increase revenue through an increase in production left little option but to persuade its neighbours to reduce production in favour of a higher price. Kuwait, on the other hand, increasingly began to see its long-term interest in a fruitful economic relationship with the West as its overseas operations grew and its oil production capacity proved sufficient to satisfy revenue needs at a lower price.

The growing tension between Iraq and Kuwait in 1989 and 1990 climaxed in Iraq's invasion of Kuwait in August 1990. How the political situations in the Persian Gulf states will evolve in the aftermath of the invasion and the subsequent war against Iraq necessarily remains uncertain. What is certain, however, is that strong cohesion on oil policies is unlikely to obtain.

Oil and the economies of the Middle East

Oil revenues and economic growth are fundamentally linked in the oil-exporting states of the Middle East. The investment of oil revenues has had a particular impact on their economies which distinguishes them from other Third World countries. First, the economic development plans of the oil states tend to concentrate on high-technology investments in the energy and energy-intensive industries. Secondly, surplus revenues tend to be ploughed back into investment in public services and infrastructure, which, given the cyclical nature of oil markets, generally results in 'bust and boom' construction cycles. Thirdly, the more traditional forms of economic activity, such as agriculture and handicrafts, tend to shrink as a result of labour migration to other sectors and to cities.

However, these broad trends cannot in themselves explain the different ways in which oil revenues have affected the economic structures, and determined the economic strategies, of the Middle East. To do this, a useful distinction can be made between the 'desert-oil' and 'oil-plus' economies of the region. These distinctions are made on the basis of population, land availability and non-oil investment opportunities.

'Desert-oil' describes those Middle East economies—Bahrain, Kuwait, Libya, Oman, Qatar, Saudi Arabia and the UAE—with slim or non-existent traditional resource bases, the result of little cultivatable land and small indigenous populations. This category may be further divided between large countries with geographically disparate settlements—namely Libya, Oman and Saudi Arabia—and the remainder, which are essentially city-states.

'Oil-plus' economies—Algeria, Egypt, Iran, Iraq and Syria—have large populations and rich agricultural resources. They have diverse sources of income linked closely to the productivity of the indigenous population. This provides opportunities for investment in sustainable types of production rather than in sectors linked to finite energy resources. The 'plus', therefore, refers to the resources accruable to those economies with a diversified resource base.

The relative importance of oil to the Middle East's economies can be gauged in several ways. Here, three of many possible measures are employed to determine the similarities and differences in the impact of oil revenues on the structure of the economies. These are: the ratio of GDP per capita to oil revenue per capital; oil exports as percentage of total exports; and the composition of non-oil GDP.

First, a high ratio of GDP per capita to oil revenue per capita implies either that the economy has successfully employed oil revenues to diversify its sources of income or that the economy had diverse sources of income before oil revenues became important. Of the Persian Gulf producers the three highest ratios are those of Saudi Arabia, Iraq and Bahrain, with 5:2, 4:9 and 4:5 respectively (1988 figures). In the case of Saudi Arabia, the ratio may be overstated as the enormous interest derived from accumulated oil revenues and the effect on non-oil income of oil revenue investment has not been included in the measure of annual oil income from exports. As an 'oil-plus' economy, Iraq's high ratio requires no explanation. However, Bahrain's high ratio accurately conveys the large investment that has been made, not only in energy and energy-intensive industries but in offshore banking and services.

The second measure—oil exports as a percentage of total exports—is used to determine the extent to which non-oil investments have led to the production of tradeable goods and services. With the exception of Bahrain and the UAE (for which the information available is insufficient to draw firm conclusions), the dependence of the Persian Gulf on oil to generate foreign currency earnings ranges from 88% to 99% (1988 figures). Despite the oil price shocks and subsequent increase in income over the 1970s and early 1980s, investment has failed to produce tangible results in the form of exports. Bahrain, with only 78% dependence on oil exports in 1988, has fared slightly better but still has a long way to go.

Having established that the non-oil GDP sector has not generated exports it is illuminating to look at the composition of this sector and so to gauge the reasons for this. As expected, the percentage share of agriculture in the non-oil GDP of Middle East economies conforms to the logic of the initial economic category of each state. The 'oil-plus' economies have the greatest percentage share, the large 'desert-oil' economies the second largest, and the small 'desert-oil' economies the smallest (around 2 to 3%). However, another distinction, not apparent in these percentages, stems from the different attitudes to agricultural investment. In the 'desert-oil' economies investment is made in capital-intensive agricultural pro-grammes, such as the wheat programme in Saudi Arabia, to encourage exports. By contrast, in the 'oil-plus' economies, agricultural means remain largely traditional.

The share of industry in non-oil GDP needs careful interpretation as the relative weight of industry is not indicative of its absolute level and, more importantly, the energy-related composition of that share. In fact, despite the small share of industry in Iraq, Oman and Saudi Arabia it is precisely these 'oil-plus' and large 'desert-oil' economies that have the greater diversity of non-hydrocarbon based industries—food processing, textiles, consumer durables, immediate goods, transport equipment, mechanical and electrical machinery, and appliances.

An obvious common feature between all types of Middle East oil economies is the small share of agriculture and industry relative to the share of the 'tertiary' sector, which includes all commerce, infrastructure and services in non-oil GDP. Why?

From this view of the structure of the Middle East's economies it seems that government investment of oil revenues has not created a real and sustainable resource base. Two factors, both extraneous to oil, have worked against them. The first is the sparse real resource base throughout the region, especially in the desert-oil economies. However, even in the oil-plus economies, where there are relatively greater opportunities for investment, the large indigenous populations have reduced the impact of oil revenues on a per capita basis. The second factor, which is often overlooked, is that until 1973 most Middle East countries were still rela-tively poor. In spite of the fact that Iran produced ten times more oil than Egypt in the 1960s, Egypt nonetheless led Iran in terms of many develop-ment criteria. From this perspective, and given the huge land expanses and disparate nature of the population in some countries, even creating the infrastructure necessary to economic development so quickly can be viewed as a success. Furthermore the nature of oil revenues makes it difficult to redistribute them to the population in a way conducive to economic development. The income derived from oil is unrelated to the cost of its production and therefore accrues directly to government. This delinks the productive effort and generation of income in the economy and has significant economic and political ramifications.

In the desert-oil economies, for example, the high per capita revenue generated by oil exports has had a marked effect on the potential for economic development. Governments know that distributing oil wealth among the population tends inevitably to reduce economic incentives; oil wealth is not always conducive to economic effort. In the 'oil-plus' economies, with oil revenues per-capita generally much smaller, economic incentives remain more potent. Equally, however, with less to go round, there is a natural tendency for these governments to distribute principally to reinforce their own power bases. The resulting inequalities tend inevitably to encourage social and political tensions. The Iranian revolution of 1979 is one such example.

The redistribution of oil revenues for the purposes of economic development must also be balanced against the public demand for quality services and security. The diversion of funds to public services is especially marked in the desert-oil economies, where the indigenous population have come to expect a high standard of living. More often than not, medical and education services, for example, are free, while the necessary staples of life, such as electricity, food, water and gasoline, are subsidised. A parallel development in desert-oil economics is the encouragement of inefficient bureaucracies as a result of the need to reward political loyalties.

The ownership of such rich natural resources brings with it the need for security. This need is particularly marked in the Persian Gulf, which has been the focus of so many political crises. Sadly, the huge expenditures on defence and security services made by most oil-exporting countries in the Middle East are at once unavoidable and useless.

Robert Mabro

Appendix 1   MIDDLE EAST POPULATIONS AND GNP

	Population	*GNP per capita in US dollars*
Algeria	25.36m (1990)	2,450 (1988)
Bahrain	486,000 (1990)	6,610 (1987)
Egypt	50.74m (1989)	650 (1988)
Iran	53.92m (1988)	1,690 (1986)
Iraq	17.06m (1988)	2,140 (1986)
Israel	4.82m (1990)	8,650 (1988)
Jordan	3.17m (1989)	1,500 (1988)
Kuwait	2.04m (1990)	13,680 (1988)
Lebanon	2.8m (1988)	N/A
Libya	4m (1990)	5,410 (1988)
Morocco	24.5m (1989)	750 (1988)
Oman	2m (1990)	4,200 (1989)
Qatar	371,863 (1987)	11,610 (1988)
Saudi Arabia	12m (1988)	6,170 (1988)
Sudan	25.56m (1987)	340 (1988)
Syria	11.3m (1988)	1,670 (1988)
Tunisia	7.75m (1988)	1,230 (1988)
Turkey	50.67m (1985)	1,434 (1989)
UAE	1.6m (1988)	15,720 (1988)
Yemen	12m (1987)	540 (1988)

Appendix 2   DEFENCE SPENDING

	Total expenditure (in millions of US dollars)	*As percentage of GNP*
Egypt	4,145	11.5
Iran	20,160	12.6
Iraq	13,900	20
Israel	3,620	22
Jordan	540	13.2
Oman	2,075	22.8
Saudi Arabia	17,750	18.2
Syria	3,480	17.7
Turkey	2,400	5.9
UAE	2,328	6.4

All figures are for 1985

Appendix 3 THE ARAB–ISRAELI CONFLICT: key documents

1 The Balfour Declaration
2 November 1917

Dear Lord Rothschild,

I have much pleasure in conveying to you, on behalf of His Majesty's Government, the following declaration of sympathy with Jewish Zionist aspirations which has been submitted to, and approved by, the Cabinet.

His Majesty's Government view with favour the establishment of a national home for the Jewish people, and will use their best endeavours to facilitate the achievement of this object, it being clearly understood that nothing shall be done which may prejudice the civil and religious rights of existing non-Jewish communities in Palestine, or the rights and political status enjoyed by Jews in any other country.

I should be grateful if you would bring this declaration to the knowledge of the Zionist Federation.

Yours sincerely,
Arthur James Balfour

2 UN Resolution 181(II)—excerpts only
29 November 1947

Plan of Partition with Economic Union
Part I   Future constitution and government of Palestine

1. The Mandate for Palestine shall terminate as soon as possible but in any case not later than 1 August 1948.

2. The armed forces of the mandatory Power shall be progressively withdrawn from Palestine, the withdrawal to be completed as soon as possible but in any case not later than 1 August 1948.

The mandatory Power shall advise the Commission, as far in advance as possible, of its intention to terminate the Mandate and to evacuate each area.

The mandatory Power shall use its best endeavours to ensure that an area situated in the territory of the Jewish State, including a seaport and hinterland adequate to provide facilities for a substantial immigration, shall be evacuated at the earliest possible date and in any event not later than 1 February 1948.

3. Independent Arab and Jewish States and the Special International Regime for the City of Jerusalem, set forth in part III of this plan, shall come into existence in Palestine two months after the evacuation of the armed forces of the mandatory Power has been completed but in any case not later than 1 October 1948. The boundaries of the Arab State, the Jewish State, and the City of Jerusalem shall be as described in parts II and III below.

4. The period between the adoption by the General Assembly of its recommendation on the question of Palestine and the establishment of the independence of the Arab and Jewish States shall be a transitional period.

Part III City of Jerusalem

The City of Jerusalem shall be established as a *corpus separatum* under a special international regime and shall be administered by the United Nations. The Trusteeship Council shall be designated to discharge the responsibilities of the Administering Authority on behalf of the United Nations.

The City of Jerusalem shall include the present municipality of Jerusalem plus the surrounding villages and towns, the most eastern of which shall be Abu Dis; the most southern, Bethlehem; the most western, Ein Karim (including also the built-up area of Motsa); and the most northern Shu'fat, as indicated on the attached sketch-map (annex B).

The Trusteeship Council shall, within five months of the approval of the present plan, elaborate and approve a detailed Statute of the City which shall contain *inter alia* the substance of the following provisions:

1. *Government machinery; special objectives.* The Administering Authority in discharging its administrative obligations shall pursue the following special objectives:

(a) To protect and to preserve the unique spiritual and religious interests located in the city of the three great monotheistic faiths throughout the world, Christian, Jewish and Moslem; to this end to ensure that order and peace, and especially religious peace, reign in Jerusalem;

(b) To foster co-operation among all the inhabitants of the city in their own interests as well as in order to encourage and support the peaceful development of the mutual relations between the two Palestinian peoples throughout the Holy Land; to promote the security, well-being and any constructive measures of development of the residents, having regard to the special circumstances [of the two] peoples and communities.

3 UN Resolution 242
22 November 1967

The Security Council,

Expressing its continuing concern with the grave situation in the Middle East,

Emphasizing the inadmissibility of the acquisition of territory by war and the need to work for a just and lasting peace in which every State in the area can live in security,

Emphasizing further that all Member States in their acceptance of the Charter of the United Nations have undertaken a commitment to act in accordance with Article 2 of the Charter,

1. **Affirms** that the fulfillment of Charter principles requires the establishment of a just and lasting peace in the Middle East which should include the application of both the following principles:

i. Withdrawal of Israel armed forces from territories occupied in the recent conflict;

ii. Termination of all claims or states of belligerency and respect, for and acknowledgement of the sovereignty, territorial integrity and political independence of every State in the area and their right to live in peace within secure and recognized boundaries free from threats or acts of force;

2. **Affirms further** the necessity

(a) For guaranteeing freedom of navigation through international waterways in the area;

(b) For achieving a just settlement of the refugee problem;

(c) For guaranteeing the territorial inviolability and political independence of every State in the area, through measures including the establishment of demilitarized zones;

3. **Requests** the Secretary-General to designate a Special Representative to proceed to the Middle East to establish and maintain contacts with the States concerned in order to promote agreement and assist efforts to achieve a peaceful and accepted settlement in accordance with the provisions and principles in this resolution;

4. **Requests** the Secretary-General to report to the Security Council on the progress of the efforts of the Special Representative as soon as possible.

4   UN Resolution 338
21 October 1973

The Security Council,

1. **Calls upon** all parties to the present fighting to cease all firing and terminate all military activity immediately, no later than 12 hours after the moment of the adoption of this decision, in the positions they now occupy;

2. **Calls upon** the parties concerned to start immediately after the cease-fire the implementation of Security Council Resolution 242 (1967) in all of its parts;

3. **Decides** that, immediately and concurrently with the cease-fire, negotiations start between the parties concerned under appropriate auspices aimed at establishing a just and durable peace in the Middle East.

5   Joint Letter From President Sadat and Prime Minister Begin to President Carter

The President   March 26, 1979
The White House

Dear Mr President:

This letter confirms that Israel and Egypt have agreed as follows:

The Governments of Israel and Egypt recall that they concluded at Camp David and signed at the White House on September 17, 1978, the annexed documents entitled 'A Framework for Peace in the Middle East Agreed at Camp David' and 'Framework for the conclusion of a Peace Treaty between Israel and Egypt'.

For the purpose of achieving a comprehensive peace settlement in accordance with the above-mentioned Frameworks, Israel and Egypt will proceed with the implementation of those provisions relating to the West Bank and the Gaza Strip. They have agreed to start negotiations within a month after the exchange of the instruments of ratification of the Peace Treaty. In accordance with the 'Framework for Peace in the Middle East', the Hashemite Kingdom of Jordan is invited to join the negotiations. The Delegations of Egypt and Jordan may include Palestinians as mutually agreed. The purpose of the negotiation shall be to agree, prior to the elections, on the modalities for establishing the elected self-governing authority (administrative council), define its powers and responsibilities, and agree upon other related issues. In the event Jordan decides not to take part in the negotiations, the negotiations will be held by Israel and Egypt.

The two Governments agree to negotiate continuously and in good faith to conclude these negotiations at the earliest possible date. They also agree that the objective of the negotiations is the establishment of the self-governing authority in the West Bank and Gaza in order to provide full autonomy to the inhabitants.

Israel and Egypt set for themselves the goal of completing the negotiations within one year so that elections will be held as expeditiously as possible after agreement has been reached between the parties. The self-governing authority referred to in the 'Framework for Peace in the Middle East' will be established and inaugurated within one month after it has been elected, at which time the transitional period of five years will begin. The Israeli military government and its civilian administration will be withdrawn, to be replaced by the self-governing authority, as specified in the 'Framework for Peace in the Middle East'. A withdrawal of Israeli armed forces will then take place and there will be a redeployment of the remaining Israeli forces into specified security locations.

This letter also confirms our understanding that the United States Government will participate fully in all stages of negotiations.

Sincerely yours,

For the Government of Israel: For the Government of the Arab Republic of Egypt:

Menachem Begin   Mohamed Anwar El-Sadat

Appendix 4   THE IRAN–IRAQ WAR

UN Resolution 598
20 July 1989

The Security Council

1. Demands that, as a first step towards a negotiated settlement, Iran and Iraq observe an immediate cease-fire, discontinue all military actions on land, at sea and in the air, and withdraw all forces to the internationally recognized boundaries without delay;

2. Requests the Secretary-General to dispatch a team of United Nations Observers to verify, confirm and supervise the cease-fire and withdrawal and further requests the Secretary-General to make the necessary arrangements in consultation with the Parties and to submit a report thereon to the Security Council;

3. Urges that prisoners-of-war be released and repatriated without delay after the cessation of active hostilities in accordance with the Third Geneva Convention of 12 August 1949;

4. Calls upon Iran and Iraq to co-operate with the Secretary-General in implementing this resolution and in mediation efforts to achieve a comprehensive, just and honourable settlement, acceptable to both sides, of all outstanding issues, in accordance with the principles contained in the Charter of the United Nations;

5. Calls upon all other States to exercise the utmost restraint and to refrain from any act which may lead to further escalation and widening of the conflict, and thus to facilitate the implementation of the present resolution;

6. Requests the Secretary-General to explore, in consultation with Iran and Iraq, the question of entrusting an impartial body with inquiring into responsibility for the conflict and to report to the Security Council as soon as possible;

7. Recognizes the magnitude of the damage inflicted during the conflict and the need for reconstruction efforts, with appropriate international assistance, once the conflict is ended and, in this regard, requests the Secretary-General to assign a team of experts to study the question of reconstruction and to report to the Security Council;

8. Further requests the Secretary-General to examine, in consultation with Iran and Iraq and with other States of the region, measures to enhance the security and stability of the region;

9. Requests the Secretary-General to keep the Security Council informed on the implementation of this resolution;

10. Decides to meet again as necessary to consider further steps to ensure compliance with this resolution.

Appendix 5 THE GULF WAR: key UN resolutions

1 UN Resolution 660
2 August 1990

The Security Council,

Alarmed by the invasion of Kuwait on 2 August 1990 by the military forces of Iraq,

Determining that there exists a breach of international peace and security as regards the Iraqi invasion of Kuwait,

Acting under Articles 39 and 40 of the Charter of the United Nations,

1. **Condemns** the Iraqi invasion of Kuwait;

2. **Demands** that Iraq withdraw immediately and unconditionally all its forces to the positions in which they were located on 1 August 1990;

3. **Calls upon** Iraq and Kuwait to begin immediately intensive negotiations for the resolution of their differences and supports all efforts in this regard, and especially those of the League of Arab States;

4. **Decides** to meet again as necessary to consider further steps to ensure compliance with the present resolution.

2 UN Resolution 661
6 August 1990

The Security Council,

1. **Determines** that Iraq so far has failed to comply with paragraph 2 of resolution 660 (1990) and has usurped the authority of the legitimate Government of Kuwait;

2. **Decides,** as a consequence, to take the following measures to secure compliance of Iraq with paragraph 2 of resolution 660 (1990) and to restore the authority of the legitimate Government of Kuwait;

3. **Decides** that all States shall prevent:
a) The import into their territories of all commodities and products originating in Iraq or Kuwait exported therefrom after the date of the present resolution;
b) Any activities by their nationals or in their territories which would promote or are calculated to promote the export or trans-shipment of any commodities or products from Iraq or Kuwait; and any dealings by their nationals or their flag vessels or in their territories in any commodities or products originating in Iraq or Kuwait and exported therefrom after the date of the present resolution, including in particular any transfer of funds to Iraq or Kuwait for the purposes of such activities or dealings;
c) The sale or supply by their nationals or from their territories or using their flag vessels of any commodities or products, including weapons or any other military equipment, whether or not originating in their territories but not including supplies intended strictly for medical purposes, and, in humanitarian circumstances, foodstuffs, to any person or body in Iraq or Kuwait or to any person or body for the purposes of any business carried on in or operated from Iraq or Kuwait, and any activities by their nationals or in their territories which promote or are calculated to promote such sale or supply of such commodities or products;

4. **Decides** that all States shall not make available to the Government of Iraq or to any commercial, industrial or public utility undertaking in Iraq or Kuwait, any funds or any other financial or economic resources and shall prevent their nationals and any persons within their territories from removing from their territories or otherwise making available to that Government or to any such undertaking any such funds or resources and from remitting any other funds to persons or bodies within Iraq or

Kuwait, except payments exclusively for strictly medical or humanitarian purposes and, in humanitarian circumstances, foodstuffs;

5. Calls upon all States, including States non-members of the United Nations, to act strictly in accordance with the provisions of the present resolution notwithstanding any contract entered into or licence granted before the date of the present resolution;

6. Decides to establish, in accordance with rule 28 of the provisional rules of procedure of the Security Council, a Committee of the Security Council consisting of all the members of the Council, to undertake the following tasks and to report on its work to the Council with its observations and recommendations:
a) To examine the reports on the progress of the implementation of the present resolution which will be submitted by the Secretary-General;
b) To seek from all States further information regarding the action taken by them concerning the effective implementation of the provisions laid down in the present resolution;

7. Calls upon all States to co-operate fully with the Committee in the fulfilment of its task, including supplying such information as may be sought by the Committee in pursuance of the present resolution;

8. Requests the Secretary-General to provide all necessary assistance to the Committee and to make the necessary arrangements in the Secretariat for the purpose;

9. Decides that, notwithstanding paragraphs 4 through 8 above, nothing in the present resolution shall prohibit assistance to the legitimate Government of Kuwait, and calls upon all States:
a) To take appropriate measures to protect assets of the legitimate Government of Kuwait and its agencies;
b) Not to recognize any regime set up by the occupying Power;

10. Requests the Secretary-General to report to the Council on the progress of the implementation of the present resolution, the first report to be submitted within thirty days;

11. Decides to keep this item on its agenda and to continue its efforts to put an early end to the invasion by Iraq.

3 Resolution 678
29 November 1990

The Security Council,

1. Demands that Iraq comply fully with resolution 660 (1990) and all subsequent relevant resolutions, and decides, while maintaining all its decisions, to allow Iraq one final opportunity, as a pause of goodwill, to do so;

2. Authorizes Member States co-operating with the Government of Kuwait, unless Iraq on or before 15 January 1991 fully implements, as set forth in paragraph 1 above, the foregoing resolutions, to use all necessary means to uphold and implement resolution 660 (1990) and all subsequent relevant resolutions and to restore international peace and security in the area;

3. Requests all States to provide appropriate support for the actions undertaken in pursuance of paragraph 2 of the present resolution;

4. Requests the States concerned to keep the Security Council regularly informed on the progress of actions undertaken pursuant to paragraphs 2 and 3 of the present resolution;

5. Decides to remain seized of the matter.

Appendix 6   ETHNIC FACTIONS IN LEBANON

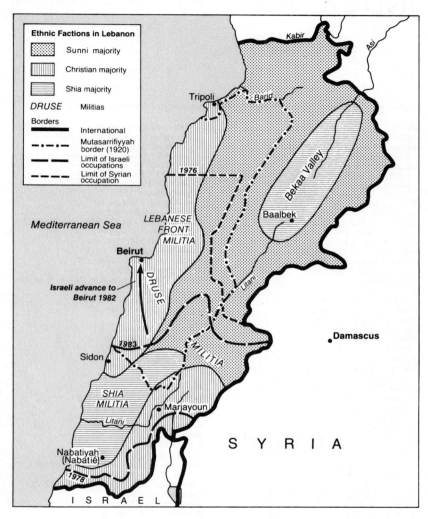

Ethnic Factions in Lebanon

Sunni majority

Christian majority

Shia majority

DRUSE   Militias

Borders

International

Mutasarrifiyyah border (1920)

Limit of Israeli occupations

Limit of Syrian occupation

INDEX

*(Entries and numerals marked in **bold type** denote a section/chapter devoted to the subject.)*

THE CRYSTAL PRISON

BOOK TWO OF
THE DEPTFORD MICE TRILOGY

ROBIN JARVIS

A Peter Glassman Book
SeaStar Books
New York

FOR THE REST OF MY FAMILY,
WHO NOW LIVE WITHOUT
THE LIGHT OF MY FATHER

Text and illustrations © 1989, 2001 by Robin Jarvis
Afterword © 2001 by Peter Glassman
Jacket illustration © 2001 by Leonid Gore

First published in Great Britain
by Macdonald Young Books Limited, London.

SEASTAR BOOKS
A division of NORTH-SOUTH BOOKS INC.

First published in hardcover in the United States in 2001 by SeaStar Books,
New York. Published simultaneously in Canada by North-South Books,
an imprint of Nord-Süd Verlag AG, Gossau Zürich, Switzerland.
First SeaStar Books paperback edition published in 2002.

Library of Congress Cataloging-in-Publication Data

Jarvis, Robin, (date)
The crystal prison / [written and illustrated by] Robin Jarvis.
p.   cm. – (The Deptford mice; bk. 2)
Sequel to: The dark portal.
Summary: When Audrey, a spirited town mouse, reluctantly keeps a promise to accompany a black
rat to the country, she witnesses the return of a supernatural evil she thought had been destroyed.
[1. Mice–Fiction. 2. Rats–Fiction. 3. Supernatural–Fiction. 4. Conduct of life–Fiction.] I. Title.
PZ7.J2965 Cr 2001   [Fic]–dc21   2001034423

The text for this book is set in 11-point Walbaum Book.

ISBN 1-58717-107-4 (reinforced trade edition)
1 3 5 7 9 RTE 10 8 6 4 2
ISBN 1-58717-161-9 (paperback edition)
3 5 7 9 PB 10 8 6 4 2

Printed in U.S.A.

For more information about our books, and the authors and artists who create them,
visit our web site: www.northsouth.com

CONTENTS

THE DEPTFORD MICE

Audrey Brown

Tends to dream. She likes to look her best and wears
lace and ribbons. Audrey cannot hold her tongue in an
argument and often says more than she should.

Arthur Brown

Fat and jolly, Arthur likes a fight but always comes off worse.

Gwen Brown

Caring mother of Arthur and Audrey. Her love for her family
binds it together and keeps it strong.

Arabel Chitter

Silly old gossip who gets on the nerves of everyone in the Skirtings.

Oswald Chitter

Arabel's son is an albino runt. Oswald is very weak and
is not allowed to join in some of the rougher games.

Piccadilly

A cheeky young mouse from the city,
Piccadilly has no parents and is very independent.

Thomas Triton

A retired midshipmouse. Thomas is a heroic
old salt—he does not suffer fools gladly.

Madame Akkikuyu

A black rat from Morocco. She used to tell fortunes until her
mind was broken in the chamber of Jupiter.

Kempe

A traveling trader mouse—he journeys far and wide selling
his goods and singing lewd songs.

The Starwife

A venerable old squirrel who lives under the Greenwich Observatory.
Her motives are good, but her methods are cruel.

THE FENNYWOLDERS

William Scuttle or "Twit"
A simple fieldmouse who has been visiting his mother's kin.
Twit is a cheerful fieldmouse who looks on the bright side.

Elijah and Gladwin Scuttle
Twit's parents. Gladwin is Mrs. Chitter's sister, but ran away from Deptford
as a youngster, when she found Elijah injured in the garden.

Isaac Nettle
A staunch Green Mouser. He is a bitter, grim figure, but many
of the fieldmice listen to his ravings.

Jenkin Nettle
A jolly mouse who suffers at the paws of his father.

Alison Sedge
A country beauty who flirts with all the boys. She is
vain and loves to preen herself.

Young Whortle, Samuel Gorse,
Todkin, Hodge, and Figgy Bottom
Five young friends who delight in climbing the cornstalks
and seeking adventure.

Mahooot
A wicked barn owl who loves mouse for supper.

Mr. Woodruffe
A very sensible mouse who has been elected to the honorable position
of The King of the Field.

Nicodemus
Mysterious spirit of the fields who is trying to get free from limbo.

The Green Mouse
A magical figure in mouse mythology. He is the essence of all
growing things, whose power is greatest in the summer.

THE DARK PORTAL

The Crystal Prison is the second book in the story of the Deptford Mice, which began with The Dark Portal. *In Book One, Audrey and Arthur Brown, two innocent town mice, are drawn into the sewers beneath the streets of Deptford in search of Audrey's mousebrass—a magical charm given to her by the Green Mouse, the mystical spirit of spring. Deep within the underground tunnels, the two mice discover the nightmare realm of Jupiter, the unseen but terrifying lord of the rats.*

Audrey and Arthur are helped by a number of characters: Oswald, a sickly albino mouse often mistaken for a rat; Twit, Oswald's cousin and a simple country mouse; Piccadilly, a cheeky young mouse from the city; and Madame Akkikuyu, a black rat who ekes out a living peddling potions and telling phoney fortunes.

The Deptford Mice discover that Jupiter is concocting a terrible plan—to release the Black Death upon London once again. However, with the help of the Green Mouse, the mice confound Jupiter's plot and lure him out of his lair. To their horror, they discover that Jupiter is not a rat at all, but a monstrous cat, grown bloated and evil by years of hatred in the sewers.

Audrey throws her mousebrass into Jupiter's face; it explodes and sends the giant cat tumbling into the deep sewer water. As he struggles to save himself, the souls of his many victims rise out of the waves and drag him down to a watery death.

SMOKE OVER DEPTFORD

It was a hot day in Deptford. A terrible stench hung over the housing estates, and increased as the sun rose higher in the sky. It was strongest on a building site near the river. There the air was thick and poisonous. The builders themselves choked and covered their faces with their handkerchiefs.

At the edge of the site next to the river wall was an untidy pile of yellowing newspapers. They lay in a moldering heap amongst the loose bricks and spreading nettles. It was here that the stink began.

One of the builders came trudging up. His worn, tough boots waded through the weeds and paused at the newspaper mound. A scuffed toe tentatively nudged some of them aside and a dark cloud of angry, buzzing flies flew out. Revealed beneath the papers was the rotting body of a horrific giant cat.

*   *   *

Jupiter was dead. The evil lord of the rats had met his end weeks before in the deep, dark sewer water. His immense body had sunk to the muddy bottom, where underwater currents pulled and swayed his corpse this way and that. Slowly he rolled out of the altar chamber and through a submerged archway.

Into the tunnels he had drifted, turning over and over in the

1

water. One minute his grisly unseeing eyes would be staring at the arched ceiling above and the next glaring down into the cold dark depths. As he rolled over in this way his great jaws lolled open, lending him the illusion of life. Like a snarling demon he turned. But he was dead. For some days Jupiter bobbed up and down in the sewer passages until stronger forces gripped him and, suddenly, with a rush of water he was flushed out into the River Thames. The gulls and other birds left him well alone, and for a while all fish abandoned that stretch of the river.

One night nature took a hand in ridding the river of the dreadful carcass. A terrible storm blew up: the wind and the rain lashed down from the sky, and the river became swollen and crashed against its walls with shuddering violence.

On one such surging wave was the corpse of Jupiter, carried along until with a thundering smash the wave smote the wall and the cat's body was hurled over onto the building site.

*   *   *

The builder who had found him hurried away quickly but soon returned dragging behind him a great shovel caked in cement. With a grunt he lifted the sagging corpse into the air. Jupiter's massive claws dangled limply over the sides of the shovel and what was left of his striped ginger fur blazed ruddily in the sunlight.

Surrounded by the thick buzzing cloud, the builder stepped carefully over to the site bonfire and tossed Jupiter into its heart.

The flames licked over the cat greedily. For a while the fire glowed purple and then with one final splutter there was nothing left of the once mighty lord of the sewers.

Only a thick dark smoke that had risen from the flames remained, and this stayed hanging stubbornly in the air over Deptford for two days, until a summer breeze blew it away on the third morning.

CHAPTER ONE

THE SUMMONS

Oswald was ill. As soon as the white mouse had returned from the sewers he had felt unwell. When the small group of mice who had confronted the terrifying Jupiter had emerged from the Grill and climbed the cellar steps, Oswald's legs had given way and sturdy Thomas Triton had carried him the rest of the way. Although the albino coughed and spluttered, no one realized how serious his condition would become.

For weeks he had stayed in bed. At first the mice thought he had merely caught a cold, and his mother Mrs. Chitter had fussed and scolded him over it. But the cold did not improve and his lungs had become inflamed so that when he coughed the pain made him cry. Steadily he grew weaker. Mrs. Chitter tended to him day and night, and made herself ill in the process, until she too became a poor reflection of what she had once been.

Oswald's father, Jacob Chitter, had moved his favorite chair into his son's room next to his bed. He held his son's paw throughout, shaking his head sadly. Oswald was slipping away;

3

bit by painful bit the white mouse became more frail. Then one day Mrs. Chitter could take no more. As she was carrying away the soup that Oswald had been unable to swallow, the bowl fell from her paws and she fell heavily to the floor—soup and tears everywhere.

From then on Gwen Brown took charge of Oswald and his mother while Twit, the fieldmouse, looked after his uncle, Mr. Chitter.

All was silent in the Skirtings. The empty old house was filled with quiet prayers for the Chitter family. All the mice helped as much as they could: those on the Landings forgot their snobbery and offered food and blankets. Gwen Brown's own children, Arthur and Audrey, collected all the donations and messages of goodwill, and it was the job of a gray city mouse, called Piccadilly, to keep everyone informed of Oswald's condition.

All the mice owed a great deal to this small group of friends. It was they who had finally rid them of the menace of Jupiter, and all their lives were now easier. No more did they have to dread the cellar and the strange Grill, which was the entrance to the dark, sinister rat world. All the cruel rats had been killed or scattered and a mouse could sleep soundly at night, fearing no sudden attacks or raids. Only the older mice still looked at the cellar doubtfully and would not pass beyond its great door.

So, when they had been told of Jupiter's fall—and when they finally believed it—there was tremendous excitement and they had cheered the brave deeds of these mice. But now the youngest of the heroes was dying.

*   *   *

Piccadilly swept the hair out of his eyes and got out of bed. The sunlight shone on the city mouse and warmed him all over, but he hardly noticed it. For the moment, he was sharing a room

4

with Arthur, and Audrey was sleeping in her mother's bed, as Gwen was at the Chitters' all the time now.

"Arthur," Piccadilly whispered to the snoring bundle, "wake up." He shook his friend gently.

The plump mouse on the bed blinked and drew his paw over his eyes. "How is he?" he asked directly.

Piccadilly shook his head. "I've just got up—how was he last night when you left him?"

"Bad!" Arthur swung himself off the bed and stood in the sunlight as was his custom. He stared at the clear blue sky outside. "Mother doesn't think it will be long now." He sighed and looked across to Piccadilly. "Will you stay here, afterward?"

The gray mouse sniffed a little. "No, I've made up my mind to stay just until . . ." He coughed. "Then I'm off—back to the city."

"We'll miss you, you know," said Arthur. "I won't know what to do around here when you've gone. I think Twit's decided to leave as well . . . afterward." Arthur turned back to examine the summer sky and then remarked casually, "I think Audrey will miss you most, though."

Piccadilly looked up curiously. "She's never said anything."

"Well you know what she's like: too stubborn to say anything! I know my sister, and believe you me, she likes you a lot."

"Well, I wish she'd tell me."

"Oh, I think she will when it suits her." Arthur stretched himself and rubbed his ears. "He doesn't even take the milk anymore, you know. Mother can't get him to drink it and if he does, it won't stay down. Maybe he would be better off . . ." his voice trailed away miserably.

"I'm dreading it," murmured Piccadilly. "These past few days he's sunk lower an' lower—I don't know what keeps him going."

Arthur touched him lightly on the shoulder. "Let's go and find out."

5

Audrey was already up and waiting for them. She had not bothered to tie the ribbon in her hair as she usually did and it hung in soft chestnut waves behind her ears.

Outside the Chitters' door they stopped, and Arthur glanced nervously at the others before knocking. They waited anxiously as shuffling steps approached on the other side of the curtain.

The curtain was drawn aside, and the small features of Twit greeted them solemnly. He looked back into the room, nodded, then stepped out and let the curtain fall back behind him.

"He's still with us," he whispered. "'Twere touch 'n go for a while last night: thought we'd lost 'im twice." The fieldmouse bit his lip. "Your mum's all in; she's 'ad a tirin' time of it. What with 'im and Mrs. Chitter, she's fit to drop."

"I'll tell her to lie down for a bit." Arthur nodded.

"And I'll take over," added Audrey. "You look like you could do with a rest as well, Twit."

"Well, Mr. Chitter, he just sits an' mopes, his wife an' son bein' so bad. I can't do anything with 'im." Twit wiped his brimming eyes. "Heck we tried—me an' your mum, but all three of 'em are slidin' downhill fast. I really think this be the last day—no, I knows it. None of 'em'll see the sunset." Big tears ran down the fieldmouse's little face. He was exhausted and felt that all his efforts had been a waste of time—this branch of his family was about to wither and die.

Audrey bent down and kissed Twit's forehead. "Hush," she soothed. "Piccadilly, put Twit in Arthur's bed. I'll wake you if anything happens," she reassured the fieldmouse.

"Thank 'ee," Twit stammered through a yawn, and he followed Piccadilly back to the Browns' home.

Arthur turned to his sister. "Right," he said. "I'll tackle Mother, you see to the Chitters. I'll come and help once Mother's gone to bed." Gingerly he pulled back the curtain.

It was dark beyond: the daylight had been blocked out for Oswald's sake.

Arabel Chitter's bric-a-brac was well dusted, her pieces of china ornament, bits of sparkling brooches, and neatly folded lace shawls and headscarves had all been seen to by Gwen Brown. Mrs. Chitter had always been house-proud and if things were not "just so" she would fret.

Arthur and Audrey slowly made their way to Oswald's room. Arthur coughed quietly and their mother came out to them.

"Hello, dears," she breathed wearily. Dark circles ringed her brown eyes and her tail dragged sadly behind her. "No ribbon today, Audrey?" she asked, stroking her daughter's hair. "And you, Arthur, have you had breakfast?"

"Have you, Mother?" He took her paw in his. "No, I didn't think so. Come on, you're going to get some sleep." He would hear no protests and Gwen Brown was too tired to make any.

"Audrey, promise me you'll wake me if . . ." was all she managed.

"I promise, Mother."

"Yes, good girl. Now, come, Arthur, show me to my bed or I'll drop down here."

Audrey watched them leave, then breathed deeply and went inside.

Illness has a smell all of its own and it is unmistakable. Sweet and cloying, it lingers in a sickroom, waiting for the patient to recover or fail. Audrey had grown accustomed to this smell by now, though it frightened her to enter the room.

It was a small space almost filled by the bed in which Oswald lay. Beside him on a chair was Mr. Chitter, his head bent in sleep. He was a meek mouse, devoted to his wife and son, but this had broken him.

Oswald was quite still. His face was gaunt and drained, paler now than ever before. His eyelids were closed lightly over his dim pink eyes. His fair albino hair was stuck close to his head and his whiskers drooped mournfully. The blankets were

7

pulled up under his chin, but one of his frail paws was wrapped inside his father's.

Audrey felt Oswald's forehead: it was hot and damp. A fever was consuming his last energies, burning away whatever hope there had been for him. Sorrowfully she picked up a bowl from the floor. It contained clean water and a cloth, and with them she began to cool his brow.

Next to Oswald's bed, on the wall, was a garland of dried hawthorn leaves, which he had saved from the spring ceremony and preserved carefully. He had adored the celebrations and was impatient for the following year, when he too would come of age and be entitled to enter the mysterious chambers of summer and winter to receive his mousebrass. To Audrey it seemed long ago that she had taken hers from the very paws of the Green Mouse. She thought of him now, the mystical spirit of life and growing things. How often she had prayed to him to spare Oswald! Now it looked as if nothing could save him.

There was a small table near her and on it were some slices of raw onion. Mrs. Chitter believed this would draw out the illness from her son, and out of respect for her wishes Gwen Brown made sure that the onion was fresh every day. Audrey only regarded this superstition as one more addition to the eerie smell of illness.

A movement on the pillow drew her attention back to the patient.

Oswald's eyes opened slowly. For a while he gazed at the ceiling, then gradually he focused on Audrey. She smiled at him warmly.

"Good morning, Oswald," she said.

The albino raised his eyebrows feebly and tried to speak. It was a low, barely audible whisper and Audrey strained to hear him.

"What sort . . . of day is it . . . outside?" His sad eyes pierced

her heart and she struggled to remain reassuring when all the time she wanted to run from him sobbing. She could not get over the feeling that it was mainly due to her that Oswald was so ill.

"It's beautiful, Oswald," she said huskily. "You never saw such a morning! The sky is as blue as a forget-me-not and the sun is so bright and lovely."

A ghost of a smile touched Oswald's haggard cheeks. He closed his eyes. "You never did get your mousebrass back," he murmured.

"Yes, I did, for a short while. You were so brave, getting it for me amongst all those horrible rats."

"I don't think I shall ever get my . . . brass now," he continued mildly. "I wonder what it would . . . have been."

"The sign of utmost bravery," sobbed Audrey. She held her paw over her face.

"I'm so sorry, Oswald," she cried. "This is all my fault."

"No, it had to be done . . . Jupiter had to be destroyed. Not your fault if . . . if I wasn't up to it."

"Don't, please! Just rest. Would you like some milk?" But Oswald had already fallen into a black swoon. Audrey cried silently.

A gentle, polite knock sounded. She dried her eyes and left the sickroom, pausing on the way to the main entrance to look in on Mrs. Chitter, who lay asleep in another room. Arabel's silvery head was old and shriveled. It was startling to see it against the crisp whiteness of the pillows. But at least she was asleep and not fretting. Audrey crept away and made for the entrance.

"Oh, it's young Miss Audrey!" Sturdy Thomas Triton looked faintly surprised to see her when she drew the curtain back. "I was expectin' your mother, but if you aren't the very one, anyway." The midshipmouse pulled off his hat and asked gravely, "How's the lad this morn?"

10

"No better, I'm afraid—we don't think he'll last much longer. Mother's resting just now: she and Twit have been up all night."

"Aye," muttered Thomas grimly, then he furrowed his spiky white brows and considered Audrey steadily with his wise, dark eyes. "'Tis a sore thing to bear—losing a friend," and an odd far-off expression stole over him, "'specially if you think it's all your fault. That's a mighty burden, lass! Don't take it on yourself—guilt and grief aren't easy fellows to cart 'round with yer, believe you me."

Audrey turned away quickly. Thomas's insight was too unnerving and she cringed from it. "Would you like to see him?" she managed at last.

Thomas fidgeted with his hat, rolling it over in his strong paws. "Lead on, I'll look on the boy once more."

When they came to the sickroom he hesitated at the doorway and changed his mind. "Nay, I'll not enter. I've glimpsed the lad and that's enough. I've seen too many go down with fever to want to witness it again. He were a brave sort whatever he may have said to the contrary. A loss to us all. I see the father has not moved—is the mother still abed?" Audrey nodded. "That's bad! A whole family wiped out by sickness and grief. Well, how's little Twit bearing up?"

"Oh, you know Twit. He always tries to be bright and jolly. You never know what he's thinking deep down."

"Yes, you're right there. I like that fieldmouse—reminds me of someone I knew once—best friend I ever had. Twit's mighty fond of his cousin there—it'll be a tragic blow to his little heart."

A soft footfall behind them made them both turn sharply—but it was only Arthur.

"Hullo Mr. Triton," he said politely. "Audrey, I've managed to put Mother to bed and she's asleep now, but I think Piccadilly's having trouble with Twit—he needs to rest, but won't settle. He can't stop worrying!"

"Right, I'll get him out of that," said Thomas firmly, and he fixed his hat back on his head. "Come with me, miss, and you milladdo, stay here. I'll see to my young matey." The midshipmouse strode from the Chitters' home with Audrey following.

"Mr. Triton," she said, catching up with him. "What did you mean before when you saw me and said I was the very one?"

"It wasn't just to see poor Oswald that I came," he explained as they entered the Browns' home, "but to see you as well."

"Me?" asked Audrey, puzzled. She had not spoken to the midshipmouse very much during the brief times that he had visited the Skirtings, and she wondered what he was up to.

"Aye, lass," he continued. "I've a message for you."

She looked blank as Thomas Triton charged into Arthur and Piccadilly's bedroom.

The city mouse was trying to get Twit to stay in bed. He had heated him some milk and honey, but the fieldmouse would not rest. When Thomas barged in Twit grinned in spite of himself.

"How do!" he said.

"Ahoy there, matey," Thomas said sternly. "What you doin', lyin' in yer bunk on a day like this?" The midshipmouse winked a startled Piccadilly into silence. "Get up, lad, there's folk to see!"

"But he's only just gone to bed," exclaimed Audrey.

Without turning around to look at her, Thomas said, "You, miss, had better make yourself presentable. What has happened to your hair?"

"I . . . I didn't put my ribbon in," stammered Audrey.

"Then chop chop, lass. Go do whatever you do do to make a good impression. Someone wants to see you."

"Who's that then, Thomas?" asked Twit, curiosity banishing the weary lines around his eyes.

The midshipmouse feigned astonishment. "Why, the Starwife, lad—didn't I say?"

Twit's eyes shone with excitement. "What? Her that lives in

Greenwich under those funny buildings I saw when the bats flew me over?"

"Aye, matey. First thing this morning, when it was still dark, I had a message from herself delivered by one of her younger jumpy squirrels–took me a long time to calm him down. They are a watery lot! Well the gist of the story is," Thomas now turned to Audrey, "that the Starwife wants to see you, Miss Brown, and she won't be kept waitin'. I've come to fetch you, and milladdo here is welcome to join us."

For a second Twit's heart leaped, but when he thought of Oswald it sank down deeper and lower than ever. Sadly he shook his head. "I can't come, Thomas. Oswald won't see the end of the day–my place is here."

The midshipmouse put his paw on Twit's shoulder. "Lad, I promise you we'll be back for that time. If Oswald leaves us, I swear you'll be at his side."

Twit blinked. He trusted his seafaring friend so much, yet how could he be so certain? Thomas's eyes bore into him and under their solemn gaze the little fieldmouse felt sure that he was right.

"I'll just go an' have a quick swill," Twit said, running out of the bedroom.

Audrey stared at Thomas and began to say something when a stern command from him sent her dashing off to find her ribbon.

Thomas Triton sighed and smiled at Piccadilly. "I'll not keep them away long. The easiest bit's been done–I've got them to go. Your job's not as simple. Pray to the Green Mouse that the Chitter lad hangs on till we return!"

CHAPTER TWO

THE STARWIFE

Thomas Triton led a flustered Audrey and Twit across the hall. Through the cellar door they slipped and jumped down the stone steps beyond. Thomas strode through the cellar gloom to the Grill.

Wrought in iron with twirling leaf patterns, this had always been an object of fear and dread. And, indeed, when Jupiter the terrible god of the rats had been alive it had possessed strange powers.

Now Audrey shivered as she stood before it, recalling how she had been dragged through the Grill by an evil band of rats. Twit backed away from it slightly. He remembered the horrible effect that the black enchantments had had upon Arthur. Only Thomas dared to touch the Grill.

With a hearty laugh he looked at the others. "Jupiter is dead," he reminded them. "Whatever forces were lurking in or beyond this grating are long gone." As if to prove it, he banged an iron leaf with his fist. "The spells are as cold and lifeless as the mangy moggy who made them." The midshipmouse

14

chuckled and squeezed himself through the rusted gap in the Grill.

"This is the quickest way to Greenwich," he said, popping up on the other side. Audrey and Twit still hesitated, so Thomas pulled a silly face. It looked so ridiculous that they couldn't help laughing. Perhaps the Grill was an ordinary metal grating after all. Audrey and Twit crawled through the gap and joined Thomas.

Down into the sewers they went. Although it was a hot summer day in the outside world, here it was chill and damp. Audrey had forgotten how bleak it all was. So many ugly memories were kindled by everything around her; the musty, stale smell of the dark running water, the slippery slime on the ledges, and the weird echoes, which floated through the old air. Around every corner there was a dark memory.

Thomas sensed her unease and remarked casually, "I use the sewers quite a bit now. I never get lost, me. I can find my way home on a black foggy night with no moon and my hat over my eyes." Twit chuckled softly, and Audrey was grateful to the midshipmouse; he took her mind off things.

"Now there ain't no more rats down 'ere," Twit piped up, "there's no danger of us gettin' peeled, is there, Thomas?"

"'S right, matey."

"But won't others arrive and take over where Jupiter's rats left off?" Audrey asked, doubtfully looking over her shoulder.

"No, rats are mostly cowardly," answered Thomas. "Only the fear of Jupiter gave them a false sort of courage. Ask that city mouse—he'll tell you how cringy they are in the city. You just have to cuff 'em about the head if they start gettin' uppity."

Audrey felt relieved. Like Twit she found the midshipmouse to be a comforting figure. He was so sure of himself that it rubbed off onto everyone he was with. Audrey's thoughts returned to Oswald lying in his bed. She shook her head to dispel that image and tried to think of something else. "Tell me about the Starwife, please, Mr. Triton," she asked.

"She'm the grand dame of the squirrels," put in Twit.

"Yes, but what can she want of me?" asked Audrey, baffled. "I'd never heard of her before."

"Maybe," said Thomas, "but she's obviously heard of you. Somehow the name Audrey Brown has reached her ancient ears. Rumors spread quickly—she must have heard about Jupiter's downfall and wants to know all the details of it."

"Yes, but you were there as well Mr. Triton. You could have told her, surely?"

"True, I was there on the altar when that old monster was sent to his watery grave—but you did the sendin' remember, and it was your mousebrass that toppled him."

"What shall I tell her then?" Audrey asked nervously.

Thomas whirled around. "Why the truth, lass, and nothing but that! Don't go addin' bits or leavin' stuff out, or your ears'll ring for weeks after. It's plain speaking in the Starwife's drays and chambers—and that only when you're spoken to."

"Have you seen her then, Mr. Triton?" pressed Audrey, desperate to know as much as possible about the strange personage she was about to meet.

"That I have," he replied cautiously. "When I first came and settled around here I was summoned to meet her." Thomas grew grave and added, "There were matters that I needed to talk to her about." He stroked his white whiskers and cleared his throat. "I've been hurled around by tempests on angry, foaming seas and nearly got drowned twice, but I don't mind telling you that I've never been so skittish as when I went to her drays. And I was shakin' even worse when I came out of them!"

Twit whistled softly. He couldn't imagine sturdy Thomas being afraid of anything. What a creature this Starwife must be! "What did she do to you, Thomas?" he asked wide-eyed.

"Well, I went in there, knees-a-knockin'. I'd heard many a strange tale of the Greenwich Starwife, and only an idiot would go into her chambers unabashed. Well, down some tunnels I was took and there behind a fancy curtain was the Starwife. Oh, she saw right through me, knew everything about me—what I'd done, what I hoped to do—uncanny that was. I think I made a right tomfool of myself in front of her. She weren't impressed with her new neighbor at all. Still, I came away feeling better, but I ain't clapped eyes on her since."

"And this morning you got a message from her about me," added Audrey.

"Yes, that surprised me no end." Thomas paused and looked at Audrey. "In fact, it's so rare an occurrence that I'd be careful, if I were you, Miss Brown."

Audrey was worried. She imagined the Starwife to be as bad as the rats. Her thoughts must have showed plainly on her face, for Thomas added, "Oh, she won't eat you, but the Starwife has motives of her own. She never does nothing for nothing. Sometimes she can be as subtle as Jupiter himself, and that's what I'm puzzled about. So I say again just watch yourself."

"You don't encourage me, Mr. Triton. I'm not sure if I'm looking forward to this. I'd rather go back to the Skirtings."

"Too late for that, miss. Here we are now."

They had come to the end of the sewer journey and a small passage lay before them, at the end of which bright sunlight streamed through the holes in a grate.

Thomas led them down it and they followed him to the outside world.

The mice stood outside Greenwich Park. Before them the green lawns stretched away up to the observatory hill. The sweet scent of freshly mowed grass tingled their noses.

Twit breathed it in deeply. "Oh," he sighed, "that do lighten me heart."

The fieldmouse leaped into the mounds of drying grass cuttings. Gurgling with delight he burrowed down into the soft damp darkness where the fragrances tugged at his memories and visions of home swam before him. Snug in the grass cave, Twit's tiny eyes sparkled. The city was no place for him—he belonged to the open fields where corn swayed high above and ripened slowly in the sun until it burned with golden splendor.

The grass rustled above his head and the harsh dazzle of midday broke around him.

"Come on, matey!" Thomas laughed, parting the cuttings. "Not far to the Starwife now."

Twit scrambled out of the mound, wiping his forehead with a clump of the sweetest, dampest grass. Audrey smiled at him as he rubbed it into his hair.

"Luvverly," he exclaimed, "I feel bright and breezy now." She had to agree: the fresh, clean scent of the grass cleansed her nose of the smell of the sickroom.

"We better catch up with Mr. Triton," Audrey suggested. "Just look how he's marching off."

"I'm thinkin' old Thomas ain't happy about meetin' that there Starwife again."

"Well, I don't want to meet her a first time. She sounds like a right old battle-ax. I'm telling you, Twit, no matter who she is, I'm in no mood for a bad-tempered old squirrel."

"Oh, I am," cried Twit. "Anything to be out of those dark rooms for a while."

They ran after Thomas, skirting around the tangled roots of the large trees. Gradually the three mice made their way up the hill.

Thomas's brows were knitted together in concentration. They avoided the paths and kept on the grass, obeying their instincts of survival—out of sight, out of danger.

The farther up the hill they went the more thoughtful and quiet Thomas became. By the time they were halfway up he was positively frowning, and his tail switched to and fro irritably. Audrey caught his mood and stayed silent. Only Twit chirped up now and again, gasping at the view and remembering when the bats had flown him over this very hill.

Presently the Observatory buildings drew near. How high they were with their onion-shaped domes and solid walls! They sat proudly on top of the hill, fringed by railings and thick rhododendron bushes.

"Look," called Twit suddenly. "In those bushes there. No, it's gone now."

"What was it?" asked Audrey.

"A squirrel," explained the fieldmouse. "It were watchin' us—didn't half give me a shock. There it was a-starin' straight at me—gray as ash then *poof*! It darted away as speedy as anything."

"How long do you think it had been watching us?" asked Audrey, slightly unnerved. She had never seen a squirrel before.

Thomas glared into the bushes. "They've been keeping an eye on us ever since we stepped into the park. Thought they were being clever, but I spotted them a-spying and jumping from branch to branch over our heads. Let them scurry and keep her informed of our progress. Like a spider in a wide web she is, gathering news—you'd be surprised at what she hears," he added grimly.

Audrey twisted the lace of her skirt between her fingers. "Mr. Triton," she began nervously, "I don't want to see her now. Please can we go back?"

"No, lass," Thomas sighed, shaking his head. "She has summoned you and you've come this far. Don't let an old jaded rover like me frighten you now. Courtesy must be kept and you never know—maybe the old boot's mellowed since last I saw her."

Twit giggled at Thomas's description of the Starwife. "I can't wait," he babbled excitedly.

"Right ho, matey," said Thomas, "let's take the cat by the whiskers." The midshipmouse ducked under a railing and scampered up the bush-covered bank. Audrey and Twit followed.

Thomas Triton stooped and sat down in the mossy shade of the dark-leaved rhododendrons.

"What are you doing?" asked Audrey in surprise. "I thought we were going to find the Starwife."

"We've come as far as we can on our own," said Thomas solemnly. "I'm waiting for our escort."

Twit blinked and peered around them. The shadows under the thick bushes were deep. "I don't see no ones," he whispered. "Where is this escort, Thomas?"

"Oh, they're here," replied the midshipmouse dryly. "I'm just waiting for them to find their guts and show themselves."

Above their heads amongst the leathery leaves nervous coughs were stifled.

Audrey glanced up. "What are they doing?" she murmured fearfully.

Thomas stretched and yawned, then he lay back and rested his head on the spongy moss. "This is where we have to wait till one of them plucks up enough nerve to come down and lead us farther. Could be hours."

"But we can't wait too long, Thomas," urged Twit, thinking of Oswald.

The midshipmouse eyed Twit for a moment. "You're right, matey. I'll not be idle while the Chitter lad's fadin' fast." He sprang to his feet, then in one swift movement snatched a small stone off the ground and flung it into the air.

Up shot the stone into the canopy of rhododendron. A surprised yell came from the leaves. Thomas jumped nimbly to one side, and with a crash of twigs, a gray lump dropped to the ground.

"Oh, oh!" cried the furry bundle in panic.

"Peace, squire!" calmed Thomas. "We have no time for your

20

formalities today. Forgive me for speeding up the proceedings."

Twit stared at the terrified squirrel before them. It was young and its tail was strong and bushy. The squirrel's face was small, but his large black eyes seemed to be popping out of his head. He looked at the three mice in fright.

Thomas waited for him to find his voice, making no effort to conceal his impatience during the squirrel's stammerings.

"But ... but ..." the squirrel began, "three ... there are three of you—we ... I ... thought there would be only two." He regarded Twit uneasily.

"This is my good young matey William Scuttle," Thomas roared in a voice that made the squirrel shrink away. "Where I go, he goes." He laid his paw firmly on the fieldmouse's shoulder.

"She won't like this ... she won't like this—not at all, no."

"That's enough!" rapped Thomas. "I'll face whatever squalls she throws my way, but we'll not sit here becalmed by your dithering. Lead us and have done."

"The ... the girl first," instructed the squirrel timidly. "The mouse-maiden is to follow me."

Audrey nearly laughed at the anxious gray figure, which hesitated and twitched before her, but she remembered her manners and tried to remain serious. She stepped in line behind her escort.

"Good ... good," he muttered, and with a jerk of his tail he bounded through the bushes. The mice followed him as quickly as they could.

Into the leafy clumps they ran and there, in the shadows, were a dozen other squirrels all fluttering and trembling with fright. Their escort was laying into them as the mice approached.

"Why didn't you?" he scolded the others crossly. "Leaving me all alone to deal with them."

'ell, we weren't to know," they answered meekly. "But you did so very well, Piers," some added. "Sshh, here they are now." They fell back as the mice entered.

"Ermm . . . this way," the escort said shakily, and he set off again.

The crowd of squirrels watched them leave and they turned to one another tut-tutting. "She won't like that will she? Three of them, I ask you. He ought to have said something. The look that little fellow gave you . . . little savages they are . . . makes me shiver all over. Who's going to tell her then? Don't be soft— you know she doesn't need us to tell her anything, she has her own ways of finding things out."

Audrey followed the escort's bushy tail as it bobbed before her. Through lanes of leaves it led her, under arches of twining roots and past startled squirrel sentries who disappeared in a flash of gray. The bushes grew thicker overhead and no daylight filtered down. Suddenly a great oak tree appeared at the end of the green tunnel and the escort vanished down a dark cleft in the trunk.

Audrey paused, wondering how far down the drop was. She braced herself and with her eyes closed tightly leaped into the black hole.

Down she plunged until she landed with a soft jolt on a bundle of dry leaves and ferns. Audrey rolled to one side as Twit came down, whistling and laughing.

"It smells in here," sniffed Audrey.

"Only oak wood and leaf mold," said Twit, staggering to his feet.

They were in the base of the old oak's trunk, hollowed out by years of squirrel labor. Small wooden bowls hung on the walls and these were filled with burning oils. The light they gave off was silver and flickering, illuminating the smooth worn oak with gentle, dancing waves.

"It's as cold as the sewers down here." Audrey shivered.

Twit sat beside her and brushed the leaves off her back. "I have heard some in my field at home as do call squirrels tree rats," he whispered.

A muffled crash and a mariner's curse announced Thomas's arrival.

"I'd forgotten about that drop," he muttered, rubbing his back. "Where's that nervy chap gone to now?"

"I don't know," said Audrey. "There are some openings over there–are they the roots of this tree?"

"Aye, we are in the heart of the squirrel domain and here the Starwife lives, but there were Starwives before this oak was an acorn and before this very hill was made. The Starwives go back a long way."

Just then the escort came bounding back. "What are you waiting for? Come, come," he implored, "she is impatient. Hurry now!" He scurried away down one of the openings.

Audrey and Twit set off after him. "I wish I'd brought some rum with me," murmured Thomas to himself.

Down the narrow passages the mice followed the squirrel. Deep into the earth they seemed to be going. After a short while Audrey noticed something other than the silver lights twinkling ahead. It was a richly embroidered banner hung across the width of the passage. The background was a dark blue and over it was stitched a field of twinkling stars that reflected the light of the lamps around them. As Audrey examined the stars more closely she saw that the silver thread of which they were made was in fact tarnished by great age.

The escort paused and bowed before the banner.

The three mice waited apprehensively. Audrey and Twit stared at each other and wondered what lay beyond this elaborate partition.

A strong, impatient voice snapped from the other side. "Bring them in, Piers–stop dawdling, boy!"

The squirrel jumped in fright. "Oh, madam, forgive me!"

He clutched one corner of the banner and popped his head through as he drew it aside. "By your leave, madam, may I introduce . . ."

"Show in the midshipmouse first!" commanded the voice.

The squirrel looked back at Thomas and said, "Come through when I announce you."

Thomas grinned at Twit. "Battle stations!" he remarked wryly, dragging the hat from his head.

"By your leave, madam," the squirrel had begun again, "may I introduce to you, midshipmouse Thomas Triton."

"Triton," called the other, sharp voice, "come in here."

Thomas scowled as he straightened the red kerchief around his neck and strode through the banner.

Audrey held on to Twit's paw as they waited for their turn.

With a rising dislike for the voice she presumed was the Starwife's, Audrey tried to keep calm.

"So, seafarer," said the voice on the other side of the banner. "It has been a long time since last I saw you in my chamber."

"Yes, ma'am," came Thomas's awkward reply, "too long."

"The fly has kept away from the web as best he might. But now you could say that the old boot is on the other foot."

Audrey gasped. How did the Starwife know that Thomas had compared her to a spider and an old boot? Whatever her sources, it was unkind and downright rude of her to taunt Thomas with his own words. Audrey felt herself becoming angry.

The midshipmouse was coughing to cover his embarrassment. He was a mouse of action, not words, and the respect he had for the Starwife and his own code of honor would not allow him to answer back.

"I hear you've settled down in your retirement at last," the voice began once more. "No more nightmares to haunt you?"

"No, ma'am, not since my last visit when you were kind

24

enough to give me those powders. That particular ghost has been laid to rest."

"It should be so. Though wounds of the heart and mind are the hardest to heal. You seem to be on the right path at last."

"I have taken your advice, ma'am, and not taken to the water once in all these years."

"Let it be so always, Thomas or . . ." the Starwife's voice dropped to a whisper and Audrey could not catch what she was saying. She considered all that she had heard. Evidently there was something in Thomas's past that he had not spoken about.

A loud sharp knock brought her up quickly. The escort peered around the banner.

"Bring in the fieldmouse," called the Starwife sternly. "I'll teach him to tag along when he's not invited."

Twit looked at Audrey in dismay. "She ain't magic is she?" he asked. "I don't want her to turn me into no frog or stuff like that."

"You stand up to her," Audrey told him. "Don't let her walk all over you."

"Master William Stutter!" announced the escort. "Scuttle!" corrected Twit angrily as he pushed past. Audrey tried to glimpse what was beyond the banner, but the escort pulled it across and tutted loudly.

"The very idea!" he said tersely.

"So, country mouse," greeted the Starwife coldly. "You have come to visit me have you?"

"If it pleases you, your ladyship," Twit's small voice piped up.

"It pleases me not at all," she snapped back. "Who are you to presume a welcome in my chamber? A lowly fieldmouse before the Starwife!"

"Now look 'ere, missus," Twit protested.

Audrey was very angry. How dare that old battle-ax pick on little Twit like that? After all he had been through lately he deserved more than to be shouted at by that rude creature. She stood tight-lipped, her temper flaring.

"Please, ma'am," came Thomas's voice, "it's my fault. I brought the lad—he needed the break. Times are bad in the Skirtings."

"Silence, Thomas," ordered the Starwife. "I know of the Chitters and their son. True the lad needed a rest from those dark rooms but what of you, midshipmouse?"

"Ma'am?"

"I sense a strong bond has grown between you and young Scuttle. I find myself wondering why—a lone wanderer such as you taking friends on board at your time of life. Who do you see in him, Thomas?"

"Ma'am, please . . ."

"I see you walk a dangerous rope, midshipmouse. Reality and memory ought never to entwine so closely! Beware your dreams and forget what has passed."

"I try, ma'am."

"Enough! Piers—fetch the girl." The loud knocking began again.

Audrey prepared herself and the escort pulled back the banner. "Follow me, please," he said stiffly.

Audrey smoothed her lace collar and stepped into the Starwife's chamber.

After the cramped tunnel it was like walking out into the open, for it was so spacious. Suspended from the ceiling above were hundreds of small shiny objects, colored foils, metal lids, links from silver chains, and polished pieces of glass. All were hung in a certain order, and for a moment, Audrey thought their pattern familiar but could not place it until she realized that, like the banner, they represented all the constellations of the heavens.

Below this dangling chart sat the Starwife.

"Miss Audrey Brown!" the escort pronounced.

"Come here, girl. Where I can see you."

Audrey moved toward the Starwife. She was an ancient squirrel perched on a high oaken throne carved with images of twisting leaves and acorns. Audrey had never seen anyone like her before. Age seemed to smother the Starwife. It was a miracle that she could move at all. Her fur was silver and patchy, and her muscles were wasted, falling in useless rolls beneath fragile dry bones. The Starwife's eyes were a dull gray and over one of them was a thin white film like spilled milk.

In her gnarled, crippled paws she held a stick and it was this that Audrey had heard knocking on the wooden floor. The Starwife had sat there with that stick for so many years that it had worn a definite trough in the floor.

Around her neck hung a silver acorn, the symbol of her knowledge and wisdom.

Behind the throned figure Audrey could see a deep darkness, which the lamps were unable to illuminate, except for now and again when a silver flash shone out brilliantly. It was curious, but before she had a chance to look farther, an impatient tapping of the stick brought her attention back to the Starwife.

"How do you do?" Audrey asked, dropping into a formal curtsy. The Starwife made no reply, so Audrey repeated herself, a trifle louder than before.

The ancient squirrel shifted on her throne and sucked her almost toothless gums. "I'm half blind, girl, but not deaf yet." She gazed at Audrey with unblinking eyes and sniffed the air.

Audrey did not like the Starwife one little bit. She looked over to where Thomas and Twit were standing and grimaced at them. No way would this squirrel intimidate her. "Rude old battle-ax," she thought to herself. She didn't see why she had to be on her best behavior if the Starwife had no manners of her own.

For several minutes Audrey remained silent and motionless under the continuing stare of the Starwife until the prolonged silence became embarrassing for her. It occurred to her that maybe the squirrel had nodded off like some old mice did in the Skirtings. Once more she thought of Oswald and felt that this was a waste of precious time.

"Excuse me," she began politely, "but we can't stay long, I'm afraid."

The Starwife blinked and opened her mouth. She rose shakily in her throne and her joints cracked like twigs. The stick pounded the floor indignantly. Thomas put his hat over his face and the escort began to stammer idiotically.

The Starwife switched her stare from Audrey to him. "Piers!" she barked, "get out, you imbecile!" The escort looked around uncertainly, but at that moment the Starwife threw her stick at him. It struck him smartly on the nose and he fled howling from the chamber.

The Starwife eased herself gingerly back down onto her throne and gave a wicked chuckle. She relaxed and turned once more to Audrey. "You must think me a rude old battle-ax," she said calmly. Audrey flushed—it obviously wasn't safe to think in front of this creature. "I do have manners, but it's so rare that I find anyone worth practicing them on. You must forgive me, child."

"Why did you send for me?" Audrey asked.

"There are two reasons, Miss Brown. Firstly, I desired to speak to the one who sent Jupiter to his doom. Tell me all you know and all that happened on that glad day."

Audrey breathed deeply, not sure where to begin. Then she recounted all that had happened to her since One-Eyed Jake had dragged her through the Grill up to the time she had thrown her mousebrass at Jupiter. Throughout her tale the Starwife kept silent, nodding her head on occasion as if she understood more than Audrey about the events. When she had finished Audrey stepped back and waited for the other to comment.

"A dark story you have told, Miss Brown, with more horror than you know. There are certain things contained in your nar-

rative that I had no knowledge of. Of course I knew all the time that Jupiter was a cat. I recognized the body he concealed in the darkness behind those burning eyes of his. A two-headed rat monster—rubbish, as I always maintained. But other things do surprise me. That episode in the pagan temple where Jake murdered Fletch, now that is disturbing—Mabb, Hobb, and Bauchan are old gods and it frightens me to think they are but newly worshiped. Who can tell what folly will come of that?" The Starwife raised her head and gazed distractedly at the star maps.

"Your pardon ma'am," said Thomas softly. "You mentioned two reasons for wanting to see Miss Audrey—may we know the second?"

"Oh, I'm sorry, Triton," she replied, and it seemed to Audrey that the Starwife was just a harmless squirrel older than nature had ever intended her to be.

"Fetch me my stick will you, lad," she motioned to Twit. The fieldmouse ran to retrieve it from the floor. He bowed as he presented it to her. The Starwife received it gratefully. "Thank you, lad. It is more than a missile with which I bruise my subjects' stupid heads—I would not be able to walk without it."

"And now," she sighed, turning to Audrey once more, "you shall know the other reason why I brought you here." She banged the stick on the floor loudly and waited for the young squirrel to return.

"Ah, there you are, Piers. Don't be afraid. I promise not to throw it anymore today."

"Did you wish for anything, madam?" asked the squirrel doubtfully.

The Starwife nodded and told him, "Bring in our guest."

Piers disappeared once more.

"It's over a week ago now," she began, "that our sentries spotted someone skulking in our park. The sight of this creature was fearful to behold and all fled before it. Nearer to my

30

realm it drew. I could not get a word of sense from my guards—such a state they were in. 'A gibbering ghost,' they called it. I gave them a clip around the ear and told them they would be the gibbering ghosts if they didn't bring the creature to me." The Starwife allowed a slow smile to spread over her face.

"Did they bring the ghost?" asked Twit breathlessly.

"Oh yes, they did right enough, but it was no ghost. They caught her in their nets and she was in a terrible state."

"She?" asked Audrey in surprise.

The Starwife narrowed her misty eyes. "Yes, her ribs were like roots poking through the soil and her belly was taut as a bark drum. She had not eaten for many days, but she still managed to put up a hearty resistance. Seven of my sentries still have sore heads."

"So who was she?" Audrey broke in. "What did she want?"

"She wanted nothing, but I made her drink some milk and with that some life seemed to return to her dead eyes. I questioned her but could learn very little. In fact, Miss Brown, you have told me more about my guest than she has herself."

"*I* have?" Audrey could not believe it. Slowly a vague suspicion began to dawn on her.

"Yes, for she is known to you—can you not guess? I see you suspect."

Audrey's heart was fluttering with apprehension and dread.

Behind the banner, coming down the passage she could hear Piers returning—his quick, nervous footsteps were unmistakable, but alongside came a clumsy flapping of large ungainly feet and with them there was a voice.

"Go to see squirrel boss lady, oh yes."

Audrey's mouth fell open and she inhaled sharply.

The banner was thrust aside and Piers scampered into the chamber followed by . . . Madame Akkikuyu.

CHAPTER THREE

THE BARGAIN

Audrey backed away as Madame Akkikuyu entered.

Once she had been a beautiful rat maiden, but her looks had faded with the cruel blows life had dealt her. When Audrey had first met her, Madame Akkikuyu had been a fortune-teller who also dabbled with poisonous love potions. But she had always craved genuine magical powers and that is how Jupiter had corrupted her into his service. It was Madame Akkikuyu who had delivered Audrey to him. Even then she had still been a striking figure—her fur a rich, sleek black and her eyes dark and fathomless.

Audrey pitied the fortune-teller now. As Madame Akkikuyu dragged her feet toward them they could plainly see that the rat had nearly starved to death in the past weeks. Her skin hung baggily off her frame and her fur was molting away in ugly patches. Only the tattooed face on her ear looked the same. Around her shoulders she still wore the old spotted shawl, and strapped about her waist she carried her pouches of dried leaves and berries. In one large bag was her crystal ball.

Madame Akkikuyu stumbled up to those gathered around the throne and grinned sheepishly up at the Starwife. With a shock Audrey saw something terrible dancing in the rat's eyes—Madame Akkikuyu had lost her mind.

"Welcome, Akkikuyu," said the Starwife warmly. "There are friends of yours here."

The rat gazed distractedly at the mice. She did not recognize the sturdy one with the red kerchief around his neck, but then she hardly knew anything anymore. Her head was in such a muddle these days, ever since . . . no, she could not remember when. There was a closed door in her head that she could not open and she knew that all the answers were locked behind it . . . and yet for some reason she was afraid to discover the truth.

Her memory was as patchy as her fur. She knew the crystal ball and the pouches of leaves were important to her, but she did not know why. Since these nice squirrels had taken her in she had sat with the crystal in her hands many times and admired it—how the light curved over its perfect round surface and how it soothed her. She regarded it as her most precious belonging.

Occasionally a vivid image of some past time would flit over her eyes and she would snatch at it, then hold it dear without knowing what it was. There was one scene where the sun beat down harshly and there was sand between her toes, and water all around. She felt as though she were traveling a great distance, and when she looked down at her claws they were young.

Two other things she remembered. The first was a rat with one eye who faded into ash. Indeed, in with her herbs she had found an eye patch. It was frustrating not to know what this meant and most nights Madame Akkikuyu wept long, bitter tears.

The last memory was the one that she feared the most. She was in a vast echoing chamber, and in front of her were two candles and, between them, an archway, which she could not force herself to look into. This was the key to unlock that door, but she was terrified to discover what lurked in there.

Madame Akkikuyu looked at Twit–the face of the little field-mouse stirred nothing in the jumble of her memories. Finally she turned to Audrey.

The fortune-teller froze. Yes, she had seen that young mouse before, somewhere. A confused array of images crowded in. Audrey was standing before her, but it seemed as though a ball of fire separated them. This was suddenly swept away and an overwhelming sense of guilt washed over her. As she continued to stare at the mouse her own voice spoke to her from the past. "Mouselet. You, me–run away. Leave dark places, hide and be happy."

A tear rolled down Akkikuyu's sunken cheek–what had happened to that wonderful plan, she wondered? That was what she wanted now, to go away and have peace in a quiet spot where the sun shone. Swallowing the lump in her throat she said, "Mouselet, Akkikuyu know you. Why did we not go to distant places and sleep in summer sunlight?"

Audrey felt uncomfortable. She knew why. The rat had been taking her to Jupiter when this idea had first gripped her. Akkikuyu had weighed up all the unhappiness she had suffered and would have escaped with her when Morgan, Jupiter's henchrat, had interrupted them and Madame Akkikuyu had been forced to carry out her orders. Audrey had felt sorry for the rat even then but all the more so now. She could not answer her question.

The Starwife tapped her stick and all looked to her. "Akkikuyu," she began, "you have been my guest for nine days now and are free to remain, yet I sense that there is a yearning in you and you feel you are unable to stay here."

The fortune-teller bowed her head. "Oh, wise boss lady, you see into Akkikuyu's heart." She closed her eyes and clasped her claws in front of her as though in prayer. "You so kind to Akkikuyu. You give food and shelter when others throw stones. Akkikuyu never forget you, sweet bushy one, but mouselet and me, we special—she and I promised. We go away together—we friends."

Audrey spluttered and lifted her head, but the glitter she saw in the Starwife's eyes silenced any outcry she might have made.

Gently the old squirrel held out one arthritic paw to the fortune-teller.

The rat took it, careful not to hold too tightly. The Starwife bent down and patted the rat's claw.

"Peace, Akkikuyu," she said. "You shall go with your friend, but first you must make ready. The day after tomorrow you will leave. Go now to your room and prepare."

Madame Akkikuyu wept with joy and moved to embrace Audrey. The mouse backed away, horrified.

"Hurry, Akkikuyu," cut in the Starwife. "Run along now. There is much to do."

"Yes, yes, Akkikuyu go at once," chuckled the rat gleefully as she ran from the chamber.

When she had left, Audrey turned on the Starwife angrily. "That was the cruellest thing I've ever seen," she stormed. "Why did you build her hopes up like that?"

The Starwife sat back in the throne and heaved a sigh. "What is it I have done wrongly, girl? I merely told her a fact."

"But what will happen when she finds out that I'm not going anywhere with her?"

The stick began to tap the ground slowly. "She will not find out any such thing, for one simple reason—you are going with her."

Audrey laughed. "Not on your life."

The stick crashed down. "Silence!" raged the Starwife. "I will not be spoken to in such a manner. I have told Akkikuyu,

35

now I am telling you. You and she will depart the day after tomorrow."

Thomas Triton stepped up beside Audrey and put his paw on her arm. "Take care, miss," he whispered. "She can make you do anything she wants."

Audrey glared at the old squirrel. Was this the real reason she had been summoned? Or was this a punishment for her rudeness before? One thing was certain, however. Nothing would make her go anywhere with Madame Akkikuyu.

Thomas spoke to the old squirrel. "Ma'am," he began politely. "Where are they to go, the rat and this girl? And how are they to get there?"

The Starwife pointed her stick at Twit. "This lad does not belong around here," she said. "He knows it and was about to go home before his cousin fell ill. What better place for Akkikuyu than a remote field to spend the rest of her days in?"

"You have to be joking!" Audrey remarked, shaking her head in disbelief.

"Never was I more serious," the old squirrel replied, a deadly tone in her voice. "The day after tomorrow you, young Scuttle, and Akkikuyu will leave."

Suddenly, Twit piped up, "But I can't go yet, missus—poor Oswald . . ."

"The Chitter boy will die before this day is out," she said flatly.

The fieldmouse cried out in dismay.

"Silence!" the Starwife demanded. "You thought so yourself, remember. Late this afternoon the Chitter lad will reach the crisis point and pass away."

Twit sobbed uncontrollably. "How do you know? He might not."

"This I have seen," snapped the Starwife irritably. "Look behind my throne. Behold the Starglass!"

The mice peered around the carved oak throne and there,

as tall as three mice, was a flat disk of black, polished glass set in a carved wooden frame. It was this that Audrey had glimpsed before. Over its surface silver flashes flickered and in its midnight depths swirled a multitude of vague and distant images.

"It is my life," explained the Starwife quietly, "and it has been the life of every Starwife before me. Our most precious and most powerful possession. With it I have looked into the heart of the rat Akkikuyu and found no evil. That is why she must be taken away from this place. She must not remember what happened in the sewers and never must you mention the name Jupiter to her—it would unhinge her totally. There is only this one chance of redemption for her—are you the one to deny her this, child?"

Audrey thought for a while. Finally she said, "I am truly sorry for her—but why must I go?"

"Because she will feel safe with you. Somewhere in her mind you have become linked with this notion of safety in the sun. Only you can lead her away. She will go with no one else." The Starwife stared intently at Audrey as if willing her to accept the heavy burden she was offering.

Audrey looked at Thomas, but he was staring at his feet. She wondered what he was thinking. Had he known about this? No, he had suspected none of this—she was sure of that.

Twit was drying his eyes and saying, "Why must we go so soon? We won't have time for . . ."

"I think one day is sufficient for the necessary arrangements to be made and undertaken," the Starwife replied coldly.

"What about Mr. and Mrs. Chitter?" pleaded Twit. "They'll need me to help them get over . . . it all."

An icy glint appeared in the old squirrel's eyes. "They will not need any comfort after tonight," she said darkly. Twit choked and buried his head in his hands.

Audrey felt cold. She stared grimly at the Starwife. How could anyone be so unfeeling? She put her arm around Twit's

37

shoulder and spoke softly. "Don't you listen to her. I'm not going anywhere with that rat–no one can make me do anything I don't want to." Thomas raised his eyes but said nothing.

"So, you still refuse," the Starwife remarked dryly.

"I do. There's no way I would ever do anything for you now."

The Starwife tapped her stick and called for Piers. The young squirrel had been waiting silently at the entrance of the chamber. Now he jumped to attention.

"Madam?" he asked eagerly.

"Fetch it, Piers."

The young squirrel became agitated and flustered. "But my lady," he whined. "You know the consequences, my lady."

"I said fetch it!" she roared, the stick pounding on the floor. "There is more to this than you know."

Piers bowed and dashed off through the banner.

The Starwife tilted her head and smiled at Audrey triumphantly. "So, there is nothing I can do to make you take Akkikuyu away?" she almost chuckled as she said it.

"Nothing," answered Audrey firmly. She eyed the Starwife warily. Who could tell what she might try next?

Piers came bounding back. In his paws he carried a small cloth bag tied tightly at the neck. "I have it, madam," he puffed.

The Starwife's smile disappeared and for a moment she looked sad and dejected. "Thank you, Piers," she said as he handed it over. He stopped to kiss her paw. "Help me down now," she asked. "Mr. Triton, could you take one arm and Piers the other?"

The midshipmouse rushed to help. Carefully they eased the Starwife off the great chair. Her face screwed up as her old bones creaked and the stiff, dry joints ground together noisily.

"Thank you," she said to both of them when finally she stood on the floor.

"I curse this old body of mine–it grows worse with every winter."

"That is because you do not sleep properly, madam," said Piers unexpectedly.

"There is too much to attend to—how can I sleep? Now, the Starglass. Come along, young Scuttle, it needs the relative."

She hobbled slowly with her stick to the rear of the throne until she stood before the Starglass. There she leaned on the stick heavily and eyed Twit solemnly.

"Stand in front of me, lad," she told him, "and take this in your paws." She gave him the cloth bag and placed her own paws on his shoulders. "Now, hold your arms out straight— that's right."

"No, Twit," said Audrey violently. She had watched them curiously and now she was afraid of what the Starwife might do to him. "Don't trust her!"

"Ignore her, boy," rapped the Starwife crossly. "Do as you're told!"

Twit looked from Audrey to the Starwife. What was he to do? Was the old squirrel going to turn him into something dreadful after all? Audrey's face was anxious and frightened; the Starwife's was set and stern. But what about Thomas, his friend and hero, what did he think?

"What'll I do, Thomas?" asked the fieldmouse.

The midshipmouse gave him a smile and reassured him. "It'll be all right, matey—I know what she's doin'. She won't hurt you."

"That's good enough fer me," said Twit, greatly relieved. "Don't worry, Audrey, Thomas says there ain't nothin' to fear." Audrey hoped he was right, but then she noticed Piers turning away, a troubled look on his face.

"Go ahead, missus," called Twit, holding out his arms as straight as he could.

Before the Starglass stood the two figures, mouse and squirrel. The Starwife whispered under her breath and the silver lamps on the walls grew dim and went out. Only the flashes over the black glass lit the chamber now and as the Starwife chanted the light grew brighter.

Twit opened his eyes wide as he witnessed the strange squirrel magic happening before him.

From the depths of the dark glass he saw the night sky–only the stars shone a hundred times brighter. Presently the light from them gleamed stronger and the stars drew nearer. Twit gasped. It seemed as if the whole sky was about him now. In a blaze of blue and silver the stars leaped out of the glass and whirled all around. The chamber had vanished, and only he and the Starwife were left amid the burning heavens.

Twit heard the Starwife's voice calling into the sky and felt her old paws on his shoulders. Suddenly the bag in his paws grew heavy and all the starlight seemed to be sucked down into it. At the same time he felt two sharp pains in his shoulders as the Starwife gripped too tightly.

Twit stifled a cry of surprise as a fierce tingling sensation shot down his arms, as if a thousand ants were crawling over them, stinging as they went. The tingle traveled to his paws and then seemed to enter the bag.

"Enough!" cried the Starwife. "It is done." She released Twit and blew on her paws as if to warm them. Then she groped for her stick.

Twit blinked. He was back in the chamber again and the lamps were lit once more, but the Starglass was dark and impenetrable. He shook himself and whistled softly.

Piers ran forward and took the Starwife by the arm. She seemed feebler than before, and older–if that was possible.

Audrey did not understand what had happened. She had heard the old squirrel mumbling strange words and seen Twit's face light up in awe, but then a bright flash had dazzled her. It seemed to have come from the bag, but she was not sure. Now the Starwife was breathing hard and clinging onto Piers.

When she had regained her breath, the Starwife turned to Audrey and said, "Before, I told you to take Akkikuyu away to young Scuttle's field. Well, now I am asking you. Will you take her?" Her voice was cracked and hoarse, she seemed to have no strength left in her at all.

Despite herself, Audrey felt sorry for her, but still she said, "I've told you, nothing will make me go."

"So you said—I remember. Well, girl, what if the life of your friend Oswald depended on it?"

"That's unfair. Oswald's ill—nothing can save him."

The Starwife interrupted with a fierce striking of her stick. "Wrong!" she shouted. "What is now in that bag can restore his health."

Twit looked at the bag in his paws. "Really, missus?" A broad grin spread across his face.

"I don't believe you," said Audrey cautiously.

The Starwife sighed, too tired to reply.

"Oh, it's perfectly true," Piers remarked, speaking for her, "and it costs dear."

Thomas Triton nodded. "It'll do what they say, lass."

Audrey began to believe them. "That's marvelous," she said happily, "Oswald will be well again."

Piers had been trying to get the Starwife back to the throne but she pushed him away from her and pointed the stick furiously at Audrey. "If!" she cried.

Audrey did not understand.

"You may take that bag away with you and cure your friend and his parents only if . . ."

Then she knew. "You mean if I agree to take Akkikuyu away."

The Starwife nodded. The triumph was plain on her face.

"So if I said no, even now you wouldn't let us take that bag away with us?"

42

"The bag would be useless. The bargain must be kept or the Chitters will perish."

"But I made no such bargain," Audrey protested urgently.

The Starwife regarded her coldly. "I made the bargain, child—I always do."

Audrey thought of poor Oswald lying in his bed perilously close to death. Then she saw Twit's little face turned expectantly to her. "I have no choice, then," she said. "The day after tomorrow I will take Akkikuyu to Twit's field."

"I knew you would," replied the Starwife. "Piers, show them out, the audience is at an end."

"But, madam, let me help you into your throne first."

"Get out, you fool—if I weren't so tired I'd throw this at you again," she snapped, waving the stick menacingly.

"This way, please!" Piers called from the other side of the banner.

Thomas bowed before the Starwife. "May we meet again," he said to her.

"You stay in your ship and leave me alone," she answered shortly.

"Thank 'ee, missus." Twit laughed when he stood before her. "This bag do make me so happy. I be fair burstin'."

"Get out, you country simpleton," said the Starwife. But she had a smile on her face as she said it.

When it was her turn to say good-bye Audrey looked at the old squirrel with intense resentment. She was glad to be leaving at last. Thomas had been right. The Starwife never did anything for nothing. She had known all along that Audrey would agree eventually. "Remember, child," she said, "the bargain will keep. If you cure him this afternoon but later refuse to go with Akkikuyu then the fever will return and strike him down once more. This bargain is for life, girl. As long as Akkikuyu lives you must remain with her."

It was a chilling prospect and Audrey felt a cold dread grip her heart as she realized the doom that the Starwife had decreed for her. She shivered. "You are cruel," she said, though wanting to say more. "Why is that fake fortune-teller so important to you? She's only a rat after all."

The Starwife looked steadily into her eyes. "And does that make a difference, child?" she asked with scorn. "To me you are just a mouse—and a very rude mouse at that."

"Well . . ." Audrey stammered.

"Well, nothing. Listen to me. I have seen in the Starglass an important future for Akkikuyu. Exactly what that may be I cannot be certain, but I do know that she will make two choices in her life. Her decisions will undoubtedly affect us all. It may seem harsh to you, but I want you to be with her all the time—good may come of it. I pray so anyway." She closed her eyes wearily and waved the mouse away from her. "Now leave me. I am too drained—you have been an expensive guest to entertain." The Starwife turned her back and laboriously limped to the great oak chair.

Audrey left the chamber deep in thought, but as the banner swept down behind her the Starwife raised an eyebrow and said softly to herself, "Can she be the one?"

In the passage Twit was asking Piers, "What does I do with this bag?"

"Steep it in hot water and when it is cool enough make him drink, then call his name three times. Remember, you must never open the bag."

"Oh, I won't!" Twit was nearly back to his old self. Hope was filling his little chest and that was all that mattered.

Audrey caught up with them. "But Oswald can't bring himself to drink anything," she reminded Twit.

"He will drink this," said Piers haughtily. So saying, the young squirrel led them up through tunnels they had not seen before, along winding passages with the light of the silver lamps glimmering about them. Soon the soft lights became mingled with a brighter radiance. It was the sparkle of sunlight streaming through green leaves.

"There it is!" said Piers, halting suddenly. "I will go no farther. Once you pass through those leaves you will find yourselves in the park once more. I presume you will be able to find your way from there?" he added sarcastically.

"Oh, I think we can manage it," put in Thomas.

"Well, go straight back to your holes," retorted Piers pompously. "You will be watched."

"By your ferocious sentries, no doubt." Thomas arched his brows and a flicker of a smile wandered over his face.

"Indeed," said Piers, greatly agitated. "They are there to make sure you leave in an orderly fashion—we don't want riffraff cluttering up our park."

Thomas laughed heartily. "And what would your brave lads do if we did leave in a disorderly fashion—pelt us with daisies?" Twit joined in the laughter.

The young squirrel pursed his lips and eyed them disdainfully. When he was able to be heard he loftily told Thomas, "When you have finished with the bag, you, midshipmouse, must return it to us. Tonight at the latest. Now good day to you!" he dismissed them curtly.

The mice made their way to the opening and crawled out between the leaves. As Audrey stepped out into the sunlight, she turned to see Piers for one last time. For a moment she blinked blindly as her eyes adjusted to the brightness and then, through the leafy gateway, and partly hidden in the comparative darkness of the tunnel she saw the squirrel watching them intently. What a strange race they were, these bushy-tailed creatures, running around in a constant state of nervous fluster—all except the Starwife, of course. Audrey shivered in spite of the afternoon heat as she thought of the old half-blind animal seated on her throne in the heart of the hill, weaving her cruel webs for everyone.

"He's making sure we go quietly," whispered Thomas in Audrey's ear. "Let's go back to the Skirtings and leave this hill far behind us."

Audrey continued to stare moodily through the leaves. "I hate squirrels," she decided, and pulled such a grim face that Piers scurried farther into the shade.

"Come, lass," Thomas told her, "we've a pleasant task ahead of us."

"Yes," agreed Twit, "we're off to make Oswald well again."

Audrey finally tore herself away from the leaf-covered entrance but hesitated before following the others. She looked at how happy Twit was and felt guilty because she was unable to join him. It should have been a time of celebration for them all, but the Starwife had denied her that. The day after tomorrow she would have to leave with that awful Madame Akkikuyu and set off for a horrible field in the faraway country.

"I don't want to leave Deptford!" she cried to herself.

A DRAFT OF STARLIGHT

In the Skirtings, Oswald's condition was failing fast. His face had a deathly pallor and his temperature was soaring. Sweat beaded his forehead and ran glistening down his hollow cheeks.

Arthur watched him fearfully. "Go and rouse Mother," he told Piccadilly quickly. "I think this is it." The two mice exchanged hurried, meaningful glances, then the gray city mouse dashed out of the sickroom.

Arthur knelt beside his stricken friend. "Oh, Oswald." He sighed sadly. He took the albino's frail, hot paw in his own and waited.

Shortly, the muffled sound of hushed voices came to Arthur's ears. Evidently, curious mice anxious for news were gathering outside the Chitters' home. There was soon quite a commotion and Arthur could hear Piccadilly's voice above the clamoring queries.

"Put a lid on it and let Mrs. Brown through there. I'm sorry we can't tell you more. Blimey!" Piccadilly's exasperated voice floun-

47

dered amongst the good-natured and well-intentioned questions.

Arthur smiled grimly to himself at Piccadilly's situation—coping with gossipy, fussing housemice was something he had not encountered in the city.

The outer curtain was drawn aside and Gwen Brown squeezed in. She had escaped the prying neighbors, although a covered bowl had been thrust into her arms. She shook herself and entered the sickroom.

"Piccadilly told me he's worse," she said, moving quickly to Oswald's bedside. She felt the albino's brow and studied his face. "Yes, this is the crisis," she sighed. Gwen turned to her son and drew him to her. "I'm afraid he hasn't the strength to fight it. This will be the end. How is Mr. Chitter?"

They both looked at the figure asleep on the chair. Jacob Chitter was pale and weak—he appeared as ill as Oswald.

"I looked in on Mrs. Chitter before," whispered Arthur. "She's as bad as he is."

"Yes," nodded Gwen. "The lives of this family are all tied together. As Oswald fades—so do they. It's so terrible." She laid the covered bowl, which she had been carrying, on the low table next to the pieces of raw onion.

"More ointment from Mrs. Coltfoot?" guessed Arthur. "A bit late for that now."

"Let's not presume the end before it's come," breathed his mother. "We must continue as before. Audrey and I will see to Mrs. Chitter, you see to . . ." She paused and puckered her brow as Arthur bit his lip. "Arthur?" she asked. "I haven't seen Audrey since I woke up . . . and Twit wasn't in his bed when I looked in on him. Where are they?"

Arthur gritted his teeth, then took a long deep breath while he shuffled his feet awkwardly.

"Arthur!" demanded his mother sternly.

"Well you had just gone to sleep, so we didn't like to disturb you," he began earnestly.

48

"Who's we?"

"Well, us and Mr. Triton."

"Mr. Triton!" Gwen Brown exclaimed. "What did he want?"

"He took Audrey and Twit to Greenwich," said Arthur nervously.

"To Greenwich? Oh, Arthur, what's got into the old fool's head? And why did you let them go? I'm surprised at Twit–up and leaving like that."

Arthur waved his arms and tried to calm her down. "But it wasn't like that! He promised they'd be back in time and Twit needed to get away for a bit. Mr. Triton can be very persuasive, you know," he added lamely.

"Oh, I'm sorry I snapped, Arthur." Gwen smiled apologetically. "I do remember Mr. Triton's way–he's a forceful one, there's no denying. I suppose they didn't have time to think what they were doing when he arrived. But why take Twit and Audrey to Greenwich? Audrey hardly knows him, for one thing, and it isn't like her to be interested in boats and such."

"Oh, didn't I say?" put in Arthur quickly. "Mr. Triton brought a message from someone called the Starwife. She apparently wanted to speak with Audrey."

Gwen Brown was taken aback. "The Starwife! Let me see now . . . yes, I do seem to have heard of her. Oh, dear–what can she want with our Audrey? I don't like it, Arthur. If I had been awake I would not have allowed her to go. Just wait till I see that midshipmouse–I'll bend his ear for him."

The afternoon crept by. The hot sun veered west and the evening clouds gathered lightly about the horizon.

In the hall of the old house many mice were gathered: Algy Coltfoot and his mother, the two Raddle spinsters, flirty Miss Poot, and many more had mustered together to see how the Chitters were faring. It was as if some instinct had told them that the end was near for that family. A dark shadow lay over all their hearts.

49

Poor Piccadilly was getting impatient with them all. They kept badgering him for information and they evidently considered his bulletins too few and scanty in detail. Just when the city mouse felt like punching a couple of stupid, nosey heads, Master Oldnose, disturbed by the row, strode out of his rooms and waded through the crowd.

"Now then, now then!" He clapped his paws and looked around crossly.

Master Oldnose had been the tutor of most of the mice present, and their memories of him with his ears white with anger awoke their old respect for him. Voices were hushed and silence fell.

Master Oldnose eyed everyone severely—even those mice who were older than him respected him and held their tongues. Besides his school duties, Master Oldnose was the mousebrass maker and that was a position of great honor.

Now he surveyed them all and waited until he was satisfied.

Piccadilly flicked the hair out of his eyes.

"Ta, mister, they were gettin' out of hand."

Master Oldnose bristled at being called "mister" by this uncouth and obviously ignorant city mouse but decided to pass over it. "You, boy," he addressed Piccadilly. "What is the meaning of this riotous gathering? Explain yourself." He stood with his paws clasped firmly behind his back and rocked slightly on his heels awaiting a reply.

"It's the Chitters, mister. Oswald's in what Mrs. Brown calls 'the crisis' and she an' Arthur are doin' their level best for 'em, but this lot aren't happy with just knowin' that and won't shift."

"I see." Master Oldnose glared at the crowd as if they were children. "Go about your business—there is nothing more for you to learn here."

The mice stirred and mumbled feebly, and the two old maids fluttered shyly and hid their mouths behind nervous paws. Algy coughed and put on his most stubborn face. Nobody moved away.

"Tough luck, mister." Piccadilly grinned cheekily. "I thought you had 'em then."

"We only want to know how they are," said a small voice. It was Tom Cockle. "We owe the lad a lot, you see, and well—I've been stewin' all day, not knowin' how he was doin', so I come here, and blow me if there wasn't a blessed crowd already."

"That's right," broke in Mrs. Coltfoot. "Algy an' me were terrible restless—poor Oswald, I had an awful feeling about today." Murmurs of agreement ran through the crowd.

"We're not doin' any harm," continued Tom. "We're sorry if we were a bit rowdy, but we're not budgin'."

Even the Raddle spinsters nodded. Master Oldnose sighed. He could see that today he would not be obeyed. Indeed, *he* had been sitting in his workroom unable to concentrate on the unfinished mousebrasses before him. He was quite prepared to remain with the others now and wait for news. Everyone expected the curtain to be pulled to one side at any moment and to see Gwen Brown's tearful face appear and relate grave, tragic words. All eyes were fixed on the curtain and even Piccadilly was forced to turn and stare at it glumly.

The evening drew closer. Outside, the day was still warm and the sun had not yet disappeared, but no mouse took any notice.

Eventually, the mice on the Landings crept down the stairway and stood, silent and depressed, with the Skirtings' folk. Time stole by—only the breathing of many mice disturbed the blanketing stillness.

All at once, confusion broke out. Cries of alarm rippled through the crowd. Piccadilly looked around. The Raddle spinsters, as usual, had the same expression on their faces. Even in panic they were identical. No one seemed to know what was happening. Master Oldnose scowled. The disturbance seemed to emanate from the back of the crowd near the cellar door. He gulped and wondered with dread what had crept out of that dark place. Something was forcing its way through the assembled mice. Master Oldnose drew back in fear.

"Out of my way!" shouted a gruff voice. "Let me through there!"

Piccadilly managed a smile—he knew that voice.

"Hey! Avast there." A blue woolen hat bobbed into view amongst the sea of startled mice.

Master Oldnose was relieved, but glowered as he saw Thomas Triton emerge from the crowd. "Mr. Triton," he declared, "what means this rude interruption?"

Master Oldnose was not fond of the midshipmouse, for on the few occasions they had met, Thomas had flagrantly disregarded his authority.

"Evenin', Nosey!" greeted Thomas cheerily.

Master Oldnose's mouth dropped open as he watched the midshipmouse barge past him. Thomas ruffled Piccadilly's hair on his way then nipped behind the Chitters' curtain.

Excited whoops then came from the crowd. "How do, Algy! Hello, Algy's mum!" called a small but unmistakable voice. It was Twit, finding it more difficult to get through the crowd than the midshipmouse had done.

Master Oldnose came out of his sulk and looked up quickly.

"What you got in that bag, Twit?" asked Tom Cockle.

"Oh, you'll see, Tom, you'll see." Twit blundered out of the assembled mice, carrying the Starwife's bag as high as his little arms could manage.

"Hello, William," said Master Oldnose warmly. "Are you feelin' well, boy?"

"The best I ever did!" And as if to prove it Twit burst into a fit of joyful laughter.

The crowd thought he had gone potty and sighed and tutted

with disapproval. Audrey had been following Twit unnoticed by everyone, but now she stepped out and took his paw.

"He really is fine," she explained to them all, and hurried the still giggling fieldmouse into the Chitters' rooms.

"Audrey?" Piccadilly stopped her. "What *is* going on? Why were you so long and why is Twit acting so barmy?"

"He's just happy because Oswald is going to get well," she answered.

Piccadilly looked at her doubtfully. "Come off it," he whispered. "There's no way to save him now."

"Oh yes there is," said Audrey in a strange, somber voice. "There's *one* way to save him." She turned suddenly and ran through the curtain.

The city mouse stared after her. He could have sworn he had seen tears in Audrey's eyes. But if Oswald was going to be cured, why was she so unhappy?

In Oswald's sickroom excitement charged the air. Thomas had told Gwen Brown about the Starwife's bag and she was already boiling some water.

Oswald lay still and silent on the bed like a broken statue of cold marble. He was unaware of everyone around him. He felt so weak that even breathing seemed a dreadful labor. It was as if he had been falling down a deep black well: gradually the light at the top had grown fainter and more distant, until he accepted that there was no way out for him. Down he sank into the blackest night imaginable. He could hear nothing but the darkness filling his ears and closing in around him. How easy it was to sleep and forget everything, all he had known and all he had been—to be one with the rich velvet blackness.

Mrs. Brown came into the sickroom carrying a bowl of hot steaming water. Twit was about to drop the bag in when he hesitated. Was this a cruel trick of the Starwife? He glanced around at his friends and at once drew heart from Thomas's wise, whiskered face. The bag plopped into the bowl.

At once the steam snaked higher and filled the sickroom completely. All who breathed it in felt refreshed and tingles ran all the way down their tails.

A silver light began to shine in the room. In his chair Jacob Chitter stirred in his sleep. Small stars gleamed through the steam and once again Twit felt as if he was swept up into the bright heavens. Only this time Oswald was next to him and there seemed to be music everywhere. As he looked at his cousin the fieldmouse gasped. For a moment it seemed as if he could see the Starwife lying in his place, but the vision was snatched away and Twit could see that it was indeed Oswald lying there.

"The water is cooler now," said Gwen. "Twit, dear, see if he will drink it."

Twit took the bowl from her and knelt beside Oswald. He used one paw to raise his cousin's head and tilted the bowl slightly with the other.

At first the water simply touched Oswald's lips and trickled down onto the pillows.

"Come on, cuz," cried Twit urgently. "Drink it!" Everyone held their breath and watched. More of the precious water spilled onto the pillows. The albino looked dead.

Twit's paw trembled as he feared they were too late. The pillow was very wet now and there was not much left in the bowl. Thomas lowered his eyes and removed his hat. Mrs. Brown buried her face in her paws.

"Oh, Oswald," the little fieldmouse cried. "Oswald, Oswald." Twit's little heart was breaking. And then Oswald's lips moved.

"Look!" yelled Twit. 'He be drinkin'." Oswald swallowed the liquid and then opened one eye feebly. He gazed at them all and managed a smile.

"Hooray!" shouted Twit, skipping around the room. "Hooray!" He took Mrs. Brown's paw and dragged her into the dance.

Thomas stepped up to Audrey and said softly to her, "I'll be off to Greenwich later to return the bag. No doubt I'll be told details of your departure. She won't leave anything to chance—everything will be planned and organized."

"Mr. Triton, I have to go, don't I?" said Audrey. "I am the price of all this, aren't I?"

He nodded regretfully. "Alas, miss, I'm afraid you are. Forgive me for taking you to her. I am truly sorry."

Audrey smiled at him. "It isn't your fault, Mr. Triton—she would have done it with or without you."

They were interrupted by an impatient knocking on the wall. Everyone paused and listened.

"Where's my milk? What's all that noise? Can you hear me, Jacob?" Mrs. Chitter was in fine form by the sound of her.

Jacob Chitter jumped to attention in his chair. "Yes, dear. Of course, dear, I . . ." he paused suddenly as he noticed his son smiling up at him. "Oh, Oswald," he said, and burst into tears.

Gwen Brown led the others out of the sickroom. Thomas hung back and collected the small cloth bag.

On the way out to the hall Gwen looked in on Mrs. Chitter. She was sitting up in bed fussing with her hair. "Oh, Gwen what is going on in there?" she asked. "What does my husband think he's doing, the old fool?"

"Arabel," cried Mrs. Brown. "Oswald is better! It's all over now."

Mrs. Chitter dabbed her eyes and gave thanks to the Green Mouse. "Well if that isn't the best news I've ever heard," she sobbed. "You see, Gwen, I told you those pieces of onion would do the trick."

In the hall Thomas was telling an awestruck crowd about Oswald's recovery. For a short time they simply blinked at the midshipmouse—not sure if they had heard him properly and then with one voice they cheered.

"My word!" exclaimed Master Oldnose.

"Let's celebrate," called Tom Cockle.

Audrey felt miserable and dragged her feet back home. Arthur was munching away in the kitchen and getting crumbs everywhere.

"Isn't it terrific?" he mumbled, with his mouth full.

"Oh yes, Arthur, I couldn't be happier for the Chitters." Her voice fell and she sat down heavily.

Arthur swallowed and licked the crumbs around his mouth, forgetting the ones clinging to his whiskers. "What's the matter?" he asked seriously, sensing his sister's mood.

"Didn't Mr. Triton tell you?" she asked wearily.

Arthur sat down beside her and said fearfully, "Tell us what? You're all right, aren't you? You're not coming down with what Oswald had, are you?"

"Oh no, Arthur—nothing like that. My fate's much worse than that," she said morosely. "It's the miracle cure of the Starwife."

"That was amazing wasn't it—really magic stuff that was."

Audrey stared at him steadily. "It had . . . conditions, Arthur. We could only take the cure *if* I agreed to go with Twit to his field the day after tomorrow *and* . . . take Madame Akkikuyu with me."

"Audrey! That's terrible. I thought that ratwoman was dead." Arthur thought deeply for a moment then brightened. "But Oswald is cured now—they can't make you go if you back out now, can they?"

"I'm afraid so. Oswald and his family will fall sick again if I don't stick to it."

Arthur put his arm around her. "Don't worry, Sis," he soothed. "I'll come with you. I promise. How long do you think it will take to get there and back?"

"But that's just it." Audrey wept. "I shan't be coming back— I've got to stay with Akkikuyu forever."

Arthur gasped. "But that's dreadful. Oh, how shall we tell Mother?"

"I don't know," sobbed Audrey.

"My dears!" Mrs. Brown was standing in the doorway, tears falling down her cheeks—she had heard it all.

She wrapped her arms around Audrey and kissed her. "There must be a way," she whimpered. "Oh, what would your father do if he were here?"

An apologetic cough sounded behind them. "Forgive me, good lady," said Thomas self-consciously. "I came to tell you about the party the rest of your Skirtings' folk are arranging, but I see you are busy. Excuse me."

"No wait, please," called Gwen desperately. "Mr. Triton, you seem to know this Starwife better than us. Is there any way she would release Audrey from this horrible bargain?"

Thomas's eyes were grave beneath his frosty white brows. "No, ma'am. I'm sorry, but the Starwife clings to a bargain like a limpet to a stone. She does not make idle threats either: that family will surely perish if Miss Audrey does not go." The midshipmouse fumbled with the cloth bag in his paws. "I must leave now," he said, tugging the edge of his hat. "I have to return this, you see. No doubt you will see me in the morning if I guess rightly about the messages I'll find waiting for me." He turned and left the Skirtings and began the journey back to Greenwich.

"If it's all right with you, Mother," ventured Arthur, "I'd like to go with Audrey to make sure she's safe."

"I don't need looking after," said Audrey indignantly. "Just you stay here with Mother!"

"Listen, silly," argued her brother crossly. "I can go with you, make sure you settle in, then come back and tell Mother how you're doing."

"Oh," said Audrey—she could see the sense in that.

So could Mrs. Brown. "That's a very good idea, Arthur," she said, and hugged them both tightly.

Meanwhile, Algy Coltfoot and Tom Cockle had brought out their instruments—whisker fiddle and bark drum—and soon the strains of a melody came floating in through the hall.

Gwen Brown made her children wash the tearstains from their faces. "It may sound silly of me," she said, "but I don't feel as though you'll be away too long. Let's regard this evening as a sort of grand going-away party. We'll all be together again soon, you see."

Audrey and Arthur agreed—for her sake—though in their own hearts they doubted her. Audrey went to fetch her tail bells, which she had not worn for weeks. She felt that tonight was a good occasion to wear them once more.

In the hall the other mice had not been idle. To celebrate the Chitters' return to health, food had been brought out and decorations festooned the walls. Algy and Tom played "The Summer Jig" and their audience danced and clapped heartily. Between tunes Mr. Cockle slipped out a bowl of his own berrybrew and quaffed it down happily, hoping his wife wouldn't see. Mrs. Coltfoot was being congratulated on the success of her ointment, and the Raddle spinsters were tittering on the stairs as usual.

Into this mirth came Twit. He was immediately grabbed and hauled into the dancing—until someone called for him to play on his reed pipe. The fieldmouse darted away to fetch it.

It was a joyful chaos of noise and laughter. Soon the tensions of the last weeks were forgotten—forgotten by everyone except Audrey.

Perhaps this is the last time I shall wear bells on my tail or have a ribbon in my hair, she thought. With a rat for company I shan't need to look nice.

"Come on, Audrey," said Arthur, suddenly interrupting her thoughts. "There's some terrific food here. Mrs. Cockle and Mrs. Coltfoot have been busy." Arthur dragged his sister over to a crowded area where a cloth had been spread on the floor and laid with biscuits, cheeses, soft grain buns, jam rings, and a large bowl of Mrs. Coltfoot's own specialty—Hawthorn Blossom Cup. Gwen Brown was chatting mildly to Biddy Cockle.

"Here she is," Arthur told his mother. "I found her over there all dreamy and sorry for herself."

Gwen linked her arm in her daughter's. "Try to be happy, my love," she said. "It'll be all right, you'll see!"

"Where's Piccadilly?" asked Audrey suddenly. It occurred to her that he knew nothing of the bargain. Perhaps he would come with them to Twit's field—it might not be so bad after all if the cheeky city mouse came too.

"Piccadilly was over there before with the dancers," said Mrs. Brown, relieved that Audrey had snapped out of herself.

Audrey left her mother behind and went in search of the gray mouse. The musicians were now playing "Cowslips Folly," a lively dance in which a ring of boy mice rushed around a central circle of girl mice and chose a partner from them. Audrey hovered at the edge of the dancing. She saw Piccadilly choose Nel Poot three times. Miss Poot was evidently enjoying all the attention and she was brazen enough to wave at Audrey!

At first Audrey was amused—everyone knew how dotty Nel Poot was. But when Piccadilly chose her a fourth time the smile twitched off Audrey's face and her foot began to tap bad temperedly. What did Piccadilly think he was doing?

"Cowslips Folly" ceased and the musical trio went to see if there was any food left. Audrey watched the dancers break up, but before she could turn away, Piccadilly caught her glance, excused himself from Nel, and sauntered over.

"Did you want somethin'?" he asked her. "Only Miss Poot thought you were trying to get my attention."

Audrey answered casually. "Yes, I did as a matter of fact. I just wanted to say good-bye to you and take this opportunity to thank you for all you have done for me and my family."

"You gone soft in the head?" Piccadilly laughed. "What you on about?"

"I'm leaving," said Audrey, enjoying the moment. "Arthur and I are going with Twit to his field on a visit."

Piccadilly's face fell and his shoulders drooped sadly. Audrey bit her lip and cursed her stupid tongue.

"I see," he managed. "I hope you have a nice time," he muttered, staring at the ground miserably. "When was all this decided?"

"Oh we decided as soon as Oswald got better," she said. "We're going the day after tomorrow. You can come and wave us off if you like." How could she be so cruel, she wondered. Had the Starwife put a spell on her too?

Piccadilly raised his head as if stung. He stared at Audrey incredulously, then with anger said, "Sorry, ducks, but I'm goin' back to the city tomorrow."

"Oh," gasped Audrey.

"Well, Whitey's better now, ain't he, and there's nothin' to keep me here is there?"

"I suppose not," said Audrey in a small voice. She wanted to tell him of the terrible bargain that she had to keep—surely he would not think she was cruel then. "Piccadilly . . ." she began.

"Listen to that," he said, cocking one ear to the band. "That's the Suitors' Dance and I promised Miss Poot." The city mouse left her and Audrey's eyes pricked with wretched tears.

The rest of the evening swept by merrily. Nobody noticed Audrey slipping away to her room with her paws over her eyes.

Slowly the party broke up. Those from the Landings yawned and made their way up the stairs. The Raddle sisters tittered at Tom Cockle, who was sound asleep and snoring loudly with an empty bowl of berrybrew at his side. Biddy Cockle scolded and shook him, then with some help from Algy, Tom Cockle staggered home singing at the top of his voice

about a mouse called Gertie. Biddy was not amused and made him sleep in the spare room for three days afterward.

Eventually, Piccadilly was left alone in the hall. "I must go tomorrow," he told himself miserably. "Back to the grit and grime of the city." He bowed his head and wept silently beneath the crescent summer moon.

A MEETING AT MIDNIGHT

It was not yet dawn. The grayness of night lingered reluctantly in corners and doorways. Somewhere, behind the tall tower blocks and council estates the sun rose slowly over the hidden horizon and the night shadows shrank deep into the earth for the rest of the day.

Piccadilly quietly rose from his bed and put on his belt. He checked to see that everything was where it should be: small knife—yes, that was there—mousebrass—yes, the belt was looped through it securely—and finally, biscuit supply—well, the leather pouch was there, but it was empty. He wondered if Mrs. Brown would mind if he took some of her biscuits. It might take a long time to walk back to the city. Piccadilly frowned—it would seem like stealing to take without asking, but he wanted to slip away without any fuss—maybe he ought to leave a note. He crept into the Browns' kitchen.

The biscuits were next to the crackers, so Piccadilly took two of each, broke them into small pieces and slipped them into his pouch. He looked around for a bit of paper to write on. Then he wondered what he could write—it needed a long explanation to tell Mrs. Brown why he was going, but how could he put into words all that he felt?

In the end, Piccadilly simply wrote: *"Have gon back to the city. Thank you for having me. Have took some biskitts hope you don't mind—Piccadilly."*

He was not very good at writing. Long ago he had neglected his schooling for more exciting adventures. Now he regarded his handiwork with some doubt. Would anyone read his note? His handwriting was unsteady and he had pressed too hard with the pencil. He pulled a wry face. "I bet Audrey can read an' write perfect," he grumbled to himself.

Outside the house a sparrow began to sing to the new day. Piccadilly looked up quickly. It had taken longer than he had intended to write that note. Now he had no time to spare. He propped the piece of paper on the table, tiptoed out of the Browns' home, and passed through the cellar doorway. Quickly he scrambled down the cellar steps and through the Grill into the sewers.

The morning stretched and shook itself. The clouds were few and wispy—it was going to be another blazing June day.

When Audrey woke, her mother handed the note to her. She read it quietly and with dismay. "Has he really gone?" she asked.

"Yes, love," said her mother. "Arthur has looked every-where."

"Oh, it's all my fault," was all Audrey was able to say.

She ate her breakfast dismally as she thought about Piccadilly. Her heart told her that she was the reason he had gone off without a word. When Arthur came in she avoided his accusing eyes and went to start her packing.

Arthur was unhappy too. He had begun to consider Piccadilly as his best friend and he guessed that Audrey had something to do with his abrupt departure. It was about time she stopped playing games with everyone. Ever since poor old Piccadilly had arrived she had used him, made him feel guilty for surviving the horrors of the rats when their father had not. She had sent him into peril with Oswald down into the rat-infested sewers to look for her mousebrass and had never really apologized for that. She really was a silly lump. To cheer himself up Arthur went with his mother to see the Chitters.

In the sickroom even the air felt healthier. The sickly smell had gone completely. Oswald was propped up in bed with a great smile on his face as Twit told him funny stories. Mrs. Chitter was up and about, chiding and tutting, finding dust where there was none and rearranging all her ornaments. She herded Gwen Brown into the kitchen, where she demanded to know all the latest doings of everyone in the Skirtings.

Arthur sat himself on the end of the bed next to Twit and waited for a tale to end. Idly he looked about the room. Something was missing, something that had seemed such a fixture that now it was gone he couldn't think what it could be. Oswald saw his puzzled expression and laughed.

"Father's gone to bed finally," he said. "It does seem odd without him in here, doesn't it? I wanted to get up today, but Mother wouldn't let me. She says I'll be here for at least two weeks—or until she's satisfied with my health."

"You'm in bed forever then," giggled Twit, holding his feet and rocking backward.

"Twit says he's going home tomorrow and that you and Audrey are going too—I'm so jealous, Arthur. I wish I could go too."

Arthur caught a quick, cautionary glance from the field-mouse and understood that Oswald had not been told about the Starwife's bargain.

"Still . . ." continued the albino, "I suppose my hayfever

would have driven me crazy in the country. I can't wait for you to come back and tell me all your adventures."

"I will," said Arthur.

"Of course we shall all miss cousin Twit, but he says he might come visiting again. I'm going to be terribly bored all alone here, but I suppose I should count myself lucky, really."

A knock sounded outside and the patter of Mrs. Chitter's feet accompanied by the clucking of her tongue came to them as she went to see who it was. There were some muffled words, which the three friends were unable to catch, but presently Arthur's mother popped her head into the sickroom.

"Arthur dear and Twit, could you step out here for a moment, please?"

Soon Oswald was left alone to stare at the table covered in raw onion.

Outside Twit and Arthur found Thomas Triton. He grinned warmly at the fieldmouse and began.

"I've come from the Starwife," he said. "Plans are slightly changed. You leave tonight—seems the old dame can't get none of her folk to escort the ratwoman down to the river in the daylight, so tonight it is."

"Oh, dear," sighed Mrs. Brown. "Arthur, fetch Audrey—she has to hear this."

"Wait, lad, I already told the lass. I went there first y'see, thinkin' you'd all be there like," the midshipmouse explained. "Seems there's a merchant chappy the Starwife's persuaded to take you to my young matey's field."

"A merchant mouse?" asked Twit.

"Aye, lad, he's a sort of peddler—sells and trades things. Well, it seems he knows everywhere along the river, stocks up in Greenwich, then takes his goods 'round to out-of-the-way places."

"Well, I ain't never seen him afore in my field," said Twit.

Mrs. Brown had been frowning deeply. Now she suddenly said, "Would this peddler be Mr. Kempe?"

Thomas looked surprised. "Why yes, ma'am, that it is—how do you know of him?"

"Why, he comes here in the autumn to see Master Oldnose on mousebrass business. Yes, he seems respectable enough. . . . I think I'll feel a lot happier knowing my children are in his paws."

Thomas agreed. "Just so, ma'am. Well, as for tonight, I shall lead milladdo here and your two children down to Greenwich Pier where Kempe will meet us. There we shall all wait until the rat arrives with those fidgety squirrels."

"About what time will this be, Mr. Triton?" asked Gwen.

"Midnight, if it pleases you, ma'am."

"Oh, Mr. Triton, it does not please me—not at all. Still there is much to be done. Arthur, come with me. Are you packed yet, Twit?"

"Bless me. I clean forgot about that," admitted the field-mouse.

*　　*　　*

The rippling river was dark, and cool air drifted lazily up from its shimmering surface. It was a clear, clean night pricked all over by brilliant stars. Greenwich Pier huddled over the lapping water like a tired old lady. Its timbers were creaky, its ironwork rusted, and yellow paint flaked and fell from it like tears. Daily trips departed from the pier to see the landmarks of London from the river, and in the summer many crowded the benches and ice-cream stands. But now it was still and dark, its gates were closed, and the visitors had all deserted the pier for gaudier delights.

The only sound was the water breaking gently against the

supports and slopping around a broken wooden jetty nearby.

There were no lights on the pier at night, all was dim and gray—a place of alarming shadow.

Audrey held on to her mother's paw. They had come through the sewers once more, led again by the midshipmouse. She watched Arthur and Twit run ahead to explore the deep pools of darkness and shuddered. She was cold, but her mother had knitted her a yellow shawl and she pulled it tightly over her shoulders.

All the mice were carrying bags packed with provisions, blankets, and personal treasures. Audrey's arms ached with the weight of hers and she was glad when Thomas said it was not much farther. Somewhere, in amongst the folded clothes, was a dried hawthorn blossom. Oswald had given it to her when she said good-bye to him that evening—it was one of those he had saved from the Spring festival.

Gwen Brown was savoring every moment with her children, storing up the sound of their voices for when she was alone.

Twit and Arthur ran ahead once more, swinging their baggage happily. After some moments they came rushing back, their faces aglow with excitement.

"Thomas," squealed Twit eagerly, "there be somethin' up there. We done heard it."

"Yes," joined in Arthur. "Someone's singing." The little group of mice edged forward cautiously. In the shade ahead nothing could be seen, but gradually a voice floated to them on the night air.

It was a merry, hearty sound, first singing, now humming.

> Poor Rosie! Poor Rosie!
> I'll tell you of poor Rosie,
> The tragedy that was Rosie
> And why she died so lonely

Coz for all her looks her armpits stank,
The suitors came, but away they shrank
Far away from Rosie,
With their paws tight on their nosey.

Twit spluttered and laughed helplessly as the song continued. Gwen Brown gave Thomas a doubtful look. The midshipmouse shrugged and hid a smile.

"Who is it, Mother?" asked Audrey.

"That is Mr. Kempe," Gwen replied dryly.

Thomas coughed and shouted. "Ahoy, Mr. Kempe! Come out so we may see you! And before your verses become too colorful, remember there are tender ears here."

From the shadows a great clanking noise replaced the song, as if some metal monster had been roused from sleep. Audrey waited with wide eyes wondering what this Mr. Kempe would be like.

"Are you the party bound for Fennywolde?" came the hearty voice.

"That's right," Twit piped up, "that be the name o' my field."

"Why, that sounds like a fieldmouse."

"I be 'un."

The clanking drew nearer and into the dim light stepped one of the strangest figures Audrey had ever seen.

There was a mass of bags, pans, straps, and buckles mounted on a pair of sturdy legs and somewhere amongst all this madness was a furry round face and two small beadlike eyes. It was friendly and welcoming, and Audrey warmed to Kempe immediately—especially as he said, "Bless my goods, two beautiful ladies and I knew nought of it. A curse on my palsied tongue that you should hear it yammering away like that. But 'tis the lot of the lone traveler to sing when he's on his tod. Forgive my verses, dear ladies." The clanking began again as he attempted to bow.

69

Gwen Brown smiled as she accepted his apology. "You just keep your songs tucked away while my daughter travels with you, Mr. Kempe," she said.

"Oh, please," he protested, "there's no 'Mister,' plain Kempe I am—no titles, no end pieces! Kempe, and that's all."

Audrey was staring in fascination at his bags. Poking through the sides there were glimpses of fine silks and silver lace, and strung around the handles of his pans and around his own neck were beads of every type and variety—pear-shaped droplets done in gold, green leaf patterns threaded on a single hair from a pony's mane, little charms worked in wood and hung on a copper wire, and chains of fine links from which dangled tears of blue glass.

"I'll trade anything for anything," he continued, catching Audrey's eye. "Well, young lady—see anything that tickles you? I see you like fine things, with your ribbon and all that lace. Why, I've got such an array of ribbons in here—enough to make rainbows jealous. Take your pick, and all I ask are those wee bells on your tail."

"But these bells are silver!" Audrey exclaimed. "They're worth more than all your ribbons."

"Alas for sensible girls," he sighed. "Still, you can't blame a mouse for trying."

Thomas chuckled and introduced everyone to the traveler.

"What a fine party we'll be making to be sure, sailing up the river together, leaving the fume of the city behind us. A pity you'll not be joinin' us, Mrs. Brown, but have no fear. I'll keep one eye on my goods and the other on my charges." He turned to Thomas. "And you, Mr. Triton, sir, sorry I am not to have your stout company on board, I bet you know many a worthy tale."

"That I do," replied Thomas, "though not all are comfortable to listen to."

"Still, I'll wager we'd not get bored with you on hand."

"Oh, I don't think you need worry on that score, Kempe, my

boy." Thomas smiled. "Have you met your other traveling companion yet?"

"Why no, that's the truth of it, but I had word from herself what lives up yon hill—the batty old squirrel."

"What did she tell you exactly?" asked Thomas, smiling.

"To be here tonight, at this hour, to guide certain parties to Fennywolde—they being your own good selves and one other, a special lady." He turned to Gwen Brown and confessed. "To be honest I thought my luck was in and you were she—alas, it seems not." He clapped his paws together. "So where is this other of our jolly group?"

Thomas considered Kempe for a moment and said, "Has the Starwife promised you anything for your services?"

"Why no, sir." He seemed surprised. "Why 'tis only a simple task and I'll have the pleasure of it, such fine young fellows a trader never had to journey with! I'd do it for nought . . . but now you mention it, herself made me give my traveler's oath not to change my mind—ain't that funny now?"

"Not really," said Mrs. Brown, "not when you know who this lady is. The Starwife has used you like she has used my daughter—deviously."

Kempe looked at the mice before him and grew concerned at the expressions on their faces. "Why, there you go worrying a body—kindly tell me who this lady is."

But even as he spoke they all heard voices, one loud, the other timid.

Madame Akkikuyu strode onto the pier followed by two squirrels.

"Mouselings!" cried the rat, dropping her many bags and flinging her arms open.

Kempe's face sagged and it seemed as if all his goods drooped as well. Audrey ducked quickly behind her mother, avoiding Akkikuyu's attention.

"We travel at last," the fortune-teller exclaimed triumphantly.

"Off to sun and rest—together forever."

"Why the batty old she-divil," bellowed Kempe, cursing the Starwife and shaking his fist at the two terrified squirrels. "My traveler's oath an' all—for this, this . . . lump of a rat. I be conned outright."

One of the squirrels braved a reply. "The bargain with you must stand," he said, dodging a blow from a pan. "If not, all the river will know of your falseness."

The trader stood still, but his face looked as though it would burst. "A traveler depends on his reputation and the goodwill of others—why, if his traveler's oath is doubted he goes out of business."

"Just so," replied the squirrel smartly.

"A plague on you," called Kempe angrily.

Thomas intervened. "Now look, squire," he said to Akkikuyu's escort. "You've done your delivery, now tell your mistress it's all working well for her. Get you gone before this chap cracks you both one."

The squirrel stroked his tail smugly and glanced casually around for his silent comrade—but he had already run away. That was enough. The squirrel jumped in the air and dashed after him.

"They sure are slippery, Thomas," said Twit.

"So," said Kempe sourly, "here we are with that baggage to join us. A pretty lot we are, to be sure."

"Yes," said Thomas briskly. "And if I'm going to get some sleep tonight I've got to take Mrs. Brown home first. Make your farewells please—it's time to go."

Gwen held Audrey in a desperate embrace. "You will come back, Audrey, my love—I know it."

"I hope so, Mother, I wish I was as sure as you." She tried not to cry, but her eyes were already raw and swollen from Piccadilly's departure.

Gwen turned to her son. "Now, Arthur," she said, "you look

after your sister and come home when you can." She hugged and kissed him, much to his embarrassment.

Thomas Triton turned to Twit. "Well, matey," he said awkwardly, "there's no denyin' I'll miss your cheerful face around here. Ever since you dropped on my ship we've got on famous." He fumbled with a flask that was slung over his shoulder and thrust it into the fieldmouse's paws.

"What is it, Thomas?" asked Twit.

"Just a little something for your journey—and to remember our first meeting by."

"Will you come visitin' one day, Thomas?"

The midshipmouse shook his head. "No, Woodget—not by water, you know I can't go that way again."

"What did you call me then, Thomas? It's me, Twit, remember?"

The midshipmouse looked flustered and apologized for getting muddled. Twit laughed and said it didn't matter. "I reckon I'll be poppin' this way again some time," said Twit. "I bet there's a bundle of stories you've still to tell me."

"Maybe, matey, maybe."

Then Madame Akkikuyu, who up till then had been gazing earnestly up at the stars, hugged Mrs. Brown. Gwen gasped but found nothing to say.

"Oh, mother of my friend, good-bye," Akkikuyu breathed with feeling. "And you old salty mouseling, farewell also."

Thomas cleared his throat and hurriedly waved "Cheerio" before she had a chance to hug him. Then he led Gwen Brown away from the pier.

The three young mice sadly watched them go. "Well," began Kempe. "I'll show you our trusty vessel."

"Are we to leave tonight?" asked Audrey.

"No, missey," said Kempe above the jangle of his goods. "The boat sets off in the morning, but we've got to settle down."

74

"I shall be near my mousey friend," declared Madame Akkikuyu, stooping to collect her things. Audrey looked at Arthur and grimaced.

Kempe took them farther along the pier to where the river splashed through the planks under their feet. A large tourist cruiser was moored at the edge and it bobbed gently up and down bumping against the pier.

"There she is," said Kempe. "Our transport—well one of them, anyway. Now up this rope here and we'll be on deck."

"Easy," cried Twit, and scampered up the mooring rope in a twinkling.

"Akkikuyu do that also." The fortune-teller hauled herself onto the rope bridge and clumsily made her way along with her thick tail flicking behind her.

"That's right, missus," grinned Kempe. "Don't go fallin' in now—we wouldn't want to lose you!"

It was Arthur's turn next; he stared at the rope warily. "I'm not usually very good at balancing," he admitted. "I can climb, but . . ." he looked despondently at the sloshing water below—it seemed green and cold, and he did not want to land in there.

"Come on now laddie, just don't look down."

From the boat Twit watched them and laughed, "Come on, Arthur. If you spend any time in my field you'll have to learn to climb stalks. But I suppose you'd have to lose some weight first."

"I'm not fat," protested Arthur.

"Course not—you great puddin'."

That settled it. Arthur virtually ran up the rope and began scuffling with the fieldmouse, who was helpless with giggling.

Now it was Audrey's turn, but she stepped onto the rope nimbly and was soon aboard—straight into the welcoming arms of Akkikuyu.

"Clever mouselet. Akkikuyu knew mouselet could do it."

Whistling a quick tune, Kempe ambled up to them, balancing with perfect poise on the rope, his many goods not affecting him whatsoever.

"Now follow me, fellow travelers," he said once he was on deck. They strode over the boards and between wooden benches to where a steep flight of wooden steps plunged darkly down into an invisible blackness.

"Down here," called Kempe, briskly jumping onto the first step.

Silently they all descended. Twit followed Kempe. Then Arthur went, followed by Audrey, and Madame Akkikuyu brought up the rear.

Audrey tried to hurry down the steps as quickly as she could. Close above she could hear the rat's claws clicking as they caught on the steps, and Akkikuyu's croaky muttering breaths. Once the fortune-teller's tail brushed against Audrey's face in the dark and the mouse cried out in alarm, nearly falling off the steps altogether.

"Hush, mouselet," the rat cooed, "only the tail of Akkikuyu— fright not."

When they were all at the bottom of the steps, Kempe lit a small candle and they looked around them.

It was a storage hold. Oil drums and tarpaulins surrounded them, thick black rope snaked across the floor, and a stack of folded wooden chairs was piled precariously in one corner. It smelled strongly of the river and of stagnant, neglected pools.

"This is where we bunk tonight," said Kempe brightly as though he was used to much worse accommodation. "And tomorrow we'll hide here under the tarpaulin out of the way— until we change boats."

"Change boats?" repeated Arthur. "Why? Doesn't this one take us to Twit's field?"

"Bless you, laddie, no. Whatever made you think it did? I'm sure I said. Never mind. No, three vessels will bear us on our way. That's the joy of the traveler, hopping from boat to boat.

Knowing which one goes where and when. Why, I know the sailing time of everything along the whole great stretch of Grand Daddy Thames, from the biggest ship to the smallest barge."

They put their bags down and Kempe disentangled himself from his rattling goods. Without them he seemed a much smaller figure.

Madame Akkikuyu hugged her knees and muttered happily to herself.

Audrey did not like the hold: it was stuffy and more like a prison than anything she could imagine. The small flickering candle flame brought no cheer to the gloomy place and the rocking of the boat made her feel sick.

Arthur and Twit sat near Kempe, each lost in his own thoughts. The fieldmouse delved into his little bag and brought out his reed pipe. He put it to his lips and blew absentmindedly. He was thinking of his home and wondering if it had changed in all the months he had been away.

Arthur listened wistfully to the slow, solemn notes from the pipe. He too was thinking of Twit's home. What had Kempe called it—Fennywolde? Strange how Twit had never called it by that name before—it was always "my field" or just simply "back home." Arthur wondered what he and Audrey would find there.

The haunting music stopped and after a short while Twit's little voice gurgled with pleasure. "Good old Thomas!" he cried. He had remembered the little flask, which the midshipmouse had given to him, and pulled the cork out. The exotic smell of rum met his twitching nose.

Kempe was sorting through one of his bags, pulling out scraps of material and stuffing them back again. He hummed quietly to himself—it had been a busy week for the traveling mouse, deals had been made, a good bit of trading done down Tilbury way, and in Greenwich itself earlier that evening he had done a nice little deal with a Norwegian mouse from a ship docked near that old power station. Seven little wooden charms he had got in return for two spoons and a length of buttercup yellow satin. It was these small charms that Kempe was looking for–he was sure he had put them in this bag. Ah–yes, there they were. Kempe fished them out and examined them in the candlelight.

"Oooh," admired Twit, "they'm pretty. Can I see 'em proper?" Kempe inspected the fieldmouse's paws for dirt, then, when he was satisfied, handed the little carvings to him one by one.

All were figures of mice delicately done in boxwood. Every detail was correct down to the suggestion of fur. There were running mice, old wise-looking mice, pretty damsel mice curtsying and dancing, and an angry mouse with a sword in his paw.

"They're terrific," said Arthur, peering over Twit's shoulder.

"To be sure, they're right dandy little things," nodded Kempe. "Chap I traded with says he got them from a holy mouse what lived up in some mountain or other–not that I believed him like, probably knocked them up himself, but I took a fancy to 'em."

"I ain't never seen so neat a bit o' carvin'," said Twit, handing them back. "We never had nothin' like that in my field."

Kempe raised his eyebrows and shrugged. "In Fennywolde– I'm not a bit surprised. I never go there."

"Why not?" asked Arthur.

"Got chased out only time I did go," Kempe replied, shaking his head. "Some pious feller it was, babbling about frippery and vanity."

"What do you mean?" pressed Arthur. "What's wrong with what you sell?"

"Why, nothing! I have the finest selection on all the river. But you see–and begging your pardon, youngster," he said to Twit, "there are some in this world who think we come into it

78

empty-handed and should leave that way, with no decoration or little luxury to cheer us along. And they don't like those of us who deal in these indulgences."

"But I still don't understand why," said Arthur, confused. "What harm can your wares do?"

Kempe raised his hands in a gesture that showed he too had asked that question many times.

It was Twit who answered. Slowly he said, "Because they go against the design of the Green Mouse." He spoke the words as though he was repeating something he had heard many times.

"Twit!" exclaimed Arthur in surprise.

"Staunch Green Mousers," put in Kempe darkly, "fanatics too busy livin' in fear of the Almighty to enjoy his bounty."

Arthur stared at the fieldmouse. "But you never said," he stammered, "I thought your field was a happy place."

"Oh, it is," Twit assured him quickly. "Most of us don't think and reckon things like that. It's only a few what's hot against 'owt different an' such."

"Really?" Arthur was slightly annoyed. "What do you think that few will make of Audrey with her bells and lace?"

"Oh, they won't take to her," agreed Kempe. " 'Specially that pious feller what chased me—if he's still there."

"Oh, he be there all right," confirmed Twit glumly. "Old Isaac still goes into a fume and temper when it comes to the Green Mouse design."

"What do you make of this, Audrey?" asked Arthur, turning around. But his sister was not there—nor was Madame Akkikuyu.

*   *   *

The night breeze had made Audrey feel better. She hated being cooped up in that dreary, musty hold. She had left everyone engrossed and climbed the steps once more. Audrey leaned against one of the railings along the deck and gazed up at the bright stars. The sloshing of the water and the motion of the boat lulled her senses and the rich green smell of the river was brought to her on the breeze. She closed her eyes and a calm descended on her.

"Mouselet."

Audrey jumped at the sound of that voice behind her. Akkikuyu had followed her from the hold. The rat's black eyes were gleaming.

"The night—she is beautiful. See the stars—how they burn." She raised her claws to the heavens and spun around. "Oh, mouselet," she cried. "Finally we are together and we shall never be parted."

Once more Audrey felt a wave of compassion flow over her. Madame Akkikuyu was really a creature to be pitied. Audrey decided that the Starwife must be right—all the rat's wicked memories had indeed been forgotten. Madame Akkikuyu was little more than a harmless mouse child dressed in a rat's skin.

From the other side of the river a dog howled, breaking the peace of the night.

Akkikuyu traced a wide circle in the air with her claws and drew her breath.

"Wolf sees death and gives warning," she muttered. "Akkikuyu must not linger in dark places—listen to the wolf voice, 'Beware,' he says, 'old Mr. Death walk near.'" She pulled her spotted shawl tighter and kissed her dogtooth pendant. Whatever else she may have forgotten, Akkikuyu's instinctive belief in the supernatural remained.

Turning to Audrey, the rat added, "Akkikuyu have many treasures, mouselet. Things she not understand, powders in pouches, leaf and herb in bundles, secret packets that do smell most strange, and a terrible trophy of a kitty head." She frowned as she looked into the swirling water, as if all her answers lay there. "What they all about? Why for Akkikuyu keep such grislies? Was she doctor to have bowl for pounding and mixing? A darkness is behind Akkikuyu—too black to see." Her voice trailed off as she sighed with regret.

On impulse Audrey said, "Don't worry, leave the past alone—look to the future, Madame Akkikuyu. There will be answers enough for you there."

"Oh, mousey, how good it is for you to be such a friend." The fortune-teller grabbed Audrey and because the mouse pitied her she did not struggle as the other hugged her tightly. Large rat tears ran down Audrey's neck.

Arthur, Twit, and Kempe peered over the top of the steps.

"We've a tidy way to go before we get to Fennywolde," said the traveler slowly. "We had better keep an eye on that Madame there, bad business to be sure. You can wash a rat and comb a rat, but it will still be a rat. You can't trust 'em!"

"We know that," said Arthur.

"What I says is," continued Kempe, "nourish a rat and one day it will bite your head off. Just you watch her when you get to your field, young laddie—rats is always trouble."

*   *   *

It was much later that night when they had all bedded down in the hold that it really began.

The mice were sleeping soundly. Arthur's soft snores rose and fell with a steady rhythm. Kempe twitched his whiskers as he dreamed of pearls and silks flowing through his trader's paws. Twit, as always, was curled up in a circle, looking for all the world like an addition to Kempe's wooden carvings. Audrey had untied her ribbon and her hair spread around her like a fine network of fairy webs.

Nearby, Akkikuyu grunted as she wandered through her own dark dreams. She was sprawled amongst her bags and sacks, and occasionally her face would screw itself up into an expression of pain and her tail would beat the tarpaulin with heavy, agitated smacks. She rolled over and over, shaking her great head and mumbling to herself.

From somewhere in her dreams a voice seemed to be calling to her: "Akkikuyu! Akkikuyu—are you there?"

In her sleep Madame Akkikuyu groaned aloud. "Yes, I am here," she muttered, as if in answer to the unseen thing of her dreams. "What do you want? Who is it? Leave me alone."

For the rest of the journey along the river the night was to become a time of dread for Madame Akkikuyu—a time when the nameless voice invaded her sleep to call her name unceasingly.

CHAPTER SIX

FENNYWOLDE

The sunlight spread across the growing corn and cast deep charcoal shadows under the elm trees. The field was a large one—a mass of green, rippling like the ocean as the wind played over its surface and murmuring with lovers' whispers as the breeze sighed through it. The corn soaked up the sun, drank its gold, and grew tall.

The field was bordered on one side by a deep ditch that fed a pool at the far end where the hawthorn grew thick and impenetrable. But now the ditch was dry and the mud at the bottom was cracked and studded with sharp stones. Along the side grew the tall elms and one solitary yew, dark giants rearing high over the swaying grasses and stretching into the fierce blue.

To the left of the ditch was a meadow. Too small and difficult to plow, the meadow was rich in the glossy show of buttercups and flowering grasses. An enchanted scent hung over the place—a perfect blending of wild perfumes, so strong that you could almost taste them. Beyond the meadow was a great clump of oaks, fully in leaf, like green clouds come to rest on the earth.

This small land was what the fieldmice called "Fennywolde" or "the land of Fenny"–he being the first mouse to have lived there many years ago. It provided them with everything they needed: an abundant supply of corn, berries from the hawthorn, water from the pool, and brambles for autumn brewing. In the winter the steep banks of the ditch provided excellent shelter, and there were numerous tunnels and passages under the roots of the elms, which had been dug a long time ago by venerable ancestors. Secret holes to hide from the bitter winds and escape the midwinter death, places to spend chill dark days, and spacious halls to store supplies.

During the summer it was usual for the fieldmice to move out of their tunnels and take up residence in the field–to delight in climbing the tall stalks and nibble the ripening corn. So far, however, the inhabitants of Fennywolde had remained in their winter quarters. Only during the day would they dare venture into the field, and woe betide any mouse not safe in the tunnels at dusk. A terror was hunting in the night.

* * *

Alison sauntered through the meadow lazily. She was a beautiful country mouse, her strawberry blond hair hung in two creamy ponytails behind her ears. Her fur, like the fur of all fieldmice was reddish gold, but Alison's held a secret glint that dazzled when it caught the sun. She was a curvy young mousemaid with an impish pout and large brown eyes. Her skirt was of simple cotton stitched around with humble rustic embroidery. At her breast a mousebrass dangled–a sickle moon with a tiny brass bell–the sign of grace and beauty. And this was the trouble. Alison had received the charm a year ago and it had gone straight to her head.

She flirted with the boys, flicking back her hair and flashing her eyes at them, promising sweetness. They had all fallen for her: Todkin, Hodge, Young Whortle, and even skinny Samuel had been victims of her careless, dangerous glances. Those slight tosses of her head and devastating grins had been practiced and scrutinized in the mirror of the still pool where she spent most of her days preening and rehearsing her powers.

The warm afternoon, mingled with the dry rustle of the grasses, was a potent drug. Alison slumped on the ground, face upturned. The seeding grass heads bobbing overhead seemed to be bowing before her beauty. She fanned herself with a buttercup, allowing its rich buttery aura to wrap around her.

"Poor Dimsel," mused Alison in a throaty whisper. "Face like a cow's behind and wit to match." She laughed softly and stretched. "Dear Iris, legs like a redshank and not a curl in her hair." She passed her paw through her own crowning glory and made a mock appeal to the world in general. "But, friends, let us not forget Lily Clover, she has the grace of a swan—but she do stink like a fresh steaming dunghill." They were the names of Alison's rivals and she spoke of them with casual disregard, because today she had decided she had surpassed them all. It was clear in her mind now that she had no equal anywhere.

A bee droned in and out of the clear patch of blue above. "Old Bumble knows." Alison laughed, and her voice rose high and flutey. "He do know it! Bees go to honey and I be the sweetest thing by far." She rolled over and spied a forget-me-not pricking through the grass stems. Reaching out, she plucked it mercilessly. After weaving it into her hair she paraded up and down for her invisible audience. She contemplated whether she should return to the pool to assess the impact of the flower, but then her mouth curled and she set off purposefully.

*   *   *

Jenkin kicked the hard ground and scratched his head. He was carrying a large bundle of dry wood and felt like throwing it all into the ditch. His friends Hodge and Todkin were in the field practicing their stalk climbing while Samuel and Young Whortle had gone off to quest the oaks beyond the meadow.

Jenkin was tired and fed up–his father made him work hard. "Waste not the hours the good Green gives" was just one of the rules drummed into him.

Suddenly his mousebrass reflected the sun full into his downcast eyes. He dropped the sticks and rubbed them. For a moment he was blinded. It was a brass of life and hope–a sun sign. His father, the local mousebrass maker, had forged it specially with him in mind and was gravely pleased when Jenkin managed to choose it from the sack two springs ago.

"Ho, there! Jolly Jenkin!" came a clear voice suddenly. "Why for you rubbin' your eyes? Do I dazzle so much?"

Jenkin blinked. As his eyes readjusted through the misty haze of light he could just see Alison strolling toward him out of the meadow. Her fur was a fiery gold and there was buttercup dust glittering on her face. In her eyes there were dancing lights.

"Is that you, Alison Sedge?" he ventured, doubting his vision.

"Might be," she answered, staying just within the fringes of the meadow grass. "Then again I might be the goddess come down from the moon to torment you with my beauty."

Jenkin snorted. "Pah! You don't half talk addled sometimes, Alison Sedge. Just you mind my dad don't hear you goin' on like that. He'll tell your folks, he will."

"Pooh." She stepped out onto the hard ground.

Jenkin eyed her again. She had certainly changed in the past year–why, before she had been given that mousebrass they had been firm friends. He had even thought that perhaps . . . He saw her eyebrows arch in that infuriating way of hers. She had guessed what he was thinking about and tossed her head.

"Like my flower?" she asked huskily.

"Look better in the ground," Jenkin replied shyly, turning away from those eyes that held those dangerous lights. "Why don't you go show Hodge?"

"I may," Alison answered mildly. It amused her to flirt with the boys and see how she set them at odds with one another. How easily they could be confounded by a sideways glance or a sweet smile. It was Jenkin, though, whom she enjoyed teasing most. He was so serious and solemn and when he was with his father she reveled in disconcerting him. In fact, if her pride and vanity had not swelled so much she would quite happily have married Jenkin. He was by far the most handsome mouse in Fennywolde. Now, though, she enjoyed dangling him on a string with all the others, tempting and rejecting with soft, mocking laughter.

An impatient voice rang out over the field. "Jenkin! Where are thee, lad?"

He jumped up and hastily retrieved the bundle of sticks. "That be my dad callin' for me." Jenkin began to run to the ditch, past the bare stony stretch and up to the cool shade of the elms.

Isaac Nettle stood stiff and stern outside one of the entrances to the winter quarters. He scowled as his son came panting up to him. He was a lean mouse whose face was always grim and forbidding—no one had heard him laugh since his wife had died. His eyes were steely and solemn, set deep beneath wiry brows in a sour face.

"Where did thee get to?" he snapped. "Idling again, I'll warrant. Come here, boy."

Jenkin set the wood down before his father, watching him warily.

"What's this!" bellowed Isaac. "The wood is green. How am I to burn that! We should choke on smoke!" He grabbed his son by the neck and raised his hard paws to him. "I'll beat sense into thee yet, boy, and with the Green's help I'll cure thee of thine idleness."

Jenkin knew better than to protest. He gritted his teeth and screwed up his face. His father's paw came viciously down on him. Jenkin gasped as he opened his eyes; the blow had been a severe one. The blood pounded in his head and the side of his face throbbed with pain.

Isaac raised his paw again and smacked his son across the head once more. He spared no effort, so that Jenkin sobbed this time. "Thou must learn," exulted his father. He hit him one more time to emphasize his words.

Jenkin staggered on his feet when Isaac had finished. His head was reeling and already he felt a swelling around his eye. In his mouth he tasted the tang of iron and knew that his lip was bleeding. Soon the shock would wear off and he would be left with a dull ache and painful stinging.

"Now what have thee to say?" rumbled Isaac.

"I . . . I thank thee, Father," stammered Jenkin, holding his sore lip.

"We shall pray together," intoned Isaac to his son. "Midsummer scarce a week away and still we live in winter holes. 'Tis a judgment on us all. The Green is angry. There are those in our midst who have offended thee, Lord. Heathen loutishness creeps in. Give your servants strength to drive out the vain pride that you despise. Let us walk free at night once more." He dragged Jenkin inside.

From a safe distance Alison had watched it all. She had flinched as she saw Jenkin suffer those three terrible blows. Everyone in Fennywolde feared Mr. Nettle. His temper was dreadful, but he commanded the authority and respect due to a mousebrass maker. Several times Jenkin had carried the bruises given to him by his father and no one dared do anything about it—indeed Mr. Nettle was not the only staunch Green Mouser in Fennywolde.

Alison walked up to the ditch. She knew that Isaac classed her as one of the offenders in the field. He sermonized at her whenever he saw her. She thought of the miserable night that lay before Jenkin: he would have to kneel on a painfully hard floor next to his father for hours praying to the Green Mouse for deliverance and forgiveness. Alison sighed and told herself that she must make sure to be kind to Jenkin the next time she met him—why, she might even let him kiss her. She chuckled at the notion and looked about her.

The evening was growing old, and clouds of gnats were spinning over the barren stretch of ditch. It was time for her to go home.

She turned on her heel and made for one of the other entrances to the winter quarters.

"Alison Sedge," came a distraught voice. She looked up quickly and noticed a group of six worried mice. A plump harassed mouse bustled over.

"Hello Mrs. Gorse," greeted Alison politely.

The mouse brushed a long wisp of hair out of her red-rimmed eyes and asked, "Have you seen our Samuel?"

Alison shook her head. "Why, no, Mrs. Gorse. I think he went off with Young Whortle this morning."

"Oh, dear," murmured Mrs. Gorse. "I was hoping you might know where they were. Mr. and Mrs. Nep are asking everyone in the shelters. If they don't come back soon . . ."

Alison turned toward the meadow and stared at the grasses intently. It was getting dark and no mouse was safe above ground then.

*   *   *

Samuel Gorse was close to tears. He held on tightly to his friend and tried to pull himself farther under the oak root.

It had been a magnificent day. The morning had been so fine that he and Young Whortle Nep had decided against joining Todkin and Hodge in the field and planned an adventure.

"Warty," as Samuel was fond of calling his friend, was always full of terrific ideas. Last year he had built a raft and together they had sailed it along the ditch, fending off imaginary pirates and monsters from the deep. This year, though, the ditch had dried up and they had been forbidden to sail the raft on the still pool as it was too deep.

Young Whortle was older than Samuel, though not as tall. "Right, Sammy," he had said that morning. "If Jenkin's too busy an' Todders an' Hodge are set on climbin' today, then it be up to us to take what thrills the day has to offer."

So they sat down and thought seriously about what they could do. They had already explored the field this year and the ditch promised little in the way of adventure in its parched state. They had been to the pool once or twice, but Alison Sedge was always there teasing them. Alison Sedge had been declared dangerous territory by them both, so the pool was out of the question, with or without the raft.

While the two friends contemplated the day's destination Young Whortle had raised his head and seen the oaks in the hazy distance.

"Aha!" he cried, jumping to his feet and assuming a triumphant pose. "The oaks, Sammy. We shall quest the oaks and see what secrets they keep." So off they went, passing a dejected Jenkin and waving cheerily to him as they entered the meadow.

Now Samuel shivered. Fear chilled him and his teeth began to chatter.

"Sshh!" whispered Young Whortle close by. "It'll hear you."

What a situation they had landed themselves in. All had been going wonderfully. They had charged through the piles of last year's leaves, which still filled the hollows near the oaks, and had played hide-and-seek behind the roots; then Young Whortle had suggested that they attempt a climb.

"Don't go frettin', Sammy," he had said. "We won't pick a difficult tree and we won't go too high—promise."

"But, Warty," Samuel had protested, "shouldn't we be getting along now?"

"Bags of time yet! Sun ain't low enough to think on going back. Come on, give us a leg up."

So up an oak tree they had climbed. It was gnarled, knobbly, and ideal to climb. Footholds were plentiful and there were lots of low branches to run along and swing from.

Then Samuel had noticed the hole.

"What's that up there?" he had asked, pointing higher up the tree trunk. "Looks like some sort of big gap in the bark."

Higher they had clambered. Samuel had been determined not to look down and had kept his eyes strictly on his paws. Eventually, Young Whortle had drawn near to the hole.

"Seems like the tree's hollow here," he had called down.

"Wait for me!" Samuel had pulled himself up to his friend's side. Together they had peeped over the brink of the hole.

Inside all had been dark . . . but their sharp eyes had picked out something in the gloom. Something terrible . . .

Samuel shrieked and nearly fell off the tree. Young Whortle's eyes opened very wide and he gave a funny sort of yelp. Here, in the oak, was the frightful thing that had kept the fieldmice below ground this year—a large and very fearsome barn owl.

It was fast asleep amongst some old straw, but it stirred when the mice gasped in fright. Lazily it opened one eye and puffed out its soft feathery chest.

Quickly Young Whortle and Samuel ran down the tree. They slid and slithered, scraped their knees and broke the skin on their paws scurrying down it.

As Young Whortle jumped from the lowest branch a great

shadow fell on him. Quickly he yanked Samuel to the ground and ducked under one of the roots.

Seconds later sharp talons scored the ground where they had been.

Now here they were, two small frightened fieldmice cowering in terror from a dreadful enemy.

"Be it still up there?" asked Samuel in a tiny voice.

"Aye, Sammy, prob'ly sat on one o' them low branches just a-waitin' for us to make a move."

"Oh, Warty, I'm whacked," whimpered Samuel. "It's gettin' so dark now an' I haven't eaten for ages: just listen to my belly!"

"I hear it an' so can the owl most like. Put your paws over it or somethin'."

"I can't! I be starved."

"So be yon owl, Sammy, an' I don't want to be no bird's breakfast."

Samuel tried to control the growls and rumbles coming from his stomach. He was a thin mouse—"too thin," some said. The likes of Alison even called him "skinny Samuel." His mother was most perturbed by his weight, but no matter how much he ate he never got any fatter. " 'Tis his age," Old Todmore said of him. "Too much energy—he'll plump out afore he's wed." Now the thought that he would make a poor breakfast brought Samuel no comfort at all.

"We can't stay here," he said softly.

Young Whortle patted his friend on the shoulder. "Right," he said decisively. "I got me an idea."

"Smashin'!" Samuel brightened instantly. "I knowed you'd think o' somethin'. What be the plan?"

"Well," Young Whortle kept his voice low in case the owl was listening, "if I throws a stone yonder," he pointed behind them to a patch of ferns and bracken, "it just might fool Hooty up there an' distract him long enough for us to make a dash for them hollows full o' leaves."

"You're barmy!" exclaimed Samuel. "No way will that work. He's crafty he is. He'll spot that trick for sure an' we'll be runnin' straight down his gizzard."

Young Whortle said nothing. Instead he picked up a good paw-sized pebble and threw it for all he was worth. The ferns rustled and swayed as it crashed through them.

"Now!" he hissed, grabbing Samuel by the arm.

The fieldmice darted from under the root. Samuel ran as fast as he could, too terrified to look up in case he saw the owl rushing down to meet them—talons outstretched.

And then they were at the edge of the hollows, and with one leap they dived into the heaps of dry leaves.

"It worked!" Samuel cried. His heart was racing and his ears flushed with excitement.

"I told 'ee we'd have adventures today," said Young Whortle. "Now we'll have to be careful. He won't have liked that trick and it might make him anxious to get us."

"So what now?"

"We tunnel through these here leaves till we're at the point closest to the meadow. Then you just run like crazy."

Samuel gulped nervously, but their first success at owl-foxing heartened him. "Lead on, then," he said.

In the leaves it was easy to believe that it was autumn again. The smell of the dry decay was the very essence of that season. The leaves crackled over and beneath them as they pushed their way through. The sound filled their ears, like the noise of a greedy consuming fire. The mice moved quickly. Like moles they scooped the leaves out of the way with their paws and kicked them backward with their feet. Through the leafy ceiling the owl could be heard hooting irritably. It froze their hearts and made them move faster than ever.

Suddenly there was an explosion of leaves and twilight shone down on them.

"He's dive-bombing us," wailed Samuel. He looked up and

could see the owl soaring above, gaining height for the next dive.

"We'll have to zigzag and hope he misses us," shouted Young Whortle, burying himself in the leaves once more.

Samuel jumped in after him, and they madly dashed from side to side.

The owl tore into the leaves close by and gave an angry hoot at finding his talons empty. "Hooo mooouses, I'll get yoooou!" he bellowed furiously. The owl beat his great wings fiercely and rose high above the treetops. He stared with his great round eyes at the leafy hollow and glided on the night airs, silent as a ghost. There—a movement.

He dropped like a stone. With murderous intent he descended. He'd show them! How dare they wake him then hide and play silly tricks.

The owl skimmed the surface of the hollow with his talons, churning up leaves and twigs in the chaos of his wake.

Samuel and Young Whortle had managed to dodge that onslaught—but only just. Samuel lost the tip of his tail and the pain was terrible. Blood poured out of it and made him feel sick.

Young Whortle was near to panic himself. Both mice were tired now, but the owl had been asleep all day. Young Whortle wished they had stayed under that oak root after all. Even in the dim light he saw how pale Samuel had become, and in horror he noticed his friend's wounded tail. He knew then that they would not survive the next attack; they were exposed and too tired to move fast enough.

An insane idea gripped him suddenly and in a wild frenzy Young Whortle scrabbled amongst the muck of the floor until he found a stout twig.

Samuel was too groggy and near to fainting to question his friend. He watched Young Whortle bite the twig and strip away the bark with his teeth, gnawing like a demented demon. Then high above he saw the dark sinister shape of the owl plummeting toward them.

The owl had licked the blood from his talons and was cackling to himself, eager for the kill. The blood was warm and it tasted wonderful. The first mouse of the night was always the best and he had been unable to find any for months. But now, oho! Two lovely mice for him to swallow.

The cool night air streamed over his flat face as he hurtled down, legs stiff and talons glinting under the light of the first stars.

He had them in his sights—wise of them to stop running. "Ooooh mooouses." He chuckled, licking his beak in anticipation.

"FENNY!" bawled a voice. The owl blinked, and as he bore down on the mice one of them jumped up and drove something sharp into his left leg.

"Ooooww!" screeched the owl, floundering in the air with the shock. He rose up, shaking his head in disbelief. How dare they! The audacity of it! The owl was really furious now. Screaming with rage, he plucked the twig from his leg with one deft movement, spat it out, and glared down. This was serious; insult and injury—that had never happened to him before and he was deadly in his wrath.

"Mooouses!" he cried in a bitter cold voice. "Mahooot will find yooou!"

Young Whortle had wasted no time. As soon as he had wounded the owl he had dragged the wilting Samuel out of the hollow and pulled him toward the meadow.

How they managed he never knew. Samuel had lost a lot of blood and kept swooning. But fear kept them going and suddenly they were in.

Tall grasses surrounded them. Young Whortle knew, however, that it would take more protection than the meadow afforded to save them from a determined owl.

Samuel panted heavily. He felt very weak and his legs were like water. He tried to focus his eyes, but everything was blurred. Young Whortle's voice came to him urgently, calling his name.

"Sammy! Come on, we've made it to the meadow, but Hooty's still after us."

As if in agreement, a frightful screech came down out of the night sky.

Samuel felt himself tugged at roughly. "Leave me, Warty," he mumbled. "Too tired, you go."

"Shut up!" Young Whortle gripped his friend none too gently and shoved him farther into the meadow.

They stumbled and staggered along, flinging themselves to the ground when they felt a shadow pass overhead.

"What's he doing?" Young Whortle asked himself. "Why doesn't he strike? He must know where we are. Why doesn't he get it over with?"

A wicked cackle told him the reason. The owl was tormenting them, letting them know the full meaning of fear before the kill.

"Mooouses," he called, "Mahooot sees yoooou." A dark wing swept over the tops of the grass.

Young Whortle bowed his head in defeat. He could run no more and even if he could the owl would snatch him before he made it to the ditch. The dark wing soared over again; this time battering down the grass.

Next time, thought Young Whortle desperately. "This is it, Sammy," he said, "I'm sorry this adventure has ended so badly."

Samuel shook his head feebly. "Not your fault, Warty." He held out a thin, trembling paw and Young Whortle clasped it tightly. Together they waited for the end.

Down came Mahooot, the owl. He smashed through the

grass and landed in front of the fieldmice.

"Ohooo, mooouses!" he said wickedly, narrowing his baleful, round, tawny eyes into evil slits. "Piece by piece will yooou slide dooown." He stepped nearer and opened his sharp beak. "Mahooot learn yooou tooo behave."

The owl shot out a talon and grasped Young Whortle by the shoulder. The small mouse squealed in pain as Mahooot drew him near to his waiting beak.

Samuel felt his friend's paw being dragged out of his own, but he was too far gone to be frightened of the sinister night bird about to feast on them.

Young Whortle saw through his tears the ghastly beak open. He felt the iron grip of the talons squeeze even tighter. The musty breath of the bird swept over him and he swooned. Mahooot sniggered. He was about to pop the fieldmouse's head into his beak when . . .

"Aiee! Aiee!" screamed a strange voice. "Aiee!"

Mahooot blinked and glanced up. Who was that disturbing his breakfast? The owl swiveled his face around but could see nothing. He grunted irritably and turned his attention back to the mouse.

"Aiee!" A stone came flying out of nowhere and stung Mahooot right on the beak.

"Whoooo? Whooo?" he began ferociously. He unfurled his wings but kept a tight hold on Young Whortle.

Great clumping footsteps came rushing toward them. Mahooot twitched with uncertainty—he would take to the air and see who this intruder was. His wings opened out and he began to flap them. He decided to leave the thin mouse behind, this one would do, he could eat it at his leisure in the oak tree.

"Aiee, beaky hooter!" came the voice. "Put down the mouselet!" Into view, crashing through the meadow, came a large ratwoman with a shawl around her shoulders and a bone in her hair. It was Madame Akkikuyu.

Mahooot eyed her doubtfully and rose into the air; he didn't like rats.

"Help!" squeaked Young Whortle, dangling from his talons.

The rat leaped up and grabbed the owl's other leg, bringing him sprawling to the ground with an astounded screech.

Madame Akkikuyu hopped onto Mahooot's back and dealt him a great thump with the bone from her hair. "Let go, feathery one, free mouselet."

The owl twisted under her and scrabbled at the ground in a bewildered frenzy. Another *thwack* hit his head. "Oooow!" he roared.

Madame Akkikuyu laughed out loud, then thrust the bone back in her hair and proceeded to pluck the owl.

Mahooot's screeches were deafening, and he turned his head to snap at the rat.

"Oh no, fowl one." She laughed, giving the slashing beak a swift smack with her claws.

Clouds of soft, pale feathers floated into the air as the raw bare patch on Mahooot's neck grew larger. Madame Akkikuyu began to hoot herself, mocking him as she tore out large clumps of feathers and threw them before the owl for him to see.

Suddenly Young Whortle was free. The talons opened and he staggered over to Samuel, where he fell unconscious.

Mahooot writhed and managed to scramble upright. Madame Akkikuyu clenched her claw and gave him a powerful punch. He staggered backward and she flung her arms around his neck and bit deeply into his shoulder.

That was enough for him. The owl let out one last hoot of pain, shook the rat off his back, and rose shakily off the ground—but not before a hail of stones and twigs battered him as Madame Akkikuyu jumped up and down with glee below.

"Scardee Birdee!" she shouted, sticking out her tongue at the receding dark shape in the sky. The fortune-teller smiled,

then rushed over to the fieldmice and inspected their wounds. "Poor mouseys," she cooed sadly, "very bad they are." She fumbled in one of the pouches that hung around her waist and brought out a broad-leafed herb. With it she dabbed Young Whortle's punctured shoulder and then with some more, bound Samuel's mutilated tail.

Madame Akkikuyu stepped back and sat down with a bump. How had she known what to do? She looked into her pouches and knew the properties of all the herbs in it–most of them were deadly. "Oh, Akkikuyu," she gasped breathlessly. "What memories are you waking?" She looked at Samuel's tail and it seemed to dissolve away, and in its place was a rough rat's tail, stumpy and with an old rag tied at the end. From out of the past a coarse voice said, "Just don't get in my way, witch!"

Madame Akkikuyu shuddered and all her instincts told her not to delve into her past too deeply. Yet she began to wonder, just who was she and why did she carry all these weird objects and powders around with her?

A sound from the real world reached her ears and she broke out of her brooding. The others were coming; already she could see the torches flickering. Silently she waited for them and reflected on the past days.

*   *   *

The journey to Fennywolde had been uneventful, but it had been so wonderful to be with her friend Audrey, to know that they were going somewhere pleasant in the sunshine. She had not stopped counting her blessings and hugged herself with pleasure.

It had taken three different boats to get this far, and Mr. Kempe had guided them all the way. He had been a little stand-offish to her, but she was very grateful to him for taking the trouble to lead them here. This afternoon they had all waved good-bye to him and set foot on dry land once more. From there that funny little fieldmouse, Twit, had led them, pointing out local features and telling amusing stories. Madame Akkikuyu had reveled in the company of her friends. They turned from the river and followed a little stream, which divided and became several small brooks. The one they followed soon became a dry ditch. There they found a crowd of worried-looking mice staring across a meadow.

Someone had gone to fetch Twit's parents and they nearly hugged the breath clear out of him when they saw him. But the celebration had been short-lived. An owl screeched over the meadow and all the mice gasped; some had tears in their eyes. It was explained that two youngsters were missing. Akkikuyu saw the owl circling and knew it was about to strike. To everyone's astonishment she had dropped her bags and stormed into the meadow, calling out a challenge. Yes, what a day it had been—if only the nights were as good. She had come to dread the empty darkness and the fear it brought her.

"Over here!" came the babble of voices. Madame Akkikuyu wrenched herself back to the present and got to her feet.

The meadow was lit by little burning torches carried by a host of fieldmice. They hurried toward her and she threw open her arms in welcome. The mice came and stared at the scene before them with open mouths.

There were the two youngsters lying, dead for all they knew, on the ground, and the peculiar ratwoman was boldly waving her arms about. Covering everything was a layer of downy feathers like a light fall of snow. They gazed at Madame Akkikuyu dumbly, not knowing what to do.

Mrs. Gorse pushed her way to the front and ran to her son's side. She wept over his damaged tail and kissed his forehead.

"He need rest," advised the fortune-teller. "I make broth to heal tomorrow."

Young Whortle's parents came squeezing out of the crowd

101

and knelt beside their son. Slowly his eyes opened and he managed a weak smile for them. Then he lifted a finger and pointed at the rat.

"She saved us, Dad," he said. "Saved us from the owl she did."

"Thank you," said Mr. Nep gratefully to Madame Akkikuyu.

The crowd cheered until she flushed with pleasure. Then to her great surprise and enduring delight, they picked her up and carried her on their shoulders, although it took eight of the strongest husbands to manage this feat. Others helped to take Young Whortle and Samuel back to the winter quarters.

Arthur and Audrey could not believe their eyes. Here they were, newly arrived in Fennywolde and Madame Akkikuyu was being feted as a heroine. Everything was happening so quickly. They hadn't had a chance to meet Twit's parents yet.

Arthur stood amongst the feathers and shrugged. "I'd never have believed it," he said flatly.

"She is remarkable," said a voice behind them. They turned around and saw a fieldmouse sticking a feather in his hair. "Even my father approved of her," he added. "Oh, sorry, my name's Jenkin. You're the ones who came back with Twit, aren't you?"

"Yes," replied Audrey. She liked the look of this mouse and he had been the first one in Fennywolde to speak to them so far. "I'm Audrey and this is my brother, Arthur. What's been going on here?"

"Oh, an owl's kept us in our winter quarters all year. We daren't go out at night coz he'd catch us an' eat us. But it looks like we've done seen the last of him for a while." Jenkin beamed at them and Audrey noticed an ugly bruise on his ear and that his lip was badly swollen.

"You've been in a fight," she said to him.

Jenkin turned quickly away and said, "We better get goin'– the others are nearly home now." The rows of bobbing torches had dwindled in the distance. "Follow me," he told them, and set off back to the ditch.

"You embarrassed him," Arthur hissed at Audrey, "Why can't you mind your own business?"

"Why should it have embarrassed him?" protested Audrey. "I shouldn't think he's trying to keep the fact a secret. Did you see the state of his bruises?"

"Yes, I did, but I've had worse. Anyway, we must follow him now, I don't want to spend our first night here tramping through the fields lost. Come on."

At the ditch, the fieldmice put Madame Akkikuyu down and the husbands wiped their brows wearily. The fortune-teller gazed about her, enraptured. She could not remember ever feeling like this before—she wanted to burst with joy.

By the time Arthur and Audrey arrived she was speaking: "Owly not come back in hurry, if he do—Akkikuyu bite him again."

There was thunderous applause and some mice cried, "We can move into the field at last!" and "Hooray for the ratlady!"

Then other voices called, "Where be Mr. Woodruffe? He's got to declare the field open." The mice looked at one another and muttered agreement. Hastily a young mouse ran into the shelters to fetch him.

At the Spring Ceremony every year the fieldmice elected a "King of the Field." This year the honor had gone to Mr. Abraham Woodruffe—a well-liked and respected mouse who so far had been unable to enjoy his high office, being stuck in the winter quarters all the time.

The mice waited for him and excited expectation charged the cool night air. Audrey and Arthur sensed their mood and they too grew impatient. Audrey began to fidget and started to look around at the fieldmice. It was the first chance she had had so far to view them properly. There were fat mice, thin mice, some tiny ones with large pink ears and long twitchy tails but no tall mice. Except perhaps . . . yes, on the far side of the crowd Audrey saw a lofty mouse. She stared at him curiously: what a grim face he had! It seemed as if his face never saw a smile. Idly she wondered who he was and then, next to him, she noticed Jenkin, who to her surprise and lasting embarrassment was looking straight at her. Audrey coughed and turned quickly away. She felt her ears burn with her blushes and hoped it would not show under the torchlight.

Audrey tried to compose herself and gazed fixedly ahead, hoping that her ribbon was tied properly. However, she could not resist having a crafty peep around to see if Jenkin was still looking at her.

As casually as she could manage, Audrey turned, but Jenkin was speaking with that tall mouse now. She was amused to find that she was disappointed, and smiled broadly at herself until she saw something that made her cough and turn away again.

A girl mouse was glaring at her–glaring with real hatred in her eyes. Audrey could feel them boring into the back of her neck. She could not think who the girl was and asked herself if she had done anything to deserve it.

"Oh, what the heck!" she said to herself in a low determined whisper and looked back at the girl. Alison Sedge was still eyeing Audrey with a face like thunder. Their eyes met and Miss Brown gave her her most insolent, pretty smile, then turned away.

Suddenly a hush fell on the gathered fieldmice as Mr. Woodruffe stepped out of the winter quarters. He was a jovial mouse and seemed quite ordinary except that on his brow he wore a crown of plaited corn. Mr. Woodruffe raised his paws and began solemnly.

"May the field be blessed and may the goodwill of the Green Mouse follow us therein."

"Amen to that!" called out Isaac Nettle, but he was drowned out by the frantic cheers of everyone else.

Mr. Woodruffe waved his arms for silence and continued. "I have been told of the daring bravery shown 'ere by our guest." He bowed to Madame Akkikuyu. She pointed her foot and managed a curtsy back. "And as 'King of the Field,'" he went on, "it is my pleasure to offer her the freedom of Fennywolde, for surely she is a messenger of the Green Mouse come in our most desperate hour."

There were shouts of agreement from the fieldmice. Arthur and Audrey stared at each other. Isaac Nettle nodded his head gravely.

"And now," shouted Mr. Woodruffe, "you may all enter the field!" He stood aside and the fieldmice scurried past him.

"Make the Hall," they yelled happily.

Soon only Mr. Woodruffe, Madame Akkikuyu, Audrey, and Arthur were left standing by the ditch, and the field was filled was joyous calls and mysterious sounds.

Mr. Woodruffe looked at the Deptford mice and smiled. "So you are Twit's companions. Come, he is below with his folks. I think we can interrupt them now. You look like you could do with a good sleep. The field is no place for you tonight. The work would keep you awake."

"Please, sir," Arthur asked, "what work?"

"Hah, you'll see tomorrow, lad." Mr. Woodruffe turned to Madame Akkikuyu and raised his eyebrows. "Will you join us below, ma'am? We would be most honored."

The fortune-teller grinned at him and came over to give Audrey a big hug.

"Yes, Akkikuyu come, she not leave her friend. First Akkikuyu find bags. You go, I follow."

The three mice left the rat to find her things and entered the winter quarters.

Madame Akkikuyu was left alone in the dark. In her mind she relived the thrilling moments of glory, and the thrill that those cheers gave her. What undreamed wonders there were in the world and how her heart swelled with pride to think that all these mice honored her!

As a tear fell from her furry cheek, Madame Akkikuyu knew that she had never been so happy before. Tonight, she thought, would be a good time to die, while she was happiest. The fortune-teller sniffed. No, with her friend there would be many more times such as this—if not greater. Madame Akkikuyu blew her nose on her shawl, then cast about for her bags.

It was too dark to see them. The sky had clouded over and the moon was hidden. She stooped down and groped for her things. It was so quiet. The noise of the mice in the field had died down or they had moved farther away, out of earshot.

"Akkikuyu!"

Madame Akkikuyu paused and tilted her head to one side.

"Akkikuyu!"

There it was again. A distant, echoing voice calling her name. It had troubled her on the river but no one else seemed to have heard it. Madame Akkikuyu despaired. Tearing at her hair, she shook her head violently. "Leave me!" she wailed. "Go away. Akkikuyu not listen!" And she ran up the side of the ditch and down into the shelters.

CHAPTER SEVEN

THE HALL OF CORN

The sun brimmed over the tops of the oak trees and its dazzling, early rays moved slowly over the meadow, pushing back the gray dawn and creeping toward the field. The corn seemed to stir at the sun's warm touch and stretched as high as it could. Fennywolde awoke.

Audrey rubbed her eyes and gazed sleepily at the low, rough ceiling. She was in a small room in the winter quarters, that part lived in by the Scuttles. The room was bare—there was no decoration on the lumpy earth walls, no flowers, drawings, ornaments—nothing. Only a small tallow candle flickered miserably in one corner and Audrey looked at it thoughtfully. She was sure she had blown that out before she had gone to sleep. Someone must have been in to relight it. Yes, on the floor near her bed was a bowl of water for her to wash in. That was a kind thought and one which Audrey felt she needed.

She dragged herself out of bed and began splashing the drowsiness and grime of the past few days away.

"Is that you awake now, Audrey?" came a friendly voice just

outside the room. "Well, breakfast's ready when you are."

Audrey finished dressing and smoothed the creases out of her lace. She tied a new ribbon in her hair—a parting gift from Kempe, then she slipped her bells onto her tail and went into the breakfast room.

Again it was bleak and bare with only a table in the center and three stools around it. Mrs. Scuttle pattered in carrying a bowl of porridge.

Audrey and Arthur had been surprised when they first saw Mrs. Chitter's sister. She wasn't a bit like that gossipy old fusspot. Gladwin Scuttle was a brown housemouse, as they were. She was slender with short chestnut hair, graying at the crown, and a thin, delicate face. Around her neck she wore a prim starched collar. Audrey thought that she must have been quite lovely when she was younger.

"Where's my brother and Twit?" asked Audrey between mouthfuls.

"Gone out with Elijah," replied Mrs. Scuttle, settling down on a stool and beaming warmly. "Oh, and your . . . er . . . friend, Madame—what was it?"

"Akkikuyu," prompted Audrey, "but she's not exactly my friend, you know."

"Well, I did wonder. I came from Deptford too, remember, and I know how horrible the rats were there. I'd watch her if I were you, wouldn't trust her an inch despite her doings last night."

Audrey wondered about that. "That's what Kempe said, but you know I really do think she's changed. She really is trying her best."

"Hmm," Mrs. Scuttle sounded doubtful. "Still, I suppose I shouldn't judge her too harshly. My William's been telling me all about you and her and . . . ," here she lowered her voice to a faint whisper, " . . . Jupiter."

"Please," begged Audrey, "you mustn't mention that name

108

to Madame Akkikuyu. She can't remember a thing and it might just be too much for her."

"Oh quite, dear . . . I can keep mum. I don't suppose my sister has learned how yet–no, your smile gives that away. So, Arabel's not changed a bit, I thought William was being too polite when I asked him about her. Still it was good of her to look after him all this time."

Audrey finished her breakfast and then said, "You never did tell me where Madame Akkikuyu had gone."

"Oh yes, why there I go again–forgetting things. I tell you, dear, my head's like a sieve these days. Oh . . . where was I?"

"Madame Akkikuyu."

"Yes, such an odd name. Well, you should have seen how much she ate this morning, and I'm sorry, but her table manners are dreadful. Anyway, after making a right mess she ups and goes outside hauling one of those big bags with her. What does she keep in them, do you know?"

Audrey nodded. "They're her herbs, powders, mixing tins, and other stuff like that."

"Well. William did tell me how she's supposed to be a fortune-teller, I didn't like to ask her myself–I find that sort of thing very frightening."

"Oh, it's all right," assured Audrey. "She doesn't do any of that anymore. I think she just carries that junk around with her out of habit. You don't have to worry, she's not likely to start brewing up spells now."

Mrs. Scuttle put her paws on the table and stared at Audrey. "But my dear! That's precisely what she is doing. That's where everyone's gone. She's making a healing broth, so she says–for Young Whortle Nep and Samuel Gorse."

"What!" spluttered Audrey, aghast. "But she doesn't know how. She'll probably poison them with what's in those bags of hers." She jumped up from the table and ran out of the Scuttles' rooms.

The winter quarters were a series of drab tunnels with family rooms leading off the main passages. There was no decoration anywhere, just the dismal tallow candles flickering on the walls. Up the tunnel Audrey hurried and sped out into the fresh air.

She followed the sound of voices and ran along the top of the ditch overlooking the bare stony stretch. There were all the fieldmice and in the center was Madame Akkikuyu.

Her brewing pot was over a crackling fire and she stirred the bubbling contents with the bone from her hair. Occasionally she delved into one of her pouches and threw some leaves in the boiling mixture.

The fieldmice watched her with keen interest and admiration. Audrey spotted Arthur and Twit and pushed past the others to reach them.

"Mornin', Audrey," greeted Twit brightly.

"Hello," she mumbled. "Arthur, what do you think you're doing letting her do this? It's bound to be poisonous."

"What am I supposed to do?" asked Arthur crossly. "She'd already started by the time we got here."

"But she might poison one of those boys," Audrey said. "I can't let her carry on." She forced her way through the fieldmice to the front.

"My," whistled Twit, "your Audrey ain't one for standin' by."

"That's what worries me," said Arthur.

Audrey went to the fortune-teller's side and tugged her elbow fiercely.

"Mouselet!" cried the rat gleefully. "You sleep well, yes? Akkikuyu look in on you before she go. You sleep like twig." She put her arm around the mouse and Audrey squirmed.

"What are you doing?" she asked. "You don't know what those herbs and powders are for."

Madame Akkikuyu gave a deep fruity laugh. "But, my mouselet, Akkikuyu remember now—leaves make you better, heal wounds. They strong nature magic."

110

"But they're poisonous," hissed Audrey.

"No, no," tutted the fortune-teller, "some leaves bad, yes, Akkikuyu chuck them, she knows those that heal." She gave the potion one last stir and declared to the fieldmice, "Is ready, come–take to the poorly little ones."

Mrs. Gorse stepped forward and looked apprehensively at the steaming thick broth bubbling away in the pot.

"Come, come," encouraged the rat, beckoning with her claws.

Mrs. Gorse held out a wooden bowl and Madame Akkikuyu scooped some of the potion into it.

"Take to boy, make him drink all. He get better soon."

Audrey rushed over to Mrs. Gorse. "Don't take it to him," she implored, and a murmur of surprise rippled through the fieldmice. "Madame Akkikuyu isn't well herself. She doesn't know what she's put in there, it might make your son worse."

Mrs. Gorse blinked and regarded the bowl with suspicion. The crowd muttered and stirred uneasily.

"Mouselet!" exclaimed the fortune-teller in a shocked tone. "Why you say such fibs? Akkikuyu knows–she not moon calf. Potion good–take to boy," she insisted.

"Well," began Mrs. Gorse uncertainly.

"See," cried Madame Akkikuyu, and she took the bowl from her and drank down the whole lot.

The crowd fell silent and stared at her wide-eyed.

Madame Akkikuyu swilled some of the potion around in her mouth before swallowing. She knitted her brows and Audrey looked up at her, fearfully expecting the rat to keel over or for her claws to drop out. The fortune-teller licked her lips and simply said, "Need salt." She sprinkled some into the pot.

That was enough for the fieldmice. They broke out into a peal of applause.

"But that doesn't prove anything," Audrey tried to make herself heard.

Mrs. Gorse took the bowl again and filled it herself. "Listen, young lady," she said to Audrey, "this Madame Akkikookoo saved my Samuel last night and that's good enough for me. It's wicked of you to say such things about her."

Audrey was speechless. It was no use. Mr. Nep came forward and took a bowl for Young Whortle, giving her a very disagreeable look in the process.

"This potion keep," shouted Madame Akkikuyu. "If mouseys seal it in jar, potion last till spring."

"My Nelly's got jars," said Mr. Nep. "You come with me, missus, we'll see to our boy then root some out for 'ee."

The crowd cheered as Madame Akkikuyu followed Mr. Nep to the shelters. The rat waved regally as she passed by. As the fieldmice dispersed and went into the field, Arthur and Twit came over to Audrey. Arthur was shaking his head.

"A right idiot you made of yourself there, you soft lump," he said. "I've never seen anyone make such an ass of themselves before."

"Stow it, Arthur." Audrey was in no mood for brotherly criticism.

"Never mind," piped up Twit. "Maybe Young Whortle and Sammy will get better."

"I wouldn't bet on it," said Audrey. "They can't say I didn't try and warn them, can they?"

"Aye." Twit laughed. "But you made a right pig's ear of it."

Audrey could never be angry with Twit and she sighed loudly. "Oh, you're right, both of you. What a fool I must have looked to them." She laughed at the thought of it. "Oh, well, what shall we do now?"

"There's the Hall to see," Twit said. "They've been at it all night—me dad's gone to see it already."

"The Hall?" asked Audrey mildly. "What's that?"

"Oh, you'll see soon enough." Twit chuckled, leading them away from the edge of the ditch and into the field.

*   *   *

Jenkin held tightly to the cornstalk. He could see Todkin a little farther away and behind he heard Figgy humming to himself. Jenkin waved at Todkin and a little paw was raised in answer.

"Jenkin," a familiar voice called up to him. He looked down and on the ground below, Alison Sedge was peering up at him with a paw shielding her eyes from the sun.

"What you wantin'?" he shouted down to her.

"To talk to 'ee," she answered. "Come down—me neck's startin' to ache."

"Darn her," grumbled Jenkin as he nimbly descended the stalk. It was the only free day he had had for weeks. His father had told him to celebrate the Green Mouse's bounty in the field and he was only too happy to do so. He did not want to waste his time with Alison Sedge.

She waited patiently at the base of the stalk for him and twisted her hair coyly. Suddenly Jenkin was at her side. "Mornin'," she said.

"Don't tell me that's all you wanted to say, Alison Sedge," he puffed.

"No, just bein' p'lite that's all," she told him sniffily. "'Ere, what you got that feather in your hair for, Jenkin Nettle?" She reached over to pull it out. "Let me put it in mine—suit me better."

He stepped quickly aside. "You go pick yourself another flower," he said, irritated. "This is my good-luck charm, this is."

"Luck is it?" she asked in surprise. "What does your dad say to that?"

"Nothin', cause I ain't told him and don't you either." He licked his sore lip and Alison had enough tact to change the subject.

"What I really come to tell 'ee is about the ratwoman and the girl that came with her."

"Oh yes?" Jenkin tried to disguise his interest.

"Had a right old dingdong, they just did. There was that Mrs. Akky Yakky a-makin' a potion to heal Young Whortle and Skinny Samuel when that girl comes bargin' up and rants on about it bein' poison."

"Was it?"

"No, she's barmy." Alison sniggered. "That rat up an' drank some an' she didn't snuff it. Made that town mouse look real daft, she did."

Jenkin looked past her, and curious, Alison turned around. Toward them came Arthur, Twit, and Audrey. "Well, here she is herself," said Jenkin. "Shall I ask her if she is potty for you?"

"Pah," said Alison, tossing her head. "I ain't stayin' to talk to no loony. I'm goin' to meet Hodge—see if he wants to come to the meadow with me."

"Suit yourself." Jenkin grinned as she hastily departed.

Arthur and Audrey had never been in a cornfield before. They gazed about them with great interest. It was like a thick, dense wood of stalks. If the fieldmice had not made pathways they would have had to struggle and fight their way through like explorers in a jungle. They craned their necks to see the tops of the stems where the young ears waved gently in the breeze. Bright red poppies were tangled in the field and Audrey gaped in wonder at the gorgeous flaming flowers. It was a more beautiful place than she had expected.

"Look," said Twit presently, "there's Jenkin. Hoy there, Jolly Jenkin!"

"How do," he said shyly with his eyes on the ground. "Where you goin' then, Twit?"

"Arthur and Audrey ain't seen the Hall yet," Twit replied. "I was jus' takin' 'em there. You on sentry, Jenkin?"

"Sentry?" asked Arthur.

"We don't leave the field unguarded once the Hall's been done," said Twit. "There's a great ring of lads circling the Hall keepin' a look out for enemies."

114

"Where?" put in Audrey. "I haven't seen anyone so far."

"Hah, miss." Jenkin laughed. "You ain't been lookin' proper." He pointed upward. "How's things, Figgy?"

"Fine so far!" came an answering call from above.

"There's someone up there!" gasped Arthur. "He's at the very top of the stalk."

"Where else would you sentry from?" asked Jenkin, highly amused.

"I'd love to do that," Arthur said as he stared upward.

"Have a go, then," urged Jenkin.

"Old Arthur won't make it," tittered Twit, "not with his tummy."

"Huh!" snorted Arthur, stepping up to the nearest stalk. He hesitated. Now that he had to climb it, the stalk did seem very high.

"Go on, then," encouraged Jenkin, "ignore Twit."

Arthur frowned and breathed deeply. Then, with a loud grunt, he jumped up and grasped the stem with his paws. He dangled in the air like a caught fish, winning another giggle from Twit. Arthur tried to climb, passing paw over paw. The stalk wobbled and swayed treacherously.

"Wrap your tail around it," advised Jenkin.

Arthur tried, but once his tail had gripped the stalk it refused to budge anymore.

"I'm stuck," he cried, and with a thud he fell to the ground.

Twit rolled around, his sides aching. Even Audrey laughed and Arthur glared at them both—after he had shaken some of the dust out of his fur.

"Shall we show you how it's done?" offered Jenkin. "Twit?"

Twit wiped the tears from his eyes and stood beneath the stalk Arthur had tried to climb. "Ready?" he asked Jenkin.

Jenkin, standing under another stalk, nodded. "First to the top," he said. "Say when, miss."

Audrey counted them down. "Three, two, one—go."

115

The fieldmice shot up the corn as if they had wings. Their legs and paws were a blur and their tails spiraled around the stems faster than anything she had seen. It was Jenkin who won—just a second before Twit.

"Beat you at last." He waved triumphantly.

"I be out of practice," panted Twit, "this time next week I'll leave you standin'."

Arthur regarded them enviously, wishing he could do half as well. Jenkin slid down quickly, eyed Audrey bashfully, then said to Arthur, "Don't worry—you'll soon learn. Come see me after you've been to the Hall if you're willin' an' we'll get you up a stalk afore the end of the day."

"If only I could," Arthur sighed in disbelief.

"Anyway, you best get goin'," said Jenkin, "soonest there, sooner you can come back." He looked up, Twit was still enjoying being at the top of the corn. "Been a long time since he sat up on sentry," murmured Jenkin. "Thought he were dead, you know—we all did. He's a good bloke, but a bit simple."

"He doesn't get into fights," remarked Audrey sternly, "and I bet he's done more in his life than you ever will."

"Never said he hadn't!" Jenkin refused to be provoked. "All I'm sayin' is, there's some in Fennywolde who don't respect the Scuttles—say Twit's a dimmy and more besides. Not me—I like him. I reckon he's too good-natured, though. Folk take advantage and think he's daft. That's all."

"I think," said Arthur breaking in, "that one day Twit might get pressed too hard, and he may surprise a few around here if that kind nature of his snaps."

Twit slid down the stalk. "Oooh, that did me good," he said, beaming from ear to ear. "Ain't nothin' like it for blowin' the cobwebs away. You ready to see the Hall now? Come on, then."

They left Jenkin behind and he flashed up his stalk and resumed his sentry duty.

Deeper into the field went the three friends until the dense

116

corn around them began to thin out more considerably and appeared to form a corridor, the ceiling of which was made by twisting together the ears of corn from opposite "walls." It began to look very grand and imposing.

"This be the main way to the Hall," Twit informed them in a hushed, reverent tone. "This be what they all were doin' last night."

"It's very clever," remarked Arthur.

Twit chuckled. "Just you wait."

"What's that ahead?" asked Audrey as they turned a corner.

"The great doors," Twit answered.

At the end of the corridor there were two large doors made completely from tightly woven corn stems. They reached up as high as the growing corn itself, and on either side of them were two fieldmice who carried themselves importantly–they were the door guards.

"Mornin', Twit," greeted one of them.

"Hello, Grommel, how've you been keepin'? Your back still playin' you up?"

"Somethin' chronic, Twit lad. These your town friends?"

"Right enough. This here's Audrey Brown and this be her brother, Arthur. I be takin' 'em to see the Hall."

"Then pass, friends," said the door guard, and he stood aside, pushing open one of the large doors.

Audrey and Arthur stepped through and blinked.

The Hall of Corn was immense. It was wide and long, and clumps of corn had been left standing at regular intervals, giving the impression of mighty pillars–but the Hall was open to the sky. At the far end, on a wickerwork throne, sat Mr. Woodruffe–able at last to take up his plaited scepter and govern the Hall as every King of the Field had done since the time of Fenny.

Many fieldmice were bustling about, building large spherical structures halfway up the corn stems.

117

"What are they doing?" asked Arthur.

"They be our summer quarters," replied Twit gleefully. "You never slept till you spent a night in a fieldmouse's nest—not on the ground, but halfway in the sky," he added dreamily.

It certainly was very grand. Audrey was overcome by the industriousness of the Fennywolders. All this had taken only one night to accomplish. She was amazed.

"There's me dad," said Twit suddenly, and he ran over to where Elijah Scuttle was working. He had built a good large nest for him and Mrs. Scuttle and was in the process of completing a slightly smaller one.

"How do, Willum," he nodded to his son. "Thought 'ee an' Master Brown could share a nest."

"Terrific!" said Arthur.

"Don't be doin' it too high, though, Dad." Twit laughed. "Old Arthur can't climb too good."

"Now, now, Willum," chided his father softly. "You knows I do make your mam a straw ladder every year—I'll do 'un for Master Brown too."

Mr. Scuttle was a pleasant fieldmouse. He looked like an older version of his son, except there were creamy whiskers fringing his chops and on his shoulders there were two white scars where no fur would grow. He did, however, have the same mischievous twinkle in his eye.

"And what about you, missey?" Elijah addressed Audrey. "I'm not sure if you want to sleep with your ratty friend."

"Oh no, Mr. Scuttle," gasped Audrey, horrified, until she realized he was teasing her. He grinned and said, "I'll make 'ee a real pirty nest for one, so she can't squeeze in."

"Thank you," said Audrey, greatly relieved. The thought of having to share a nest with Madame Akkikuyu was too terrible even to joke about.

"Look," began Arthur. "I better go back and find that Jenkin chap—I'm not going to be the only boy using a ladder—what would everyone say?"

"I'll come with you, Arthur," said Twit. "I got me some practicin' to do." So the two boys went off, laughing and jostling each other.

Audrey decided not to join them. "Is there anything I can do, Mr. Scuttle?" she asked.

Elijah looked surprised, then pleased. "Aye, missey," he said delighted. "See you over there." He pointed to a pile of moss and soft grass picked early that morning by a robust group of mousewives. "That there," he continued, "is what we do line our nests with—featherin', we calls it. Makes 'em real comfy and soft it do—you could fetch some if you're willin'."

"Certainly," said Audrey. She made her way over to the heap of feathering—although she could see no feathers in it whatsoever.

She passed beneath half-made nests where husbands not as deft as Mr. Scuttle cursed as the weave fell apart. She wanted to learn more of the families who shouted cheerfully to one another from nest to nest and drew the very young children up on straw ropes. Some stout wives who refused to be parted from the bed linen were taking sheets and pillows into the nests with them. Audrey walked by one group of children who were all sitting down, listening with eyes agog and breaths held to an old mouse brindled white with age telling them stories. It was Old Todmore—the storyteller of the field, and today he had a new tale to tell. Most of the children had been in bed the night before so had missed the excitement of Madame Akkikuyu and the owl and were now listening to the story, thrilled and captivated.

"Well, there's poor Young Whortle Nep with this great deadly owl about to chew off his head when crashin' through the meader comes the answer to our prayers—Madame Ak . . . Akky . . .?" Old Todmore was finding it difficult to get his

119

tongue around the fortune-teller's name.

"Stop a-doin' that Abel Madder!" he said, vexed. "Now where was I? Oh, aye, well, crashin' through the meader comes the answer to our prayers–Madame Ratlady."

Audrey did not know whether to be amused or alarmed at how the fieldmice considered Madame Akkikuyu to be their savior. She wondered how those two young mice were faring after drinking that potion.

Finally she reached the heap of feathering and gathered some spongy moss in her arms. Three other girl mice were there doing the same. They smiled at her nervously.

"Hello," said Audrey.

They nodded their heads in reply.

"I'm Audrey Brown," she persisted.

One of the girls who had a mass of coarse, straight red hair said, "You be Twit's friend."

"That's right."

"Saw you last night with another towny."

"That's my brother, Arthur."

"Arthur is it?" cooed one of the others.

"Aye, Dimsel, and only a brother," said the first.

"Tush you," cried the one called Dimsel, nudging her friend.

The girl who had not yet spoken pushed the others aside and said, "How do, Audrey. I be Lily Clover. This one with the nose of a Hogpry be Iris Crowfoot."

"Hogpry yourself," shoved Iris.

"And this be Dimsel Bottom, she's mad keen on your Arthur."

"Oh, Lily!"

"It's true, ain't it?"

"Well!"

Audrey laughed. She liked these three and she wished Dimsel the best of luck concerning her brother. For a while they chatted amiably, then Iris said, "We best be goin', our mams'll take on so if we don't 'ave the featherin' done soon."

As they left Lily turned and asked Audrey, "You met Alison Sedge yet?"

"No—I don't think so."

"Well you just mind when you do—got claws has our Alison." Lily cast a lazy, lingering eye over Audrey's ribbon and lace before she said, "Aye, you watch out, me dear." And with that she left.

Audrey wandered back to Mr. Scuttle. He had started work on her nest now and he called down to her.

"Leave it down there, missey, if'n you're not sure of your stalk paws yet."

Audrey waved to him, then fetched some more.

The morning turned into lunchtime and merry wives brought out cheese and hot fresh bread for their hardworking husbands.

Gladwin Scuttle appeared with her arms laden and Arthur and Twit were following eagerly. They sat down and munched happily, Mr. Scuttle swilling down the bread, which stuck in his throat, with some blackberry ferment and telling his wife how he was progressing. It was hot work and he was glad of the rest. He sat with his back to a stalk, his ears beetroot red.

Mrs. Scuttle passed a critical eye over her bedroom for the summer and nodded satisfactorily, then told her husband to help some of the others she had seen whose attempts at nest building were pitiful.

"Ah," said Elijah, "Josiah Down won't never learn if'n I always do it fer 'im. Never has patience with the framework, that's what does it."

"Well," tutted Gladwin, "I passed Mrs. Down just now and she did ask me to mention it to you."

"Reckon I'll pop over later on," he promised.

All around, the light, happy sound of fieldmice talking,

relaxing, eating, and laughing filled the air. Audrey lay on her side and watched the inhabitants of Fennywolde content in their element. The Hall of Corn was near to completion. Nearly all the nests were finished and it was interesting to see the different styles. Some were perfectly round, others egg-shaped; there were small ones and those large enough to need supporting by many stalks. Yes, the Hall was a marvelous place and Audrey could not wait to sleep in her nest and see the stars shining through the small entrance.

The midday sun glittered on the dust from the straw, which swirled in a fine mist over their heads. It made everything look hazy and unreal.

Twit saw her gazing around and said, "You should see it when the corn is really ripe, then it looks as if the entire Hall is made of gold."

"It is marvelous," she sighed. "Grand yet simple as well." She wondered if the fieldmice would decorate the Hall properly with garlands of flowers and chains of daisies. In a small way it reminded her of the chamber of spring and summer that she had entered in Deptford when she had received her mousebrass. As she thought of it an idea came to her.

Just then their lunch was disturbed by a cheer from some of the families and calls of "Hooray."

Audrey strained to see. There was Jenkin coming through the doors and with him was Young Whortle.

The families rushed up to him to see if he was really all right. But apart from some nasty bruises and a bandage over his shoulder he seemed fine.

"It was that potion," he said. "Didn't taste too good but made me sit up and take notice. Sammy's gettin' better too—that rat-lady reckons he'll be up an' about in a few days."

The crowd murmured in wonder and praised Madame Akkikuyu's skill in healing.

"Where be she now?" asked one of them.

"Why she's with my mam a-bottlin' that stuff to keep for next time someone gets ill," replied Young Whortle.

"That's a turn-up for the books," whistled Arthur when all the commotion had died down. "Who'd have thought that goo actually worked?"

"Well, I didn't, for one," said Audrey. "I look an even bigger idiot now, don't I? Oh, well, rather that than have one of those two get poisoned."

Lunch was over and Elijah climbed up to the nest again, taking some feathering with him. Mrs. Scuttle tidied up and went to the still pool to wash the bowls. Twit scurried up and helped his father.

Arthur was eating the last bit of cheese absently. Then forgetting to wipe his whiskers, as usual, he pulled Audrey to one side and told her.

"Look, Twit's been telling me about Jenkin—you really mustn't tease him anymore about those bruises, you know."

"Why ever not?" demanded his sister curiously.

"Because his dad gave them to him. Apparently, Mr. Nettle often hits Jenkin—thinks it's good for him."

"Oh," stammered Audrey, "I feel terrible now. Why doesn't his mother do something?"

"Because she's dead—died when he was born, apparently, and no one else likes to interfere with Mr. Nettle—he's the mousebrass maker, you see."

"Poor Jenkin."

"Yes—so just be a bit nicer next time, eh?"

"Of course, Arthur."

"Well," Arthur said, changing the subject, "this afternoon I'm going to crack climbing one of those dratted stalks if it kills me. What are you going to do?"

"Oh, I've had an idea to make something for the Hall."

Arthur regarded her doubtfully. "What sort of 'something'?" he asked.

"A corn dolly. You know, like the ones at home in the chambers of summer in the Spring Ceremony. I'm surprised they haven't already got some here."

"Maybe they don't know how–I didn't know you did, either."

Audrey shrugged. "Easy. I watched the Raddle sisters once."

Arthur considered the idea for a moment, then said, "Yes, that sounds nice, you could present it to Mr. Woodruffe when you've finished and let him decide where to hang it." He looked around to see if any crumbs had fallen on the floor but was disappointed, so he went off to talk to Jenkin again about his climbing.

Audrey picked up some thin straws and began to plait them together.

It was more difficult than she had thought. The plaits were impossible to keep even and free from ugly gaps. However, eventually Audrey became more adept with the straw and her confidence grew.

She intended to make something simple to begin with–a bell shape perhaps, but as the straw flicked between her fingers her ambitions for it soared.

Audrey decided that the figure of a girl would be best, with corn ears for arms and a dress of bunched stalks.

The afternoon wore on. The dolly grew larger under her fingers, far larger than she had intended. Some mouse children who had been running around playing chase stopped and watched her. They had never seen anything like it before and Audrey talked to them happily as she made it.

Alison Sedge wandered into the Hall. Hodge had walked with her to the meadow, but she was in such a sulk that he had left her and gone to join Todkin on sentry.

Alison was thinking about Jenkin and the look that he had on his face when he saw that town mouse. It was uncomfortably hot and Alison was in a bad mood with the world. She decided to go to the still pool to bathe and admire her reflection.

She had just been gathering some wild rosemary to rinse her hair with when she decided to see how the Hall was coming along and if her father had finished her own nest.

It was as she crossed the Hall that she noticed a small crowd of children near the Scuttles' nests. And there, in the center of all the attention, was that town mouse! Curious and irritated, Alison tossed her head and strode nearer.

The dolly was now taller than Audrey, its head was a loop of plaited straw and she was busily straightening it as at the moment the whole thing had an amusing drunken air about it.

The children were watching everything Audrey did keenly. Alison quietly drew close and observed the scene acidly. She looked at the town mouse's silver bells tinkling on her tail and noted with envy the lace dress. Alison glanced down at her own simple frock, which seemed shabbier by comparison, and pursed her full lips.

The dolly was getting better every minute and Alison saw the admiring looks Audrey was getting from the boys who went by. Young Whortle was leaning out of the large Nep family nest positively ogling.

Alison regarded Audrey coldly, then a slow smile curled over her mouth and she spun on her heel and ran out of the Hall.

There, the dolly was finished. Audrey was very pleased with the final result, even though it was much larger than she had anticipated. The plaiting had worked well and only the Raddle sisters would be able to criticize it—but they were not there.

"What's it for?" ventured one of the children shyly.

"It's a decoration," said Audrey. "Will you help me take it to Mr. Woodruffe?"

Eagerly, small paws helped her lift the corn dolly and carry it to the wicker throne. Mr. Woodruffe watched them approach with a puzzled look on his face.

Audrey and the children put the corn dolly down and curt-syed and bowed before him.

"Can I do something for you, lass?" he asked.

"Please, sir," she began, "I have made this corn dolly to decorate your Hall."

The King of the Field laid his staff of office on his knee and leaned forward to inspect the dolly.

"It is most . . . unusual," he remarked jovially. "I wonder, could you teach our young ones to make such things?"

"Why yes, sir, they seem to enjoy watching me making this."

"Very well," declared Mr. Woodruffe, "you, Miss Brown, shall . . ."

A sudden commotion interrupted him. The doors of the Hall were thrust aside and Isaac Nettle stormed in.

He rushed over to the throne with a face as black as thunder and no one stood in his way—they had seen that mood before.

Isaac pointed a shaking finger at the King of the Field and cried, "What heresy is this? What sin have thee welcomed, Woodruffe?" He flung his arms open wide and yelled to the sky. "Forgive thy subject, Almighty, that he should have fallen into such folly."

"Isaac!" muttered Mr. Woodruffe sternly. "What's all this about?"

Mr. Nettle glared around at Audrey. "Pagan idolatry! Brought hither by this unclean creature."

Audrey was astounded at his passion. She had never seen anyone so angry before and some of the children began to cry.

"It's only a decoration," she protested.

"Silence, fiend of the deep cold," ranted Isaac. "Thy craft speaks for itself. It is a blasphemous effigy and mocks the design of the Green Mouse. Oh, Great One, do not let us pay for the misguided deeds of the ignorant. She is the scum of the vile cities, the cream of the sinners—not one of your true servants. Punish us not for her wrongdoing."

"Now look here!" fumed Audrey, her astonishment boiling to anger. But he would not listen to her.

"Shun the image maker," he cried to the mice who were gathering to see what was going on. "See how she wears her vanities!" he flicked her ribbon with contempt.

"Don't you touch me!" she shouted, outraged.

By now everyone in the Hall was watching them. Twit dropped his feathering and slid down the stalk.

"Beware the maker of dolls. Repent ye or the vengeance of the Green shall smite ye down." Isaac moved nearer to the corn dolly and raised his fists to smash it.

"Don't you dare!" cried Audrey, pushing herself between him and the figure of straw.

"Away, profane one!" roared Isaac, shoving her roughly. Audrey stumbled and fell backward.

Twit reached Isaac before he had a chance to smash the dolly and stood glaring up at him, his eyes smoldering with a frightening fire that none had seen before.

"Get thee gone," warned Mr. Nettle harshly.

Twit was breathing hard. No one had ever known this mood in the little fieldmouse and the crowd gasped and wondered at the outcome. Twit's teeth flashed as he bared them and put up his fist.

"You oughtn't to have done that," he shouted, trembling with emotion. "Try it again an' I'll do fer you."

Isaac stared at Twit and bawled, "See how the heathens taint your subjects, Lord. Out of my way, simpleton."

Twit stood his ground and an alarming, unpleasant growl came from his throat.

Arthur and Jenkin came running into the Hall. Word had spread around the sentries about what was happening.

They saw Isaac raise his hard paw to Twit. "Father!" shouted Jenkin. "No, you mustn't."

Arthur sped over to Audrey and helped her up while Jenkin swung on his father's arm.

"Nettle!" bellowed Mr. Woodruffe. "That is enough. I will not allow you to spoil the Hall of Corn."

Isaac threw him a foul glance, but he persisted.

"Listen to me. I am your king! I am the law here."

Isaac faltered and put his arm down slowly, all the while staring steadily into the level eyes of Mr. Woodruffe.

"I cannot allow this behavior," continued the King of the Field.

"I do but honor the Green and keep His laws."

"Maybe, but you offend me!"

"Then I shall not enter here again," Isaac roared. He whirled around, snatched up the corn dolly and strode off crying, "This abomination has stunk before the Green Mouse long enough." And he carried it out through the doors before anyone could stop him.

"Consider yourself banished from the Hall till your temper cools," the king called after him.

All the fieldmice relaxed and muttered, shaking their heads. Then mothers came and fetched their children away from Audrey.

Elijah Scuttle came puffing up red-eared and worried for his son. Twit, though, had calmed down.

"You all right?" he asked Audrey. She nodded and thanked him. Twit let out a great sigh of relief.

"I'm so sorry," stuttered Jenkin to both of them. He was dreadfully ashamed of his father.

"Oh, Jolly Jenkin," Twit brushed the incident away as his humor returned, "thank 'ee for comin' quick—I nearly let fly then."

"Oh, dear," Audrey said to Arthur, "I seem to be getting on the wrong side of everyone here, don't I?"

He tried to reassure her. "But it wasn't your fault, I'm sorry about your corn dolly—you spent such a long time on it."

"That doesn't matter," she said, "I'm just glad no one got hurt. That could have been very nasty then. Twit really took everyone by surprise, didn't he?"

"Maybe," remarked Arthur thoughtfully, "I suppose it's this terrible heat as well." He frowned suddenly.

"What is it?" asked his sister.

"Just this," he began slowly. "How did Mr. Nettle know you were making a dolly? He passed below us in the field and he was angry before he got here."

"That is strange," agreed Audrey.

From her nest, Alison Sedge watched them with a satisfied smile on her pretty face.

CHAPTER EIGHT

THE VOICE

Arthur made it to the top of a stalk at last, to the cheers of Twit and Jenkin. He could barely see them as night was falling and already its shadows were gathering about Fennywolde.

Arthur gazed over the top of the field. The silver light of dusk played over the rippling corn ears so that it really did look like a shimmering sea and he, Arthur, was floating on it. It was a bizarre feeling. Now he began to understand the love that fieldmice have for climbing.

"Come on, Art," called up Twit. "I don't want to stay down here all night—I wants me bed."

Arthur tried to slide down as he had seen his friends do, but he scraped his paws and bloodied his heels, then landed with an undignified "bump" on the hard ground.

"Did 'ee like it?" inquired Jenkin.

"It's just wonderful up there," enthused Arthur, scrabbling off the ground. "Could I be a sentry, do you think?"

"Wait till tomorrow, Arthur." Twit yawned.

"I'd best be off now," said Jenkin. "I'd like to stay with Figgy

131

and the others on sentry, but my dad wouldn't like that."

"Will those mice be on sentry all night?" asked Arthur, surprised.

"'Course," replied Jenkin. "No good havin' sentries if they go home at night."

"Well, shouldn't we stay?" Arthur addressed Twit.

Twit yawned again. "Oh, come on, Art," he said sleepily. "If I do sentry tonight like as not I'll drop clear off and bash me head in—I was up all hours last night a-talkin' to my folks. Let me have one good night's sleep an' we'll do a ghoster tomorrow."

"Well," Jenkin began, "if I don't go now I'll be in for it. 'Night, lads."

"Hope your dad's calmed down now," Twit ventured.

Jenkin licked his sore lip and nodded. "So do I. Oh well, I'll probably have a lot of praying to do when I get back, that's all. See you tomorrow hopefully." He ran off out of the field.

Arthur watched him go until the night swallowed him. "Will he really be okay, do you think?"

"Should be," Twit answered. "It's not him Isaac's mad at. Now, we gonna get some shut-eye tonight?" They made their way through the corridor to the great doors.

*   *   *

In the Hall of Corn all was calm. Nearly all the mice had gone to bed to try out their new nests and here and there orange lights showed through the openings as they settled down. Some fieldmice were talking, enjoying the refreshing change of a night spent under the sky without having to dread an owl attack. The hum of their chatter mingled with the quiet snores of sleepers, which in turn blended with the rustle of the corn.

The summer stars shone down onto Audrey's face. Her nest

was snug and warm, and the moss that lined it was soft and scented. She nuzzled down into the cool fragrant feathering, which smelled of the green earth and shady forests. It was at times like these, when the peace and beauty of Fennywolde were overpowering, that she thought it might not be so bad to spend the rest of her days there.

She closed her eyes and, breathing heavily, sunk deeper into her bed.

Suddenly the world seemed to quake. The nest shook violently from side to side. Audrey was jolted out of her short velvet sleep and hurled about. What was happening? She tried to cling onto the round walls of the nest and staggered to and fro, unable to keep her balance. The bells, which she had removed from her tail, jangled and rattled around the nest like beads in a baby's rattle.

A claw appeared over the opening and then everything went dark.

"Mouselet?" Madame Akkikuyu squeezed her huge head through the tiny hole, blocking out the light. She looked at Audrey. "Why mouselet in here?" she asked curiously. "No room for Akkikuyu to sleep—come down, mouselet, and we sleep on ground together."

"No!" answered Audrey sharply. "This is my bedroom now and it's not big enough for two."

Madame Akkikuyu insisted. "But, mouselet—little friend, Akkikuyu not like be alone in dark. Night has voices, they speak to her," the rat whimpered. "Besides, Akkikuyu not well—she need friend, need mouselet to help."

"What's wrong with you?" demanded Audrey sternly.

"Akkikuyu's ear—it aches and pounds."

"Why don't you go and make yourself some potion or other," Audrey suggested.

"Have tried, mouselet," assured the fortune-teller. "Akkikuyu

133

has rubbed on bramble leaves and said the charm, she has made the paste of the camomile flower but still it hurts. I am frightened, mouselet."

"Look," said Audrey, too tired to continue. "Why don't you get some sleep. It might be better in the morning and you could ask Mr. Scuttle to build you a nest tomorrow next to this one."

But Madame Akkikuyu merely stared back at her with the eyes of a scolded dog, hurt and confused. "Come down," she asked one last time, "for Akkikuyu sake."

"No," Audrey said, and she hated herself immediately.

The fortune-teller looked crestfallen. She stuck out her bottom lip and said sullenly, "Akkikuyu go—she sleep on ground alone, poor Akkikuyu." She pulled her head out of the nest and began to climb down again.

Audrey leaned out and saw the diminishing bulky figure reach the ground. In the darkness of the Hall floor she could just make out the spots on the rat's red shawl and they quickly bobbed away.

"Oh, she can please herself," mumbled Audrey. "I never promised to stay with her all day and night, did I?"

She remained leaning out of her nest for some time. Fennywolde was cooling after a hot day. The wind had dropped to a whispering breeze, which brought sweet fragrances out of the meadow.

Presently the muffled sound of voices drifted up to her. It was Twit and Arthur returning at last. Their nest was above hers and slightly to the left. She waited for them to climb up.

Out of the gloom appeared two little paws and then Twit's head popped up.

"Hello, Audrey," he said, drawing level with her. "You comfy in there?"

"Yes, it's lovely, your father's very clever."

"Reckon he is—oh!" two plumper paws had emerged and grabbed Twit's tail tightly.

"Shove up!" shouted Arthur.

Twit giggled, then said good night to Audrey before vanishing into his nest.

Arthur came into view, climbing the stalk determinedly. His tongue was sticking out as it always did when he was concentrating.

"Arthur," said Audrey when it looked as if he would continue up without noticing her.

Arthur flinched in surprise. "Hello, Sis," he said, startled. "You still awake, then?"

"Yes—I had a visit from Madame Akkikuyu."

"Didn't try to get in did she?"

"Yes, but it was too small. I sent her away in a sulk and I wish I hadn't."

"Oh, blow," said Arthur. "If she goes running off at the slightest thing, well . . ."

Audrey interrupted him. "But, Arthur, she said she wasn't well and she mentioned that voice of hers again."

Arthur scoffed. "She's going batty—none of us heard that voice on the boat, did we? Yet she swore blind she had. I wouldn't worry about it, Sis, really. Now look, I'm sorry, but I've got to go—my paws are killin' me, hanging on like this. See you in the morning."

"Good night," Audrey called after him as he wriggled into the nest above. She withdrew into her own bed and sank into a deep, untroubled sleep.

*　　*　　*

Madame Akkikuyu wandered through the field miserably. Her right ear ached terribly and her best friend had not done anything to help. She kicked stones belligerently and felt sorry for herself.

She soon left the field behind and walked along the edge of

135

the ditch, cursing her ear and rubbing it vigorously. How it pained her. A constant dull throb pulsed inside, like the worst toothache imaginable. It was almost bad enough for her to want to run to the lonely yew tree and chew on its deadly poisonous bark.

Bit by bit the pain increased.

"Oooh," whimpered the fortune-teller despairingly.

Madame Akkikuyu sat down at the stony stretch of ditch and buried her head in her claws, moaning to herself. The pain had only begun when the sun set, and as the night became darker and cooler it grew more intense.

"Akkikuyu."

The rat looked up quickly. She could see no one—only the ghostlike moths fluttering overhead.

"Akkikuyu!" repeated the voice.

The fortune-teller wailed loudly. It was that voice again—the one that had haunted her from Greenwich.

"Leave me!" she cried.

"Akkikuyu," the voice persisted. It was stronger than it had been on those previous occasions. It was a strange, sickly sweet voice, which made her shudder.

"Listen to me," it said softly.

"No," snapped the rat. "Never, Akkikuyu not want to go round bend. Leave me."

"Listen to me, let me help you."

"No, you not real—Akkikuyu barmy, she hear voice when nobody there."

"But I am real, Akkikuyu."

"Who are you then?"

"My name is—Nicodemus," whispered the voice, "I am your friend."

"Then why you hide?" asked Akkikuyu, glaring suspiciously at the shadows, which seemed to have closed around her. She rubbed her head. She had seen something out of the corner of her eye and thought it was a spider dangling from her hair.

"I do not hide, Akkikuyu," crooned the voice of Nicodemus. "I am here."

And to her everlasting horror Madame Akkikuyu saw who it was that spoke to her.

"Aaaghh!" she screamed, getting to her feet in panic. But there was nowhere to run. On her right ear the tattooed face was moving and talking. The old ink lips were opening and closing and the drawn eyes were staring straight at her.

"Aaaghh!" she screamed again. She thought she had finally gone out of her mind. "Akkikuyu is cracked! Oh poor Akkikuyu," she sobbed.

"Listen to me, Akkikuyu," Nicodemus ordered. "Trust me, you are not mad."

"Stop, stop," whined the rat. "Stop, or Akkikuyu murder herself. This cannot be. Inky faces do not talk—they are doodles on skin, not real peoples."

The face on her ear began again. "Akkikuyu, listen, I am merely using this tattoo to talk to you. It is a channel through which you are able to hear me. I am really far, far away."

The fortune-teller ceased her sobs. "What are you?" she asked slowly.

"I am a spirit of the fields," said the tattoo, smiling. "I am the essence of the harvest, the sunlight on a distant hill, the splendor of a golden meadow, the heady perfume of the hawthorn in bloom."

"Why you speak to Akkikuyu? Spirits not supposed to talk to feather or fur."

"Because, dearest lady, I am trapped. Caught in a void—a horrible limbo where nightmare spirits of darkness dwell. I must escape. You must help me, I must return to the fields ere I perish for eternity."

"How you get trapped?" asked the fortune-teller doubtfully.

"That is a long and frightening tale, which I cannot relate.

137

Help me, Akkikuyu–give me sweet liberty."

She considered his entreaty, then shook her head. "No," she answered plainly. "Akkikuyu is mad–you not there–she imagine all this, so shut up."

"What proof do you need, woman?" demanded Nicodemus sternly, and in his impatience his voice faltered and became ugly. "You must release me."

"So you say," said Madame Akkikuyu, "but how is this to be? Akkikuyu have no great magicks to work for you. She know only herbs and medicines to make mouselings better."

The voice shouted, "But I can teach you, Akkikuyu. All the forces of nature are mine to command. You could learn from me secret knowledge known to none of your kind–just think of it." The voice lulled and coaxed most invitingly.

Madame Akkikuyu thought hard. A yearning awoke inside her–it seemed to be a very old feeling nudged to the surface by Nicodemus's promises. Magical power, he would give her that! The hunger for it, which welled up inside her, felt so new, yet also strangely familiar. Nicodemus's voice began again.

"You could be a queen, Akkikuyu," the tattoo went on, "mighty above all others."

Madame Akkikuyu seemed to come out of the illusions he was weaving about her.

"Tach!" she snorted. "Akkikuyu not believe in magic. Power of herb yes, and rule of fate yes, but not magic. Tricks and tomfool nonsense."

The face on her ear screwed itself up with impatience. "Do you want a demonstration? Very well. I shall show you what can be done and what powers can be yours."

"What you do?" inquired the fortune-teller expectantly.

"Look down there!" said Nicodemus. "At the bottom of the ditch!"

There, lying on the stones where Mr. Nettle had thrown it were the remains of Audrey's corn dolly.

"Go down there," instructed Nicodemus. The fortune-teller did as she was bid and made her way down the side of the ditch, hanging onto the tufts of coarse grass, which grew up its steep banks.

The dolly was in four pieces, testaments to Mr. Nettle's passion. The head and arms had been torn from the dress section.

Madame Akkikuyu tutted to see the damage. She had heard of Audrey's corn dolly from Young Whortle.

"Straw lady bust," she said aloud.

"Then join it together, Akkikuyu," said Nicodemus craftily. "Put back the head and fix in the arms."

"No," said the rat, "Straw ripped. She not go back together now."

"Then put the pieces where they belong and I shall do the rest," beamed the face.

Madame Akkikuyu arranged the arms and head around the body in their correct positions and stepped aside.

"Now," said Nicodemus, "with the bone from your hair draw a triangle around it. Good, now throw open your arms to the night and repeat after me—only make sure you do it exactly."

They began the invocation to the unseen spirits of the world.

"Come, Brud. By slaughterous cold and searing ice I call thee. Come out of the shadows, awake from your empty tomb and walk amongst us. I entreat thee, make whole again your effigy."

Madame Akkikuyu repeated all the words and watched the corn dolly in fascinated silence.

All around them the grasses and leaves began to stir and rustle, beating against each other like applause. Inside the triangle the moss that grew over the stones writhed like clusters of angry maggots and burst open new shoots like green fireworks. Everything living within that area grew and bloomed a thousand times faster than normal. Then, as Madame

Akkikuyu stared in disbelief, the severed stems of the corn dolly's grain arms twisted and coiled into the body section. The plaited head put out a tentative wiry tendril like a bather testing the water, then rooted itself onto the shoulders.

"Aha," squealed Madame Akkikuyu, "dummy repaired."

"Quite," said the tattoo matter-of-factly. "Are you convinced now, Akkikuyu?"

The rat nodded quickly, "Oh yes, Nicodemus, my friend—you real, Akkikuyu not bonkers." She hugged herself as she gazed at the completed figure of straw.

Nicodemus continued. "Would you like to see more?"

"More?" repeated the rat. "How so?"

"This has been a mere child's trick, Akkikuyu, compared with what you could achieve under my learned guidance."

"Tell me more," said the fortune-teller, eager to see other wonders. "Akkikuyu want to see more."

"Very well," the voice muttered softly, "step nearer to the straw maiden. Enough—do not touch the triangle. Now we need blood."

Madame Akkikuyu backed away. She did not like the sound of that. "Blood?" she queried cautiously. "Why for you want blood, and where from?"

"To give the doll life," announced Nicodemus. "Blood is a symbol of that. Just three drops are needed. I daresay you could nick your thumb and squeeze some out."

"Give doll life!" exclaimed the rat wondrously. "You can do such? You are very strong in magicks, field spirit. Quickly show Akkikuyu."

She took out her small knife and made a tiny cut in her thumb.

"The blood must fall on the straw," Nicodemus told her as three crimson drops were forced out onto the corn dress.

"Now stand back," commanded the voice.

Madame Akkikuyu did so and felt a thrill of fear tingle its

way along her spine and down to the tip of her tail.

"Hear me, oh, Brud!" called out Nicodemus. "Give this image life–let sap be as the blood on the straw. Pour breath into its empty breast and let stems be as sinew."

A deathly silence descended over the whole of Fennywolde. The fieldmice shifted uncomfortably in their soft nests as a shadow passed over the sky. Birds shrank into their feathers as they roosted in the tops of the elms and feared the worst. A hedgehog in his den of old, dry leaves felt the charged atmosphere and curled himself into a tight ball of spikes. Down came the shadow, thundering from the empty night on the back of the wind. The treetops swayed and the leaves whipped around. The grass in the meadow parted as the force fell upon it and traveled wildly through, flattening and battering everything in its path. It rushed toward the ditch and went howling down into it.

Madame Akkikuyu stood her ground as the unseen fury tore at her hair and pulled her shawl till it choked her.

And then all was still.

The fortune-teller lowered the claws she had raised against the ravaging gale and looked down at the dolly.

"Command it," said Nicodemus.

"I . . . I?" she stammered.

"Who else? It will obey none but you."

Madame Akkikuyu swept back the hair, which had blown over her face, and peered again at the corn dolly. "Up," she ordered meekly.

One of the grain arms gave a sudden twitch and the rat drew her breath sharply.

"Up!" she said again with more force.

The straw figure flipped itself over, rustling and crackling. It leaned on its arm and jolted itself up until it stood before her.

The fortune-teller took some steps around the dolly and waved her arms over it just in case someone was tricking her with cotton threads. But no, the corn dolly was alive!

141

"Instruct it to bow before you," suggested Nicodemus.

"Bow," said the rat.

With a snapping and splintering the corn dolly bent over and bowed.

"Hee hee," cackled Madame Akkikuyu, joyfully jumping up and down, her tail waving around like an angry snake. "It moves, it moves," she called. "And only for Akkikuyu, for she alone. See how it dances."

She pointed to the figure and jerkily it moved from the confines of the triangle, making odd jarring movements. Its dress swept over the stone floor like the twigs of a broom as it pranced in a peculiar waltz. The arms quivered in mockery of life and the loop head twisted from time to time as though acknowledging an invisible partner. It was a grotesque puppet and Madame Akkikuyu was its master.

The corn dolly tottered this way and that, buckling occasionally in a spasm that might have been a curtsy and shaking its dress with a dry papery sound. Madame Akkikuyu capered around with it, beckoning and following, teasing and pushing, until finally she panted, "Stop!" and the straw dancer became motionless.

"So," began Nicodemus in a pleased tone, "you must choose, will you help me?"

"Yes, yes," she crowed gladly.

"Excellent, Akkikuyu. We must prepare for the spell that will release me from this endless darkness where I am imprisoned."

She was eager to learn more and asked, "What do we need Nico? I fetch, I get."

"Hah!" The tattoo laughed. "First I must teach you, and there are many ingredients to find—some will not be easy, others will. There is a ritual involved in the breaking of my bonds, and everything must be perfect."

"Trust me, oh spirit. Akkikuyu no fluff." As she said it she thought her own voice came to her out of the past.

142

"Come then, let us talk away from this ditch. Only the hours of night are afforded to me. That is the only time I may speak with you, Akkikuyu, so spend your days wisely and make no exertion that may tire you out ere night falls."

She agreed and promised to rest for most of the daytime from then on. As she climbed up the bank the fortune-teller glanced back at the corn dolly and grinned as she thought of the powers that would soon be hers. What would her mousey friend have to say to this, she wondered.

CHAPTER NINE

MOLD TO MOLD

It was another baking-hot day. Audrey awoke to a blazing blue sky empty of cloud. She rubbed the sleep from her eyes and peeped out of the nest.

The Hall of Corn was glowing with light. The sun shone down on the stems, and those stout wives who had insisted on taking their sheets were shaking them vigorously outside the nests, waving them like dazzling flags of surrender.

Old Todmore passed below, swaggering on his bowed legs and nibbling a straw. He took up his usual position in the Hall and watched the world hurry by.

"Bless the Green for morns like this," he sighed, stroking his whiskers.

Tired sentries came into the Hall blinking and yawning, while those newly awake ran to take their places.

"Where's our Hodge?" a small mouse-woman asked Figgy.

"Haven't seen him," was the sleepy reply.

"Well, I'm not takin' his breakfast to him. Sentry, sentry– that's all that boy thinks about."

Arthur poked his head out of his nest. He was covered in bits of grass and moss. "Mornin', Sis!" he said brightly. "Breakfast's ready–didn't you hear Mrs. Scuttle calling?"

"No," replied Audrey, "but I'll be down in a minute." She retreated back into her nest, but after breathing the fresh air of the outside world the atmosphere in her bedroom seemed stifling. She decided that nests were lovely places to spend a night, but in the daytime they were like ovens.

As soon as she had dressed and brushed away some stray bits of straw she clambered out and descended the ladder Mr. Scuttle had made for her.

On the ground below, Gladwin Scuttle had spread a clean cloth and laid out the breakfast things. Arthur was well into his third helping when Audrey arrived.

"Mornin', missey," greeted Elijah. "And how did you sleep last night?"

"Very well, Mr. Scuttle, thank you."

Mrs. Scuttle patted the cloth by her side and said, "You sit down here, dear, and tell me what you think you'll be doing today."

"I think I'd better find Madame Akkikuyu," Audrey answered glumly. "I was a bit nasty to her last night."

"Hey, Sis," Arthur butted in, "I'm going to be a sentry today. Twit's going to present me to Mr. Woodruffe and they do a little ceremony or something," he added with his mouth full.

"That's right," agreed Elijah, "you'll be made to swear an oath of allegiance to Fennywolde for the rest of your days."

"But, Arthur," Audrey pointed out, "you can't promise that. What about Mother? You said you'd go back."

Arthur looked ashamed. "You're right. Do you know, I hadn't thought about home since I've been here–aren't I awful?"

"Never you mind," consoled Elijah. "I'll pop over an' have a word or three with Mr. Woodruffe–we'll see if'n we can't bend the rules a tiny bit." He got to his feet and set off in the direction of the throne.

The doors of the Hall opened and in came Madame Akkikuyu. She looked tired and she trudged along with heavy limbs. The families of fieldmice waved and nodded to her as though she were a dear old friend, and Mr. Nep bowed politely as she walked by.

"Here comes trouble," observed Arthur dryly. "Good morning, Madame Akkikuyu," called Audrey, trying to be as nice as possible. "Did you sleep well—how's your ear today?"

The fortune-teller gave her a weary glance and mumbled. "Akkikuyu not sleep—she busy all night finding root and herb for mousling potions." She showed them her claws, which were caked in soil and dirt. "Ear better," she added grudgingly.

"Sit down and have something to eat, Madame er . . ." offered Gladwin kindly.

Madame Akkikuyu grabbed a whole loaf and shook her head. "Akkikuyu not sit—she off to sleep."

"Oh," said Mrs. Scuttle. "Well, when my Elijah gets back I'm sure he'll make you a nest of your own."

"No," the rat declined sharply. "Akkikuyu no like mousey house. She go find place to sleep."

"Akkikuyu," said Audrey, "if you like we can go for a walk or something later."

The rat regarded Audrey for a moment and shrugged. "Maybe," she replied, and stalked away, tearing the bread into great chunks and gulping them down as she went.

"Oh, dear," said Gladwin.

"She ain't happy with us mouselets," remarked Twit lightly.

"This is all my fault," admitted Audrey. "I'm not turning out to be a very good companion for her, am I?"

Arthur munched thoughtfully on a crust. "You know," he began after a while, "Madame Akkikuyu is a lot more independent than she was when we set off—haven't you noticed? I don't think she needs you anymore, Audrey. I do believe she's settled in here better than we have."

"I ought to be relieved," sighed his sister. "It's funny, though—I feel just the opposite, as if I've betrayed her."

"Don't be soft," Arthur told her. "You came all this way, didn't you?"

"Well, let her down then," argued Audrey. "I haven't been much of a friend to her, have I? She thought we were best friends—I think I failed her in that."

"Pah!" declared Mrs. Scuttle. "Rats and mice being friends! I never heard of such a thing!"

They waited for Audrey to finish nibbling her breakfast, then Elijah came puffing back.

"It's all fixed and sorted," he informed Arthur. "We put our heads together, such as they are, an' we come up with the answer."

"So I can still be a sentry?" asked Arthur.

"Aye, lad, you can be a sentry for as long as you likes—till you goes home."

"Great!" shouted Arthur, dancing around. "When can I start?"

"Right now, if you're willin'. Mr. Woodruffe's a-waitin' on you."

So, with great excitement, they all went over to the wicker throne where the King of the Field sat with his staff of office on his knee.

"A blessed Eve to you." He smiled warmly.

They all bowed and curtsyed to him, and Audrey contrived to whisper into Mrs. Scuttle's ear, "Eve?"

"Midsummer's Eve, child," Gladwin murmured back.

"So, Master Brown, you wish to become a sentry and guard our Hall from enemies. Is this so?" said the King of the Field.

"Yes, sir," said Arthur keenly.

"Majesty!" hissed Twit.

"Yes, Majesty," corrected Arthur.

"Who presents this mouse to the King of the Field?" asked Mr. Woodruffe solemnly.

"I do, Majesty," chirped Twit. "He is a friend of mine and a braver lad you never did see." He found it hard to stifle the chuckles as he described Arthur to the king. He had to follow the correct procedure, which had been unchanged for countless years.

"Now you must swear loyalty to me, your king, and the land of Fenny."

Arthur nodded to show that he understood.

"Raise your right paw, Art," prompted Twit. "Now hold this hawthorn leaf."

"The hawthorn represents virtue and honor, Master Brown," explained Mr. Woodruffe. "But it is also the sacred tree of the Green Mouse and we shall name him as a witness. Are you ready to be sworn in?"

Arthur's lips had gone dry and he swallowed a lump in his throat. He wished his father was alive to see this. "Yes, Majesty."

"Repeat after me," commenced Mr. Woodruffe. "I, Arthur of the brown mice, visitor from the gray town, do most solemnly swear by holy leaf and in the Green's name to protect the Hall of Corn from any evil, though my life should fail in the attempt, till by His Majesty's leave I am released from service."

Arthur breathed a sigh of relief as he finished the last sentence.

Elijah nudged his wife. "That's the bit we put in," he told her proudly.

"Now, young sentry," began the king briskly, "you may go about your duty. Have you been taught all the signals and alarms yet?"

"Why, no, Your Majesty."

"See to it, William Scuttle," ordered Mr. Woodruffe with a twinkle in his eye.

They all bowed and curtsyed again and as they were leaving Twit said to Arthur, "They're real simple when you knows 'em. Blackbird cries and funny whistles–that sort of stuff. We usually use them to tell each other when it's dinnertime, though. Mind you, the most important alarm of all and one you must never use 'cept in the direst need is to yell *Fenny* at the top of your voice."

Audrey resumed her conversation with Mrs. Scuttle. "Will you be celebrating the Eve tonight at all? We do in the Skirtings."

"I remember, yes, we have a bit of a party. This afternoon all us mums and all the girls are going to make some bunting. There's a lovely group of rose trees over by the hedge and we thread the petals onto a string. It does look jolly."

"Could I come along?" asked Audrey. "I can't imagine anything more boring than watching my brother climb a stalk all day long. I haven't a clue why he wants to do it."

"Hah," said Gladwin. "You sound like you've lived in Fennywolde all your life. We can't understand why the menfolk love it either. Anyway, you'd be most welcome, dear. Oh, there'll be such a time tonight! In the excitement of William returning and the Hall-making going on, I clean forgot all about the Eve myself till Elijah asked about it last night."

The sun was climbing higher in the brilliant sky. The heat hammered down and Audrey felt dizzy.

"Is there somewhere cool I could sit, Mrs. Scuttle?" she inquired, wiping her forehead.

Gladwin tutted and scolded herself. "Why, there I go, forgetting myself again–when I first came here I was limp as a lettuce for weeks. Housemice aren't used to all this sunshine. Mind you, I can't remember it being quite so hot as this before."

She gazed around at the merry families with their plump, pleasant wives and red-eared husbands. This is what she had given up her old home and family for and she had never once regretted it. Suddenly she clicked back to the present and looked at Audrey sheepishly.

"Oh, dear," she flustered, "there's me wandering off again. You want to get cool, don't you, dear—well the best place I used to go when I felt a bit off with the heat was the still pool."

"Yes," said Audrey, "Arthur told me that's where you get all your water from."

"Now the ditch has dried up we have no choice. You should see poor Grommel trying to carry a full bucket of water with his bad back—poor thing."

Mrs. Scuttle eventually pointed to where the pool was. "Just follow the ditch and you can't miss it."

Audrey set off. She went through the great doors of the Hall and walked straight into Jenkin Nettle.

"Hello, miss." He grinned.

"Oh," muttered Audrey, blushing. "Good morning Jenkin," she added lamely.

"You looks nice this mornin', miss," he said, enjoying the situation.

Audrey giggled and thanked him. "But I always try and look this nice for Arthur." And she sauntered out of the field with Jenkin's eyes following her admiringly. The younger children were playing dust slides near the elm roots.

"You'll catch it when your mothers see you." Audrey laughed.

The grubby children considered her for a moment, wondering whether they ought to say anything in reply, but cleaner, older sisters grabbed them by the paws and dragged them away whispering at them.

"No, Josh you mustn't—you know what Mam told you 'bout that one."

Audrey was taken aback. Evidently, Mr. Nettle's outburst

yesterday had been the chief topic of Fennywolde gossip. Audrey was surprised that so many had actually believed his ridiculous accusations.

"Still," she shrugged, "it takes a long time to make friends, and time is something I'll have plenty of here."

She carried on along the ditch, past the elms and the winter quarters and an entrance where the sound of Mr. Nettle hammering on the mousebrasses rang out in time to his deep voice booming out hymns to the Green Mouse.

Soon she found that she had wandered into a patch of dismal shade and she shivered to herself. Rearing high above her was the lonely yew tree, the frightening tree of death. Its branches poked out like bony fingers and sharp claws. She hurried on, past that place—it was much too eerie and dark for her liking. No grass grew in its shadow and no birds sang in its branches.

The floor of the ditch began to get softer. Instead of dry choking dust it had become a rich brown mud, which yielded under her little pink feet like a dark fruitcake that had been cooked too quickly. The surface was crusty yet underneath it was still gooey and spongy.

It was a sign that she was not far from the pool. Soon her footprints began to fill up with water as she passed. She pushed through the trailing leaves of an ivy creeper and found herself staring into the still pool. It was as if she had crossed the threshold into another world, a cool, silent place where magic was almost visible. The harsh sunlight was filtered through the layers of bright new leaves and dappled the water with great splashes of shimmering green, which in turn were reflected back and bounced around once more. Dragonflies in their polished emerald armor flashed over the water's surface chasing gnats. Fine trails of bubbles slipped through the water then burst silently, too small to make a ripple. The still pool was a beautiful place.

Audrey stared, not even daring to breathe in case everything should disappear—so much did it look like a fairy grotto. The edge of the pool was fringed with plants: water plantains, horse-tails, and yellow rattles grew there. Behind one clump a husky voice began to speak.

"Alison Sedge—you are the loveliest thing in creation."

Audrey looked up, startled.

"You are lovelier than the flowers in your hair. Just look at you. That hair, the goddess would be proud of it."

Audrey put her paw over her mouth. She wanted to laugh. It was a girl's voice that spoke.

"Those eyes—they're luscious, they are. A boy could drown in those."

Audrey crept around the plants to see who it was—it didn't sound like any of the girls she had met the day before.

"Those lips—don't you want to eat them up, lads? A finer cherry-red pair of lips there never were, won't someone pick them?" Now there came a sound of pretend kissing.

Through the leaves Audrey saw Alison Sedge. She was gazing at herself in the water, enchanted by her own reflection. Her thick hair hung down either side of her face, nearly touching the water. This was the reason Audrey did not recognize the girl immediately. She decided that it was rude to stay there without letting the mooning fieldmouse know she was there, so she coughed politely.

Alison Sedge whipped around and stared in horror at Audrey, embarrassment, shame, and surprise all registering in her beautiful eyes.

"I'm sorry for intruding," said Audrey. "I'm Audrey Brown— a friend of Twit. I don't think we've met." And then she remembered, this was the girl who had glared at her that first night when Madame Akkikuyu chased away the owl.

Alison composed herself and groomed her ponytails back behind her ears.

"Saw you other day," she said mildly.

"Oh, when?" asked Audrey, not seeing the trap.

"When that ratwoman made you look real stupid." Alison tittered.

"Oh!" was all Audrey could find to say.

"Your brother know Dimsel's after him?" asked Alison, her subtle mind moving on to a different subject.

"Erm . . . no," replied Audrey, trying to keep up with the shifting conversation.

"Not much of a catch—either of them," remarked Alison outrageously.

Audrey choked and spluttered. How rude this girl was! She could find nothing to say in reply. When she did manage to recover her wits, Audrey caught Alison running a critical eye over her dress and collar. This was better; Alison's plain frock was no match for them. The other girl sniffed and looked away.

Oh no, thought Audrey, and she gave her tail a slight flick. The silver bells tinkled sweetly.

Alison jumped in surprise and stared at them coldly. Then she smiled and fiddled abstractedly with her mousebrass—it too tinkled: maybe not as sweetly, but it was enough to draw Audrey's eyes to it. She recognized the sign of grace and beauty and rolled her eyes heavenward.

"You not old enough to have a brass, then?" queried Alison.

"I did have one," said Audrey, "but I lost it."

"Careless," the other observed coolly.

Audrey did not feel like explaining about the altar of Jupiter to Alison, so she said nothing.

"Young Whortle's better now." Alison changed the subject again.

"Yes," said Audrey—this was another dig about her foolish display yesterday morning. Well, she thought, if that's all you can throw at me, go ahead.

"Skinny Samuel's gettin' better too," resumed Alison.

Audrey decided to join in this little game. In an innocent voice, she said, "That Jenkin's a nice boy, isn't he?"

The hit went home and Alison scowled. Through clenched teeth she managed to say, "The Nettles are all barmy. I'd have nothin' to do with 'em."

"Oh, I don't know," sighed Audrey demurely. "Jenkin's always sweet to me."

"He's like that to all the common sort," spat Alison. She didn't like it when someone got the better of her and was not used to her remarks thrown back with added sting. "I had to tell him to stop pesterin' me," she added.

"Said I looked nice this morning and always calls me 'miss.'" Audrey held out her paw to examine her nails—something she never did usually.

Alison pursed her lips, then arched her eyebrows craftily and said, "His dad's loony too—wonder how he knew 'bout your daft dolly, though?"

Audrey understood at once, and for her the game ended.

"Can be dangerous livin' in the country if'n you're not used to it," droned Alison. "And try an' take what don't belong to you."

"Oh, I'm quite safe," said Audrey defiantly and with an edge to her voice. "You see I don't scare easily—if I come across a snake I don't run away."

"Really?" Alison sounded bored and unimpressed. "You'd get bitten then."

"Oh no," Audrey assured her calmly. "You see Madame Akkikuyu and I are best friends. I'd get some of her potions and shrivel that snake up." She brought her face close to Alison's and added darkly, "Either that or I'd choke it with my bare paws just for the fun of it."

Alison backed away—she did not like the look in Audrey's

eyes. She tossed her head and said, "I can't waste my time here all day."

"Yes." Audrey smiled. "I saw you wasting your time before."

Alison huffed and flounced off.

Audrey shook her head. So that was Alison Sedge! Lily Clover was right–she did have claws; it might not be wise to get on the wrong side of her, but it was too late now.

Audrey lay back and enjoyed the tranquil magic of the pool in peace.

*   *   *

The morning turned to lunchtime. On sentry duty, Arthur's stomach began to growl. He looked over to Twit and signaled that he was about to climb down.

Twit waved back cheerily but made it clear that he was quite happy to stay on duty a little longer.

Arthur scrambled down the stalk and went in search of food.

A narrow path veered away from the main corridor and he wondered if it was a shortcut to the Hall. It seemed to go in the right direction, so he took it and began to whistle one of Kempe's songs.

He stopped in his tracks. Something was wrong–he could feel it. Cautiously he continued farther along the path. What was that in the way up ahead?

"Oh no," muttered Arthur under his breath. He ran over to the dark lumpy shape, which sprawled awkwardly over the ground. At his feet was the body of a mouse.

For a couple of minutes Arthur could only stand and gape, shock freezing his limbs. Then he knelt down and bravely laid his paw on the sad little body. It was stone cold. The mouse must have been lying there for hours. Gingerly, he turned the body over, and squealed in fright. It was Hodge. He recognized him at once. But it was not just that which upset him. Hodge's face was ghastly to look on. Like a mask of horror, the eyes were popping out, and the mouth was fixed in a wild and silent scream. It seemed almost as if Hodge had died of some terrible fright. But Arthur could see savage marks on his throat and his neck looked pathetically thin and squashed.

Slowly it dawned on him. Hodge had died of strangulation—someone had murdered him.

Now the cornstalks seemed to hem Arthur in and the whole place took on a sinister aspect. His skin began to crawl. He gulped and gazed around fearfully. What if the murderer was still there somewhere, hiding and watching him? What if even now it was coming to get him?

Arthur yelped as panic got the better of him. Never before had he been so frightened. "I've got to get out!" he squeaked and ran up the path again, stumbling and falling in his haste.

"FENNY! FENNY!" he cried out desperately. Voices were raised at once in answer to the urgent call. Arthur picked himself up from the ground, took no heed of his bleeding knees and ran straight into Jenkin. The fieldmouse stared at Arthur's terrified face and gasped.

"What is it?"

Arthur hid his eyes and began to shake all over.

Jenkin shook him urgently. "Tell me, Arthur, what is it?"

Arthur pointed up the path. "Hodge," he said thickly, pointing back up the path.

Jenkin dashed to see. "Don't look at him," cried Arthur after him. It was too late. Jenkin cried out in horror.

Other sentries came running. Twit was the first. He stopped in surprise when he saw Arthur's expression.

"Art?" he began curiously. "What is it? Why, you're tremblin' all over."

A group of sentries gathered around. Arthur would not let

them pass. They were all anxious to know why the major alarm
had been used.

Eventually Jenkin came staggering back–his face matched
Arthur's and he was weeping.

The sentries murmured and looked at one another nervously.

"It's Hodge," sobbed Jenkin. "He's dead."

The sentries opened their mouths and shook their heads in
disbelief. Twit looked fearfully at Arthur, who was trying to say
something.

"No!" he shouted violently. "He's been murdered!"

*   *   *

A grim, silent group made its way to the Hall of Corn. Mourners
lined the corridor and the sound of lamentation was heard
everywhere in Fennywolde.

Jenkin, Young Whortle, Todkin, and Figgy carried the body
of their friend on their shoulders. A white cloth had been
placed over Hodge's face by Jenkin so that no one would have
to look on that grisly horror again.

Grommel and the other guards opened the great doors and
let the group in. Word had spread quickly through the field, and
the grief of Hodge's parents was terrible to hear and to see.

Elijah came and took Arthur to one side. Twit disappeared
into his nest and brought out the flask given to him by Thomas
Triton.

"Here, Art," he said gently, "drink some of this."

Mr. Woodruffe held up his staff of office and cried angrily,
"What creature has done this? We must not rest till the fiend is
captured. Summon everyone into the Hall at once!"

For those who had not already heard the tragic news,
Jenkin placed a piece of straw between his thumbs and blew
hard. A high screech echoed over Fennywolde and all who
heard it clutched their mousebrasses fearfully and ran to the

Hall. Isaac Nettle dropped his hammer and abandoned the forge.

Soon everyone was there except Audrey. The Hall was buzzing with grief and anger as the mice held on to their children tightly and called for the murderer to be found.

Isaac learned from his son what had occurred and turned to the king furiously.

"See?" he raged bitterly. "Now do you see what happens when you turn your back on the Green's holy laws. He has been swift to show His anger."

"Silence, Nettle!" stormed Mr. Woodruffe. "I will not have you say such rubbish in front of Hodge's parents."

"Thee must all pray—pray hard and beg the Green's forgiveness for having allowed the heathen into our midst." He whirled around and pointed an accusing finger at Arthur. "Where is thy sister—the blasphemer?"

"Isaac!" roared the king before Arthur could answer. "I will not allow you to turn this into one of your prayer meetings! I have a search party to organize and you could attend to Hodge there."

Mr. Nettle calmed a little and regarded the body grimly. "Verily—I shall order the service."

As Mr. Woodruffe dispatched fieldmice to search the field, Arthur turned to Twit and said, "I wish I knew where Audrey was. This is another thing for Mr. Nettle to jump down her throat about. Did you see the faces of some in the crowd? They were agreeing with him!"

"Here's Akkikuyu, Arthur," Twit warned as the rat strode into the room.

"What goes on?" she asked. "Who make all the noise and hullabaloo? They wake Akkikuyu." Then she saw Hodge's body and tutted sadly. "Poor mouselet—he beyond Akkikuyu's help."

"He was strangled," said Mr. Woodruffe gently.

"Who did so?" she asked in astonishment. "I give *them* a throttling."

"We are about to try and find out," said the king gravely.

"Poor, poor mouselet," she sighed. "No more cheeses for you."

"Arthur," ventured Twit, looking at the fortune-teller, "you don't think?"

"What . . . Akkikuyu?" said Arthur. "No, she was too shocked when she saw Hodge just then. I don't think it was her. . . . Good grief, no, it couldn't possibly have been."

Alison Sedge watched everything in horror. She could not take her eyes off the body. That lifeless thing had once been a boy she had flirted with and lured into the meadow. Now the thought of it made her ill.

The painful wails of Hodge's parents were unbearable to her. She stumbled to her nest and bit her nails nervously. A dreadful thought had come to her. She recalled Audrey's words at the still pool: "I'd choke it with my bare paws just for the fun of it."

Alison was scared—should she tell someone or would the town mouse punish her? She wondered what Hodge had done to warrant his horrid reward.

The ceremony was held that afternoon in a shady area kept tidy for such purposes. As the body was lowered into the ground Mr. Nettle intoned, "Receive this innocent soul, Almighty. He is beyond our care now. Take him to thy bosom and cherish this small servant of yours. Mold to mold, body to Green."

Arthur's head felt thick and fuzzy. The search parties had found nothing unusual—only Audrey asleep by the pool. Now she stood next to him looking down into the grave.

Hodge's parents cast a hawthorn leaf and his favorite flower into the grave. Then Mr. Woodruffe led them away in silence.

"We'll have to double the sentries," said Jenkin as they walked away. "If some maniac is still out there we don't want him to strike again. And don't you go off on your own again, miss," he said to Audrey.

"I shan't," she answered. It had been a nasty shock to wake to a different Fennywolde, one full of grief, anger, and fear. She could feel the whole atmosphere of the place had changed.

Gladwin Scuttle linked her arm in Elijah's and went home. No one felt like celebrating the Eve of midsummer now, and the rose petals that had been gathered were left to rot.

Madame Akkikuyu looked back to where Isaac was filling in the grave. Night was drawing closer and she rubbed her ear thoughtfully.

CHAPTER TEN

MIDSUMMER'S EVE

Audrey stared out of her nest and up into the gathering dusk. Everyone in Fennywolde had gone to bed early, trying to blot out the tragic day with sleep. Even so, Audrey could hear the sound of weeping. She lay back on her moss bed and reflected on the death of Hodge and its implications. Was it now dangerous to walk alone in the field? Was the murderer of Hodge still at large out there? And what manner of creature was it, anyway? Some of the fieldmice had come to the conclusion that the beast had been a wandering rogue whom Hodge had surprised. But after all the searching, the general feeling was that whoever had done this atrocious deed had undoubtedly escaped and was now far away.

"Ain't been nothin' like it since that old owl was around," Old Todmore had observed gravely.

The mood of the fieldmice was one of unease. Audrey had noticed that now—more so than before—the simple country mice shied away from her and looked quickly at the ground if she smiled at them. It was almost as if they thought that she had brought this tragedy down on them. She wondered if they pointed at her in secret and muttered nonsense about jinxes and the like. It was certainly good fuel for Isaac Nettle's sermons on the importance of prayer to the Green Mouse. Audrey found all this too tiresome and worrying to dwell on, so she turned her thoughts to other things.

Was Piccadilly safe in the city? She wished he was here; he'd give Mr. Nettle something to make him sit up and scowl at. She almost laughed as she tried to imagine what Piccadilly would have said, but the smile faded on her lips with the thought that the gray mouse must surely think badly of her. She had been too horrible to him for him to think anything else.

Audrey shifted uncomfortably and tried to redirect her thoughts. An image of Jenkin sailed brightly before her eyes. It was hard to believe that he was the son of sour-faced Mr. Nettle. What a fine young mouse Jenkin was! In some ways he reminded her of Piccadilly. Audrey fell asleep with the two mice filling her thoughts.

The night stars wheeled over Fennywolde. Silvery moths flew up and rode the secret breezes. The hedgehog waddled out of a leaf pile and roamed along the ditch searching for mouthwatering delicacies. The moon rose full and bright, and somewhere in a patch of deep shade Nicodemus muttered to Madame Akkikuyu of potions and spells and their mysterious ingredients.

Audrey stirred in her sleep and gradually became aware of a faint sound pulling her awake. A distant lilting music caught her ears, and despite its faintness her heart yearned to follow it.

She opened her eyes and rubbed her brow drowsily. It was an achingly beautiful melody hovering just on the edge of being heard. Audrey tilted her head and wondered where it was coming from. It haunted and enchanted her, beckoning with sweet invisible fingers.

Audrey quickly determined to find the source of the music. She slipped out of bed and turned to look for her dress. She paused and blinked: from her bag of clean clothes and personal treasures a dim light was shining.

Apprehensively, Audrey pulled open the neck of the bag and peered inside. A creamy glow at once illuminated her face and she gasped in wonderment and surprise. She put in her paw and drew out the sprig of hawthorn blossom that Oswald had given to her, back in Deptford. Tonight it was a thing of magic. The petals of the blossom, which for many weeks now had been so dry and yellowed with decay, were as fresh as the day they had been picked—only now they shone with a clear and supernatural light of their own.

Audrey could only stare at it in amazement. Yet it seemed to be the most natural thing in the world—for tonight was the Eve of Midsummer, and almost anything was possible. A thrill of expectation ran through her body as, holding the blossom before her, she left the nest and clambered down the ladder.

In the Hall of Corn nothing stirred. The nests, which lined its long walls, were dark and their entrances gazed at her blindly. The moonlight cast weird shadows all around her, and the breeze moved them so that the black shapes waved mysteriously in the gloom.

The thought of poor Hodge and his unknown assassin crossed Audrey's mind, but she managed to suppress her fear. She just had to follow the strange music. It seemed to tug her along, and she noticed that the light of the hawthorn blossom grew brighter if she went in a certain direction. Using this as a sort of magical compass, Audrey passed out of the Hall and into the wild tangle of cornstalks. Through the field and along the ditch Audrey was led, a will other than her own driving her feet toward the source of the music.

She crossed the ditch and made for the still pool. It seemed that the tune was coming from there, and as she looked a twinkle of light glimmered from behind the surrounding hawthorn bushes.

She hesitated, breathing softly. This was it—the source of the wonderful sound. The light of the blossom in her paw welled up suddenly like a star fallen from heaven. Audrey felt a pang of fear; now she was there she wondered what lay beyond the hawthorn bushes. What would she see when she drew back the branches?

Audrey bit her lip and for a moment wanted desperately to run back to her nest, but it was too late for that now. Slowly, she pulled the branches to one side.

There in the hawthorn grotto were all the mice of Fennywolde. They were arranged in a semicircle around Mr. Woodruffe and all were silent and bowed. Audrey glanced up and saw why they were all so hushed and reverent. She fell to her knees and cried out in surprise.

Floating above Mr. Woodruffe, like a dense cloud of growing things, was the Green Mouse.

He was at the height of his midsummer power and mightier than when Audrey had seen him in the spring. His fur was lush and green as grass, and on his brow he wore the crown of wheat. Here and there, fiery mousebrasses blazed out from his coat of leaves. Indeed, Audrey could not tell where his coat ended and the hawthorn thicket took over, for little green lamps had been hung all around, and they increased the wondrous quality of the place.

The Green Mouse was smiling kindly at his subjects, his long olive green hair cascading down like a lion's mane, and sparkling mousebrasses kindling a green fire in his noble eyes.

Audrey bowed her head. When she dared to look up she found that the Green Mouse was looking straight at her.

Those eyes, which she had never forgotten, now shone on her once more. Slowly the Green Mouse beckoned to her and

timidly Audrey moved toward him. He held out his great paw and she kissed it.

"We are pleased with you, little one," came the huge voice. Audrey flushed and hung her head. "There are still dangers you must face," the Green Mouse told her. "Be brave, my brassless one. I shall take care of you while I can, for spring and summer are mine to command. Remember that the Green fails in autumn and is dead for the winter." He furrowed his immense brow and shook his great head. "Let us hope my protection will not be needed in the bleak months to come, and the summer will end as we pray it will." The Green Mouse smiled and it seemed as if it was daytime. The lamps blazed back at him and Audrey realized that they were not lamps at all but shining leaves. The more he smiled the brighter they became, and the more others began to shine. Soon the entire grotto was filled with a blinding glare of green.

"Now," the Green Mouse addressed all the Fennywolders, "be not sad in heart, for verily I know your grief. Let peace fill your troubled hearts! Forget the pain of your sorrows." He raised his paws and his voice resounded around the grotto: "Tonight is the Eve, when I am in full glory, so let my light dispel your shadows."

The fieldmice cheered and began to dance in time to the music. Audrey looked around her and noticed Arthur and Twit. She rushed over to them. They were staring at the Green Mouse in wonder.

"Oh, me," sighed Twit heavily.

"Heavens," muttered Arthur.

They welcomed Audrey and then laughed, simply because they felt so light and giddy. Twit pranced around and took hold of Audrey's paw and pulled her into the rest of the dancing mice. Shyly, Dimsel Bottom sidled up to Arthur and smiled up at him. Arthur coughed nervously but was soon dancing with her.

Audrey glanced around at the assembled mice. There were Twit's parents staring deeply into each other's eyes as they whirled about sedately. Lily Clover was locked in the embrace of Todkin, and even Samuel Gorse was there, completely re-covered from his mauling by the owl. At the edge of the crowd Audrey could see Jenkin holding paws with Alison Sedge—then he kissed her!

Audrey was so surprised that she stopped dancing. "Well, I never!" she exclaimed.

Twit followed her glance, "Aye, tonight they're together. In the magic of Him all resentments are forgot."

And Audrey realized in a flood of understanding that this was how it should be. Alison and Jenkin were meant to be together.

Audrey and Twit left the dance and wandered around the pool. There they saw Isaac Nettle sitting alone with a scowl on his face. He did not seem to see them—nor indeed any of the things going on around him. He merely sat and prayed sourly.

The chatter and laughter hushed and an expectant silence fell on the fieldmice. The Green Mouse bowed his great green head and raised his paws.

"Join us, Lady!" his voice boomed. "Grace our celebration with your holy presence."

Audrey looked up, holding her breath. The Green Mouse was beseeching the White Lady of the moon to come down.

In the sky above, through the fluttering, glimmering haw-thorn leaves, the silver moon shone out brightly. A slight wind sighed through the branches as a faint mist flowed down to the earth and threaded its way past the fieldmice. Those it touched gasped and felt refreshed. A rich perfume came with it, and here and there tiny moonbeams twinkled and glowed in its depths.

"Oh my," said Twit as the mist reached him, and tears rolled down his little face.

The White Lady floated around the gathering and the Green Mouse lowered his eyes.

Audrey stared at the milky mist in disbelief. Now and then the wind moved it and she saw glimpses of something within. There was a fold of dress revealed for a moment, richly encrusted with pearls, and the toe of a silken slipper. The White Lady said nothing to the fieldmice, but the mist shifted in what might have been a bow to the Green Mouse. He too bowed, then pointed to the water of the pool. The mist rose up and curled around in a wide arc, then it poured down onto the pool's surface and vanished. The Fennywolders saw only a reflection of the night sky and the creamy circle of the moon shimmering in it.

"Drink," the Green Mouse instructed them.

The fieldmice cautiously went to the water's edge and cupped their paws together.

"It's like wine," shouted Young Whortle excitedly, and all the mice gasped in wonderment as they drank the moon mead.

Twit smacked his lips thoughtfully, "You know," he declared, "that beats old Tom's rum, paws down."

Only Audrey did not drink the magical water. She sat at the edge of the pool, staring into its dark mirror and fancied she saw shapes swirling amongst the stars. Slowly the shapes turned to pictures: she saw a long dark tunnel with bright lights at the far end of it and there, running for all he was worth was a familiar gray figure—it was Piccadilly. Audrey cried out in surprise. Piccadilly was being pursued by a horde of rats! Another image took over; it was all white, a landscape of frost and ice. Stretching far and wide, the snowy wasteland moved beneath her as if she were a bird flying. Something dreadful was in the sky, but she was unable to make out what it was. A glittering spear shot down at her, and the white ground lurched below and sped up toward her. Audrey felt herself hurtling down, the ribbon was snatched out of her hair, and she hit the ground with a tremendous crash.

*   *   *

Another hot, beautiful day began.

Audrey found herself curled up in her nest. For a moment she stared up at the woven ceiling blankly. She was unable to remember how she had gotten there. The previous night was still so vivid in her mind that the bright sunlight confused her. The sprig of hawthorn was lying next to her—dry and brittle once more. Audrey picked it up and held it against the light, try-ing to remember how the blossom had looked the night before.

It was the uncomfortable heat that made Audrey finally lean out of her nest.

"It's hotter than yesterday," Arthur's voice came up to her. Audrey waved lazily down at him. The Scuttles were having their breakfast. She dressed quickly and descended the ladder, eager to discuss the marvels of the Eve.

"Wasn't it magnificent?" she cried, running to them.

Elijah Scuttle gazed at her dumbly. "What were, missey?"

"Last night, of course, Mr. Scuttle! Wasn't the Green Mouse wonderful?"

Elijah and Gladwin exchanged puzzled glances.

"The Green Mouse, dear?" asked Mrs. Scuttle.

Audrey looked surprised, then laughed. They were teasing her. "Yes," she persisted excitedly, "when the Lady came down and everyone drank the magic water."

There followed a painful, embarrassed silence broken only by Arthur coughing nervously. Twit began to giggle and tickled Audrey mischievously.

"What you on about, Aud?" The little fieldmouse chuckled happily. "You been at old Tom's rum?"

Audrey stared at them. So they weren't teasing her after all! They did not remember a thing about last night. She opened her mouth to argue but saw Arthur giving her a warning glare from behind his breakfast.

Irritated and confused, Audrey quickly drank her milk. The terrible heat did not help her growing bad temper, and she pressed her forehead with her fingers, saying thickly, "I'm sorry, it's too hot for me here. I must go to the pool—I feel dreadful." She wanted to get away from them, so she could be alone and think this through—last night seemed too real to be a dream, so why did they know nothing about it? She got up to leave.

"Poor dear," tutted Mrs. Scuttle, "it does take some getting used to."

Arthur crammed the last of his porridge into his mouth, mumbled to the others, and ran after his sister.

"Well, I never did," remarked Elijah, highly amused. "That girl do take the biscuit for fanciful ideas. Hobnobbin' with the Green Mouse an' all. You'm got some quaint friends, Willum."

But Twit was staring after the Browns with concern.

*   *   *

"Wait, Sis," Arthur yelled, puffing behind Audrey.

She stopped and turned to wait. When he reached her he took hold of her arm and stared hard.

"Look, are you really feeling okay?"

"Yes, Arthur," she answered simply, "it's just the heat. I can't stand it."

He scratched his head and pressed his lips together. Finally he burst out, "What was all that rubbish back there, then?"

Audrey looked at her brother for some moments and shook her head. "You really don't remember anything at all?"

Arthur pulled his "don't try that on me" face and said crossly,

"Don't be daft, there's nothing to remember. We went to bed early last night: that's all that happened—not this Green Mouse stuff."

"But he was there, Arthur," she insisted passionately. "He was there—larger than life—and so were you and everyone in Fennywolde. I'm not going bonkers, believe me."

"Oh, Sis," he sighed sadly, "how can I? If it's what you want to believe, then fine, but just do me a favor and don't mention it to anyone else. You'll end up embarrassing you, me, and the Scuttles. So just keep a lid on your fairy stories, eh?"

Audrey was too angry to say any more. She spun around and strode away. How could they all have forgotten about it? A disturbing doubt crept into her mind. What if she was going barmy after all? In this stifling weather maybe even that was possible.

She made her way as fast as she could to the still pool. With her heart in her mouth she pushed through the hawthorn and entered the dappled shade.

There was no sign or trace of anything that might reassure her and prove that the Green Mouse had been there. Audrey sat down heavily and stared at the water. She was glad that Alison Sedge was not here today.

* * *

Arthur and Twit left breakfast to go on sentry duty. Arthur was excited as he would have to stay up all night on watch.

Twit nodded to Grommel as they passed through the great doors. "How do," he said.

"Mornin', Twit," greeted Grommel as they went by. "Watch this," he called after them, and proceeded to bend down and touch his toes. "It's me back," he explained, seeing their puzzled faces. "That Madame Ratlady gave me an ointment to rub on and I feels brand new."

They congratulated him and continued on their way. "Can she get any more popular?" asked Arthur.

After a short while Twit ventured, "Arthur, what did Audrey mean before?"

Arthur shrugged. "I think Audrey had a dream, that's all. Where are we going to start today?"

But Twit would not let the matter drop. "I dunno 'bout dreams–ain't too impossible–her seein' the Green Mouse. She done so afore, you know."

"So she says, but if you expect me to believe all that claptrap . . . why, she's always making things up!"

Again Twit persisted. "And our Oswald–when I was sittin' with him, he said somethin' 'bout seein' the Green Mouse in Jupiter's chamber."

"Oh, pooh!" scorned Arthur. "Oswald wasn't well, he was saying all sorts of daft things. I'm not interested in Audrey's silly stories and I'm surprised at you–don't go encouraging her, for heaven's sake. Look, there's Jenkin. Let's go join him."

The matter seemed to be closed. Twit chewed the inside of his cheek thoughtfully, then ran after his friend. The watch began.

*   *   *

Madame Akkikuyu waded through the deep leaf piles near the oaks. Her bag was stuffed full with fresh herbs and wild flowers, the ingredients for a special potion. Nicodemus had instructed her to collect them the night before, but there were some things that Madame Akkikuyu had trembled at the thought of getting. Nicodemus had been very persuasive.

"Listen, Akkikuyu, and remember well," he had told her. "I shall tell you how to free me from the black limbo where I am imprisoned. There must be a great spell to unfetter me and bring me back. Look how the land needs me. It is dying,

174

Akkikuyu! When I am released I shall cause the rain to fall and restore the water to the thirsty land and heal its burns."

Madame Akkikuyu had thought that was a very admirable thing, so she had asked him, "Tell Akkikuyu what she must do to release you."

"There must be a potion," Nicodemus had begun quickly, "and it must be the distillation of many things—but are you ready for this, Akkikuyu?"

"Yes, Nico," she had stated firmly.

"There will be herbs and flowers, which only bloom on moonless nights," the voice on her ear had continued, "and other things that are necessary but you may find difficult to gather."

"Akkikuyu get anything," she had claimed hastily.

"Good," Nicodemus had declared, "then fetch me a frog and boil away the flesh till only the white bones are left."

"No!" the fortune-teller had cried, appalled. "Akkikuyu no kill poor froggy—she good and kind."

"Believe me, Akkikuyu," the voice had wheedled, "it is only because this is so urgent that I would ask this terrible thing of you. If this is not done then no rain will fall and all the frogs are sure to perish—better one die than all."

Madame Akkikuyu had been forced to agree with his reasoning, and Nicodemus had told her to find him a frog the very next day. She looked down at her bulging bag and grimaced; there was no frog in there yet—she still demurred at murder, and had collected all the plants instead. She wondered if Nicodemus would scold her when night fell. Everything seemed muddled when he was not there to reassure and guide her and everything seemed so much less important in the daylight.

She trudged up the dell and wandered about the roots of the oaks, wiping her face with her shawl.

"Too hot," she moaned to herself. She squinted at the tattoo on her ear, but it was still. "Hah, old Nico—he not like the heat. He not see me in daytime."

She surveyed the leafy world around her and spotted some strange chalky-looking objects scattered about the base of one of the oaks. She went over to examine them.

"Hmm," she mumbled, prodding one with her claw. It was gray and dry and broke open at her touch. "Hooty cough-ups," she remarked with disdain.

They were owl pellets, tight little bundles of bone and fur that had been swallowed greedily by the owl as he devoured his prey, only to be regurgitated later when he had been unable to digest them.

"So owly still here," muttered the fortune-teller. She looked up the tree and saw the dark hole in its trunk. "Just you stay away from my mouseys," she threatened, shaking her fists, "or Akkikuyu come pluck you again."

She thought she heard a frightened hoot in response and was satisfied. It was time to find a shady place to sleep. Her nightly lessons with Nicodemus were leaving her with no energy for the following day. Madame Akkikuyu yawned widely and lumbered off to rest.

MAGIC AND MURDER

As the afternoon wore on, the fieldmice gathered in the Hall of Corn to discuss the unusually hot weather.

"Tain't natural," remarked Old Todmore, squinting at the sky. No rain fer weeks now. Mark my words, young 'uns, there's somethin' very wrong 'bout all this."

The ground had become like stone and here and there long cracks had begun to appear. The corn in the field looked dry and some of the stalks were withered and sickly—an omen that did not go unnoticed by the anxious mice.

Waves of disquiet now coursed through Fennywolde, building on the unease left by Hodge's death. The tired and anxious Fennywolders took to looking nervously over their shoulders at the slightest noise.

Isaac Nettle, accustomed to the great heat of his forge, peered out over the field and declared to those willing to listen, "The fires of the infernal are at work here. Repent ye and crave pardon from the Almighty Green." And Mr. Woodruffe was too tired and overheated to stop him.

177

Some mice swooned in the swelter and all throats were burned by the hot breeze. Many spent the day by the still pool, leaving a large space between themselves and the strange town mouse who had brought the odd weather with her.

Eventually the day burned itself out and the early stars pricked the evening sky. The fieldmice clambered into their nests, relieved that the long, uncomfortable day was over and worried about the next. They cast themselves on their beds and fell into exhausted faints rather than sleep.

In some of the little round nests, plaintive voices were raised in prayers for rain. "Please, oh Green, deliver us from the sun. Bring down the rain."

Madame Akkikuyu passed through the field with a satisfied grin on her face. She had been nosing around the top end of the ditch where the mud was still spongy, and after much searching had found a dead frog.

It was a bit old and whiffy, but Madame Akkikuyu felt very pleased with herself. She had managed to keep her promise to Nicodemus without killing anything. How clever she felt! He would be very pleased with her—no need to mention how it was acquired. She hurried along, eager to put the grisly object into her pot so that the skin could be boiled away, ready for the night's instruction.

As she was walking through the Hall of Corn, a voice called down to her from one of the nests. Hastily the fortune-teller thrust the frog into her bag and glanced upward.

Young Whortle's father came scurrying down and stood beside her.

"Forgive me, dear lady," said Mr. Nep apologetically, "but I have a . . . well . . . er . . . something to say to you."

Madame Akkikuyu narrowed her gleaming black eyes and closed her claws tightly over her bag. "Akkikuyu listen," she said at last.

Mr. Nep first looked down at his feet, then twiddled his

thumbs and wiped his face in embarrassment. Finally he blurted out, "Can you make it rain?"

It was not what Madame Akkikuyu had expected and she was dumbstruck for a few moments. But Mr. Nep babbled on.

"Oh . . . we're so desperate! You've shown yerself to be wise in the craft of healing, so some of us set to thinkin' that mebbe you had other . . . skills. There, I've said it."

The rat considered him for a while and said, "You want rain magic? Akkikuyu no witch or cloud dancer—she healer."

Mr. Nep looked aghast. "Oh, I have offended you. Please, no such insult was meant. It's just that even the pool is getting low in water now and well—we're getting very worried."

Madame Akkikuyu smiled. She liked it when the fieldmice came to her for assistance. A warm tingle shot up her tail and she puffed out her chest. She rubbed her tattooed ear thoughtfully and told Mr. Nep, "Akkikuyu try—no promise."

"Oh, thank you," he said, his face relaxing "I'll tell my Nelly, she'll be so relieved. We don't know what we'd do if it weren't fer you." Mr. Nep scampered back to his nest.

"A difficult promise to keep," came a soft whisper.

The rat jumped in surprise.

"What are you going to do about it?" her tattoo continued.

"You . . . you heard, Nico?" ventured the fortune-teller nervously.

The voice of Nicodemus mocked her. "Oh yes, I heard. You want to help these little creatures by bringing rain to them." The voice suddenly changed and became full of anger. "How dare you give such promises! Who are you to offer them the power of nature? The power of life-giving rain is not yours to give, it is the province of we land spirits."

"Akkikuyu only want to help poor mouseys," she whined.

The tattoo snarled back, "Don't bother to lie, I know you, Akkikuyu—perhaps better than you do yourself. I can see into your soul, and you wish to rule these poor fieldmice."

"No," she protested immediately, "I likes them."

"Twist and turn all you like, but you cannot escape the truth. You want them to become dependent on you—to run to you for the slightest thing until they are your subjects, enslaved to your evil will."

Madame Akkikuyu sobbed. "That false. I not like that, mouseys know—they love Akkikuyu; she their friend."

"You have no friends," snapped Nicodemus savagely. "Put your trust in me alone. The mice are using you—can you not see that? They take from you all the time, what do they give in return? Nothing."

The fortune-teller fled from the Hall. But at the edge of the ditch Madame Akkikuyu sat down and wept. "I like mouseys," she blubbered through her great salty tears.

"Then give them the rain you promised," muttered Nicodemus.

"I can't," she wailed unhappily. "Akkikuyu not powerful enough. Mouseys will laugh at me and say I cheap trickster."

"You should have thought of that before," scolded the voice.

"Nico," she began, "Nico, can you not make it rain? Only tiny bit, not much?"

"But I have already told you," said Nicodemus sternly, "until I am freed I can do nothing. My powers are useless!"

"Then Akkikuyu is washed up—mouseys not believe in her anymore."

The soft voice in her ear whispered to itself and the painted eyes closed meditatively. "There may be a way," the voice began slowly. The rat sat up, excited and eager.

"Tell me quick," she insisted. "Akkikuyu will help, best she can."

Nicodemus sounded uncertain. "Are you ready, though?" he asked doubtfully. "What is required might make you tremble."

"Akkikuyu not afraid," she affirmed, and to prove it she

flourished the dead frog from her bag. "See, I bring this, like Nico ask."

"I asked for it yesterday, Akkikuyu, yet this creature has been dead for more than three days. Do you think you can trick me?"

"No . . ." she answered feebly, letting the dried frog clatter down the steep bank and smash on the stones below.

"I must have absolute obedience, Akkikuyu," demanded the voice. "Absolute! Do you understand?"

"Yes, Nico!"

"Then swear—on your soul, to obey me in all things."

"I . . . I . . ."

"Swear!"

"Akkikuyu . . . Akkikuyu swear—on soul." She hung her head and said no more. The tattoo smiled an unpleasant, triumphant grin.

"Excellent," resumed Nicodemus, "now we may proceed. The essence of rain lies in the invocation of two elements, air and water. As I am trapped you must work the spell for me. I shall tell you what to do and let us hope some rain will fall." The voice dropped to a low whisper as Nicodemus said, "For these elements we must use symbols to call upon the necessary forces—if I was there I could do it myself."

"Symbols?" asked the fortune-teller, detecting something sinister in the whispered tone. "What symbols?"

"Something that represents the elements," said the voice. "For water a fish will be most suitable."

"And for air?"

"A bird," declared the tattoo wickedly. "At the bottom of the field in the hedge you will find a blackbird's nest. Bring the bird back here."

"Alive?" asked Akkikuyu hopefully.

Nicodemus just laughed at her.

Madame Akkikuyu set off for the hedge in misery. Would her triumph in getting the rain to fall be worth the life she was about to take? At the hedge she peered up into its dark, brambly depths. It was quite difficult to see anything in there at all at nighttime, but eventually she discovered it. Gingerly the rat squeezed through the thorns and began to climb.

The blackbird was still and silent; its feathers were fluffed out and the tiny beadlike eyes were firmly closed. Only its gentle heartbeat stirred its breast.

Madame Akkikuyu pulled herself up and looked at the bird fearfully. She thought about what she had to do and her heart beat faster. The bird looked so peaceful that tears sprang to her eyes again.

"I cannot," she whispered hoarsely.

"You must," came the voice in her ear. "One swift blow and the creature will be dead. It will feel nothing! Think of your mouse friends and the rain you can bring them."

So Madame Akkikuyu slowly raised a quivering claw and shakily drew the bone out of her hair. Then, closing her eyes tightly, she brought it crashing down on the nest.

At the ditch she lit a fire under her pot and pushed the feathery body into the bubbling water.

"And now, a fish, Akkikuyu," ordered Nicodemus, not letting her think too long about what she had done.

So the fortune-teller went to the still pool and stared long at the dark water, taking no notice of the grim reflection that gazed back at her with accusing eyes. Suddenly a string of tiny bubbles rose to the surface. With a great SPLASH she smacked her claw down and scooped out a spout of water. Within it a little fish was wriggling. As she caught it in her other claw Nicodemus said to her, "Well done—but listen, Akkikuyu, do you hear?"

The fortune-teller stood still and waited. A faint croaking was just audible amid the rustle of the hawthorn leaves.

On Nicodemus's instruction she crept around to a clump of water iris in time to see a small brown frog leap into sight and hop away from the pool.

"Catch it!" screamed Nicodemus. "We still need one and this will be fresh."

Madame Akkikuyu ran after the little frog and pounced on it.

Breathlessly she made her way back to the ditch and her bubbling pot. Hurriedly she dropped the fish into the boiling potion and repeated the spell after Nicodemus.

"Here me, folk that dwell in the spaces between the stars," he began. "I abjure all light, darken the sky, bring down the rain—in the name of Nachteg I command it, for you know who I am."

There was a silence and the rat looked up expectantly. But the tattoo said, "Now you must kiss the frog, Akkikuyu, and the spell shall be complete."

Grimly Madame Akkikuyu returned to the edge of the ditch and picked up the limp, slimy body. She gritted her teeth and kissed its head.

Nicodemus sighed and the first spots of rain pattered down.

In the Hall of Corn the fieldmice were disturbed in their sleep. They nuzzled and snuggled deep into their moss beds but could not escape the incessant drumming overhead. One by one the mice were roused from their beds and popped their heads out of their nests to see what the noise was.

"Rain!" they cried out with glee. "It's raining! Hooray!"

They abandoned their nests and danced around in the Hall with their faces upturned.

Mr. Nep gasped in wonder at the miracle, woke his wife, and went down to tell everyone. "It's the ratlady! I asked her to make it rain and she has! What a marvel she is. We must go and thank her." The fieldmice joyously trooped out of the Hall to find Madame Akkikuyu. The door guards went with them.

Sleepily, Audrey leaned out to see what the fuss was. A large drop of rain fell with a *plop* on her nose. She wiped it off and looked into the drizzling sky.

"Hello, dear," said Mrs. Scuttle, descending the ladder close by. "My, what a wonder! Everyone's saying that your ratwoman has made it rain. They've all gone to find her–imagine. Elijah and I are going to follow them–I don't think I'll sleep anymore tonight, and it will be light soon." She let the rain fall on her gladly. "Oh, it seems like years since the last drop we had. Are you coming?"

Audrey shook her head. Here was another feather for Madame Akkikuyu's cap. Wearily she sighed, "Give her my regards–but I'm going back to bed."

"Oh, well, you know best, dear."

*　　*　　*

At the ditch they found Madame Akkikuyu beaming broadly. Her potion pot was now empty and the fire was out.

"Mouseys," she said welcomingly, throwing open her claws. "Akkikuyu bring rain as promise."

"Astounding," cried Mr. Nep, shaking her vigorously by the claw. "Truly wondrous–well done." Everyone joined in to praise her, until Madame Akkikuyu flushed with pleasure.

But the celebrations were short-lived. The rain suddenly stopped.

"Won't be no more rain out of that sky," said Old Todmore, examining the heavens.

He was right. The magic rain shower had finished, and Madame Akkikuyu shook her head in dismay–it certainly wasn't worth the murders she had committed that night.

"That spot o' water won't have done much good at all," observed one mouse sorrowfully. "Ground's too dry to soak it up. It's not long afore sunrise an' all that rain'll steam off soon. Bah—darned waste o' time."

The Fennywolders tutted sadly. All their high hopes had been dashed. Now they felt more flat and miserable than ever. All agreed, however, that Madame Akkikuyu had done her best, better than any of them could have done, but this didn't get them anywhere.

Madame Akkikuyu glanced at the tattoo on her ear, but Nicodemus was silent—it was too near daybreak for him. She wondered if he had known how short the shower would be. She left the mice and sat by herself on the steep bank and cried regretfully.

*   *   *

Young Whortle was making his way through the field when dawn's gray light crept over Fennywolde. He was a heavy sleeper and was surprised to find himself alone in the nest that morning. He knew nothing of Madame Akkikuyu's rainmaking and none of the others had returned yet.

He had gone through the great door wondering where Grommel and the other guard had gotten to.

"Funny," he said to himself, "where they all gone, then?" He put his paws behind his back and began to hum a jolly tune. He felt much better now and his shoulders only gave him an occasional twinge. Secretly he hoped that he would have scars like Mr. Scuttle, as proof of his bravery.

A mist was rising as the meager rainfall turned to vapor. It was thick and white, and soon, without realizing, Young Whortle wandered out of the main corridor.

"Oh, curse this fog," he muttered crossly. "I wish Sammy was here with me." He rubbed his shoulders for they had begun to ache in the damp mist. He looked up suddenly. He ought to be out of the field by now, but the white, swirling mist billowed around him. He was hopelessly lost.

Something moved in the corner of his eye. He turned quickly and the mist pressed around closely. "Hello?" he called brightly, "someone there, then?" There was no reply, only the rustle of the cornstalks. Young Whortle shrugged and put the movement down to the swirling of the mist. He set off again in no particular direction, knowing that sooner or later he'd come across some familiar landmark. The mist grew thicker and flowed over his plump face.

"This is a daft nuisance," he muttered and began to whistle a tune that Hodge had taught him. The tune died on his lips as he remembered his dear friend. He had been found murdered in this very field. . . . Something rustled behind him—and it wasn't just the cornstalks. Young Whortle walked a little faster. He wanted to stop and take a look. But what if it was something horrible waiting for him, with long sharp teeth and pointed claws? Young Whortle shivered. He knew he was giving in to panic.

The rustling sounded again—only this time it was on his left. He yelped and stared wildly around him. Suddenly he broke into a wild, panic-stricken run, deeper and deeper into the field, not caring where he went just so long as he was away from the horror that lurked in the suffocating mist.

He crashed headlong through the dense stalks, squealing out loud. Sharp stones bit into his pink feet till they bled, and coarse leaves razored through his paws. "Oh no," he whimpered as he felt his breath rattle in his chest, "I can't go on much farther."

His legs crumpled beneath him and Young Whortle lay panting on the hard ground. He was a small, frightened animal, totally alone in a turgid sea of mist. He had never felt so forlorn. Even when the owl was after him at least he had known what he was up against. But this was different. Here the danger hid out of sight, waiting to strike when its victim least expected.

He strained his ears for some minutes but could hear nothing.

"Wait till I tell Sammy this," he told himself in a voice louder than he had intended. "He won't half laugh! 'Things you get yourself into, Warty, 'he'll say."

Young Whortle got to his feet, his legs still a bit wobbly. He scratched the top of his head and tugged the little tuft of hair that grew there. Then he froze.

Thin, long fingers appeared out of the mist and came for him. As he yelled for his life he felt something tighten around his neck.

"FENNY!" he screamed desperately, "FEN—"

Only the cornstalks rustled in reply.

*   *   *

Arthur looked up. He was sure he had heard something. He and Twit were the only sentries left on duty—the others having gone to see Madame Akkikuyu with the rest of the fieldmice.

Arthur looked across at his friend, who was swaying happily on a corn ear. "Did you hear that, Twit?" he shouted.

The fieldmouse gazed over with a blank look. "What be the matter, Art?" he called back.

"I'm not sure . . . but I think I heard the alarm."

Arthur tried to pierce the low mist with his eyes. He felt ill at ease. Something dreadful was happening down there—he was certain of it.

"I'm going to raise the alarm myself," he told Twit decisively. "I don't like that mist down there—it could hide anything. It's creepy." He cupped his paws around his mouth, keeping a tight hold on the stalk with his legs and tail, and called out "FENNY!" as loud as he could. Twice he repeated the cry, then both he and Twit climbed down.

"Should we wait fer the others?" asked Twit anxiously. Now he was on the ground, the mist was up to his chest and writhed over him like a living thing. In the dark places of the field the mist looked deeper.

"No time," said Arthur firmly, "come on."

They left the corridor path and plunged into the wild places of the field.

"Is it Hodge's murderer, do you think?" asked Twit quietly.

"Might be," answered Arthur gravely. "We should have brought a stick or something just in case."

"Here," Twit pressed a stout staff into Arthur's chubby paw. "Thought they might come in handy," he explained.

"Good thinking," praised Arthur, greatly cheered. "The two of us should be able to handle whoever it is."

"Or whatever," added Twit timidly.

Arthur gulped. "We," he said, trying to sound brave, "we've fought off a band of bloodthirsty rats before now."

"Yes, but there was five of us then and only three of them," observed Twit glumly. Arthur brandished his stick before him like a sword, cutting through the dense mist only to have the gaps fill up again thicker than before.

"We'll be all right," he said aloud, but his feigned confidence fooled no one. "Just don't think of anything frightening, Twit. What would old Triton say if he could hear us, eh? Something like 'lily-livered landlubbers' I bet. And what about Kempe? Why don't we sing one of his bawdy songs to make us feel better and get rid of all this gloom?" Arthur cleared his throat. "Rosie, poor Rosie . . . why aren't you singing, Twit? Twit?"

Arthur spun around, but his friend was gone. Only the mist met his gaze and closed in on him. From far away—or so it seemed, he heard the little fieldmouse call his name anxiously.

Twit had stumbled over a stone and in that instant had lost his friend. The mist poured in around him and he was alone.

"Arthur!" he shouted meekly. "Where are you, Arthur?" But

the fog swallowed his tiny voice greedily. His cries dwindled to murmurs and then into silence. Twit was afraid. The stick he held trembled in his paws as he tried to make his way through the corn. He was totally lost. For all he knew he was going around in futile circles. Then he began to hear the noises.

The fieldmouse paused and waved the stick about him in a frenzy. "There . . . there's five of us here, matey, so clear off sharp!"

The stems crackled and snapped to his right. He ducked and darted off to the left. Now it was in front of him, rustling and scraping, coming ever closer. It was going to get him—to murder him as it had done with Hodge. Twit turned to flee again, but the noise seemed to be all around him now. His courage left him and he stood still and howled sadly, "Please, no!" but the thick milky mist muffled his voice.

Long twiglike fingers emerged out of the fog like ghosts. Twit tried to fend them off, but it was all in vain. A plaited loop was pulled over his ears and caught him around the neck.

"EEEK! HELP! FENNY!" he squawked as the loop began to tighten and strangle him.

"Help . . . Fenny . . . Help . . ." Twit choked on each word and scrabbled at his throat. It was no use. The loop continued to throttle him and Twit fell senseless to the ground.

"Twit!" bawled Arthur, smashing through the stalks. "Twit!" He thrashed the air with his stick but could see no one. The fiend had slipped silently away.

"Twit," moaned Arthur as he knelt by his friend's side. "Oh, Twit, don't be dead." He cradled his friend's head in his paws and listened for a heartbeat.

A faint murmur fluttered in Twit's chest, and Arthur wept. Slowly, the mist began to disperse.

Gradually Twit came to. His breathing was labored and he touched his neck tenderly. There were big black bruises forming all around his throat. He grinned at Arthur shakily.

"Reckoned I were a goner then, Art," he croaked.

"You'll be fine now," assured Arthur. "We ought to get out of here while we can. Look, the mist's thinning." He helped Twit to his feet and they staggered off.

"Did you see who it was?" asked Arthur curiously.

Twit shook his head slowly. "No, Art . . . but it were uncanny. All I saw was something that looked . . . looked as if it were made totally out of straw."

HUNTERS IN THE NIGHT

When Arthur and Twit hobbled into the Hall of Corn, they found a throng of mice waiting for them. The Fennywolders had heard Arthur's alarm call but had had no idea where to go, so they had assembled in the Hall and waited.

Arthur breathlessly explained what had happened to him and Twit, and Mrs. Scuttle hurried over to help her son.

The fieldmice shook their heads, stunned that this could happen again. Mr. Woodruffe stepped onto the throne and raised his staff for silence.

"Now we know," he declared, "the creature—whatever it is, is still at large. We must search the field once more."

As the fieldmice went to find weapons, Mr. Nep came rushing out of his nest with a pale, frightened face. "My son," he cried, "my son has gone."

"Has anyone seen Young Whortle?" asked Mr. Woodruffe grimly. All the fieldmice shook their heads, and a chill entered the Hall. "Then we must look for him also," he said, "and let us

192

hope he has only gone exploring again."

A large party of strong husbands set off through the field, wielding sticks and cudgels. Arthur was too tired to join them—he had been up all night and desperately wanted some sleep. He even declined the offer of breakfast.

A group of wives who had been left behind chatted together dismally and clutched at their mousebrasses. All were fearful.

Suddenly one small child asked its mother, "Are we all going to die, Mam?" Nobody answered. But the tension was broken and a hysterical mousewife burst out, "Who is doing these things? What have we done to deserve this?"

Just then, Mr. Nettle came into the Hall followed by Jenkin. "Perhaps the villain is amongst us!" he shouted above the hub-bub.

This was too much for the worried mice. A ripple ran through them, and they looked at their neighbors suspiciously. Why, it might be any one of them.

"What do you mean, Nettle?" asked Mr. Woodruffe sternly.

"All I say is that though ye search ye will find nought. Maybe the foul one is one of our folk, playacting behind a fair mask."

The crowd stirred uneasily and murmured to one another.

"Now just wait a moment," said Mr. Woodruffe. He feared that something nasty could happen if Isaac was allowed to go any farther. He did not want the fieldmice to be at odds with one another. "You're talking out of your hat, Nettle," he said. "We were all at the ditch with Madame Akkykookoo when this happened, so it can't be any of us."

The crowd sighed with relief.

Isaac Nettle shook his head and gazed upward. "Were we all present, I wonder?" he said loudly.

Everyone followed his glance and the murmurs began again. There, climbing out of her nest, was Audrey.

"I think perhaps one was not with us," uttered Isaac darkly.

Arthur sprang forward in spite of his fatigue. He saw what Mr. Nettle was driving at. "Rubbish!" he growled angrily. "Not even you believe that."

Mr. Nettle's face was stony, and the crowd's mutterings grew louder.

Jenkin stepped up to his father. "Dad," he pleaded, "you know Miss Brown's not to blame."

Isaac turned on his son and struck him violently across the face. "What dost thou know of yon painted sinner?" he bellowed, but Jenkin merely glared back at him with a face full of anger, then turned and walked away.

Isaac strode after his son.

"Listen to me all of you!" boomed Mr. Woodruffe, commanding their attention again.

"If there are any among you who are foolish enough to listen to old Nettle's rantings then I warn you now. There are stiff penalties for those who disobey the King of the Field. Let none of you lay a paw on our guests from the town. Now go about your business or wait for your husbands to return; only clear the Hall."

The crowd shuffled away grumbling and whispering.

Audrey had watched all this with curiosity. She had not the faintest idea of what was going on, but caught several hostile glances aimed at her from the crowd. The fieldmice moved away from her when she passed them, as though terrified of what she might do to them. She quickly made her way to the throne and asked Arthur, "What's going on? What's happened?" Quickly Arthur told her about the creature that had tried to choke Twit.

"Arthur," she said when she had made sure that Twit was all right, "I don't like it here—these mice don't like me. They think I'm some sort of devil—and quite frankly they give me the shivers too. You wouldn't believe some of the stares they were giving me then. I felt as if they would tear me apart given half a chance."

Mr. Woodruffe put his arm around her shoulder. "Now lass, don't you fret none. They're a friendly lot in Fennywolde, really. It's just that right now they're scared, what with the weather and Hodge's murder and now poor Twit this morning. They need to feel safe, and if that means they have to stick the blame on some outsider, then that's what they'll try and do. Don't worry, though, I'll not let them—I've a cooler head than most, but it's a tricky job with old Isaac sticking his tuppence in. He knows how to get them riled, he do, and it's a shame, but he don't like you, and once he's got somethin' in his mulish head that's that."

Audrey was not comforted. The day was another scorcher, but she stayed away from the still pool for fear of confrontations. Instead, she helped Mrs. Scuttle with small tasks and jobs that did not really need to be done, but it kept her busy and out of folks' way.

Arthur and Twit slept all day, so Audrey had no one of her own age to talk to. She felt bored and lonely, and the Hall of Corn began to feel like a jail. Once she spotted Iris Crowfoot carrying a bowl of water for her mother. Audrey waved, but Mrs. Crowfoot scolded her daughter for daring to smile back. How could anyone think that she was connected with the murder of Hodge? It was too ridiculous for words! Audrey would have laughed at their silliness if she was not so worried and afraid.

*　　*　　*

Alison Sedge sat in the meadow weaving a necklace of forget-me-nots. As she worked, she mulled over her suspicions. She hated Audrey with all her heart. She wished that Mr. Nettle had struck her instead of Jenkin—Alison would like to see Audrey's lip swell up like a blackberry. That would spoil her fairy looks! She cursed the ill fortune which had brought the town mouse to her field—just when she was having a bit of fun with the boys too. It had been a good start to the summer, she had been admired by everyone, and had flirted with everyone.

Suddenly Alison shuddered. A horrible thought occurred to her. One of her suitors now lay under the earth: if she had been nicer to him on that fateful day would Hodge still be alive now? Young Whortle was missing as well—she hoped he was safe. If things got any worse there would be no boys left for her to flirt with.

The meadow grass rustled close by. Alison sprang to her feet and backed away nervously.

"Who's there?" she asked.

"Oh, is that you, Alison Sedge?" It was Jenkin's voice and he sounded none too happy at meeting her.

Quickly Alison sat down again and struck her most casual and alluring pose. "Over here, Jolly Jenkin," she invited huskily.

He came into sight through the silvery flowering grasses, and Alison beckoned him over. His eye was purple and the lip was bleeding again.

"Oh, Jenkin," she cried in alarm. "You look awful, this is a real baddun this time. You rest there," she added kindly. "I'll go fetch some water to bathe that eye in."

But Jenkin wouldn't have it. "I'll be aright in a bit," he explained.

"Is it very sore?" she asked. His eye was an angry bluey purple and she could actually see the lip throbbing. Alison wanted to throw her arms about him and make it all better. This was what she wanted, and at that moment she realized that all her flirting had simply been a waste of time. Time that should have been spent with Jenkin.

"Oh, Jenkin," she said, moving closer, "Your dad's horrible

to you—p'raps it's time you left him an' built a nest of your own in the Hall."

With his good eye Jenkin regarded Alison coolly. Her creamy hair brushed against his arm and her breath smelled of wild strawberries. There had been a time—not long ago, when he had prayed for her to be near him like this, but not now. He stood up and moved away.

"Were my fault these," he said, meaning his bruises. "I oughtn't a mentioned Miss Brown—my dad don't like her."

Alison was slightly vexed. He had interrupted her just as she was about to kiss him. "I don't like her either," she snapped. "She ain't right in the head an' I think she's got somethin' to do with Hodge."

"Pah," snorted Jenkin, "you'm just jealous. Not even my dad really believed that rubbish, he just said it to make her look bad."

"But, Jenkin," protested Alison. "She told me, she said that she'd choke anyone what got in her way."

"Shut it, Alison, don't bother." Jenkin turned and looked away. "Y'see," he confessed shyly, "I likes Miss Brown a heck of a lot and nothing you can say will change that."

He left Alison on her own. She twisted her fingers around the necklace she had just made and tore it off. In a cascade of tiny blue petals Alison Sedge wept bitterly to herself.

*   *   *

Audrey lay in her nest staring at the starry sky. Everyone had gone to bed—everyone except for Arthur and the other night sentries. Twit was not allowed to join them till he was fully recovered. His throat was still sore and his voice was hoarse and croaky.

Audrey wondered how much longer she could go on living in Fennywolde if the hostile atmosphere continued. Her job as

companion to Madame Akkikuyu was more or less over now—
she had only seen the rat briefly that day at lunch, but she was
so popular with everyone that they had only said a few words
before someone grabbed the rat and invited her to join them.

There was one thing that really puzzled Audrey. Madame
Akkikuyu looked different. For some time she had not been
able to put her finger on what it was. Then she realized. The
fortune-teller was no longer black—her fur was changing color!
Now she was a sleek chestnut and it seemed to get lighter with
every day. It was most peculiar, but the Fennywolders believed
that it was the country air and sunshine that was the cause.

Madame Akkikuyu certainly looked very different from the
pathetic creature Audrey had seen in the Starwife's chamber.
She had grown strong and if not fat, then well padded.

Her thoughts were interrupted by a small, polite voice whispering under the nest entrance.

"Miss Brown," it said.

"Who is it?" she whispered back.

"It's me—Jenkin."

"Oh," Audrey was surprised, "what do you want?"

"To talk to you—meet me down here when you're ready."

Quickly she pulled on her clothes and tied up her hair with
her best ribbon. What could Jenkin want at this time of night?
It had to be very important. She climbed down the ladder and
stood before him. Even in the pale moonlight she could see the
marks left by his father's hard paw.

His eyes lit up when he saw her. "You always do look nice,"
he said.

"Thank you." She blushed. "What is it you want?"

Jenkin looked around furtively. "I can't tell 'ee here," he said
shyly. "Can we go somewhere a bit privatelike?"

"Yes, all right," she consented, extremely curious. Jenkin
led her out of the Hall of Corn by a small side entrance, taking
care that the sentries did not see them.

"Why all this secrecy?" she asked him.

"My dad's forbid me to see you," came the reply in a hushed voice. "He says you're a town heathen who don't know good from bad."

Audrey felt that there was quite a lot she could say about Mr. Nettle, but for once, she held her tongue and let Jenkin continue.

"He tells me you ain't worth a crumb, that you're wicked all through an' that since you've come here we ain't had nothin' but misery an' death."

This was quite enough! Audrey felt herself near to exploding. "If that's all you've got to tell me I might as well go back now. I've got a brother who can tell me all that and more besides, thank you very much. In fact, if I don't go now you'll find yourself with another black eye."

To her astonishment he laughed. Not an unkind, mocking laugh, but a gentle good-humored chuckle. "Reckon you could do it too," he said. "But don't go yet—not till I've had my say. Look, we're all right here now. There ain't no one to listen."

The moonlight fell on his fine hair, and for the first time Audrey noticed that he had combed it. He swallowed hard and began.

"I told you what my dad thinks," he lumbered on awkwardly, "cos that don't matter to me no more. I'm never goin' back to him or our winter quarters—I've left."

"Good for you, Jenkin," said Audrey, not yet seeing what he was driving at. Was that berrybrew she could smell on his breath?

"Tomorrow I shall start a-buildin' a nest around the Hall," he told her proudly, the stars sparkling in his round, excited eyes. "What I'm sayin', Miss Brown—Audrey is . . . well, I'd like you to share that nest with me. Cos I loves you and wants . . . to wed you. . . ." He stared at her hopefully, then uttered something under his breath, "Darn I forgot!" and quickly he knelt down on one knee. "You don't have to answer straight away like–think it over."

Audrey was bewildered. A proposal of marriage was the last thing she had expected, and it took some time for it to properly sink in.

"You really want to marry me?" she sounded shocked and slightly amused.

"More than anything–that's the Green honest truth." He watched her intently with wide, trusting eyes like a baby.

Audrey's heart went out to him. The plain truth was that she did not love him, but a strong desire to see Piccadilly again grew in her.

She knelt down beside Jenkin and took his paw in hers. "Oh, Jenkin," she said slowly, "I'm sorry, I don't want to hurt your feelings, but I can't accept. I'm extremely flattered, but no– you see, I now know that I love another. I never realized it before."

Jenkin hung his head. Audrey felt so sorry for him, but she remembered the Eve of Midsummer and knew that Alison was meant for him.

"There is someone who cares for you very much," she said, trying to break through his barrier of sullen silence.

"Who's that, then?" he asked miserably.

"Alison Sedge," Audrey replied, and she squeezed his paw tightly.

"Tuh," sniffed Jenkin, "she don't care for no one but her-self," he answered thickly.

"Was she always like that?"

"No–there was a time when me an' Alison went around together quite a bit, but then she got her mousebrass an' every-thing changed."

"Then it can change again, Jenkin," urged Audrey. "Forget about me–I'm just getting in the way of the two of you. I know that you and she are meant for each other. Truly."

There was such a ring of certainty in her voice that Jenkin looked up at her and for a second caught a flash of green fire flicker in her eyes.

He gasped and Audrey kissed his cheek. "You just wait," she said, "you'll be the one giving her the runaround, only don't make her suffer too much—I've already made that mistake."

"Have I made a fool of myself?" asked Jenkin bashfully.

Audrey smiled. "Not at all. It's nice to know that not everyone in Fennywolde thinks I'm a monster." But as she said it the hairs on the back of her neck tingled.

Suddenly the cornstalks were thrust aside and something crashed toward them.

Audrey could not believe her eyes and Jenkin fell back in fear. The corn dolly she had made was lurching toward them! No longer was it the trim, neat figure she had woven but a mass of tangled, twisted stems—bent with hatred and evil spells. The arms, which had been pretty corn ears, had grown long and wild with spiky fingers, which clutched at the air greedily and waved around full of menace.

The nightmare figure staggered toward them, its twiggy fingers outstretched, ready to catch them.

Jenkin acted quickly.

He grabbed Audrey's paw and dragged her away just in time. "Come on!" he yelled.

Audrey snapped out of her trance and they stumbled off through the field, the figure pursuing them closely. It scraped its untidy skirt over the stony ground and flayed the air with its thin arms, groping for them. Its plaited loop head twisted from side to side, seeming to sense rather than see where it was going.

Jenkin and Audrey ran in blind terror with the papery crackling sound rustling close behind. Audrey slipped and quick straw fingers grasped at her heels. "Aaarh!" she squealed as they dragged her back and the figure loomed over her, lowering its plaited loop purposefully.

Jenkin beat the straw with his fists and the fingers released Audrey and grabbed him. The loop slipped over his head, but he ducked and nipped off with Audrey.

"Not far to go till we're out of the field," he called to her, "then we should be able to go faster."

Audrey leaped over stones and dodged the stalks that blocked her path. Her tail bells jangled wildly as the clutching fingers searched for her hungrily.

"Quick, Audrey, hurry!" Jenkin had reached the edge of the field and turned around to help her.

She glanced over her shoulder and cried out. The corn dolly bore down on her, sweeping over the stony ground at a terrific speed. It raised its spindly arms and brought them knifing down.

Audrey felt herself yanked backward. Jenkin had hold of her and he carried her clear of the field.

"Look Jenkin," she gasped, "it isn't following us."

Jenkin put her down and stared back. The corn dolly remained within the confines of the field, its arms upraised.

"Why isn't it chasing us?" asked Jenkin nervously.

"Maybe it can only live in the field," suggested Audrey. "Perhaps it needs to be amongst the growing corn to come alive."

"It's horrible," said Jenkin shivering. He frowned; the thing seemed to be waiting for something to happen. It reared back the loop head as though sensing another presence. Jenkin moved his eyes from the straw figure, up to the tops of the dark elms and out into the starry sky. . . .

"Get down," he yelled, and roughly pushed Audrey to the ground. It was too late to save himself.

A pale, silent ghost slipped out of the night sky and snatched

him up. Jenkin squeaked in pain as Mahooot scooped him up in his vicious talons. He saw the ground disappear below him and heard the owl cackle to itself wickedly.

"Foood, foood, lovely mooouses."

Audrey saw the owl swoop into the darkness over the meadow and heard Jenkin's frightened voice fade away.

Then Audrey screamed.

The corn dolly rustled its pleasure and slunk back into the shadowy cover of the field.

On sentry, Arthur recognized his sister's voice and soon everyone in Fennywolde was awake and lighting torches. They ran in a blazing line to see why she was making that fearful noise.

Audrey was on her knees when they found her, staring across the meadow with big dark eyes that were dreadful to look on. Arthur shook her to stop the piercing screams.

"What is it, Aud?" he asked wildly.

Without seeing him she pointed out into the sky and said weakly, "The owl! The owl has got Jenkin."

The fieldmice cried out in dismay, but from their midst, one figure stepped forward into the circle of torchlight. It was Jenkin's father. None dared look at him. His face trembled with emotion and his lips turned white.

"Jenkin lad," he said, sounding as if he had been stabbed. He turned on Audrey and his eyes burned at her accusingly. He raised a quivering finger and pointed. "You have done this, you!"

Before she could reply, out of the crowd stepped Madame Akkikuyu. The rat took a torch from one of the fieldmice and held it above her head.

"So," she shouted and all looked to her. "Mousey boy got by owly. What you do?"

"What can we do?" asked Arthur bitterly.

204

"Go fight the mangy bird!" she cried, whirling the torch around. "Come, mouseys, we go to save him!"

The fieldmice cheered her as she led them down the banks of the ditch like a general. Mr. Nettle followed like a sleepwalker.

Arthur and Audrey were joined by the Scuttles. "Arthur," Audrey whispered to her brother, "Jenkin and I were chased out here by a terrible thing! It was . . . it was my own corn dolly, Arthur! It must have killed Hodge! It tried to kill us too! What can I do?"

Arthur gulped. There was no use doubting her. Twit had been attacked by something made of straw that morning. "Look," he said, "don't mention this to anyone yet–you're in enough trouble already. What do you think they'll do if they find out your figure has come to life and murders people?"

They hurried after the lights of the rescue party. Twit took Audrey's paw and patted it.

In the empty glade near the field only one mouse was left. It was Alison Sedge. She watched the torchlight dwindle in the distance and shook her head. Her sobs were silent and her heart broken. She ripped off her mousebrass and flung it away.

*   *   *

Madame Akkikuyu led the fieldmice through the dark meadow. She whooped and shouted challenges to the owl, and the fieldmice took heart at her courage. They came to the oak trees and the rat thrust her torch into the earth.

"Stay here, mouseys," she told them. "I go to hooty!"

"Find my boy!" begged Mr. Nettle.

"Kill the owl," chanted the fieldmice, and Arthur and Twit were alarmed to hear them. They spoke not as individuals but as a great, many-headed creature with a hundred fiery eyes eager for blood. Only Twit's parents and Mr. Woodruffe did not join in. They hung back and put their paws to their mouths fearfully.

Madame Akkikuyu began to climb the tree. It was easy for her. Her claws sank into the soft bark and she ascended swiftly.

"I get you, hooty," she snarled angrily. "I tell you leave my mouseys be."

She pulled herself up to the hole in the trunk and announced herself.

"Hooty. Akkikuyu here again."

"Whooo?" came a hollow voice.

"Akkikuyu—the owl rider and neck plucker. I have mattress need stuffing!" She laughed and pulled the bone from her hair.

Sounds of agitated scrabbling issued from the black recess. Mahooot was trapped and he knew it.

"Ha!" bawled Akkikuyu, springing across the threshold and stabbing the bone in front of her.

Mahooot had been lying in wait for her, intending to bite her head off as soon as it poked through the hole in the tree trunk. He darted forward, but she brought the bone crashing down on his open beak. It crunched and chipped, and Mahooot hooted in agony.

In a foul temper he shot out a deadly talon and snapped it tight around the fortune-teller's neck. She wailed in surprise and dropped the bone as he dragged her into the darkness.

"Not so fast, hooty," she yelled, and kicked the owl in the stomach.

"Oooof!" moaned Mahooot as the air rushed out of him and he collapsed, wheezing, on the floor.

Madame Akkikuyu shrieked with laughter and disentangled herself from his clutches.

She retrieved her bone and brought it smashing down on the talon that had gripped her. The sharp claws splintered into a thousand bits.

Mahooot roared in his pain and Madame Akkikuyu crowed with delight. Then she dealt the other foot a devastating blow and danced about.

The owl lunged at her in a mad rage. He knocked her off balance, so that she stumbled and fell backward. Then Mahooot beat her down with his powerful wings until she was overwhelmed by his feathery bulk. His body crushed her and he bent his flat head to nip with his damaged beak. He pulled out a quantity of her thick hair until Madame Akkikuyu squawked shrilly. That was it! This owl was getting above itself.

"Enough hooty," she said, spitting feathers out of her mouth.

Mahooot cackled and continued to squash her. She thrashed her tail from left to right, so he bit it and the blood oozed out. Madame Akkikuyu gnashed her teeth. He had gone too far.

"Dooown, yooou doxsie!" he hooted, reveling in her suffering. "Mahooot is yooour dooom!"

Madame Akkikuyu blew a muffled raspberry underneath him and managed to pull an arm loose. With one swipe she punched Mahooot savagely under his beak. He staggered backward and she was free.

Nimbly she stepped out of the dark hole and ran along the branch outside.

"Nyer, nyer," she taunted him, waggling her bottom at the hole. "Come out, hooty, Akkikuyu thrash you good an' proper."

In a cloud of soft white feathers Mahooot left the hole. He spread out his enormous wings and reared himself up to a towering height.

"Die!" he boomed in a chilling voice.

"Oho," chuckled the fortune-teller, "not yet owly, Akkikuyu not ready to snuff candle—you play her game now." She slipped her claw swiftly into the bag slung over her shoulder and pulled out a small cloth pouch.

Mahooot made a ravaging dive at her. The rat flung the

pouch at him and a poisonous concoction exploded in his face.

She smartly stepped to one side as Mahooot floundered past. His eyes were stinging and he could not see. The smell of burned feathers fouled the air.

"Ooow!" he screeched in panic as he fumbled along the branch on his broken talons. "Mahooot is blind, ooow."

Madame Akkikuyu poked and teased him mischievously, until he could bear this monstrous ratwoman no longer. The owl flapped his wings and rose shakily into the air.

The fortune-teller let him go unmolested.

Mahooot spiraled around, unable to see where he was going. Then, with a dull thud, which smashed more of his beak, he flew into a tree trunk. Mahooot fell to the ground, bouncing off the branches.

"A fine sight to see," said a voice in the fortune-teller's ear. "What a heroine you are. The darling of Fennywolde."

"Nico," she welcomed, "I thought you not come tonight."

"I have been busy elsewhere," said Nicodemus, "but come, we must talk, you and I, for it is time you learned of the spell that will release me."

"Wait," said Madame Akkikuyu as she remembered Jenkin, "I have mousey to find."

"The lad is dead!" said Nicodemus coldly. "Now step into the owl's hole, Akkikuyu, and I shall tell you what must be done."

*   *   *

As Mahooot came crashing down out of the high branches the fieldmice who were waiting below cheered wildly and rushed forward.

"Stop, wait!" ordered Mr. Woodruffe, but they surged past him like a river and began to hurl stones at the dazed owl and beat it with their sticks.

"This is obscene," shouted the King of the Field. But they did not hear him. They only heard the gasps and cries of Mahooot as they tore at him. "They've gone mad," said Arthur, appalled.

Mr. Woodruffe turned and hid his head in disgust, then threw down his staff of office. "They will not listen to me anymore and I want nothing more to do with them. They are not mice tonight–they are the nastiest kind of rats."

"It's far worse than it ever was at home," said Audrey. They walked away with Mr. and Mrs. Scuttle. Fennywolde had become an evil place to live.

*   *   *

In the owl's nest Madame Akkikuyu listened as Nicodemus began.

"It is a mighty spell which we dare to attempt, Akkikuyu," he said. "Are you brave enough for it?"

"Yes, Nico."

"Then this is what we need. You must build a fire and feed it with the herbs I shall tell you to gather. Around this fire you must say the words of release and cast into the flame a mousebrass."

"A mousebrass, Nico–why so?"

"All this shall become clear to you, yet it must be a special mousebrass, it must be made in hatred and be a sign of destruction and death."

"Where I get such a dangler?"

"That also I shall tell you. All has been arranged. Wheels have been set in motion, Akkikuyu, and the time for the ritual is soon. At the time of the ceremony, however, I must be protected from the heat of the fire for I shall be vulnerable for a while. I must project my essence to a place of safety. Look in your bag–there you will find a vessel suitable for me."

Akkikuyu rummaged around inside her bag until she found what Nicodemus meant.

"You mean this, great one," she muttered, reluctantly taking out her most prized possession. The moonlight curved lovingly over the smooth glass ball that the fortune-teller had brought with her from Deptford.

"Excellent," he crooned delightedly. "That is most suitable! Have it with you at the fire's edge—only remember, Akkikuyu, that once the spell is complete you must smash your prize to release me. I do not want to spend another age imprisoned in there."

"I promise, Nico," she said with regret as she stroked her beautiful crystal ball.

"And one more thing, Akkikuyu. There must be an exchange of souls or the spell will be useless."

The fortune-teller trembled. "Souls? What am I to do this time?"

"There must be a sacrifice to the flame," Nicodemus whispered. "My essence will cross over to your world, and a soul must cross back in return. We must cast into the fire one who is not protected by a mousebrass."

"Who you think of?" she asked warily.

The reply was snarled back at her: "The one who has abandoned you, Akkikuyu, the one who spurned your friendship and tried to make a fool of you in front of everyone."

"No," cried the rat in dismay.

"Yes!" hissed Nicodemus. "She is unfettered by the Greenlaws and bound to no one. It must be her. You are sworn to obey me—throw Audrey Brown into the fire!"

"Mouselet!" Akkikuyu wailed miserably.

CHAPTER THIRTEEN

A WITCH AND A FOOL

The sun rose over Fennywolde to announce yet another feverish day.

Twit rose and leaned out of his and Arthur's nest. The Hall of Corn was unusually quiet–but not calm. He could almost feel dark forces surging through the field like evil water, and a half-forgotten memory awakened in him.

"Blow me," he said to himself.

Behind him, in the sweet mossy darkness, Arthur's drowsy voice mumbled, "What is it?"

The fieldmouse scratched his head and said, "I just remembered somethin', Art."

"If it's about last night I don't want to know," came the weary reply.

"Well it has somethin' to do wi' last night," admitted the fieldmouse, "but really I was just thinkin' of those bats back in Deptford."

"Oh, Orfeo, and . . . who was it?"

"Eldritch."

"That's right—what made you think of them?"

"Well, when they took me a-flyin' through the roof an' into the sky, they showed me some wild critters—they were 'orrible and mindless. I only just recalled that Orfeo askin' me if there were any of the—how did he put it—any of this 'untame breed' in my field. I said as I didn't know of any."

"So?" Arthur was baffled. "What made you think of that now?"

Twit turned a worried face to his friend, "Don't you see, Art? The bats knew. They was warnin' me!"

"What, against wild cats here?"

"No," said Twit gravely, "against my own folk here. Last night, Art, they weren't mice—Mr. Woodruffe said so, they were just like that 'untame breed' in the city. Horrid beasts with no thought 'cept killin'. I'm afeared for Fennywolde. What'll happen next?"

*   *   *

Madame Akkikuyu looked down into the ditch and prepared herself. Her task today was not pleasant, but she had sworn on her soul to obey Nicodemus. She mopped her brow with a corner of her shawl and set her jaw determinedly. She hated the idea of what she had to do, but Nicodemus would not be pleased with her if she failed him today.

She marched from the edge and strode to the elm trees where she hoped to find Mr. Nettle. A mousebrass was needed and he was the only one who could make it. Her problem would be persuading him.

Isaac Nettle, grim and steely eyed, was hammering a piece of metal in his forge. The ruddy glow of the forge fire shone on his fur and glinted off his drooping whiskers. But that was the only light in the gloomy place. Even in Isaac's heart there was darkness. Only grief and loss filled him. He pushed himself into his work passionately, smiting the red-hot metal with his hammer, trying to blot out his sorrow with the effort. Fiery sparks flew and scorched his skin, but he was thankful for them. He wanted to feel pain and be punished: for Jenkin, the shining joy of his sour life, was gone, plucked out of existence.

The ringing of his hammer was so loud that he did not hear the knocking at the door. He continued to beat the yellow metal till it was flattened, then, with a pair of tongs, he plunged it into a bucket of cold water. It was only when the steam had cleared that he noticed the ratwoman standing quietly by the door.

Madame Akkikuyu nodded at him. "Morning," she said.

Isaac grunted. He did not want to talk to anyone this day—or any other for that matter. He turned back to the fire and raked the embers together.

"I say morning," the fortune-teller repeated.

Isaac looked at her with unfriendly eyes. "Leave me!" he growled.

She shook her head. "You lose boy last night. You need talk—get it off bosom, Akkikuyu good listener, she hear your woe."

For a moment his face was impassive, but suddenly he broke down. Like a wall of glass his defenses shattered. Mr. Nettle wept openly.

"Jenkin, Jenkin, I've lost you, my son. I loved you and I never told you—not once."

Madame Akkikuyu took Mr. Nettle in her arms and patted him gently on the back. "There, there," she soothed, "that right, let it out. Tell Akkikuyu."

"Oh, Meg!" he cried. "Look after our boy, he's with you now."

"Meg?" asked Akkikuyu, "She your wife, yes?"

Isaac nodded feebly. "Meg died when Jenkin was born. I always blamed him for that—I loved her so. And now I've lost him too. I don't know what I'm going to do. I'm so sorry, lad, if you can hear me. Forgive your father!"

"Shhh," hushed Akkikuyu, pushing him gently onto a stool, "in the great beyond all things are forgiven—he knows now."

Mr. Nettle calmed down. When his last sniffs were over he thanked the rat shyly. "Verily, thou art a messenger from the Green, come in my darkest hour. And last night also—you did what no other dared, you tried to save my son. I thank thee for that. Truly thou art blessed!"

Madame Akkikuyu shrugged off these compliments. "Yes, I try, but was too late. What a shame your boy out last night. Why he not here safe with you?"

Isaac's face tightened and he became stern and grim once more. "It was the town mouse!" he spat bitterly. "It was she who lured my son away." He had forgotten now that it was his beatings that had driven Jenkin away from him.

"Aaahh, yes," muttered the fortune-teller, "Miss Audrey! Tell me Nettley, why did your boy meet her last night outside the field? And why she not there when Hodge was found, and where is the other boy?"

Mr. Nettle rose and scowled. "It is she!" he declared. "Ever since she came here there has been nought but pain and death! She has brought it!"

"Quite so," agreed Akkikuyu. "And tell me this! That mousey is of age, so why she no wear a mousey dangler?"

Mr. Nettle looked at her wildly. He had never noticed that, and he the mousebrass maker. "She should have one," he gasped. "Every mouse receives a brass when they come of age."

Madame Akkikuyu rushed in with her explanation. "Maybe Green Mouse think she not worthy of such a gift."

"My Lord!" Isaac exclaimed, staggering back. "Where were my wits? Why had I not thought of this? She must be evil indeed for the mighty Green to deem her unfit for a mousebrass. What manner of creature can she be?"

"A witch!" snapped Akkikuyu. "Why else your corn wither

in the ground and mouseys die young? What black powers she brung to your fair field, Nettley?"

Isaac was incensed. "What can we do? We must confront her and cast her out."

"No," said the rat hastily. "We must pray to the Green, see what he thinks." She narrowed her eyes and peered at Isaac through their narrow black slits. "Maybe," she began, as though working out a plan, "maybe you should make a special mousey dangler that will bring ruin on the mouselet. Make it with curses and surely the Green will hear you."

Isaac looked doubtful. He took his position as mousebrass maker extremely seriously. He considered the suggestion but declined.

"I will not presume upon my Lord," he explained. "I will not anger him by making a brass of my own design. I must know it to be his will."

Madame Akkikuyu sighed, but there was one more trick up Nicodemus's sleeve. He had been prepared for Isaac's piety and had instructed her to take him to the owl tree and wait there.

"Nettley," she said, "it hot in here, I go for walk. Come join me, leave your danglers and talk with Akkikuyu."

Isaac was unwilling: others in Fennywolde might see him and he did not want that. As if she understood this, Madame Akkikuyu added, "We not go to Hall, we walk in meadow!" Mr. Nettle agreed and he followed her out of the forge.

As they walked Madame Akkikuyu pointed out plants and reeled off their good—or bad—qualities. Mr. Nettle tried to listen and pay attention, but his mind was elsewhere. Inside, he was seething. The thought of Audrey Brown, that odious town mouse who had wrought so much grief and harm, inflamed him and his fingers itched for his hammer. What could be done with her? Her crimes were too great to go unpunished. If she was a witch then there was only one way to deal with her. He wondered if the Fennywolders would agree with him.

When Mr. Nettle next looked up they had left the meadow and he drew a sharp breath. Madame Akkikuyu had steered him toward the oaks and the sight of them brought the pain of his loss back to him.

"Why are we here?" he questioned her with a faltering voice.

"Oh, me!" said Akkikuyu, trying to sound shocked that she could have been so thoughtless and unsympathetic. "Silly Akkikuyu—her head not screwed on today. Come Nettley, we go from here." She moved back a few paces and observed Isaac keenly. He seemed to have seen something near one of the roots and he made no attempt to follow her.

"Look!" he said, "There's a shining thing over yonder. What can it be?"

Akkikuyu squinted in the direction he was pointing. The fierce light of the sun was reflecting off something down there. Isaac walked up to the great root cautiously.

"Oh no, Nico," she breathed to herself, "not this—he suffer enough."

When Mr. Nettle reached the great root he fell to his knees and shrieked. Madame Akkikuyu ran over to him and looked over his quaking shoulder.

There on the dusty ground was an owl pellet, one of those tight little bundles of fur and bones. Sticking out of it was Jenkin's mousebrass.

The sign of life blazed in the sunlight as Mr. Nettle wrested it free of the pellet. Then he turned his face on the fortune-teller and cried, "I shall make that brass, and may eternal damnation fall on that town mouse. For every stroke of the hammer shall be a curse and malediction—may she suffer for the agony she has given to me and my son."

Madame Akkikuyu smiled soberly—Nicodemus would be pleased.

*　　*　　*

The morning passed and the afternoon crept up. The rings of Mr. Nettle's hammer sang over Fennywolde.

The atmosphere in the Hall of Corn was terrible. Arguments broke out for the slightest reason. Old Todmore yelled at the children who were pestering him for a story and told them he had better things to do. One of the young boys kicked his stick and ran away.

"Come back 'ere, Abel Madder," fumed Old Todmore, "I'll clout you one!"

Dimsel Bottom and Lily Clover were seen quarreling and they had to be separated when plump Dimsel flew at her friend in a shocking fit of rage.

Josiah Down kicked the family nest to pieces while his wife called him a no-good cheddar head.

All this was watched in fearful silence by the Scuttles and their guests. They kept well away from the rest of the fieldmice and looked at one another in disbelief. What was happening to everybody?

Audrey decided to go to bed early that night. She sat in her hot nest with her knees tucked tight up under her chin. She was frightened. Several times that day she had heard her name mentioned in high, disapproving voices, and when Mr. Nep went by he actually spat on the ground when he saw her.

*　　*　　*

Alison Sedge was restless. She did not want to go to bed. All day she had lain in the shade by the still pool, thinking of Jenkin. She remembered their happy days together before she had received her mousebrass, but that was gone now and good riddance. She wore no flowers around her neck anymore and had not once gazed at her reflection. Her hair was forgotten and

217

neglected in two untidy plaits. She had not eaten all day.

Twilight came. Reluctantly, Alison picked herself up and ducked under the hawthorn branches. She passed over the ditch and entered the field. The corn was silent. No wind rustled its ears or rattled its stalks. Their long black shadows fell on Alison like the bars of a prison. She became increasingly uneasy. The field was an eerie place. She had never noticed how impenetrable those dark shadows were before. Alison gulped nervously as she remembered the murderer that hid in here, throttling unwary mice who wandered around alone. How could she be so stupid?

A noise startled her. The corn moved behind and a crackling rustle moved toward her.

Alison did not wait to look. She ran deeper into the field toward the Hall of Corn, but the rustling grew louder. It was ahead of her now and she could see dim shapes before her. Alison wheeled around and sped back toward the ditch, missing the path in her haste.

Suddenly she tripped and stumbled. She put out her arms to save herself but landed on something soft.

Panting heavily, Alison lifted her face—and stared into the blank eyes of Young Whortle. She had fallen on top of his discarded body. Alison leaped up and screamed at the top of her voice.

In the Hall of Corn the fieldmice were once more disturbed by the alarm call. What could be the cause this time?

They lit their torches and fled out of the great doors.

"What is it?" asked Audrey as Twit slid down past her nest.

"Another alarm," he answered, "we must all go—come on, Aud!"

They followed the other mice. Arthur had been on duty and slid down a cornstalk as they ran by. "Wait for me!" he puffed.

The fieldmice ran along the ditch, fearing the worst. Had another tragedy occurred? Then, crashing out of the field came

218

Alison Sedge. She ran to her mother's arms and squealed.

"It's Young Whortle—he's dead. I found his body in there."

Mr. and Mrs. Nep held onto each other for support. "Where is he?" cried Mr. Nep, preparing to enter the field.

"No, don't go in there," shouted Alison, "there's something after me—it nearly got me."

The fieldmice made angry noises and lifted their torches high above their heads. "We must find it!" they declared. "We must put an end to this murder!"

Before any of them could move, there came a splintering and rustling sound. Out of the field, silhouetted against the sky, was the evil corn dolly.

Its looped head jerked from side to side as if it were sniffing the air. Then it began to advance stiffly toward them.

The fieldmice gasped and staggered back in horror.

"It's that doll thing!" some of them muttered. "How is it moving like that? It is bewitched."

Isaac Nettle came out of his quarters and beheld the scene with a mixture of horror and satisfaction. The straw figure was truly an abomination, yet surely now there would be no doubt that the town mouse was to blame for everything. Here was the proof of her witchcraft.

The corn demon marched awkwardly on and the mice fell back before it. Its wild arms were raised and its twiggy fingers twitched eagerly.

From the dark shadows near the ditch Madame Akkikuyu observed the scene with interest. "See how I let the mice do our work for us," whispered Nicodemus. "We shall see what they do with Miss Brown."

The demon struck out with its arms and caught hold of Dimsel Bottom. She squeaked with fright as it drew her near its lowered head.

Isaac raced up to the thing and dealt it a savage blow with his hammer. The corn dolly buckled as the hammer plunged into the straw, but it reared itself up again immediately and with one powerful arm swept Mr. Nettle off his feet and flung him to the ground.

"Save us, Green Mouse!" he wailed.

The thing was unstoppable. It placed its head over Dimsel's and the plait began to tighten. Arthur rushed out and pulled the hideous thing off and Dimsel sped away.

The fieldmice were driven back, terribly afraid. "Where is that town mouse?"some began to ask, and the call was taken up by all of them. "Where is the town mouse? Where is the town mouse?"

At the rear, Audrey held Twit's paw in terror. Out of the crowd Mr. Nep saw her and cried, "There she is. Bring her forward."

Feverish paws grabbed Audrey and pulled her away from Twit and the Scuttles. Through the mass she was dragged and shoved until she was pushed out in front of her creation.

Audrey could not escape. She tried to turn back, but angry paws and bodies barred her way. Arthur tried to help her, but found that his arms had been grabbed and the mice were holding on to him fiercely.

The corn dolly swept up to Audrey and lowered its head again. Audrey screamed, "Stop. Stop."

The figure jerked up quickly and lowered its arms. Then, to her everlasting horror, it bowed before her and fell lifeless to the ground.

The crowd stared at it with wide eyes and then Mr. Nep said, "It obeyed her."

"Witch," hissed the mob, "witch, witch, witch!" They circled around Audrey menacingly.

Try as he might, Arthur could not struggle free, and at the back, Twit could not break through the crowd.

Isaac Nettle came striding forward booming, "The town mouse is a witch. She has insulted the Green Mouse by weaving idols, and conjured spirits to give life to her hellish work. Three of our folk have died because of her. What do we do with a witch?"

"Burn her," cried the crowd.

"No," whimpered Audrey as they tied her paws behind her back. "I'm not a witch!"

But her voice was drowned out by the cries of the angry mice.

Isaac picked up the motionless corn dolly and cast it down into the ditch. Then he hurled a blazing torch after it and the figure immediately burst into flames. The loop head blackened and withered into a wisp of oily smoke.

The fieldmice pushed Audrey to the edge of the ditch and the glowing ashes rose up and curled around her ankles.

"Burn, burn!" they repeated excitedly. Two strong husbands lifted her up and swung her out over the flames.

Madame Akkikuyu covered her face with her claws and trembled. Nicodemus laughed triumphantly. All was going wonderfully.

"STOP THIS!" Mr. Woodruffe wrestled forward angrily. "You must all stop this!" He pulled Audrey out of the mice's paws and she clung tightly to him.

Isaac thundered in and whirled Mr. Woodruffe around. "Go back to your nest, Woodruffe. You are not our king now. Let us do what must be done. The witch must die!"

"But you can't burn her, Isaac. It's unspeakable!" He appealed to the crowd, "Surely you cannot have sunk so low to allow this. Never has a mouse been burned in Fennywolde. As for you, Nettle, I'm surprised. This has the smack of paganism in it."

The fieldmice looked anxiously at their leader. Mr. Woodruffe was right, they had never burned a mouse before. "But what are we to do with her?" asked a frightened Mrs. Nep.

Isaac snarled and yanked Audrey from Mr. Woodruffe's grip.

"Then she shall hang!" he proclaimed. "Let her choke, just as her creature choked Hodge and Young Whortle." He signaled to the crowd and they swarmed along the ditch, with him at their head and Audrey stumbling at his side.

"We've got to do something," said Arthur when his captors released him. "Will they really hang her, Mr. Scuttle?"

"'Fraid so, lad," he answered in dismay. Gladwin wrung her paws together.

"We're not done yet, boy," said Mr. Woodruffe. "Come on!" They ran after the angry crowd and pushed their way through.

Twit remained behind. He had never felt so useless in all his life. He was too small to do anything useful. He wished that Thomas Triton was there—he would have shown these mice a thing or two with his sword. But the midshipmouse was not there and there were far too many fieldmice to fight against anyway. This needed a cool head and lots of wits. Twit, the simple country mouse, had neither. He was the one with "no cheese upstairs," the butt of every joke. Now the life of a friend was in danger and he could think of nothing to help.

Suddenly he gasped. "Could I?" he asked himself. "Would it work?" There was only one way to find out. He rushed forward.

At the yew tree a tight circle of mice had formed. In the center were Mr. Nettle and Audrey. Her wide eyes were rolling in terror and their whites were showing. A straw rope had been slung over the "hanging branch" and a noose had been tied in one end.

Mr. Woodruffe barged in followed by Arthur. "This must not happen!" he cried. "Execution must only be as a result of a trial and only then if the accused is found guilty."

"We know she'm guilty," yelled Mr. Nep. The crowd roared their agreement.

"This is against the Greenlaws!" continued Mr. Woodruffe.

Isaac held out a trembling paw. "Thou knowest full well the respect and honor I hold for the mighty Green. I would not do this thing if the law did not permit. It is you who have forgotten the law, Woodruffe. Did not Fenny himself declare that all witches must be put to death?" The mob roared again and waved their torches. "Bind their paws so they may not interfere!" commanded Isaac.

Both Arthur's and Mr. Woodruffe's paws were tightly bound and strong arms were clenched about their necks.

"No, no," wailed Arthur. "My sister's not a witch–believe me."

Madame Akkikuyu left her place of shadow and moved toward the yew. "Quickly, Akkikuyu," said Nicodemus. "I must see! The girl must not die by hanging, she must be alive when the flame takes her. If you can cut her down before she is dead we may still be able to perform the spell. But hurry, and keep away from those torches, the heat of them is agony for me." The fortune-teller hurried forward, a confusion of loyalties whirling around her jumbled head.

Mr. Nettle put the noose around Audrey's neck and pulled the knot down tightly. Then he took hold of the other end and began to draw it down. Arthur closed his eyes.

Yelps and squeals broke out of the crowd and the mice jumped as something bit and clawed its way through. It was Twit. He didn't care how he got past. He ran into the ring, and before anyone could stop him he had slipped the rope from Audrey's throat.

"Leave her be!" roared Isaac, looming over him with his paw raised.

A smoldering green fire seemed to issue from Twit's eyes and Isaac faltered. "I come to claim her!" Twit shouted at the top of his voice. "I claim her in the name of the Green."

"How dare you blaspheme!" growled Mr. Nettle. "She is for the noose."

"Do you forget your own laws, Nettle?" Twit barked back at him. "What laws?"

"The law of the gallows," snarled Twit.

"The gallows law," repeated everyone in astonishment–surely Twit was not that stupid.

Mr. Woodruffe reminded Isaac as he stood, searching his memory. "The gallows law runs thus," he said. "Any may invoke the law of the gallows–if a willing spouse can be found beneath the hanging tree then the accused, whatever the crime, will be reprieved."

"A spouse!" mocked Isaac. "Who would marry a witch?"

"I will," said Twit proudly. "I invoke the law and offer my paw in marriage to Audrey Brown."

The crowd rippled in discontent and Nicodemus hissed in Madame Akkikuyu's ear.

"No! The girl must not marry–it will bind her up in the Greenlaws and she shall be useless to me. Stop this now."

The fortune-teller entered the circle, but instead of obeying Nicodemus she said, "Mousey must marry–follow the law of your Green. Join the two before you feel his anger." In the center of all the fieldmice the tattoo dared not move on her ear, but it glared at her venomously.

"Imbecile!" it whispered harshly.

Isaac stared at the rat in disbelief. He had made a brass for the destruction of Audrey at her request. Why was she changing sides now? "But she is to blame!" he said blankly. "Are you telling me now that she must go free?"

"She must, it is the law!" demanded Twit. "I call on the Green Mouse to witness all that goes on here. He shall know who disobeys him."

The crowd murmured. There was no getting away from it. If Twit married Audrey then she could not be hanged.

"No," cried Mr. Nep as he sensed their doubt. "We cannot let her go unpunished. My son is dead."

It was Isaac who answered him. "Silence, Nep. The way has been shown, though it grieves me no less than you. We must obey the law or we ourselves are guilty. But hear me, tomorrow we shall drive Twit and the witch to our borders and banish them. Then if any find them crossing our lands they have the right to do with them as they see fit. They are outcasts." He turned back to Twit and Audrey.

"Now, take the witch's paw in yours, William Scuttle," said Mr. Nettle.

Twit looked at her. She was much calmer now and she stared back at him with gratitude. "Do you mean to go through with it?" she asked him.

"If'n I don't marry 'ee, Aud, they'll lynch yer," he replied.

"I don't know what to say," Audrey mumbled.

"Just say 'yes' an' save yer neck," advised Twit.

"Kneel ye," ordered Isaac, "and humble thyselves before the Green Mouse." Audrey felt someone cut the ropes that bit into her wrists and she dropped to her knees beside Twit.

"Dost thou, William Scuttle, take unto thyself this mouse, Audrey Brown? To cherish through the winter and revel with in the summer? Forswearing all others until the grass grows green over you both?"

"I does," said Twit.

"Who blesses the husband?" asked Isaac. It was usual at mouse weddings for both the bride and groom to receive a blessing. This could not come from their families. It was usually friends who performed the task, but at this torchlit marriage everyone wondered who would dare bless the union of a witch and a fool.

"I do," said a solemn voice, and Mr. Woodruffe shook off his guards. He wriggled his paws free of the ropes and stood before Twit.

"May the Green bless and protect you," he said with feeling, and he placed his right paw on Twit's shoulder.

"Thank 'ee," replied Twit gratefully.

Then it was Audrey's turn.

"Dost thou, Audrey Brown," intoned Isaac bitterly, "take unto thyself this mouse, William Scuttle? To cherish through the winter and revel with in the summer? Forswearing all others until the grass grows green over you both?"

Audrey tearfully thought of Piccadilly. Sobbing she uttered, "I do."

"Who blesses the wife?" Isaac looked around. No one said anything. He smiled. There might be a hanging yet, for no marriage was complete without the two blessings, and he who blessed the groom could not bless the bride as well.

Arthur gazed at the fieldmice pleadingly. "Please, someone, anyone, don't let Audrey die." But the mice shuffled their feet and hung their heads.

Isaac chuckled and was about to pronounce the ceremony void when a figure stepped up to Audrey.

"I bless mouselet!" declared Madame Akkikuyu. Isaac glared at her, but the fortune-teller came and knelt before her friend and said tenderly, "May his mighty Greenness bless and protect you for always, and may you forgive Akkikuyu. Remember that she love you and want you to be happy in summer light—it's all I ever wanted, my mouselet." She leaned over to kiss Audrey's forehead.

"Thank you." She wept.

A big tear streaked down Akkikuyu's nose. "Ach! I always blub at weddings."

Isaac concluded the ceremony.

"May the Mighty Green join these two together, through winter, harvest, youth, and age. Let no creature come between them for now they are under the Green's great mantle." He sucked his teeth and said, "Rise, Scuttle and Scuttle."

"You better be gone before midday tomorrow," shouted Mr. Nep, "or I swear I'll hurl you both into the fire myself. The crowd began to disperse, and drift back into the field.

Twit's parents rushed forward and hugged their son and

daughter-in-law. Gladwin was tearful, but Elijah was proud. "There's another Mr. and Mrs. Scuttle around here now." He beamed.

"Not for long, though, Dad," said Twit. "Aud may be my wife, but I don't 'spect her to stay wi' me." He turned to the new Mrs. Scuttle and said softly, "'S all right, Aud. I know you aren't keen on me in that way, so p'raps it's best if'n you go home tomorrow, eh?"

"What about you, Twit?" Audrey asked. "And I can't go home anyway—what about Oswald and the Starwife's bargain?"

"Let's go and have something to eat," suggested Arthur, "then we can decide what to do."

Under the yew tree Madame Akkikuyu stood alone, sniveling into her shawl and drying her eyes.

"You fool," rebuked Nicodemus. "You interfering cretin! We might have had the girl if you had not blessed her. My plans are ruined now—Audrey Brown has been tied to the Greenlaws, the spell cannot work."

"Mouselet name Scuttle now," checked Akkikuyu sadly, "and I glad you not use her—she my friend. Akkikuyu not have many friends, mouselet only one."

The tattoo writhed with frustration. "Curse you—you Moroccan ditch drab. The spell I have prepared needs a female sacrifice, one who is of age but has no mousebrass. Am I to be marooned in the abyss till the end of time?"

Madame Akkikuyu stared out along the bank. There sat Alison Sedge, miserable and dejected. She had longed for Audrey's death and now her enemy lived and was married. With Jenkin dead, Alison knew she would never marry.

Akkikuyu frowned as Alison stood up. No mousebrass hung from her neck.

"Nico," she whispered. "Akkikuyu find another."

The tattoo stared out and grinned. "Excellent. We shall perform the ritual tonight. Prepare the girl for sacrifice."

CHAPTER FOURTEEN

THE SACRIFICE

Alison Sedge kicked the tufts of dry, scruffy grass and turned to follow the others back into the field.

"Hoy, mousey, wait for I."

The rat's voice startled her. Crossly she waited for Madame Akkikuyu to come out from under the yew tree.

"What you want?" asked Alison rudely. She did not like Madame Akkikuyu—she blamed her for bringing Audrey to Fennywolde in the first place.

The fortune-teller approached, smiling sweetly. "Let me help poor mousey," she said. "Ah, but mousey has lost pretty dangler. Where it go?"

"I got rid of it!" snapped Alison. What business was it of the rat, anyway? "What do you mean you could help me?" she added in a sullen tone.

Madame Akkikuyu walked around the girl and sprinkled fragments of yellow leaves over her. In a secret, low whisper she said, "I have spells, mousey, bring disaster on your enemies."

The mouse regarded her through the screen of fluttering

leaves. What was she up to? wondered Alison. "What enemies?" she asked stubbornly.

The rat moved closer. "Those who rob you of suitors—those who get in your way, sweet mousey. Jumped-up girls not as pretty as you."

"You mean that town mouse?" she interrupted. "Yes, I don't like her, but if you hadn't blessed the marriage back then she'd have danced the gallows jig. What are you going on about now, you barmy so-and-so?"

"Akkikuyu stop hanging, yes, because that too quick and easy for her. She too evil! She put spell on Jenky boy to make him fall for her. She led him into open and let Mahooot make him owl bait."

Alison exploded with rage. "Is this true? I ought to go and tear her apart! All that butter-wouldn't-melt routine. I hate her. I knew my Jenkin didn't really fancy her. Tell me what I can do."

The fortune-teller grinned. Alison Sedge had been an easy fish to catch. It would be easy throwing her on the fire—how could she loathe her mouselet so much?

"Akkikuyu will cast spell. You help, go get wood for bonfire." Alison hurriedly ran to collect some sticks.

"Well, Nico," the rat began, "what you think?"

"She is perfect, Akkikuyu," gloated the voice, "did you feel her spite and anger? They are strong, raw emotions. Her life essence will be most eagerly received by the gatekeepers of the abyss. Tonight I shall be free again."

Akkikuyu cleared a space on the high bank. She gathered some stones and arranged them in a circle, leaving it incomplete so that she could enter. She waited for Alison to return, then, once all the wood they needed was within, she sealed the ring with them inside. "Now, mousey," she said, "we must not break through the stones till spell complete." She began to build the bonfire. From her bag she pulled out the skull of the frog she had killed and placed it at the heart of the framework. Then around it she sprinkled the magical herbs and flowers that she had carefully gathered at night. At last the fortune-teller announced that all was ready. She stood back and admired her handiwork with Alison. It was a tall pyramid of dry branches and twigs, a satisfying result to her labors.

"Light it," urged Alison, "cast your spell."

Nicodemus chuckled to himself. "Give her the crystal," he muttered to Akkikuyu.

The rat brought from her bag the glass globe and caressed it lovingly with her claws. "Stand there and hold this!" she told Alison.

Alison took the smooth globe in her palms and gazed at it wondrously. What a marvelous mysterious object! How lovely it was with those swirls of color in its center.

"What is it?" she gasped.

"It is my delight–my peace," Akkikuyu replied sadly, "and soon it must smash."

"Will you light the fire now?" asked Alison. She was feeling impatient and wanted to get on with the ceremony.

Akkikuyu nodded. "Yes, I light fire, but first my Nico must be safe from heat."

"Nico?" asked Alison suspiciously. "Who is Nico?" She stared around her, trying to see who Akkikuyu was talking about.

"I AM NICODEMUS!" cried the tattoo triumphantly. Alison whirled around, then stepped back in alarm.

"The face! The face on your ear–it moved, it spoke!" she spluttered aghast.

Nicodemus mocked her: "I move–I speak. Hah hah hah."

Alison had had enough. She turned and tried to run from the circle of stones, but a wall of invisible force prevented her escape. She howled in dismay, but Nicodemus laughed all the more.

"Mousey not leave now ring complete," tutted Akkikuyu.

"You not listen, mousey. Now, Nico we must begin, yes?"

"Truly," said the voice, still chuckling as Alison twisted and turned around the circle in vain. "I shall project my essence into the heart of your crystal, there shall I be safe from the heat of the fire. I hope that I shall still be able to talk to you, but my powers will be much weakened by the glass." The tattoo screwed up its ugly face and became quite still.

A black cloud moved over the stars. Alison stared at the crystal in her paws and saw a pinprick of cold blue light glimmer there. Slowly it began to pulse. The light grew and filled the globe until the crystal shone like a star fallen to earth. The glass became freezing to the touch, yet Alison could not let go. Breathlessly and with great difficulty the voice spoke again, it was nearer, yet somehow it echoed hollowly. "Quickly, Akkikuyu," it said with an effort, an edge of fear creeping into it, "light the fire now! The spell must be completed soon, or the keepers of the gate will draw me back and bind me ever stronger. I have but a little time here unless the exchange is made." Akkikuyu lit the bonfire.

The wood was so dry that it kindled easily, and soon the flames leaped up greedily. The heat singed her whiskers and scorched Alison's face, but the crystal remained icy to the touch.

"Aaagghh," said the voice, "even here I feel the fire! You must hurry. Throw in the mousebrass, Akkikuyu."

The fortune-teller fished out the brass that Isaac had made for her. It was a twisted, ugly thing, made in a spirit of hatred and vengeance. She cast it into the white-hot heart of the crackling flame.

"Hear me, Arash and Iriel," cried Nicodemus. "I send you a soul in my stead. A female unprotected by the Greenlaws. Accept her and let me go free."

A deep rumble boomed in the night. Thunder was approaching. On the horizon, fingers of lightning zigzagged down between heaven and earth. A freezing gale blew up, but protected by the circle of stones, the bonfire remained unaffected. Madame Akkikuyu threw some powders into the blaze and a ball of blue flame burst into the darkening sky.

"Prepare the vessel, Rameth, so I might live again." Nicodemus screamed above the clamoring storm.

Akkikuyu hurled more powder into the flame. A blue column of smoke shot up into the air. The fortune-teller was frightened. She had not expected anything like this at all. If it carried on, the fieldmice would come soon to see what was going on. She winced and clutched her stomach. Something was happening to her . . . something dreadful . . . A terrible pain ripped at her insides. She doubled over in agony, and as she did so, she caught sight of her own body, and cried out in horror.

Her fur was changing color. Instead of being a sleek coat of black, it was now a bright marmalade orange with dark stripes. The secret, closed doors of her mind were forced open and she bellowed with fear as she remembered the past, and saw through Nicodemus's disguise.

Nicodemus laughed amid the thunder and as he did so his voice changed—it became deeper, more sinister, and absolutely evil. He crowed his triumph with insane jubilation.

"Yes, Akkikuyu," sneered the great deceiver, "it is I, your master returned. JUPITER has come back from eternity."

"No!" she yammered plaintively. "You Nicodemus, spirit of field—Jupiter dead."

"Hah hah—I am the father of lies, Akkikuyu, you know that. You have helped to release me, I shall not forget. I intend to reward you with the highest honor that is mine to give."

"What honor?" she asked in horror.

"You have opened the door of death, Akkikuyu," he congratulated her, "but my old body has been destroyed. *You* shall be the new host for my dark spirit."

"Nooo!" Akkikuyu tore at her hair and tried to flee, but like

Alison she could not break out of the stone circle.

"You cannot escape," tutted Jupiter. "Do you not listen? Continue with the spell!"

"Never," she cried, and slumped to the ground in a desperate heap, cringing from that terrible snarling voice. But unseen forces gripped her and the rat was dragged to her feet. Her claws were forced into her bag and a will outside her own guided them to the next ingredient. The powders were thrown into the flame.

"Hear me, Ozulmunn—bind her to me."

Akkikuyu's eyes stung and their black orbs trembled. A thin film of gold closed over them until only narrow slits were left. Her ears were pulled out of shape and she felt her tail grow thick, stripey fur. Jupiter's evil spells were changing her into a cat!

She threw open her mouth to scream but all that came out was a pitiful *meow*. Madame Akkikuyu clapped her ginger claws over her mouth to stop the terrible noise.

"Now, Akkikuyu, throw the girl into the fire, then smash the globe!" commanded Jupiter.

The rat's feet dragged themselves toward Alison.

The mouse had witnessed everything with incredulous despair. She cried for pity as the striped ginger rat lurched toward her. But there was nowhere to escape.

"Throw her in, Akkikuyu!" Jupiter ordered severely.

Madame Akkikuyu blinked her tawny eyes and took hold of the mouse.

"Please, please!" begged Alison as the rat pulled her toward the flames.

The lightning flashed and crackled overhead. Thunder shook the ground, and Jupiter laughed.

"Please don't throw me in," pleaded Alison. "Please, have pity on me!"

With her golden eyes it seemed to Akkikuyu that for a

234

moment Audrey stood before her. "Mouselet," she said, "go, run free."

"I can't," Alison wailed.

Jupiter heard them and scoffed. "You, girl, have no choice. You have an appointment with the keepers of the gates of hell. Dispatch her, Akkikuyu."

Madame Akkikuyu thought of the eternal torment that lay before her should Jupiter take possession of her body. She let go of Alison and shouted, "Mouselet, my friend! It is I who have choice. I will not serve you again! Akkikuyu is free!" With one terrific leap, Madame Akkikuyu cast herself into the middle of the fire.

The rat's ginger fur became black once more. . . . As the blaze roared up, Akkikuyu's voice was heard one last time from the heart of the flames, "Akkikuyu tried so hard, mouselet. . . " and with that she died.

A bolt of lightning struck the circle and blasted the stones apart. Alison dropped the crystal and fled through the gap, escaping into the field.

The bonfire spluttered, the flames leaped higher, and the tumult of the storm drowned out Jupiter's voice calling from the glowing crystal.

"The sacrifice has been made and They are satisfied. Release me child, release me. I am Jupiter, Lord of all Darkness! I command you to break open the globe!" Without his tattooed eyes he could not see that there was no one to hear him.

Bright, fiendish sparks shot out of the fire and fell within the cornfield.

Before long, the corn was ablaze.

The terrible spirit within the globe called out in pain as the fierce heat scorched the glass. The bonfire toppled over and fell with a flurry of burning ashes on top of the crystal. Jupiter's furious cries were muffled.

*   *   *

In the Hall of Corn, the Scuttles, Arthur, and Mr. Woodruffe had decided that Audrey and Twit should go back to Deptford to tell the Starwife what had happened.

The rest of the fieldmice were mumbling and talking to each other in low voices. Some of them were repenting their hasty actions while others were sorry the town mouse had got off so lightly.

Suddenly a cry made everyone turn around. All the sentries were in the Hall; none had seen Alison Sedge crashing through the field. She burst into the Hall of Corn and shouted, "It's the ratwoman—she's working for a devil, *she* is behind all this."

But before anyone could question her farther, another voice yelled out, "FIRE!"

All heads turned again. The sky was aglow and black plumes of smoke blew toward the Hall. Hot ash started to rain down and the Fennywolders squeaked in panic.

"To the still pool!" declared Mr. Woodruffe, jumping onto the throne. "Fly as fast as you can. Save yourselves."

The fieldmice streamed out of the great doors and through the corridor. They were met by the ravaging fire devouring the corn at a terrifying rate.

The Fennywolders could not escape that way—they were beaten back into the Hall of Corn by the blaze, and with a splintering *whoosh* the great doors collapsed behind them.

"We're trapped!" cried the mice.

It was getting difficult to breathe, as the air was sucked up by the flames.

One of the nests caught fire and began to burn furiously.

"Over here," bawled Arthur, "it hasn't reached here yet." Everyone ran to the Scuttles' area, and Twit guided them out through a narrow channel of choking smoke. It was so thick and hot that it burned the eyes and filled the lungs. Old

Todmore coughed and spluttered in the blackness.

"Where we goin', you daft lad? I can't see," he wheezed.

"I knows this way in me sleep," Twit called back to him.

The ears of corn above burst and spat down fiery missiles.

"Come on," shouted Arthur, trying to sound calm, "nearly there."

The babies gagged and cried, turning their tiny pink faces away from the glaring flames. Elijah and Gladwin clutched each other's paws tightly as they crouched beneath blazing arches.

The heat was furnace-hot and the tips of tails sizzled, while delicate ears roasted.

A few times Twit hesitated, doubting the way. His whiskers smoked, but the noise of the inferno, coupled with the lightning, confused him.

"This way," he decided, crossing his fingers. He dived through a wall of smoke and found himself in the glade. "C'mon," he shouted.

Soon everyone was there and they hurried over to the hawthorn bushes and dived into the pool.

"Hang on," said Arthur. "Where's Audrey?"

"Not with me, Arthur," said Gladwin, getting worried.

"I think she was with Mr. Woodruffe," Elijah muttered.

"But I haven't seen him either," Arthur cried.

"Then she must be still in there," said Twit, looking back at the field. The fire was out of control.

"Nothing could live in that," murmured Arthur grimly.

"Oh, Aud," said Twit.

When the fieldmice had left the Hall, Audrey and Mr. Woodruffe heard a faint cry. They hurried back and found Isaac Nettle lying on the ground. He had been overcome by the smoke.

"Get on yer feet, Nettle," snapped Mr. Woodruffe. He pulled the mouse up and slapped his face firmly.

"Let me be," whined Isaac miserably. He sagged down again. "Let me rest."

"Oh no, Nettle, you've done too much harm this night to fizzle out now, you old goat," said Mr. Woodruffe, hauling him away.

"Will he be all right?" asked Audrey anxiously as she looked desperately around at the burning Hall.

"Aye, lass, if we can get him out in time. Now come on, Nettle, use yer legs."

"No," cried Isaac suddenly. "The brass, my son's brass, it was in my paw. Where's it gone?"

"It must be back there," said Audrey.

"Leave it, Nettle."

"I must have it, I must. Jenkin, my lad!" He struggled wildly with them.

"If you go back in you'll suffocate," shouted Mr. Woodruffe. "Stay here! I'll go."

"No," yelled Audrey.

Mr. Woodruffe charged through the thick, clinging smoke and searched for Jenkin's mousebrass.

There came a fierce roar as a line of burning nests crashed down behind. They formed a fence of fire between him and the others. He was trapped.

"Mr. Woodruffe!" called Audrey.

"Go child, while you can," he yelled. "You can't save me. Take Nettle out of here."

More nests tumbled between them and Audrey fled tearfully away.

Mr. Woodruffe made it across to his wicker throne and sat on it just as the blazing walls caved in on him. The king died with his field.

Audrey tugged furiously at Isaac, who was singing in a mad voice. The way was practically impassable now. Terrifying sheets of fire raged on either side of the path.

239

"Glory to the Green," raved Mr. Nettle insanely. "See his blossoms grow."

It took all of Audrey's failing strength to make him follow her, and the ground scorched her feet badly as she dragged him to safety.

"Please, this way, Mr. Nettle," she implored.

"What flowers are these?" Isaac asked, staring up at blazing cornstalks. "Come, Jenkin, see this fair garden. What wonders have we here?"

"Please, Mr. Nettle," she cried, yanking at his paw. The flames swallowed the path behind them.

"With red roses and orange blossom—how bright they are," marveled Isaac. He coughed painfully.

Audrey pushed him farther along. Her hair smoldered and she discarded her lace collar so she could breathe.

They came to the end of their journey. A massive wall of flames reared up before them. Audrey sobbed: they could go no farther. They were cut off.

"Praise be to Him who makes the flowers," ranted Isaac.

Audrey fell to her knees. The fire roared on every side and blazed overhead. She looked around dizzily and gave up. Audrey fainted.

"Blessed be the new leaves of the hawthorn," rejoiced Mr. Nettle.

Thunder split the sky and the clouds were rent apart. Heavy rain teemed down with torrential force. The pool filled and flooded into the ditch while the blazing field hissed and seethed.

*　　*　　*

Audrey opened her eyes. There was a low, rough ceiling over her head and she was in a small bare room. It was the Scuttles' winter quarters.

"Hello, Aud!" Twit was sitting by her side.

She smiled at him. "How did I get here?" she asked. "There was fire everywhere. I thought I was done for—what happened to Mr. Nettle?"

"He's sleepin'. We found him an' you when the rain put the fire out. We all thought you were dead, but you were only in a swoon. You was lucky this time, Aud."

"Yes." She pulled her fingers through her singed hair and remembered. "Mr. Woodruffe, did you find him?"

Twit looked at the floor sadly. "He didn't make it, Aud. And we found somethin' else." The little fieldmouse fidgeted with his toes.

"What else?"

The fieldmouse raised a pale face. "Akkikuyu's dead—she burned in her own bonfire."

Audrey shook her head. "Poor Akkikuyu—are you sure?"

He nodded hurriedly. "Ain't no doubt there."

Audrey burst into tears. She had started out hating the rat but had grown fond of her funny ways. The memory of last night's wedding ceremony and Akkikuyu's blessing flooded back. "Oh, Akkikuyu, I'm sorry," she wept.

Twit patted her hand. "Leastways you're free of that bargain now Aud. You can go home. Oswald is safe."

"Yes," she sniffed, "the bargain is over." She stared at Twit and said, "But you're my husband now, Twit. I can't leave you."

Twit reassured her, "Now don't be daft, Aud," he said, "we both know I only married yer to stop yer gettin' hanged. I told 'ee you don't have to stay. Go back to Deptford—it's where you belong."

"And you?"

Twit shrugged. "A fieldmouse belongs in a field," he told her. "I'll stick around, providing my banishment's been lifted, and help with the clearing up. A nasty mess—very nasty."

"You know," whispered Audrey, "you're not as cheeseless

as folk make out, William Scuttle. You're a very wise mouse, indeed. I'll miss you." She kissed him.

"Aw," he puffed, turning bright red and twisting his tail in his paws. "I reckons I'll come back one day to see me wife an' have a chinwag with old Thomas over a bowl of rum."

Gladwin Scuttle bustled in. Her hair was tied up in a scarf and she wore a white apron. "Oh, you're awake, Audrey," she said. "Well, that is a relief. I'm just on my way to help with the cleanup. Half the tunnels are flooded by the rains and it's still pouring. No, don't you get up, young lady. You stay there for at least a week. You hear me?"

Audrey laughed.

It took nearly a week for the cleanup to end. The tunnels had been flooded with sooty water and this left everything grimy and unpleasant. One of the first things the fieldmice did was start redecorating. They stained the walls with berry juice and decked flowers everywhere. The drab years had passed and in his sickroom, Isaac Nettle, recovering from his madness, accepted the way of things. He even strung nutshells together and painted them bright colors. He was a changed mouse. Many of the children were ill with smoke sickness and Samuel Gorse left his room to visit them and cheer their spirits by acting out, with Todkin and Figgy's help, the story of Mahooot the owl. Figgy played the part of Young Whortle, who was sorely missed by them all.

Arthur arranged the burials of Mr. Woodruffe, Young Whortle, and Madame Akkikuyu's remains.

It was the first time Audrey was allowed out of doors and she was stunned at what was left of the field.

All was charred and ugly. The corn had disappeared, leaving unlovely, spiky stubble poking out of the ground. Rain puddles were coated with ash, and everything was drab and dismal. It seemed that the whole world had turned dark and gray.

The King of the Field was buried on a drizzling morning near the rose trees. The fieldmice raised a mound over him, and Isaac carved a beautiful crown of hawthorn leaves from a single piece of wood. Into it he inscribed the words: "We have lost our king whose light shone on our darkness."

He laid the monument on the top of the mound, and fresh flowers were placed there every day.

Young Whortle was laid to rest next to Hodge. Mr. and Mrs. Nep mourned the loss of their son for the rest of their lives.

The Fennywolders could not decide where to put Madame Akkikuyu. Some thought that she ought not to be buried at all, but be thrown to the birds. Most fieldmice, though, remembered her eagerness to please and the bravery she showed with Mahooot. So it was decided to lay her to rest under the hawthorn around the still pool. There it was hoped she would find peace at last. Audrey, swallowing back her tears, insisted that the remains of the fortune-teller be placed in a patch of ground that the sunlight touched. So the branches were cut back, and as the earth was piled over her grave the sun appeared in the wet sky and a pale, slender ray shone down upon the last resting place of the fortune-teller.

"It's all she ever wanted," wept Audrey.

The still pool became known as "the witch's water," and in years to come, youngsters would go there to cast offerings into it and beg for wishes. And sometimes, on certain summer evenings, when the last flickering beams of the setting sun touched a particular spot—wishes did indeed come true.

In Fennywolde the cleanup finished, and Audrey began to think of going home.

Arthur was upset at the thought of leaving. He had gained everyone's respect, and now they knew that Audrey was innocent the mice had warmed to her too. A veil seemed to have been lifted, and they became the good-natured creatures they had always been.

Finally the day dawned when it was time to leave. Audrey kissed Elijah and Gladwin good-bye.

"Tell my sister to stop poking her nose in where it's not wanted—she did that when she was a child, you know."

"Fare'ee well, lass," said Elijah.

It was time to say good-bye to Twit. "I'll miss you, William," she said thickly, her eyes brimming with tears. "I'll never forget you."

"See you, Aud," he replied brightly, but the twinkle had left his eye forever. "Say hello to Oswald for me, an' thank Thomas for his rum. Take care now."

"I will. Good-bye." She kissed her husband for the last time.

Arthur said his farewells briskly. "Cheerio," he said, waving to everyone who had come out to see them off. Dimsel Bottom slunk away and stared after him sorrowfully.

Brother and sister set off. Twit raised his paw, but his voice croaked hoarsely, "'Bye!" He tried to wipe the tears from his eyes, but they would not stop. "I did love 'ee, Aud," he whispered.

Arthur Brown and Audrey Scuttle became two specks on the horizon, making for the river. When the farewell cries of the country mice had finally dwindled into nothingness, the two town mice looked back for their friends, but they had already traveled too far. All they could see as they gazed back toward the cornfield were the elms rising high above the ditch and the yew tree spreading darkly behind them. This picture stayed in their minds long after. But although they both vowed to return one day, neither ever saw the land of Fenny again.

CHAPTER FIFTEEN

SUMMER'S END

It was the last day of summer. The breeze was fresh and cool, the sun was a pale disk in the sky. The leaves of the elms were past their best and had that tired, old look, which suggests the coming of autumn. Some of them were already curling up and turning gold.

Alison Sedge sat on the edge of the ditch, lost in thought. She no longer took great care of her appearance. Her hair needed brushing and she let it fall in tangled, untidy knots over her face. Her dress was shabby—but why should she care? In her mind she was with Jenkin. They laughed together and smiled at each other in a dreamworld she greatly cherished. Alison lived for such dreams now. She no longer tossed her head or flashed her eyes, and she never listened to compliments from boys. In fact, such compliments had ceased. Alison did not bother about that, for in her mind's eye she was the way Jenkin liked her.

She turned the black thing over in her paws. She had found it buried in a pile of ashes and cinders. Her find was scorched, blackened, and pitted but not broken. She raised the crystal of Madame Akkikuyu up to the sun, but it was too black and opaque to allow her to see within.

It was some months now since the town mice had left Fennywolde and returned to Deptford. Alison had kept out of their way. How fickle everyone was to begin liking that horrid girl after everything she had done. But no, it was the ratwoman who had caused all the evil wasn't it? Alison was confused. Her thoughts were really too full of Jenkin to dwell on other subjects for long. But there was something about this globe—it had something to do with . . . oh, she could not remember anymore.

"Curse you, Audrey," she spat, and discarded the black sooty ball. It began to roll down the steep bank. . . .

Alison struggled to her feet and walked away. She was oblivious of the light noise behind her, and did not hear the glass crack and then smash on the sharp stones at the bottom of the ditch.

Unwittingly, Alison had completed the spell that had caused so much suffering. While she dreamed of a time long before, when she and Jolly Jenkin had been happy together, a hideous great shadow rose up from the ditch behind her.

Jupiter soared into the sky—free at last from the crystal prison.

AFTERWORD

B Y   P E T E R   G L A S S M A N

Power-hungry rats, nature-loving mice, mystical bats . . . In *The Dark Portal*, Robin Jarvis delights readers with not just one, but three unforgettable animal societies. By creating characters with human motivations and personalities flavored by their essentially animal natures, he offers a strikingly original, totally absorbing fantasy world.

Of course, tales about animals who act like people have been told as long as people have gathered to listen to stories; Aesop's fables, some of the oldest stories in western culture, are filled with such animals, as are many tales from African, Asian, Inuit, American Indian, and Aboriginal cultures.

In the nineteenth century, when literature for young people blossomed in Great Britain, many books included animal characters who could talk—such as those in *Alice's Adventures in Wonderland*—but none featured animals subsisting in their very own societies. Then, with the dawning of the twentieth century, came the debut of the Peter Rabbit books by Beatrix Potter. Although without distinct societies or customs, the

247

animals in these stories wore clothes and misbehaved like adventurous children (and suffered the consequences!). Soon after, Kenneth Grahame's *The Wind in the Willows* was published, and the animal fantasy novel truly came into its own; for in this story, Rat, Mole, and their friends lived quite apart from human society (although people resided nearby).

After the publication of *The Wind in the Willows*, animal fantasy books became móre popular. In the early 1920s, Hugh Lofting introduced the Doctor Doolittle books, while A. A. Milne created the Winnie-the-Pooh stories, and Felix Salten wrote *Bambi*. The following decades saw the publication of such classics as Walter Brooks's Freddy the Pig books, George Selden's *The Cricket in Times Square* and its many sequels, the Newbery Medal–winning *Mrs. Frisby and the Rats of NIMH*, and James and Deborah Howe's *Bunnicula*. And, of course, there was the phenomenal success of Richard Adams's *Watership Down*.

In *Watership Down*, Adams re-ignited interest in what Kenneth Grahame had created nearly seventy years earlier—a fantasy story in which animal communities had their own distinct rules, customs, and lore based on their animal nature, yet tinged with human qualities. In the wake of this surprise best-seller, many authors wrote animal fantasies aimed at the adult market, but few met with much success.

Then in 1986, a novel by British radio performer and writer Brian Jacques was published, in both Great Britain and America. Almost overnight, on both sides of the Atlantic, readers young and old were caught up in the saga of *Redwall*. Its heroic animal characters gave fresh life to what had been thought a dead literary form—the swashbuckler—and its success helped revive American publishers' enthusiasm for animal fantasy. In the past, more attention had been given to humorous tales like *The Cricket in Times Square* and *Bunnicula*, but *Redwall* had shown readers' appetites for serious adventure stories featuring animal protagonists.

In 1989, Robin Jarvis's *The Dark Portal,* an animal fantasy unlike any other, was published in Great Britain. With its sinister characters of Jupiter and the rats who scurry to serve him (as well as their evil plotting against one another), the novel has a tinge of the occult darkness found in the writing of such masters as Edgar Allen Poe, H. P. Lovecraft, and M. R. James. But countering this blackness are the farseeing bats, who possess mystical visions of the future, and the loving mouse communities, who cherish their mouse brasses and their belief in the living spirit of spring, the Green Mouse. This careful blend of good and evil, combined with compelling mythology and powerful rituals, made *The Dark Portal* and its two sequels—*The Crystal Prison* and *The Final Reckoning*—best-sellers in Great Britain.

The summer it was first published, I was lucky enough to come upon *The Dark Portal* during a trip to London. Over the following years, every so often I would run into another person who had read and admired this series. When S. E. Hinton (the award-winning author of *The Outsiders, Tex, Rumble Fish,* and *That Was Then, This is Now*) asked me if I had ever heard of the Deptford Mice books, I told her how much I had enjoyed them, then asked her how she came to know about them. She replied that her son had discovered the books when they were in Britain and that they had quickly become his favorites at the time. And she, like all who knew them, couldn't understand why they weren't available in the United States.

Well, finally, they are. At the dawn of this new century, the Deptford Mice books are here for us to share and enjoy. Thank the Green!

Peter Glassman is the owner of Books of Wonder, the New York City bookstore and publisher specializing in both new and old imaginative books for children.

ROBIN JARVIS was born in Liverpool, England, and studied graphic design in college. He worked in television and advertising before becoming a full-time author and illustrator. It was while working at a company that made characters for TV programs and advertising that he began making sketches of mice. From these drawings, the idea for the Deptford Mice was born. *The Dark Portal*, short-listed for the 1989 Smarties Book Prize in England, was followed by two more titles in the series: *The Crystal Prison* and *The Final Reckoning*. Mr. Jarvis currently lives in Greenwich, London.

LOOK FOR THE OTHER BOOKS IN

THE DEPTFORD MICE TRILOGY

BOOK ONE
THE DARK PORTAL

In the sewers of Deptford, there lurks a dark presence that fills the tunnels with fear. The rats worship it in the blackness and name it "Jupiter, Lord of All." Into this twilight realm wanders a small and frightened mouse–the unwitting trigger of a chain of events that hurtles the Deptford Mice into a world of heroic adventure and terror.

BOOK THREE
THE FINAL RECKONING

The ghostly spirit of Jupiter has returned, bent on revenge. Struggling to survive in an eternal world of ice and snow, the Deptford Mice are worried: the mystical bats have fled from the attic, and underground a new rat army is growing. With food short and no sign of spring, the mice know that desperation is close at hand. And few, it seems, might live to tell the tale.